TJIDENG REUNION

A Memoir

of

World War II on Java

by

Boudewijn van Oort

Acknowledgements

This book could not have been written without the help of friends. I owe a mountain of debt particularly to those who shared the experiences described herein. They not only furnished me with valuable anecdotal material, but also had the patience to read my draft and suggest improvements: Bart van Nooten (who also provided me with information from the Bandoeng Adres Boek), Emmy de Visser, Ank de Ridder, Elsa Kleist, Eduard W. J. Kerkhoven and Marguerite Ruys deserve my gratitude. The latter two persons kindly shared with me unpublished memoirs written by their relatives (Elly Soeters-Campioni and Charlotte Kerkhoven). I owe a debt to my wife, Nancy, who patiently let me pursue this work and proofread the text, and to Merrie-Ellen Wilcox for superb assistance in turning my scribbles into a presentable document. In addition, I received much appreciated encouragement from Anneke Bosman, Tony van Kempen (who brought me into contact with travel companions on the MV *Straat Soenda*), Jan van Dulm and Herman Bussemaker; the latter shared with me information on pre-war Dutch diplomacy and also kindly brought me into contact with Dutch archival material. I am indebted as well to Petrie Leroux of the National Library of South Africa, who meticulously scanned old newspapers for relevant articles.

The writing of this book presented a peculiar challenge: for a three-year period, March 1942–May 1945, covering our internment in Bandoeng (now Bandung) on Java, there is almost no contemporary surviving written material describing the lives of some fourteen thousand fellow citizens. I have been able to find just one document providing a reasonably continuous account of events, the diary of a sixteen-year-old girl.[1] By way of contrast, several diaries survived from our second camp in Batavia (now Jakarta). Remaining source material is fragmentary, with conflicting and inconsistent dates, mostly committed to paper decades after the events described, but including a small number of surviving unpublished fragmentary contemporary accounts. Compiling from this a coherent chronicle of the internment experience and providing broader wartime context have been the major challenges. I owe especial gratitude to Susan King, who kindly read through my initial scribbles, and gave me a sense of direction.

---

[1] Anneke Bosman.

A Note on Spelling and Language

Since my tale spans several continents in a different era, I have had to grapple with concepts and place names that may be unfamiliar to the modern reader.

To tell a tale about the interaction of diverse peoples without using foreign words would sadly impoverish it. I have done my best to introduce foreign words in such a way that their meaning either becomes clear from the context or is accompanied by an explanation. A glossary has been appended for reference.

Geography presented a second challenge. I could not expect all readers to be familiar with the geography covered by this story, and therefore maps have been included.

Place names have presented a third challenge. As a result of the decolonization process following World War II, many place names mentioned in the book have changed since then, sometimes more than once. To adopt a completely modern nomenclature for these place names would detract from the atmosphere I am endeavouring to recapture and would moreover create confusion for those readers who have at least some familiarity with the circumstances described. Tjideng, for instance, was a notorious women's and children's camp, but today the name only refers to the drainage canal it is named after, "Cideng." The pronunciation has not changed, and in both cases reflects the "ch" sound in the English word "church." The camp is gone, but its story remains significant, while the smelly canal still drains part of Jakarta, a city we knew as "Batavia." Whereas Batavia was a distinctly Dutch colonial city, Jakarta is a modern Asian one. I am describing a colonial period and hence adhere to the old name—that's what we called it.

I finally need to explain the voice of this tale. Much of it took place when I was scarcely conscious as a human being—I was too young and my personal recollections of much of this period is fragmentary and disjointed. I grew up in a turbulent historic period, and that experience certainly has left its mark, but describing it does not fit comfortably within the bounds of this story. Many sources have been used to develop this account, and family discussions years later provided the important overall framework.

Boudewijn van Oort
Victoria, British Columbia
June 2008

MAPS

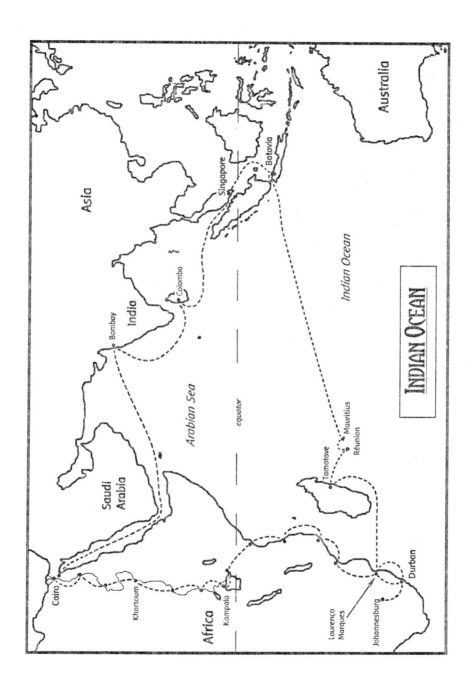

INDIAN OCEAN

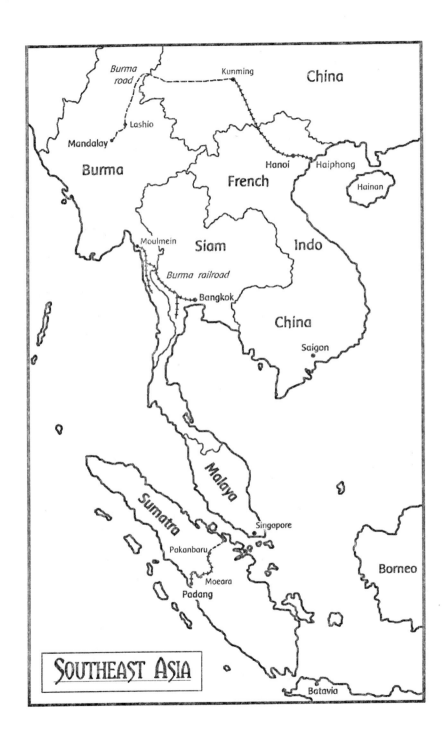

Burma road

Kunming

China

Lashio

Mandalay

Burma

Hanoi

Haiphong

French

Hainan

Moulmein

Siam

Indo

Burma railroad

Bangkok

China

Saigon

Malaya

Sumatra

Singapore

Pakanbaru

Moeara

Borneo

Padang

SOUTHEAST ASIA

Batavia

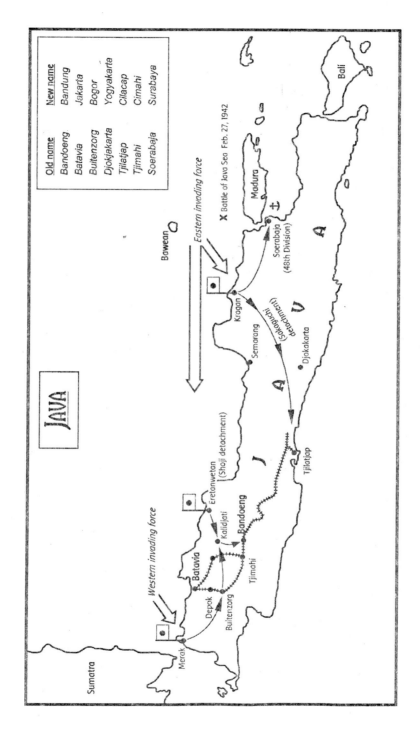

JAVA

Old name	New name
Bandoeng	Bandung
Batavia	Jakarta
Buitenzorg	Bogor
Djokjakarta	Yogyakarta
Tjilatjap	Cilacap
Tjimahi	Cimahi
Soerabaja	Surabaya

Eastern invading force

X Battle of Java Sea Feb. 27, 1942

Bawean

Bali

Madura

Soerabaja
(48th Division)

Krogan

(Sakaguchi)
detachment

Semarang

Djokakarta

Western invading force

Eretonwetan
(Shoji detachment)

Kalidjati

Bandoeng

Batavia

Tjimahi

Tjilatjap

Depok

Buitenzorg

Merak

Sumatra

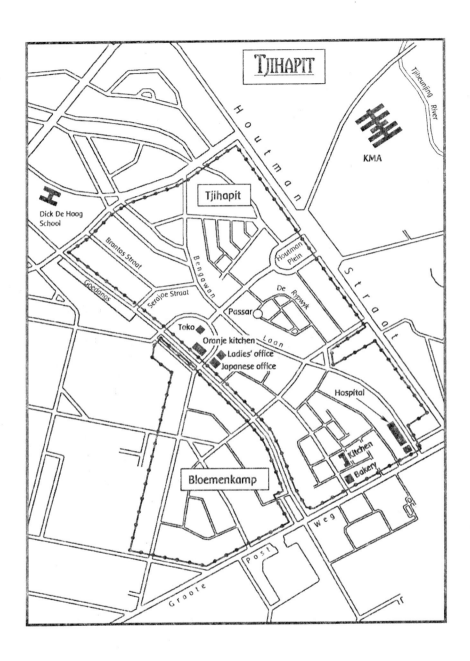

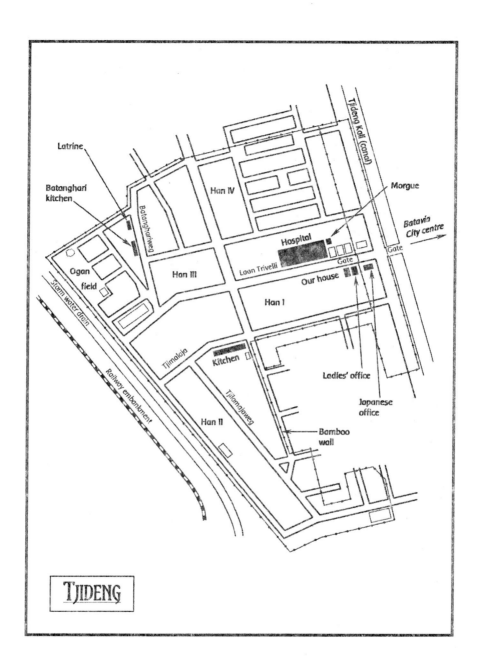

PROLOGUE: APRIL 1990

"Boudy, will you please say something about your father at the funeral tomorrow?" Henny, my stepmother, made this request as she returned from the kitchen with after-dinner coffee. I was seated in my father's easy chair, an uncomfortable experience, because on previous visits he had always sat there. This time Henny had pointedly ushered me to his former seat from the moment I arrived at her house.

Her plea caught me off-guard, as my reveries had strayed from his unexpected death the previous day, back to our distant and tumultuous past, which I had only recently begun to ponder. I suppose that this is a common phenomenon for those of us reaching an age when it is obvious that our own life has run the major part of its course. I had reached that stage and had started to wonder how it was that I had become who I was, how my own background had in turn forced me to adapt to new challenges in a given way. My plans and hopes for the future had, up until now, been more important than reflecting on the past, even though the past would not easily let go, especially at night, when demons from my childhood often disturbed the rest I craved after a busy day. Mostly I had been a passive individual, caught up in the maelstrom of World War II, unable to comprehend the significance of what was happening. The Pacific war ended officially on August 15, 1945, but we who became trapped in it still had to register our own ending, to slay our personal dragons. My parents, along with some other adults, emerged from that conflict with an additional burden: they had failed to anticipate the course of world affairs that became so disastrous for them. Having survived, they vowed never to get caught in such currents again, and yet did not want to dwell on the horrors of the past. "I want to forget the past; the future interests me more," was how my father had put it in 1945.

But I had grown curious, and he had been the only person left with whom I could discuss the events that had shaped our destiny. Others had died long ago, and now he was gone as well.

Henny's request shook me out of this train of thought.

"Yes," I replied automatically, while putting the cup down on the armrest of the chair to ponder this challenge. It was my father's role in this drama that I needed to touch upon at the next day's ceremony. A meaningful address at the funeral was impossible unless this critical period of his life, his ups and downs, his triumphs and his bitter disappointments, were somehow conveyed to those in attendance. In my estimation he was a remarkable man.

Earlier that afternoon I had arrived after an eight-hour journey from Victoria to say goodbye to my father; that was the way Henny put it when she phoned me to break the news of his passing. One could hardly say that his death was unanticipated—he was eighty-two years old—but it had occurred in hospital while he was being readied for a minor operation. Although I was deeply saddened by his departure, it was at the same time a relief that he had gone so peacefully, for the last year of his life had been marred by bouts of depression and aches and pains.

Even on the journey from Victoria this question of the past had preoccupied me. The ferry crossing from Horseshoe Bay, west of Vancouver, across Howe Sound to Langdale must be one of the most breathtaking forty-minute voyages in the entire world, yet this time I ignored the magnificent scenery of majestic coastal mountains still capped with snow. As I stared vacantly out of the ferry window, thoughts about what lay ahead were periodically interrupted by reflections on the events that had brought us to Canada.

When the ferry made its final approach to the dock, tracing a broad, foamy arc over the still, dark waters of Howe Sound, I could clearly see Henny standing, sadly alone, beside the car ramp. She looked serene, a remarkable woman, I thought. I knew how much my father and Henny had meant to each other, and I was relieved that she had taken his passing so well. As we walked silently to her car, she handed me the keys.

"Can you please drive, Boudy?"

I knew that Henny had learned to drive only late in life, after she had married my father, and that she disliked driving and felt more comfortable in the passenger seat, even if it was in her own vehicle; I dutifully took the keys, got in the driver's seat and started the engine, while she got in on the other side. We drove towards the Sechelt Hospital so that I could pay my last respects to my father, and then we returned home, to what had now become Henny's house, for supper and to discuss the next steps.

The more I pondered Henny's request, the more I warmed to the challenge of honouring and celebrating his life before the hundred or so guests who were expected to come to the funeral. There was so much that I wanted to say to his friends and to Henny, but above all I wanted to share an anecdote: my first conscious encounter with him in September 1945, when I was the seven-year-old son he did not recognize, and dared not approach for fear it was a mistake. That dramatic, emotion-charged image was still crystal clear in my mind and now haunted me. Thus my thoughts, aided by sips of coffee, were distracted by memories of a distant past.

After coffee, I began to mull over the task facing me. In order to make a small speech I needed to jot down some ideas, but where on earth could I start? His relation to me as a father, interrupted by a dramatic three-and-a-half-year hiatus, was what I obviously needed to touch upon, but Henny could not help me with this. It was the time before she arrived in our lives, the time when my mother had still been alive, that needed to be addressed most of all. Henny understood this very well; a few words from that perspective was what she certainly expected from me.

As I sat in the chair, with a pad of paper on my lap and a pencil in my hand, I looked around this room so deeply permeated with my father's spirit: he had designed the room, indeed the whole house, had sawn and dressed every piece of wood, lifted into place the massive roof beams above my head, and hammered in every nail in the building. He had made much of the furniture as well, the big easy chairs, the coffee table with antique Dutch tiles salvaged from a farmer in Drenthe[1] who had been seized by an urge to modernize his beautiful old dwelling. The smell of my father's cigar smoke still perfumed the room, as though he could return at any moment. On the wood-panelled wall above me hung the old Friesian clock, calmly ticking away the hours with a wonderful soothing rhythm, as it had done for almost three hundred years. There was no other sound.

The clock had been in our family almost since the day my father was born, and it was a miracle that we still owned it. The clock had first started to tick two hundred years before my father's birth, and it was still going strong in spite of obvious wear and tear. The brass covering of the lead weight was now a bit crumpled, and part of the painted lead decoration was gone: a lead mermaid had lost her tail and a lead lion had lost its head, while the gilt paint had lost its glitter. The voluptuous wooden mermaids on either side of the dial could do with a cleanup to reveal their bright colours, but the clock still ticked and tocked, and that it could do so was owed to my father's ingenuity. Every now and then the chain would slip over a worn brass sprocket, and the brass weight bounced up and down. A spring hidden by a piece of copper tubing now joined the weight to the pulley hanging from the chain. That spring arrangement had been an innovation of my father's, an attempt to prolong the functional life of this very old clock by absorbing the shocks as the chain slipped over the worn sprocket. And indeed the pendulum, the heart of the clock, was not the original one; one could not miss the awkwardly shaped piece of brass, with holes lacking purpose, that swung out with each tick or tock. After the war, when through a miracle we and the clock had been reunited in South Africa, the original pendulum was missing, and so my father improvised a new one with some wire and a piece of salvaged brass. That had been his first piece of handy-work after leaving the prison camp.

1: A province in eastern Holland.

My thoughts were interrupted by Henny returning to the living room from downstairs; she was bearing an old binder, a Lever Arch File that had once been used in an office and a parcel wrapped in crumpled brown paper.

"Boudy, you may want to go through this album, and this package may also have meaning for you."

Henny then went to the bookcase, saying, "There's something else here that you may find interesting."

While she was thus engaged, I placed the unfamiliar package on the floor in order to concentrate on the familiar binder; it was the old family photograph album containing black and white photographs pasted onto thick green cardboard; most of the photos were from the pre-war days. Suddenly it dawned on me that I did not know how this photograph album had survived the war. All things considered, this too was a miracle, for we had emerged from the prison camps with next to nothing.

In the meantime, Henny had returned with an unfamiliar book, a paperback, in her hands, which I added to the pile on the floor beside the chair.

Leafing through the album, I glanced over some old postcards and souvenirs from visits to exotic places: Bombay, Cairo, Java. There were also prints of etchings, perhaps from an exhibition my father had attended, or perhaps they were even older—grandfather's? Tucked among the pages, I found an envelope containing letters I had never seen before. One letter had been written in pencil on fragile, yellowed paper torn from a school scribbler in the familiar neat, rounded handwriting of my mother. There were also letters written in ink by my father. Obviously considered precious by whoever had placed them in the album, these letters were dated September 1945. They merited study.

Many of the old photos were familiar to me: images of my parents, of me, of Juf (my nanny), Emmy and Edu, and the houses we had lived in; but I had not looked at the album for almost half a century, and I was immediately struck by the tale the photographs seemed to tell. One of the photographs, of a tropical river valley on Java, was partly freed from the paper. Lifting it up, I noticed my mother's pencilled handwriting on the back: it read "Serajoe *Rivier Juli,* 1941." I remember living in Serajoestraat,[2] but I could not remember a river of that name. Perhaps many of the pictures had been thus annotated by her prior to being glued onto the green card. The photographs prompted memories from my childhood; it clearly was a treasure trove. What other secrets lay forgotten, tucked away in a box, down in the basement?

"Henny, I think there used to be some more pages. Do you know where they might be?"

"No, your father never looked at this album while I was married to him."

---

2. Serajoe Street in English, but today called *jalan* Seraju.

I could understand that. To do so would have been painful for him and embarrassing for her. And yet much of the household she now commanded was full of reminders of my mother. The awful, cheap crockery, clearly not dishwasher proof, that we had bought when we first arrived in Canada was still in use. For some reason my father had been attached to those plates, and Henny had stoically humoured him by continuing to use them. She had always been extremely sensitive to other people's feelings.

Henny emerged from the kitchen with a couple of silver bowls filled with peanuts, placing one on my armrest and the other by the chair where she planned to sit. Those bowls! How I had taken them for granted all those years, and how special they really were. My mother had always referred to them as the "Djokja bowls," souvenirs from a vacation trip; they also had miraculously survived our internment. They were made of silver, gracefully shaped like an eight-petalled flower, each petal in turn decorated with embossed floral motifs, a triumph of exquisite Javanese craftsmanship. Reflected in the silver I suddenly caught a mirage, a ghostly image of my mother's beautiful face, her dark hair, her blue eyes, her quiet smile.

Shaken, I leafed further through the album, now struck even more by the vicissitudes of our lives. My parents and even Henny had suffered so many setbacks in their lifetimes, and yet they had always bounced back, carrying me along. I stumbled onto a picture of my father, my mother and me, taken in 1945 on the beach in Durban. It was Christmas and the beach was full of holidaymakers; the casual observer taking in the festive scene would have concluded that we too had come here for a week's relaxation. No one would have suspected that this bedraggled threesome in their ill-fitting swimsuits were refugees from one of earth's hellholes. It was a bizarre scene. My mother looked happy and relaxed. She had successfully navigated my seventy-three-year-old nanny, Juf, and me, her son, through a terrible period of deprivation, disease and anxiety. Now she was back where, before the war, her married life had begun in such a wonderful way. My father also smiled, but the grim legacy of a bloody encounter with an iron wrench, swung in anger at his face by a Japanese prison guard, was clearly visible, and he was much thinner than he had been before the war; although only thirty-nine years old, he looked at that time as though he were in his sixties.

And then I remembered the other items she had given me. I picked up the paperback and examined its cover. It had a photograph of a man in distress, the author, one would think, and its title was *Indonesische Overpeinzingen*,[3] by Sutan Sjahrir.

"Where did this come from?"

"Edu gave it to your father, on our last visit."

---

3. *Indonesian Musings.*

I found a coloured photograph inside, used perhaps as a page marker. It was a picture of my father standing in front of an elegant house. I showed the photograph to Henny for an explanation.

"Oh yes," she replied, "I took that picture when we visited the house he had built and never lived in—in Bandung. The people who were living there were very nice and let him see the place—the experience had moved him deeply."

The book seemed to be a sort of a diary written in prison. Someone had marked a passage:

> I note that unconsciously I have grown accustomed to think as little as possible in terms of time. That is probably so because so little happens, making the increments of time so lacking in content that one is scarcely able to differentiate between them. I believe that there is a second reason for this, namely that my stay here is indeterminate. I think that all the other prisoners here know exactly what the date is, they know day by day how many years, months and days they remain locked up before regaining their freedom.[4]

I wondered whether Edu, my father's dear friend who had gone through so much with us, had marked that passage, but Henny did not know.

I then reached for the brown paper parcel, opened it and pulled out a blue and white piece of cloth. At the top was embroidered in black thread, "Tjihapit 18-10-2603." I was dumbfounded, for I could not recall when I had last seen this humble item: it must have been 1945. With a lump in my throat I recognized my mother's needlework—and that weird date; that must have been Juf's seventieth birthday.

With difficulty I brought my thoughts back to the present and the task at hand; so much had happened in our lives. Pondering, I stared out through the great living room windows at the tall fir and cedar trees that marked the edge of my father's property. They were silhouetted against a late spring evening sky. I had at times suggested that the trees could be thinned out, to let more light into his beloved house, but he had always stoutly refused. Those trees were his "cathedral."

It was getting late, and there was much to do in the coming two days. I began to scribble some notes, an attempt to give the funeral guests a brief coherent review. But as I wrote, I knew that after the funeral I would

---

4. Sjahrir was a political prisoner in the Netherlands East Indies, and was therefore not charged with a specific crime, nor given a specific sentence.

immediately set off on a much larger quest. How did this all come to pass? How and why did we make that convoluted journey from a modest cottage on the highveld of South Africa to a chalet on the wooded West Coast of Canada?

1. MAY 10, 1940

When my father, Boudewyn A. J. van Oort, stepped out of the Chevrolet on Friday night, my mother, Wilhelmina, immediately knew something serious was amiss: he was earlier than usual. He strode up the gravel path to the veranda steps waving a newspaper in an agitated fashion; he was almost unable to express himself coherently.

"Wil, Wil, call Juf—did you not hear the news? Holland has been attacked by the *moffen*," he shouted.[1]

As he stumbled up the steps of our veranda, he unfolded the special late edition of the *Rand Daily Mail*, the paper he usually bought on his way from work in Roodepoort. Its headline screamed, "HOLLAND AND BELGIUM, NAZIS' NEW VICTIMS—SUDDEN INVASION." An entire page was devoted to the shocking news and the reactions from various world capitals.

My mother had only shortly before driven home to Lombardy East from an afternoon's game of tennis and had not bothered to turn the radio on. She hurried to the back of the house to call Juf, and returned to my father saying in an overwrought voice, "We must contact my family—must send a telegram."

Just then Juf appeared. She was an old-fashioned soul who preferred not to listen to the radio at all and in any case understood no English and only the little Afrikaans that she could relate to Dutch. Besides, we had to be careful with our electricity consumption: the batteries did not have unlimited capacity. When Juf heard the awful news she shook her head in disbelief. "Oh, oh, oh," she wailed. "It can't be true. How could the Germans have done that to us?"

"We'd better go right away into town before the post office closes!" my father urged. "Let's see, Wil, we need to send one to Zwolle, and I must get one to Jurrema, and perhaps we should also send one to Bets." After a search for the address book, my parents had a short discussion on what should be said in the telegram to Jurrema, the accountant who managed Juf's pension; my father wondered whether there was time to safeguard those investments.

"What can we say to your parents," he thought out loud.

"Let's think about that on the way to town."

They hurried out to the car and left in a cloud of dust, as my father raced to cover the five-mile trip to Germiston before closing time. When they returned an hour and a half later they could reassure Juf that they had succeeded, but

---

1. *Moffen* is a derogatory term for Germans.

only just, because of the huge lineup at the telegram counter. My father was spluttering about "uncooperative post office workers, who refused to stay on after six."

"There was a scene when some who had come after us were unable to get their telegram off," he recounted to Juf. "I authorized Jurrema to do whatever he thought best for the family."

As if struck by a bolt of lightning, our peaceful life on the Transvaal veld had been shattered by events over five thousand miles to the north. That's how our adventure began, a story I heard over and over again, years later, when my father and mother reflected on our troubled past.

Lombardy East

The house my father built for himself in 1936 stood in splendid isolation in a new district called Lombardy East, part of the municipality of Germiston, a gold-mining town ten miles southeast of Johannesburg (figure 1). In those days the grassy veld landscape surrounding the house stretched to the horizon, uninterrupted by any other manmade intrusion. Only a nearby clump of bluegum trees marked the former presence of a farmhouse.

This region of South Africa was referred to as the Transvaal Province, a name one will no longer find on a map. It was the land immediately north of the sluggish, westward-flowing Vaal River, so named by the Boer settlers of the nineteenth century because of its muddy colour; from its banks the grass-covered veld rose northward to the height of land formed by a rocky ridge called the *Witwaters Rand* (white waters ridge, because of its quartzite rocks). Beyond the Rand the land gradually dropped down through dense, thorny acacia bushland to the banks of the eastward-flowing Limpopo River, which marked the northern boundary of the province and of the country. Today the southern part of the former Transvaal is called Gauteng, and that is where one can still find Lombardy East. Mpumalanga, Limpopo and Northwest Province cover the remainder of the former Transvaal. To many this land was then affectionately known as "*die ou* [the old] Transvaal."

Today's traveller, visiting the area where my story begins, would not recognize the landscape I am trying to depict, for so much has changed: the air is no longer so clear, the endless vistas are interrupted by power lines and smoking factories, and Lombardy East is just a suburb lost in a vast sprawling city.

At the time the air of Lombardy East was alive with seed-eating, chirping finches, weaver birds, and the "flap," an ungainly black bird with an oversized tail and a bright red ring around its neck, laboriously flapping from bush to bush. Occasionally, a white cattle egret, or tick bird, would pass through, looking for tick-infested cattle. The emptiness and expanse of the land lent it a beauty all its own. A mile above sea level the air was always clear, in spite of a few new industrial plants to service the great gold mines that then drove the economy. Here and there *koppies* interrupted the gently undulating grassland. These were small rocky hills strewn with rounded boulders, where stunted, thorny acacia trees, with their fine feathery green summertime foliage, could grow along with a variety of small shrubs. Because of their abrupt rise above the veld they reminded the Boer settlers of upturned teacups, or *koppies*. Even in winter, when the vegetation was dormant, the lonely vastness was hauntingly beautiful in pastel shades of mauve, rose and ochre, with always a brilliant blue sky overhead. Only in the occasional gully, or *vlei*, grey-leafed eucalyptus trees might indicate the presence of an isolated farm. For a brief period in the summer, when the infrequent rains came, the grasses would burst into life and display a rich green, but for most of the year the grasses appeared dead, coloured russet near their base and blending upwards to a pale straw hue. Mixed in with the grass were clumps of *khakibos*,[2] threatening the unwary wanderer with its seeds—tiny black needles armed with three sharp spikes that could prick exposed skin or adhere like a black mass of insects to one's socks. The veld was crisscrossed by dusty footpaths or game trails; they seemed to start nowhere in particular and led to an equally indeterminate destination. Whether such trails had originally been carved by man or beast was impossible to determine. Clearly, the trails had been there for a long time, but the dominant form of life they guided was undergoing rapid change—the vast herds of antelope of former times had given way to people, both black and white, along with their horses and cows.

In the summer, between November and January, the morning sky filled with puffy white clouds, drifting with the breeze, and growing to towering shapes as the day wore on, casting stark shadows over luminescent, undulating but endless veld, marking the contours of the land with their gliding motion. When these thunderclouds grew, their billowy whiteness towering high into the sky, a pungent smell of ozone, the promise of rain, would fill the air. Oftentimes the rain barely reached the ground. From a distance, it appeared as sheets of grey, ragged curtains descending from the dark clouds in a broad sweep down towards the earth, but melting into nothingness before reaching the thirsty land. The Afrikaans farmers described this phenomenon evocatively as *die reën sak uit* (the rain is dropping down). But it could also drench the ground, causing flash floods that would carve out the steep-sided *donga*s, the gullies feeding little rivulets. Occasionally there might even be hail but this was rare. Sudden violent storms could occur; they were accompanied by ferocious lightning flashes and thunder that would roll and echo among the *koppies* and

---

2. *Tagetes minuta*, a member of the Marigold family.

occasional *kranse*, the wreaths of higher cliffs that here and there broke the gently rolling prairie landscape.

In the winter months, especially August when the land had dried out, veld fires often swept across the landscape. The heat would sometimes carry aloft clouds of black ash, the charred remnants of vegetation, and flocks of birds would rise and shriek their anxiety. Behind the advancing front of the fires there would remain a blackened landscape with occasional embers glowing for some time, releasing thin wisps of smoke as an afterthought. The fires could end as mysteriously as they started, perhaps halted in their march by a *donga*, where there was no vegetation. In the spring, after a bit of rain, green blades of fresh new grass could then make a startling appearance between the blackened remnants of the previous year's growth.

At night, the magnificent sky was always clear, dark, yet sparkling with the myriad stars forming the Milky Way. Of the constellations, the Southern Cross stood out. No one could stand on the veld at night and not be filled with awe and wonder at the sheer magnificence of this earth and the universe it occupies. For immigrants arriving from the flat, windswept landscape of Holland so often covered by low, monotonous, lead-grey clouds, this land was breathtakingly bright, beautiful and exhilarating.

My father, an architect, had designed and built his house within a year of arriving from Holland, the country of his birth, which he left not because he was destitute, but because of his need to be usefully employed. Holland was still in the depths of the Depression, and although he could afford to take a somewhat relaxed view regarding the necessities for survival, thanks to the hard work and thrift of his deceased father, he needed purpose; South Africa with its expanding gold production had beckoned to him. Upon his arrival, the municipality of Roodepoort, another gold-mining town some ten miles to the west of Johannesburg, had promptly hired him as town architect. The house my father then built for himself was of modest size, but attractive and comfortable. It had a whitewashed brick exterior and a white corrugated asbestos roof. There were two verandas, one at the front of the north-facing structure to take advantage of the winter sun (this being in the southern hemisphere), and another around the east side of the house giving access to the master bedroom. My father always felt that the bedroom should, if at all possible, be positioned so that the morning sun would cheer its drowsy occupants. Both verandas were paved with a green polished concrete that the Bantu "houseboy" would wax to mirror-like smoothness. We called such a veranda, a common feature of homes, permitting the residents to enjoy the fresh air while shaded from the hot sun, a *stoep*. Towering above the house and behind it stood a windmill for the domestic water supply. The location of that water well had been selected by the driller using his divining rod; a second attempt had been unnecessary, thereby proving the potency of this humble device.

There was a second building, providing accommodation for the servants. Its roof was also crowned by a windmill, an electricity generator capable of keeping the glass-cased batteries of a thirty-five-volt system fully charged. The electricity supply was adequate not just for lights, but also for a radio-gramophone. Being able to listen to his collection of 78 rpm records, especially those of Bach and Mendelssohn, was important to my father. Coal provided for the remaining domestic needs—the kitchen stove, a water heater, and the living room fireplace for chilly highveld winter evenings.[3] The house, though isolated, was self-contained and well appointed.

By the front *stoep* a newly-planted lantera bush quickly bore a profusion of orange and red flowers, but the rest of the garden then consisted of an expanse of stony dirt fringed by a fence and adorned with a lawn that barely covered the soil. In South Africa the climatic and soil conditions did not allow for the English concept of lawn, but a hardy variety of grass had been identified that did not grow three feet tall and that might even benefit from the attention of a tolerant lawnmower. Shortly after the house was completed, my father had contracted a gardening firm to plant thousands of young grass plants with the help of a team of Bantu labourers. The plants had now begun to send out lateral shoots in an attempt to cover the unplanted patches of soil. This my father proudly called his "lawn."

The struggle to embellish the house with such a modest garden was testimony to the fact that the original description of the land as "a farm" required etymological latitude in order to apply a distinctly European agrarian concept to this piece of rural Africa. A century before the land had readily supported huge herds of zebra and gnu, but with difficulty it now fed cattle, whether belonging to the white man or the Bantu. Flanking the fence was the beginning of a hedge that gave refuge to various forms of wildlife, including snakes and large lizards. Neither of these were particularly attractive animals to have around the house; both were dangerous, the first because of its venomous bite, the latter on account of its powerful tail. A large dog to keep the unwanted wilderness guests at bay was therefore another essential part of the household.

To the west of the house, there was the remnant of a plantation of Eucalyptus trees, providing shade and a windbreak, an invariable feature of all farms on the highveld. These trees had been partly cleared away to make space for a neighbour's house. From the veranda the view to the northwest was glorious; there the veld dropped gently to a distant *vlei*, where, after rainstorms, a small stream flowed over a stony bed. Beyond the *vlei* the land rose again to

---

3. A dramatic scarp separates the "highveld" of the interior of South Africa from the "lowveld" bordering the Indian Ocean.

the horizon. Johannesburg, the great city, lay well out of sight beyond another rise. However, on a clear day one could just catch a glimpse of wisps of smoke from the Alexandra township, the rather dreary and, later, notorious *lokasie* (shantytown or "location") where many of the black labouring masses of Johannesburg were living.

Johannesburg, dominating the landscape with its skyscrapers, had, within the astonishingly short period of fifty-one years, waxed from a huddle of miners' shacks to a city of a million. Together with the other mining towns of the Rand and the numerous farming communities elsewhere, they gave a distinctly European appearance to this portion of what was otherwise known as the "Dark Continent." So overwhelming had the influx of European immigrants and culture been that very few saw South Africa as anything other than a European country at the southern tip of Africa that happened to also accommodate a much larger Bantu population. The bloody "kaffir wars" that had been fought in the early part of the nineteenth century were largely forgotten, so decisively had the Bantu been defeated. But the European invasion had also robbed the Bantu of their traditional pastoral way of life, with the white farmers fencing in the land they now claimed as their own. A huge migration had then commenced, bringing hungry Bantu men and women to the cities to do manual labour either as domestic servants or in the rapidly growing industries. Mostly these Bantu now lived in the crowded shantytowns like Alexandra that sprang up around all the towns and cities; these were areas where Europeans never ventured. The Bantu men who worked in the mines lived in "mine compounds" resembling military barracks.

On July 14, 1937, my father married Wilhelmina Boland in the old Amsterdam town hall. He knew her as "Wil." That the wedding took place on the day when the French celebrate the fall of the Bastille had been seen by my father as a propitious coincidence, but my mother reckoned that it might help him remember his wedding anniversary. The courtship preceding the marriage had of necessity been short, since my father had secured from his employer only two months' leave to visit the land of his birth.

When he brought Wil to her new home the house was not exactly empty, for aside from the servants there was Juf, my father's sixty-four-year-old nanny, who had in effect become a family member (figure 2). Her name was derived from the Dutch *mejuffrouw* (miss), a childish modification of a more formal title that had long since been forgotten; now it was simply her name. Juf, tragically widowed within a year of her own marriage, had taken on the position of nanny shortly after my father was born, when his mother tried to resume her career as a voice teacher at the *conservatorium* of Amsterdam. Four years later his mother contracted tuberculosis and died; thereafter Juf became a permanent household fixture, inadvertently becoming the only mother my father had ever known.

13

She was a kindly soul, a nineteenth-century figure, very religious in a quiet, upright, Lutheran sort of way. She was slightly built, with long black hair tied in a bun on the back of her head, and she never went out without a black straw hat modestly adorned with unobtrusive, almost invisible imitation daisies and forget-me-nots. She was in perpetual mourning, not only for her late husband, who had also died of tuberculosis, but also for her deceased former employer, who had treated her with love and respect. Grandfather van Oort had moreover ensured that she would have a pension. After emigrating to South Africa and getting established, my father had invited her to join him because of his attachment to her and also because she had almost no personal ties in Holland. Juf had left Holland after she had supervised the clearing of my deceased grandfather's house and had accompanied on the ocean voyage to Cape Town the antique furnishings my father had inherited. Once in her new home, she had taken on household responsibilities as before, which, given the inevitable presence of domestic help, were not onerous.

My father's marriage had not changed this arrangement at all. With Juf in charge of the household, my mother had been able to dedicate her energies to making the transition from immigrant to contented resident of South Africa. This was achieved by enjoying an active social life: there were the tennis clubs, numerous dinner parties and picnics. Her conversion from a recently trained and newly employed secretary, enjoying the pleasures of a vibrant cosmopolitan Amsterdam, to life on the wide open veld of South Africa, was dramatic, but there is no evidence that this was anything other than a huge thrill for her.

And then she became pregnant. On August 25, 1938, Dr. Willie Liebenberg assisted my mother with my journey from the womb into the world. By all accounts the trip was a normal one, though my father afterwards commented that his son "looked like a skinned rabbit." After childbirth my mother had immediately been able to rely on an experienced nanny. Pregnancy had therefore caused only a brief interruption in her social life, in those days the birthright of all white South African women.

Dr. Liebenberg was a big man of Afrikaner stock, with a face deeply etched by the sun and dry winds of the Orange Free State *plaas* (farm) where he had grown up. He was more than just our family doctor; he was also a friend who had given my parents a beautiful zebra skin for a wedding present. He had shot that zebra himself on his *plaas*. In those days wild animals often shared grazing with domesticated cattle on the immense farms. My father had first met the doctor in Holland, where he had gone to study medicine. During his student days at Leyden, he had spent his vacations with relatives who happened to be clients of my paternal grandfather; that is how we got to know Dr. Liebenberg. Such academic exchanges were more common in those days, assisted by the learning of *Hoog Hollands* (High Dutch) in South African schools. After 1930

Afrikaans had become the official second language, and the teaching of Dutch ceased.

There nevertheless remained strong historic ties between the Netherlands and South Africa. A Dutch presence in Southern Africa had first been established to provide a halfway station for ships making the six-month journey from Holland to the spice islands of the Far East. But over time a settlement consisting partly of adventurers and partly of refugees from Europe's devastating religious conflicts had grown at the seemingly uninhabited Cape of Good Hope. These people did not see themselves as temporary residents waiting for an opportune time to return to Europe, but had made the place their home. My father had gone there, like generations before him, looking for a better future, but once arrived, became a member of a distinct Dutch first-generation immigrant community.

Many of the pleasant social diversions my parents enjoyed in those years were directly related to this community and its close links with Holland. For instance, towards the end of 1938, KLM, with a well-deserved reputation for technical leadership in the realm of air transport, stirred the Dutch inhabitants of South Africa with national pride when it introduced the latest in aviation transport, the twin-engined DC-2, on the route from Amsterdam to Johannesburg. While its European rivals were still dutifully adhering to aircraft built by their respective domestic industries, KLM had decided to sever its historic links with Fokker and opted for the new all-metal planes now coming off the Douglas assembly line in the United States. This thirty-passenger silver bird offered the very latest in comfort and speed. The plane that inaugurated the new service was christened *de Reiger* (Heron), a name shared with one of the three Dutch East India Company ships that in 1652 had arrived at the Cape of Good Hope to establish the first European colony. A huge welcoming party had assembled at the Johannesburg airport to witness the inauguration of this improved link with Holland. My parents' excitement was increased by the anticipation of seeing an old friend, Jan Butner, himself a pilot, who had joined this historic flight. The plane arrived shortly after a late summer's thunderstorm had swept over the veld, leaving puddles on the grounds of the airfield; it emerged suddenly from among towering cumulus clouds and dropped down smoothly on the far end of the Johannesburg airfield. As the aircraft taxied to the terminal building where the crowd stood waiting, a brisk wind caused ladies' skirts to flap. After the plane had come to a halt, the welcoming party streamed onto the field to greet the passengers and crew emerging from the cabin.

Ambassador van Lennep had come all the way from Pretoria for this historic event and attempted, in a hopeless struggle with the gusting wind, to deliver a short welcoming address. He then took the flight captain into town to meet the leading figures of Dutch business interests. Those left behind were invited to board the plane and admire the comfortable rows of seats on either side of the central gangway and the instrument-laden flight deck. My parents had organized a small reception at Lombardy East for Jan Butner, who would board the return flight on the following day. The party was joined by Jan's friend Viruly, the co-pilot who later became a well-known author, as well as by Joost and Ruth Wesselo, a young Dutch couple who made their living in Johannesburg as professional photographers. A photograph of the occasion appeared in the *Nederlandse Post*, a newspaper circulating among the Dutch community of South Africa.

With such diversions, life could only be described as good. Fragrant flowers grew outside the bedroom window and an interesting assortment of wild animals gave periodic reminders that, in spite of all the domestic comforts provided by our house, we still lived in a wild land. Giant lizards, two to three feet long, required occasional attention from the garden boy armed with his rake. More serious was a cobra invasion; one once made its way into the house, startling my mother as she was doing her hair in front of the mirror. She noticed a tickling on her legs, looked down and stared into the hypnotic eyes of a large poisonous snake. She kicked and screamed, and the snake went flying over the slippery bedroom floor. Within seconds the garden boy appeared with his rake and dispatched the snake to the ever-after. He well knew the habits of snakes, since he had spent his childhood in a mud hut in Zululand; cobras travelled in pairs, and therefore the cobra's mate was somewhere in the garden. He went out to look for the mate, which he duly found among the shrubs, and so he dealt with the second threat.

But this existence was idyllic only in a superficial way. Below the pleasant, social surface there were rumblings of discontent within the country. It was a bit like the earthquakes that frequently affected Johannesburg and other gold-mining towns like Roodepoort or Germiston. When deep below the ground the wooden mine props and remaining rock pillars in the mined-out areas could no longer withstand the weight of the overlying rock mass, a gentle tremor would rattle teacups in the kitchen cupboards of the overlying suburbs, as the mine roof and floor suddenly converged. No one was alarmed, for this was a normal, almost daily, occurrence. Occasionally a chasm would open up in one of the Johannesburg streets, where the mine workings had come too close to the surface. This nuisance required patching to permit resumption of traffic; the civic authorities had become rather good at this. Yet, with reflection, one knew that the geological forces at work deep down below the ground were tremendous, and one could only hope that the miners themselves were at a safe distance from this area of subsidence and that no one got hurt.

The bitter memories of the Boer War, Lord Kitchener's internment of Boer women and children in concentration camps and his policy of farmhouse burning, were still fresh in survivors' minds. The Peace of Vereeniging of 1902 had resulted in humiliation and hardship for the defeated party; it was flawed in the eyes of the vanquished and could be characterized as an ominous foreshadowing of the disastrous peace negotiations of Versailles in 1919. Hubris is seldom far away when victory seems absolute.

And yet in a way, the Boer resentment was curious. The Boers had lost the war but won the peace, a truth that eluded them owing to their enormous propensity to quarrel among themselves. The main lasting impact of the war had been the creation of the Union of South Africa from the two former British colonies, the Cape and Natal, and from two former Boer republics, the Transvaal and the Orange Free State. Soon thereafter, in 1910, South Africa became a self-governing dominion with universal white male suffrage, its democratic credentials on par with other Western democracies of that period. More than sixty percent of the electorate was Afrikaner, and it was their kinsmen who dominated the new Union Parliament from the start. But the Boer War had left the Afrikaner population deeply divided into three distinct groups: those who wanted to encourage the adaptation by Afrikaner society to the economic and social changes sweeping the world; those who were prepared to collaborate with the British, provided traditional Afrikaner culture could be protected; and those who sought to turn the clock back, undo the Boer War, and send packing the British and the mine bosses who were blamed for starting the war.

For the time being, governance of the land was dominated by political interests dedicated to forging a new relationship between the English and Afrikaner communities. The "Fusion Ministry" was a coalition of two distinct political parties, each led by an Afrikaans Boer War hero. The Prime Minister, General James Barry Munnik Hertzog, better known as "JBM" Hertzog, leader of the Nationalist party, drew his electoral support from predominantly rural Afrikaners, preoccupied with their cultural identity, which they sought to protect under the umbrella of the British Crown and Commonwealth. The other side of the Fusion Ministry was led by General Jan Christiaan Smuts, who headed the South Africa Party. He drew electoral support from the urban areas and their educated Afrikaners, as well as from their predominantly English-speaking inhabitants. The lingering charisma Smuts and Hertzog possessed provided them with grudging support from their Afrikaner constituents, thus enabling them to pursue progressive policies that seemed to play into the hands of the industrialists. One source of formal opposition was a tiny "Dominion Party," suspicious of each sign of increased independence from Westminster. More worrisome was the vehemently anti-British opposition group formed around the personality of Dr. Daniel F. Malan, a Dutch Reformed Church preacher hell-bent on undoing the outcome of the Boer War. Malan employed rhetoric and a simple, clear vision for the future that looked to a romanticized past for guidance. He also had close links with *Die Burger*, a Cape Town

Afrikaans language daily broadsheet that was far from shy in expressing outspoken anti-British attitudes.

The years immediately preceding the outbreak of World War II fell under the dark shadow of another historical event, the commemoration of the Great Trek. In 1837, independently minded Calvinist Afrikaans farmers opted to escape the unwelcome restrictions imposed on them in the Cape and Natal colonies by the British colonial government, or simply sought land that they could call their own. They packed their families and belongings into *ossewa* (ox wagons) pulled by a span of oxen, and headed north to establish their own Utopia in the largely empty plains of the highveld. There they founded the Orange Free State and the Transvaal Republic, and decreed that all towns should have a main street wide enough to permit an *ossewa* to turn around. They referred to themselves as *Voortrekkers*, and many towns in South Africa to this day have a main street called Voortrekker Street.

To commemorate the centenary of this event, a magnificent monument was to be built outside Pretoria, the nation's capital. On December 16, 1938, the cornerstone was laid; this occasion had been preceded by a huge replay of the "Great Trek," with wagons coming from every part of South Africa, complete with men and women decked out in quaint period costumes. My parents drove to Pretoria to witness some of these festivities; the women were dressed in long calico dresses and wore white poke bonnets, while the gentlemen paraded around under their broad-rimmed hats and sported bushy beards. The air was thick with smoke from huge *braais* (barbecues) and there were plenty of folk-dancing displays. But aside from this jovial scene, my parents could not help noticing the disturbing underlying political machinations that gave the entire event a sinister twist.

Malan and his ultra-Nationalists had managed to hijack the event by imposing rigid control over the political credentials of those conducting the ceremony. The government had agreed to finance much of the construction of this huge monument, but its leaders were banned from attending in an official capacity. General Hertzog, the Prime Minister, withdrew himself to his *plaas*, and General Smuts, the Attorney General and Deputy Prime Minister, attended, but only as a simple Afrikaans citizen. They had been excommunicated for failure to be properly republican. The event coincided with the founding of a secret Afrikaner society, the Ossewa Brandwag. The term *brandwag* could be interpreted as "sentry." The Ossewa Brandwag leader, Dr. Johannes van Rensburg, had acquired a great admiration for the purposeful direction German society had taken since 1933, and he made it clear that his aim was to establish an authoritarian one-party state.[4] Underlying all of this was the widespread fear of the time: the spread of Bolshevism.

---

4. *Eastern Province Herald,* May 29, 1942.

Thus the upheavals far to the north, from well beyond the crocodile-infested Limpopo River, even beyond the lands inhabited by the dark-skinned people of Africa, were having a profound impact on life in South Africa. The arrival on the German electoral scene of Adolf Hitler had supplied fresh fuel to the smouldering embers of the Boer War; Hitler's decisive action, undoing the perceived injustices of the Versailles treaty, found a sympathetic response in South Africa, where a number of Afrikaners were agitating to undo the perceived injustices they had suffered, and in both cases Britain was portrayed as the aggressor.

Hitler's demand for the return of the former German colonies, among them South West Africa (today's Namibia), stoked these fires further; SWA, as the latter colony was commonly referred to, had been mandated to South Africa in trusteeship by the terms of the Versailles Treaty. Hitler's rhetoric of German victimhood, widely broadcast via radio Zeesen, had elicited a sympathetic response from the South African government, allowing new German settlers to arrive in SWA—not only augmenting the existing colony, but incidentally bringing along with them Nazi propaganda and enthusiasm for paramilitary organizations, and moving South Africa out of the British and into the German sphere of interest. By April 1939, German agitation in SWA had reached such a pitch that General Smuts had to send three hundred troops to put down a rebellion, a *putsch*. The difficulties were not just in South West Africa; there were as well open hostilities between pro-Nazi and anti-Nazi demonstrators in Johannesburg itself. Suddenly Hitler's recent machinations in Europe, the infamous *Kristalnacht* of November 1938 and his callous treatment of Czechoslovakia the previous month, took on an alarming local dimension, with South West Africa becoming a portal for the threat of German domination.

With so much controversy, there was a need just to carry on living. In a country as empty as South Africa, it was relatively easy to do this and to escape the nasty political conflicts, which in any case were confined to the cities; out on the veld, in Lombardy East, life remained peaceful.

Emmy and Edu

By early 1939, my parents could once more resume the adventurous trips they had enjoyed before my arrival. The quintessential South African experience was a visit to the Kruger National Park on the eastern border of the Transvaal. Juf had no interest whatsoever in wilderness expeditions and preferred to remain at home to look after the baby. Gus Giesler, a friend, had suggested a trip to the game reserve for the August bank holiday, when the bushveld trees were bare, permitting good game spotting, and the risk of malaria was absent. He had offered seats in his newly acquired Ford sedan to another recently arrived immigrant couple, Edu and Emmy, who had just become engaged. Little did my parents know at the time how our future lives would become intertwined. My parents were keen to join the party and accommodation was arranged at Pretorius Kop, one of the park rest camps.

On Thursday evening the party assembled in Lombardy East to begin the night-long journey to the park gate. Before departure there had been time to meet the new trip-mates. Edu was an easy-going, jovial party man employed as a sales representative by Philips, the Dutch electrical firm. He was tall and thin as a beanstalk; he had a perennial smile on a face strongly marked by a prominent aquiline nose, and a voice that regularly broke like that of a teenage boy. His fiancé, Emmy, was a cheerful dark-haired schoolteacher recently arrived from Holland; she gave the impression of being strict in the classroom of the private institution where she gave French lessons. The two men, my father and Edu, and the two women, my mother and Emmy, soon discovered that they had much in common and were instinctively drawn to one another. The two men had both disappointed their fathers by failing to pursue academic studies at Delft, the technical university, and both were extremely sociable. Both women had graduated from the gymnasium (Dutch high school providing a classical education), but had seen no merit in going to university, preferring a quick road to economic independence away from a restrictive family environment.

Before departing they made last-minute checks to ensure that the canvas water bags were properly filled and attached to the car antennae, and that the spare tires were in good order. They then said goodbye to Juf and set off on the road eastwards from Germiston and along the neighbouring gold-mining towns, Boksburg and Springs. Here the gravel highway passed through a landscape that harboured only vast farms, barely able to provide subsistence on the arid land; asphalt roads were rarely encountered and then only in towns. Bridges across rivers were equally rare, the usual stream crossing consisting of a concrete causeway flanked by low concrete pillars to mark the inundated roadway, when the stream was in spate—these were tricky crossings to make at night. At Waterval Boven, a sleepy farming town, the road began its long descent over an escarpment from the highveld to the lowveld. In the lowveld the countryside was dotted with Swazi *kraals*, clusters of three or four round mud huts with conical thatched roofs, with only the embers of dying fires marking their existence at night. The landscape was wild and untamed. Shortly before dawn the party arrived at the park gate, a largely symbolic structure that served to mark an otherwise invisible line through the bush.

After spending an entire Friday slowly driving through the park along its narrow, sandy bushveld roads, ever on the lookout for lions and other less common forms of game, they made their way to Pretorius Kop, arriving just before sunset and the closure of the camp gate. Here a night's shelter was provided for the party in *rondavels*, the round, thatch-roofed huts modelled after the local native dwellings, though more substantially built. Since there were no electric lights in the camp, they had to hurry to get the barbecue pits going before dusk had given way to night; after that, the only light available was from candles or the hissing spirit lamps, enough illumination to consume the meal of *boerewors* (farmer's sausage) and *mielies* (sweet corn) washed down with beer. As darkness descended, animal and bird noises filled the air with magical and mysterious sounds, interrupting the low voices of the holidaymakers as they drank their coffee by the light of the dying embers. The moon rose late that night, but when it finally shone it cast a wondrous soft white light over the roofs of the *rondavels* and the broad canopies of the camp's acacia trees.

Far away to the north, in Europe, relentless War once again was on the move, destined to upset our idyllic life; on September 1, 1939, Hitler's armies invaded Poland. It was this event, and Smuts's subsequent successful but highly controversial parliamentary plea for a declaration of war on Germany, that propelled him into the role of Prime Minister and caused his ally, the aged General Hertzog, to retire from politics to his *plaas*. At the same time this development undermined Smuts's own support among the Afrikaner voters, while the smashing of Poland made further hostilities inevitable.

On December 16, 1939, South African society nevertheless set about celebrating Dingaan's Day with its usual enthusiasm. This national holiday commemorated a Boer victory over a huge Zulu *impi* (warrior) attack at the battle of Blood River of 1838, and conveniently initiated the annual Christmas holiday season. Since Dingaan's Day fell on a Saturday that year, schools and many businesses took the Friday off. For many it was a time to head to Durban and the Indian Ocean beaches along the Natal coast. For my parents it was an opportune time to explore the Natal mountains, the Drakensberg. Here, along the western border of Natal province, the escarpment that marked the eastern edge of the high interior plateau took on dramatic proportions, where the grass-covered slopes abutted against the base of a towering wall of ochre sandstone, which was overlaid by a thick tier of dark purple-grey basalt cliffs. At Mont Aux Sources, these cliffs formed a majestic amphitheatre. From the hostel, one could wander along narrow footpaths through land covered with tall waving grasses and up and down the valley of the sparkling Tugela River and its tributaries. An immense solitude reigned here, broken only by the cries of the birds.

They returned after a one-week stay, bubbling with enthusiasm. My mother tried to describe to Juf the grandeur of the setting.

"The hostel is set below a huge amphitheatre, you know, high cliffs in a great arc. You can have no idea how beautiful the setting is."

"Is it not dangerous—won't they fall down?"

"Oh no, we walked on the footpaths and had picnics by mountain streams," my mother added.

"Are there no snakes?"

"We didn't see any, but they warned us to be careful with rock climbing: when you reach up to a rocky ledge there is always a risk of putting your hands on a puff adder sunning itself," then adding hastily, "but we did not do that."

"Did you not see the snake skin in the cave, where we saw the Bushman's paintings?" my father asked.[5]

"No, but those paintings were beautiful—they seemed so fresh, as though the Bushmen had only just made them. And the view from that cave was breathtaking—I am sure we could see the Indian Ocean."

"No Wil, that's impossible; the coast is almost a hundred miles away."

"That was a nice *braai* the hostel organized on the banks of the Tugela river, wasn't it? I hope the photos turn out."

"I just wish the roads could be made better. That stretch through the Free State, this side of Bethlehem, was terrible."

"Oh, Juf, something funny happened on that road—"

"Wil—," there was a note of concern in my father's voice, but my mother, unperturbed, carried on. "Bou was driving, trying to avoid the corrugations, when we caught up with a native riding a bicycle. He must have been drunk, because he was weaving all over the road. There was a lot of sand on the road as well—" she giggled, "and—"

"Wil, Wil—"

"Bou suddenly had to swerve to avoid the *kaffir*, and turned left, off the road and went straight through the fence of a Free State farm. When we came to a stop on the veld, we discovered that not a single strand of barbed wire was broken—some had gone over the roof and some under the wheels, but the drunk *munti* was pedalling twice as fast, raising a cloud of dust," she laughed.

"No flat tires—just some scratches on the paint," my father added reassuringly.

"How did you get back to the road?"

"It took a while to find a good stick to help lift the wire. By the time we were back on the road the native was gone."

Thus life continued into 1940 much as it had ended in 1939. Early in the new year another Dutch acquaintance made an appearance at our house: Jacob (Jaap) Nunez, a Jewish Dutch journalist and a good friend of my maternal grandfather, came on a brief visit to South Africa. It was the last we saw of him:

---

5. The Bushmen were hunters, also called the San people. Formerly widespread throughout Africa, today they inhabit only the Kalahari desert.

two years later he was arrested by the Gestapo as a resistance fighter and interned in Auschwitz.

War's Echo in South Africa

As far as we were concerned the Second World War began on May 10, 1940, with the dreadful news that Holland had been invaded. For the Norwegians and Danes, hell began on April 6, 1940. Historians, on the other hand, will argue that the war really began on September 1, 1939, when Hitler's Panzer divisions crossed the Polish border and his Luftwaffe rained destruction on Warsaw; the following intervening period was referred to by many as the "phoney war." However, for the Spanish, the war had only just ended, and for the Chinese it was the fourth year of suffering. It is all a matter of perspective.

In South Africa, the vicious political furor that was sparked by the invasion of Holland was extraordinary; it seemed to have injected the ongoing simmering domestic conflict with an explosive power. My father became worried that the Boer War would be resumed, a perfectly understandable fear given the venom with which the English and Afrikaans media attacked one another. The real conflict lay almost entirely within the Afrikaner community and its perpetual obsession with its soul and sense of destiny. The Afrikaans media levelled its most virulent attacks on its kinsmen and leaders, who had "sold out" to the British and were now supporting calls for active intervention to thwart the ambitions of Hitler.

One correspondent, writing from London in the English press, noted, "It may now be regarded as an incontestable fact that the Germans are in a most desperate mood and are prepared to violate every moral law in order to extricate themselves from their dreadful and unenviable position and make a gambler's reckless throw for final victory."[6] On the same page the paper dismissed the "old excuse" given by the Germans that all they were doing was "protecting Dutch and Belgian neutrality." The Cape Town daily, *Die Burger,* gave these events a different spin by describing the military invasion as a situation involving "diplomatic discussions" between the Netherlands and Germany. That this form of diplomacy was accompanied by paratrooper landings and bombardment of Amsterdam's Schiphol airport was not mentioned.

The *Johannesburg Star* sought to explain the internal divisions within the Afrikaner community; it correlated contrasting South African attitudes towards Hitler with exposure to, or isolation from, "foreign" and therefore "enlightened" ideas. *Die Burger's* editorial writer found this most offensive and

6. *Cape Argus,* City Late edition, May 10, 1940.

concluded that in the eyes of the *Star* "someone who has not visited a British university is an inferior creature." The paper, a staunch mouthpiece for the political aims of Malan and his ultra-nationalist "malanite" clique, saw in these European developments a rhetorical opportunity to demonstrate the traitorous behaviour of Smuts, the Afrikaner with a degree from Cambridge.

On Saturday, May 11, Malan was ready to strike. That edition of *Die Burger* quoted in full the speech made on the previous day by General Smuts, who had referred to the Netherlands soil as "holy" because so many of his fellow citizens had Dutch ancestry. In a lengthy editorial the newspaper attacked the sentiments expressed by Smuts under the heading, *"Nederland en Suid Afrika."* Its opening sentence said it all: "The sympathy of the entire *Afrikaanse volk,* who themselves have experienced the might of an all-powerful country, is extended to each and every small nation that becomes the victim of aggression from a superpower..." But then, using rhetorical gymnastics, the paper asked, "Who was the aggressor and who the victim?" *Die Burger's* sympathies clearly lay with Hitler. A number of days later, angry letters began to appear on the editor's desk from such prominent Afrikaner intellectuals as the poet W. E. G. Louw, who on May 14 complained, "One wonders how the leading Afrikaans daily in this country, in judging this matter, could not even for one day rise above the disputes of our domestic politics."

My parents concluded that the Dutch immigrant community had become a catalyst for the deep-seated hostilities within the South African body politic. At the same time their concerns were drawn to the strife in Holland. From the moment news of the German invasion arrived, Dutch consulates had, according to the papers, been "overwhelmed by telephone calls and visitors, announcing a spontaneous outpouring of patriotic support and concern on the part of the large Dutch immigrant community in South Africa."[7] On Monday, May 13, the Dutch embassy posted media notices calling for meetings of Dutch nationals to be held in cities where there were consular offices, including Johannesburg, Cape Town, Pretoria, Bloemfontein and Durban.

Years later, my father ruefully recounted the subsequent events. He had gone to Johannesburg, where the town hall meeting room had been booked for the occasion; the response on the Rand had been enthusiastic, filling the room to capacity, a response that perhaps was assisted by optimistic front-line reports of German setbacks. The commercial attaché, J. M. Donker, presided over the packed assembly from a podium, having as a backdrop the Queen's portrait swathed in red, white and blue banners. After a rousing rendition of the *Wilhelmus* (the Dutch national anthem) and a threefold "Long live the Queen," he updated them on the situation in the Netherlands. Donker assured his audience that "although the German army has made significant territorial gains,

---

7. *Cape Argus*, special edition, May 10, 1940, p. 11.

it was now meeting with firm resistance." He elaborated this claim by asserting that "flooding the lowlands is having the desired impact, and counterattacks behind the advancing German front are effective. Germany is experiencing greater resistance than it had nine months earlier in its conquest of Poland."[8] Spontaneous offers of help, to enlist with the Dutch defensive forces and repel the German invader, flooded the podium. A number of people had even expressed an interest in going "home" at their own expense to join the Dutch army. Donker told his audience that further statements and instructions for making good the offers of assistance could be expected shortly from the Dutch legation in Pretoria.

These spontaneous offers of help from Dutch nationals now residing in South Africa caught the attention of Dirk de Geer, the Dutch Prime Minister, but before de Geer and his colleagues had had a chance to discuss the matter, the Netherlands surrendered. The bombing attack on Rotterdam, and threats of more such attacks, had forced the Dutch government to capitulate a mere five days after the onset of hostilities. The Royal family managed to flee across the English Channel, accompanied by the Prime Minister and his Cabinet. Queen Wilhelmina was now a refugee, as had been Kaiser Wilhelm, who, only twenty years earlier, had come knocking on her door for shelter from the winds of change then blowing through Germany. She had now offered him a seat on her airplane to England, but he had decided to take his chances with his countrymen. The historian Liddell Hart concludes that the Dutch defences had not succumbed to an overwhelming military might as initially thought, for the German attack on the Low Countries had been under-resourced, though daring. Dutch resistance was stronger than anticipated and Hitler therefore ordered the bombing of Rhine bridges near Rotterdam and the city itself. A detailed account of the Rotterdam bombing raid did not appear in the South African papers until almost a week later, when the Dutch embassy issued a statement claiming the deaths of one hundred thousand citizens, an estimate later reduced to nine hundred.

Wholesale bombardment of civilian targets was a relatively new and frightening development made possible by advances in aviation technology. This tactic had first been used in 1937 at the Basque village of Guernica during the Spanish civil war, but had been refined to devastating effect during the bombing of Warsaw in the first two weeks of September 1939. Arial bombardment offered an effective new technique for spreading terror among the civilian population, thus hastening the surrender of defending forces.

The Netherlands behind enemy lines! This unexpected and calamitous turn of events stunned the Dutch community in South Africa, creating consternation

---

8. *Cape Argus*, May 14, 1940, p. 5.

and confusion. At a stroke, we were cut off from family and friends. The spontaneous emotional offers from Dutch expatriates to return home to defend the fatherland now took on an entirely new perspective: the need to form, on foreign soil, a liberating army. However, such a course of action seemed unrealistic to many. With Hitler controlling the European coastline, from the northern tip of Norway to the English Channel, and with the German Wehrmacht on an apparently unstoppable march south through Belgium towards France, a permanent change in political geography appeared to be in the making. What's more, my parents and their friends had become stateless within the astonishing space of one week.

Almost immediately, world attention was drawn to the remnants of the considerable Dutch empire. Media pundits argued that Germany was in no position to seek dominion over the Netherlands East Indies, or NEI, as these territories were commonly referred to. References were made to United States and Japanese concerns about maintaining the status quo in the Far East, but the significance of this arcane diplomatic utterance was not understood in South Africa, and why should it have been? The NEI was so very far away.

Other distressing ramifications of the calamity that had befallen the Netherlands was of more immediate concern to employees of the numerous affiliates of Dutch companies in South Africa. Were they now working for companies fully controlled by the Germans? The Dutch government-in-exile, that is to say the Queen and her Cabinet, immediately passed legislation to prevent the overseas mercantile wealth of the Netherlands from legally falling into German hands. Fortunately, a list of companies registered in the Netherlands, along with the addresses of their corporate headquarters, had been quickly tracked down in the Dutch legation in London. The government enacted the transfer of official headquarters from addresses in occupied Netherlands to new addresses in various colonial territories; in addition, the huge Dutch merchant marine fleet was placed under the control of shipping agents in New York. This move was designed to facilitate the efforts of President Franklin Delano Roosevelt to dispense material assistance to Britain and France, but without formally abandoning the American policy of neutrality, a move for which his electorate was not yet ready. The enormous overseas wealth of the Netherlands could now be placed at the disposal of Britain and France in the struggle against Germany.

It was not just the Dutch who were motivated to enlist. The invasion of the Netherlands also assisted General Smuts in his year-old attempt to bolster the South African armed forces. By Wednesday, May 15, the English press could crow about a "rush to enlist on the Rand," but the rift within the Afrikaans community continued to grow. The *verkramptes* (diehards), who had until recently found succour in the idea of Germany's being declared the enemy of Britain and therefore "their friend," were continuing to have difficulty reconciling recent developments in the Netherlands with this pro-German position.

Whereas the South African media had been mesmerized by the fall of the Netherlands, other countries did not share this perspective. In Canada and the United States, it was the fate of Belgium that received the most attention, since it was on Belgian soil that so many Canadian and American soldiers had fought and perished during the First World War; the fate of the Netherlands barely merited mention. *Time* magazine, the American weekly publication, raised the unpleasant prospect of the rapid German advance meaning "that contrary to earlier American assumptions of World War Two [a name recently coined] being a protracted affair, it would end sooner rather than later, leaving the United States to face on its own two threatening naval powers: Germany across the Atlantic and Japan across the Pacific."[9] It pointed out, as an afterthought, the strategic value of the NEI and Malaya (today part of the federation of Malaysia), both now falling under increased Japanese influence. The United States was to an overwhelming degree dependent on rubber and tin imports from these two countries. Snidely, the magazine referred to the Anglo-Dutch "Tincoons" who ran a tin cartel.

The perspective from Australia was different again; her closest neighbour was the NEI, and events in the Netherlands had therefore been followed with great interest. Australia saw Singapore and the British presence there as the main guarantor of her own security, but the NEI provided Australia with a vital telegraph and air transportation link to Singapore. The Australian media now dwelt on the fact that Japan, an ally of Germany, was heavily dependent on the NEI for vital raw materials, and they expressed fear of a Japanese occupation of the Indonesian islands.

On Monday, May 17, *Jonkheer* W. F. van Lennep, the Dutch Minister in Pretoria, published a formal request for Dutch nationals of military age to support the liberation of the Netherlands, but from a puzzling location:

> Dutch reservists and those liable for military service who voluntarily wish to proceed to the Netherlands Indies at the expense of the Netherlands Indies government, should immediately make their intentions clear by means of a telegram to the Dutch embassy in Pretoria. All volunteers will receive a telegram from the Netherlands embassy, which can be presented to the South African railways to procure a second class rail ticket to Durban. Volunteers should present themselves at the Dutch consulate in Durban on or before May 22.[10]

---

9. *Time*, May 13, 1940.

10. *Cape Argus*, May 17, 1940.

The call to arms gave volunteers only five days' notice to resign from their jobs, dispose of personal effects, and head east. However, many of those who had earlier announced their willingness to enter military service had expressed a clear preference for service in Europe rather than the Far East. The notice moreover begged the question of how service in the army of the NEI was relevant to the liberation of Holland. There was no hint of an explanation. The significance of the word *liable* in the news announcement was not immediately clear either. It smacked of conscription, but how could a government-in-exile, no longer assisted by its police and judicial system, enforce any of its laws, when the citizens to whom the directive was addressed resided in sovereign foreign lands? Similar calls went out to the extensive Dutch immigrant communities in the United States and Canada; since the United States was neutral, Dutch subjects resident in that country were encouraged to enlist in Canadian army units, which were then being expanded.

The South African government immediately signalled its support for the Dutch position by providing £100,000 to help its "cousins"—that is to say the exiled Queen and her Cabinet, now housed in London. General Smuts hoped that this step would help strengthen the support for his policy of Imperial solidarity amongst the moderates of the Afrikaner community. He also obtained, despite vehement opposition from Malan and even jeers at British impotence, parliamentary approval to form a volunteer army, the *rooi lussies* (red strap) brigade; distinctive vermillion shoulder tabs distinguished this military unit from others that were mandated only for defence or for internal security. These tabs were intended to make it quite clear that service away from South African soil was entirely voluntary; conscription of South African citizens was ruled out.

The Dutch government was pressuring its Dutch nationals in South Africa to enlist in the army and unseat a powerful entrenched tyrant, while the South African political landscape was being shattered by riot and rebellion. It was a trying time for my parents and the rest of the Dutch community: what should they do? The daily flood of messages directed to the embassy in Pretoria offering voluntary military assistance had waned significantly as the grim truth of the rapidly evolving military situation in Europe sank in. Instead of offers of help, questions were now raised: Can my passport be renewed? Can I still register my newborn child as a Dutch citizen or will he become a German citizen? How can I contact my sick and dying parents? I am here on vacation, but I must return to my business, what should I do?

The questions were endless. The embassy staff therefore arranged more meetings, and this time both of my parents attended. My father had long ago placed his Dutch financial affairs in the hands of kindly old Mr. Jurrema, my grandfather's former accountant, but the instructions he had telegraphed a few days before might no longer be workable: my father, too, had urgent questions. The meeting was well attended, but the atmosphere had become sombre and the Dutch national anthem now, more than ever, sounded like a funeral dirge; events of the last few days had dimmed the patriotic fervour of the group.

Donker, stiffly formal, deeply conscious of the gravity of the situation, once more presided. He opened the proceedings by providing a short recapitulation of the events of the past week, and then discussed the question of rebuilding the armed forces. He assured his audience that the government would be able to muster the financial resources to equip and train recruits; besides, units of the Dutch army were still active in the field, on the islands and lowlands in the Scheldt estuary straddling the Belgian border. All Dutch men had in the past served in the military, so training would not be a huge concern. Holland's new ally, Great Britain, had promised assistance, and discussions were also under way with the Canadian government for the establishment of training facilities in that country (where Her Royal Highness Princess Juliana and Prince Bernhard were now accommodated).

The mention of the young royal couple prompted a spontaneous "Long live the Princess!" Donker was gratified to note that the Dutch living in South Africa had retained their affection and loyalty for the Royal Household. The commercial attaché then went out of his way to cast perspective on the situation. He optimistically noted that the disaster in the Netherlands was unlike those in other European countries, since the Netherlands was still engaged in a battle to recover its lands and was in action alongside that of the British. Fortunately, most of the proud Dutch navy, comprising three light cruisers, eight destroyers and twenty-three submarines along with smaller craft, was at the time stationed in the NEI. A few naval units stationed at den Helder, the North Sea naval base, had also managed to escape. The attaché implied with these assertions that Britain and France placed great store in the Dutch contribution to the struggle with Hitler. This brought him finally to the question of military service, and with a touch of pomposity he announced, "The Crown would react favourably to its nationals choosing to serve in the South African volunteer corps, but in due course expected to form a Dutch military unit in England."[11] Then he drew attention to the Netherlands East Indies. "May I remind you that the Netherlands may have fallen, but its overseas possessions are still in effect under the Netherlands Crown and the defence of those territories needs strengthening."

The request for volunteers to join the Royal Netherlands Indies Army—the KNIL, as it was referred to in Dutch—was curious. What was the threat? Donker explained that Japan might be tempted to benefit from the fall of the Netherlands by taking over Dutch colonies, as it had at the end of the First

11. *Cape Argus*, May 18, 1940.

World War by taking over German colonies. "It would have to take the Indies by force, but that would obviously be difficult," he added. He promised that "reinforcement of the defence of the Indies would ensure a powerful deterrent, a manifestation of resolute determination." The KNIL was clearly a force to be reckoned with; it had a 150-year history of maintaining the peace throughout this immense island empire. The Dutch Crown had moreover been assured of support by the considerable British and French forces in the area.

Laughter broke out in the audience at the thought of a Japanese attack on the NEI; such an attack was really preposterous. My parents admitted as much in later discussions. Who could take the Japanese seriously? They were a strange, inscrutable people with slant eyes that would prevent serious marksmanship and their bandy legs would prevent decent performance as infantrymen, while their technology was all imitation. The Western world in 1940 still seemed invincible and the military goings-on in the East were likened to pantomime productions, or a real-life version of *The Mikado*. Everybody had conveniently forgotten the Russo-Japanese War of 1905, when an Asian country had inflicted a humiliating defeat on a Western power.

Someone asked whether the KNIL could perhaps be used to liberate the Netherlands. This question was not answered; the worthy attaché undoubtedly had other pressing issues on his mind: would he be able to continue functioning in his present capacity now that the Dutch taxpayers were supporting the ambitions of Hitler? He might have to find more modest accommodation. He might also have been privy to the discussion that had recentl' taken place around this topic within the Dutch Cabinet in London: the idea of liberating the Netherlands with Indonesian troops had been dismissed on the grounds that political difficulties could be anticipated should such a liberating force contain too many brown faces.

Donkers concluded his plea for manpower assistance by once again cautiously raising the spectre of conscription. He commented that such steps were of course not expected to be required, given the enthusiasm so far displayed for coming to the assistance of the fatherland, and he left the issue at that. It was late and he was sure everyone needed to go home to ponder the terrible situation and the appropriate response for Her Majesty's loyal subjects. He closed the proceedings by stating that all other questions should be submitted in writing to the Dutch legation in Pretoria, and answers would be provided at the earliest opportunity.

Few among the Dutch community stopped to contemplate or question the credibility of Donkers' assuring the continued sovereignty of a colony *sans* an imperial power. The absurdity residing in that assurance was left unexplored by the South African press. The Netherlands had become embroiled in war, but the Indies were peaceful: there the Imperial tricolour still proudly snapped in the wind on the flagpoles. However, the Dutch Cabinet in London was divided over the prospects for reversing the disaster of May 15. The Prime Minister, de Geer, was so skeptical of this possibility that he tendered his resignation to Queen Wilhelmina later that summer and returned surreptitiously to German-occupied Holland.

After the meeting, my parents were invited by Gus Giesler, with whom they had shared the occasional trip to Kruger National Park, to come to his house for drinks and a discussion with other compatriots. Gus, a coffee merchant, and his wife Liesbeth had become well established in South Africa and had just moved into a lovely new home on Corlett Drive in one of the better, leafy northern suburbs of Johannesburg. About twenty guests had turned up, including Edu, his fiancé Emmy, and our photographer friends, Joost and Ruth Wesselo.

My father mentioned his reaction to recent events. "Wil and I are thinking about going to the Indies."

"How can you do that? You mean to take the whole family?"

"Oh yes."

"But why? What difference will it make?"

"The government seems to think it will make a difference; they may also get heavy-handed."

"D'you really think they will impose conscription?"

"They might, and besides, the place does not sound so bad."

"I think it's a good idea," said Ruth with enthusiasm. "I know Bandoeng well: it's a great place—in fact, the whole of Java's wonderful."

"Were you born there?"

"No, but I grew up in Bandoeng. It has a wonderful climate."

"Is that where you met Joost?"

"No, we met in Holland."

"And how about you and Ruth?" This question was directed at Joost.

"I would be disqualified on medical grounds," he answered. "I had polio as a child."

"That's true," responded Ruth. It was not easy to surmise whether this statement was uttered with a sense of relief or of disappointment at not being able to come to the aid of the Queen.

"I'm going," said Edu. "I've already made arrangements and told my landlady."

"What about Emmy?"

"She'll come later, after the school term has finished in July."

"What about Philips; will they grant you leave of absence?"

"They say they can't. Eindhoven won't permit it."

Everyone knew that Eindhoven was synonymous with the headquarters of the Philips electronics firm, for which Edu was working, but Eindhoven was now in German hands. Edu, however, did not appear to be overly worried about his financial future; besides, he had family in the NEI. They were well-heeled and he was sure that he would be fine. He turned to my father, asking, "Well, van Oort, so you're coming too?"

"We've thought about it, but we must sell our house."

"Man, are you crazy, and what about Juf?"

This comment came from another gentleman, our next door neighbour, Dirk Schoenzetter, who had come to know Juf quite well since they moved into their house the previous year. My father turned to him and replied that she was willing to go as well.

"I was surprised that no one at the meeting raised the possibility of Germany invading South Africa. South West Africa is a lot closer to Bremen than the Indies."

"Yes, and the Brownshirts over in Windhoek would gladly give a helping hand!"

"The malanites[12] would roll out the red carpet, all the way to Pretoria!"

"D'you think that de Geer will be able to impose conscription here in South Africa?"

"Jannie Smuts seems keen enough to push South Africa into the war, but I don't see him ever imposing conscription."

My father then began to discuss practical matters. Joost would help, and so would our neighbour, Mr. Schoenzetter. The furniture would have to be stored, temporary accommodation found and passage booked. He needed to appoint a Power of Attorney to look after the property sale. "We need to find a good home for Pittah," my mother anxiously added. "I'll miss that dog."

"Have you looked for passage?" Edu asked. "I've already got a berth on the *Boissevain*. It's leaving Durban next week."

"My brother is the captain on that ship," Ruth interjected. "Please give him my love."

"The consul suggested a KPM[13] ship," my father responded. "They provide a regular service between Durban and Batavia."

"Those are cargo boats," Mr. Schoenzetter objected. "Wouldn't it be better for Juf to travel on a proper passenger liner like the *Boissevain?*"

"No, Juf is quite happy with the idea," said my mother. "Besides, I think that a cargo boat will be fun."

Most of those present opted to stay behind in South Africa.

That same day, South African media attention had focused on a thorny issue: granting leave of absence to Dutch nationals who had offered their services to the Dutch government. The South African government had issued instructions to South African businesses to be lenient with South African nationals

---

12. Dr. Malan's political followers.

13. *Koninklijke Pakket Maatschappij*, based in Batavia, Java.

volunteering for overseas duty, and General Smuts had also gone out of his way to urge employers to be equally lenient with the Dutch volunteers. My father had already discussed his ideas with his employer, the municipality of Roodepoort, but he viewed the situation differently; he let them know that he planned to make a permanent move out of the country, and that it was unlikely that he would be back, since the entire household was going with him to the Indies, as the Netherlands East Indies was commonly referred to. The municipality raised no objection to his leaving at short notice.

For many others, who only saw the move to the Indies as a temporary arrangement and were working for Dutch affiliates, it was difficult to obtain unpaid leave. Regardless of the paper transfers made by the Dutch Cabinet in London, their head offices remained firmly in German hands, adding complexity to their situation. Enough news had leaked out of Poland, Norway and Denmark to make it clear that the Third Reich would impose its will on its new subject peoples with ruthless brutality. Should news reach the head offices in the Netherlands that Dutch subsidiaries in an enemy country were lending material assistance to the Allied cause, terrible reprisals might fall on colleagues, friends and family. From this perspective the hasty transfer by the government-in-exile of the addresses of Dutch corporate head offices was meaningless.[14]

To the best of my knowledge, ours was a unique contribution: the shipment of an entire household across the Indian Ocean, in response to the call to arms, was unmatched by anyone else. Our fellow travellers were mainly single men, some to be followed at a later date by sweethearts or families.

The trip to the Indies for a family of four, including bulky antique furniture, would be expensive and it was certain that the NEI government would not be prepared to reimburse us fully. My parents arranged to leave our household effects temporarily in the care of friends, with the request that they organize shipment to the Indies at a later date. First of all, a proper new home, suitable for accommodating the antique furniture, would have to be acquired. A KPM freighter was due to arrive in Durban from the Orient on or around May 24, and could accommodate twenty passengers. We would have to present ourselves in Durban on May 25.

In the meantime, the first party got under way. The train carrying Edu and forty-one compatriots left Johannesburg's Park Station on the evening of Tuesday, May 21. The next morning's *Johannesburg Star* covered the exciting event, accompanied by a photograph showing Edu waving farewell from a train window (figure 4).[15]

---

14. Conscription for the Dutch army was implemented three months later and enforced by the South African government (de Jong, *Het Koninkrijk der Nederlanden in de Tweede Wereldoorlog*, Vol. 9, 696).

15. *Rand Daily Mail*, May 22, 1940.

Jonkheer van Lennep, representing the Queen, was able to confirm that 130 volunteers had so far answered the call to the colours (out of an estimated total of 2,300 eligible for military service).[16] Upon the arrival of the first group in Durban the party, now decked out with patriotic red, white and blue ribbons, was welcomed by F. Heckman, the Dutch consul and trade commissioner. Some made clear their love for the house of Orange by wearing orange ribbons as well. Most of the volunteers had come from the Rand, although about forty had also arrived from Cape Town. Two days later, this first contingent of volunteers set sail from Durban on the *Boissevain*.

That same day, Guderian's Panzer division completed its remarkable dash for the Belgian coast, reaching le Crotoy, a channel port at the mouth of the river Somme. It soon became obvious that England, too, might now come under attack, while a curtain of silence had descended over the Netherlands. That Rotterdam had suffered horrendous damage was known, but what about the fate of loved ones? Bets, my father's widowed sister-in-law, lived in Rotterdam: had she been hurt? Was she still alive? There was no way of finding out. Nor was there a way of informing friends and relatives in the Netherlands that we were on the move to the East. It was several years before my grandfather and grandmother found out through a Red Cross notice that we had left South Africa.

During this eventful month, the media began to puzzle over another development: the United States Congress had been apprised of the possibility of developing a new explosive device thousands of times more powerful than TNT. It was noted that recent experiments in Germany, France and Denmark had demonstrated the possibility of splitting the uranium atom using slow-moving neutrons. This exercise was thought to create an energy profit of 6,000,000,000. What that meant was not explained, but it sounded impressive. The key challenge was to isolate the particular isotope of uranium in sufficient quantities to initiate the process. A team of scientists from the University of Minnesota and the General Electric laboratory had managed to isolate small amounts of this form of uranium using a time-consuming technique. University scientists, interviewed by the press earlier in the month, therefore admitted that such a development was theoretically possible but impractical. Now word had

---

16. A total of 170 volunteers turned up to serve in the Indies (de Jong, *Het Koninkrijk der Nederlanden in de Tweede Wereld Oorlog*, Vol. 9, 704).

come from a Swedish laboratory that a newly invented thermal diffusion method of separating U235 from U238 was eleven thousand times faster.[17]

---

17. *Time*, May 20, 1940.

2. TO JAVA

Our adventure began on May 25, 1940, a mere twelve days after the Dutch ambassador had broadcast his emotional appeal for help. That night the train taking us to Durban began its journey from Johannesburg's Park Station.

During the previous few days my father had resigned from his job, found a buyer for our house, arranged for all the furniture to be sold or placed in temporary storage with friends, and delivered Pittah, the dog, to its new owners. The sale of the house had been arranged remarkably quickly because the dwelling, in a rural setting, was charming and the price was reasonable; legal details of the transaction would be completed after our departure. We spent our last night in the home of friends, who took us to the station the next afternoon. There was a brief, minor panic when my father discovered that his passport was no longer valid, but the Dutch embassy was most helpful in arranging an extension at short notice. He had obtained passage on the KPM freighter, *Straat Soenda*, named after the Sunda Strait separating Java from Sumatra; it was scheduled to arrive in Durban that night. All we could take with us on the journey were three cabin trunks, because accommodation on the *Straat Soenda* would be tight.

Such a prompt response to the ambassador's request from a family of four would have been unthinkable if my father had not had the good fortune of possessing a healthy bank account. The cost of the journey would, according to the ambassador, be partly refunded by a grateful NEI government and we could expect immediate reimbursement upon arrival, reflecting such a spontaneous and selfless offer of service in defence of the State and its citizens, including those currently dwelling under the menacing might of the Third Reich. The day before our departure the Dutch minister plenipotentiary, Jonkheer W. F. van Lennep, had publicly commended the volunteers for their patriotism, making clear his understanding of the anxieties created by having to leave loved ones or property behind. The departure from the station was, like the one a few days earlier, a festive affair, enlivened by an army of well-wishers once again outnumbering the volunteers. The call to action had released a wave of goodwill and there was a sense of adventure in the air. We left in good spirits.

The journey from Johannesburg to Durban would take all night, and to make the trip easier my father had booked a compartment for the four of us. While we retired to the dining car for an evening meal, the train staff converted our seats to four bunks. Winter was approaching, and as we departed from the city and gathered speed en route to Heidelberg, a trail of smoke and steam drifted over the land through the rapidly cooling evening air. Outside the carriage window, a bleak, almost treeless, dry eastern Transvaal landscape slipped past, marked off by endless lines of barbed wire fencing stretching into the distance. The flatness of the landscape was relieved by the rocky outline of the Suikerbosrand, a mountainous ridge silhouetted against the western horizon. There followed a brief but spectacular South African roseate highveld sunset, casting lengthening shadows from the occasional bluegums, and with the *koppies* silhouetted against the crimson and vermillion sky. By the time after-dinner coffee was served, the sun had completely set, and over the dark highveld landscape an immense moonless autumn sky sparkled with the Milky Way.

We returned to our compartment through the chilly corridors of the gently rocking train to find the carriage heating turned on, making our compartment cozy. After Heidelberg, where the train took on additional passengers, we stopped at the farming town of Standerton, perhaps for another passenger, and then proceeded to the Natal border at Volksrus, another farming community. Thereafter we slept to the clickety-clack of the train wheels.

The next morning, the train steward knocked on our carriage door with the cheery news that tea and biscuits awaited us. Someone raised the window blind to reveal the dawning of a subtropical morning. During the night the train had descended several thousand feet from the highveld and down the length of the province of Natal. We crossed the Tugela River near Colenso and finally, beyond Pietermaritzburg, entered the Valley of the Thousand Hills, wonderful rolling grassland now coloured pale yellow and ochre under the early morning sun. It was dotted here and there with clusters of grey-coloured, grass-domed Zulu huts along the narrow streams. This was the final leg of the journey, the approach to Durban.

With the help of a fleet of taxis, our party made its way to the harbour, where the *Straat Soenda* lay awaiting its passengers. At our arrival, captain Koning came to the head of the gangway leading up from the quay and welcomed us on board. An assistant, acting as purser, gave us details of our accommodation. That a woman in her late sixties was part of the passenger list came as a surprise, but Juf assured him that she was more than fit for the journey.

That same evening our ship slipped its moorings from the Durban quayside and was nudged into the middle of the harbour by two tugs before being towed towards the open waters of the Indian Ocean. At the end of the breakwater stood a lighthouse, which, with its beam of light, periodically swept the city, the coastal dunes and the Durban beach and its pier. Here the ship let go of the tugs and gradually gathered speed, setting a course northeastwards along the

Natal coast towards Portuguese Lourenço Marques (today's Maputo). That evening we enjoyed a festive meal in the small dining room. It was an occasion to get to know our fellow travellers and the ship's officers, and the party was aided by liberal quantities of duty-free wine and brandy.

The *Straat Soenda* was one of a fleet of ships operated by the KPM. Since 1935 three of this company's ships had been engaged in a regular service between Saigon and Durban, carrying sugar, rubber and hardwoods from Southeast Asia to South Africa and returning with coal. Our vessel, having joined the fleet in the previous year, was modern and comfortable and could muster a respectable speed of sixteen knots. It provided quality accommodation for seventeen *salon* passengers. Since our party numbered nineteen, two passengers had to be lodged with the crew. I was the only child on board, and aside from my mother and Juf, there was only one other female passenger.

During our first breakfast at sea, my father suggested that a photograph be taken of the party (figure 5). Later that morning we all assembled on the bow of the ship. Juf, standing next to my mother, held me in her arms, while the breeze caught my shock of curly blonde hair. Bessie Fischer stood next to her while her husband John crouched behind a ship's bollard. My father took the photograph and therefore is not in the picture.

Our family of four survived, though for Juf it was a close call; she was almost sixty-seven years old when the photograph was taken. Rein Jessurun was, at age thirty-six, the oldest male travelling companion. He had left his wife and son behind in Cape Town with the intention that they would n due course follow him to the Indies. Since he had the most extensive military experience, he had become the unofficial spokesman for our group. Jessurun would suffer wounding, escape imprisonment, continue to fight, survive the war, achieve the rank of Lieutenant Colonel, and be decorated for bravery at the highest level, only to perish in an accident in May 1949, while attempting to re-establish peace under the Dutch Crown. He was buried in the military cemetery at Menteng Rulo, near Cilitan on Java. Justinus Jacob Leonard Heldring had come to South Africa to study at Stellenbosch University, where he had excelled in swimming. Alas! his swimming skills would not prevent him from drowning four years later. And then there was Helmer Siegers. He had had high hopes of serving his fatherland in a military capacity, but upon arriving in the NEI found that there was no immediate need for his services, and returned to his banking profession in Bandoeng. In due course he was called up, joined the KNIL as a sergeant, saw brief action, was imprisoned and later packed on a ship destined for Japan as a slave labourer. Owing to Allied naval action he ended up in Singapore in Changi Prison. He survived, and after the war returned to South Africa, where he married and rejoined civilian life.

It was a jolly group photograph, which miraculously survived the war.[1] The optimism betrayed by the faces in it are testimony to the enthusiasm of another era. Spirits among the crew and passengers were high and the voyage was for us an adventure, with stopovers to pick up and drop off mail and cargo at such fascinating Indian Ocean ports as Lourenço Marques, Tamatave on Madagascar, and French colonial island possessions Reunion and Mauritius. Between those journey-breaks our days were spent rolling at a leisurely pace over the iridescent blue of the Indian Ocean, which was marked here and there by swarms of Portuguese man-of-war (large jellyfish with their white "sails"). The journey was about five thousand nautical miles, requiring two weeks.

Unbeknownst to us, our departure from Durban had prompted a curious diplomatic exchange on the other side of the world. The Dutch minister plenipotentiary in Tokyo, Major General J. C. Pabst, was summoned to the Japanese Ministry of External Affairs, where he was confronted with evidence drawn from South African newspaper reports that military recruits were heading towards the NEI. A program of military build-up there was not considered by the Japanese government to be consistent with either the policy of neutrality avowed by the Netherlands government-in-exile, nor American assurances of status quo maintenance. The notion of Japan, with its army of almost a million men, describing the movement of two hundred volunteers as a "military build-up" was faintly ridiculous.

Related concerns troubled His Excellency, the Honourable Tjarda van Starckenborgh Stachouwer, Governor General of the NEI, and our future protector on behalf of Her Royal Highness Queen Wilhelmina. On June 4, 1940, when we were more than halfway to our destination, he shared his growing anxieties with the Minister of Colonial Affairs in London in a telegram, using the following clipped but unmistakably clear language:

> From reliable, secret sources, suspicions are repeatedly aroused by Reuter reports about large credit transactions with America, the landing of allied troops in the Dutch West Indies, rumours of departure of disguised military personnel from Singapore to the Indies, the recruitment of volunteer servicemen in South Africa, and formal joining of the Indies to the Sterling block. In addition, tendentious reporting by the Japanese consul is thought to be aimed at disturbing the good relations, and provision of encouragement to radical political groups in Japan for the demand of an altered foreign policy with respect to the Netherlands Indies.[2]

---

1. The identity of our other travelling companions and their fate is unknown.
2. Manning, *Documenten betreffende de buitenlandse politiek van Nederland*, Nr. 63.

The telegram reveals the nervous state of senior government personnel in the NEI, where the activities of the sizeable Japanese community were being closely observed. His Excellency was at the same time resisting overtures from the Australian government to seek closer military co-operation.[3] Japanese trade was important for the Indonesian economy, and economic welfare helped keep Indonesian nationalist aspirations under control. He was in a bind.

The situation was, moreover, confusing because it was not clear who called the shots in Japan; a substantial portion of young Japanese military officers were impatient with the slow, convoluted steps of diplomacy and demanded action. The war in China was not going smoothly, partly because of interference from the United States, while Japan's immense navy lay under-utilized. With Britain and France preoccupied with their own survival, the odds in terms of naval supremacy in the western Pacific had now shifted in Japan's favour. But America's ambivalent position was a key source of concern to Japan: the United States was not formally allied to China, but its sympathies lay with the Chinese in their struggle against an invading Japanese army. Claire Chennault, a former US air force major, had for instance taken on the task of training Chinese pilots.

Japanese relations with the Netherlands had for centuries been exceptionally stable, and the NEI had become the source of key raw materials for Japan's rapidly industrializing economy, especially oil. Ambiguity had now crept into this situation: on the one hand the Netherlands was under seemingly permanent German control, while a Dutch government-in-exile, allied with Britain, was reinforcing its military presence in the NEI, and courting favour with the United States, a thorn in Japan's side ever since 1853 and the days of Commander Perry's "most extraordinary confrontation in modern history."[4] It was extraordinary because the "black American ships" lying at anchor in Edo Bay were able, through advanced American military technology, to force the feudal Tokugawa regime to open Japan to American trade. This latest development, with the Netherlands seeking closer ties with the United States, could only be interpreted as another anti-Japanese move by a Western nation.

The ship's company, on its gentle journey to the Indies, had reason enough to be oblivious to unfolding world events: there were no newspapers, while shortwave radio reception was erratic; our isolation was glorious. During the day, the sky was blue, while the burning tropical sun was rendered tolerable by the cool, refreshing breeze caused by the ship's eastward progress. The sea was often glassy, its smooth surface broken only by the ship's bow lazily rising and falling and periodically throwing up a foamy spray. Sometimes there were clouds in the sky, but rarely did we have rain. Every now and then porpoises leapt ahead of the ship's bow, breaching the water's surface with effortless ease

---

3. Herman Bussemaker, personal communication.

4. Buruma, *Inventing Japan*.

and seemingly guiding our course; overhead, the wind sang a haunting melody through the rigging of the ship's masts and the antennae wires. To port or starboard, schools of flying fish frequently left the water, skimming skilfully and with utmost grace over the ship's bow wave, escaping the pursuit of sharks and dolphins below the surface. At night, the ship's wake would light up with the phosphorescence of plankton, causing a streak of light along the ship's hull, where the steel plates and rivets brushed past the foaming water, and leaving astern a white glowing trail stretching to the horizon. Overhead in the early evening a breathtaking display of stars dominated the nighttime sky, until the silver sickle of a waning moon rose over the ship's bow and the eastern horizon: it was magic.

On the afternoon of June 10 we passed through the ship's namesake, the Sunda Strait. Captain Koning pointed out the low, barely visible silhouette of Krakatoa,[5] the volcanic island that at the turn of the century had blown up with such a spectacular and devastating explosion that it could be heard up to three thousand miles away. A small plume of white steam rose from its middle, "from *Anak* Krakatoa, the child of Krakatoa," he explained. Late that night, we reached the roads of Batavia and dropped anchor to await daybreak and the arrival of a pilot and tugboat to take us into the harbour.

Tandjong Priok, June 11, 1940

The next morning the loud, clanking rattle of the anchor chain being winched up penetrated the dining room while we were enjoying our breakfast of coffee, boiled eggs, ham, cheese and freshly baked bread. Soon we again felt the gentle throb of the engines, the welcome rhythm of the ship once more under way. From the deck, a low profile of land punctuated by palm trees was visible on the horizon. While we were eating, a small boat had delivered the pilot and was now, as it were, leading the way towards land; ahead of us a tug lay patiently waiting. When we drew alongside, deckhands passed a huge ship's hawser down for the Indonesian tug crew to make fast to a towing bollard. Once more the ship's engines fell silent, as the tug slowly pulled our vessel into the sheltered waters of Tandjong Priok, the modern harbour for the city of Batavia. Another tug came, with a large, ragged cushion made of woven rope over its bow, resembling a huge bushy moustache. The tug placed its cushioned bow against the ship's side and nudged us to a quay, where a welcoming party stood assembled under the morning sun. It was a splendid sight—a military band with instruments that glistened gold and silver drawn up beside some bemedalled officers, all smartly turned out in white tropical uniforms, contrasting with the

---

5. On maps denoted *Krakatau.*

colourful dresses of two ladies armed with huge bouquets of flowers. The moment the ship's hawsers were looped over the bollards, the band struck up a nostalgic Boer War tune, "Sarie Marais," creating a wild wave of enthusiasm among the ship's company, and soon the band found itself accompanying an impromptu choir on board the ship.

When the ship had been secured and a gangplank arranged, we descended onto the quay and listened attentively to a stirring but brief welcoming address by Lieutenant Colonel W. C. A. Sol, describing himself as the local area commander and introducing his companions, his wife, Colonel W. Schilling, commander of the First Infantry Regiment and Colonel Schilling's daughter. He commended us for our spontaneous gesture, anticipating that we would serve proudly and valiantly under the Netherlands' flag and, if necessary, defend the Netherlands East Indies. One or two Indonesian workmen, helping with the heavy work of securing hawsers and manhandling the gangway, listened with rapt attention; they were clearly impressed by the pomp of this ceremony.

Jessurun, our unofficial leader, took the opportunity to express our collective gratitude for the extremely warm and friendly reception. Thereupon Sol's wife and her young companion distributed orange rosettes to the party. A final touch was the offer of a bouquet of red, white and blue flowers to my mother and Bessie Fischer, though unfortunately, through an oversight, not to Juf. Juf was not offended, but rather relieved, for she was unpretentious and would have been embarrassed by such a gesture from the wife and daughter of senior military officers. Someone began to shout "Hurrah for the Queen," and everyone joined in for two more "hurrahs." This paved the way for a rendition of the stately but grave Netherlands' national anthem. Fortunately, given the limited patience of the youngest member of the party in the oppressively hot, humid atmosphere under a merciless equatorial sun, this homage to patriotism was restricted to three stanzas.[6]

A couple of reporters wanting to interview the "South Africans" then arrived. This caused awkwardness on the part of Colonel Schilling, for there was a brief but unmistakeably unpleasant exchange of words between him and one of the journalists. Jessurun, on the other hand, expressed surprise at discovering that we were the first arrivals from South Africa. One of the officers present was able to explain that the *Boissevain*, carrying Edu and his companions, had taken a more circuitous route, stopping at larger Indian Ocean ports, such as Mombasa and Bombay. While some pictures were being taken, a comment about "pushy reporters" escaped from the mouth of Lieutenant Colonel Sol, perhaps an ominous forewarning of things to come.

In later interviews, the authorities were pained to admit to the reporters that whereas single young men were welcome to join the local army units, older

---

6. Out of a total of fifteen stanzas.

married couples with children and grannies were perhaps unsuited to the needs of the Indies. Clearly the diplomats in Pretoria had somehow failed to convey to the Dutch community in South Africa the needs and expectations of the Indies. Perhaps their patriotic emotions had overwhelmed an objective assessment of military requirements. The subsequent news that the government's promise to pay for the ocean trip had (unknown to us) been qualified by the need to have such payments approved in advance by Dutch authorities in South Africa imparted a further source of discomfort. We were nevertheless assured that the issue would be resolved (passage had been prepaid for other groups of volunteers departing at a later date). The promise of payments, alas, was never made good, not because of bureaucratic stumbling blocks, but because war and defeat twenty-one months later terminated the approval process before all the necessary steps had been taken.

After dealing with very brief customs and immigration formalities, the newly arrived "South Africans," as we were called, eagerly bought copies of local newspapers at the harbour kiosk to bring themselves up to date on events in Europe. The news was not good—the mighty French army had lost several divisions and the French government had fled Paris, while the outlook for Britain was gloomy.

But suddenly the news-starved readers were also exposed to a different slant on matters of public concern. The NEI had been in a state of growing tension for some time, the main concern being internal security. During the previous three decades, growth of the Indonesian nationalist movement had precipitated periodic bouts of political unrest, invariably met by heavy-handed government repression. The sudden disappearance of the Netherlands had added constitutional confusion to the complex social and political framework of the NEI, but only a small number of people interested in these matters grasped this last fact; for the majority in all races nothing of significance had changed.

For years, the Indonesians had been overawed by the apparent unity of purpose of the Dutch community, contrasting dramatically with the tribal rivalries of their own complex feudal society. Dutch had become the official language of governance and together with an efficient administrative and legal system had (with the help of a small but well-disciplined army) imposed a form of unity on three thousand inhabited islands.

This had impressed the indigenous groups, more than ever aware of their Asian shortcomings, particularly in the light of the ongoing "fraternal" conflict between China and Japan and perhaps their not being familiar with European history. Leyden-educated Sutan Sjahrir, one of the more thoughtful Indonesian nationalists, at that time languishing in a prison under preventive detention as a "troublemaker," lamented that Indonesian "intellectuals" like himself were mostly merely individuals with a diploma or degree, and lacking the European propensity to become men of letters; their intellectual achievements were limited not by defective intellect but by lack of exposure to intellectual stimulus. To him the shortcomings of his fellow Indonesians were only too obvious.[7]

News of the invasion and capture of the Netherlands within the short space of a week, now broadcast throughout the archipelago by means of radio and newspapers, had suddenly revealed the Imperial Dutch power to be remarkably fragile, not only in a military sense, but also socially. The defeat by the Germans of what had been portrayed in the hysterical media as the "invincible Dutch army" was attributed to "fifth columnists" and traitors. "How the Teutonic barbarians misjudged the quality of the Netherlands army," proclaimed a special May 13, 1940, edition of the *Indische Courant & Soerabaiasch Handelsblad*, a daily from East Java. The subheading elaborated with the words, "in spite of months of military preparation, the effect of the German offensive was minimal." The *Bataviaasch Nieuwsblad* that same day assured its readers that "the German invasion had been beaten back." Two days later, the readership had to be informed that the Queen and her Cabinet had fled the country. The local Dutch press, reflecting the paranoia of its readership, could only rationalize such an abrupt change of fortunes by invoking the impact of traitors. With the collapse of the Netherlands' defences attributed to collaborators rather than to an imbalance in military capability, a demand for reprisals against persons who might play a similar role in the Indies became inevitable. The European population in the Indies had always been suspicious that the Netherlands' government had been too soft on dissent and had not appreciated the importance of a strong army in the colonies. Here, there was no debate about the importance of law and order, and a partial mobilization of the *Landstorm*, a militia unit, had been declared to emphasize this point. The main perceived danger lay within the country.

The subsequent and totally irrational witch hunt for "Nazi sympathizers" and "collaborators" was in full progress when we arrived in June 1940. Within days, some 2,400 men of German extraction or having suspected Nazi sympathies had been rounded up. With no investigation as to the level of threat posed by these neighbours and fellow citizens, they and a few German nationals were imprisoned on an island called *Onrust* (Restlessness). A number of declared NSB[8] members were interned at Fort van den Bosch, at Ngawi in eastern Java. They probably distinguished themselves from the remainder of the Dutch population only by being more open about the need to keep nationalist movements under firm (European) control.

Let me clarify that the term "nationalist" here had a different meaning from that held in South Africa or in Europe. In South Africa and Europe

---

7. Sjahrir, *Indonesische Overpeinzingen.*

8. Nationaal Socialistisch Bond—a political organization espousing Nazi policies.

"nationalism" suggested preoccupation with the defence of a culture, preferably by an authoritarian government; in an extreme case it involved protecting a race, especially the superior Teutonic one, against degenerate foreign influences. In Indonesia it reflected a quest by a few well-educated members of the huge indigenous population for equality with the European colonial masters. A somewhat related sentiment was nurtured by equally well-educated Dutch compatriots who regarded the Indies as their ancestral home and viewed arbitrary rule by a distant government as irksome; for them there was a need for devolution of political power.

The unpleasant situation recently created with the wholesale arrest of "Nazis" was aggravated by the fact that the internment facilities, intended originally for indigenous "troublemakers," left much to be desired.[9] These reprisals caused the Dutch ambassador in Washington to address a note to his superiors in London wherein he complained about the adverse impact they were having on Roosevelt's attempts to swing American public opinion over to a declaration of war on Germany.[10] The matter was so indefensible that the Governor General, undoubtedly prodded by the Minister of Colonial Affairs in London, felt compelled to gingerly take "corrective action," a delicate task given the ease with which his European countrymen on Java, excited by events in far-away Europe, classified fellow citizens as "unpatriotic." The witch hunt revealed the Dutch community to be as fragmented as the traditional Indonesian community had always been, and thus the myth of European superiority, widely held by educated Indonesians, was abruptly undermined. However, aside from the handful of Indonesian nationalists among their number, no one else in the population as yet saw it that way—the well of interracial goodwill on Java was deep.

What did my parents make of it? The controversy in the press sounded very similar to what had gone on in South Africa, but here the threat from Germany seemed remote and the recent lengthy boat journey had driven home the isolation of this island from any source of external threats. The real source of concern precipitated by the outbreak of war in Europe was the economy, and this issue got much attention in the media. Germany had been an important source of manufactured goods, but this trade had now ceased. With indications of Japanese sympathy for the German cause, the very important raw material export trade with Japan had become a source of anxiety—would Japan now secure for Germany a back door access to strategic raw materials? The logistical challenge such a trade would involve was not discussed, but the concern was

---

9. Zwaan, *Nederlands Indië 1940–1946: Gouvernementeel Intermezzo 1940–1942.*

10. Ambassador H. F. L. K. van Vredenburgh, letter to Minister of Colonial Affairs, London, May 15, 1940, in Manning and Kersten, eds., *Documenten betreffende de Buitenlandse Politiek van Nederland.*

heightened by Japan's declared intention, announced within ten days of the capitulation of the Netherlands, to increase its access to exports from the Indies, especially oil. Diplomatic discussions began promptly. Hubertus van Mook, Director of Economic Affairs, now dealing with the economic fallout of war, later described the situation:

> The Indies was at that moment a house that had lost part of its roof through a storm. Everyone was working sixteen hours per day in order to repair the roof, while Japan was banging on the front door to demand that the occupant hand over the keys and all the possessions.[11]

A key to maintaining internal peace was the ability of Dr. van Mook and his colleagues to keep the raw materials export–driven economy healthy. It was not just trade, but the entire monetary system that had come under strain now that the NEI guilder, suddenly severed from the Dutch guilder, was cast adrift and the first signs of inflation had been noticed. Suggestions made about redirecting Indonesian exports towards the United States sounded good on paper, but changing centuries-old trade patterns was not easily accomplished at short notice. Japan remained an important trading partner.

Any reference to a military threat from Japan was totally absent from the local newspapers, and the media devoted hardly any space to developments in Japan, let alone its protracted and vicious war in China. It was, to be fair, an awkward situation, given the importance of the trade with Japan and of the prominent Chinese population in the cities of Java. The distance separating the NEI from Japan was vast. Air travel with Japan had not yet been established, and ships of the Java-China-Japan Line required a full month to make the scheduled return journey between Soerabaja and Kobe.

In the Netherlands Indies' southern neighbour, Australia, some observers were not sleeping so soundly. The Australian historian, Manning Clark, noted that:

> Since the days of the defeat of the Russians by the Japanese in 1905, a few in Australia had predicted that the day would come when the Japanese would threaten the survival of European civilization in Australia. The Tanaka memorial of 1927, which put Australia on the list of areas to be conquered by Japan, the Japanese attack on Manchuria in 1931, and the police incidents in Shanghai un 1937, kept these fears alive.[12]

To this day it is unclear whether or not the memorial,[13] attributed to the belligerent Prime Minister Giichi Tanaka of that time, is an authentic document

---

11. Bijkerk, *De Laatste Landvoogd*, 26.
12. Clark, *A Short History of Australia*, 258.
13. An alleged long-term Japanese plan of conquest.

or was merely a Chinese forgery; this uncertainty is beside the point, as the historian Herbert Bix makes clear: "Starting around 1928 Hirohito and his reign became associated with the rediscovery of *hakko ichiu*, an expansionist belief that imparted new dynamism to Japanese nationalism."[14] Underpinning *hakko ichiu* was the widely held view that Japan "must grow or die." Religious concepts supported this. Since Emperor Hirohito was a deity, it followed that he had to be king of the entire world. Those peoples who did not see the inevitability of Japanese leadership according to this world view needed to undergo thought-training, if necessary by force. Any other ideologies, threatening to undermine the very foundation of Japanese society, would be fiercely resisted by the Emperor's army. The Tanaka document spelled out with chilling accuracy a program of Asian conquest that appeared to predict the trends of Japanese military activity between 1927 and 1940.

The editorial of the *Sydney Morning Herald* for June 11, 1940, the day we arrived in Tandjong Priok, discussed the possibility of a Japanese attack on Australia. The threat posed for the NEI was obviously greater and well known, because a lengthy article appearing in the April 22, 1917, issue of the *New York Times* had made clear the Japanese view, fortified by Japan's successful campaign against Russia twelve years earlier, that the NEI ought to be a Japanese colony, to be bought or taken by force. Why the Japanese threat got so little public attention in the Indies is a mystery.

When the welcoming ceremony on the Tandjong Priok quayside had ended, Colonel Schilling made a short speech explaining that our immediate destination would be Bandoeng, "for acclimatization and integration within the military structure," as he put it. "Before you go," he continued, "we have arranged a typical Indies welcome for you at the non-commissioned officer's mess hall—there you will be given a light lunch. A bus will take you there and your personal possessions will be sent to the station. Could you please ensure that your bags are all accounted for? We will distribute your travel warrants for the next stage of your journey after lunch." Turning to Captain Koning he added that the latter would also be welcome to attend the reception.

With this, Colonel Schilling signalled to a bus and truck, waiting at a respectful distance, to come closer. Our personal possessions had in the meantime been placed on the quay by Indonesian stevedores. Each item had been labelled with the first letter of our family names on a large sticker, allowing the stevedores to place our suitcases and cabin trunks in order. My mother went to check that our luggage was all accounted for under the *o*'s, while my father made sure that Juf's suitcase was indeed under the *e*'s, since her family name was Eisenberger. We got into the bus, which was stifling hot in spite of all its

---

14. Bix, *Hirohito and the Making of Modern Japan*, 201.

windows being wide open, and soon commenced our journey out of the dockyard, past railway tracks, sheds and oil storage tanks.

The drive into Batavia took about half an hour. At first the straight road led us through a rather dreary marshy landscape. A broad drainage ditch on one side of the road gave the landscape the semblance of being Holland's polders transferred into the tropics, with here and there a palm tree breaking the monotony of the flat horizon. We came to the outskirts of Batavia, a chaotic mixture of shacks, houses and shops, the latter festooned with oriental characters. There was a curious dissonance between the name of this sprawling city, a clear reference to a northern province of the once great Roman Empire, and the first impressions of this hot, humid, dusty and predominantly Chinese city.

The bus took a side road leading away from the sea, and eventually entered a more congenial part of town, where a mixture of every type of vehicle imaginable crowded the roadway. The traffic portrayed a stratified society with, at one extreme, elegant roadsters, the latest automotive products from the United States, Germany and Britain, driven by chauffeurs in snappy white uniforms, and at the other, half-naked men walking barefoot, their bodies glistening with perspiration and carrying goods in two baskets suspended from the ends of a long bamboo pole slung over their shoulders. There were carts piled high with tropical produce and hawkers selling snacks from handcarts on bicycle wheels. Here and there along the road were temporary stalls, where women were selling fruits, vegetables, cooked snacks, chickens, ducks, basket work and earthenware utensils. A stream of colourful humanity filled the sidewalks—native women in their sarongs, coolies with their grass hats, Indonesian gentlemen smartly turned out in Western suits, other men in loin cloths. The smells of charcoal fires and pungent spices wafted in through the open windows of the bus. Batavia looked like an extraordinarily cosmopolitan city, dominated by Dutch and Chinese architecture.

We arrived at an elegant, neoclassical, whitewashed building, set a little way back from a broad street, here canopied over by tall graceful trees. A short, broad flight of steps led up to a colonnaded portico with bamboo matting suspended from the ceiling to provide additional shade; there a soldier in smart tropical uniform was standing guard. An officer, awaiting our arrival, ushered us into the building and towards a large room hung with military memorabilia, because the Dutch East Indian Army had a long and illustrious history maintaining a *pax Neerlandica* on these islands. Under the watchful gaze of Queen Wilhelmina's austere regal bust, a long table had been set in anticipation of our arrival, but some men rushed off to find a provisional stool arrangement for the infant, since the non-commissioned officers' mess had not expected to cater to the needs of children. Soon a number of smiling *djongos* (waiters) appeared, in white robes and neatly folded head cloths, to serve the assembled party *nasi goreng*, a spicy fried rice dish. This was accompanied by copious quantities of ice-cold beer to wash down the *pedis* (hot, spicy) food. My parents thought it was delicious, though it was not to everyone's taste. The regimental band had followed us here and was entertaining us with the strains of popular dance tunes: it was a festive welcome. Our host, seated at the head of the table, pressed us to spare no time in seeking future enjoyment of a *rijst tafel* (rice table), an expansive "typically *Indies*" dinner. Best of all, he thought, was the sight of an almost endless queue of servants, dressed in ornate native costumes, bringing to the table every conceivable Indonesian delicacy.

"It sounds like Trimalchio's feast, if you ask me," my mother observed, thinking back to her Latin classes in gymnasium, when she and a couple of friends had secretly secured a copy of Petronius' racy text describing the decadent orgies of Imperial Rome. Later on we learned that the *rijst tafel* was a colonist's extravagant invention.

After lunch an officer announced instructions for the next stage of our journey: the trip to Bandoeng. "Please pick up your travel warrants at the front desk," he announced, pointing to an officer who had just then taken up a position by the exit. "That officer has made arrangements for conveying all of your personal belongings to Bandoeng, where you are expected to present yourselves at the military headquarters tomorrow morning at eight o'clock. *Bon voyage*, ladies and gentlemen."

"How long will the trip take?" someone asked.

"About four hours. You will take the 1:50 train—It's a nice trip," he added as an afterthought.

"What accommodation will we be able to find in Bandoeng?"

"There's a list of hotels and boarding houses among your papers. Each person has been issued a voucher to cover initial expenses, and you will also find five guilders to pay for the taxi fares and other incidental costs." This brought the party to a conclusion with, one must admit, a favourable impression of Dutch colonial administrative efficiency. Jessurun then stood up to thank Captain Koning of the *Straat Soenda* for his hospitality and we all got ready to leave. My father and John Fischer had decided that in their case a hotel was essential and the two approached the officer to seek help.

"Can you recommend a decent hotel in Bandoeng?" Fischer asked.

The sergeant major thought for a minute as he looked at us, and answered, "I would try the Savoy Homann, if I were you." He beckoned to see the documents we had been given and pulled out a booklet with photographs of hotels on its front cover. The booklet was called *Guide to the Netherlands Indies*, and under the section "Bandoeng" he pointed out the ad for the Savoy Homann. "It's new and not far from the station, on the Groote Postweg [the Great Postal Road]," he explained. "I'm sure you will enjoy Bandoeng. Its climate is most agreeable."

We followed the others onto the bus, which had become even hotter and more stifling, and the bus departed on its short journey to the railway station. Here my father and the other men lined up at the ticket office to exchange the travel warrants for second-class train tickets, and we made our way towards the station platform. The enthusiasm of the small party of travellers was such that the unbearable early afternoon temperature and humidity of the city were ignored, while the very purpose of our coming, to "strengthen the defences," was completely forgotten.

The short time waiting for the train allowed the travelling companions an opportunity to inspect the booklet that had been handed out. Fischer soon found the train timetable and was able to explain that the train journey would take only two and a half hours: this was the fast train, making only two stops. The booklet also carried other interesting information, including settling-in requirements for new arrivals, postal and telephone rates, city maps and some brief historical summaries, all written both in Dutch and English. It stated that Java, our new home, was the most populous and most richly endowed island of Indonesia, or "Nusantara," as it was once called. The archipelago, stretching from the northwest tip of Sumatra to New Guinea, included thousands of islands of unparalleled beauty. Lofty volcanic peaks towered above dense, lush tropical forests, and sheltered on their lower slopes and plains prolific agricultural enterprises, from rice paddies to sugar cane fields and vegetable plots. Frequent volcanic activity made the land especially fertile through a steady supply of minerals to the earth's surface. The islands were home to intelligent, creative and above all culturally diverse people. The archipelago was steeped in history and was fondly referred to by its inhabitants as the "land crowned by the rainbow." It was on Java, the crown jewel of this "Emerald Girdle," that the hugely successful Dutch commercial empire had been launched in 1596.

Soon the train, whose journey had started in "lower Batavia," the old town, drew into the station and we took up seats in the second-class carriage, while our luggage was loaded onto a goods wagon at the rear of the train. "Did you see the fourth-class carriage?" someone asked with a chuckle. "It's packed with people, but also chickens—I thought I even saw a goat."

A stranger standing on the platform near us overheard this and commented, "That is why it's called *klas kambing*—they call goats *kambing* over here."

As the train left the city, an exotic landscape began to unfold before our eyes. We passed distant *kampongs*, settlements where the indigenous people lived in houses with walls made from bamboo poles and woven bamboo matting and sheltered by *atap* (palm leaf) roofs. What a contrast this landscape formed to the land we had left behind. Whereas the Transvaal had consisted of wild and untamed scrubland wilderness, where the impact of human activity was jarring and isolated, Java appeared to be gentle, a land where humanity had evolved over the millennia in harmony with a vigorous, fecund nature. The pastel hues of the highveld, the distant purple hills, the ochre grasslands, the ubiquitous thorny acacia and the rusty rocks of our former home were now replaced by luxuriant greens of palms, gently swaying bamboo fronds, and here and there vivid splashes of vermilion on flame trees. The coastal landscape was mostly low-lying and flat. The teeming life on Java, where every acre of flat land was under artful cultivation, contrasted with the immense spaciousness and utter loneliness of the South African veld.

After about an hour the train made a brief stop in a smaller town called Tjikampek. Then the land became more undulating, and soon we made a second stop at a larger town called Poerwarkarta, a sort of regional centre, to judge by the large modern buildings. After leaving this centre, the train headed into more mountainous terrain and had to negotiate a tortuous path with several tight curves: here the slopes along the river banks were too steep for agriculture and were covered by dense rain forest, a seemingly impassable tangle of vines, air roots and weirdly shaped plants. But where the land sloped at a gentler angle, remarkable neatly terraced rice paddies outlined with geometrical precision the contours of the landscape. These marvels of agriculture shimmered green and blue in the sun and were tended by women who stood knee-deep in the water with their sarongs tucked up, planting or harvesting rice and shielded from the sun by broad conical hats made of thinly sliced, delicately woven bamboo. Occasionally we saw a man in a loin cloth working a plough pulled by a water buffalo through a paddy. According to the guidebook this bounteous land could provide several rice crops per year. Here and there was the more familiar sight of sugar cane fields, and everywhere tall coconut palm trees, often with gracefully curved stems, marked the edge of a narrow dirt road or a footpath between the rice paddies. Around the perimeter of each small *kampong* grew clumps of banana palms and papaya trees, the latter laden with oval fruit at various stages of ripening. Hunger seemed impossible in this land. In the shade of those trees, half-naked children smiled and waved, while chickens scratched in the dust. The landscape was enchanting.

We arrived in Bandoeng, on time at half past four, and a taxi took us to the Hotel Savoy Homann, which was fortunately able to offer two good rooms. Most of our travelling companions sought accommodation elsewhere because this hotel was reputed to be pricey. It had opened its doors only the previous year and boasted the very latest in comforts. Located in the heart of the city on a broad east–west thoroughfare, it was most convenient for an initial exploration of our new environment. My father was impressed by the architecture of the building, which was in an attractive art deco style that had also become very popular in the Netherlands. The four-storey building was for most of its length set back from the road, except for a wing at its eastern end that projected out towards the road. A tall tower stood beside the elegant entrance, providing a sort of homing beacon visible from most parts of the city. It was soon obvious that all of Bandoeng was immensely proud of this new edifice that gave the city such a distinctive, European character. So, on an upbeat note, we began our sojourn in the NEI, seeing nothing around us but the fabulous sights of an apparently peaceful and harmonious paradise.

The next day's newspapers provided prominent coverage of our arrival in Tandjong Priok. On the front page of the *Java Bode* appeared a photograph of John and Bessie Fischer with the caption, "It must have been encouraging for them to have been welcomed so warmly to *Indie*." The article drew attention to the fact that "South Africa was the only Allied country where Germans had not all been imprisoned." The curious composition of our party of volunteers had attracted comment as well—there were not just able-bodied young men, but also women, and even a child and a grandmother. The reporter noted how a curly-haired blonde two-year-old had caused amusement for the two ladies of the welcoming party, but discomfort for the two army officers, who had not been forewarned about the full details of our group and were ill-prepared to deal with the situation.

More interesting by far was the second article appearing on the same page; this clearly was the work of the editor, C. A. de Vries, a man fluent with the pen, equipped with a mind capable of lofty thoughts, but also a master of sarcasm. The article painted a somewhat more elaborate but imaginary picture of the welcoming ceremony for our party of nineteen. It referred to the imagined presence of the NIROM, the Netherlands Indies Broadcasting Service and the imagined recordings made of our arrival for broadcast throughout the Indies "that very night," including comments about the "love for our Queen." However this was all "fantasy," as the writer explained in his final paragraph:

> Please, honoured reader, make no attempt to listen tonight to such broadcasts; this entire report is based on fantasy. The only fact is that a KPM ship arrived bearing the first group of volunteers. The press had not been alerted, neither had the NIROM. And if we ourselves had not had access to information sources, we would still not know of this event. Then the Indies public might in due course have been informed by means of a government communiqué of this historic national event, an event that was ideal for stimulating patriotic fervour.[15]

The reader could not escape the clear message that the government had, as usual, displayed hopeless incompetence in stimulating the level of patriotic fervour that the times demanded.

---

15. *Java Bode,* June 11, 1940.

The editor should be forgiven, however, for being unaware of the nervousness his writing would cause the Dutch envoy in Japan, Major General J. C. Pabst, who would once again be summoned to the office of the Japanese Minister of Foreign Affairs in order to be reminded that the transfer to the Indies of Dutch nationals for military service was contrary to the avowed policy of strict neutrality and could be interpreted as having anti-Japanese intentions. Little did the editor know that the reluctance of the government to publicize the arrival of our handful of volunteers was deliberate, and that in the opinion of the Governor General, his Excellency Jonkheer Tjarda van Starckenborgh Stachouwer, people in glass houses should refrain from hurling stones. The editor, like everyone else in the Indies, had nothing but contempt for Japanese sabre-rattling.

The Governor General knew better; although denied direct contact with the Netherlands legation in Tokyo, he had his own local sources of intelligence and he was sensitive to the fact that the Japanese legation in Batavia paid the closest attention to all media reports—his task was not to shatter the illusion of our utter security.

That was the only occasion on which the flow of volunteers from South Africa found mention in the local media. After our brief moment in the limelight, we were discreetly ignored and forgotten by our countrymen. Well, not quite forgotten. Abdul H. Nasution, who years later rose to the rank of general in the Indonesian army, shortly after our arrival got his earliest military training at the Military Academy in Bandoeng, where he noted with surprise a "South African" contingent among his classmates.[16] At least a future Indonesian nationalist leader had taken note.

A week later, on Wednesday, June 19, the passenger liner *Boissevain* arrived in Tandjong Priok and Edu disembarked and sent a telegram to his sweetheart Emmy, still in South Africa. Also on board was Tony van Kempen, a former employee of the Holland Africa Line shipping company. In his case, volunteering for the KNIL (Royal Netherlands Indian Army) involved the unpleasant sacrifice of severed relations with his employer. Tony moreover had to press hard to find a suitable spot in the KNIL, since his military training in the Netherlands had been inconsistent with the Indies' needs. He finally got acceptance as a fighter pilot and completed his training when the war broke out. He survived internment and after the war returned to South Africa. In July another ship, the passenger liner *Tegelberg*, brought a third group of volunteers. In all some two hundred Dutch citizens made the journey from South Africa to Indonesia. A more exact number of such Dutch patriots is, alas, not available.

---

16. Beynon, *Verboden voor Honden en Inlanders.*

After breakfast and a quick read of the newspaper, my father reported to the KNIL headquarters and was promptly appointed to a position with the Engineering Branch. His office was located on the Borneoweg,[17] where he reported to Colonel F. F. Blok and was offered the position of "Supervising Architect." His immediate task would be to supervise the design and subsequent construction of the KMA (*Koninklijke Militaire Akademie* or Royal Military Academy). This project had become essential, since the traditional military training establishment at Breda in the Netherlands was now in German hands; in this way the NEI had gained de facto independence from the fatherland and would now have to look after its own defence and security needs.

Since the threat of invasion was unthinkable, the country could afford to be mesmerized by developments in Europe. An extraordinary fundraising campaign had just been initiated all over the archipelago to collect money for Spitfires, to assist with the defence of Britain and thus pave the way for the liberation of Holland. Enhancing the military capability of the Indies by expanding its own tiny air force was not considered a pressing need. Nevertheless, for my father, being placed in charge of such an important project was flattering and ensured a good start to our new life in the Indies.

Having sorted out the employment situation permitted my parents to find their social feet; they both knew people who had in previous years moved from Holland to the Indies, and tracking them down became an immediate preoccupation. The hotel receptionist was able to assist by lending my mother a copy of the *Bandoeng Address Boek*, an annual publication issued by the Bandoeng municipal authorities. She quickly found a reference to Mr. Mandersloot, living in a nearby district called Tjioemboeloeit (now Ciumbuluit); she thought that this might perhaps be the person my father had known from his Sunday school.

"Where is Tjioemboeloeit?" she asked.

The hotel receptionist produced a colourful map of Bandoeng and pointed to a built-up area some distance out of town, to the north.

"It's a nice district," she said. "It lies on the slopes of the Tangkuban Perahu."

"What's that?"

"Oh, that's our volcano," the receptionist answered airily before adding, "It's still active, you know, but not very." She liked being able to impress foreign visitors with her casual attitude towards such nearby sources of destructive power. People from Holland, ("the old country") were always going on about the destructive potential of the sea; well, here on Java "we had molten rock and fire."

---

17. The Dutch word *weg* means "road" or "way."

The address book also had an entry for Mr. Weeda, a name my mother had recalled from her childhood days, when her father and Mr. Weeda sometimes played chess—this might well be that man's son, Jan, who had emigrated to the Indies. His name was linked to a rubber plantation called Argasari, but it was not identified on the Bandoeng map. The receptionist did not know where the plantation might be, for there were so many in the district; she suggested that my mother should contact the plantation office by telephone. After waiting patiently for a telephone line to be free, my mother succeeded in leaving a message requesting that Mr. Weeda call us. That evening my father managed to phone Mr. Mandersloot and found to his joy that it was indeed his old acquaintance. This was an enormous stroke of luck, because years before my father had lost contact with this school friend and only through rumour had heard that he might be in Bandoeng. Mr. Mandersloot immediately invited us to stay with them. "Let us welcome you to Bandoeng, the Paris of Java," he added with a hint of pride. My father explained that he had not come by himself, but had a wife, child and granny in tow. "That'll be no problem," came the response. He and his wife were childless, and had ample room for accommodating a family of four. My father accepted the generous offer gratefully. Daily contact with established residents would facilitate the process of settling down in a strange new environment; besides, the hotel was indeed expensive.

He then started to sort out his financial situation, organizing the transfer of the remainder of his savings and the proceeds of the house sale from South Africa to Java. This would take time, for the economic difficulties of the thirties had left a legacy of convoluted and lengthy international financial procedures. The bank manager was confident that the problems could soon be solved, given the steps being taken to transfer the NEI guilder into the Sterling Block and thereby rendering the two currencies freely exchangeable. A bank loan for buying a car could be arranged immediately, however, and by Thursday my father had purchased a new Opel sedan. It was a German vehicle and therefore perhaps no longer so easily supplied with spare parts, but there were few alternatives. The car salesman moreover had assured my father that future spare parts requirements would be of no concern, since the car was manufactured by the huge General Motors Corporation and America was not at war with Germany. The car gave us the freedom to explore our surroundings and find suitable rental accommodation. Our relocation from the rather grim gold mining town of Germiston, in South Africa, to a city calling itself the "Paris of Java" began to look like a very positive step, and the future looked bright.

Tjioemboeloeit

Two days after arriving in Bandoeng, we left the hotel and found our way to the Mandersloot residence in Tjioemboeloeit. Since we anticipated a short sojourn there, we left some of our large cabin trunks in the hotel for safekeeping. The Mandersloot residence was easy to find, being located on one of two main roads leading north out of town. It was Saturday and Mr. Mandersloot was home to welcome us and introduce himself—Jaap—and his wife, Miep, to us. Colonists were always happy to offer accommodation to newcomers, who would bring news and provide a pleasant distraction from the rather close-knit, gossipy European community. With servants to clean and prepare the rooms, guests caused minimal inconvenience. Many European homes in Bandoeng and elsewhere in the Indies had moreover been augmented with a guest cottage, referred to as a *paviljoen* or a *dependance*. They provided accommodation for visiting friends like us, or could conveniently be rented out to individuals not yet ready to acquire a home of their own. Aside from the additional income, such arrangements could also contribute extra security from petty thievery during absences on vacation, which in the case of "home leave" to the Netherlands might last for several months. The Mandersloot family kindly offered us such temporary accommodation; it was admittedly rather crowded for the four of us, but it was more congenial than the stiffly formal hotel rooms. On that late Saturday afternoon, my parents could thus finally relax on the porch with tea and biscuits, and after sundown look forward to a home-cooked Indonesian meal, consisting of *bahmi* (an Indonesian noodle dish) washed down with ice-cold beer.

Tjioemboeloeit was a very agreeable community, positioned quite a bit higher up the slopes of the Tangkuban Perahu than Bandoeng. Jaap pointed out the volcano to us; its broad dome dominated the northeastern horizon, and one could clearly make out a plume of steam, illuminated by the afternoon sun, rising from the crest. To the south, beyond green fields and a large fish farm, its waters sparkling in the late afternoon sunshine, lay the northern outskirts of Bandoeng. Tjioemboeloeit consisted of a collection of whitewashed villas with terracotta roofs set on spacious properties in what might be described as an upscale "bedroom community." Nearby was the very grand Villa Isola, built by a media magnate; it gave the area status ("We live just around the corner from Villa Isola, you know"). My mother, years later, recalled these wonderful first impressions with evident nostalgia—it was what she meant when referring to *tempo dulu.*[18]

After the tea things had been cleared away the *djongos* brought out roasted peanuts to gently ease our way to dinner, while my parents admired the view of

---

18. *Tempo dulu* means "the old days."

the setting sun, dipping towards the horizon through a rapidly clearing sky after a brief, refreshing rainfall. This was, according to our hosts, a common afternoon feature of the Preanger climate. "The Preanger," Jaap explained, "is the name of the broad fertile upland valley where Bandoeng is located. The Preanger is ringed by volcanoes," he continued. "You can perhaps just make out Malabar, far to the south, and beyond it lies Papandajan—very active."

As dusk rapidly descended into a tropical night, revealing a magnificent jet-black sky sparkling with millions of stars, a wonderful peace enveloped us. But then, my mother later recalled, "Strange sounds emerged from the living room through its open doors. First there was a whirring sound—rrrr, rrrr, rrrr—followed by a sound like tokeh, tokeh, tokeh. I thought it was a child's toy, you know, one that you wind up, but that would be strange because the Mandersloots had no children. Then Miep told me it was a gecko called a *tokeh*. By day they hid behind cupboards and pictures, and at night they ran out along the picture rails and caught insects."

Out in the dark, beyond the garden gate, distant fires became visible in the *kampongs* scattered over the valley, and one could hear the occasional barking of a *kampong* dog sensing an intruder, perhaps a feral pig, trespassing on its domain. A gentle warm breeze now wafted up from the valley, carrying with it traces of the rich scent of honeysuckle and frangipani from the gardens. Miep then ushered us to the dining room, explaining that the air outside could become quite cool at night, requiring a sweater or jacket.

After dinner our hosts told us a bit more about the area. The Preanger, stretching below Tjioemboeloeit and to the south, was the floor of an ancient lake created by what was thought to have been a spectacular eruption of the Tangkuban Perahu, perhaps a thousand years ago. "What you see now," Jaap said, "is the smouldering rump—it has eleven small craters." The eruption spewed forth so much dust and ash that the river, which drained to the north around the west flank of the volcano, had become blocked and formed a temporary lake. Looking at the hulk of the volcano, with its small plumes of steam always visible in daytime, drew one's attention to the awesome subterranean power that threatened the peaceful scene of the Preanger. South Africa's landscape was ancient by comparison, and volcanic activity had stopped long ago, but here on Java one had daily reminders of the volcano's immense and sudden destructive capabilities; and yet at the same time it provided the source of the region's fertility. The very earth here seemed to be alive, and one could understand why the inhabitants of these lands thought it was the home of powerful spirits.

"Yes," continued our host, "and there are legends associated with the mountain—how it got its name: Tangkuban Perahu is the Malay for 'overturned boat'—but—"

"Jaap, that's not right, it's a Sundanese name," Miep interjected.

"—you know," he continued, slightly changing the subject, "this Malay, or *pasar* Malay you hear around us, is only spoken in town. On the plantations, away from town, they speak Sundanese—Malay is not much of a language," he added.[19]

The legend, Jaap told us, related to a young Sundanese prince called Sankuriang, a renowned hunter who had been fathered by a demigod. Sankuriang's mother, Njai Dayang Sumbi, was the beautiful only daughter of the Prince of Galuh, who reigned in these parts long, long ago. One day Njai bade Sankuriang to go hunting for deer and he set off, taking with him a dog for companionship, being unaware that this dog was his demigod father. He was unsuccessful in his hunt and, so as not to disappoint his mother, killed the dog and brought it back. That evening they enjoyed a meal with the spoils of the hunt.

"That sounds a bit like Oedipus," my mother interjected.

"Hmm," said Jaap, but then after a brief pause continued, "A long time later the mother noticed the absence of the dog. When she discovered what had happened, she grew so agitated that she lost self-control and hit her son so hard on his temple that he fell down, bleeding. Upon hearing this, the king banished Njai from the Kraton, the royal dwelling, and she wandered all over the land. Her son recovered from his wounds and several years later, while roaming in the forest, spied a beautiful woman with whom he fell in love. His love was returned and the two agreed to get married, but the day before the wedding the young woman accidentally uncovered, while stroking his hair, the site of Sankuriang's head wound. Rather than reveal her identity as his banished mother, she devised a ruse to avoid the unacceptable marriage planned for the following day and told him that he had to prove his devotion to her by building a boat large enough to hold the wedding party and damming the Tjitarum River to fill the valley with water so that the boat could float. All this had to be done before dawn the following morning."

"I wonder whether this had anything to do with the former lake in the Preanger—the volcanic eruption?" my father mused.

"Perhaps," Jaap answered before continuing his tale. "Sankuriang laboured all night and managed to fulfil the task, helped by the spirits and gods, who built a huge dam across the valley. As dawn broke and the mother saw her son expectantly seated in the huge boat floating on the newly formed lake, she had to resort to a second trick to avoid the marriage. She invoked the might of the great god Brahma to undermine the dam, which subsequently burst, and in the following catastrophe the huge boat got shipwrecked and ended upside down on a raised piece of land. And that is how the Tangkuban Perahu came to be."

---

19. The language now spoken in Indonesia is referred to as *Behassa Indonesia*, and some of the spelling conventions have changed from what was in those days used under the guise of "High Malay."

"You know," continued our host after a short pause, "There are many more such tales among the people of Java, especially among the Javanese themselves."

"They are not the same as the Sundanese?"

"No, the central and eastern portion of Java is their land, but they really dominate this island and always have."

"They speak a different language?"

"Yes, a very difficult language to learn."

"It really is a collection of languages, isn't it?" Miep interjected.

"Yes," agreed Jaap. "The language depends on the social rank of the persons engaged in the conversation—you can easily insult someone before you realize it."

Java sounded fascinating.

In the following days, Miep helped my parents find a house to rent. It stood in a modest neighbourhood, but was immediately available and clean. We would be able to move in on Monday, July 1.

During the remaining weeks in Tjioemboeloeit, Miep introduced us to friends and helped us find doctors. One of these was Ank de Ridder, the wife of Miep's dentist and also his assistant; she came by to say hello. She was a tall, beautiful woman who had grown up in the Indies but had married her husband, Ben, in the Netherlands. My parents were furthermore introduced to a surgeon, Dr. Marius Poortman, and his wife, Hanna.

Miep finally helped us move into our new rental home. With her assistance my mother hired a *grobak*, a flatbed two-wheeled cart pulled by a horse and led by an Indonesian man, to get our cabin trunks, still stored at the hotel, to the house. In our new home the zebra skin was unpacked and with great ceremony hung from some hooks on the wall in the living room.

While my parents were establishing a new household in this far-flung outpost of the Dutch Empire, Emperor Hirohito and his entourage were scheming to destroy it. He was looking for ways to extract Japan from its self-inflicted difficulties, especially with the United States.

That the NEI happened to play a key role in this daisy chain of relationships was not self-evident to the public inhabiting the splendid archipelago, and obviously caused not the slightest anxiety in my parents or their friends. During these first months of our stay in paradise my parents were far too preoccupied with the drama unfolding in Europe to have time for events in backward Asia.

The underlying problem was the "China Incident," as Emperor Hirohito put it, though most outside observers who cared to look, and certainly the Chinese themselves, saw the struggle as a bloody war of aggression. By calling this struggle an "incident," United States Congress–sanctioned economic reprisals could be avoided; at risk were Japanese imports from the United States of scrap iron and aviation gasoline. This careful choice of words was an expedient method for circumventing inconvenient legislation, but perhaps contributed as well to a future misconception that war in the Pacific would not break out until the attack on Pearl Harbor. The war in China was dragging on, even though the Japanese army was employing the most heinous and ruthless tactics to subdue the Chinese.

Adding to the murkiness of the situation was the political confusion within Japan itself. "Nothing is what it seems in Japan," was the opinion of a *Time* magazine correspondent:

> The Emperor is a Divinity and yet Japan is not an absolute Monarchy. Every general is responsible to the Emperor, and yet the army does as it wants. In the last three years the Japanese government has seemed totalitarian and yet it actually has been unmitigated chaos.[20]

His was an astute observation: in Japan, decisions with strategically important ramifications were made in the name of the Emperor by impetuous army officers in the field. Thus Japan had blundered into the China conflict and now sought to paper over the conflict with notions of "Asian Economic Co-Prosperity." This incoherent policy was accompanied by a bewildering sequence of Japanese Cabinet changes in search of an escape from its costly self-inflicted predicament.

Trade between Indonesia and Japan had also grown during the first half of the twentieth century, stimulated by Japan's rapid industrialization. Indonesia became an important supplier of raw materials such as tin, bauxite, agricultural produce and oil, while becoming a buyer of Japanese manufactured items. But the colonial opinion-makers in Indonesia treated developments in China and Japan with equal disdain, and the conflict in China therefore created minimal interest.

In the United States it was different. There the China conflict aroused criticism by a public stirred by the books of Pearl S. Buck, and the Japanese therefore had to tread warily to avoid those sentiments precipitating embargoes on its American trade: the longer the China "incident" lasted, the greater the risk of an American backlash. A United States trade embargo would almost certainly find an echo in the NEI, given the Netherlands government's anxiety to gain United States military support for the war in Europe. Japan faced a nightmare scenario.

One reason why Chinese resistance was so stubborn was the continuing ability of China, though cut off by Japanese troops from its own coastal ports,

---

20. *Time,* July 22, 1940.

to acquire new supplies via two important routes: the recently completed Burma Road, connecting Chunking to the Bay of Bengal, and the Haiphong railway line, linking Chunking to that city in French Indochina.[21]

The outbreak of war in Europe had suddenly supplied Tokyo with new options for satisfying Japanese military ambitions without necessarily provoking reprisals from the two adversaries it feared most: America and Russia. On June 19, 1940, the day France sued for a ceasefire with Germany, Japan demanded that Britain close down the Burma Road and that French Indochina halt immediately all further transshipment of military supplies via Haiphong. Japan backed this ultimatum with a show of force on the Indochina border.

French Indochina Governor General Georges Catroux sought support for thwarting the Japanese ultimatum, but neither the Vichy regime nor Washington could or would respond, and thus, under duress, he agreed to negotiate with General Issaku Nishihara.[22] The French Minister of Colonial Affairs, Albert Rivière, took offence at the rapid capitulation by Catroux, and sent him a stinging rebuke. Catroux fired back his own denunciation of the French armistice and was subsequently relieved of his responsibilities.[23] He eventually joined the French resistance under de Gaulle, but in the meantime stretched out the negotiations with the Japanese, while waiting for Admiral Jean Decoux to take over his functions. Winston Churchill, under pressure from his Governor General in Hong Kong who was confronting a Japanese army, also caved in to Japanese demands. Thus the two best supply lines to China were severed before June was out, and this Japanese gamble paid off.

The commencement shortly thereafter of the Battle of Britain, another likely German success, seemed to offer another pain-free opportunity for Japan to achieve its "Southern Advance" objectives, the Dutch and British colonial possessions along with their riches in raw materials. The key military impediment to Japanese expansion was the huge US Pacific fleet, based on Hawaii, but with each German victory, influential voices in Washington, seeing Hitler as the greater threat and advocating appeasement of Japan, urged President Roosevelt to move the Pacific fleet to the Atlantic.

The dramatic change in the European situation brought about by the capitulation of France had an immediate impact in Japan. In that country a generation had grown up thrilled during their childhood by the boy-hero war adventure stories of Ichiu Miyazaki, and his "hot-blooded novels" (*nekketsu shosetsu*)[24] portraying an ultimately glorious future Japanese naval victory over the United States. Subconsciously these stories served to avenge the humiliation

---

21. A third supply route was from Russia, but it was ineffective.

22. Japanese names normally have the family name precede the given name. In this book the Western practice is followed (given name first).

23. Lerner, *Catroux*.

24. Griffiths, "Militarizing Japan."

Japan had suffered at the hands of Commodore Matthew Perry in 1854, and in addition built on Japan's successful war against the Russians in 1905: securing for Japan unchallenged leadership in Asia seemed a God-sanctioned quest. The army got Emperor Hirohito to dismiss Prime Minister Mitsumasa Yonai, who resisted allying Japan with Germany.[25] Prince Fumimaro Konoe's new administration gave less voice to those well-informed about US industrial and military potential and more voice to those on the streets of Japan clamouring for action. On August 1 Japan accordingly presented France with a new ultimatum, demanding military privileges in French Indochina. For a month France struggled with the choice between accommodation and resistance, while the battle of Britain was nearing its climax, and as Japan stationed an aircraft carrier in the Gulf of Tonkin in support of a hundred thousand Japanese troops massed on the French Indochina border, confronting French troops lacking any form of air cover. On September 1, 1940, France signed the inevitable agreement with Japan, letting Japan incorporate French Indochina into Japan's Co-Prosperity Sphere, while retaining as a fig leaf for hiding this disgrace a Japanese promise to honour French sovereignty, thereby leaving French troops to confront the growing independence movement within French Indochina.[26] This signalled the death of French, British and Dutch interests in Asia.

These disturbing developments in a "sister colony" located less than eight hundred miles across the South China Seas from strategically important Borneo and its oil fields hardly drew press commentary in the Indies. But then the oil production centre of Tarakan was more than a thousand miles from Batavia; it is difficult to keep tabs on what the backyard neighbours are up to when one's backyard is so vast. Singapore, less than a hundred miles from the Sumatran coast, was assumed to be the key barrier to any military threat, especially from distant Japan. This feeling of security among the educated inhabitants of the NEI was augmented by the fact that "their" country was still fighting alongside Britain and her Commonwealth partners, while the French had given up.

Japanese Prime Minister Konoe, like an artful spider expanding its web, now initiated a diplomatic move to achieve for the NEI what had been procured for French Indochina: incorporation into Japan's exclusive, all-embracing, Tokyo-centric economic trade sphere. To this end he handed the Dutch ambassador in Tokyo a request to send to Batavia a trade delegation led by General Kuniaki Koiso. For the time being the Dutch government bought

---

25. Bix, *Hirohito and the Making of Modern Japan.*
26. Dreifort, *Myopic Grandeur.*

breathing space by refusing to deal with Koiso on account of his previously expressed criticism of the Dutch regime in Indonesia.[27]

---

27. Bijkerk, *De laatste landvoogd.*

3. WE SETTLE IN

While these diplomatic skirmishes were taking place, my parents were fully preoccupied with settling in to their new home: they first had to register their planned residence address with the municipal authorities, a standard practice in the Netherlands, and then attend to the other essential administrative requirements as spelled out in their guidebook. In due course our names would thus appear in the *Bandoeng Address Boek*, even while the demise of that admirable document was being planned in Tokyo.

The house we had rented faced the short, east–west–running Serajoestraat, named after a large river in central Java (figure 6). A proud number 1 was displayed on the masonry pillar beside the driveway. A small distance beyond the garden wall to the west was the intersection with Riouwstraat, a major thoroughfare forming a broad arc around northeast Bandoeng; it was shaded by a canopy of flame trees set in broad grassy verges, giving the street a grand, spacious aspect, and incidentally shielding our house from traffic noise. A short walk southward along the Riouwstraat brought one to an agreeable semicircular park called the *Oranje Plein*,[1] which had a small concession stand shaded by a large flame tree. Here Juf and I would often come during the coming months.

The neighbouring house on the other, eastern, boundary occupied a corner lot, where Brantasstraat, named for another Javanese river, ran northward from Serajoestraat. This neighbourhood of bungalows and more modest duplexes was loosely referred to as "Tjihapit" (today spelled *Cihapit*), deriving its name from a rivulet that flowed southward through it.

A number of blocks to the northeast, near the city boundary, the municipality had recently built a low-cost housing project, confusingly called the Tjihapit "model" or "demonstration" *kampong*. The name therefore was somewhat ambiguous.

The modest but comfortable single-family dwellings in our immediate neighbourhood, all enjoying small but adequate front- and backyards, had been constructed during the previous two decades, and their residents were mainly drawn from the ranks of junior officials of the railways and postal service. A feature of the population was its racial diversity. What the residents had in common was being Europeanized, and having well-established local roots, even

---

1. In Dutch cities the word *plein* can refer to any open public space, paved or grassy.

though their appearance might suggest distinct European or Asian ethnic backgrounds.

Our house had lofty ceilings, a roof covered with pantiles, a somewhat neglected front lawn with one or two tropical bushes, including the omnipresent poinsettia and *kembang sepatu* (hibiscus), and a backyard with the ubiquitous banana palm and a papaya tree. Most houses had a low garden wall around the front of the property—the one for our dwelling was built of basalt blocks, a building material readily available in this volcanic region. The lower portion of the house was also clad with the same material, but the remainder of the walls were whitewashed. The windows were fitted with shutters, hinged on the wall at either side of the window frame. These shutters could be closed while still permitting air to circulate if the windows themselves were left open; above the windows were more ventilation slits. At night, protection from mosquitoes was provided by a *kelambu*, a net covering the bed. Those were the days before air conditioning, and ample ventilation was essential for daytime coolness.

A few days after taking possession of the house, my mother visited Tjioemboeloeit for tea and asked Miep how she should go about hiring a servant. "There is an office downtown where they can help you," Miep replied as she went to her desk to find a scrap of paper and pencil. "Don't hire one of those guys wearing a black hat," she advised, while scribbling an address. "They're nationalists. When you hire a *djongos* make sure he is wearing an *ikat kepalla.*"

"What's that?" asked my mother.

"A head cloth," Miep replied. "By the manner of its folds you can tell from what part of Java he comes and also that he is a good man. It's the traditional form of dress," she added as an afterthought. My mother was not yet ready to consider a *djongos*. The *babu* my mother subsequently hired was a slightly built Indonesian woman, who referred to herself as "Iti" and was swathed in a sarong of batik (the typical printed fabric from Java); her black hair was neatly tied in a bun at the back of her head and she spoke some Dutch. My mother and Juf quickly discovered that Indonesian servants were easier to manage than the Bantus of South Africa, because in Indonesia the work of the servant was a time-honoured profession rather than an adaptation from a form of slavery, whether through intertribal warfare or the white man's form of industrial bondage. No sooner had *babu* Iti clapped eyes on me than she decided that I would be her charge. That is the way it always was in the Indies, but Juf objected, and *babu* Iti had to make do with more mundane kitchen, laundry and house-cleaning duties.

Once this had been settled, Juf found the changed living arrangement most agreeable. In South Africa, she had been housebound, for she had never learned to drive a car, an essential requirement in the New World. In Bandoeng she was once more living in civilization. This was a modern, European city and accordingly a church stood within walking distance from our house. If she wanted to go further afield and a bus or tram was not convenient, she could take a *sado*,[2] a horse-drawn cart on two wheels, or a *betja*, a tricycle with room for two passengers and pedalled by an Indonesian who was invariably fond of ringing his bicycle bell, "tingaling, tingaling." Passengers were always nicely shielded from the sun or from the rain by a canopy. Undoubtedly Juf would meet kindred spirits at church. At Lombardy East she had missed these social and religious diversions.

In her earlier position as my father's nanny, before and during the First World War, she had been expected to pay due attention to the Christian aspects of child-rearing, because grandfather's household had close though perhaps somewhat superficial links to the Lutheran church. My great-grandfather, who had also been an architect, had assisted the Church with the maintenance of its buildings in Amsterdam, and my grandfather had continued that service. My father, on the other hand, had developed a certain detachment from "organized religion" (as he put it) and had long ceased to be comfortable in a church, though he held deep spiritual convictions that transcended any particular set of Christian beliefs. Had he been a student of literature, he would have been an admirer of the philosophy of people like Goethe or Wordsworth, for he held a deep reverence for nature. My mother, by way of contrast, had grown up in an agnostic, if not outright atheistic, environment. Her father was a great admirer of the Bloomsbury group, of people like Bertrand Russell, Lancelot Thomas Hogben and George Bernard Shaw, and he described himself, if pushed, as "agnostic" even though he owned a Bible; grandmother Boland, his wife, was a devout atheist and refused to touch a Bible at all, as though it were bewitched. As a result, my mother succeeded in reaching adulthood without ever having set foot in a church. Juf consequently faced a formidable challenge in guiding my young soul, for in terms of religious outlook, there was a distinct split in the attitudes of the childminder from that of the child's parents. She bore this burden stoically, but now could once more look forward to church attendance on Sundays, at least without inconveniencing the rest of the family.

Early in August my father received good news from his bank manager: since the Indies had finally joined the Sterling Block, it now was possible to transfer his savings from South Africa, thereby opening up the prospect of buying a piece of land and planning for the building of a new house. He immediately began to look for a suitable building plot near Tjioemboeloeit, the area that had made such a favourable impression when we first arrived in Bandoeng.

---

2. The term *sado* was derived from the French *dos à dos*, or back to back.

My parents quickly made new friends in this sociable environment. My father got to know people in the building trade, such as the civil engineer Theo Aalbers, also working on the KMA complex, and his wife, Mien. The fact that they had a son my age added to the value of this new friendship. Via the Mandersloot family we were introduced to Dr. A. J. Jochems, a family physician. Dr. Jochems had his practice at his home in Tjiliwoengstraat, conveniently located a few blocks to the north of where we lived. He had a friendly wife, also called Emmy, who doubled as his assistant. With the household settling down so quickly and smoothly, my parents could congratulate themselves on the excellent move they had made.

Unease in the Indies

Although life in our new home was unfolding in an agreeable manner, there were hints of discontent in society, which were finding guarded expression in the pages of the Malay language press. These periodicals showed more interest in developments elsewhere in Asia than did the European press, but their editors had to be circumspect to avoid any hint of disloyalty to the Dutch Crown. Indonesian nationalists agitating for independence and self-determination found Japan's proposed "New Order" appealing, not so much because of the message, but rather the source of the message: they had no interest in replacing a Dutch colonial regime with a Japanese colonial regime, but a rapidly industrializing Asian country on the other hand was a source of inspiration. Given centuries of European colonial dominance in Asia, deep-seated feelings of Asian inferiority had arisen, and this tended to find expression in reference to Japan, the vigorously growing industrial power, as being "*bung*," the "big brother of the immature Indonesians." The Indonesian weekly *Pemandangan* (Panorama), for instance, reflected this in its July 11 edition: the slogan "Asia for the Asians" was attractive in the eyes of its editor, but he was saddened by the "fraternal struggle between China and Japan." My parents could not read Malay, and like their friends, read one of the Dutch language dailies, which tended to focus on the reports coming from Europe and especially from Britain, now alone confronting the German menace.

The issue of independence was repeatedly raised in the proceedings of the *Volksraad*, the Consultative Assembly, not just by the Indonesian representatives, but by the Dutch as well. Since the capitulation of Holland, the Netherlands Indies had acquired a *de facto* independence that now seemed to warrant an appropriate constitutional adjustment. A major hurdle was the issue of citizenship, a delicate topic given the widespread conviction that the military disasters in Europe were primarily caused by the activities of so-called fifth columnists, false neighbours: the slightest allusion to ideas not driven by blind patriotism were likely to be branded as "traitorous."

Citizenship constituted a devilishly complex legal issue because the government had for years implemented a policy of multiple, and therefore unequal, civil rights, largely in deference to demands for ethnic-specific laws. The idea behind this arrangement was not to create discrimination, but rather to apply the principle that everyone should be judged according to his own concept of law.[3] It was a marvellous exercise in multiculturalism, but now led to complications: who could or should serve in the army? A tiny minority of the NEI population had citizenship and the right to hold a passport; there was no such thing as an NEI citizen. The promise of independence for Indonesia's eastern neighbour, the Philippines, added ammunition to nationalists' arguments. In late August, Wiwoho, an Indonesian *Volksraad* member, had put forth a formal motion that both this topic and the granting of greater powers to the *Volksraad* be seriously considered.

War had focused many minds on this matter. In British India there were complaints about lack of representative government, while its citizens were expected to join the army. The French had demanded that French Indochina should play a part in liberating France, and there similar qualms were raised about reciprocity of rights and obligations.[4] In the Indies the Dutch community was unwilling to seriously consider the matter of defence or the idea of fielding an army to liberate Holland because of the disturbing issue of citizenship it raised. The mighty British fortress at Singapore was a convenient, unquestioned source of security. There was no need for placing reliance on unreliable "*inlanders*," as natives were then described; changing the constitution therefore had to wait. The historian, Bernard Vlekke, describes the situation thus:

> The Netherlands government, strongly supported by Dutch public opinion, both wanted to proceed slowly and to delay further political concessions until the Indonesian peoples would be ripe for a larger measure of self-government. It was never said what qualifications a people must have to be ripe for self-government and this policy of the colonial powers to make themselves the sole judges on this matter of being ripe for self-government must have been both irritating and insulting for the dependent peoples. These peoples might well complain that they were treated like schoolboys who are being told that they will have to pass a difficult examination, but who are not informed about the subject they must study to prepare for the examination.[5]

---

3. Vlekke, *Nusantara*, Ch. 15.

4. Duiker, *The Communist Road to Power in Vietnam*.

5. Vlekke, *Nusantara*, 364.

Everyone in the Advisory Council agreed that citizenship was a complex issue. In September 1940 the Visman Commission was therefore called into being: the single Chinese, three Dutch and three Indonesian delegates were charged with studying the matter, which they did over the following sixteen months, completing the job by the time war broke out, after which the study was forgotten.

The Cabinet in London moreover made it clear that any constitutional adjustments would have to await the end of the war, when a Dutch Parliament could, after proper debate, sanction such a move. And so the entire issue of reform became stalemated at a time when Hirohito was promising elegantly simple deliverance from foreign oppression.

A military threat from Japan had no credibility in the West, given Japan's poor reputation as an industrial power and its seeming isolation in the immensity of the Pacific Ocean. The Japanese navy was not mentioned in the press. Our own existence on an island added to our sense of security. What the man in the street saw were cheap, crudely manufactured Japanese goods; this impression was misleading.

In mid-August the Japanese military had successfully combat-tested a piece of their rapidly expanding technology: twelve Mitsubishi *A6M Reisen*, popularly known as the "Zero fighter," flew their first sortie, providing cover for a bombing raid over Chunking, the Chinese seat of government. This was the culmination of a three-year, top-secret project. Ironically, *Time* magazine devoted space during the following week to the state of Japanese aircraft manufacturing: "Planes have improved," its correspondent wrote. "The best types are mostly built under licence from foreign designs."

The first prototype of the new plane, designed to outrageous specifications, began its tests eighteen months earlier on March 23, 1939:

Just after seven o'clock that night, two oxcarts emerged from the gates of the Nagoya Aircraft Works of Mitsubishi Heavy Industries, Ltd. Each cart was heavily laden with a large cargo shrouded in canvas. Slowly the carts moved north, following the street car tracks along the main street of the city of Nagoya. The oxcarts belonged to the Onishi company, contracted for this job by the Nagoya works of Mitsubishi. The two drivers holding the bridles of the oxen each held a lantern in his hand. Four heavers paced alongside the carts, guarding the loads. At the head of the ponderous little procession walked Seiichiro Tamura, transportation supervisor of the materials section of the aircraft works. A security guard brought up the rear.

The drivers and heavers had an idea of what was on the carts. The front one was loaded with an airplane's wings and the front part of its fuselage. The second cart carried the after part of the fuselage with a horizontal stabilizer and an engine section. The teamsters knew this because it was routine to disassemble a completed airplane into wings and fuselages for transport to the Kagamigahara Airfield of Gifu Prefecture, forty-eight kilometres away. Transportation companies such as Onishi were regularly employed to make the trip there. On this night, however, the drivers and heavers had a vague awareness that the load on their oxcarts was of unusual importance. This is because Tamura, the transport supervisor, would not otherwise be accompanying them. The oxcarts moved along the main street. On the uneven, stony road, the iron-rimmed wheels ground and rattled loudly. The loads swayed heavily. Progress was slow. It would take twenty-four hours, including a few hours for a rest, to cover the forty-eight kilometres to the airfield. It seems astonishing that a modern, high-speed fighter should be carried to its test field on an oxcart, but despite objections, the Nagoya Aircraft Works had no other choice. In the first place, the Nagoya works had no adjoining airfield of its own. Then there was the fact that methods of transportation alternative to oxcarts had proved inadequate. Trucks had been tried...however, the roads were so rough that aircraft carried on trucks had been damaged by strong shocks and vibrations. Horse-drawn carts had also been tried...but the possibility of stampede made it too risky to entrust delicate aircraft fuselages to horses. In the transport of aircraft, avoiding damage was the first priority, and in the circumstances, only the slowness of an oxcart offered an acceptable margin of safety. Tradition added some dignity to the oxcart, besides. As the carts creaked through Nagoya, they passed in front of the east gate of the Atsuta shrine. Tamura and the guard stopped there and made a bow before resuming their posts at the front and rear of the procession.

The journey was being made by night not just to avoid the high traffic density of the day in Nagoya. There were strong security concerns, too. The greatest danger, however, was a disturbing rumour at the aircraft works that the windows of the U.S. Consulate at Nunobiki were almost always open slightly when oxcarts loaded with planes passed by. As Tamura passed he watched the consulate's darkened rows of windows with a stiff expression. None were open...the consul was a sound sleeper. [6]

The next evening the oxcarts reached the vast airfield, where technicians assembled the plane and commenced testing the craft. By early 1940 it was clear that the aircraft would exceed the original requirements for speed, manoeuvrability and range. This was, needless to say, not the first triumph of the Japanese aircraft industry; its predecessor, the Claude, was almost as good

---

6. Yoshimura, *Zero Fighter*, 1–3.

as the Zero fighter and much better than anything the Allies had. On September 13, 1940, the new fighter was tested in combat on another bombing run to Chunking, and proved its capability to devastating effect, when thirteen Zeros annihilated an opposing force of twenty-seven Chinese Polikparov I-15s and I-16s, the pride of the Soviet Union.[7] The Zero had no match (Allied or German) in terms of speed, firepower, manoeuvrability and range until late in the Second World War.

US Major Claire Chennault, stationed in China as an air force advisor to Chiang Kai-shek, was alarmed by what he saw over the Chinese skies, and submitted a report to the American government in which he predicted disaster for American and British air forces. His report was greeted with disbelief, and the Japanese accordingly were able to continue testing and improving their new plane without precipitating increased Allied effort. While the Zero was proving its worth over the skies of China, the airborne attack on Britain was reaching a crescendo. On August 27, 1940, Japan, confident of an imminent British defeat, urged its citizens in the United States to return home, and two days later, Japan and Vichy France signed an agreement recognizing Japanese interests in French Indochina. This agreement gave Japan permission to build airfields; thus Japan had advanced one more step further south.

In the meantime Japan had been doggedly pursuing its NEI trade initiative, finding in Minister of Trade Ichiro Kobayashi a delegation leader acceptable to the Dutch government; on September 12 he arrived on board the *Nissya Maru* at Tandjong Priok, accompanied by twenty-four assistants, including four military officers and a large contingent of curious journalists. He was met with great pomp on the quay by Dr. H. J. van Mook, the Director of Economic Affairs. This was the first time such a high-ranking Japanese official had visited one of *dai* Nippon's most important and oldest trade partners. On his arrival Kobayashi reminded the press of "the friendly trade ties between the two countries that had lasted for three hundred years." His expectations were very high and entailed acceptance by the Indies government of Japan's economic leadership and political dominance in the region. His nine detailed demands (not given publicity) read like an ultimatum: to call this a "trade mission" was an understatement. The talks got off to a rocky start when it became clear that Minister Kobayashi preferred to conduct his discussions in German, to which van Mook objected, and discussions could therefore only commence after someone found an interpreter fluent in English and Japanese.[8]

The governments of New Zealand and Australia watched these proceedings with alarm. They viewed the NEI government's reluctance to abandon its flimsy neutrality with suspicion. Should the Japanese now secure greater access

---

7. Deighton, *Blood, Tears and Folly*, 516.

8. Bijkerk, *De laatste landvoogd*, 27.

to the Indies, it might compromise the security of Singapore and the two Dominions.[9] Van Mook had inadvertently been thrust into the front defence line of the Dominions as well as the British and Dutch colonies.

The key objective of Kobayashi's quest was to secure increased access to raw materials—above all a six-fold expansion of oil deliveries to Japan. Van Mook reacted to this alarming request by summoning to Batavia the managing directors of the two large oil companies then active in the Indies, Baron van Eck of the Shell Group, and Stan Kay of Standard Vacuum. But when Kobayashi examined their detailed proposals he was disappointed to learn that the quality of the crude petroleum offered was not suited for the manufacture of aviation fuel, Japan's most pressing need. Kobayashi could afford to be patient, for he anticipated soon being able to celebrate the fall of Fortress Britain within the grand state dining room of the Governor General's neoclassical palace facing Waterloo Square in Batavia. He would occupy the *place d'honneur* at the head of the table.

War Is in the Saddle

While van Mook was entertaining his demanding Japanese guests, our life in Bandoeng happily muddled on. We were aware of the delegation's presence, but were shielded from the full nature of the Japanese demands and were of the opinion that the delegation did not deserve the attention it was getting. The population, one might say, was in a state of blissful ignorance.

My parents and our fellow citizens of the Indies were, if anything, self-confident and upbeat, a situation allowing Queen Wilhelmina to offer King George VI enough money, collected by her loyal subjects, to purchase forty Spitfires and eighteen Hudson bombers. The next day, September 20, the Queen's speech was broadcast three times, always accompanied at its close by a rendition of the Dutch national anthem, the *Wilhelmus*. How proud everyone was. The residents of the Indies were doing their bit to defend Britain and to evict the Hun from the Netherlands. Another Spitfire collection was promptly launched and gifts flowed in from the Chinese merchants, from Indonesian teachers and Sultans, and from the Dutch. This outpouring of generosity demonstrated quite clearly to the ruling classes that the Indonesians "loved the Dutch." It never dawned on us that those Spitfires might possibly be more useful for the defence of Java (assuming that they could have been made available by the hard-pressed British).[10]

9. Governor General of New Zealand, telegram to the British Secretary of State for Dominion Affairs, September 7, 1940.

10. About 100 were purchased; most were given Indonesian names (Morgan and Shacklady, *Spitfire*).

Two days later, while the Queen's broadcast was still a hot topic of discussion in the *Societeit Concordia*, which was located downtown in a very well-appointed building and known to its exclusively European *totok* (no mixed race) members as *de Soos*, Japanese troops took action on Tokyo's gamble. They crossed the French Indochinese border and took control of some French military bases. This action would help speed up suppression of the rebellious Chinese, who had so far not appreciated the benevolent nature of Nipponese rule, but it also paved the way to the south. *Time* magazine noted that "War was in the saddle and headed south to Thailand, Malaya and the rich curve of the Netherlands Indies, scattered islands as though a careless Creator had dashed a hamper full of especially rich soils and raw materials off the continent of Asia into the southwest corner of the Pacific."[11]

Governor General Admiral Decoux had not willingly admitted the Japanese troops and the Vichy government had again sought assistance from Roosevelt, and again this was declined. Roosevelt was fully preoccupied with the coming presidential election for an unprecedented third term of office and he was facing a formidable challenge from Wendell L. Willkie, a man with great charm, but who was, in the eyes of Roosevelt, "a fascist."[12]

Decoux's difficulties in French Indochina caused no comment in the Indies press, but Tokyo's broadcast three days later (September 27, 1940) announcing Japanese membership in the "Tripartite Pact" certainly changed matters. It was a fateful step for Japan because the country had now irrevocably severed its former ties with Britain and had firmly allied itself with Hitler, in the confident belief that Germany would conquer Britain. President Roosevelt retaliated by embargoing scrap iron and oil exports to Japan, thus making a German victory essential for Japan.[13] Only then could Japan gain access to the oil and other resources of the NEI and British Borneo without undue risk of war.

In the Indies the public response to the Tripartite Pact was not one of fear but of outrage, because it provoked suspicion that delivery of its raw materials to Japan would now ultimately end up in German hands. How this might be achieved in practice was not discussed. Top-secret discussions got under way between senior military personnel of the Indies, Britain and Australia, but were hampered by an inability to acquire military hardware.[14]

The Japanese gamble did not pay off. As October wore on, the threat to England of a German invasion receded, allowing the government of the NEI to stiffen its resistance to Kobayashi's demands, but by now Japan had become committed to war in the Pacific in order to regain access to essential raw materials and to realize the aspirations of the firebrands in its society. No one

11. *Time*, September 16, 1940.

12. Davis, *FDR: Into the Storm*.

13. Black, *Franklin Delano Roosevelt*, 645.

14. Bussemaker, "Australian-Dutch Defence Cooperation, 1940–1941".

among the European public in the Indies seemed to connect the dots: a recent history of Japanese expansion, Japanese media demands for more, a bloody war in China, unprotected French and Dutch colonies, Britain fighting for its life, and a huge Japanese trade delegation in Batavia. There was no discussion about the vast disparity between the Japanese forces on the one hand, and the pitiful forces available to the defenders of Malaya and the NEI on the other hand. In the public eye, both in the Indies and in Australia, the naval base at Singapore had taken on such mythical proportions as to render objective assessments impossible. With the Battle of Britain won, a sigh of relief was audible in the Indies, but the crisis facing Japan had deepened and therefore the threat of a Japanese invasion of Java had increased.

Life in the towns and cities and on the numerous coffee, tea, sugar and rubber plantations of Java remained agreeable and relaxed. It was hard to imagine a better existence than that enjoyed by the Europeans with their good salaries and their servants. Years later, an Indonesian diaspora would look back from new homes in foreign lands to pre-war Java as a former "paradise," a Garden of Eden.

My mother got absorbed by the social life, which in a city like Bandoeng was even more congenial than it had been on the Transvaal veld. There was the *de Soos* as well as the tennis club, and numerous tea and cocktail parties. The Opel car allowed us to do some more exploring of the surrounding areas. Not far outside of Bandoeng stood the Dago *Thee Huis* (still called by that name today, meaning "tea house"). It was a popular Sunday's outing up the Dago Road on the east bank of the Tjikapundung River. A visit to this charming destination helped us celebrate Juf's sixty-seventh birthday on Sunday, October 20. Beyond Dago, the road followed a route along the east flank of the Tangkuban Perahu through the Tjiater (today Ciater) Pass, leading to the hot springs on the north flank of that mountain. Stopping at the tea house on the return journey from a visit to the hot springs, one could enjoy delicious Dutch pastries on a terrace shaded by the broad leafy canopy of a rain tree (*abizia saman*), while enjoying a splendid view over the Preanger Valley and the distant, blue volcanic peaks marking the southern extent of the valley. A swimming pool offered a refreshing dip, while a paddling pool amused the small children.

During the weekdays my father was fully occupied with the construction of the KMA complex, for which a large site had been acquired on the eastern outskirts of Bandoeng; he found the work unexpectedly rewarding. The only satisfaction my father had derived from his year of compulsory military training in the late twenties was making new lifelong friends who shared his interest in music and had joined him in a chamber music ensemble. Apart from that incidental benefit, the experience had been boring, if not outright unpleasant.

His attitude towards the military was commonplace in Dutch society. In April an attempt had been made on Java to muster the volunteer home defence forces for training, but many of its members failed to turn up. Exercises of this nature were dismissed as "playing soldier—a waste of time." The disaster overwhelming the Netherlands weeks later had abruptly changed this sentiment, and my father sensed that his work was important and valued.

Among the inhabitants of Java there was an elevated atmosphere of war fever, but absolutely no sense of fear about invasion. Local military attention was focused solely on two fronts: internal security, given the threat of fifth columnists, and the heightened need to become self-sufficient in terms of training and weapons procurement. Support for and confidence in the military was based on two premises: the military threat was internal, and it lay well within the capabilities of a military force drawn almost exclusively from the ranks of the small European and Eurasian society. And even then, no one thought of any island other than Java. Of course there was Sumatra, but it lay almost within sight of Singapore, and in the case of Borneo only the oil towns, Balikpapan and Tarakan, merited concern. Perhaps the archipelago was so huge that no one dared to consider the challenge of uprisings anywhere beyond Java. People talked about "fortress Java," but that was a relative concept. On Java there was a military presence, whereas the remainder of the archipelago had almost nothing. Questions of such magnitude could not be answered and therefore it was pointless asking them.

Two days after Juf's birthday, Kobayashi announced that he had been recalled to Tokyo "to celebrate that country's birthday, the 2,600th anniversary of the creation of the Nipponese Empire by the Sun Goddess." The trade talks had so far yielded almost nothing and Kobayashi could not hide his disappointment as he was ceremoniously accompanied by van Mook to his ship in the Tandjong Priok harbour, where he gave a short speech:

> The Japanese delegation wishes to call the attention of the Netherlands delegation to the fact that the negotiations between Mr. Mukai [the Japanese oil expert] and the two petroleum companies have led to proposals with a wide difference in quantity and quality from those of Mr. Mukai. The proposed quantity of aviation gasoline and crude oil promised to Japan is as good as nihil.[15]

His trip was not, however, entirely in vain. Beginning in November, Japan would operate the Japan Ocean Bonito and Tunny Company in the Indies. With a fleet of five hundred fishing vessels it operated from sixty-five fishing stations strategically located around the archipelago.[16] Most of the mission

---

15. Fabricius, *Brandende Aarde*, 15.
16. Zwaan, *Nederlands Indië 1940–1946: Gouvernementeel Intermezzo 1940–1942*, 245.

stayed behind, under the leadership of Kenichi Yoshizawa, former Minister of External Affairs. The trade discussions *per se* were fruitless, but the delegation's time was well spent, acquiring detailed information about the political situation and defensive works, and paving the way for a future regime change.

There continued to be available a remarkable well of goodwill in support of the Dutch presence among the peoples of the Indies, accompanied by confidence in the Netherlands' ability to ensure the welfare of its subjects. The *Suara Semarang* (Voice of Semarang), a Malay-language weekly illustrated magazine published in a city of central Java, wrote on November 3, 1940, "We do not understand why our government is treating the Japanese with so much honour, while the Japanese press never ceases to display its hatred for the Netherlands Indies and exhorts us to rise up against the Netherlands."[17]

My parents explored their new surroundings with enthusiasm. Through Edu they had been introduced to other members of the Kerkhoven clan. One of Edu's uncles had been a major driving force in the establishment, some twenty years earlier, of the huge and successful tea plantations around Bandoeng, and visits were arranged to Gamboeng, one of his magnificent estates. This plantation was one of the oldest in the area and was located south of town on the north flank of a dormant volcano. This plantation epitomized the elegance of colonial life, with its grand main dwelling, richly appointed with luxurious furniture; the beautifully laid-out gardens, vibrant with the colour of tropical flora; and, to ensure that the estate was kept in first class order, an army of servants and workers. Gamboeng was one of four or five plantations managed by him and his partners. The wealth generated by these enterprises had, over the previous twenty years, begun to make its presence felt in Bandoeng through various philanthropic initiatives, and the owners could count themselves as the elite of society. Another plantation, Malabar, remains today a tourist attraction, but under new management.

All told, there were about sixty such estates in the vicinity of Bandoeng, mainly located around the edge of the plateau, where drainage was better. Tea was the dominant crop, but here and there rubber and coffee plantations could also be found.

We also regained contact with Jan Weeda, a family acquaintance on my mother's side, and his wife Vera; years earlier they had emigrated to the Indies to seek their fortune and now lived on a rubber plantation, where Jan was the administrator. They had three young children: a girl and two younger boys. My mother had only met Vera once before, at her wedding to Jan. "Were you not enrolled in a secretarial course when you came to our wedding?" Vera asked. My mother gave her a brief account of how she had met my father. Later Jan

---

17. Zwaan, *Nederlands Indië 1940–1946: Gouvernementeel Intermezzo 1940–1942*, 71.

took my parents on a short walk through the rubber plantation and the shed where the latex was collected in vats to congeal into brown rubbery sheets.

"It's a nice surprise seeing you here," Jan commented, "but why did you leave South Africa? We had heard from home about your wedding, and by all accounts you were heading for a very nice life over there in the land of plenty."

"We were told that the defences here in the Indies needed strengthening," my father replied. "They also threatened us with conscription if we did not go as volunteers."

"Things are pretty quiet here," Vera murmured without conviction. "Oh, we have a few troublemakers like everywhere else, but they are locked up. The *inlanders* [natives] are really nice people and they do not like the troublemakers either. They trust us."

"The *inlanders* know which side their bread is buttered on; the economy has so far survived the war in Europe, and we have a pretty good administration," Jan added, sounding confident.

"What about the Japanese?" asked my father. "They seem to be pushy."

"The Japs have their hands full in China, and the Russians beat them up a couple of years ago, and you know what happened in Finland in 1939, so you can see..." and Jan's words trailed off as he bent over to pick a bright red hibiscus flower. My father had to admit that was true. The Finnish resistance to the numerically superior Russians had been breathtaking, while the Russians had recently dealt a decisive blow to the Japanese on the Manchurian border: the Japanese threat could not really amount to much.

"The Indies is now a bit like South Africa, a sort of Commonwealth country, is it not?" my father asked.

"The GG certainly has more powers, and you now hear more from the *Volksraad* [the Advisory Council]. That's a good thing because the Hague was always meddlesome," Jan said with a note of derision.

"What's the *Volksraad* all about?"

"They can approve the budget, and can propose laws or changes to laws. There are sixty members, half of whom are *inlanders*, so you can see how progressive we are over here. Are there any *kaffirs* in the Parliament of South Africa?"

"No." My mother had to agree that the Indies by comparison were progressive. "Are the native members elected to the council?"

"I think twenty are elected by the Sultans," Jan answered. "The other ten are appointed by the Governor General—isn't that so, Vera?"

"Sultans?" my mother interrupted. The concept of "Sultan" sounded exotic to her.

"You should see their palaces," continued Jan. "You would be amazed— elegant gilt coaches, impressive thrones and grand paintings of themselves in their regal splendour. They're well-off."

"How lucky we are to be here," my father mused. "D'you think you would like to return to Holland to retire?"

"We could not stand it. Holland is so *burgerlijk* [bourgeois], though we would like to go back for a visit," Jan responded.

"Some come here just to make money and then want to return home; they never leave the city to see the land, and will only eat Dutch food. We call them 'pea soup eaters'," Vera sniggered. "The *inlanders* call them *Belanda totok*."

"In a way that's true, Vera," Jan interjected, "but *totok* means 'pure blood.' Look at someone like van Mook. He is *totok*, but he calls himself an *Indische jongen* [an 'Indian boy']. He is born and bred here." Thus we were introduced to more of the racial subtleties of Java.

"I guess any Hollander born in this country is suspected of having some *inlander* blood," Vera mused.

Sir Stamford Raffles, who had administered the colony on behalf of the British government for six years in the early part of the nineteenth century, had already noted this trend—the Dutch population becoming just another permanent facet of the local scene—in direct contrast to the British presence in India, always a transient phenomenon in terms of individuals. The upper crust of Dutch society kept to themselves, but a large portion of the Dutch population had over the preceding centuries intermarried with Indonesians, resulting in a spectrum of ties. Raffles had then already noted that "Dutch society" was overwhelmingly Eurasian.

"Have you travelled around at all?" asked Jan.

"No, we have been too busy settling down."

"You must go and see the Borobodur, and on the way you can visit Djokjakarta [today Yogyakarta]. The Sultan's palace is sometimes open to visitors. You will be amazed—Oh yes, and don't forget Buitenzorg."

"And don't forget the *wajang* performances," Vera added.

"What are they?"

"Beautiful puppet shows—a sort of shadow performance on a white sheet, and usually there is a *gamelan*, a Javanese orchestra, providing music."

"And you mentioned Buitenzorg. What is that?"

"Magnificent botanical gardens, over a hundred years old, on the road to Batavia—a nice trip, well worth the effort."

St. Nicholas, 1940

It was a curiosity of the Dutch colonial experience that although the colonists were quick to import Dutch ideas in the plastic arts and civic administration, no attempt was made to impose the Dutch language or other forms of Dutch culture on the nation. Dutch was the language of official business and a small but growing number of Indonesians were given a full Dutch education, albeit with the option in certain schools of distinctly Asian subjects, such as one of the Chinese or Javanese languages. 'Institutions of higher education in the Netherlands and within Indonesia had become accessible to these young people. For these Indonesians, the "Europeanization" was so intense that nationalists like Sukarno would, years after independence, still converse with colleagues in Dutch and until his dying day swore exclusively in Dutch. But the use of Dutch was not expected of anyone beyond a narrow circle around government, and sometimes was even considered presumptuous by the Dutch elite.

The Dutch, on the other hand (my parents included), quickly learned to speak some *"pasar"* Malay, a level of fluency required to purchase meat, eggs, fruit or vegetables at the local market, or *pasar*. They subsequently modified their own language by incorporating Malay words. In those days Malay was a convenient but hardly universally spoken language, and accordingly it was difficult to find a Malay grammar or dictionary in the bookshops: traditionalists among the indigenous population preferred to speak Javanese, Madurese or Sundanese. A popular vehicle used by new arrivals to inculcate the language was a rhyme, easily learned (today's equivalent being the ubiquitous traveller's phrase book). The rhyme taught fifty or so of the most common verbs, nouns and adjectives. Its opening lines went:

Bintang are stars and *boelan* is month
Lari means to run and *bendiri* is to stand
Laoet is the sea and *bumi* is the land
Tjuri is stealing and *harga* is the worth...[18]

The result was not so much fluency in a new language as the incorporation into spoken Dutch of Malay words. One no longer ate a banana, but a *pisang;* goodbye was *tabé*, spicy food was *pedis*; to pilfer was to *tjoep*, which might happen to some duck eggs (*telor bebek*) or chicken eggs (*telor ajam*) at the *pasar;* while any emphasis was obtained by the use of *betul* or *betul-betul* (abbreviated form $betul^2$—that is to say, "*betul* squared," conveniently borrowing from mathematical notation). The fight against mosquitoes and malaria was conducted with the help of a *kelambu* (a mosquito net) and *obat njamuk* (mosquito coils, though the word *obat* was also used to signify "medicine"). In that way, the Dutch language itself morphed into a sort of new pidgin language, unintelligible to those newly arrived from the Netherlands.

Dutch festive traditions were, on the other hand, enthusiastically introduced. December arrived with the celebration of that quintessential Dutch event, the visit of St. Nicholas. Young school children had been practising their

---

18. Beynon, *Verboden voor Honden.*

Sinterklaas songs in kindergartens, and on the eve of St. Nicholas, the fifth of December, dutifully placed their shoes (clogs were preferred) near the front door in anticipation of the good Saint leaving behind a present during the night when good little boys and girls were asleep. A ceremonial procession with Saint Nick on his dappled grey mare accompanied by "Black Peter" had been organized by some neighbours. As they passed through the neighbourhood, children lined the streets and congregated at their school to witness the event. Black Peter (and how black his face was!), dressed in a colourful sixteenth-century costume, hauled cookies out of a large bag he was carrying and threw them on the sidewalks and lawns. These were scooped up by children jumping around like little frogs, oblivious to the hygiene challenge this posed; one could not grow up in the tropics without a strong constitution. At the local school St. Nick, appropriately enthroned, determined which child had been good and which child naughty by ceremoniously consulting an impressive book, on which his long white beard sometimes rested. He dispensed warnings against bad behaviour and distributed more toys along with copious quantities of chocolates and cookies for the good boys and girls; the boys and girls were always good. Older children entertained him with skits drawing upon recent school events and the lively tales and legends of these magnificent islands.

As the end of the year approached, peace and prosperity reigned on Java and the remainder of the archipelago, and those who governed this island realm could congratulate themselves on having navigated successfully through a trying period. First the Depression of the 1930s and then war breaking out in Europe, leading to currency instability and trade disruptions, particularly with Australia, until admission of the NEI guilder to the Sterling block allowed trade with Australia to resume.

Just before Christmas the Indies provided Britain with money for another twenty-four Spitfires, and a day later it transpired that rebellious Aceh had, on its own, collected money for an additional Spitfire with contributions from all population groups. How pleased and surprised everyone was at such a gesture from such an insurrectionary corner of the empire. It was a splendid expression of solidarity with the Crown.[19]

However, the Governor General and his advisors were not oblivious to the threat posed by Japan, and after January 1941, regular secret discussions took place between Dutch, British, Australian and American military representatives. In March funds were found for the construction of a munitions factory and for mechanising the army: thus neutrality had surreptitiously been abandoned. To the participants of these meetings the threat of conflict with Japan was clear, but the discussions were "bedevilled with obstacles and unknown factors": the

---

19. Zwaan, *Nederlands Indië 1940–1946: Gouvernementeel Intermezzo 1940–1942*, 246.

potential area of operations was so vast, and the diversity of possible Japanese attack scenarios so great that an action plan defied definition; besides that, the conflict in Europe absorbed all military resources. Japan's ability to launch a multi-pronged attack was not considered.[20]

Among the citizens of Bandoeng the need for more defence had become a daily topic of discussion, but no one wanted to exaggerate the problem. A voluntary *Stadswacht* modelled on the British Home Guard had been launched in 1939. In each of twenty-three major cities (mostly on Java) such a local defence force, staffed by volunteers who could demonstrate good knowledge of their community and would be able to react speedily to a parachute attack—or more likely, the action of fifth columnists—now existed; they were drawn from all sectors of the population and totalled seven thousand men and women.[21] Now a call went out for voluntary contributions to make available the half a million guilders required to properly motorize these brigades, for the key to their success was rapid deployment to areas where the realm was being threatened, and for this, trucks, motorbikes and some armed troop carriers were required. It was a step in the right direction, a small step, though some questioned the need for equipping a "home defence force" with capabilities for transportation to trouble spots away from "home": that seemed to be a contradiction.

The authorities also decided to develop a reserve officers corps, the only qualification for entry being possession of a high school diploma. Approved applicants were then subjected to a vigorous short-term training assignment. Previously, membership of such a corps would have consisted exclusively of reservists from the Netherlands who happened to be in the Indies, where they obtained specialist training for service under local conditions. Now fresh recruits were sought among the various populations of the Indies. A key requirement was attainment of fluency in Malay so that in future these officers could command units of indigenous soldiers who might be recruited in time of need. Popular opinion held that the country was now "well on its way to achieving a higher degree of preparedness."

The upbeat atmosphere was sadly depressed by the untimely death, on January 11, 1941, of forty-seven-year-old Mohammed Husni Thamrin, one of the representatives in the *Volksraad*. At Christmas he had been placed under house arrest for yet again demanding Indonesian independence (but with a Dutch form of Commonwealth status) and his death was now attributed to suicide. He had been born in Batavia, where he received his Dutch high school diploma, after which he took on a clerical position with the KPM. He soon became active in politics, serving initially in a local government council; in 1938 he was appointed to the *Volksraad*, whose chairman, J. A. Jonkman, now

---

20. Thomas, *Battle of the Java Sea*, 35.

21. *Java Bode*, January 23, 1941.

observed that this sad event "cast a deep shadow over the council chamber." Today, one of the main roads passing by the *Lapangan Merdeka* (freedom square) in Jakarta perpetuates his name as a martyr of the independence movement.

But war was inexorably moving closer, creating a mild sense of unease on Java. The seemingly carefree ocean voyage we had enjoyed a scant six months before now was attended by risks. Our friend Edu had accordingly heaved a sigh of relief when his sweetheart Emmy arrived safe and sound. Shipment to Java of our possessions remaining in South Africa had to be postponed. During the last month or so, ships plying these waters had mysteriously disappeared, often after being diverted from their route by distress calls. In November two ships, the Norwegian oil tanker *Ole Jacob* and a British freighter, the *Automedon*, disappeared in rapid succession. This was troubling.

The loss of MV *Automedon* was noteworthy since it contained among its cargo top-secret military assessments of the situation in the Far East addressed to Commander-in-Chief Far East, Air Chief Marshall Sir Robert Brooke Popham. That document may well have ended up in Japanese hands: it set out a likely sequence of steps the Japanese would take to attain their objectives and indicated the inability of Britain to thwart such steps, and in so doing spelled out the vulnerability of Singapore defences. Why this secret document was sent in this insecure and slow way is a mystery. Alan Matthews suggests the following:

> The most feasible theory attached to this deliberate action concerns itself with the British War Cabinet and their possible desire to ensure the entire Appreciation could not be discussed at the Singapore Defence Conference of October 1940. Particularly as documented evidence alludes to the War Cabinet having deep reservations that any pessimistic disclosures within the Appreciation could prelude a detrimental reaction on recent requests to Australia and New Zealand for reinforcements to be sent to the Middle East.[22]

General Tomoyuki Yamashito of the Japanese General Staff, on the other hand, completed a tedious train journey through Siberia in time to celebrate Christmas in Germany, where he wanted to study Germany's Blitzkrieg tactics at close hand; soon he would put those lessons to good use, thereby earning the nickname, "Tiger of Malaya."[23] As a result he missed the second Tokyo visit by members of the Hitler Jügend, who had offered the Japanese so much inspiration during their previous visit when they scaled sacred Mt. Fuji while

---

22. Mackenzie, *German Armed Merchant Raiders During World War Two.*

23. So famous had he become as to threaten his seniors in Tokyo: he was reassigned to an obscure position in Manchuria.

singing anti-communist songs. Their visit was used to inaugurate a Japanese counterpart, *dai Nippon seishonendan*, to inspire Japanese youth in a similar way.

In the meantime General Yamashito's compatriots in the Indies were diligently pursuing their diplomatic objectives, bringing the Indies completely within the Greater East Asia Co-Prosperity Sphere. Early in the New Year, Foreign Affairs Minister Yosuke Matsuoka dwelt on this latter concept during his address to the *Diet* in Tokyo. The Dutch government-in-exile could not let this challenge pass unnoticed, and on January 31, 1941, the ambassador in Tokyo, Major General J. C. Pabst, lodged a formal protest informing the Japanese Minister of External Affairs that the Netherlands refused to admit the inevitability of the Indies forming part of a Greater East Asia Co-Prosperity Sphere. Chuichi Ohashi, the assistant minister, responded to Pabst's complaints by pouring scorn on "comments from a government-in-exile," and ensured that this message got wide media coverage. The press in the Indies gave this news item full front-page attention on the following Monday, February 4, 1941.[24] "How could the Japanese government belittle the Dutch government, while agreeing to negotiate with its representatives?" was the rhetorical question posed. The situation was deemed so bizarre, so puzzling, that it called into question the veracity of the source of this information, the Japanese news agency Domei. The newspaper innocently concluded, "There must be a mistake."

On Friday, February 6, 1941, Emmy and Edu were married in a little church in a charming north Bandoeng residential area; Edu's older brother, Rudolf, and his wife, Charlotte, had made their home on the Bouwmanlaan available for the event. It was a glittering social occasion, with Emmy in a flowing white gown and veil and Edu resplendent in his white tropical officer's uniform amidst a sea of gaily dressed well-wishers bearing gifts and flowers. After the service my parents went outside to take up a position near the road so that my father could get a good 8 mm film shot of the couple emerging from the church. As the strains of Mendelssohn's wedding march filtered to the outside air over the hubbub of voices, the newly-wed couple appeared on the church steps, where members of Edu's regiment, resplendent like the bridegroom himself in their white tropical uniforms and their black *kepis*, had lined up, forming an honour guard with their swords raised to create an arch under which Emmy and Edu slowly made their way, while two small boys, the children of Rudolf and Charlotte, scattered flower petals over the ground ahead of them. The happy couple entered a car and left for a short honeymoon in one of the mountain resorts.

---

24. *Java Bode*, February 1, 1941; *Ochtendblad*, February 4, 1941.

In the meantime my parents' house building plans had moved ahead. They had bought a building site north of Bandoeng, in a new district called *Dennelust*, or "Pine Grove," a nice name for a fancy residential suburb with distinctly upmarket pretensions. It was a most agreeable piece of land, with a splendid view over the Preanger valley; on a clear day the Malabar volcano beyond the city could just be discerned. Not only would we have a wonderful view from the front of the house, but it would also face the cooler southern breezes that occasionally wafted up the valley. My father had surveyed the land and completed the design for an elegant two-storey villa, and had negotiated a building contract.

With the tenancy contract for the Serajoestraat house soon to expire, the time was ripe to seek a more convenient, short-term rental accommodation. Through an acquaintance, my mother heard about Mrs. Raken, a widow who had just bought a new house but was unable to move in as yet, and for whom a short-term rental would be fine. The house stood in a new residential area on the northwestern edge of Bandoeng and we could take possession on the first of May. An added bonus was my father's ability to readily visit the building site on his way home from work. In his opinion an architect had to closely supervise a building project because contractors were likely to cut corners if given the chance.

On Friday, April 4, my father celebrated his thirty-third birthday. The following Sunday, Edu and Emmy came over to help mark the event. In addition, they hoped to relive their recent wedding by looking at the 8 mm film and promised to tell us about the wonderful sights they had seen on their honeymoon. So upbeat was the atmosphere that my father unpacked his violin and played a rendition of his favourite Bach piece, the Air on a G string. He had not played his violin at all in South Africa, but here in Bandoeng, he might be able once more to find partners for a trio or a quartet, and perhaps my mother could be interested in playing the piano. "Wil, we must get you a piano in the new house, a grand piano!" he exclaimed.

That year Easter fell on April 19. The house foundations had not yet been laid, so why not make a short trip into the interior of Java? My parents had heard so much about the fabulous scenery that lay beyond the Preanger and Juf gladly agreed to stay behind to look after the household while they were gone. The trip was a huge success and they brought back wonderful stories and photographs.

"We crossed the Serajoe River—our street was named after it," my mother enthusiastically related to Juf. "It was beautiful, with big trees along its banks." Now they could understand why the city fathers had chosen to name a city road for this stream. When Emmy came by to hear about the trip, my mother told her about their volcano adventure: they had been allowed to descend onto the crater floor of Merapi which had been dormant for a while: what had been a lake of molten rock was now congealed, and while the rock was still too hot to walk on, one could nevertheless traverse the caldera on a temporary wooden path.

"When we walked on that path we could feel and see the rock bending under our weight," my mother, who had found it rather scary, recounted. "The path led us to one of the fumaroles where hot, smelly gases escaped from a crevice."

"Did you get to Borobudur?"

"Oh yes, it was magnificent! They are still excavating part of it. It's an immense monument of ornate stone work describing—what was it, Bou?"

"The Mahayanian Buddhist Holy Way, I think."

"Yes—in a spiral fashion around a temple complex made to resemble a lotus flower, according to the guide. We also visited Kalasan, Hindu I think, and Mendut."

She reached for an ornate silver cigarette case on the coffee table and offered a cigarette to Emmy.

"Where did you get that beautiful cigarette case?"

"Oh yes, I had forgotten," she said, as she got up and went to a cupboard. She brought out some silver bowls to show Emmy. They were, like the cigarette case, exquisitely crafted and decorated with stylized flowers and plants. "These we bought in Djokjakarta, from a shop next door to the Sultan's palace," my mother explained.

The trip was an amazing and memorable experience, and served to heighten my parents' conviction that their move from South Africa to Java had been wise. One of the curiosities they encountered on this journey was a bridge made entirely of bamboo spanning a narrow gorge. It was as daring a piece of civil engineering as it was elegant, and my father took a snapshot to help find out more about its origin. After he returned to Bandoeng, he showed the image to his new friend, the civil engineer Theo Aalbers, who told him that the bridge had been designed by a Javanese engineer recently graduated from the Technical College in Bandoeng, but who had since forsaken engineering for politics and was now in jail.

"He was a bright engineer," continued Theo, "but unfortunately Sukarno got diverted to bad ways and became a troublemaker."[25]

What a wonderful, romantic country this was, so blessed with the bounties of nature, crowned by such a venerable, ancient civilization, a country mostly of content, happy people with their songs and puppet plays and their beautiful carvings; my parents felt that they, too, had caught a glimpse of paradise.

---

25. Like many Indonesians, Sukarno had only one name.

We Move House

Our new home, Professor Eykman*weg* (way) 17, was a much more agreeable residence than the one we had just vacated. Professor Eykman, after whom this road had been named, was a nineteenth-century Dutch scholar who had been overwhelmed by the fascinating botanical wealth of the Indies. He had been a recognized expert on the pharmaceutical properties of certain tropical plants, and for that reason this road continues to honour his name to this day.

The recently built house stood on the south side of the east–west–running road along the northern edge of Bandoeng; the open field across the road was earmarked for a future housing development. Only two or three houses were located to the west of our dwelling, but to the east, where the Professor Eykman*weg* intersected the main road leading south to the city centre, there were more houses. Behind the house lay the spacious treed grounds of a large hospital complex, then known as the *Instituut* Pasteur, but now called the Hassan Sadikin Hospital.

The only one who regretted the move was Juf, because she once more felt restricted in her ability to get around. No longer could she walk to a nearby square or the church with her little charge, and an independent shopping trip now required the use of a bus or a *betja*. Juf, however, was not one to complain, and she knew that the next move, to *Dennelust*, would bring us into even greater isolation. The new address made it easier for my father to keep a close watch on the construction progress at *Dennelust*, located only three kilometres further to the north. At that time, the road where our future home was located was unnamed; today it is called *Jalan* Kapiten Tandean. In the evening, on his way back from work, my father could, with little inconvenience, make a detour to the building site before coming home for supper.

Although our new home was more spacious than the one we had just vacated, the garden remained modest. The main dwelling was set back some thirty feet from the road, which was partly shaded by a row of royal palms.[26] A gravel driveway, skirting the western edge of the lot, gave access from the road to a garage attached to the house. The front of the house had a large veranda, from which French doors led into a living room and the adjacent dining area. There was a small backyard, completely enclosed by whitewashed masonry walls to provide privacy and dissuade petty thieves or stray animals from trespassing. With time, those whitewashed walls would become green with mildew from the frequent rains and then supply nourishment for *keongs* (large snails). A separate building provided accommodation for *babu* Iti and for *koki*, a cook. *Babu* Iti had moved with us from the Serajoestraat home, but *koki* had recently been hired.

---

26. *Roystonea*, a native of the US Gulf Coast.

Sitting on the veranda we could relax, sipping afternoon tea, while letting our eyes feast on the magnificent unobstructed view of the Preanger valley. The open land in front of the house sloped gently down to the small, meandering Tjikakak River, flowing southward past Bandoeng into the Tjitarum River. On the distant banks of that little stream, there stood a clump of bamboo and banana plants, marking the location of a small *kampong*. In the early morning, when the air was fresh and clear, one could make out the huddle of *atap* roofs, set off by their dung colour among the greenery. Further to the north, beyond that river and the crest of a low rise of land, lay the hazy blue silhouette of the Tangkuban Perahu, with a thin wisp of steam rising from its broad crest. If one looked to the northwest, one could just make out the peaks of volcanoes flanking the Puntjak Pass, the route followed by the main road to Buitenzorg, site of the Governor General's residence and the famous botanical gardens.

Out here on the edge of town, one was somehow more aware of the weather than downtown. Typically, morning daybreak came abruptly after a cool night. The warmth of the sunlight streaming down from a blue sky was therefore always welcome. As the day progressed and the air temperature rose, fluffy clouds would accumulate around the mountains and grow by early afternoon into monumental towering masses of billowy castles in the sky, their bases becoming darker and darker as the day wore on. Eventually the clouds would shed their watery load, first with a few large drops and soon with a downpour that could within minutes convert a lawn into a shallow lake. Such showers were localized, and a clear line would often delineate the land being drenched from that remaining dry. It was exciting but at the same time scary standing on the veranda, sheltered from the rain, and seeing gusts of wind tearing at the palm fronds of the trees lining the road. If between the sheets of rain one caught sight of the bamboo clumps in the distance, one could see them swaying wildly, and one wondered how the *inlander*s living in the *kampong* fared. When the rain stopped the air would carry a wonderful, intensely pungent smell of ozone.

No one wore raincoats. Those who wanted to stay dry would have to find shelter or carry an umbrella. Sometimes one would see an *inlander* hurrying along with a banana leaf used as a makeshift umbrella; in the tropics, getting wet was no hardship. The rain would eventually stop and the sun would break through, and in no time one was once more dry and refreshingly cool. By late afternoon, the remaining clouds would shrink, leaving little puffs of pink and orange in the evening sky. The Bandoeng climate was very pleasant indeed, notwithstanding the frequent showers.

By this time the major building project my father had worked on, the KMA complex, had reached an important construction milestone. Celebrating completion of the wooden roof-frame had been a long-standing tradition of the building trade, and for this occasion leading figures of the project gathered in front of the future entrance for a formal photograph (figure 7). Most were dressed in their tropical regalia: white shirts, shorts and pith helmets.

Construction at *Dennelust* proceeded satisfactorily, and Theo Aalbers, the contractor, promised that the house would be finished by Christmas 1941, if only the Sundanese coolies would stay on the job! My father had quickly sized up this distinction between the casual labourers of Indonesia and the ones he had previously encountered in South Africa. In South Africa food was scarce, the soils were poor and the rains were infrequent; here on Java, the land was unbelievably fertile. The Javanese economy was at that time partly dependent on rice imports from the outlying islands, but *kampong* fruit trees such as banana and papaya could produce an almost limitless supply. Every *kampong*, moreover, had its population of pigs and ducks, chickens and roosters. The Sundanese workers of the Preanger, happy-go-lucky as ever, saw no real benefit in toiling for the white masters any longer than required to earn enough money to purchase a *strootje* (cigarette), as my father put it. For him and his colleagues, charged with important construction projects and timelines, this casual attitude to work caused frustration. My father would sometimes complain about the indolence of the *inlanders*.

My parents' plans for shipping to Java the furniture left behind in South Africa were looking more dubious than ever, given the recent loss of more ships in the Indian Ocean: in March the KPM ship *Rantau Panjang* had disappeared, and speculation was rife that German U-boats were now active here.[27] In May 1941, the German army had overrun the Balkans and invaded North Africa with the clear intent of denying Britain the use of the Mediterranean and access to Middle Eastern oil supplies. There even seemed to be a threat that the German army might reach the Indian Ocean shore.

The local press had taken note of the increased military activity, and began to raise questions about Allied co-operation, thus prompting the Foreign Minister to announce that a Common Defence Front was in place, running from Singapore via the Indies to Australia. On May 10, a "huge" (according to the press) military show of force was staged to commemorate the fall of the Netherlands, to emphasize the determination with which we were striving to free Dutch soil from foreign oppression, and to reassure the inhabitants of Java. The march-past (reported in great detail in all the papers) included all available military and quasi-military units, to wit: infantry, the bicycle brigade, the armoured brigades, the horse-mounted cavalry, and the women's transport auxiliary. A fly-over of fighters and bombers demonstrated the growing air power. We had certainly noticed the increased level of military activity, because

---

27. A heavily armed German ship disguised as a Dutch merchantman was responsible.

our house on Professor Eykmanweg lay under the flight path of incoming air traffic to the Andir airfield, located two kilometres to the west. Air traffic in those days was so infrequent that it constituted an entertainment for young and old rather than being a nuisance. Not only did the occasional DC-3 or DC-5 make an approach, but now, thanks to the increased interest in military activities, we also saw a few military aircraft, such as the American-built Curtis Interceptors, recently delivered and stationed at Andir, and Tiger Moths, used for training a newly established volunteer air corps. Among these trainees was our South African compatriot, Tony van Kempen. Thus war fever had finally reached the Indies.

An authoritative newspaper article, however, gave readers tremendous comfort about "the state of our defences." The headline read "Singapore is capable of holding out for a long time," and its subtext read, "lessons taught by tiny Malta." Colonel Fredric Palmer, a military history expert, elaborated with the following encouraging words:

> The prophet who claims that Singapore should be capable of holding out for two or three months, would be advised to extend his estimate by a factor of ten—even twenty to be on the safe side, should it even be possible to conquer this mighty fort.[28]

The justification for this bold statement was the extraordinary resilience demonstrated by the "tiny, rocky island of Malta" against the might of the Italian and German air forces. The key to success, according to this military expert, was the small size of Malta, facilitating a concentrated defence. The Colonel discussed the possibility of Japanese invasion of Singapore, and pointed out how much more difficult such a venture was than the German attempt to invade Britain. The English Channel was only twenty-five miles wide, but the distance between Japan and Singapore was 2,900 miles, thereby providing more than enough early warning. Because of the daunting terrain of Malaya, Palmer discounted the possibility of the Japanese invading Singapore via the Jahore causeway joining the island to Malaya. He added that there was no risk of fifth columnists, since there were few Japanese in Singapore, and "the Chinese population was far too busy earning money to be detracted by promises of a new order in Asia." How reassuring that analysis was!

That same evening Colonial Affairs Minister van Kleffens gave a radio address in which he once again turned down Indonesian requests for constitutional discussions "until after the war." It was a momentous occasion, because this was the very first time a person charged with that high office of the Crown had actually visited the loyal NEI, the Crown Jewel of the imperial possessions of the House of Orange.

---

28. *Java Bode*, May 9, 1941.

Our free time was occupied with more outings to the pleasant surroundings of Bandoeng. We made the trip to Buitenzorg (today's Bogor) and its famous botanical gardens. The scenic road taking us northward in the direction of Batavia passed over the breathtaking Puntjak Pass, flanked by steep, heavily forested slopes marking the northwestern boundary of the Preanger valley. From there the road led down among the coffee and tea plantations covering the lower, northern slopes of the volcanic backbone of Java. As we approached the lowlands around Batavia, the landscape gave way to more serene, undulating countryside. In 1817 the botanical gardens had been added to the existing grounds around the Governor General's palace by Casper Georg Carl Reinwardt, a German scientist recruited by the Dutch government for this task. The botanical garden had been proposed by Sir Stamford Raffles, the English gentleman serving as Governor General of the Indies during the Napoleonic interlude. Near the entrance was a cenotaph, placed there by Raffles to honour his deceased wife, Olivia. Inscribed thereon is the following verse:

Oh thou who ne'er my constant heart
One moment hath forgot.
Tho' fate severe hath bid us part
Yet still forget me not.

The gardens had extensive walkways; a huge variety of trees, shrubs and flowers, including numerous colourful orchids and spectacular bougainvillea; large ponds with giant *Victoria Regina* water lily pads "big enough to support a new born baby," my father claimed; and the world's largest flower, the bizarre, one-metre-wide stinking *Rafflesia*.

On June 14, 1941, the Japanese trade envoy, Yoshizawa, received a telegram from Tokyo ordering him back home. Two days later he broke this surprising news to his host, Dr. van Mook, forgetting to tell him that it was the promise of the future German onslaught on Russia, confided to the Japanese ambassador in Berlin, that had rendered valueless to Tokyo prolongation of the diplomatic charade in Batavia. Van Mook accompanied Yoshizawa and his companions past a uniformed honour guard to a Japanese ship lying in the Tandjong Priok harbour. Yoshizawa thanked his host profusely, but thought it undiplomatic to mention his hoped-for early return to Java's verdant shores—in a modified capacity. The inhabitants of the Indies were glad to see the delegation retrace its steps to Japan, but failed to sense the sinister significance.

A month later news filtered through that Japan had occupied French military bases in southern French Indochina.[29] Tokyo knew, thanks to the top-secret papers acquired from the doomed ship *Automedon*, that Britain would not

_____

29. *Java Bode*, July 24, 1940.

consider this as a *casus belli*. Having secured in advance compliance from the Vichy regime, Japan could peacefully disembark at Cam Ranh Bay forty thousand Japanese troops who were then able to make their way unopposed into Saigon by bicycle. Since the Japanese continued to rely on the heavy-handed French colonial rule to maintain peace, the stage was set for the communist-led uprising after the Second World War.

It was Hitler's attack on Russia that prompted Tokyo to take this gamble, even though the previous gamble, based on Hitler's expected conquest of Britain, had not paid off. With Russia fully occupied on its western front, Japan had gained some freedom of manoeuvre in Asia. The occupation of Indochina sent a shock wave around the world, for the Japanese now had a secure base of operations two-thirds of the way from Tokyo to the Indies. The United States and NEI responded by imposing a full embargo on the shipment of oil and other raw materials to Japan. This dramatic response forced the Japanese to measure the time available for conquest of the NEI in terms of its dwindling stocks of oil and other strategic materials. Japan had boxed itself in.

Edgar Snow, an American correspondent for the *Daily Herald*, the largest newspaper in the British Empire, was adding the final words to his book, *The Battle for Asia*, predicting, "It would only be on the gamble of successfully grabbing those [European] colonies before exhausting her own reserves that Japan would go to war against Britain and America."[30]

Snow had a poor opinion of Japanese conscripts, attributing this to the feudal nature of the Japanese army, but admits that it could provide Japan with an army of six million. He observes as well "that Japan's successes have been built solely on her immense technical and armament superiority rather than on the Japanese conscripts,"[31] and that "she at present enjoys an advantage over the European colonial powers in the east, who still hold their possession fundamentally by sea power, which is itself inferior to Japan's."[32]

The difficulty the Europeans living on Java had in comprehending the gravity of the situation is curious. The appearance of Japanese troops in French Indochina prompted the newspapers to express concern about Japanese intentions, but not in terms of a military threat to the Indies. The *Java Bode* of July 24 printed pictures of the meeting between French Admiral Jean Decoux and Japanese General Raishiro Sumita. In the accompanying text, the comforting point was made that "the Japanese occupation will not violate French Sovereignty." A month later, the periodical *Geef Acht!* (Attention!) published a lengthy article, complete with a map of French Indochina, with the heading, "What is Japan's Strategy?" The article concluded that Japan was planning an invasion of Thailand. The map did not include Malaya or the Indies

30 Snow, *The Battle for Asia*, 379.

31 Snow, *The Battle for Asia*, 383

32. Snow, *The Battle for Asia*, 380.

within its frame, suggesting thereby that a military threat to these two colonial possessions was inconceivable. In the accompanying text the breaking-off of trade discussions between Japan and the Indies was attributed to the refusal of the Indies government to kow-tow to Japanese assurances that exports would not be sent through to Germany. That these goods were of strategic importance to Japan itself was not considered.[33]

Observers in the NEI were not alone in this respect. A British military attaché, accustomed to assessing an army by its "polished buttons and precise foot drill," was unimpressed at seeing the Japanese troops on parade "in baggy uniforms" in Tokyo.[34] It was one thing for the Japanese troops to be allowed to enter French Indochina, and quite another to have to attack a European army and navy armed with modern weapons. The risk of a Japanese strike was discounted because of the vigilance displayed by the patriots of the NEI against fifth columnists such as the NSB. There would be no equivalent to a Vichy regime in the Indies!

Early in July it nevertheless was agreed that a limited "non–Dutch citizen" militia would be created, although some Indonesian *Volksraad* members wished to see exclusive use made of "native Indonesians" (no Chinese or Arabs) on a hugely expanded scale. They also wanted to ensure that such military service would only take place "on the home front." The government, however, saw no benefit in "creating an army of a million." Selective recruitment from only one racial group "would result in an imbalance with air and naval power, and would be as utopian as it was unnecessary."[35] Training for non-commissioned officer positions was open to all who spoke Dutch, and a substantial number of Indonesians presented themselves. For the Indonesians, who mostly took for granted the need to remain loyal to the Dutch Crown and for years had been chafing at the limited employment opportunities, this came as a welcome improvement.

By September, the papers could reassure the public that the United States' defence preparations in the Pacific were making excellent progress, and that the United States would likely gain future access to Singapore. What's more, the KMA complex was ready for use. Defence matters, in other words, were well in hand. At that same time the Japanese War Council defined its pre-emptive strike southwards in terms of simultaneous attacks on Malaysia, the Philippines and Hawaii. This would be a naval operation and thus finally justify the immense expenditures incurred over the previous decade. All that was needed for final plan approval by Emperor Hirohito was assurance that Japan would emerge victorious against the much more powerful United States. Admiral Isoroku Yamamoto's suggestion that a humiliating defeat of British and Dutch

---

33 *Geef Acht!*, August 23, 1941.

34. Deighton, *Blood, Tears and Folly*, 584.

35. *Java Bode*, July 2, 1941.

forces at the hands of a lightning Japanese strike would destroy the American will to fight back was gladly accepted by almost everyone in the Emperor's circle of advisors. It was the sort of logic that appealed to the Japanese mind, which set great store on the superior Japanese "spirit" as a secret weapon. Withdrawing from China, Japan's only alternative option, was unthinkable. Diplomatic talks with the United States would continue, but since they occurred against a strict deadline, they were doomed to be pointless; meanwhile, preparations for war went into high gear. There was no need for an elaborate attack plan on the Indies: we would be like lambs led to the slaughter.

We continued to enjoy the pleasant domestic life of Bandoeng, with daily trips to the *pasar*, the wonderful market stocked with the most exotic sights and smells: live fish in tanks, chickens, eggs, vegetables of every conceivable description, earthenware goods, pots and charcoal stoves, bags of rice, fruit in abundance, pungent spices such as curry and the *tjabe rawit*—tiny, red peppers that set one's tongue on fire. Occasionally, we also went along the footpath through the *alang* grasses of the field in front of our house down to the nearby *kampong* to buy eggs or a chicken for dinner. Here, sheltered by the bamboo bushes, stood a cluster of huts, artfully made of bamboo poles and *gedek* (woven bamboo strips) walls and *atap* roofs. The densely clustered bamboo trees looked formidable with their thick, smooth, yellow and grey stems. The ground around the houses was bare and the *kampong* looked neat. Children ran around half-naked and the chickens, little "*kampong* hens," scratched busily in the dirt. We could always count on diminutive *babu* Iti to lead the way and assist with the bargaining in her patient and cheerful manner.

As November reached its end, the magnificent house at *Dennelust* was nearing completion; the interior had been painted, but the parquet floor still needed to be laid; we were waiting for the final touches (figure 8). In Dutch society, birthdays are very important and my father had hoped to celebrate my mother's twenty-seventh birthday in our new home, but sadly, inevitable construction delays had made this impossible. So instead Emmy and a number of lady friends joined us for tea and tasty Dutch pastries on the veranda of our rented home on the afternoon of Wednesday, November 26. When my father and some of the ladies' spouses came home, they injected new life into the party, augmented by stronger drinks.

In the evening, after the guests had left, my parents and Juf sat on the veranda enjoying the cool night air. The moon was half full, only occasionally obscured by a small cloud, and only the sounds of a *tjitjak* scurrying around looking for insects disturbed the quiet. As yet, there were no street lights on Eykmanweg and so the view in the distance was crystal clear. Small charcoal fires could be seen glowing in the *kampong* by the river and, if one looked very closely, the dark outline of the distant mountains stood out against the wonderful tropical night. Overhead, the stars sparkled like diamonds. My parents were discussing the final stages of house construction and what furnishing plans they should make. A gentle breeze occasionally stirred the palm fronds of the trees along the road.

That night, thousands of miles to the north, a large number of men had sprung into action. Aided by a cloud cover that would obscure these activities from unwanted eyes, a large Japanese naval task force commanded by Rear Admiral Chuichi Nagumo weighed anchor from Tankan (Hitokappu Bay) in the southern Kurile Islands. The fleet, consisting of six aircraft carriers equipped with 423 aircraft, two battleships, three cruisers, nine destroyers, and eight accompanying tankers, left on a southeastward course—destination Hawaii. Simultaneously, Japanese pilots were readying their planes on Formosa for an air attack on Luzon, while General Tomoyuki Yamashita was assembling his troops in French Indochina for an amphibious operation against Malaya and a Japanese army Division was preparing to move in on Hong Kong.

Two days later Tony van Kempen and his fellow fighter pilots were instructed to remain on the air base, since intelligence had revealed that a large Japanese naval force had set sail for an unknown destination.

Once more the December 5 St. Nicholas festivities were in full swing in Bandoeng. For many, the weeks prior to the event were consumed with devising skits, wrapping personal gifts in the most elaborate fashion, or composing for loved ones verses of poetry to commemorate light-hearted events of the past year.

A day later a celebration took place on the coast of Borneo. On December 7, the cruiser USS *Marblehead*, accompanied by four destroyers and a tender, all part of the small American Asiatic fleet stationed in the Philippines under the command of Admiral Thomas C. Hart, lay in the bay of Balikpapan, one of the important oil-producing centres of the NEI. Admiral Hart, knowing that war was imminent, remained in Manila on his flagship, the USS *Houston*.[36] Such naval visits were not uncommon and offered a convenient opportunity for the ships to stock up on fuel. The previous night, the American crew members had attended a reception in the Balikpapan *Soos* in traditional "Indies" style; the party had lasted until the early hours of the morning, and the lower ranks had also had a good time on shore, judging by the number of children from the *kampongs* surrounding Balikpapan running around the next day with white sailor hats on their heads. More festivities at the club were planned for the evening, this time taking advantage of the hospitality of the US navy. Evidence that Uncle Sam was prepared to be a good host was amply demonstrated by the provisions already ferried to shore by the various quartermasters. The party was

36. Thomas, *Battle of the Java Sea*, 38.

on the point of commencement when one of the senior officers announced that the crew should return to their ships immediately. In great haste, bunker oil was loaded and the flotilla headed out to sea.[37]

---

37. Fabricius, *Brandende Aarde*, 52.

4. WAR

The morning of Monday, December 8, 1941, began normally enough. The citizens of Bandoeng were reassured by morning newspaper reports that "although tension has increased in the Far East on account of recent mysterious events, the ABDA (American-British-Dutch-Australian) front is in a state of preparedness."[1] The support for this expression of confidence was based on the government announcement that the NEI had invited the Royal Australian Air Force to station planes on "Indies soil" on Timor and Ambon. The newspaper article was accompanied by a helpful map showing French Indochina and Thailand, it being assumed that a Japanese invasion of Thailand might be next.

The previous week's story about the mysterious disappearance of the Australian cruiser, HMAS *Sydney*, travelling from the Sunda Strait to Fremantle, had certainly increased public unease, while leaving the public uncertain as to whom to blame. News that the *Kormoran*, a converted and heavily armed German freighter disguised as a Dutch vessel, had also been sunk in that area, apparently by the *Sydney*, combined with the fact that the Australian government had waited almost two weeks before publicizing these shocking events, to the mystery added contentions of a nasty political cover-up.

In spite of all this, we were still enjoying the aftermath of the St. Nicholas festival. Emmy, whose Christmas school holidays had started, came over in a *betja* to enjoy morning coffee with my mother. The two women were seated on the veranda, still giggling over the absurd presents they had given their husbands on Saturday. My mother had purchased a music stand for my father, and had wrapped it up in a package to disguise it as a handsaw. Emmy had disguised her present, a fancy cigarette case, as a machine gun. The men had been too busy with their work to have time for such elaborate surprises, though my father had managed to compose an amusing poem to accompany his gift, a house key.

At a stroke all was changed. It began when the NIROM radio announcer interrupted a program of religious discussions to declare that the Governor General would address the citizens of the Netherlands East Indies. As tension had been high, Juf, who happened to be near the radio, immediately called my mother and Emmy in from the veranda. His Excellency, Tjarda van

---

1. *Het Ochtendblad*, Dec 8, 1941

Starckenborgh Stachouwer, then announced in solemn tones that war had broken out in the Pacific; he gave few details beyond the fact that an American naval base at Pearl Harbor had been attacked and that the Netherlands East Indies had immediately declared war on Japan. It was a short address, lasting no more than a minute, followed by a rendition of the *Wilhelmus*, the national anthem.

As though struck by lightning, Juf stammered, "We have declared war?" Her emphasis lay on the word "we." It was a most bizarre idea. "O jee, o jee," she wailed.

"Where's Pearl Harbor?" My mother looked puzzled.

"Haven't you got an atlas?"

"Yes," my mother answered, "in South Africa. Perhaps our neighbours know."

When they returned to the veranda they noticed Mrs. Boot out in front of her house, a couple of doors down the street, having an agitated discussion with our neighbour, Mrs. Hannay; they had heard the news as well and Mrs. Boot's husband was a lieutenant in the KNIL: she knew that Pearl Harbor was on Hawaii, an unbelievable distance from Japan.

That evening, when my father came home, my mother asked him whether he had heard the shocking news. "Of course," he answered. "The news flashed through the office, but no one could figure out what's going on. Colonel Blok said that we had declared war on Japan, but Japan only attacked American positions."

"The Governor General said that Japan was crazy—stark raving mad," my mother offered. "He said that Britain is also involved, and that Japan would attack the Indies."

My father had brought with him the evening paper, with the news that Hawaii and Manila had come under air attack. "Look here," my father observed as he pointed to a small news item describing an air raid on Singapore and troop landings on the Malayan coast near the Thailand border. "That's why Britain's involved but the Indies has not been attacked."

"It's unbelievable—how could those bastards do this?" he growled. "They must indeed be crazy—even Hitler did not do something so stupid."

"Are we in danger here?" Juf asked anxiously.

"Of course not. The Japs have been cut off from their supplies—they'll soon run out of fuel, and their planes and ships are no match for ours."

"What about Australia?" my mother wondered thoughtfully.

"Australian troops are already fighting in the Middle East," my father answered.

My mother went to get the morning paper from the veranda, where she had been reading it while waiting for Emmy to arrive, and pointed out the news item she had seen but not read. "Something to do with Australia," she muttered, as she scanned the pages. She soon found what she was looking for, a report that the Royal Australian Air Force had just been given landing rights on Timor—and she read out loud, "This move will assist Britain in her task of patrolling the immense marine area stretching eastward from Malaya, and between the Indonesian archipelago and the southeast coast of Asia. Yes," she added after a pause, "the Australians are bound to get involved as well." Although it all came as a terrible surprise, there was a weird sense that this development had been anticipated by the government.

"I don't understand this," my mother muttered, pointing to the paper in my father's hands and the headline: "NETHERLANDS INDIES DECLARES WAR ON JAPAN."

"We have not been attacked, so why should we declare war?" she asked.

"That's exactly the point made by Colonel Blok," my father responded. "We are not allied with Britain nor the United States." It took a while for the crazy situation to sink in.

"Oh dear," Juf wailed. "This sounds frightening—just like 1914. Why could we not have remained neutral?" she whimpered, shaking her head from side to side.

"Don't worry, Juf, the Japanese are mad," my father repeated reassuringly. "They can't get far."

The Governor General's radio address was reproduced in full below the headline, and was accompanied by a photograph of His Excellency, dressed in his splendid viceregal uniform, lavishly decorated with gold braid, his face bearing an expression of supreme but quiet self-confidence in the invincibility of Western imperial power and prestige. Was this unprovoked declaration of war a manifestation of confidence that the arms at the disposal of the Governor General would provide the British and the Americans with valuable although so far unsolicited support—or was it something else? It was flattering, though, for this declaration seemed to confirm for the NEI a more independent status than that of a mere colony.

Seven hours after the commencement of war operations, Emperor Hirohito had signed a declaration of war against Britain and the United States, but a declaration of war against the Netherlands was absent because the Japanese government continued to hope the NEI would change sides of its own volition.

Confidence in the invulnerability of Western might had five days earlier been reinforced by the arrival in Singapore of the battle cruisers HMS *Repulse* and HMS *Prince of Wales*. This event was given prominence on the front page of the *Java Bode* of December 3. Not mentioned was the mishap of the third vessel earmarked for Far Eastern service, a modern aircraft carrier desperately needed, but which unfortunately had run aground off Jamaica and had to be repaired.

Henceforth issues around constitutional reform and self-determination were relegated to the back pages of the newspapers: the war drama now unfolding to the north of us as well as the worries about fifth-column activities commanded our full attention. The changed tactic of the Japanese government drew special press comment: hitherto Japan had exploited weakly defended positions of Asian countries to achieve a painless conquest, the French Indochina invasion being the latest example. Now Japan had challenged the super-power, America, as well as Britain, a step considered as bizarre as its previous forms of aggression had been opportunistic: Japan was an enigma.

The shock of the Japanese attacks soon wore off. For the first few days all the action took place far away, in Malaya against the British and in the Philippines against the United States; there seemed to be no further activity around Hawaii and as a result we could breathe a bit easier. "The Japs will soon be pushed back into the sea by Britain and the US," my father confidently predicted.

The departure from Andir of a squadron of Brewster bombers to support the British was also reassuring. Surely this madness would soon be put to an end, now that the feudal Japanese were confronting modern Western armies. In Bandoeng and elsewhere in the archipelago, all remaining two thousand Japanese citizens were promptly rounded up and dispatched to Australia to avoid a "fifth column" situation. They were then exchanged for Allied diplomatic staff in Japan, and as a result some of these Japanese businessmen were later able to return as part of the invading force in the guise of political and business experts with excellent local contacts.

The attack on Pearl Harbor nevertheless continued to dominate all discussions among our friends. The damage was spectacular though ephemeral, whereas the Japanese attacks closer to home left lasting impacts. The newspapers seemed to revel in the fact that the despicable, arrogant "Japs," with their ceaseless demands for concessions, had gone too far and had tweaked the nose of the US giant, who would quickly put them firmly in their place.

However, the government immediately ordered blackouts and imposed a curfew, an unsettling move. The windows of the houses were covered with dark paper or shuttered to prevent any light escaping at night, while street lights no longer came on; only a moon, shining through the palm leaves, illuminated the lawn in front of our house. Air-raid sirens were installed on hastily erected steel towers at various places in town. One was installed at the intersection of Nijlandweg with Professor Eykmanweg, not far from our house, and within days we could hear it wailing during practice runs. It would start softly on a low note and rise in pitch, and as the pitch rose, and as the sound from more distant sirens reached us, so rose the volume. The sound would echo around the Preanger like the howling of wolves, and then would gradually abate, its pitch and volume dropping to nothingness; this was followed, after a period of silence, by a short blast—the "all clear" signal. Initially the sound of the air-raid sirens was so startling that all activity on the streets came to a stand-still, and when the sirens stopped the silence could be deafening. Activity cautiously resumed after the all clear, but people remained subdued.

Our car was sent to a garage to be equipped with covers for the headlights. They were black, and only near the top of the headlight, where there remained a small rectangular opening, could one still see the glass. Above the hole was a flap to prevent light shining upward; it made the headlights look like a creepy eye with a heavy eyelid.

Our plans to move into the new house were now in thorough disarray. With defence activity feverishly under way, it had become impossible to arrange the final touches—securing the approvals necessary for water and electricity service, and to obtain permission for residency. Reluctantly, my father sought leave from Mrs. Raken to extend the lease on the house on Eykmanweg and the latter, herself facing an uncertain future, agreed; my parents paid the rent regularly and that was something.

On Thursday, December 11, the air-raid sirens suddenly sprang to life, bringing all traffic to a halt as people looked up to listen for the sound of approaching aircraft. False alarm! The following Saturday night, the sirens once again roared, sounding even more frightening at night, now made extra dark with the city lights off and the moon not yet risen. This, we were told, was a practice run for the civil defence organizations. Prompted by the Bandoeng town hall, my father contracted coolies to dig a deep, wide trench in our front lawn. The resulting air-raid shelter was about five feet wide and five to six feet deep, and about as long. The roof, consisting of grass turf, was supported by bamboo logs lying on supports five or six inches above the lawn; thus the structure was raised slightly above ground level and had narrow slits to provide fresh air, light, and a view of the sky. In town, school classrooms were hurriedly cleared of desks in preparation for service as emergency hospitals, while volunteers were sought for civil defence positions. The press nevertheless found grounds for optimism, and on Saturday, December 13, was able to report that Dutch submarines, operating out of Soerabaja, the naval base in East Java, had managed to sink a number of Japanese transport ships.

All of a sudden, Djojobojo legends appeared in the Malay language press: Djojobojo was a monarch who, in the twelfth century, had reigned over an east Javanese Hindu Kingdom called Kediri. This king is credited with various predictions that had a tendency to fluctuate as circumstances changed. One of these predictions now warned that the Javanese people, as punishment for their misdeeds, would for three centuries be subjugated under a light-skinned people, the people of the white buffalo: these seafaring people would come to Java to conduct trade. They would, however, get involved with internal Javanese conflicts and eventually divide the land among themselves. They would then be driven away by a yellow-skinned people, the *orang tjebol* (the yellow dwarf) coming from the north, who would remain here for only a short time, the time it takes for *djagung* (corn) to ripen or for the lifetime of a rooster—in other words, three months or three years. A *Ratu Adil* (a righteous king) would then appear, bringing this yellow interlude to an end and heralding a period of independence and progress.[2] Like all prophesies it was a wonderful mixture of metaphor, enigma and obscurity, and formed a sharp contrast to the disciplined and purposeful firestorm that had been unleashed from the north.

And so the days trundled on until December 18, when the disturbing news was published that "Terempa, a small Indonesian island, has been attacked. Damage was slight." Where did these planes come from and what were they doing? There was virtually no news from Malaya, where the "Japs" were undoubtedly being thrashed by the "Brits," nor from Luzon, where the Americans surely knew how to deal with these cheeky devils.

"Bah, it's nothing," my father scoffed. "The Jap pilot got lost and dropped his bombs to have enough fuel to get back home." That evening my mother read out loud the commentary given to the press by Major General L. H. van Oyen, who had been in the United States for military discussions and happened to be in Hawaii when the Japanese attack occurred. His return journey by commercial airline to Manila via Honolulu had been interrupted on Hawaii because of mechanical difficulties. Van Oyen reported looking "out of his Moana Hotel window on Sunday, December 7, to be pleasantly surprised by the sight of a large squadron of planes approaching—American," he thought, "— doing something unusual: engaging in military exercises on a Sunday."[3] Those morning reveries had been quickly shattered by the dropping of three small bombs within four hundred yards of the hotel. He remarked that it took some time to realize that this was an enemy attack, for "such had been the sense of security."

However, the next day the paper reported more unsettling news: attacks on New Guinea and the Moluccas.

When my father came home he found the map of the Netherlands East Indies to help him locate where the Moluccas were among the three thousand inhabited islands. He then read out loud a passage from the morning paper, "The bombs have missed their targets and the NEI air force has chased the enemy away. This is all good and well, but I would be happier if the targets were further away from us."[4]

---

2. Brugmans, *Nederlandsch-Indië onder Japanse bezetting*, Document 37.

3. *Het Ochtend Blad*, Dec 19, 1941

4. *Het Ochtend Blad*, Dec 19, 1941

The following Sunday Edu was granted a day off from his military duty and came over with Emmy to have dinner with us on the veranda. "Did you hear about the attacks on Miri?" he asked, adding, "on British Borneo?"

"No," my father answered. "What about those British ships—the *Prince of Wales* and the other one—."

"—the *Repulse*," Edu filled in. "I don't know. You would think that they would stop the Japanese. Some of our men have gone to Miri to defend the oil fields."

"Are people in the army worried about an invasion of Java?"

"No, Java is too well defended, but Thijs, my brother-in-law, the other day mentioned his plans to evacuate the family to Australia. This caused a row in my family, with my brother calling him unpatriotic. I think he is being melodramatic—we'll have this mess cleaned up soon. Just wait and see what General MacArthur will do to these baboons on Luzon."

My father and Edu could be forgiven for being puzzled by the attack on British Borneo, for the pride of the British Asian fleet, the two recently arrived modern battle cruisers, had a week earlier (on December 10) been sunk by a devastating air attack, causing the military experts to rethink their strategy and to demand more aircraft. The citizens of Bandoeng were not informed of this disaster until after the Japanese invasion, when the newspapers, now prompted by a changed propaganda slant, could present in glowing language accompanied by vivid illustrations the success of the Imperial Nipponese army in teaching the hated Western interlopers a lesson. The sinking of these two capital ships sealed the fate of Singapore and therefore also that of the Indies. More NEI air force units were hastily despatched to Malaya in a desperate attempt to reinforce the British position.

The pace of Japanese successes and Allied disasters became breathtaking. By December 20 sombre press articles suggested that women might be forced into military duty as part of the general mobilization.

"I wonder if that relative of Edu's was right, and that we should consider leaving Java," my mother thought out loud.

"How? We can't. I would have to give one month's notice, and I am sure I would be carpeted for daring to suggest this," my father responded glumly. "Besides, we can forget about *Dennelust*, and even if we got to Australia, we would be penniless. Around the office they call this 'Fortress Java'—and Singapore is still secure," he added hopefully. The remainder of the evening passed in gloomy, contemplative silence.

By December 22, most of the Philippines had fallen into Japanese hands after a heroic and bitter resistance offered by the inadequately supported American and Filipino troops. The setbacks came with bewildering speed and over an immense area. On Christmas Eve, Tarakan, the oil-producing centre on the east coast of Borneo, received its first air attack. The seven hundred oil wells, producing a crude oil so good in quality that it could be used in diesel engines without further refining, were spared along with the production equipment. That the Tarakan oil field would be a key military objective was clear and local oil company staff immediately started to prepare for the sabotage of the oil installations, while most European women and children were evacuated to Java. It was becoming obvious that something very serious was happening; everyone began to wonder what our soldiers, sailors and airmen were up to.

Every night, searchlights swept the Bandoeng sky, rarely picking out any planes, but illuminating with eerie fingers of light the water-laden monsoon clouds that lingered after the last rain storm. After dark, we sat on the veranda, and all we could see was the bright red tip of a cigarette at the neighbour's house when someone took a puff, and the white beams of the searchlights moving uneasily to and fro over the sky, which we watched with silent fascination. Everyone spoke in hushed voices, as though the enemy might be listening. No city noises penetrated this silence, and only the *tjitjaks* and *tokehs* could be heard, though occasionally a dog would bark. When the night was clear, the palm trees in front of our house were silhouetted against the sky and in the distance the looming hulk of the Tangkuban Perahu was faintly visible with, here and there, the flicker of a small *kampong* fire or the hooded headlight of a car. At other times, such quiet could be inspiring and restful, but now it had become frightening.

Christmas, never much of a celebration in Dutch society, now precipitated gloomy reflection.

"I wonder what our friends in South Africa are up to this Christmas?" my mother said at tea time. "It's been ages since we got the last letter."

Christmas in South Africa would have meant a trip to Durban, to the beach and the wonderful Indian Ocean surf. We sent my grandparents recent photographs via the Red Cross. Among them was a picture of a splendid new house with on the back the question in my father's handwriting, "Anyone interested in buying a house?"

By December 29, the tiny Tambelan Islands, halfway between Borneo and Singapore, were occupied, thus beginning the conquest of the Indies archipelago. Still the Japanese government refused to declare war on the NEI, but few could have any doubts about Japan's true intentions. By year's end, bombs had begun falling all over Borneo and an attempt was well under way to conduct a scorched earth policy in order to deny the Japanese access to the oil fields. We still found time to visit Emmy and Edu and talk nostalgically about the "good old Transvaal" and the happy times we had seen there, but the future looked bleak. Our world was shrinking: first the Netherlands had disappeared from the map, and now, suddenly, we had the unnerving feeling of becoming cut off from the world ourselves.

A New Year's Eve celebration had been planned for over a month, so notwithstanding their depressed spirits, my parents that night took the Opel for what would become its last ride. The moon was new and had set by the time they commenced their homeward journey from a dinner and dance at the *Soos*. My father was slowly driving up the tree-lined Nijlandweg, and being unable to see the road because of the blacked-out headlights, was steering the car by leaning against the steering wheel and looking up at the strip of night sky between the silhouettes of the tall, motionless Tamarind trees lining the road. My mother was also leaning against the dashboard, looking upward, as the car was passing through the intersection with the Pasteurweg, with home little more than five hundred metres further north…

Juf was startled when, in the early hours of the first of January, a strange car came up the driveway. She had anxiously stayed up until my parents returned from a party that appeared to have lasted a very long time.

My father's dark figure appeared on the driveway, slammed the car door shut, and mumbled something to the driver, who then quickly left. When my father entered the house, his clothes were soaked in blood and a pained expression marked his face. "My God, what happened?" Juf cried out. "Have the Japanese come—where's Wil?"

"An accident—Wil's in hospital—Pasteur—but I think she'll be okay." He uttered these words with difficulty, and there was blood in his mouth. My father then explained that they had not seen the other car coming from the north. "I had trouble getting Wil out of the car—the door was jammed and she was bleeding from her face."

"Nothing broken?"

"Wil has a broken arm, and my chest hurts."

"And your mouth?"

My father stuck out a bloody tongue.

"We were just by the Pasteur, and they heard the noise—came quickly—a doctor gave me a ride home."

The next day, my father, Juf and I went to the hospital around the corner to visit my mother. We were armed with a bunch of flowers and some green grapes *babu* Iti had procured first thing that morning; they were a luxury, imported at great expense from Australia. My mother tried to put a brave face on the matter: she would soon be discharged. "*Onkruid vergaat niet,*" she exclaimed laconically. "Weeds do not perish!" She came home a day later with her arm in a sling, a bruised face and a huge bandage over her eye where her forehead had been cut by the glass of the windshield; my father's tongue remained swollen, and his chest was painful. With the car gone and no prospect of getting a replacement, my father had to buy a bicycle to get to work. Our world had shrunk to the limitations of our own two feet, our ability to walk and cycle to get groceries. Trips to the Dago *Thee Huis* were ruled out; no longer was it even practical to keep an eye on our magnificent new house, now all but abandoned at *Dennelust*. It was a gloomy end to a turbulent year.

Fortress Java Falls

New Year's Day, 1942, saw the beginning of the end of our comfortable, happy life on Java. The next day British Borneo and Manila were taken and the Japanese conquest of the Netherlands Indies was under way. The end came with bewildering speed, like a devastating tsunami. For two more months we were able to delude ourselves with ideas of Western superiority, shrugging off the obvious signs that it was a flimsy façade. For two more months a degree of civil normalcy ruled over the many different peoples living on the archipelago.

On January 6, 1942, our daily newspaper speculated that General Sir Archibald Wavell would have to move from Singapore to Soerabaja. There was still a ring of self-confidence in these assertions; the journalist described Soerabaja as a "second Singapore." Upbeat newspaper articles described the frenzied activity of naval ship-building in that port, restricted, alas, to minesweepers and anti-submarine patrol boats, while the Japanese navy boasted the world's largest battleships.[5] Much was made of the fact that Indonesian workers were doing some of the skilled work and "even reading blueprints": how hard it was to adjust! The following day the *Java Bode* was able to reassure its readers, using huge headlines, that it was time for a "counterattack" on Japan: a joint effort between Australia and the NEI was in the works.[6] Delusions about the balance of military capabilities in our favour, as suggested by the news media, had reached preposterous levels. It was too late even to plan close defence co-operation between Australia and the Indies. Two weeks later, a large Japanese fleet was spotted homing in on New Guinea. Timor was clearly under threat, and Australia itself might now also fall within reach of Japanese aircraft. The deterioration of our position was absurdly rapid.

On January 9 another large Japanese invading force of forty-eight ships was sighted off the Borneo coast, heading for Tarakan, the oil-producing centre. When the Japanese troops finally overran the settlement on January 11, the sky glowed red with burning oil from the storage tanks and from the damaged, flowing wells, which once more had become "gushers" spewing flames high into the sky.

---

5. Built under immense secrecy.

6. *Java Bode,* Jan 7, 1941.

That same day Japan finally declared war on the NEI, thereby paradoxically recognizing its sovereignty as an independent state. The news that General Wavell would move his headquarters to Bandoeng followed; this city appeared to be designated as the point of ultimate resistance to invasion. The newspapers described it as a "highland fortress" that would be defended with "resolve and steadfastness" by "our Indies army."

On January 18, General Wavell arrived in Bandoeng and set up his headquarters in the Grand Hotel Lembang; it was located eight kilometres north of Bandoeng, on a plateau where the air was a bit cooler, not far from where the land began to rise abruptly toward the crest of the Tangkuban Perahu, thus providing modest shelter from Japanese planes that might suddenly invade the Bandoeng airspace. It was a very charming country hotel, with beautifully laid-out gardens.[7] General Wavell needed support staff, and so Elsa Kleist, an acquaintance of our friend, Ank de Ridder, cheerfully offered her services. "It only lasted a month, but it was fun and exciting," she recounted years later.

By the end of January, Borneo and its oil sources were effectively under Japanese control, but most of the oil installations had been destroyed, thus placing a question mark over the Japanese gamble. For them, the failure to acquire the oilfields intact was a major setback and evoked from one of its leaders a tirade of disgust, not because of the destruction of equipment, which could after all be replaced, but because of the destruction of the

> ...valuable fuel that rose from deep within the earth as a gift of the Gods, a holy gift that no mortal could appropriate, and which was the natural possession of Emperor Hirohito, whom the Gods had appointed to be ruler of all of Asia.[8]

Disgust was also accompanied by the ruthless execution of sixty-two Europeans, mainly soldiers injured during the previous campaign for Tarakan. Local villagers, including a dark-complexioned Eurasian KNIL soldier who had sought sanctuary there, were forced to witness the victims being marched into the sea and shot.[9]

The oil field damage, though at first sight spectacular, had been superficial and was quickly rectified. Prior to hostilities, annual oil production had been 7.9 million tons. During the first year of the Japanese occupation, production reached four million tons and during the subsequent year, pre-war production levels were re-established.[10] The failure of the scorched earth policy was attributable to a combination of factors. When these plans were first formulated

---

7. Hotel Lembang is still in operation today.

8. Fabricius, *Brandende Aarde,* 50.

9. Klemen, "Massacres of POWs Dutch East Indies, 1941-1942".

10. de Jong, *Het Koninkrijk der Nederlanden in de Tweede Wereldoorlog,* 11b, 508.

the aim was to implement "degrees" of destruction, commensurate with the seriousness of the threat: this left out of consideration the time factor. Thorough destruction of the subsurface equipment, thus rendering the wells beyond repair, would have taken more time than the pace of events permitted, while denying these vital supplies to the defenders themselves.

On February 15, the brave, hopelessly overwhelmed forces defending Singapore gave up the struggle, in spite of exhortations from Churchill "to fight to the death," and in spite of the growing evidence of the cruel treatment that lay in wait for them. Singapore fell, despite its huge garrison, because of lack of effective air defence; Lieutenant General Archibald Percival had to concede victory to General Yamashita.

The next day the *Java Bode*, our evening paper, carried the headlines, "Singapore has capitulated, a heavy military defeat." It called on the citizens to persevere, with the stirring message, "Let us together steadfastly carry on, in a storm and through a storm." A lengthy editorial on these events in the same paper opined that the fall of Singapore "is a lesson for the Indies." Singapore had relied on outside help for its defence, and it was now clear that "we" in the Indies would be better off relying entirely on our own capabilities. The writer concluded with the optimistic assessment that "Java will be a much more difficult nut to crack than Singapore, in spite of the absence of giant cannon, in spite of the smaller fighting force." He attributed this to the resolution of the defenders of Java, who would never be subjected to Japanese rule: "We, old and young, would rather die standing up than remain alive kneeling."[11] A noble though rather theatrical sentiment, but the fate of the NEI was sealed, and the only real remaining question was the fate of Australia.

A small group of Allied soldiers, including a contingent of Gurkhas, escaped from Malaya to Sumatra. They were soon captured, for that same day Palembang, on Sumatra, fell into Japanese hands, thus giving the latter control over the Pladju oil fields and access to an airfield close to Java. Java could now expect air attacks, and was as well denied access to its only remaining oil resources.[12]

Almost immediately air raids commenced. Every morning, when the sky was clear of clouds, air-raid sirens wailed, chasing us into our shelter, where we smelled the dank moist earth. The onset of the sudden afternoon thundershowers mercifully brought the threat to an end; then the wind would tear at the palm trees and the bamboo bushes, whipping their fronds to and fro, and rain would pelt us. A month earlier such a storm would have been frightening, but now it provided a brief respite from worse danger. No sooner had the storm abated, and the sirens' wail would again return. One would start

---

11. *Java Bode*, February 16, 1942.
12. Voskuil, *Bandoeng*, 56.

up, quickly followed by an echo from another part of the Preanger, more distant, more lugubrious. Conversations around war and peace, fears and hopes for the future, and anxiety about the fate of loved ones in far-off Europe stopped and we would listen for the ominous drone of airplane engines. When the "all clear" sounded, relief would return, as once more the buzz and chirping of the insects and their hunters, the *tokehs* and *tjitjaks*, became audible, along with the patter of residual monsoon raindrops on the veranda roof.

The Japanese air superiority was decisive: whereas the Allied Java Air Command had access to only eighty-six planes, many outdated, the Japanese had at their disposal 340 modern aircraft. We now finally began to get a first-hand sense of the military odds in Japan's favour. On Thursday, February 19, the air-raid sirens sounded in the afternoon, as they had done so many times before, and as usual we hurried into the air-raid shelter in our front yard. Then planes appeared; at first we thought they were returning Allied aircraft, but bombs exploding with muffled thuds confirmed that the war had come to our neighbourhood. Andir, the military airfield, barely two kilometres west of us, was the target for a Japanese squadron of nine bombers and twenty-eight fighters. The sixteen Dutch Hawk fighters had taken to the air in time to ward off the attack, but they were unable to prevent the destruction of thirteen planes parked and undergoing repairs. That afternoon, smoke and the stench of burning rubber and oil drifted eastwards over our house, long after the attacking planes had left, and in the evening the radio announced that one Japanese plane and three Dutch planes had come down. That same day, 1,500 miles to the southeast, Darwin, its harbour full of ships, was devastated by a bombing attack. Java was now surrounded by armed conflict.

A week later, the sirens sounded before my father had been able to leave for work, and so he joined us in the air-raid shelter. At about nine o'clock the Japanese planes once more appeared, again heading for Andir, this time with seventeen bombers and fourteen fighters, and that day another five planes undergoing repair were lost. Through the windows of our shelter, just above ground level, we could see the trails of smoke in the sky and a snow-white parachute, dropping in the fields across the road, no more than a kilometre away: it was a Dutch pilot who had bailed out.

Two large convoys of Japanese ships accompanied by two powerful Japanese strike forces were sighted heading towards Java. One convoy came from Cam Ranh Bay in French Indochina, and the other from Jolo in the Sulu archipelago between Celebes[13] and the Philippines. This news stirred the defenders of Java to desperate final measures. Given the hopelessness of the situation US Admiral Hart relinquished control of the crumbling Allied fleet to Vice Admiral Coenraad Helfrich, born and bred in the Indies and determined

---

13. Today's Sulawesi.

to fight to the death. Helfrich called for aircraft to cover his fleet of cruisers and destroyers, and General Wavell hastily rerouted to Java an American shipment of Curtis P-40 fighter planes that had arrived too late to assist with the defence of the Philippines. Of the squadron flown from Brisbane to Soerabaja, many were lost when the inexperienced pilots, unfamiliar with the geography, strayed off course and crash-landed. The remainder of the American shipment was therefore dispatched by sea, with some planes loaded in flight-ready mode on the aircraft carrier USS *Langley,* and the others, still in a disassembled state in crates, loaded on the freighter *Seawitch.*[14] Three days later, the USS *Langley,* its only air cover being a Catalina flying boat, was spotted by a lone Japanese bomber south of the Javanese port of Tjilatjap, and minutes later the *Langley* was sunk. The *Seawitch* succeeded in reaching port and its cargo of plane kits was shipped by rail to Bandoeng, where only three of the much-needed P-40s could be hurriedly assembled by the mechanics; but no sooner had this been accomplished than orders came for them to be destroyed, along with the remainder of the shipment, in order to prevent them from falling into Japanese hands.

The departure of General Wavell for Ceylon a few days later and the arrival of the Governor General in Bandoeng from Batavia caused morale to plummet. It was clear that we on Java would be left to the mercy of the approaching enemy, and that Bandoeng itself, rather than the island of Java, had now been designated as the "ultimate point of resistance."

W. H. J. Elias, a pre-war member of the administration in Batavia, was ordered to Bandoeng, and captured the drama with detail and freshness:

> War is coming, now also on Java. The inevitable farewell approaches. How much braver the women now appear to be than the men. Late at night a car turns up the driveway. A last kiss, summing up your entire life and your future, and already the car is on its way. Once more you turn around to catch a last glimpse of the loved face. Will you ever see it again? How hard the call of duty can be!
>
> A pale waning moon has just risen and throws through the branches of trees white patches on the road. The only illumination from the car comes through a narrow slit from the blackened headlights. It is quiet on the road. A single, red car tail-light appears and disappears in front of us. Far behind us glow two tiny cat's eyes from a vehicle following us. Not a word is spoken in the car because each one of us is far too preoccupied with his inner thoughts.
>
> Like the shadows of the trees we pass along the road, the memories of the years spent on Java glide through our consciousness. Will this be the end? Our thoughts go back to the past. The exotic

---

14. Tornij, 'De Seawitch bracht nog P40s naar Java."

novelty of Java, when we first arrived, later became familiar and commonplace through our daily experiences. The early responsibilities then thrust upon us reinforced the feeling of participation in the creation of something great in the Indonesian society. Life moved on with holidays on Java, Bali and with mountain climbing expeditions or restful days in the wonderful, cool mountain retreats.

Must this be the end? Will the Japanese destroy our Netherlands Indies, as a swarm of locusts destroys all? Or will the Allied victory, which certainly will come, leave something that permits reconstruction? Will we then still be able to meet and confront our Indonesian compatriots with confidence?[15]

During the last week of February, the inhabitants of Aceh on the northwestern tip of Sumatra once again rebelled against Dutch Imperial rule, and the local defensive force was now facing two adversaries. This had been the last area of the Netherlands East Indies to have submitted to Dutch rule after the bloody "Aceh War" at the close of the nineteenth century.

With much of Andir destroyed, we were suddenly relieved of air attacks and for a few days could attempt to go about our normal business. But the atmosphere remained sombre, for the newspapers could not hide the fact that Java was increasingly being surrounded by hostile forces. The grim news, punctuated by frequent, clipped military communiqués, seemed to blow over us like a never-ending storm. It was odd how the newspapers dwelt on the damage inflicted on Japanese planes and ships, giving the suggestion that Allied losses were fewer and less significant, sometimes even totally absent, and yet each new report of an island captured or the flight of refugees clearly spelled disaster. On February 26 the paper reported Japanese parachute landings on Timor, placing Darwin, only 430 miles to the southeast, under direct threat. That same day it also reported "heavy successful American bombing attacks on a large Japanese convoy."

The convoy nevertheless continued heading for the central Javanese coast, while a second convoy was ominously approaching the western Javanese coastline. The most significant defence Java had against invasion was the combined naval forces of the NEI, Britain, Australia and the United States, but the papers said little about the damage so far inflicted on these ships and their men in the defence of Borneo. It was the action over our heads that caught our attention. Those two large invading Japanese armadas were now rapidly nearing the Javanese coastline, like some great monster eager to devour its prey. So overwhelming was the Japanese strike force heading towards Bantam Bay on the western tip of Java that Vice Admiral Helfrich made the difficult decision to

---

15. Elias, *Indië onder Japansche hiel*, 28—29.

order his puny, outdated British "Western Naval Strike Force," based on Tandjong Priok, to seek the safety of the Indian Ocean. He nevertheless authorized a desperate final stand against the eastern invading fleet by his Eastern Naval Strike Force, based at Soerabaja, a port that had already suffered many bombing attacks.

On the morning of Monday, March 2, 1942, my mother opened the morning paper to see the stunning headline, "THE BATTLE FOR JAVA HAS STARTED."

Juf had come out for a cup of coffee on the veranda, and was shocked by the news. My mother read aloud the accompanying story about Japanese landings near the western tip of Java; it made for sombre reading. A smaller headline claimed that "a counterattack by our forces is expected."

"What does counterattack mean?" Juf wondered out loud.

The word "counterattack" had appeared so frequently during the last three months that it had lost significance, beyond offering us a faint glimmer of hope in an otherwise hopeless situation.

"Bou thought that twenty thousand American and sixty thousand Australian troops were supposed to reinforce our defences. Colonel Blok had told him that—I wonder where they are?" My mother's explanation did not help Juf at all.

The paper also carried a brief report on the battle of the Java Sea, the last-ditch attempt to obstruct the inevitable Japanese landings on central and eastern Java; this naval action was the only really significant opposition the Allies were able to muster. The article described "heavy losses" on both sides, but only mentioned "two Allied cruisers" having to leave the battle after "superficial damage," while "a cruiser of the Japanese Mogami class was left in flames."

During the day trucks loaded with cheerful, singing soldiers, totally unaware of Vice Admiral Doorman's hopeless battle against overwhelming odds, now thundered north along the Nijlandweg, not far from the house. We went to the intersection to have a look, encountering Mrs. Boot on the way.

"They're heading towards the Tjiater Pass[16] to reinforce the defensive works there," she explained. Mrs. Boot sounded authoritative.

That evening, when my father returned from work, my mother tried to tell him about the day's happenings, but he complained about the chaos in downtown Bandoeng.

"Red Cross personnel had arrived from Batavia but could not find accommodation—can you believe it? In the office a rumour went round that Bandoeng may have to restrict the flow of refugees for lack of space."

---

16. Today's Ciater Pass.

"We seem to have inflicted heavy damage on the Japanese," my mother commented, pointing to the morning paper, "but they still landed to the east of Rembang. It doesn't make sense."

She was right, for left unstated was the fact that the naval action that had taken place fifty kilometres north of Soerabaja had wiped out the Allied fleet, and left the Japanese navy in complete control of all the waters around Java. That encounter had become the largest naval battle since the battle of Jutland in 1916. It would be months before the scale of that Allied disaster was publicized, and then as a glowing propaganda coup by the victorious Japanese. It would be years before we began to appreciate the heroic sacrifice made by Vice Admiral Doorman and his men in the defence of Java. Although the two naval forces were almost matched in terms of number and sizes of ships, the Japanese strike force had torpedoes that worked and naval fire power that was made accurate by airborne observers. Vice Admiral Doorman, commanding the Allied fleet, had faced the Japanese with damaged ships, no agreed communication system beyond his order, "follow me," an exhausted crew and a shortage of ammunition, but with incredible bravery and grim determination. He surprised the Japanese with rapid fleet manoeuvring, confusing the Japanese gunners, a tactic Michio calls "*hi-dan undo,*" thereby delaying the inevitable disaster.[17] Of all this we were unaware at the time, and it is perhaps just as well that we did not know the scale of the defeat.

The excellent quality of the Dutch roads connecting all major cities of Java was a welcome surprise for Lieutenant General Hitoshi Imamura, commander of the 16th Imperial Japanese Army, and considerably facilitated his rapid conquest of the island. Seeing the Japanese infantry mounted on bicycles was startling to Dutch eyes. It was an effective military combination: cheap Japanese bicycles on expensive Dutch roads. Here and there, Dutch sappers had wisely arranged for the large Tamarind trees flanking these roads to be felled by dynamite to hinder Japanese advances, and Imamura's progress up the first few kilometres was agonizingly slow; unfortunately they also relied on the local Indonesian population, who may not have understood the full significance of the unfolding drama, to set off the remaining charges. Since this would also hinder the movement of local inhabitants taking produce from their *kampong* to the local *pasar*, they refused to carry out these instructions. Indonesians of that region subsequently went out of their way to assist the invading army by helping the soldiers clear away those few trees that had been felled.[18] Such enthusiasm for collaboration with the Japanese did not last long.

---

17. Noriki, *Maru Besatsu*, Utsonomiya's memoir, "Haguro Suitei", (author's translation).
18. Reid and Akira, eds., *The Japanese Experience in Indonesia*, 36.

That same Monday morning, while Juf and my mother were trying to enjoy their cup of coffee in spite of all the bad news, one of the Japanese cavalry units under the command of Colonel Toshinari Shoji completed its dash from the central Javanese north coast to overrun Kalidjati, the important military airbase, only forty kilometres north of our house. Some of the defenders managed to escape and walk back to Bandoeng, but a large part of the British unit stationed there, along with another twenty wounded in a nearby hospital, were bayoneted and beheaded. The Japanese army was in no mood to be burdened by prisoners, whether sick or healthy, and relished the opportunity to give their men some practice in their martial arts, the thrusting of bayonets into the bodies of prisoners firmly secured to the barbed wire fence, as well as the opportunity to exercise their swordsmanship on the same victims regardless of their being still alive or dead.[19] For the few who escaped with their lives, the scene was a chilling, stomach-turning spectacle; how abruptly our emerald paradise had become soaked in scarlet blood! The Japanese were inclined to see this as a manifestation of the compassionate sentiments of *bushido*, the samurai code of honour; the prisoners after all had not fought to the death or committed *sepukku* (the Japanese suicide ritual).

On March 5, the Wakamatsu group, now assisted by locally based air cover, advanced south from Kalidjati towards the Tjiater Pass on the flanks of the Tangkuban Perahu and towards Lembang, where Major General Pesman had his last line of defence. Japanese surveillance aircraft were able to pinpoint the positions on a map, which was stuffed into a metal cylinder and subsequently dropped to Wakamatsu, the commander.

We spent the next three days in our air-raid shelter, trying to make sense of the aircraft wheeling and diving to the north of us. When there was a lull in the deafening noise of plane engines, we heard the incessant, distant thuds of mortar fire.

Kalidjati, March 1942

On Monday, March 9, the sun rose through the still morning air over a frightened, tense Bandoeng. As the earth warmed, mist rose from the fields across the road from our house. The Tangkuban Perahu was silhouetted in blues against the morning sky and the wet leaves of the tall palm trees along the Eykmanweg glistened in the sunlight. An eerie, deathly hush hung over what should have been the busy start of a new week. The only sound breaking the morning stillness came from birds chirping in the palm trees lining the road.

---

19. Voskuil, *Bandoeng*, 60.

We were on the veranda, drawn out of the house by the sun and the silence. The events of the last few days seemed like a nightmare. The road, never busy at the best of times, was now uncannily quiet. Beyond it, in a distant field, little plumes of smoke could still be seen rising from where a plane had come to a fiery end. Was it one of ours or theirs? A lone *katjung* (a native boy) came into view strolling along the road. He stooped to pick up something shiny, a piece of metal, a spent shell perhaps? A plane suddenly appeared overhead and we ran out on the lawn to catch a glimpse: was it friend or foe? But there were no air-raid sirens and the plane disappeared over the hills to the east.

"I wonder what happened to those friends of Ank and Ben living near the observatory," my mother thought out loud. "That was where the fighting was, wasn't it?"

"Yes," answered my father. "There was a large defence installation on the Tjiater Pass, not far from Lembang."

We had heard the thud of bombs, seen the wheeling and diving of Japanese planes, heard the rat-a-tat-tat of anti-aircraft fire—in short, the sounds and sights of an awful conflagration. The war had come so close!

Later Ank told us of the awful death of Elsa's father, the elderly Mr. Kleist. Ank's mother had gone to stay with them, but then some KNIL soldiers established a machine gun emplacement near the house. The Japanese had targeted that emplacement and shot Mr. Kleist, standing in the entrance of his bomb shelter, right in front of the women's eyes.

The radio inside the house was blaring loudly enough for us to hear any news from the veranda. Normal programming had been replaced by music, interrupted every hour by the gruff, tired voice of General ten Poorten announcing a ceasefire and that citizens had "nothing to fear and should remain calm and carry on as normal."

Nothing to fear? There had already been reports of *rampokken* (looting), particularly to the east of us in Central Java. Bandoeng had, thanks to a strong police presence called into being as a last act of Dutch civil government, remained relatively quiet, in marked contrast to what was happening elsewhere on Java. Around the back of the Savoy Homann Hotel there was a huge pile of broken glass, the remnants of an all-night drinking binge by returning, demoralized troops. My father was wondering whether there was any point in his going to the office. What would he find there? He would have to go on his bicycle, as he had done since the new year began. Perhaps there would be news. The newspapers appeared erratically and said little, beyond giving orders not to listen to foreign radio broadcasts: such orders were of course ignored, but the news we heard was not good either, for the Japanese juggernaut seemed to be unstoppable. But what would the Japanese do in Bandoeng?

Later that day Emmy came by on her bicycle to let us know that Edu was okay. "The barracks of the 15th Battalion are full, and the men have relinquished their arms."

"Will Edu be released?"

"No, he says he's a prisoner of war, but no one knows what is going to happen. Rudolf is also there, and he told me that nothing can happen until a formal peace treaty is signed between the Netherlands government and Japan—but there is nowhere to go. Luckily, I had brought along some clean clothes for Edu, because it's a mess there."

That day a stream of refugees began to arrive in Bandoeng. They came from the coffee, rubber and tea plantations in the Preanger and even further afield, where gangs of Indonesian youth seemed to be running amok. Soon accounts of atrocities did the rounds; they were directed not only against the Dutch, but also against Chinese shopkeepers in remote villages, some of whom had been circumcised, while others had had their throats slit.[20] The refugees, some with wounds needing medical attention, arrived with just a suitcase or, in exceptional cases, with belongings loaded on a hired truck. In the days that followed, furniture and household goods piled by garden entrances became a common sight; these belongings had been unceremoniously dumped by truck drivers who had been hired to transport the possessions from plantations to town, but had misread the address, or perhaps lost it. The drivers had made sure that they were paid in advance, and under the changed circumstances could now afford to be cavalier with the quality of the service delivered. The impression of a European urban society transposed onto an Asian environment began to look like a façade; "Bandoeng, the Paris of Java" now sounded hollow.

A *betja* drew up in front of our house and a Chinese man stepped out in the early morning sun. "Bou, there's a man coming to the front door—should we call the police?" Jufs voice from the living room was trembling. The Chinese man turned out to be one of the sub-contractors who had been working on our future home, and even though the house was not quite finished, wanted to be paid. My father left the man standing on the veranda and came in to discuss the situation with my mother.

"Wil, there's going to be a run on the banks. I think it best that I make a payment to this guy, but at the same time take out as much cash as possible—then I will go to the office to see if I can get paid, so don't worry if I am late."

"How are you going?"

"I can get a ride downtown in his *betja*."

My father did not return until late in the afternoon. The banks had been overrun by worried clients, but he had been able to extract a substantial sum.

---

20. Touwen-Bouwsma, "The Indonesian Nationalists and the Japanese 'Liberation' of Indonesia."

He had also gone to the office, but found it in a state of chaos, with filing cabinets spilled over and documents hurriedly destroyed. The KNIL, his employer, no longer existed.

How could the battle for "fortress Java" have come so suddenly and ingloriously to an end? It had taken the Japanese army over two months to capture the rugged, impenetrable Malay peninsula in order to reach Singapore, while the struggle for Java had taken a week.

In the chaos of war there had been no opportunity for the citizens to be informed about the challenges faced by the military and the hopeless task that it had been expected to perform, while the role of the navy was completely forgotten. Accusing fingers were instead pointed at those immediately involved: bewildered, frightened citizens muttered about the incompetence of the KNIL, poor administration, incoherent orders, and above all, defeatism. However, the decision to capitulate, to declare the cities "open" and to turn down the suggestion of continued guerrilla warfare, had been an extremely difficult one. The fact that members of the indigenous population, outnumbering the Europeanized portion by a factor of a hundred to one, had openly sided with the Japanese made further resistance not only futile, but extremely dangerous. The do-or-die brigade was not being realistic, but then in a way the position of the European community on these islands had long ago ceased to be founded on realism; we had been living in a dream world and that dream was about to become a nightmare.

The evening paper carried an extensive communiqué from the Chief of General Staff, General ten Poorten, explaining how the Japanese army, thanks to its overwhelming command of airspace, had succeeded in penetrating into the Bandoeng highland area via the Tjiater Pass. He also explained that Bandoeng had been threatened with an all-out bombing campaign, and that this had forced him to propose a ceasefire. The paper next itemized ten Japanese demands, including "relinquishment of all arms, self internment of all military personnel, delivery to the Japanese command of all dead Japanese troops, imprisoned Japanese people and goods formerly belonging to Japanese citizens."[21] There was also a demand "to stop forthwith the destruction of military equipment, buildings, roads," and so on and for "cessation of all communication with the external world." General ten Poorten appended to his announcement a request directed specifically at the troops under his command with whom radio contact had been lost through the confusion of the previous week: they were to cease hostilities, accept the Japanese demands and confirm receipt of this order. It made for disturbing reading; the final instructions from the colonial government were "to stay indoors, and to co-operate with an

---

21. *Algemeen Indisch Dagblad*, March 9, 1942.

orderly transition of power to the Japanese authorities." The Netherlands East Indies had become part of *Asia Raja*, or Greater Asia.

Towards evening Japanese soldiers began to appear in Bandoeng. We were curious to see this strange-looking army: their funny cloth hats with neck flaps, their baggy pants, odd shoes and swords. They looked shoddily dressed compared to what we had come to expect from our soldiers; some walked, many were on bicycles, and others rode in the backs of requisitioned trucks. All appeared to be travelling very lightly equipped. We immediately had to get accustomed to the sight of foreign soldiers all over town, walking in twos or threes, with their hair cut to within a millimetre of their scalp, giving them the appearance of thugs.

It is perhaps fair to say that the Japanese invading army experienced an equally profound culture shock during the sudden forceful confrontation with such diverse peoples: it was hard for them to believe they were still in Asia. When invading the Malayan peninsula they had been amazed at the luxury of the British army camps they overran, the diversity of food supplies and the comfortable state of accommodation: what a contrast to their own conditions! A bicycle was their preferred means of transport, and their daily rations consisted almost exclusively of rice. In Bandoeng, the soldiers suddenly found themselves in an incredible paradise of roomy houses, leafy suburbs and untold luxury.

In the days following their arrival a large number of their officers gave the impression of being tourists: armed with cameras, they took snapshots of Bandoeng street scenes and children playing on roller skates, and some even attempted to have pictures taken of themselves with teenage girls. From time to time there were incidents in which a group of Japanese soldiers would invite themselves into the homes of Europeans to have a look at how these people lived: it was such a contrast to their own experience! For the hapless homeowners there was no choice but to stand back and offer their conquerors and new masters whatever it was they desired, which usually was no more than water with ice.

But at the same time chilling anecdotes began to spread about Japanese atrocities, the stomach-turning action against defeated opponents at Kalidjati and the Tjiater Pass witnessed by a few survivors. These accounts quickly changed the attitude of Europeans from contempt to hatred and fear; what a contrast for a population that had previously known Japanese shopkeepers as smiling, polite, obsequious individuals!

European hostility was also directed against some of the Indonesian population, darkly accusing well-known Indonesian nationalist politicians of collaboration with the Japanese: it was the old fifth columnist canard, now given a xenophobic twist. Such collaboration was impossible, given the rapidity with which events had unfolded, the fissiparous nature of the Indonesian population and its difficulty in burying differences in favour of an overriding objective, and the success of the Dutch regime in keeping potential leaders, such as the influential Sukarno with his oratorical skills, locked up: he was not freed by the Japanese from his prison in Sumatra until three months after capitulation, and then only by chance.[22]

For those individuals who had been frustrated by the stiffness of the colonial regime and naively took Japanese propaganda at face value, opportunism was too strong to resist. Dr. Achmad Subardjo, a lawyer trained at the universities of Utrecht and Leyden, had long been embittered by the seeming hypocrisy of a Dutch nation extolling through its learned institutions the virtues of enlightenment, while denying him influence in the conduct of affairs in the Indies. Subardjo and his supporters took the Japanese, portraying themselves as "liberators," at their word and now sought to bring about a revolution in the governance of Java by forcibly evicting the *Belanda* (the Dutch) from their positions of power. Subardjo had even worked out a "blueprint" for Indonesian self-government, which he was able to present to the Japanese authorities upon their arrival in Batavia. He had to wait only two weeks for the Japanese response.

The counterpart of opportunism is reflection. For many Japanese soldiers their quest in Southeast Asia had a strong, self-righteous moral and religious thrust. The fact that Indonesians had for centuries acquiesced to foreign domination was, in the eyes of some Japanese, indicative of moral shortcomings. The Europeans should moreover be evicted from Asia because it was not "their God-given place." One of the Japanese officers, Colonel Noguchi, used such a religious argument to explain Japanese military success:

I think these war results do not signify the inferior power of our enemy, but rather owe to our absolute indomitable power—that is to say, the power protected by *kami* [heaven]. Wherever the Nippon army and navy advance, *Tenyu Shinjo* [special providential help] always follows; you should recognize the fact and consider the reasons.

The Nippon army and navy are under the imperial command of *Tenno* [Emperor] who is the personification of *Kami* [God] so that the imperial troops are to be called the troops of God. Now you have become prisoners because of struggling against *Kami-no-Gun* [God's army] and now you are convinced of fearfulness to the marrow and became aware of unsavoury results.[23]

The religious rationale for Japanese victory was an echo of the jubilation felt when the Japanese navy inflicted a resounding defeat on the huge Russian navy in 1905. That victory was ascribed not to superior technology and strategy but

22. Zwaan, *Nederlands-Indië 1940–1946: Japans Intermezzo 9 maart 1942–15 augustus 1945*, 69.

23. Strachan (ed.), *In the Clutch of Circumstance*, 165.

to *kamikaze*, the divine wind that had saved Japan from the Mongol invasions in the thirteenth century and whose intervention proved, to contemporary Japanese, Japan's indisputable divinity and indestructibility.

Overnight we became part of Japan's New Order and saw the destruction of our familiar world; Batavia, named after a West-Germanic or possibly Celtic tribe encountered by the Romans near the Rhine estuary, would in future be referred to by the name "Jakarta." The word *Japan* was moreover considered insulting. The new head of government, Lieutenant General Imamura, commanding the 16th Imperial Nipponese Army, took up residence in the Governor General's former palace on the *Konings Plein* in Batavia to reign over Java in the name of the Emperor.

The brief interlude during which Bandoeng played a role on the world's stage, beginning with the relocation to this city of General Wavell's command, had now come to an end. Henceforth Bandoeng reverted to the role of a provincial city, remarkable only for the large number of Europeans concentrated in the area during the remainder of the war. The largest initial component consisted of about eighteen thousand prisoners of war awaiting transportation to labour camps in Burma, Sumatra, Formosa, Japan and elsewhere.

During the following months the Japanese shunted large numbers of European military and civilians in and out of the area. At its height the number of internees in the Preanger totalled forty-seven thousand men, women and children, double the pre-war total of Europeans.[24] The number of Europeans who at one time or another were captive in Bandoeng exceeded this number by a huge margin. The choice of Bandoeng for this activity was stimulated partly by the availability of the military barracks of the former colonial army, and partly by strategic considerations. The capture of the Netherlands Indies had been a key prize for the Japanese, and they assumed that evicting the Japanese from these islands would be a key Allied objective.[25] Concentrating Allied personnel, particularly men, away from the coast and in and around Bandoeng minimized the risk of their collaboration with future invading Allied forces.

Although Bandoeng had so far remained calm, other parts of Java had descended into chaos—the looting that quickly spread as Dutch rule waned and before firm Japanese control could be exercised. Imamura, however, was anxious to keep the economy in working order. The rioting youths therefore soon began to experience the wrath of the Japanese military, hell-bent on pacifying the country so that they could continue with their wave of invasion and conquest elsewhere. By Thursday the Military Police, the dreaded *Kempetai*

---

24. These statistics exclude the Eurasian population.

25. A Japanese view of the conquest of Java is presented in Zwaan, *Japans Intermezzo 9 maart 1942–15 augustus 1945*, Chapter 1.

(literally "Law Soldier Regiment"), had set up headquarters in a former Roman Catholic girl's school; it was dreaded because it behaved not like a conventional military police force, but more like the Gestapo, the Nazi secret police.

Japanese soldiers were quickly billeted in public buildings such as schools, while their officers requisitioned private homes in the luxurious northern suburbs. Several homes of our neighbours on the Nijlandweg, a road crossing the Eykmanweg a few doors down, were evicted in this manner. The former European residents could do little else but seek accommodation with friends or relatives, and in that way began a process of concentration that would continue for the coming four years.

For my parents and Juf these days were filled with great anxiety. The island of Java had become a prison from which there was no escape. *Babu* Iti remained loyally with us and, being Indonesian, provided a modicum of security—her attitude had not changed and she knew how to procure the essentials of living. But how long could we afford to pay her? *Koki* had left, and that was just as well, for now there was one less mouth to feed. At night, when it was dark, sleep would only come fitfully. We had no guard dog to alert us to the approach of strangers and so every noise from the street caused our hearts to beat with anxiety—was it a friend or a foe? Aside from the threat of marauding bands of looters, there was the uncertainty as to what we could expect from the strange Japanese army. Stories of drunk soldiers terrorizing young women regardless of race soon surfaced. It transpired that it was the Korean members of the invading force who mostly indulged in this misconduct, and the Japanese army was quick to mete out harsh punishments, thereby bringing its own troops fairly quickly under control, but presenting us with a confused image of brutality and impartial discipline. All of a sudden we had become a very small community surrounded by an ocean of hostility; our paradise had turned within an unbelievably short time into hell.

For hints of possible salvation from this predicament we became dependent on rumours. The local radio station now only broadcast Japanese orders and propaganda, but news from the outside world still reached us via clandestine listening to shortwave radio, and thus a situation arose whereby we knew more about the happenings in Europe than on Java. One of the most persistent rumours was that the Japanese army would be defeated and driven out of the Indies by the Americans "within the next three months." Was this yet another distortion of the Djojobojo legend or was it a deep-seated part of the European psyche that sought to overcome adversity through eternal optimism? It was the manifestation of this European optimism that would, in the coming months and years, drive our Japanese conquerors to distraction. This reaction they could not comprehend and indeed saw as a manifestation of European stupidity. In their eyes a nation of people, defeated so completely in

120

battle, should become utterly submissive to what was clearly a superior power: we did not fit that preconceived notion.

And what about the Americans? On March 18 General Douglas MacArthur was forced to flee from Corregidor to Australia, where, after lengthy deliberations in Washington, he was placed in charge of a limited portion of what the Americans now referred to as "the Pacific war." MacArthur was forced to share responsibility with Admiral Chester W. Nimitz, who assumed that the defeat of Japan would be a naval and not an army operation. MacArthur had a totally different opinion and soon proved his extraordinary abilities in successfully conducting amphibious landings, but liberating the NEI was from the start given a low priority, and he therefore saw no need for the appointment of Dutch officers to his staff. Washington assigned him the task of capturing the Bismarck Archipelago, using modest resources, but his own personal goal was to recapture the Philippines and avenge his defeat at the hands of the Japanese army. After that, his priority was to strut on the Tokyo stage. We on Java had become a footnote to his campaign.

By Friday, March 13, the *pasars* and some shops in Bandoeng had once more opened, but business was depressed. For anyone employed in any capacity by the former colonial regime the future looked grim, because news quickly spread that European men formerly linked to the administration in Batavia had immediately been imprisoned, as had also been the case in Singapore. So far this did not happen in Bandoeng, but it seemed inevitable given the noisy clamour emanating from the nationalists for personnel changes. Travel by Europeans was forbidden, thus slowing down the flow of refugees in search of safety. Our short-term survival seemed to be based on the money we had in our pockets, and whatever personal possessions we had that could be bartered for food. The long-term outlook was too awful to think about.

A power vacuum briefly arose in Bandoeng, encouraging strident expressions of contempt for the army of occupation, especially among European teenage boys no longer concerned about their education and with no responsibilities for family. They were not alone—on March 25 about thirty prominent members of the Dutch colonial regime had taken advantage of the interlude to discuss resistance options. They were promptly arrested, an unwelcome reminder that their position had abruptly changed from one of secure imperial governance to that of a highly visible minority with almost no friends among their numerous former colonial subjects, whom they had failed to protect from external aggression with such a spectacular loss of face. The Japanese army, for the time being at least, was not short of Indonesian eyes and ears unwilling to countenance a return to pre-Kalidjati conditions, and now, moreover, had absolute power; they immediately demonstrated their willingness to use it to counter any sign of disrespect. It would take time for us to adjust our mentality in order to survive and not become martyrs for a pointless cause; we, who had for so long imposed our values and norms on others, now had to learn to sail to a changed wind direction or suffer the consequences.

On March 15 we heard that the Aussies, the Blackforce group under the command of Brigadier Arthur Seaforth Blackburn, had surrendered. Blackburn and his men had not been bound by the Kalidjati surrender terms, but had sought to continue fighting in the mountains around the southwest of Bandoeng. This fifty-year-old former fighter pilot and recipient of the Victoria Cross at Poznières had more recently seen action in Syria, where he had accepted the surrender of the Axis forces at Damascus, and while on leave in Australia had been redirected to Java. He and his men, unable to find sympathy among the Indonesians, were finally forced to put down their arms.

The semblance of an uneasy peace on Java was exceptional, for elsewhere, over vast reaches of the archipelago stretching from Sumatra to New Guinea, Allied resistance by guerrilla groups continued for the coming months, and in isolated cases continued to the end of the Pacific war.

Imamura's New Order

The uninvited arrival of Lieutenant General Imamura in our part of the Emerald Girdle turned our world upside down; the consequences were beyond our wildest fears or expectations. A substantial number of Indonesian compatriots had looked forward to a promised utopia, going so far as to frustrate to no small degree the defensive efforts of our soldiers: they too were now in for a shock—a shock as traumatic as the one experienced by the European population.

Imamura and his imperial masters, however, found themselves facing unexpected challenges. While the invasion and conquest of Java took a mere week, the challenge of turning the conquest to a benefit for Japan was never met, and all of us suffered from the failed attempt.

From the outset the Japanese had conflicting opinions about the governance style to be adopted. Commenting on the period immediately following capitulation, Imamura writes:

> Many of the young officers insisted, "Although the administration may gradually be altered to a 'soft' one in the course of time, we must adopt an iron-handed policy at the initial stage to demonstrate the authority of the Japanese Army." However, Col. Nakayama, who was in charge of the administration, opposed this opinion. "The military administration should be directed, as is clearly prescribed in the *Outline of Military Administration in Occupied Regions*, towards the acquisition of

the hearts and minds of the people through a fair policy of virtue and dignity, the quick restoration of damaged military resources, the requisitioning of all military resources and an increase in their production."...Since we are strong, the administration is to be implemented as softly as possible.[26]

An immediate consequence of Imamura's policy was a sharp contrast between the situation in occupied Java and that in Singapore, where all Europeans had immediately been interned. Controversy around this issue persisted to the end of the war.

The Indonesian archipelago, however, had to support Japan with its economic bounty, and this demanded control. Nationalist leaders such as Subardjo, who had looked forward to acquiring positions of power they deemed commensurate with their abilities, now found themselves in competition with the strategic needs of Japan; with a war to fight, the Japanese were in no mood to be altruistic, but determined to derive immediate benefit from their recent conquest and on their own terms. On March 20 Imamura firmly took the entire Indonesian independence movement, including Subardjo's beautiful self-government blueprint, off the agenda. *Undang-undang* (Military Decree) number 3 suppressed any aspirations the nationalists might have had about *merdeka* (freedom).[27] It proscribed all Indonesian political activity and the display of the red and white "freedom flag," and forbade people to even talk of political change. Then there was the question as to what Imamura should do about the Indonesian aristocracy, the sultans, some elegantly clothed in sarongs with long curled finger nails to show that they did not need to work, and others, like the westernized Sultan of Solo, owning factories and commanding a military regiment. From their splendid palaces they had, under the colonial regime, wielded real power over the tradition-minded *desa* dwellers and the *tani* (rice farmers) and were loath to relinquish these privileges.[28] On March 23 the four self-governing sultanates were placed under direct Japanese military supervision. Whether the Indonesians liked it or not, a Japanese imperial master had replaced the Dutch one.

Imamura took up the challenge of governing Java assuming that its residents thought like Japanese—or at least ought to learn to do so. Java was, after all, now part of Japan the way the Dutch had previously assumed that it was an integral part of the Netherlands, and the process of forced assimilation into the Japanese constellation began.

An immediate change was the introduction of new currency that had thoughtfully been printed in Japan prior to the invasion. Only paper money was

---

26. Reid and Akira, eds., *The Japanese Experience in Indonesia*, 52.

27. Sluimers, "The Japanese Military and Indonesian Independence."

28. Mangkunegoro VII died in 1944.

made available, still printed in Dutch and still referred to as "guilders," but with the picture of the Queen having been replaced by a banana palm. For the next three and a half years the Japanese authorities unsuccessfully sought to replace all Dutch guilders in circulation with Japanese guilders. Any fees or taxes had to be paid to the Japanese authorities in Dutch guilders, while any government salaries or army purchases were paid in Japanese guilders. Two currencies were therefore now in circulation—a fixed number of NEI guilder notes and silver coin, as well as an inexhaustible supply of Japanese notes, including one-, five-, ten- and fifty-cent denominations. A black market in currency speculation immediately sprang up.

On March 27 we changed time zones and the calendar. Juf got the news over the backyard fence from Miss Fukken, one of the three nurses working at the Pasteur *Instituut* and sharing the house next door.

"Miss Fukken is upset with the clocks being moved forward," Juf told my mother.

"Moved forward? Really, how much?" My mother sounded bewildered.

"She says one and a half hours, to bring our time in line with that of Tokyo, but she now does not know whether this means that the hours of her shift will change or that she has to go to work long before sunrise and come home in the early afternoon. She is afraid of going to work or coming home in the dark."

"I think it is the other way round," said my father, scratching his head. "Perhaps we can borrow an atlas?"

In the tropics the sun normally rises and sets around six o'clock in the morning and evening with hardly any twilight. Henceforth the sun would rise at four thirty in the morning and set at four thirty in the evening, a curious disruption causing widespread confusion, especially for the Indonesian workers. That same day the date changed to March 27, 2602—by Japanese reckoning, their civilization, beginning in the reign of their first Emperor, Jimmu Tenno, descended from the Gods Izanawi and Izanami, was some six hundred years older than Western civilization as defined by the onset of the Christian era. The Japanese did not bother changing the calendar any further, and so, aside from the year, all other date references remained the same. The days of the week did not change, but their meaning did. A day of rest, dedicated to religious worship, whether on Sunday, Saturday or Friday, did not fit in with the Japanese custom: for them spiritual considerations would govern each day.

The next day a Japanese economic mission arrived on Java, and two days later Dutch economic experts, who had been abruptly fired two weeks earlier, were invited to return to work. Those Indonesians who, a short two weeks before, had enthusiastically taken up the positions vacated by their former masters, now had to suffer the chagrin of equally rapid demotion.[29]

As the balance of fortunes swung back, the European population began to breathe a bit more easily. It had become clear that the arrival of the Japanese troops in Bandoeng would not immediately precipitate a catastrophe of plunder, rape and murder, as had been the case in Nanking five years before and more recently in Singapore. The swimming pools and cinemas were once more allowed to open—the Japanese soldiers were in need of entertainment and Charlie Chaplin's *The Great Dictator* was then doing the rounds. Some Europeans also ventured to go to a film show, although they were scandalized by newsreels that now celebrated Western setbacks at the hands of the glorious Nipponese forces. Children on roller skates again ventured onto suburban streets, now quieter than before, but schools remained closed. On Sunday the devout once more went to church and heard sermons about the meek inheriting the earth and about loving thine enemies. Collections even resumed for missionaries in Borneo and elsewhere.

To cheer us up further, Imamura decreed that all Japanese festivals were to be observed. For the next three days *Jimmu Tenno sai*, the founding of Japan, would be celebrated with widespread display of Japanese *kokki* flags—the white flag with the blood-red sun disc, perhaps the most elegant, though by us most despised, flag in the world. Instructions were issued regarding the precise design of the flag and even the flagpole (a feature already gracing many houses in Bandoeng) which was to be painted in black and white stripes.

"This is a fine April first joke," my father grumbled, but it soon transpired that Imamura was serious. The flag response of the Bandoeng population was disappointing—in our neighbourhood some flags appeared on broomsticks stuck in the lawn—but then the radio announcer repeated the order, "The flags must be displayed," and added ominously, "an order from General Imamura."

"The people on the Nijlandweg have all flags at half-mast," my mother gleefully reported on returning from a short stroll to the crossroad, "and some of those are pillow slips with red ink stains!"

But then there came the prohibitions. In the following week all Dutch language publications were forbidden, and telephone conversations had to be conducted in Malay. This language edict was immediately greeted with a howl of derision.

"They're declaring their own rotten money illegal," my father remarked icily, pulling out of his pocket a crumpled bank note with the beautiful message in flawless Dutch, *De Japansche Regering betaalt aan toonder een gulden,*[30] on it. They won't get far with Malay when dealing with the *inlanders*." This prohibition for

29. Touwen-Bouwsma, "The Indonesian nationalists and the Japanese 'liberation' of Indonesia.

30. "The Japanese government pays bearer one guilder."

the time being did not apply in Soerabaja, on the east coast of Java, where the Japanese navy was in charge, and allowed the local Dutch newspaper to continue publication for a number of months.

Bank and post office savings accounts were frozen, and money immediately became a major concern for everyone.[31] We had been lucky, thanks to my father's ability to withdraw some of his savings before it was too late. Emmy and Edu had arrived on Java without savings. With Edu interned, and the schools closed, Emmy was immediately dependent on earnings from private lessons and charity from relatives. We took it for granted that Edu, being a prisoner of war, would be looked after by the Nipponese army, but that turned out to be an optimistic assumption. In the *Senjinkun* (Japanese Army Field Service Code), General Hideki Tojo had encouraged his troops to "live without the humiliation of being taken prisoner and die without leaving a blemish on your name." Theirs was a spartan military regime and under no circumstances should captured soldiers get better treatment than Nipponese soldiers. Allied POWs became slaves. All pensions earned from colonial government service were stopped. Of the eighty-six thousand affected pensioners, two-thirds were Indonesians, and more Indonesians were affected indirectly because all of these pensioned people had once employed one or two Indonesian servants, who could no longer be paid; thus the circle of deprivation grew.

The newly established *Kempetai* immediately began to plot the assassination of Dr. Mohammed Hatta, the deeply respected, Leyden-educated nationalist leader. This worthy economist had just been released from his recent internment as a troublemaker, and was now seen by the Japanese as a threat because of his alleged communist sympathies.

The somewhat relaxed atmosphere that nevertheless continued to prevail in early April allowed my father to venture forth from the house on his bicycle to contact friends and to make essential purchases. Above all he needed to plan for future survival: perhaps he could become self-employed? But his trips were futile, as the post office, telegraph and municipal offices were all in a state of chaotic inactivity. When he returned late that afternoon he grinned as he told my mother, "You'd better find some other things to wear."

"Why?"

"In one of the shops I heard people talking about a young woman who had been walking on Bragaweg dressed in slacks," my father recounted. "A bunch of Jap soldiers stopped her and ordered her to undress. When someone tried to intervene on her behalf, he was told that only 'bad women wear those clothes.' When she stood in her underwear the soldiers moved on and the poor woman had to seek refuge inside a shop to dress herself again."

---

31. Some major corporations had, as a precaution, withdrawn large sums of cash and entrusted it to individuals for periodic distribution among former employees.

My mother was invariably dressed in shorts during the daytime; that had been her preferred garb in South Africa, as it was here in the tropics. This was prohibited, along with the display of affection in public—these were at variance with the moral values of Japan. "I guess we have to draw the curtains before we kiss one another," my father muttered. "The windows are big and people can see us from the street." Juf shook her head and sighed, "Oh jee, oh jee, oh jee." It was something for her to invoke the name of Jesus.

Emmy had also used this relaxed situation to visit Edu in the 15th Battalion barracks. She had gone in the company of her sister-in-law, Charlotte, who was anxious to see her husband, Rudolf. Later that afternoon Emmy phoned to let us know she was coming and then made her way to our house to relate what had occurred.

"We waited a long time along the fence before someone tracked Edu and Rudolf down, and we were only allowed to talk for a short while before the Jap guards chased us away—but they told us something awful," she added, lowering her voice. She explained that some POWs had tried to escape. "They said they were hungry and had sought food," Emmy added indignantly, "but the Japs caught them, tied them to some wires, and used them for bayonet practice. One of the boys was still alive but bleeding badly and begged for someone to kill him. They're barbarians."

"Are there not international rules for the treatment of POWs?" my father wondered, with consternation in his voice.

"Rudolf said that the Japs never signed the Geneva convention. Apparently some soldiers had planned to escape and start guerrilla action, but Ru thinks that's impossible, because they would be betrayed by *inlanders*. Edu thought that this was really what those soldiers had hoped to do." Emmy then hurriedly left on her bicycle to be sure to reach her home before twilight set in.

The pauperization among the European population soon became obvious with the appearance of beggars, including young children going from door to door looking for food; cottage industries sprang up and there were rumours of prostitution. "At least the nurses in the hospitals are still employed," my mother observed after she had handed some cookies to a pair of children at the front door.

"I'm not sure," said Juf. "Miss Fukken was told that women nurses were not allowed to treat Japanese soldiers, and that she might have to leave. Patients have been sent home to make room for the soldiers." The gloomy future created tension almost on a daily basis in the house, causing my mother and even Juf to let my father's thirty-fourth birthday slip by unnoticed. A week later notices were posted all over town, labelled *Undang-undang Nr 7*: "All foreigners 17 years and older must register, for which a fee is required, and they should at the same time swear allegiance to the Japanese Emperor." Henceforth a *pendafteran* (identity card) would be required. The registration fee was high, equivalent to a week's salary, a salary we could no longer earn, and it had to be paid in Dutch guilders.

"Where can I find the money?" Juf lamented. "I lost my pension long ago."

"Tsk, don't worry Juf," my father tried to soothe the old woman, who had of late begun to burst into tears regularly.

That evening, when one of the nurses, Miss Schotanus, passed our house on her bicycle as she returned from the hospital, my mother hailed her:

"D'you understand what's going on?" asked my mother. "That registration fee is ridiculously high, isn't it?"

"It doesn't apply to me," she replied. "I was born here and have a birth certificate to prove it—in fact my father and one of my grandparents was also born on Java—I am an *Indische Nederlander*" (Dutch citizen born in the Indies). My mother conceded that it did not make sense to call someone born in the country "foreign"; there was, however, no such ambiguity in our position. Since the expected yield on Java amounted to 150 million guilders, or half of the last NEI annual budget, it was clear that this was in part a form of taxation, but it was not clear how the Japanese authorities could enforce the intimidating edict. No deadline for registration was given, and so it was for the time being ignored by almost all. However, that same day the authorities ordered all senior civil servants to report to Sukamiskin.

Sukamiskin was a huge high-security prison located not far from Bandoeng. It had previously been used to house political prisoners, or "impenitent trouble-makers," as we had called them in order to justify incarceration. These "trouble-makers" had been released with a great display of populist celebration, and the emptied cells were now filled with their former persecutors, a step of masterful irony. But this sweep caught up others as well: medical doctors, even prominent Eurasian doctors with deep Javanese roots, received this order, and to cap it off, the list included a number of Indonesian administrators. The Japanese social sieve could be as indiscriminate as the one used by the former colonial regime, when the Nazi paranoia had swept through Java. Japanese soldiers, suitably informed by the *Bandoeng Address Boek*, now turned up at homes here and there in town to enforce these orders. They forced the victims to make the long march to prison among the jeering insults of some of their former Indonesian subjects, while their meagre possessions followed in a *sado* (horse-drawn carriage). A month or so later the authorities realized the *faux pas* committed and the Indonesian civil servants were released.

On Saturday, April 18, the first American bombing raid took place over Tokyo, taking the Japanese completely by surprise; this news spread through Bandoeng like wildfire. My father brought the news home from one of his bicycle trips, and for the first time in months elation brightened the evening dinner table. Even Juf, pacifist by nature, could not help being cheerful for a change.

"Maybe they're right," my mother commented. "Maybe the Americans will throw the Japs out of Java in three months' time."

The speed with which this good news had spread through Bandoeng precipitated increased efforts by the Japanese to stop people from listening to the BBC or Radio San Francisco. Reports of horrible reprisals by the *Kempetai*, such as cutting off an ear, or worse, perforating an ear drum by driving into it a bamboo stick, began to circulate. It was clear that sharing bits of good news heard on the radio with friends was as risky as it was tempting.

The raid itself had only symbolic value as an indication of American resourcefulness and determination. It was a morale-booster after all the Allied setbacks, but bought at the expense of sending the bombers beyond their operating range and forcing them to make emergency landings in China. However, by chance the raid interrupted a strategic planning session of the Japanese High Command in Tokyo, which was debating the next military move: an invasion of Midway, Hawaii or Australia? Should Japan continue its advance or retrench now that its most urgent strategic objectives had been realized? The High Command, fearing its inability to successfully alter the psychological mindset of its troops from one of conquest to the needs for defence, had recommended a compromise, but now, as a result of the American raid, the policy swung in support of security through more territorial expansion.[32]

Notwithstanding the attack on Tokyo, Colonel Kumajiro Matsui, the newly installed Governor of the Preanger (*Priangan Shucho*), announced on April 25 with remarkable *sang froid* that we were to help Emperor Hirohito celebrate his coming birthday. Preparations were to commence immediately for three successive days of festivities in Bandoeng. Each evening the celebrations would last until nine o'clock, when curfew commenced, bringing an abrupt and curious end to the party atmosphere. The focus of festivities would be the Aloon-Aloon, a large grassy field in the middle of Bandoeng that served as a traditional gathering place. Huge rain trees marked its periphery and a nineteenth-century mosque graced its western border. Enthusiastic young Indonesian cyclists distributed pamphlets containing instructions for all households. "All residents must display the Nipponese flag from properly painted flagpoles," read the order. The civic authorities also made it clear that the upcoming celebrations would as well be an opportunity to humble the former colonial masters:

> All Dutch flags, orange ribbons, medals, distinctions, pictures of the royal family, certificates and so on, must be delivered to a central location on the Aloon-Aloon. On April 29 Colonel Matsui will be

---

32. Liddell Hart, *History of the Second World War*, 360.

honoured with parades of school children to whom Japanese flags will
be distributed. In the evening there will be a bonfire.[33]

Few Europeans cared to participate in the downtown celebration. In our
neighbourhood flags were again dutifully but sloppily displayed. On the Aloon-
Aloon, flag-waving, parading children were told to shout "*banzai!* [hurrah!]", but
some adults were shouting "*bangsat!* [scoundrel!]."

However, from our street we could see three giant balloons rising over the
downtown area, heralding another innovation: the use of celebrations to launch
political initiatives. These balloons advertised the *Tiga A* movement, offering an
outlet for nationalistic fervour under strict control of the military authorities.
Tiga A (triple A) stood for *Nippon penimpin Asia, Nippon pelindung Asia, Nippon
tjahaja Asia*, roughly translated as "Japan the leader, the protector and the light
of Asia." On notice boards the three *A*'s were arranged as a pyramid forming a
giant *A* for Asia. Indonesian wags promptly turned this into *Amerika Ampir
Ada* (America is nearly here) or *Asia Akan Ambruk* (Asia will collapse). That
evening's bonfire, consuming Dutch flags and pictures of the Queen, was
modest, but the parade of school children had been a resounding success, and
the Japanese propaganda machine could thereafter display films of happy,
liberated, flag-waving children.

Colonel Matsui used the upbeat occasion to stress to the population the
many reforms Nippon was introducing. He announced the formation of a *heiho*
(soldier assistant) regiment staffed by volunteers drawn from the Indonesian
population to operate "shoulder to shoulder with their older brothers," but he
neglected to mention that they would always serve under a Japanese non-
commissioned officer.

More significant for us was the news from Batavia. There the occasion had
been used to announce that all British men, women and children residing in the
city faced immediate internment.

So far the actions of the Japanese on Java with respect to the European
civilian population had been ambivalent and stood in contrast to their policy in
Singapore and Hong Kong, where all Europeans had immediately been
imprisoned. Japan needed the economic wealth of Indonesia, but that entailed
management continuity. Before the Dutch capitulation the Japanese
government had gone out of its way to assure civilians that they would not be
interned, but an unstated corollary was the need to secure their co-operation.
This was one reason why the Japanese had deferred a declaration of war on the
NEI until it was absolutely necessary. For years the Japanese had enjoyed a
privileged position in Indonesia and long-standing trade relations. It was the
Indonesian economy that Japan craved, not its scenery. But the continuing

33. Bouwer, *Het vermoorde land*, 66.

conflict in Western Europe and Anglo-Dutch attempts to enlist the help of the United States got in the way of this calculation.

Colonel Matsui did not forget to direct an announcement at us: the scary, costly registration process first announced on April 11 was to take immediate effect.[34]

"Wil," my father said with a sigh when he heard this, "we'll be next—those Jap promises to leave us alone are not worth a damn." What lay in store for us?

The next day he got on his bicycle to seek the advice of Theo Aalbers, who did not live far away. He returned late in the afternoon, after being held up several times by Japanese soldiers to find out what he was doing. "I had to buy some *pisang* just to show the Japs that I needed to buy food," he lamented. "Theo thinks we had better register. Others are refusing, but they have always lived here and have friends among the *inlanders*."

The following day he went to city hall, described himself as *Belanda*, gave his address and his thumbprint, and paid some money. When he returned, waiving his black thumb and his *pendafteran*, he was grinning.

"What happened?" asked my mother.

"I was told I could pay by instalments, so I only gave them the first five guilders (out of 150). Then I noticed that the clerk kept no records, and that the money disappeared into a cigar box. I should have given them a false address—it's chaos there. Oh yes," he added, "someone in town is selling counterfeit *pendafterans*, also for five guilders."

That evening Miss Schotanus stopped by on her way home from the *Pasteur Instituut* in an agitated state. My mother went to get some tea to calm her down, while my father began to talk about his *pendafteran* experience, but Miss Schotanus would not pay attention. "Listen," she said. "Things are getting out of hand. Today someone from the Borromeus hospital came looking for help because they were dealing with fifty-seven badly wounded *inlanders*. Most of them are still in the emergency ward."

"What happened?"

"The Japs broke up a fight between a policeman and some *inlanders*. I think the policeman had told an *inlander* he had parked his *bendi* [a two wheeled horse-drawn carriage] illegally."

"Where did the other *inlanders* come from?"

"*Bendi* drivers—they all picked on the poor policeman, and then the Japanese soldiers came. I believe seventeen *bendis* got totally wrecked," she added with a sigh. After a pause to take a sip of tea she added darkly, "The *inlanders* called the policeman a *peranakan*."

"What's that?" my mother asked, perplexed.

---

34. Zwaan, *Nederlands-Indië 1940–1946: Japans Intermezzo 9 maart 1942–15 augustus 1945*, 47.

"A half-caste. This is shocking—it would never have happened before. At work they think that the position of the policemen has now become impossible. They are nearly all *Belanda Indo*."

Suddenly a group of people who in the past had called themselves *Belanda Indo* to distinguish themselves from *inlander,* and usually seemed to have a lower social rank than Europeans, seemed to be vulnerable too. Born and bred in the Indies, they saw themselves as *bumi putera* (natives), but in addition to having a Dutch education, they often also had Dutch names. The societal range of these people was broad; some lived in fancy houses in town and others dwelt in *kampongs.* Some were almost indistinguishable from new arrivals from the Netherlands, and others looked thoroughly Asiatic. Now there was a hint of a wedge being driven between them and those who loudly proclaimed their Asian racial purity.

It was difficult to absorb the significance of this development. The group of people who had "*inlander* blood" to varying degrees was large, and we had become friends with some of them; it seemed to portend more future unhappiness. An immediate consequence of the *bendi* riot was the firing of all *Belanda Indo* policemen.

The growing pauperization of the citizens of Bandoeng caused the mayor, *raden* (a Sundanese aristocrat, but given his appearance, possibly tainted with stout European genes) Atma di Nata, concern. On May 7, with great fanfare, he opened a soup kitchen where a plate full of food could be had for five cents. This bit of good news was followed by the release from prison of a number of European doctors, a move partly prompted by the sinking of the *Taiyo Maru* en route from Tokyo to Batavia. A large group of trained Japanese civilian staff—a scarce resource that could not be replaced—had perished in the sinking.[35] An added concern was a serious water supply problem that had arisen for the overcrowded city. The released doctors accordingly returned to their hospitals.

Late at night on May 10, after *babu* Iti had disappeared to her room, and while my mother stood guard in the kitchen, my father was listening to the BBC. One had to be so careful—but this was the second anniversary of the invasion of Holland and there might be a special news item. When the news was finished he turned to my mother and asked, "Wil, where is the Coral Sea? The BBC announced heavy Japanese losses fighting against the Americans."

"Must be somewhere in the Pacific."

"Apparently the Japs were trying to invade the south coast of New Guinea, but the US navy seems to have stopped this," he added.

"My school atlas would have come in handy now," my mother sighed.

---

35. Lieutenant Commander Allen Joyce had made this "kill" with the submarine USS *Grenadier,* but remained ignorant of its significance until after the war.

By the next day all of Bandoeng knew about this battle and Colonel Matsui reacted by ordering the immediate registration of all radios, threatening house searches to ensure compliance. The battle was a significant setback for the Japanese, who wanted to capture Port Moresby, from which they would have had easy access to the uninhabited north coast of Australia. They were now forced to attempt to capture this objective overland via the rugged Kokoda trail.

The next day my father dutifully put our radio on the back of his bicycle and took it to the town hall, where the clerk handed him a receipt. A week later he retrieved the radio, now fitted with a metal plate displaying a registration number. At least the Japanese now would know who did and who did not have a radio.

Towards mid-May important visitors arrived from Tokyo—Army Chief of Staff Field Marshall Hajemei Sugiyama came to review the security situation on Java, since the Coral Sea disaster had forced the Japanese to once more consider strengthening front-line defences. But Sugiyama and his entourage observed that Lieutenant General Imamura was not treating the conquered Western people here on Java in a manner consistent with that used elsewhere in Southeast Asia. A casual observer wandering the streets of Batavia and Bandoeng would have noticed many non-Asian faces out and about, while many key occupations were still filled by Europeans, now designated as "Nippon workers." There were simply too many whitish faces on the street.

Of course, ever since mid-March there had been a steady stream of announcements about prominent (mainly Dutch) persons being incarcerated. Almost every week another layer of government or industry personnel were told to report to a prison, first the governors and senior civil servants, then judges, police chiefs, union bosses, heads of schools and so forth. As a corollary many of the institutions they worked for were now shut down. It was a determined attempt to systematically eliminate any sign of Western society from Indonesia. Eventually schools reopened (only for Asian students), but the curriculum changed: instead of European languages, Japanese now became mandatory, and far greater emphasis was placed on physical training. Thus the social environment we inhabited was day by day forcibly converted from a Western to an Asian society. The Japanese need to secure their grip on Indonesia nevertheless caused them to court the Muslim community, albeit within an overarching military control structure that, for the time being, muzzled doctrinal disputes beloved by the Muslim-Judeo-Christian tradition. The next wave of internment of Europeans furthermore lay just around the corner.

On Sunday, May 17, Imamura decreed that all unemployed *Belanda totok* men between ages seventeen and sixty who were not "Nippon workers" were to prepare for future internment.[36] Nippon workers would be identified by a white armband with a blood-red *kokki* symbol and their name written in Japanese characters—they were henceforth unkindly referred to as the "Red Ball Brigade," because some of their countrymen saw this as a form of collaboration. The term *Belanda totok,* however, was puzzling—some *Belanda* but not others? However, it soon became clear that the term *Belanda* in this context now meant more than Dutch born in Holland and most definitely included English, and that the accident of birthplace no longer was a distinguishing characteristic: a racial sieve was being introduced. And just to be sure that we would not forget how much Java had improved since the capitulation, Imamura ordered that all air-raid shelters were to be filled in to give the city a peaceful appearance.

A sense of panic began to grip the European community, for newspaper articles mentioned "preparations made at the LOG for future internment." This was serious. This institution, *s'Lands Opvoedings Gesticht*, until recently had been a borstal, a young offender's correctional institute.

"Are they going to put you in jail? Oh Bou, that's terrible!" Juf gasped and she disappeared into her room to wipe her eyes.

On Monday my father went to the *pasar* to get rice and returned glumly with the announcement that "all *totok* men will be interned in July, regardless of whether or not they are doing useful work. If you have some *Indo* blood in your veins or are married to an *Indo* you are okay—the Americans had better hurry up."

"Mr. Hannay thinks that the *Belanda Indo* men are also bound to be interned," my mother responded. "The other day, when I saw Emmy Jochems, she also was gloomy about her prospects. Some of her family look like typical *inlanders*, but she is afraid they will still go to Maria Stella Maris."

"That's a convent isn't it? Might be better than a jail."

During the following weeks the Bandoeng civic registry office was overrun with requests to prove parentage and confirm *Belanda Indo* status. It was a desperate attempt by the more European-looking citizens to take advantage of bureaucratic distinctions to avoid internment by demonstrating the presence of drops of Asian blood.

As we struggled with the frightening prospect of internment, June came, and with it more good news—a naval battle being waged near Midway Island was not going in Japan's favour. Numerous Bandoeng residents had heard this via Radio San Francisco or the BBC and everyone was now talking about it. The conflict of June 4, with the colossal Japanese armada, including the world's largest battleship, the *Yamato*, "saw the most extraordinarily quick change of

---

36. Voskuil, *Bandoeng*, 71.

fortune known in naval history."[37] The much smaller American defending fleet suffered losses, but the losses suffered by the Japanese navy were greater by far—the deciding factor had been superior American intelligence.

The local Japanese reaction was as dramatic as it was prompt—all Indonesian publications were henceforth forbidden save one, the *Tjahaja* (the *Light*). Colonel Matsui promptly ordered reinstallation of the air-raid sirens, reinstatement of recently filled-in air-raid shelters and the delivery of all radios to the town hall for "adjustment by technicians to prevent the listening to foreign propaganda." The local paper carried an announcement in Dutch about the dangers of listening to foreign broadcasts, "because they were lies, like the bark of distant wolfhounds too afraid to come near." The Bandoeng radio station, which was still transmitting news items in Dutch, reported the perforation of four more sets of eardrums and two executions for listening to foreign broadcasts. In addition there was a new wave of house searches for contraband and wanted persons.

Once again my father delivered the radio to the town hall "for adjustment" and came home with the news that Imamura, who had been on an inspection trip to Bandoeng, had been upset to hear that a municipal soup kitchen had been established. "He ordered it shut down immediately and arrested Poldervaart, its director."

"Why?"

"They say Imamura did not want to advertise that economic conditions are so bad."

A few days later Emmy dropped by in an agitated frame of mind; she and a couple of other soldiers' wives had gone to the 15th Battalion barracks hoping to catch another glimpse of their husbands, but Japanese guards had driven the women away. Emmy had escaped the beating, but "it was a close call," she remarked.

"Did you hurt your leg?" my mother asked, having noticed a fresh plaster behind her knee.

"Oh, nothing really, I got nicked by the point of a bayonet—an accident I think."

On June 27 the Bandoeng radio announced that "all *Belanda* will be brought together in designated areas"—ghettos, in other words. The day of my father's departure was clearly approaching, but the future for the rest of us looked grim as well.

"Emmy Jochems thinks that many *Belanda Indo* will go into hiding to avoid internment—they can count on relatives, who will definitely stay out."

---

37. Liddell Hart, *History of the Second World War*, 367.

"That's risky. In town you are liable to be found by the Jap soldiers, and Jesus, in the *kampongs* you stand the risk of being betrayed for money. The longer this lasts, the greater the risks, and if the Japs find you, they have no mercy."

"Yes, she agrees, but she has friends who may nevertheless do this."

Some Europeans sought to evade this looming fate by going into hiding, a risky undertaking. Jan Bouwer, a Dutch journalist married to a *Belanda Indo* woman, chose this route. He was wanted by the *Kempetai* in Batavia for his pre-war anti-Japanese reporting on behalf of the Associated Press, and had for this reason already fled from his home in Batavia to Bandoeng, where his wife's parents lived. In north Bandoeng they found a house possessing a large overgrown backyard, a "jungle" and that is where he spent all his daytime hours for the coming three and a half years, with his radio and his diary hidden in a hole in the ground; he remained there even after his father-in-law was interned.

With the start of July, Matsui once more ordered preparations to celebrate the "March 8 liberation of Java" with the display of Japanese *kokki* flags. It looked as though "victory celebrations" were to take place every month on the eighth day. Mayor *raden* Atma di Nata advised the *Belanda* to stay at home, and if they did need to go out, to be properly dressed and to be extra polite.

My father got his radio back and discovered that some wires had been snipped. My mother pronounced that the radio had been "circumcised," but after examining the handy-work of the technicians, my father thought that "castration" was a more apt term. However, the radio still worked and could still receive the BBC, though Radio San Francisco was no longer available.

He did not have much time to enjoy this possession, because a few days later Matsui ordered "all unemployed men between seventeen and sixty years of age, who were *Belanda totok*, to report no later than July 17 to the LOG." My father was allowed to take with him one suitcase, a *tikar* (sleeping mat) and ten guilders. The next day the *Kempetai* began systematic house searches to verify the personal information gathered by the municipal authorities. There was nothing to be done but follow orders.

On the appointed day my father said goodbye. Juf, beyond consolation and sobbing her heart out, embraced him in the security of the living room, while my mother, grim-faced, stood waiting by the side of the *betja* on the road in front of the house. As the *betja* moved down the road with my parents on board, Juf retreated to the solace of her bedroom. *Babu* Iti hung back with me near the front door; she also was having trouble controlling her emotions. That night, after my mother had returned, my father phoned, breaking all rules by speaking Dutch. "You got back alright?" he asked with a worried voice. "Theo is here, too, and he and others think this will not last long. *Hou je taai!* [loosely translated as 'Hang on!']", he concluded.

My mother's last words to him were, "*Onkruid vergaat niet* [weeds don't perish]."

Home Alone

My mother's new position as the head of our household was daunting. She had to look after a child and an elderly mother-in-law in a country she barely knew, and in a city that within the astonishing short time of four months had flipped from being friendly to being alien and threatening. Juf moreover had spent a lifetime living in the security of Dutch urban society and was unable at this late age to adjust to a radically new situation.

Most of the men my mother could trust were gone, locked away in prisons and former barracks or hunkered down in their homes, out of sight of the Japanese. The men who now might come to the front door were all to be feared—victorious Japanese soldiers, far from home, intoxicated with their unchallenged military authority and sometimes drunk on stolen booze. Worse was the threat of the rampaging Indonesian youth revelling in their release from the strictures of a discredited colonial regime.

My mother's ability to acquire the most basic necessity of life, food, was limited to the meagre savings hidden on her person, consisting of some paper money and silver coin that was no longer legal tender, and also entailed her making risky bicycle trips downtown or to the nearest *pasar*. The only source of help was friends, for the new government had no interest in social assistance. Charitable organizations were now outlawed—the Salvation Army had been disbanded because it was "an army."

There were at the time perhaps another ten thousand European women and children in Bandoeng in a similar predicament, and more in other cities and towns of Java, but for most of them a lifetime spent in this country had provided a depth of resources that my mother did not have; we had arrived a mere two years before. My mother faced an unhappy, frightening future, while her friends, from whom we were separated by distances measured in hostile city blocks, were themselves now preoccupied with their own survival. Her position was impossible and I am amazed at what she went through on our behalf.

It is a good thing that my mother did not know how futile it was to hope for rescue, for the United States, rightly or wrongly, had other priorities and was on the point of launching the attack on the Solomon Islands, three thousand miles to the east. The battle for Guadalcanal, a steamy, malarian jungle-island barely seventy miles long, would last six months and inflict the first major military defeat on the Japanese. From the Solomons the route to Japan lay through the Philippines and not through Java. If that logic had been understood in the

Indies, countless mothers would have gone crazy with desperation. As it was, the naive, ever-flickering hope for imminent salvation sustained many through the coming ordeal. For almost forty consecutive months those mothers assumed that they only had to hang on for another three months, and mentally budgeted their dwindling savings to cover that period. Thus each month, the food allowance shrank, assuming there was any allowance left.

For the time being our location on the northern fringe of Bandoeng was both a blessing and a curse. On the one hand we were far removed from the centres of commerce, the *pasars*, where staple foods such as rice, could be purchased. My mother's trek on my father's bicycle to and from the *pasar*, dealing with intervening roadblocks and checkpoints, was hazardous, not least because of the unpredictable behaviour of surly sentries demanding to see one's *pendafteran;* frequently such inspections were accompanied by rough handling or a serious beating by the thuggish soldiers. But we were also spared some of the violent break-and-entry traumas residents closer to downtown suffered. Almost everyday more refugees arrived from the isolated plantations and smaller towns, bringing with them evidence and news of atrocities directed against the *Belandas* (anyone with pale skin, for in such instances the perpetrator did not care about ancestry). Often these atrocities were carried out with the silent connivance, and sometimes even with the active encouragement, of the Japanese soldiers. It was, to be fair, a minority of the Indonesian population that had run amok; they were for the most part unemployed, uneducated young men, while their victims were the privileged ones—anyone without a distinct brown skin, including the thoroughly Asian Chinese, was considered privileged.

On the afternoon of Monday, July 20, my mother came home excited; she had been downtown trying to buy food and had made a detour via the home of Mien Aalbers, in the eastern part of town.

"Mien told me that we can see *pappie* (Dad)," she crowed as she came through the door with her shopping basket. "Apparently there are notices posted all over town and in the *Tjahaja*. Wednesday is visitor's day at the LOG."

Babu Iti helped my mother and Juf prepare a parcel of clean clothes and extra food for my father. On Wednesday the three of us squeezed onto the bench of a *betja* tracked down by *babu* Iti, who had nervously agreed to guard the house. The *betja* driver set off down the Eykmanweg, furiously pumping the bicycle pedals. He took us through the middle of town to Daendelsweg, on the southeastern edge of Bandoeng.

The LOG building, surrounded by high barbed-wire fencing, stood well back from the road; it was a single-storey edifice with an arched entranceway in the middle, leading through the building to an inner courtyard. Japanese soldiers, with sabres at their sides and rifles with bayonets in their hands, guarded the entrance by the road; one of them inspected our food hamper for contraband before letting us in. By the time we arrived, the lawn in front of the building was filled with men, women and children, and the entire scene, if one were to ignore the menacing barbed wire and the soldiers, gave the impression of a festive Sunday school outing.

"Are you being fed?" Juf inquired anxiously.

"Yes," my father replied. "The kitchen has a food allowance of seven cents per day per person."

"That's not much," my mother remarked worriedly. "But have you got a good place to sleep?"

"Oh yes, don't worry—the place is full, but so far everyone has a bed."

"How many are here?"

"I think almost four hundred, but there are rumours that more will come."

"When do you think we can see you again?" Juf asked, but my father could not answer this.

"Are you okay on the Eykmanweg?" he asked. "Perhaps you should move in with friends, maybe with Mien Aalbers."

"Mien also has family to look after," my mother answered. "We'll try to stay where we are for now. Mrs. Raken is happy enough, and this may end soon. Besides what should I do about the *babu*?"

"You may have to let her go; this war may last longer than our savings," my father replied.

"Have you heard about the Kesilir plans?"

"No, what's that all about?"

"One of the nurses next door told me that the Japs want to ship Europeans there—a sort of agrarian colony, where they can look after themselves." After hesitating, my mother continued, "She thought it was a bad idea."

"Why?"

"Kesilir is in a bad part of Java—it's in the east, and has a lot of malaria—I will try to get more quinine pills."

After spending almost three hours on the lawn, we were told by the soldiers that it was time to go. The trip back home was awful: Juf cried all the way, and my mother, seldom emotional, had trouble keeping her composure. My father had tried to be cheerful, and had maintained that the "food was good," but as we left the gate Juf remarked that my father had aged in the short time he had been there. "I do not think he gets much sleep," she said in a concerned voice.

In a hushed tone my mother remarked to Juf, "It was awful when the soldiers beat the couple who were kissing each other goodbye."

The Japanese were horrified by the European habit of showing affection in public; kissing in public could cost either or both parties a sound beating from an exploding, armed and scandalized soldier, and if such a beating resulted in bloodshed, that was neither here nor there. My mother, not demonstrative by nature, had heeded my father's warning, but for Juf, who had cared for my father since he was a toddler, the forced emotional restraint was terrible.

On Friday a truck appeared at the end of our street and stopped, and a group of Japanese soldiers emerged from the back. An officer descended from the cab and accompanied by the four soldiers strode up each driveway in turn and entered the house. Nobody came to the front door at the house next door, occupied by a widow we seldom saw, and the men all went around the back. They soon returned to the street and now it was our turn. My mother stood waiting for them by the front door with a defiant look on her face, while Juf, shaking with fright, sat on a chair in the dining room; *babu* Iti disappeared to the backyard, where her laundry tub stood. The officer, armed with a sword and a revolver in its holster, and the soldiers with rifles slung over their shoulders and shiny, sharp bayonets in place, came to the veranda and brazenly approached my mother. The officer asked her in Malay, "*Anak laki? orang laki* [husband]?— *orang Belanda?*"

My mother replied, "*Tidak ada.*"

The men ignored my mother, rudely pushed past her and went through all the rooms. Within five minutes they were gone, and had moved on to the nurses' house.

"What did they want?" Juf asked.

"They were looking for men," my mother answered, with hatred in her voice.

It was a *razzia*, a roundup of older boys and men who had thus far evaded internment.

The next morning my mother set out by herself to take more soap, clothes and food to my father, but she returned late in the afternoon with her parcel, teary-eyed. "The rotten Jap told me that he could not visit his uncle in Australia, and so I could not see Bou. The city looks awful," she added. "It's dead."

A week later, the air-raid sirens suddenly came on again and Matsui imposed a blackout at night. Miss Fukken was able to tell us that the Americans had "launched an invasion on Guadalcanal, in the Solomon islands, near New Guinea."

Once again the Japanese soldiers went through Bandoeng, this time looking for undoctored and unregistered radios. They also checked blackout effectiveness at night and we sometimes were unnerved to see the silhouette of a truck drive slowly past with dimmed lights. It was a sinister sight that momentarily caused our hearts to stop. The Japanese were clearly frightened of invasion and air attack, which in turn scared us.

In the middle of August my mother came home from a foraging expedition in the company of Mrs. Boot. The latter had heard that another three thousand *totok* men were to report to the LOG. My mother offered her a cup of tea, wondering out loud, "How can they be housed? When I visited Bou he told me that the place was designed to accommodate only eight hundred. They can't possibly do that."

Mrs. Boot shrugged her shoulders, so my mother continued, "I'm sure we will be next, don't you think?"

"No," the latter replied. "I've heard that the *Belanda Indo* men are next. The Japs are scared," she added.

"Why?"

"They're moving troops out from Bandoeng, probably to replace wounded soldiers in New Guinea or on the Solomons, and I think they are afraid of riots and losing control of this area." Mrs. Boot, familiar with the work of her husband, had an appreciation for the ease with which the indigenous population could start a local uprising. Indonesia had always been like that.

"The American offensive is having an effect," she continued.

Miss Schotanus, one of the nurses, was returning from work and, seeing the tea party on our veranda, came over with the news that there were more wounded Japanese soldiers in the hospital. It all seemed to confirm that contrary to radio broadcasts and newspaper articles claiming that the American invasion was a failure, things were not going well for the Japanese.

With these military setbacks the pressure on the European population grew: on August 17 Matsui read the riot act to the *Belandas*, who still remained at large, and the following announcement was posted all over town:

1) It is expected that all European residents, being members of a conquered people, exhibit deference to *dai* Nippon, and in particular to the Nipponese army.

The following rules need to be taken into consideration by them:

2) All rules of courtesy must be followed strictly.

(a) Provocative behaviour is unacceptable.

(b) It is permitted to leave your residence, but only for essential purposes, such as food purchases, doctors visits, etc. One must, moreover, behave properly, not spreading rumours, and they should not transgress the rules of good living.

The rule mentioned in section 2(a) may not be transgressed when going out on the street. It is not permitted to create commotion or to behave noisily in restaurants, cafés and other public places. Those who are guilty of such behaviour will be forced to pay the registration fee on behalf of poor Europeans, as a gesture of mutual aid.

3) Everywhere outside of the home, it is mandatory to express humility when meeting a member of the Nipponese army, regardless of rank. This is done by bowing.[38]

A later announcement regarding the need to bow was accompanied by the explanation that the Nipponese soldiers "who, regardless of rain or the burning tropical sun, protect European property, are the personal representatives of the Japanese Emperor."[39]

We were all now placed under a form of house arrest and when out on the streets had to contend with a new problem—paying the proper respects to the Japanese soldiers. They now manned more checkpoints, where *pendaflerans* had to be shown and explanations had to be given as to why we were on the street. And one had better bow correctly. But learning to bow to a common foot soldier was hard for us Europeans, for we were accustomed to performing this expression of humility only when confronted with royalty itself, a rare occasion indeed.

Now it must be said that in Japanese society, bowing is a very common form of greeting, and the Japanese saw absolutely no reason why we should not be as polite to them as they were to each other. But the punishment enthusiastically administered by our new masters, common soldiers, exceeded by far in severity any reasonable reflection of personal disrespect. Almost everyone had seen someone being whacked over the head or forcibly pushed to the ground for having failed to pay the proper respects to a soldier who was cycling on the far side of the street or whom the victim thought was too preoccupied with a task to pay attention. The soldier would use whatever implement came in handy, whether a sword, a stick or his hand, and obviously took great delight in this manifestation of his superb physique; besides, corporal punishment was widely accepted in Japan as a sound pedagogical technique.

Notwithstanding the doctoring of radios and the known punishments for surreptitious listening, all of Bandoeng heard that the Japanese had lost the naval engagement at Guadalcanal, and that the Americans had by August 20 captured an airfield. One could moreover not miss seeing more troops leaving Bandoeng and heading east: it seemed a safe bet that they were going to Guadalcanal. Far to the north in Tokyo there was yet another political crisis, with Shigenori Togo, the Minister of Foreign Affairs, resigning because of disagreement with the army regarding civilian administrative policy in the occupied areas, and with Hirohito setting conflicting strategic objectives while the navy kept hidden from the army the scale of its recent losses at Midway and

---

38. Brugmans, *Nederlandsch-Indië onder Japanse bezetting*, document 28.
39. van Velden, *De Japanse burgerkampen*, 58.

Guadalcanal. To crown it all, everyone considered Hirohito's wish as a command, never to be questioned as to its wisdom.[40]

A week later Mrs. Boot unexpectedly dropped by our house with a broad smile on her face. "Have I ever got a good story for you," she announced, as she stepped onto our veranda.

"Juf, you'd better come and listen," my mother shouted to the back. With all the recent bad news it was a relief to hear something more positive.

"It's crazy," Mrs. Boot began. "The Japanese had ordered an anti-invasion exercise—"

"Where? Here?" My mother sounded bewildered.

"No—in Batavia," Mrs. Boot continued, "with planes and civil defence and anti-aircraft fire. They are apparently preparing the city for a possible attack from paratroopers. Someone over there asked an *inlander* policeman what was going on and he said, '*Ada parasutis*' [paratrooper attack]. Other people heard this, but took it for factual news, and it spread through the city like wildfire. Then a radio announcer added his ten cents' worth and spread the news further, adding that Singapore and Palembang had also been bombed," she giggled, shaking her head in disbelief. "That guy is now in jail for spreading the rumour of an American invasion."

"By the way," she added on a more serious note, "I gather that the Maria Stella Maris convent is being converted to an internment facility for *Belanda Indo*—they're next." And with that parting shot Mrs. Boot took her leave and headed home.

The heightened fear of invasion sparked off more street-by-street house searches. When it was our turn the officer made himself comfortable in an easy chair on the veranda and requested ice water, sending a trembling Juf off to do his bidding, while his men ransacked the rooms. When they had gone, leaving behind an incredible mess, my mother emerged from her bedroom cursing, "*God-ver-dom-me*," almost spitting out the guttural *G* and stressing each syllable. "The rotten Japs have taken Bou's camera." Suppressing her tears with difficulty, she added, "I'd hoped to sell it."

And so August 1942 drew to a close without the usual festivities to mark the Queen's birthday, in the past the most important occasion for partying on these islands.

But on the evening of September 1, Miss Fukken, our chatty neighbour, darkly told us that the Japanese had that morning discovered a cache of weapons and a radio transmitter in an abandoned house near Lembang. "There was a fight and they caught a teenage *totok* boy and beat him, but when he arrived at the hospital he was dead."

40. Bix, *Hirohito and the Making of Modern Japan*, 457.

For the following week the Japanese stopped all vehicles entering or leaving Bandoeng and rounded up all boys fourteen and older. Hardly had this furor calmed when a systematic roundup of *Belanda Indo* men got under way. It started with the delivery of individually addressed notices for some to report to the Maria Stella Maris convent. The Indonesian messengers who had to deliver these notices sometimes found this an uncomfortable task because they were related to some of the addressees. And yet amidst all of this misery there were to be more celebrations to reinforce the myth that we were living in paradise. On September 8 we were to celebrate the six-month anniversary of the capitulation—what joy! Within a short time the Maria Stella Maris convent had become so crowded and unhygienic as to defy the imagination.

On Friday, September 11, the *Tjahaja* made it known that *Belanda* women and children in Batavia were to report to a protected area. It seemed a given that we, too, would be subject to such a ruling; it would only be a matter of time. My mother had already been gathering emergency supplies of rice and flour, both increasingly difficult to obtain, and now this hoarding appeared to be justified.

"I wonder what they mean by 'protected area'?" my mother mused.

"Tjideng is near the red light district," Miss Schotanus, who told us this news, sniggered. "They could have chosen a better area. You'd better prepare yourself—it will come here, too." This bad omen was followed by notification from the town hall that the authorities were going to make an inventory of all furniture in order to impose a wealth tax—the yield from the *pendafteran* levy had been well below expectations. And so it went, a seemingly endless stream of announcements, all designed to make our lives miserable.

Days later my mother came home from a foraging trip on the bicycle and entered the house in a very upbeat mood, bubbling with excitement. It was a wonderful change from the tension that had hung over her since my father's departure.

"On my way back I paid a visit to Emmy," she said, "and she confirmed what I had heard downtown. You'll never guess what happened—everyone is talking about it." My mother interrupted her story to light up a cigarette, a luxury now, and took a deep breath before continuing, "Roosevelt has told the Japs to get out of Java. He has threatened that if they do not leave willingly he will force them out. The Japs are busy preparing their evacuation plans."

"No, it can't be true!" Juf sounded incredulous.

Hardly had we digested this information when one of the nurses living next door popped into the house to show us a new dress she had bought.

"D'you think the American soldiers will like me in this dress?" she asked. "There was such a crowd at Gerzons—I saw a lot of my friends there."

For a few days the clothing shops in Bandoeng did a roaring trade, but the rumour soon provoked more hysterical anti-Dutch articles in the *Tjahaja*, the sole surviving Malay language mouthpiece of the occupying power. A few days later Mrs. Boot came by, waving her copy of the *Tjahaja*, and opined, "The Indonesian collaborators are running scared, too. The US and the Japs are negotiating and Roosevelt will deal with these—," and here she shook the paper in the air to emphasize her point, "—as well, just as they deserve."

So intoxicated were we by the thirst for good news that even this media diatribe was interpreted in a positive vein. A day or so later we were startled by the sight of black smoke drifting over our neighbourhood; it seemed to come from the direction of Andir, the military airfield. Was this after all related to the invasion rumour? That evening Miss Fukken told us that one of the Indonesians, accused of petty theft at Andir, had been taken to hospital suffering from severe dehydration after being tied to a telephone pole for a week. "*Inlanders* took revenge by setting fire to some drums full of oil," she added.

"How awful," lamented Juf as she glanced at the wisps of smoke still drifting through the air. By now most of us had begun to realize that the invasion story was just another rumour, more bizarre than any earlier one, and depression firmly returned.

"You can have no idea how bad it is," continued the nurse. "Have pity for the interpreters of the *Kempetai*. They are supposed to keep absolutely secret what happens there, but I had to help one of them to some *obat* to calm his nerves—he had a breakdown. I felt so sorry for the man—the things he has to hear and see on pain of death." After a short pause, she continued, "A lot of trains are going to the coast with the windows shuttered. I think they are transporting our soldiers to other areas."

"Do you think this affects the men in the LOG?" my mother asked anxiously.

"Maybe," she answered.

Then the tax-collecting campaign got under way. My mother sought out the advice of Mrs. Boot on how to deal with this issue. "I do not understand how assessing furniture is going to help them," Mrs. Boot had offered. "If they take away the furniture, who'll buy it?"

On October 9 the Bandoeng radio station broadcast a message in Dutch for the last time:

> The Imperial Japanese government is concerned for the welfare of all *totok* women and children. For those women and children who do not have a male protector, a protected area will be set aside in Bandoeng. Two such areas have been designated: Tjihapit and Karees residential districts. These areas will be ready to receive the new inhabitants by the beginning of November.

The Japanese Minister of War had laid the groundwork for this plan in April, soon after the conquest of Java, and his Confidential Report Number 1232, titled "Disposal of Enemy Aliens in Distress," included eight instructions, freely summarized as follows:

> Japan recognizes that as a result of our "Asia for the Asians policy" we will reduce the European population to paupers. A state of affairs where these minorities starve to death may not be in the long-term interest of Japan. We will initiate policies that will permit these people to fend for themselves for the time being. This will be facilitated if we round them all up and herd them together in designated areas, where we can, incidentally, keep an eye on them and prevent subversion. Should they nevertheless encounter real hardship, and demand assistance, we should ensure that such assistance is warranted. Local Japanese authorities will be best placed to make such assessments. Assistance should nevertheless not be a burden on the Japanese taxpayer but should be financed from the seized foreign bank accounts.[41]

The task of preparing the "protection areas" was assigned to the municipal town hall staff. First of all, houses in the area had to be inspected to determine the number of rooms available and a space allocation notice was then attached to the front door on the assumption that each internee would get nine square metres. Then the people currently occupying those houses had to be dealt with. Since the two areas were intended to house only enemy *totok* women and children, all other racial groups had to leave. The Chinese, *Belanda Indo*, Indonesian and miscellaneous other residents had to find alternative accommodation, regardless of whether they owned the house or not. Almost four hundred families had to be relocated, and they naturally procrastinated by seeking this or that special consideration to resist the move. The exercise therefore became a drawn-out affair.

To my mother the announcement was worrying.

"Tjihapit is a model *kampong*. I remember once walking past those houses, not far from where we used to live on Serajoestraat."

"Oh yes," Juf agreed. "I remember—just beyond the Oosterkerk [a church]. Those houses were tiny."

"Yes. They were not even made of brick and were occupied by *inlanders* and poor *Belanda Indo*. Bou had said that South African cities should consider emulating Bandoeng with such projects. He admired the mixture of traditional and modern materials used for these houses, but I don't fancy moving there."

---

41. van Velden, *De Japanse burgerkampen*, 583.

The news was unsettling and puzzling, but for the time being we heard no more of it.

As October wore on our daily lives were punctuated by more *razzias*—more house searches for men. Even a valid *pendafteran* was no longer a guarantee of being left unmolested, and whitish men's faces virtually disappeared from the streets of Bandoeng. And when it was not a *razzia* in search of men, it was the tax collector; in the last week of the month they also came to our house and made a list of our furnishings, but soon left, for our furnishings were not impressive—but again the house was left in a state of chaos.

On the first day of November we were once again told to be cheerful and festive to help Matsui and his compatriots celebrate *Meiji Setu*, the birthday of the Meiji Emperor: "All houses must display the *kokki* flag on November 3. You may keep the flags out until after November 8, the celebration of the capitulation." He would not want our feeling of joy to dissipate too soon and so he gave us notice that on December 8 we could look forward to celebrating the start of the Pacific Liberation Movement. Such prompting suggested concern on the part of the army of liberation that the enthusiasm for flag-waving among Bandoeng residents had diminished over the last few months; hardly anyone in our street bothered to hang out flags.

"Is it not risky?" Juf wondered out loud.

"The Japs are too busy rounding up *Belanda Indo* men," came my mother's offhand reply.

At the same time, good news once again swept through Bandoeng. This time it was the naval battle of Santa Cruz, southeast of Guadalcanal, where the Japanese sustained high aircraft losses and two Japanese battleships, the *Hiei* and the *Kirishima*, were sunk. The speed with which news of this setback travelled through Bandoeng again sparked reprisals from Matsui, who then became aware that the BBC was broadcasting from India on a wavelength that almost coincided with the one used by the local radio station, but the BBC transmitter was so powerful that it drowned out the local broadcasts. Matsui ordered all radios to be handed in, even those owned by Japanese junior officers.

In the middle of November directives were sent to all households in the two designated "protected areas," Tjihapit and Karees: all non–*Belanda totok* inhabitants were ordered to find alternative accommodation within a week.

The order caused consternation. Where on earth could they find alternative accommodation in this overcrowded city? And what about all their belongings? A number of these houses had been owned by the occupants, and many, including the entire Tjihapit "model *kampong*," dwellings had provided subsidized rental accommodation for those of limited means. Thus nervous tension throughout Bandoeng rose to a new pitch, and not just among the *Belanda totok* women.

"At least we do not have to move now," Juf commented. But my mother irritatedly shot back, "We have to move to that protected area." An icy silence descended on our household. Juf spent the remainder of the day in the kitchen with red rings around her eyes and *babu* Iti kept to the back of the house to stay out of the way of *njonja*. She had caught wind of what was afoot and realized that her employment would soon end.

A week later, on November 24, a messenger boy came down our street, stopping at a few houses, including ours. From the veranda my mother saw him coming up our driveway and commented sourly that perhaps he was delivering her a birthday card. He delivered two letters typed in Dutch under the pre-war Bandoeng municipal letterhead: one was addressed to *Mevr.* (Mrs) van Oort and family, and the other was addressed to *Mej.* (Miss) Eisenberger—to Juf, in other words. My mother read the letter out loud; it instructed us to move into Tjihapit the next day. The letter included a short set of instructions as to what we were allowed to take with us, which was very little: a bed and a suitcase and a chair per person. It also specified our future address. Without thinking she opened the other letter, read it, but then crumpled it up.

"*Godverdomme,*" she cursed, as Juf appeared. "We have to move—they are crazy—tomorrow!" But the address assigned was not in the model *kampong.* That was a small relief.

"Perhaps I should talk to some friends and neighbours about this," my mother thought out loud that evening. There followed a discussion around the dining room table as to what we should bring and what we should leave behind. A bed, a chair and a suitcase per person seemed an unrealistically small allowance. "You know, if Ank or Charlotte have to move they will have a terrible problem—all that furniture, their silver and porcelain dishes and those paintings. It's perhaps a good thing that our stuff is still in South Africa." Juf seemed to agree that this was a small silver lining to our unhappy plight.

"You know," my mother carried on more brightly, "perhaps we should make the move as soon as possible—we may be able to have a choice in accommodation. We might even be able to move into Mrs. Heidsieck's *paviljoen*—I am sure she was *totok*. It might be better accommodation than some of those other houses in that area, and you know, the Japs have picked two areas of town where the houses tend to be smaller."

"Did the letter not specify our future address?"

"Yes, but the town hall is a mess. They no longer know who lives where, and have even sent letters to dead persons. Nobody pays serious attention to them any more." The more she thought about it the more merit an early move seemed to have, but it was impossible to leave the house for at least another few days; there was so much to arrange.

Juf could only reply, "Oh, oh, what a situation."

It was obvious that the administrative system was in serious difficulty, with all the upheavals that had taken place. But when orders that deviated from the norms of the past came from a familiar source on familiar letterhead, there was an explosion of dissatisfaction. Hundreds of outraged women stormed the town hall and inundated helpless junior clerks, safely ensconced behind their wickets, with a barrage of complaints—the room assigned was "absurdly small" or "filthy" or the bathing facilities were inadequate. A number of women even descended on the offices of Governor Matsui to tell him that the Mayor, *raden* Atma di Nata, should be fired for "forcing so many women to live under one roof—ten to fifteen women in one house—an outrage!" The protest movement brought the municipal offices to a standstill.

Raden Atma di Nata reacted to the uproar in a characteristic Dutch bureaucratic way: he appointed a commission of seven women and three men to advise him on how to deal with the chaos. Later, the unfortunate *raden* got a rocket from Matsui when it appeared that lists of *totok* women had gone missing and had to be recompiled.

The next day my mother made the risky journey into town to buy three camp beds—folding wooden and canvas contraptions. She also dropped by the Borromeus hospital to tell Mrs. Raken, our landlady who was working there as a laboratory technician, what was happening. The latter promised to do her best to guard the possessions, including the stove and fridge, beds and a few large pieces of furniture we were forced to leave behind.

On November 27 my mother asked *babu* Iti to find a *grobak* to help us move our belongings. She gave the kindly woman a week's pay and said goodbye to her. In an act of vengeance, my mother smashed my father's fine violin to pieces to prevent it from becoming war booty. She was prescient and had quickly grasped the importance of becoming utterly objective in the fight for survival. All we took with us were some soft furnishings, the three folding camp beds, the zebra skin (a lovely reminder of happy times past in South Africa), a wall-cloth embroidered with images from popular children's' songs that had decorated my room since I was born, photographs, the Djokja silver bowls brought back from those wonderful pre-war holiday trips to central Java, and clothes. My father's Bolex movie camera, fortunately so far overlooked by the Japanese in their house searches, might come in handy as a trade item.

5. TJIHAPIT

The move from our home on the Eykmanweg to Matsui's "protected area" was a bit like a scene change in a Kafkaesque play, where logical continuity between successive events does not exist, and the final moments of one scene bear no relation to the opening of the next, and might indeed refer to an entirely different plot.

At the behest of a new Japanese military government that ceaselessly reminded us of its benevolent nature, we had vacated a house, a perfectly fine place, leaving behind the bulk of our possessions, and moved into a single crowded room in a house owned by stranger. There had been a war, but that had lasted only three months, and then the soldiers had signed an armistice, which now was nine months old. This had all happened in a country that was now seemingly at peace, and, if the new government were to be believed, that had been converted into a paradise. To emphasize these facts there had been numerous joyful celebrations to commemorate the birth of the Greater East Asia Co-Prosperity Sphere.

If it was paradise, it was nonetheless defective, for in our old homes we had lacked the protection deemed essential by that same government and therefore we needed to move somewhere where protection could be assured. The protection that we lacked was that of a male, of a husband and father, whom that altruistic government had several months earlier imprisoned for being unemployed, a fate largely prescribed by that same government.

My mother had already decided against the address assigned to us, because it would have split up the family, a prospect she had kept hidden from Juf at the time. However, Miss Heidsieck, our former neighbour, was still living in the house at 3 Serajoestraat, at the intersection with Brantasstraat, and what's more,

---

Very little documentation has survived from this, the largest women and children's camp under the Japanese occupation. The one diary I have been able to track down is that of Anneke Bosman, published privately in 1985. Since she was interned later than we were, and left Tjihapit before we did, the overlap is limited. In addition, the value of the diary is limited from a historical perspective by the fact that it was the work of a teenage girl, more preoccupied with personal concerns than with providing a chronicle of events. Aside from this there are only fragments of first-hand contemporary accounts. For a chronicle of events in Bandoeng, the diary of Jan Bouwer, a journalist who remained hidden throughout the war, is an invaluable source of information. Other information has been gleaned from various recollections committed to paper decades after the events described.

had on her grounds a separate guest cottage. "Wouldn't it be nice if we could move into Miss Heidsieck's *paviljoen*?" my mother had suggested to Juf. My mother expected some resistance from a spinster to the prospect of accommodating a small child, but she could only try. "Better the devil you know," was her motto.

The *paviljoen*, alas, was occupied, but Miss Heidsieck agreed to let us take possession of a bedroom facing the back garden; on the door was a piece of paper with "III-4" on it. "The officials claimed this room should accommodate four people, but I just used it as a spare bedroom for a guest," she said. After Miss Heidsieck's guest bed had been removed there was barely room for our three camp beds, our suitcases and a chair. Fortunately a *tuan botol* (a rags and bones man), keen to buy Miss Heidsieck's guest bed for a song, was in the neighbourhood with his *grobak*.

We had come not a moment too soon, for the next day the dining room was taken by another pair of women.

My mother and Juf did their best to make our new home *gezellig* (cozy), even though it was now reduced to the dimensions of a shared bedroom. The task was quickly accomplished because we now had so little. My mother had taken along a hammer and some nails and now once more hung the zebra skin and my wall hanging from the picture rail; both were reminders of happier days. She placed her oval portrait of my father on an upturned tea chest.

The next most important thing to do was to let my father know where we were. She wrote a short note explaining what had happened and made the two-kilometre trip to Heetjansweg, where Mien was still living, hoping that the latter could find a way of getting this information to my father in the LOG where her husband also was interned. Mien lamented that she expected to be called up as well, even though on her *pendafteran* she had claimed partial Indonesian heritage. "I have relatives who probably will stay out," she said. "They will find ways of delivering our notes."

Survival in our new home immediately became a daily preoccupation; what had previously been taken for granted had now become a challenge to our ingenuity. The gas, water and electricity provisions for Bandoeng had deteriorated and the greater demands that were now placed on these services in our crowded Tjihapit area aggravated the situation. Cooking became an immediate problem; neither the stove nor the gas supply was up to the demand placed on it by the increased population in our house. Besides, tempers got frayed when too many women were trying to work simultaneously in the small kitchen. My mother bought an *anglo* at the *pasar*; it was a small terracotta single-burner charcoal-fired stove. This was set up outside the house in the garden when the sun shone, but when it rained, it was moved onto the veranda. This was not the end of the problem; matches were no longer available. For a short while my mother used her cigarette lighter, a steel-ribbed cylinder with a wick shielded from the wind by a small adjustable cage. On one side there was a small steel grooved wheel that rubbed against a tiny flint. Thanks to years of practice lighting cigarettes she easily made the wheel turn with her thumb, causing sparks to fly towards the wick, but paper had become scarce and so she had to make do with dried Spanish moss from the trees. She then used this to light thin sticks and finally charcoal. This all took a lot of time, and a lot of lung power was needed to encourage a tiny glowing ember to burst into flame. (Some lucky people had a *kipas*, a fan made from woven bamboo strips that they vigorously waved at the embers to encourage a flame.) The lighter fluid supply did not last long and could not be replenished, and after that we had to make do with a tinder box, an old tin cigarette box that held a piece of steel, a flint and some dried Spanish moss. It became a most valuable possession. Thus we stepped back in time to an era predating the invention of matches, adopting not only the language of the indigenous people, but their traditional means of survival as well.

Toilet paper had also disappeared and henceforth the water bottle became an indispensable accompaniment on trips to the WC. One cleaned oneself with water using the index finger of one's left hand in the time-honoured Asian fashion. Our house had only one toilet, and with seven users the WC had become a popular room; with water pressure low, however, it sometimes took a long time for the flushing system to recover. My own toilet needs could for a while be accommodated with the help of a potty, a magnificent white enamelled steel affair with black trim. How lucky we were to have a potty, and what a treasured object it was to become! With the unreliable municipal water supply, any type of container was useful, for water needed to be collected when available.

In this way our scale of values changed abruptly. In Act I of our metaphorical play we lived in a city with the residue of civil amenities; in Act II we had moved in terms of amenities to a rural *kampong* and were advised to regard this as "progress." The wanton destruction of a valuable violin was soon forgotten and the possession of a lowly chamber pot cherished.

My mother was not altogether happy in our new environment. Juf, on the other hand, clearly felt more at home and relieved.

"It's very nice of Miss Heidsieck to make room for us," my mother had said, and Juf agreed, for when we first arrived she had noticed that Miss Heidsieck had a Bible on her bookshelf. For Juf the move had another silver lining. "Is the church also in the protected area?" she asked.

"Oh yes," Miss Heidsieck replied. "You mean the *Oosterkerk*? It's only ten minutes' walk from here."

"I wouldn't hold my hopes too high," my mother cautioned. "The Japs seem to be anti-Christian."

"Had you expected us?" Juf then inquired of Miss Heidsieck.

"No, I just was told to share my house with strangers—*totok*—and that was all. I wonder what happened to Mr. Hirschman and Mrs. van der Worm."

"Who are they?"

"My neighbours across the road. They are *Belanda Indo* and had to move. And poor Mrs. van der Worm also lost her pension—*schandalig, hoor!* [a scandal]," she added with a sense of outrage.

"Were you instructed to come to this address?" Miss Heidsieck asked in return.

"Yes," my mother replied.

I found out much later that she was lying. My mother had decided that the administration had become too chaotic to notice what was happening and so she had ignored the details of our assignment to Tjihapit and did not bother to inform Miss Heidsieck of the liberties she had taken with edicts from the town hall. Besides, the house was of a good quality and that was important. We had previously only understood Tjihapit to refer to the demonstration *kampong*, situated near the edge of town. What we now referred to as "Tjihapit" was more extensive and included more diverse housing.

Mayor *raden* di Atma had assured *totok* residents of Bandoeng that "their homes would be guarded" and had instructed them to leave all their house keys for safekeeping at the town hall, but no one had any confidence in these assurances. After six months of chaos they fully expected that their properties would be pillaged. My mother had locked the rooms containing our remaining belongings and had given the keys to Mrs. Raken, our landlady; others had dutifully deposited the keys in the town hall, where a huge box began to fill with bunches of keys, most of which soon lost their labels. Some individuals ignored the order and retained their keys, hoping to retrieve more cherished items from their homes once alternative accommodation had been found in Tjihapit. The instruction to bring only a "suitcase, a bed and a chair" was ignored by most.

The stream of refugees coming past our new home grew in subsequent days and Miss Heidsieck proved adept at turning people away, even when armed with her address as their destination. With Serajoestraat being one of the access roads into the protected area, we witnessed a steady stream of humanity passing by our garden wall, for we had formed the vanguard of about seven thousand women and children taking up residence in this neighbourhood. On and on they came, laboriously rolling, carrying or dragging their possessions down Serajoestraat, past us and in and out of houses in search of space that had been assigned to them or that they considered acceptable, occasionally finding both. Some came in style, with mother and children in a *sado* or a *bendi* leading the way, followed by another vehicle with the baggage. Others, wishing to bring proper furnishings, or determined not to leave family heirlooms behind, had hired a horse-drawn *grobak*. Moving house with the help of *grobaks* was a refined art in Indonesia. It did not entail packing china and clothes into cardboard boxes; entire cupboards filled with their normal contents were instead gingerly loaded onto these flat carts and slowly driven to the new address with minimum breakage or inconvenience.

Individuals came on bicycle and in *betjas* and some, who had fled the rioting and looting of the outlying districts, came on foot, miserable and tired. Those who had been far-sighted brought along a hoarded bag of rice, while no one would have dreamed of abandoning a beloved dog, cat or a cockatoo. Some mothers, facing the prospect of dealing with the needs of children, brought along their *babu*. This arrangement satisfied both parties: continued employment ensured that *babu* might still earn some money to send back to the *kampong*, where she had relatives in need; if *njonja* could no longer pay, *babu* was still housed and fed. Often close bonds of affection had arisen between the children and *babu*, and, in some cases, *babu's* services were essential for putting food on the table or to assist with shopping at the local *pasar*. One could always rely on *babu* to cut a favourable deal with Indonesian produce sellers at the *pasar*.

The entire relocation process was interrupted by the torrential downpours that commonly occurred in Bandoeng at this time of the year, adding to the misery and chaos.

The original *totok* occupants of the houses had to be satisfied with at most two rooms and the displeasure of seeing some of their former possessions unceremoniously dumped in the garden to make way for a prized piece of furniture brought from a former residence elsewhere in Bandoeng. This difficulty did not present itself in houses hurriedly vacated by *Belanda Indo* or *inlanders*; however, the departed residents had certainly not exerted themselves in leaving their former dwellings clean and tidy, but had simply abandoned whatever struck them as junk at the time, to the great benefit of the *tuan botol* with his cart, ever on the lookout for useful items. An unpleasant cleaning task awaited the new occupants. All of the tiny houses in the Tjihapit demonstration *kampong* were in this state. In many cases an attempt was made to keep a common area like a living room free for communal uses, but some houses were so modest that only an outside corridor, exposed to the weather, could serve this function.

The move into Tjihapit changed our lives in unexpected ways: we had moved into a ghetto, though no one called it that; for the first time since arriving on Java we were living in a racially and culturally homogeneous area. This was of course intended by the authorities, for the entire process had been driven by racial considerations. The *pendafterans* had required racial specification, and the internment instructions that we had been subject to had been based on that evidence and were aimed at *Belanda totok*. It was rumoured that the *Belanda Indo* population would undergo a similar yet separate isolation, though no one who gave this any thought could yet foresee how that would work. There were at least twenty-five thousand *Belanda Indo* living in Bandoeng, and it was an extremely loosely defined group of people. In our ghetto we nevertheless achieved a degree of security we had not known for months. Although the camp was a so-called "protected area" there were no signs of policemen, just a large concentration of European women and children and, aside from European teenage boys, hardly any other men.

Shortly after our arrival I went shopping with my mother at a *pasar*, newly established on Wilhelmina Street, two blocks away from our house. There, sheltered by *atap* roofs and supported by a flimsy bamboo structure, Indonesians had with miraculous speed erected stands selling all sorts of wonderful things—lemonade from bamboo canteens, fish swimming in buckets, terracotta objects, rice, vegetables, live chickens dangling upside down and tied by their feet, eggs, *gula Djawa* (the Indonesian form of brown sugar made from palm fruit), *djeruk Bali* (pomelos), *pisang* (bananas), papaya and spices. One could buy delicious packages of cooked rice with chicken, neatly wrapped in banana leaves, or some noodle dishes. However, my mother bought very little because the prices were outrageous: a single egg had become a luxury item, and a chicken cost a fortune.

On Sunday, December 6, we celebrated St. Nicholas' day, this time a very low-key affair and a pale reflection of the previous year's effort. The night before, I had dutifully set out my shoes in the dining room on Miss Heidsieck's polished floor and had placed in them a couple of sprigs of palm leaf, for alas! we had no hay for St. Nick's dapple grey mare. The next morning, I was delighted to find a terracotta pigeon with a hole in its tail in place of the leaves! There were also a chocolate and a spiced cookie. From somewhere St. Nicholas appeared, properly attired with a white beard, red cloak and a bishop's mitre and accompanied by his "Black Peter." This was a privilege we had regained. Here in the relative security of the protected area we could hold our own celebrations and ignore the ones made mandatory by Matsui in the rest of town. Children who turned up in Tjihapit in the days following the St. Nicholas feast were bitterly disappointed, because they had missed out on the fun.

In the rest of Bandoeng it was different. There the mandatory festivities began with compulsory house cleaning on November 30. Each of the next eight days had been designated for a particular purpose and announcements of wonderful new Nipponese initiatives. December 8 had been crowned by parades of flag-waving school children and stirring speeches given to an audience forced to listen (every household had to send one representative to the Aloon-Aloon). Best of all was the subsequent military parade consisting of fifteen small tanks, ten former KNIL Blitzbuggies,[1] twenty sedans and fifty Chevrolet and Ford trucks filled with a small detachment of Indonesian recruits. All we had noticed of these festivities was the flypast of three Zero fighters, outmoded versions with landing gear that could not be retracted.

This all contrasted strangely with the reality of the conflict in the Pacific, for by now the Allied onslaught on the Japanese merchant fleet had become so devastating that the Japanese navy had to economize on fuel use, notwithstanding access to the Sumatran and Borneo oil fields. This complicated the Japanese defence against American attacks on the Solomon Islands and prompted an acrid debate within Japanese military circles over the proper use to be made of the remainder of their dwindling merchant fleet; should it be used to transport vitally important raw materials such as oil, rubber and tin from the Indies to Japan or should it be used to transport reinforcements to the disastrous battle of attrition at Guadalcanal? Increasingly Emperor Hirohito had taken a direct, personal role in the conduct of the war, sometimes using his Imperial authority to overrule his admirals and generals, and urging greater sacrifices from his people. The bad news, however, was relentless and forced him to seek divine help; on December 12 he made a special two-day trip to worship at the Ise Shrine.[2] Perhaps another *kamikaze,* a holy wind, would bring relief to Japan's holy quest, just as it had so dramatically brought aid to his grandfather in the Russo-Japanese War. The visit to the Ise Shrine gave Hirohito the confidence to permit withdrawal of the remainder of his decimated army from Guadalcanal.

Everyone in Bandoeng knew that the battle for Guadalcanal was nearing an end. At unguarded moments, Japanese officers even admitted that they were surprised by the strength of Allied attacks; they had been told that it would take a year for America to recover from the setback at Hawaii, but this had proved to be wildly optimistic. When the air-raid sirens sounded on a daily basis, we in Tjihapit as well as the *kampong* dwellers knew that "*Ini bukan main*" (this was serious), but with every setback the authorities redoubled their efforts to instill in the population a positive spirit, as though sheer willpower could overcome physical odds.

From the outset Tjihapit and its inhabitants needed an administrator. Preanger Governor, Colonel Matsui, made this a high priority, for he needed a formal link between his office and the women he proposed to protect. Equally important was the matter of ensuring that the women would not undermine the Japanese authorities by, for instance, harbouring men who had escaped from one of the prison camps.

---

1. Originally "Bantam Blitzbuggy," later "Jeep"—for "General Purpose" vehicle (GP).
2. Bix, *Hirohito and the Making of Modern Japan,* 461.

This management task he assigned to a former non-commissioned officer of the KNIL, Captain Padma. He was an Indonesian who had declared a willingness to work for the Japanese army, and had the advantage as well of being able to speak Dutch. There was, however, a drawback: Matsui could not really be sure how successful a subordinate Captain Padma would be. Japanese non-commissioned officers were reliable in executing orders, but with these Indonesians one just did not know. Japanese officers, however, were for the time being unavailable and Matsui moreover knew that the task of supervising a camp full of women and children would be resisted by a Nipponese soldier.

The women themselves had also quickly realized that they would need to form a civic management structure, because Tjihapit was filthy. It was not just the recently vacated homes that posed a problem; clearly the city's department of sanitation no longer functioned as effectively as it used to, thanks to personnel upheavals and shortages of equipment. Within a week of the start of the influx to Tjihapit, a number of older women banded together to address these problems. Among the internees were several female doctors, who immediately set about organizing a provisional hospital in one of the homes, while the wife of a former KNIL officer, Mrs. Droog, took it upon herself to create and oversee a number of committees dealing with key civic services, such as hygiene, care for the sick, and accommodation. It was a matter of good fortune that Captain Padma had in his previous existence served in the KNIL under Colonel Droog, for this now provided his wife with some leverage and goodwill in dealing with Padma and facilitated the formation of an effective organization, in spite of the very wide social gulf that separated Captain Padma from "his" camp committee. From this perspective, too, life had suddenly become somewhat more orderly.

But there were problems. Almost immediately the impact of crowding and of our lopsided social environment began to be felt. The teenage boys were the first source of concern. There had been enough trouble already with impulsive, cocky, testosterone-charged young males throwing all caution to the wind and testing the mettle of the despised army of occupation. Now there was the added anxiety about all these bored young men, without school or the guidance of older men, living in close proximity to teenage girls and lonely women. Within a few weeks of our arrival, concerned mothers of girls were organizing a petition: they wanted to have the boys moved elsewhere.

The boys' mothers of course had a different view and dwelt on the positive aspects of having some sturdy lads around. Many other women agreed. The boys could fill a gap that normally would have been occupied by tradespeople and municipal workers. A good example was Rollo, the son of my father's colleague, Hansen. Rollo had been able to help his mother move to Tjihapit by providing transportation on his homemade "velo." This was a four-wheeled vehicle that he had recently made to replace his father's car, which had been requisitioned by the Japanese. For the concept and the name he had drawn inspiration from a magazine article. He had mounted four bicycle wheels on a chassis made from North American timber salvaged from the aircraft packing crates on Andir airfield, where his father had managed construction projects. At a *pasar busuk* (a flea market) he had found the steering wheel of an Austin 8. The velo seated a driver and his mate, both equipped with bicycle pedals, and behind them was a platform for passengers or goods. Rollo had completed the prototype just in time to transport his father to the LOG. Soon other boys in Tjihapit copied his example and two of these velos were now being used as ambulances.

The boy problem continued to simmer, but was increasingly overshadowed by other crowding concerns. As the stream of new arrivals continued unabated, choice in accommodation quickly evaporated and houses, often very modest houses, had to be shared by women, children and sometimes even old men from all walks of life; this soon caused difficulties. Children were noisy and rude, and sick children cried all night, whereas elderly ladies had nervous conditions and could not cope with children, and elderly gentlemen tended to become short-tempered. Miss Heidsieck found it rather difficult with me around, and would not countenance any other women burdened with children moving into her house; this caused Juf to devote her time trying to keep me occupied and out of Miss Heidsieck's way, while my mother was out looking for food, now a daily preoccupation.

On one such occasion my mother returned to find a discussion under way between some women on the sidewalk across from our house, while three young boys larked about in the front garden of the house. She joined the group, for she was keen to get to know her neighbours, hoping to find some moral support or even assistance, as she missed the comforting presence of our former neighbours on the Eykmanweg.

"The office can't do a thing," one of the women, who could not have been more than twenty years old, said with a note of resignation. "It's the town hall that organized the accommodation and Mrs. Droog thought they were useless." Then, turning to my mother, she introduced herself in a quiet voice, "My name is Amelia; pleased to meet you." One of the other women present introduced herself as Mrs. van Dijk, who, it turned out, lived in the house across the Brantasstraat from us. "My boys," Mrs van Dijk announced, indicating the three children.

"What's the problem?"

"Amelia had been assigned to a house on the Houtman *Plein*,[3] but the people already living there created a fuss," Mrs. van Dijk explained, adding, "*Schandalig, hoor.*"

"One of the women said that if I came to live there it would ruin her husband's chance of becoming the next mayor of Batavia," Amelia added.

"What?"

"Ach—" Mrs van Dijk interrupted. "Amelia has only recently arrived in the Indies as an *au pair* girl with a family returning from Holland."

"We also arrived recently," my mother commented, seeing in Amelia a person who shared some of our difficulties. "So what?"

"Her employer was a member of the NSB—how could Amelia have known that? But now Amelia is also accused of being an NSB member—can you imagine? And that woman now thinks Amelia's presence may affect her husband's career—if and when he gets released from internment. It's too crazy for words."

Amelia struck my mother as a most unlikely person to be a member of any political organization.

"Why not move in with us?" Mrs. van Dijk proposed. "The owner has been kicked out by the Japs, and the others in the house will not mind." My mother said nothing, for she was not sure how Mrs. Heidsieck would react to an alleged NSB sympathizer moving into her house; the situation was awkward enough already.

The grimness of the future we all faced had not yet become a sufficient presence in our collective psyche to permit the burial of these petty squabbles. It was as though we still could not comprehend, almost a year after capitulation, that our world had really and truly changed, and that we were not dreaming some ghastly nightmare that would end with the rise of the morning sun.

The dramatic differences in wealth among internees caused more difficulties; the rich, the newly pauperized and those who had always been poor now had to live cheek by jowl. In some houses, a family in one room might still be able to enjoy chicken with their rice, while the mother next door, with three or more children, was already destitute, and the cooking smells, admittedly from a simplified menu, wafted through the open doorways and windows.

A week or so later, Emmy turned up; the relative with whom she had sought refuge had been evicted as well. Emmy also experienced difficulties finding acceptance at a Tjihapit address. One of the ladies in the house to which she had been assigned had inquired whether she was married or single. It was undoubtedly well meant, but then the next question popped out: "And what happened to your husband?"

---

3. The Houtman *Plein* lay adjacent to the eastern edge of the built-up area of Bandoeng, facing the military grounds where the KMA complex had been built.

"He is a POW in the 15th Battalion barracks."

"Oh, so you are a soldier's wife?"—a rhetorical question posed with a distinct tone of superiority.

"I like being a soldier's wife," Emmy replied with a sharp edge to her voice, despite the fact that she was destitute, a state shared by nearly all soldiers' wives. Emmy eventually found accommodation in a house at 8 Serajoestraat, diagonally across the road from ours. From that day on, my mother and Emmy, both newcomers to the Indies, became virtually inseparable; to me she became known as "*tante* (aunt) Emmy."

By now about seven thousand people were living in a neighbourhood that previously had housed about one thousand.[4] At the same time the geographic extent of our world had shrunk. Initially we had been cut off from Europe, then from the rest of the world outside of Java, after which we were limited to the confines of a single city—and now to a small suburb in that city. We could still venture outside of the suburb to go shopping or visit uninterned acquaintances, but such expeditions had become hazardous.

By the end of December the monsoon season was well under way and each afternoon, with uncanny predictability, torrents of rain would fall from the dark clouds overhead. On such occasions, tree-lined Brantasstraat in front of our house turned into a river, with torn-off leaves and branches being swept along and piled up at the street corners. The water then sloshed along Serajoestraat and plunged into the Tjihapit *selokan*, a concrete-lined ditch passing beneath the street through a culvert. Once upon a time, before the Europeans had come, before Bandoeng existed, that water would have drained freely from the land into the Tjihapit *kali* (river), disgorging its watery, detritus-laden contents into the Tjitarum *kali* to the south. The river banks would often have overflowed, causing a *bandjir* (flood), but vegetation debris carried by the water and deposited on the surrounding landscape would soon disappear in the riot of new jungle growth. But now the Tjihapit *kali* had been transformed into a *selokan*, while houses and paved streets further interfered with Nature's ways; the consequences were spectacular. It was as though Nature were determined to sweep away with a torrent of swirling water the recent concrete and brick intrusions on this emerald isle.

Thunderclaps crashed over the rooftops, drowning the din of the rain that pounded the houses and trees; it rendered conversation impossible, so we sat quietly on the veranda, watching the atmospheric drama unfold. Later in the afternoon, the rain usually petered out, not to a drizzle but to very large,

---

4. This number is only a rough estimate, since whatever records were compiled by the municipal offices regarding the Tjihapit population are now lost. The numbers quoted are based on estimates of arrivals, departures, births and deaths, compiled three decades after World War II ended.

infrequent drops, while the clouds would dissipate and the evening sun could once more break through as it dropped to the horizon, revealing a brilliant blue sky cleaned by the recent downpour. A refreshing smell of ozone would invigorate us, and once more the insects would buzz, the crickets would chirp and the birds would twitter excitedly in the trees along the side of the road, while the *tjitjak* could commence their evening hunt for bugs. At moments like this, it was tempting to forget that we were in a war.

My mother contracted jaundice. A camp doctor was consulted, but scarce medical supplies had been requisitioned by the Japanese army and were no longer available. A Japanese doctor, a very gentle person who refused to be bowed to by European women, was made aware of the situation and advised my mother to consume leaves of sweet potatoes. The cure worked, providing her with an impressive demonstration of the powers of herbal medicines, and for years after the war she mentioned this welcome sign of some compassion from our otherwise unyielding captors. We also tried to augment our increasingly scarce food supplies by way of little gardens and my mother persuaded Miss Heidsieck to let her convert a brick flower box into a small tomato patch; my contribution to this horticultural enterprise was the contents of my potty.

But the arrival of work parties consisting of European men armed with picks and shovels, who started to dig a series of holes in the streets bordering Tjihapit was a new source of anxiety.

From Protection to Incarceration

With foreboding we watched the work being done around us; before our eyes an enclosure rapidly began to take shape, changing the "protected area" into what looked unmistakeably like a prison camp. Act II of our crazy play gave way to Act III with a dramatic scenery change.

The raggedly dressed *Belanda* labourers from the 15th Battalion men's camp in Bandoeng worked under the supervision of a Japanese soldier. They dug holes every ten feet or so in straight lines along the edge of the roads defining the boundaries of our protected area; in those holes they erected ten-foot-high stout bamboo poles. Then a number of *grobaks* appeared bearing piles of *gedek*, large panels made of woven bamboo strips that were a familiar feature of the *kampong* dwellings, where they served as walls. These panels were now attached with wire to the poles. The message presented by this activity was unmistakable: we were being cut off from Bandoeng.

Of the original roadway, only the sidewalk remained running between the *gedek* (as we called the wall) and the front garden of the houses. The *gedek* deviated from this course only at one spot along its eastern boundary, to exclude from the camp part of a convent now used by the Japanese army.

The Tjihapit *selokan* was cut into three segments by the newly built bamboo monstrosity. Its waters entered our enclosure at the northern boundary via a culvert beneath Tjiliwoengstraat, the culvert outlet being within the camp just inside the bamboo wall. From there it took no more than five or ten minutes for its waters to complete their journey through the camp, leaving via another culvert beneath the south bamboo wall and the main, east-west artery of Bandoeng, the *Groote Postweg*.[5] Neither the modest source of this stream nor its destination or role as part of a larger drainage system were evident any longer; it was just a one-kilometre stream of brown water entering the camp at one spot and leaving at another. In a strange way it seemed to symbolize our changed existence—loss of contact with our past lives, and a blank future.

Upon completion, the bamboo structure was liberally festooned with *kawat* (barbed wire) to deter escape attempts. Bamboo towers were built at strategic points, permitting the army to ensure that the wall fulfilled its function—segregating and isolating those within from those without, as though we inside Tjihapit had a communicable disease from which the remainder of the population had to be protected. By the Oranje Plein, where less than two years before, Juf and I had enjoyed such pleasant outings, an entrance gate appeared. This provided our sole glimpse of the remainder of Bandoeng to the west. Two huge *gedek* doors were now hung on crude hinges from stout poles and, as a finishing touch, were fitted with an oversized padlock.

Thus Tjihapit became a well-defined geographic concept, an enclosed neighbourhood, or, more accurately from our perspective, a huge, windowless, claustrophobic tank. For those living within the enclosure, with its increasingly oppressive overcrowding, uncontrollable urges to escape arose, if only to get a glimpse of the normal world. The name *Tjihapit* has permanently entered the historical lexicon, but if a traveller goes back to Bandoeng today, he or she will find only the drainage ditch still bearing that name, while archival material, a plaque or any sort of paper record of the camp's existence in this city, is totally absent.

At the same time the camp administration was given more structure. Two houses facing the Oranje Plein and located just inside the new bamboo wall and adjacent to its gate, were designated "offices," one for the European management and one for the Japanese overseers; its occupants were told to find alternative accommodation.

Mrs. Droog sought volunteers to help staff her office. This type of work, earning a small salary, immediately became controversial. On one hand it

---

5. Today this is called *Jalan* Afrika-Asia.

smacked of "collaboration with the enemy," but on the other hand everyone recognized it as an essential requirement. She got a sympathetic response from Dr. Lily Cramer, our pre-war paediatrician, and Mrs. Diepeveen, both recent arrivals. Mrs. Diepeveen took on the position of Camp Head and she and her two colleagues began work in establishing a functional organization.

The two camp offices soon acquired appropriate names: the one occupied by Mrs. Diepeveen and her assistants became known as the "Ladies' Office," while the one being used by Commandant Padma was referred to as "the Gentlemen's Office" or, when decorum could safely be dispensed with, the "Jap office," regardless of the ethnic characteristics of its occupants. Padma, being patient and unhurried in the typical Indonesian way, provided helpful leeway in seeing his orders properly executed. This flexibility also reflected the moderate attitude of Matsui, the Japanese Governor in the Preanger, who deserves some credit for the fact that our internment came at a later date than it did for Europeans elsewhere in Indonesia. That flexibility moreover meant that internees were still allowed limited access to their savings accounts and that shopping at the *pasar* was, for now at least, permitted.

On January 5, 1943 (2603 by Japanese reckoning), Padma ordered Mrs. Diepeveen to identify boys born before 1926 (now sixteen years old); they were to leave Tjihapit and move to a men's camp where they could be properly guarded. This caused temporary consternation among our neighbours, but was quickly forgotten, since Padma did not appear to press the matter.

Our isolation was not absolute. The *gedek* was hardly an insurmountable barrier to communication with the outside world, for it was child's play to extract strips of bamboo and make a hole large enough for an adult to crawl through. In addition, voices could easily carry through the flimsy wall, and its height permitted objects to be thrown over it. In certain parts of the wall a gap remained between its base and the ground, and through this items could also be passed in or out of the camp. For the wall to be effective it had to be policed.

Indonesian teenage boys, originally recruited for civil defence duties, were assigned the policing duties, which they performed in a lackadaisical fashion; we called them the "PBO boys" (*Pengawasan Bahaja Udara*, or Supervision Air Attack). Since they were underpaid, small bribes greatly facilitated the transmittal of notes to friends still at liberty in Bandoeng. Thus the combination of an Indonesian camp commandant and Indonesian guards somewhat mitigated the otherwise dramatic impact of the enclosure (figure 9).

We nevertheless immediately felt the emotional impact of being cut off from the remainder of Bandoeng. Although time moved on at the same pace outside as well as inside the camp, our two existential trajectories diverged. With no idea when or how this situation would end, our sense of time gradually changed; we knew that something had happened, but were not sure whether it had happened last week or last month, and the days acquired a dreary monotony. We moreover carried with us through the following years a static snapshot of the world that we had left behind. This image of Bandoeng and its society, frozen in our memories, still appeared friendly and sympathetic. As time progressed we became acutely aware of the misery and suffering we shared with our companions inside our camp, but were oblivious to the chaos emerging outside.

As a result the imagined outside world became an increasingly irresistible magnet, a phantom vision of former normality. Before the *gedek* wall was finished, a number of women seeing the "protected area" being metamorphosed into a "prison" sought freedom and escaped. The escapes were noticed, and in time the periodic dragnet operations of the *Kempetai* recovered the offenders, meting out, as a deterrent to future escape aspirations, punishment never forgotten by some and fatal to others.

A week after completion of the wall, Matsui ordered the removal of all Indonesians from within the camp. The *babus* many mothers had brought into Tjihapit now had to leave; they were even more upset by this measure than the *njonjas* were and stormed Captain Padma's office to complain. Although they were servants, they had often lived with a family for years, and had developed deep attachments to the *njonja Belanda* and especially the children. But in addition, they would now lose their livelihood in a land beset by inflation and a dying economy. Captain Padma could do nothing, and there followed tearful scenes at the camp gate as the *babus* left with their *bunkus* (bundles of possessions). However, for a time they could still return for a few hours during the day, when the gate was open. By the same token Tjihapit residents could still be granted a *surat lepas* (permission) to venture into town for visits to a dentist or a doctor, while the *pasar*, though smaller now, was also allowed to continue in Tjihapit.

Outside our camp in the rest of Bandoeng the reign of terror continued unabated, as the Japanese army sought to exert absolute control over all aspects of life: what people did, what they said and even what they thought. The forced imposition of an alien culture was a curious way of winning over the hearts and minds of the residents of Java. Dr. Lily Cramer had brought with her into camp gruesome stories of recent happenings in town.

"The sense of justice of these Japanese is indescribable," she stated one day when she dropped by for a cup of coffee.

"How so?" Emmy, who happened to be with us, asked.

"They beat up about a hundred *betja* operators, because one of them had stolen six hundred guilders from a Japanese officer."

"How could a *betja* operator do that? The Japanese soldiers always have their guns and swords with them."

"The officer was drunk, and when he got out of the *betja*, he left the money and his sword behind. The *inlander* threw the sword in a ditch and pedalled away with the money," she added with a snigger.

"Surely he went straight back to his *kampong* or *desa*."

"He probably did," Dr. Cramer agreed, "but his mates were thrashed within an inch of their lives. I heard this from a colleague at the Borromeus Hospital, where they were patched up."

"Did you read anything about this in the *Tjahaja*?" asked Emmy. "You'd think that some of the *Inlander* journalists would get upset at this treatment by their saviours."

"Yes, mention was made," continued Dr. Cramer. "Matsui said in the paper that this was Japanese justice; how could you have community spirit if individuals did not take responsibility for the entire community? He described this as a good example of how Japanese morality would benefit Indonesia."

On January 11, 1943, the *Saiko sikikan* (the commander of the 16th Nipponese army) issued a warning to the Eurasian population. The article in the *Kan Po*, the official mouthpiece, was headed "*Peringatan kepada bangsa Belanda-Indo* [foul smell from the *Belanda Indo*]." The article explained that these people were to be pitied because they were neither Dutch nor Indonesian and therefore "had no place they could call their own." The Japanese army had hoped that this population would realize its predicament and wholeheartedly support the New Order, but unfortunately some of its members had adopted the wrong attitude—they did not think like Asians. Unless this changed, the army would abandon its benevolent attitude and take hard measures.[6] It was clearly a step designed to bring the Indonesians, who tended to see themselves as inferior to the *Belanda Indo*, fully within the Japanese camp, and to force the *Belanda Indo*, who as a group had always been made to feel inferior to the "proper (*totok*) Dutch" yet constituted an important cornerstone of the economy, to become even more Japanese than the Japanese themselves, or else become outcasts.

This campaign went hand in hand with another intensified recruiting campaign for the *heiho* (soldier assistants) corp. During the previous month Matsui had relied on a city-wide poster initiative to find recruits, but this had been unsuccessful, as most Indonesian lads had had second thoughts about living in or near Bandoeng and its violent, often brutal, Japanese occupiers; they had drifted back to the relative security of the *desa* to avoid the abusive discipline of the Japanese army. But the army's need for more manpower continued to grow and so alternative ways had to be found to meet the need. Matsui abandoned the reliance on volunteers and initiated the registration of all Indonesian young men in the Preanger. Registration could conveniently be

---

6. Brugmans, *Nederlands Indie onder Japansche bezetting*, 454.

followed by enlistment. *Heiho* recruits were given two months of intensive training and then entrusted with nothing more lethal than a dummy wooden rifle.

With most of the *totok Belanda* families out of the way, Matsui next focused his attention on an ethnic mop-up operation. The *totoks*, who now became the focus, were Europeans who had married Indonesian partners; also suspect were those *Belanda Indo* women who had married *totok* husbands and had so far been exempted from internment. The genetic subtleties became quite complex.

Mien turned up with her son, Theo, and found accommodation on Brantasstraat, a door or so away from us. My mother, delighted to see another familiar face, had hurried out to greet her when she came past our front door. With the increasing crowding and chaos, finding old friends had become a matter of luck.

"I thought that *Indos* would be able to stay out of the camp," my mother said, inadvertently using the simplified name for this ill-defined population group that had suddenly attracted official attention.

"Well, I expected this from the moment they locked up Theo," she replied, adding philosophically after a short pause, "It's perhaps just as well. I just hope my mother and father can stay out."

"Is your father still employed?"

"Yes, he found a position teaching *kampong* children and thinks he is therefore safe."

So far only a small portion of the male *Belanda Indo* population had been interned, but from all accounts the conditions under which the men lived in the Maria Stella Maris convent were appalling. Distressing news leaked out about dietary and hygienic conditions that defied belief. The remaining group was huge, too large to accommodate, feed and guard, and worst of all too difficult to define. Japanese attempts to pursue this policy, assisted and encouraged by a small, radical, but outspoken section of the Indonesian population, created deep divisions in the society. All over Bandoeng posters appeared with slogans like *Awas mulut merah, awas matamata biru* (watch out for red [lipstick] mouths, watch out for blue eyes).

Part of the Eurasian population attempted to retain its freedom and its jobs by declaring a willingness to co-operate fully with the Japanese, thereby also hoping to thwart the pressure from "pure" Indonesians to completely eliminate it from the economy; to improve their credibility, some individuals started a political campaign urging all members of their group to adopt a Japanese outlook. To this group the coming Japanese victory celebration seemed a good opportunity to demonstrate its Asiatic credentials; this occasion could be used to swear allegiance to *Tenno Heika* and, with the help of banners, the shouting of slogans and enthusiastic waving of flags, demonstrate wholehearted support for the many improvements made to Javanese society by the Emperor's men. The initiative was doomed to fail in an environment where any hint of European blood was viewed as hostile both by the Japanese, fearing sabotage, and by Indonesians coveting the positions held by *Belanda Indos.*

In the meantime Matsui refined the far simpler human sieve that he had so far employed. In the second half of January he ordered Padma to purge the camp of all boys who had narrowly escaped being rounded up half a year earlier when the men were first interned. Fifty-two boys, recently turned seventeen, were identified and told to present themselves at the camp gate, where they were ordered to proceed to the Topographic Services building on Bankastraat, five city blocks to the west of Tjihapit. They had to find their own way there, walking or cycling, and thus were limited in what they could take with them. They left mostly in a cheerful mood, feeling "grown up," perhaps looking forward to a more "manly" environment or a shared adventure. One of them took along his guitar, strapped to his back. The Topographic Services building moreover did not seem threatening, like a prison, and might even be interesting. A group of mothers and siblings had gathered at the camp gate to see them off. Miraculously, about half of them returned the next day, because for now the Japanese were interested only in "big boys" who could do heavy physical work.

During the final week of January Matsui ordered several *razzias,* combing the city repeatedly in search of any *totok* or *Belanda Indo* men who had misled the authorities regarding their racial characteristics with false *pendafterans* or had gone into hiding. The deteriorating administrative effectiveness of the municipal offices rendered reliance on an administrative approach pointless; Matsui was now forced to conduct house searches, assisted from time to time by the information-gleaning capabilities of the *Kempetai.* To do this, trucks were stationed at various points in town and teams of ten or eleven soldiers, led by a Japanese officer, systematically ransacked homes, looking for people with suspicious appearance and not in possession of a valid *pendafteran;* they seldom left empty-handed, for if they could not find people they could always find things. Matsui's *razzia* squad uncovered several *totok* men, who were bundled onto a truck and locked away without an opportunity to gather personal possessions or notify relatives. They even picked up some Nippon workers who happened to be on the street doing their shopping. Consequently a number of women and children, suddenly deprived of husband or father, turned up in Tjihapit during the following weeks.

In the middle of January 1943 a conference took place in a pleasant country hotel on the outskirts of Casablanca, in newly liberated Morocco—almost but not quite on the other side of the globe. Winston Churchill had requested the meeting in order to improve the coordination among Allied forces, which he deemed essential for launching a successful invasion of Europe; recent Allied success in eliminating the German presence from North Africa had been achieved under an ad hoc arrangement. To improve this situation he requested a meeting with American President Theodore Roosevelt and Russian President Joseph Stalin. However, Stalin was dealing with a siege of two key Russian cities and declined the invitation. Roosevelt agreed to come in spite of his frail health and the political risk: an incumbent American president had never before left the United States during wartime—this was an unheard-of initiative.

The most significant achievement of this conference, aside from the fact that it had taken place at all, was the press address Roosevelt made upon its conclusion. To the invited journalists he announced that in the eyes of Britain and the United States, "victory" was now defined as the "unconditional surrender of Japan and Germany." This announcement took Churchill by surprise, but at least he knew where the phrase had originated: when confronting Brigadier General Simon Bolivar Buckner at the battle of Fort Donaldson in 1862, General U. S. Grant had demanded "unconditional surrender" of the fort. What unconditional surrender signified when applied to whole nations at war was left unexplained, but the phrase was guaranteed to resonate with the American electorate, and for the continuance of the war effort Roosevelt needed their support. A historian later described this demand as a "putrefying albatross around the necks of America and Britain."[7] In due course we would experience the significance of those words.

The mood inside Tjihapit remained relatively sanguine and upbeat. Our squabbles were minor, and we were isolated from the hate-mongering and pogroms taking place elsewhere in the city. With time, the occupants of some Tjihapit houses began to see themselves as a club, and the houses were given names such as "The Plucked Hen" or "*J'attendrai*." my mother suggested a suitable name for our house—"*Alles sal reg kom*"—made a sign with the motto on it and showed it to Miss Heidsieck.

"What does it mean?" asked Miss Heidsieck.

"It is a popular Afrikaans expression, meaning that all will come right in the end," my mother replied. Miss Heidsieck approved of this idea and my mother nailed the cardboard sign to the front door frame.

The food situation, however, was deteriorating. Part of the reason for this was the depletion of the hoards that many individuals had first brought with them. In the Rijpwijk, a set of narrow streets giving access to very humble homes in the middle of Tjihapit, a weekly *pasar* was still being held, but the choice in foodstuffs had become limited and the prices had shot up. The camp administration consequently sought to augment the food supply by making bulk purchases at more realistic prices from wholesale merchants. They tried to get

---

7. Crocker, *Roosevelt's Road to Russia*, 182.

financial assistance from Matsui but failed, and therefore reliance had to be placed on savings in the possession of community-conscious Tjihapit residents, but the response to this initiative fell short of requirements.

With the growing shortage of food, my mother decided to seek a new source of protein inside the camp—the giant snails, or *keong*s, that had been a familiar garden pest before the war. "I had escargot on my honeymoon—they were delicious," my mother explained to Juf, over whose earnest face a shadow of aversion and distrust stole. "These probably taste the same," my mother added confidently. Juf remained skeptical, however, because she had never tried such an outlandish dish. Armed with my potty, my mother and I went snail hunting, an adventure I thoroughly enjoyed. We headed for the narrow alleys that separated the backyards of houses. These passageways were flanked by six-foot-high masonry walls that had been whitewashed when first built, but, through neglect and the humid climate were now covered with green lichens, while the air smelled damp and musty. The dense vegetation flanked shallow ditches formed by rainwater run-off, while here and there stagnant puddles of water from the latest downpour remained. All in all the area provided a feast for *keong*s and we returned home triumphantly with a dozen snails and some juicy herbs that grew in the ditches, probably watercress.

My mother invited Emmy to join us and help prepare and eat the *keong*s; the latter approached the cooking task with enthusiasm. The women first boiled the snails and got them out of their shells, but they were tough, and so Emmy tenderized them by beating them between two bricks. When they were finally fried with a bit of onion, they tasted pretty good, and even Juf ventured to try one. It was a memorable change from the boring diet we usually had now—plain rice, tiny pieces of poor-quality meat and occasional bean sprouts. It was a pity, though, that over the coming months the number of *keong* diners in Tjihapit grew, rapidly wiping out the snail population.

With the March 8 anniversary of the Dutch capitulation rapidly approaching, Matsui once again ordered *raden* Atma di Nata to organize a celebration in the city. It was a coincidence that the Pacific war had also been launched on December 8; eight is such a significant number in eastern Asia, and now nowhere more so than here on Java. Eight days of festivities were planned, and once again Indonesian school children were dragooned into playing a major role as a flag-waving cheerleading squad. The festivities began on Monday, March 1. The slogan was now *"Perajaan Pembangunan Djawa Baroe,"* or "The Awakening of New Java." It was curious how the capitulation on Java was not interpreted anymore as the capitulation of the NEI regime, but merely the capitulation of the Dutch presence on Java. This was a further, not so subtle reminder that in Japanese eyes Indonesia, a country synonymous with a huge archipelago, no longer existed. The rest of the program was extensive and varied. The next day the school children were on parade, and attention was focused on public health with the help of hooting decorated ambulances; March 3 was set aside for the announcement of military exercises in defence of Java; March 4 was dedicated to sporting events. On March 5 Bandoeng's mayor, *raden* Atma di Nata, placed flowers on the graves of Japanese soldiers, and on Sunday March 7 the authorities remembered to include us in the festivities by declaring the Tjihapit camp closed, thereby completing the metamorphoses of Tjihapit from a "protected area" to a "prison"; Matsui certainly had a sense of drama. March 8, the anniversary of the capitulation, was set aside for another show of military might; this time we saw only two Zeros flying overhead, a one-third reduction in Japanese military prowess from that displayed in December. The assembled masses on the Aloon-Aloon were nevertheless reassured that Japan remained invincible.

This commemoration was an occasion for Sukarno to boost his position. In Batavia he addressed a large crowd with a stirring speech that amply demonstrated his oratorical skills. The occasion was the founding of a new organization, POETERA (*Pusat Tenaga Rakyat*, or Centre, Focus and People Power), coinciding with the celebration of the eclipse of Dutch Imperial power at Kalidjati. In a voice thundering with emotion he declared:

> Fifteen years ago we already had announced the true Indonesian nationalism, one that is broadly based, and then we employed the saying, so well known by the children of the *kampong*, "When the Chinese Dragon co-operates with the White Elephant of Siam, the Indian Cow and the Egyptian Sphinx, with the Banteng (the wild cow of Indonesia), and if that co-operation is illuminated by the Japanese Sun, imperialism will be destroyed throughout Asia."[8]

Matsui used the occasion to announce his departure for service in China and that his successor would be Colonel Komiyama, currently governor in Semarang, a city in East Java. That evening Matsui celebrated his new posting with a sumptuous dinner party for close colleagues in the Hotel Savoy Homann. A few days later his parting words to Mrs. Diepeveen, the Camp Head, were, "You will have a pleasant time with Colonel Komiyama."

For the next few weeks the *babus* were still allowed to enter the camp on a daily basis to serve their former mistresses by doing some shopping, laundry or cooking, but that too came to an end. During the subsequent weeks and months many *babus* returned periodically to the gate in the hope of catching sight of their former charges and bringing valuable supplies of fresh food, like fish or a papaya that they might have procured in the *kampong*, but over time these visits diminished in reaction to increasing abusiveness of camp guards.

---

8. Brugmans, *Nederlandsch-Indië onder Japanse bezetting*, document 407.

Ominous rumours about Colonel Komiyama, the next governor, then began to circulate through Bandoeng. It was said that he was responsible for a trail of destruction among the women's camps in Central Java.

We Get a New Governor

Komiyama's reign got off to a bad start when the *Kempetai* discovered weapons being smuggled into Tjihapit. The boys had done it.

In a camp full of women and small children, the teenage lads had so far rendered valuable service, performing tasks previously done by coolies. For instance, they provided expert demolition service where holes needed to be broken through masonry walls to secure direct access from living quarters to the garden without having to inconvenience too many of the family groups now crowding these houses. The boys also pushed and pulled carts loaded with food ordered by the administrative staff into the camp. But it was in such a food cart that the guards at the camp gate discovered a cache of *klawangs* (sables) and revolvers hidden in bags of rice. The *Kempetai* promptly swung into action, arresting eight boys, all under sixteen years of age, and immediately followed this with a search throughout Tjihapit for more weapons, finding instead two brand new motorbikes.

The rest of Bandoeng also felt the impact of this discovery; the Japanese authorities had long since recognized that Bandoeng with its large European and Eurasian population remained a trouble spot, and this experience confirmed that viewpoint. Komiyama ordered the registration of anyone with blonde hair or blue eyes, regardless of irrefutable archival evidence that they were Eurasian.[9]

He nevertheless had responsibility for the welfare of his prisoners and had been made aware of the rapidly growing food shortage. On March 20 he accordingly issued a decree that all jewellery and money had to be submitted to a central fund to purchase camp foodstuffs, stating that it was totally unrealistic to expect the Nipponese taxpayer to subsidize the feeding of a people who had maltreated Japanese residents so badly! To further demonstrate his reasonableness he recounted shocking tales about the awful things that had been done to peace-loving Japanese citizens, especially in the United States, but also in Australia, where the Dutch had banished those of Japanese citizenship who had still been living in the Indies at the outbreak of war. To assist the camp management in securing the money, Komiyama organized another larger search party, this time consisting of a number of Japanese soldiers assisted by two hundred Indonesian policemen. They were to comb the houses for money,

9. Bouwer, *Het vermoorde land*, 168.

and to do this he ordered us out on the street while groups of soldiers went through each house, opening suitcases, boxes and cupboards. When the inspection was over and we returned to salvage our belongings, it was clear that the operation had been in part a plundering effort—money had been taken, but so had items like pocket watches, jewellery and other personal effects. "The camera is gone—rot Japs," my mother shouted with tears of frustration in her eyes when she discovered the loss of my father's Bolex movie camera. As a result of this experience the mood in Tjihapit became more defiant.

Three days later shots were fired near the *gedek* and a Japanese soldier travelling on a motorcycle outside the camp received a beebee gun pellet in his behind. This outrage prompted yet another house search, and this time revolvers were found in the possession of two women, along with the beebee gun. The women were dispatched to the *Kempetai* offices, where more information and confessions could be extracted with the help of a combination of hunger, thirst, sleep deprivation, lack of hygiene, the cries and wails of other *Kempetai* victims being tortured, and long stints standing in the sun, tied to poles or forced to squat with a bamboo pole painfully held behind the knee. The *Kempetai* completed this sweep by rounding up all boys fourteen years and older, loading them on the back of a truck and sending them to a men's camp to fend for themselves.

Sadly, for some mothers the departure of the rebellious youth was a relief. They no longer would have responsibility for restraining them from upsetting neighbours, provoking the camp guards or getting involved in sexual relations. Some mothers were painfully aware that their youngsters might jeopardize their own safety and that of younger siblings through their exuberant but ill-considered actions. Quite a number of these boys, on the other hand, particularly the older ones, treated the eviction as an adventure. For them, a camp dominated by females was "unmanly." The Japanese would certainly have agreed, and some may even have seen this move as a "constructive effort" for the upbringing of young males; in Japan such treatment of youths was not uncommon. A few lucky boys were reunited with their fathers, but the majority were left to shift for themselves in overcrowded camps where food was scarce and their future was grim.

My father along with some other concerned men "adopted" a number of fatherless lads, and attempted to give them a minimal education. These activities had to be done surreptitiously because they were strictly forbidden, on pain of a severe beating.[10] The really unfortunate boys joined the slave labour parties; all of them would bear varying degrees of scarring for the remainder of their lives. In Tjihapit, we would miss their services; henceforth the heavy work had to be

---

10. My father's charge was Peter Mees; he survived the war and by chance again met his mentor almost thirty years later in Vancouver.

done by the women and teenage girls. The sight of the exodus of boys was moreover unsettling: what family member would be split off next?

Boys, even young boys, were far from immune from beastly treatment by the Japanese soldiers—this we knew full well. Amelia confided to my mother the awful things that had been done to Marius, the eleven-year-old boy living with two younger siblings right across the street from us. Shortly before entering the camp, he had been dragged by soldiers to the office of the *Kempetai* and there he had been subjected to terrible brutality in an attempt to force him to identify, from among a number of women living in his neighbourhood, the one who had provided some Australian soldiers with shelter. The Japanese had offered the boy a choice—whether he preferred to have a soldier's spit forced into his mouth, or to have his nose broken. He chose the latter, and had to suffer the forcible entry of a man's fingers up his eleven-year-old nose and to have the cartilage cracked by a twist of the man's hands. After his ordeal, the boy was hospitalized, and eventually returned to his family with his face still black and blue.[11] Now the boy was morose and sullen, sometimes sitting on the wall in front of his house with a shifty, nervous expression on his face. The word *Kempetai* thus became the most dreaded sound of the Japanese language. Its physical presence hovered outside the camp like an evil dragon that could suddenly pounce on Tjihapit, capture victims, drag them out of the camp, do unspeakable things to them and then dump the human wreckage, if still alive, back in our midst.

And yet in spite of the fearful actions of the *Kempetai*, rebellious tendencies persisted among Tjihapit residents. The more the Japanese clamped down, the more determined some women were to do as they pleased and to defy "the rotten Japs." Even though Bandoeng itself had ceased to be hospitable or safe, some women and remaining boys periodically took their chances by escaping from Tjihapit, making use of the Tjihapit *selokan* culvert under the northern boundary of the camp—"sewer rats" they called themselves. On the other side of the *gedek*, this stream flowed through a narrow park in a quiet residential neighbourhood before entering the culvert taking it under Tjiliwoengstraat and the bamboo wall to emerge within the camp. At night the culvert and the darkened, quiet, tree-lined streets on the other side became an irresistible magnet for the audacious, and some of the women used these occasions to procure on behalf of the camp essential medications from pharmacies. If they were caught, the reprisals were terrible. Sometimes we would hear gunfire at night, when a soldier saw shadows flitting through the trees between the houses outside the *gedek*, and we suspected that yet another escape attempt was under way.

---

11. An extensive personal account by Marius van Dijk van Nooten can be found in Tromp, *Four Years Till Tomorrow*.

As March neared its end, Governor Komiyama paved the way for a broadening of the internment. He decreed that communal rooms would no longer be tolerated in Tjihapit and were to be cleared of furniture. In other words, we had to prepare for more arrivals. At the same time he decreed that all *Belanda Indos* still at liberty were to be issued a new *pendafteran* and that henceforth only *Belanda Indos* who could demonstrate that their blood was at least fifty percent Asian would be allowed to work in government offices. Furthermore, the decree that partners of mixed marriages were exempt from internment was cast aside. Existing *pendafterans* that had ensured one's liberty were considered suspect and therefore were no longer valid. Any pale faces appearing on the streets had their *pendafterans*, the "freedom tickets," blithely confiscated by the Indonesian police constables. Seven hundred women still at liberty in Bandoeng were within days robbed of their *pendafterans* and promptly had to re-register.

Nobody had any illusions; Komiyama was trying to reduce the remaining presence of whitish faces on the streets of Bandoeng by fifty percent. As a practical measure it was decided to limit the genealogical consideration to three generations. If one could demonstrate that at least four great-grandparents were Asian one was judged to be amenable to Nipponization. This precipitated another rush to the civic offices to identify grandparents and great-grandparents with impeccable racial pedigrees.[12] With a history of racial intermarriage stretching back for ten generations, this was admittedly a bit rough and ready. For the dwindling number of *totok Belandas* still officially at large, the so-called "Red Ball Brigade," new armbands were also required; these individuals had no illusions about this step being anything other than a precursor to their internment as well.

Flagging Fortunes

By April 1943 unmistakable evidence of the demise of the grandiosely titled Greater East Asia Co-Prosperity Sphere had begun to appear.

Java ran short of rice, that staple food the whole of eastern Asia depends on; the island's rice harvest had been a disaster. A bad rice harvest was a misfortune that could have occurred regardless of political circumstances, but with the economy and the administrative system in ruins, the impact of this misfortune could not be offset by imports from other rice-producing regions of the archipelago or elsewhere. In order to stretch the supply, a thirty percent level of adulteration with tapioca flour was now permitted. We all bore the brunt of this misfortune and the Javanese paradise faded further into distant memory.

---

12. Under Dutch law, births and deaths were recorded by municipal authorities.

Cotton, milk and sugar were scarce as well, and Chinese merchants were as a matter of course accused of speculation and hoarding. Even the production of rubber had to be curtailed because of a chronic fuel shortage.[13] The Japanese authorities began to introduce strict price controls, hoping thereby to retain a semblance of economic stability.

Everyone also knew that the Japanese were in retreat. Sukarno did his best to mask the tide of bad news with a smokescreen of eloquent rhetoric at huge popular rallies and with slogans like "*Amerika kita strika, Inggeris kita linggis*" (we flatten America, we pulverize England). When Tunis fell into Allied hands in the middle of May and the Japanese were pushed out of the Aleutian Islands, the news flashed through Bandoeng, precipitating repeated house searches for contraband radios. However, this good news could not compensate for hunger.

Governor Komiyama's solution to the food problem in Tjihapit was to order the construction of a soup kitchen, to be staffed by the women of Tjihapit and to be supplied with food bought by the women of Tjihapit. Space for such a kitchen was available on the Oranje Plein, across the road from the two administrative offices and conveniently close to the camp gate and the Tjihapit *selokan*. Here a long, low single-storey structure gradually took shape beside a flame tree. Built with a bamboo frame clad with panels of that popular building material, *gedek*, and a roof covered with *atap*, this edifice also served to remind us that we were stepping back into time, placing reliance for a communal building on ancient indigenous technology (figure 10). The workers did not bother to remove the grass from the area where the building arose, but that grass soon disappeared as it was replaced by bare earth or, when it rained—a frequent occurrence—mud. Inside the structure a dozen or so primitive masonry fireplaces were built, over which forty-five-gallon drums could be suspended. There was no cement available so the bricks were loosely stacked to make a platform with large holes for the wood fire.

The creation of such a communal kitchen coincided with a growing waste problem, since the pre-war municipal collection of rubbish from this part of town had ceased completely. Now the smelly rotting stuff piled up in front of the houses, and the remaining teenage boys, going up and down the streets with handcarts, collected it for delivery to the Oranje Plein, near the camp gate; given the absence of shovels and buckets, this was a filthy job. An inevitable consequence of the Japanese policy of racial segregation was that the rubbish was dumped where it could then be removed by the municipal workers under the direct supervision of the Japanese guards to minimize the risk of contact between the Indonesian workers and the Tjihapit inmates. The rubbish pile now lay—conveniently, one might say—next to the kitchen, where kitchen

---

13. Sato, "Indonesia 1939–1942: Prelude to the Japanese Occupation."

waste could in future also be dumped, but also adjacent to the spot where the suppliers delivered food to the camp. Needless to say, the arrangement fell far short of the Bandoeng municipality's pre-war hygiene standards. For a while this unsatisfactory arrangement worked, though the constant presence of stinking rubbish did not enhance the attractiveness of the kitchen's alimentary production.

Fortunately the rubbish dump would in future not have to accommodate much kitchen waste because our standard of acceptability was undergoing a rapid evolution—the squeamish in our midst soon learned to be otherwise. The rubbish dump did become a serious concern later that year, when the city hygiene department was no longer allowed to enter the camp, leaving the smelly pile there, while a new pile was started right outside the main gate. That was a better place because failure to do anything about its removal could cause traffic disruption on Riouwstraat and it was no longer hidden from outside view. But it also meant more work for us, carting the rubbish through the gate and past the guards.

Early in April we moved. For some time my mother had complained to Emmy that Miss Heidsieck did not want children around her. The beginning of a new wave of imprisonment, the outcome of Komiyama's March initiative, offered my mother a convenient opportunity to make the change.

"Why not join us at 8 Serajoestraat?" Emmy had suggested. "There are lots of children there and that will keep Boudy busy."

"Is there space?"

"I share a room with some elderly ladies who would probably prefer to live with your Miss Heidsieck," Emmy replied.

It did not take much to move us. A boy was found who could help us with a cart, and within a matter of hours we had made the transition. It was a relief for all of us, even Juf, because she had become increasingly nervous about keeping me quiet and occupied, and in future she could also count on Emmy's support. By now the average population per dwelling had grown to seventeen persons. Some of the larger houses contained significantly more and the more modest dwellings fewer, but there was still room for pianos in several houses, and many people could still sleep on beds. With all the children in this house we probably exceeded twenty persons living under one roof, but we still had a modicum of privacy, with our extended family group sharing one room. And we still had a common room at the front of the house, where a coffee table stood by the window; it was usually adorned with a small vase of flowers, to cheer up the room and make it *gezellig* (cozy).

Shortly after our arrival in our new home we children got a lesson in biology. It was raining outside and so a number of us, perhaps five or six, were allowed to play in the common room. We made an astonishing discovery when a three-year-old girl had to avail herself of the services of a potty; however, she appeared to have all the physical attributes of a boy. One can only speculate on the cause of this situation; perhaps it was a mother's fear of losing her offspring? We had already had hints of the Japanese policy of sending young boys away to look after themselves. Long after the war, when survivors could reminisce with one another, some mothers admitted that they had done the opposite, dressing their daughters like sons to avoid the risk of providing the Nipponese army with staff for a brothel, only to have to reverse tactics when the announcement was made that all boys over a certain age had to leave the care of their mothers to join a boy's camp.[14]

As yet the mood in our house remained remarkably upbeat and the women devised various forms of entertainment. It was in this house that we celebrated Easter Sunday. To amuse the children Emmy and another former teacher made an Easter tableau in the common room. They had decorated the round glass-topped coffee table with miniature baby chickens, ducklings and flowers and converted part of the glass surface into a pretend pond while the children were kept out of the room. When it was ready, we were allowed into the room and crowded around the table, enchanted by the display. For this Easter occasion my mother got involved in an effort to perform Handel's oratorio, the Messiah. She found some paper and pencil and began drawing music staves to prepare copies of the various parts. However, this project remained unfinished because of the shortage of paper.

Other, less complicated forms of entertainment did take place, the most popular being the cabaret evenings. Tiny, vivacious cabaret star Corrie Vonk turned up in Tjihapit at this time. She and her co-star husband, Wim Kan, had left Holland on an artistic tour shortly before the German invasion and thus found themselves stranded in an outpost of the empire. Now they also were interned and Corrie soon got busy organizing soirées, thereby inspiring a number of other gifted women to follow suit. A number of houses had a garage that could be turned into a music hall when provided with a piano. For the following year we had a regular fare of songs and skits poking fun at our conditions and ridiculing the Japanese soldiers. Corrie Vonk would from time to time come up with a marvellous new skit and strut about our makeshift theatre wearing her top hat and tails, twiddling a walking stick and filling the room with laughter. One day she strode onto the stage holding a frying pan, and with an earnest expression on her face addressed the cooking implement with the warning, "Yeah, pan, you will soon feel the heat," a pun that caused a roar of appreciation.

A pair of gifted women with the stage name "Tholen *en* van Lier" alternated with Corrie at cabaret evenings. The songs were invariably well-

---

14. Krancher (ed.), *The Defining Years of the Dutch East Indies, 1942–1949*, 196.

known pre-war tunes with new lyrics reflecting our camp life. The audience always joined in, lustily singing the easily learned refrain. Occasionally Japanese administrative personnel turned up for such entertainment functions. They called themselves "economists," were employed by the Japanese army to act in an administrative capacity, and often had a good command of the English language, but rarely understood Dutch and therefore failed to catch the play on words. They were nevertheless pleased to see so many of their charges having such a good time under the benevolent protection of His Majesty, Tenno Heika.

Boenjamin Takes Charge of Us

On Sunday, April 18, 1943, Komiyama appointed another former Indonesian KNIL soldier, Boenjamin,[15] to replace the easy-going Padma as Camp Commandant. Komiyama ordered Boenjamin to exercise greater control over the camp, since the numerous escape attempts had given the Tjihapit women a reputation for rebelliousness and plans were afoot to increase the camp population. He also assigned a platoon of armed, newly trained *heiho* guards to replace Padma's PBO boys.

Komiyama moreover ordered Boenjamin to introduce in this camp full of European women and children Japanese administrative practices, the *tonari-kumi* system of governance. This feudal concept was not entirely foreign to the Indonesians, who had known the same idea as *gotong-rojong*,[16] but it was a novelty for us. *Tonari-kumi* entailed a pyramid-like control system for directing instructions from a central authority into each individual household; it was in no way designed to permit the upward flow of suggestions, requests or complaints. Boenjamin accordingly told Mrs. Diepeveen, our Camp Head, that henceforth she was his lieutenant, his *kaicho*, his voice in the camp. She needed to appoint *hanchos* (district leaders) for a number of *hans*, groups of neighbouring city blocks, and they in turn had to appoint *kumichos* to be in charge of each *kumi* (street); the latter in turn had to appointed a *kepalla* (head) for each household. For some reason the Japanese nomenclature broke down at the house level and we reverted to Malay.

Boenjamin was not up to the challenge. He had to manage a population of over nine thousand women with deeply ingrained independence and self-worth, in many cases supported by high educational achievements and a sense of superiority over their former servants-turned-master; moreover, during the previous three months of ghetto life, they had developed a strong sense of

---

15. Boenjamin, like many Indonesians, had only one name.
16. Bouwer, *Het vermoorde land*, 173.

tribal cohesion. The women welcomed their new Camp Commandant with disdain, if not outright defiance, assisted in this enterprise by the existence in their midst of individuals with a flair for the creative use of language. The syllables of his name, for instance, were identified as three Indonesian words for "woman" and formed the basis for a riddle: "My name has three syllables, each meaning 'woman,' but I have the shape of a man; who am I?" (Answer: "Boen-ja-min.")[17] Boenjamin reciprocated by trying to identify these women who were ridiculing him and making their life difficult; thus a running battle of wits developed. Some of the women called him obnoxious because he was trying to recruit spies amongst their number.

Outside the camp, throughout Bandoeng, similar *tonari-kumi* initiatives got under way in a concerted effort to integrate Java into Japanese society and cleanse the city of lingering Western influences. As the human dragnet repeatedly swept through town, persons who failed to pass whatever race test was being applied, whether they had the wrong appearance, ancestry or habits, were unceremoniously dumped in our midst, causing the houses of Tjihapit to become more and more crowded. Increasingly the new arrivals were *Belanda Indo* women and their offspring, along with dribs and drabs of *totok* women, who had so far evaded internment because of Indonesian family connections, being married to Nippon workers or holding an Axis passport. Some had evaded internment by hiding, only to be betrayed for the five hundred guilder reward now being offered by the Bandoeng authorities for each unmasked *totok*.

And so in May, tall, statuesque Ank, accompanied by her mother and her friends, Elsa and Mrs. Kleist, turned up in our midst. Ank had occasionally appeared in camp before, usually bringing food and always wearing her white armband with the red sun disc, but this time she brought her two boxers with her. "What else could I do with the dogs?" she asked. There were other animals in the camp, for no one willingly abandoned the family pet to wander the streets as a stray animal facing an uncertain future.

"We got orders to re-register," she explained, "and some of us were given new armbands while others were told that their services were no longer required. Without an armband the police pick you up. While Ben was at home we were able to also offer accommodation for Elsa and her mother, because we convinced the authorities that Ben was a good protector—so they had to come too."

"What happened to Ben?"

"He is in Tjimahi. The Japs confiscated his dentistry equipment."

"Do you know where Bou might be?" my mother asked anxiously.

"No," Ank replied. "I do know that the LOG is very crowded."

---

17. *Bunda* (mother), *djawi*, (cow) *Mina* (common girl's name).

"What about the soldiers, do you know anything about them?"

"Emmy, there are rumours that they will be moved overseas, and some may already have left, but no one really knows. The Japs are moving our men in shuttered railway carriages or goods wagons." This was disturbing news.

A week or two later a case of rabies was detected in a camp, and Boenjamin ordered all dogs to be killed. Ank and other desperate women then made holes in the *gedek* and chased their pets to the outside in the hope that someone in Bandoeng would look after them.

6. HARADA CLAMPS DOWN

The confusion of the war in which we had become immersed took a dramatic turn in the first half of 1943. Both Japan and the United States were reacting to the unexpected challenges and opportunities of armed conflict and both took initiatives that had unpleasant consequences for us, the helpless victims being tossed to and fro in the turmoil. Our presence on Java had become a footnote in history; we were ignored by our Allies and we were a nuisance to our enemies.

It was the new perspective in Tokyo that had the most immediate effect on us. The relentless military setbacks suffered by the Japanese caused Tokyo, in search of security, to embrace a policy shift from military aggression to reluctant acceptance of retrenchment. The *Gunseibukan,* the Japanese military administration, ordered that preparations be made for the defence of conquered territories. The Japanese army command structure on Java was accordingly overhauled, and on May 26, 1943, Lieutenant General Kumakichi Harada replaced Lieutenant General Imamura, who had been reassigned to New Guinea as a full general.[1] Harada was a more dogmatic individual than Imamura (who had repeatedly been criticized for being too easy-going with the inhabitants of Java). Harada addressed his new assignment with zeal.

Most significant of the Japanese setbacks was the death of Admiral Isoroku Yamamoto, the undisputed mastermind behind the attack on Pearl Harbor and the one person who more than anyone else could claim credit for the development of Japan's impressive naval capability. On May 21 the news of Yamamoto's death was publicized on Java with instructions to mourn his passing by flying the *kokki* flag at half-mast. The Japanese authorities broadcast that the Admiral had suffered an accident, but some romantics insisted that he had committed suicide on account of the naval setback Japan had suffered in the Coral Sea the previous year.[2] In fact, his death had actually occurred on April 17, 1943, but had been kept secret. On that day the bomber taking him on an inspection trip to Bougainville Island was attacked and shot down by two squadrons of American Lockheed Lightning Interceptors. The Americans owed this opportunity to their recent cracking of the Japanese naval communications code, and Roosevelt's authorization had been sought to shoot down

---

1. Bouwer, *Het vermoorde land*, 182.
2. Radio San Francisco had erroneously broadcast the story.

Yamamoto's plane; the Japanese might have inferred from this event that they needed a new code.

Yamamoto had been an extraordinary individual, coming from a modest background, the son of a schoolteacher but adopted by a more eminent family lacking sons; they gave him a military education. His opposition to war during the late 1930s nearly cost him his life at the hands of militarist assassins, but his loyalty to Emperor Hirohito had trumped his misgivings about the military direction Hirohito authorized, and his execution of that direction was brilliant. He could not be replaced.

The Allies, too, were facing a new situation: the German onslaught in Russia had been arrested, the Mediterranean once more made safe for Allied shipping and the Japanese advance halted. This had been achieved partly thanks to a hastily cobbled together Anglo-American joint military effort, which nonetheless lacked a formal coordinated planning structure or a coherent long-term strategy beyond the vague objective of unconditional surrender of the axis. Differences regarding the next steps to be taken in the struggle were partly resolved at a "Trident" (Anglo-American) conference in Washington, held in May 1943 to debate the options after gaining complete control of North Africa. Given Britain's considerable military presence in the Mediterranean, agreement could be reached for an assault on Europe, but in the Far Eastern theatre British and American interests diverged. Britain lacked the amphibious *materiel* necessary to bring its considerable Indian army into play in launching an attack across the Indian Ocean on the "Malay Barrier," preferably Sumatra. Repelling the Japanese was therefore left almost entirely to the Americans and their Pacific campaign, and an attack that would have a more direct bearing on our fate was thus delayed.

A curious situation had now developed. Although the Pacific war had been unleashed by embargoed Japan to secure access to the immense wealth of the Netherlands East Indies and Malaya, and although American newspaper articles discussing the situation of the NEI during May 1940 had stressed the strategic importance for American industry of export items like oil, tin and rubber, early liberation of the Indies to regain access to these supplies was not considered imperative.[3] Instead, the Philippines were to be retaken by a two-pronged thrust: from the south by General MacArthur and from the east by Admiral Nimitz. This would repair the damage to MacArthur's reputation resulting from the humiliation of Bataan. The Philippines, in turn, would open up a route north to Japan, bringing a quick end to the war. How this would affect our fate was not considered.

A Japanese war of conquest for resource-rich territories had turned into an American war of revenge for Pearl Harbor and Bataan. Even the war in China

---

3. *Time,* May 20, 1940, 73.

had diminished from strategic concern (the need to halt aggression) to tactical issue—the need to secure an airbase for attack on Japan.

Almost coincidentally, a decision taken by Tokyo in January was now given some cautious publicity in Japan; this decision had significance for our Indonesian compatriots.[4] On June 15 Prime Minister Hideki Tojo announced to the Japanese Diet that the Philippines and Burma would be offered quasi-independence, whereas Indonesia would be treated as an integral part of the Japanese nation, but with local political control.

This was a compromise between the Ministry of Foreign Affairs, which was still pursuing a policy aimed at portraying Japan as a liberator of east Asian peoples, and the Ministry of War, which saw Indonesia as a source of raw materials, therefore requiring direct rule from Tokyo. "Local political control" consisted of little more than affirmation that Indonesians would be allowed to occupy important administrative positions, subject to Japanese supervision. This awkward announcement was shrouded in secrecy to avoid giving the Allies a propaganda weapon. Another full week went by before even a hint of this policy direction became known in Indonesia; Sukarno could only with difficulty portray this as "good news" by vaguely referring to Japan's "June promises." To assuage Indonesian testiness and to ensure their continued co-operation with General Harada, Prime Minister Tojo planned a personal visit to Java.

A cruel justice was thus being meted out to both the former colonists and former colonial subjects of the NEI by the only two political powers able to make things happen in the region, the United States and Japan: no rescue and no independence.

General Harada addressed his new tasks with vigour. He had been charged with mobilizing Javanese manpower to strengthen Japanese defence capability, while keeping nationalistic aspirations under control. To achieve the first he accelerated the training of the newly formed *Seneindan* (Indonesian army units); encouraged the reopening of air-raid shelters; declared large areas of Java where invasion was expected, around Djokjakarta and Soerabaja, out of bounds to all foreign visitors; intensified the action against spies; forbade the ownership of radios; and outlined a grand plan for the disposition of all foreigners—except of course the Japanese themselves and their Chinese "brothers," provided the latter minded their p's and q's. To manage nationalistic aspirations, while placing the entire island on a war footing, he launched *Djawa bersiap* (Java preparedness) as an umbrella organization.

An impediment to Harada's task was the thorny issue of the small but important Eurasian population; were they enemy or ally? Were they Asian or European? Unscrambling the multiracial omelette of the population on Java

---

4. Brugmans, *Nederlandsch-Indië onder Japanse bezetting*, document 418.

was frustrated by the nature of this population group—impossible to demarcate, while continuing to play an essential administrative role, occupying positions coveted by poorly educated Indonesians, and by and large resisting Nipponization. They could have Dutch names or typical Indonesian names and almost all were bilingual. By default loyalty to Japan and Indonesian nationalism became a matter of skin colour. Darkening the average hue of the population visible on the street became an acute obsession, especially in Bandoeng, where deep divisions arose within the Indonesian and Eurasian communities.

The changing fortunes of war now also began to lend urgency to resolving the security problem related to interned foreigners. The three hundred separate localities where Europeans (mainly Anglo-Saxon and Dutch) had so far been herded together, scattered over the length and breadth of Java, created a mammoth guarding task. This task had been entrusted thus far to the Indonesians; but there was growing concern that they might not be reliable guards and should therefore be replaced by Japanese soldiers, a human resource in increasingly short supply. By mid-May the Bandoeng offices of the *Kempetai* had already had words with Boenjamin, our camp commandant, regarding irregularities, among them the rumour that women had escaped from Tjihapit and gone into hiding.

Logic dictated that the racial winnowing job had to be completed before the guarding task could be simplified. Forcing all of these undesirable people into a small number of manageable concentration camps would be a huge future undertaking.

Amidst these developments, we in Tjihapit continued our mundane struggle for survival, oblivious to the future threats hanging like thunderclouds over our heads.

Early in June 1943, the soup kitchen finally came into service. Mrs. Diepeveen asked for volunteers to staff the kitchen for a morning and an afternoon shift. Almost from the start my mother and Emmy, eager for the extra bit of food this would give them, joined the kitchen crew. We called it a *dapur*, but it fell well short of what we used to designate as a kitchen. It was now the only facility in camp capable of producing something resembling food. All the houses in Tjihapit had once boasted a real kitchen, with running water, a sink, countertop and cupboards for storing food, and there had always been a stove and a collection of cooking utensils such as pots, pans and meat grinders. Those individual kitchens had now all been converted to bedrooms, with the stoves and fridges having been confiscated or converted to storage devices, and fuel such as gas, coal, wood or charcoal no longer obtainable.

Our standards had slipped and our language had changed. The new communal *dapur* consisted of a bamboo shed with oil drums serving as saucepans. They were suspended over open fires that produced from the wet wood more smoke than heat. What we now called "food" we would a year before have considered inappropriate for the dog, instead calling it "waste," good for the compost heap. The adjective "delicious" had also taken on an entirely new dimension, meaning a rare break from the dreary, never-changing menu of cooked rice, *sajur* (a watery vegetable soup) and starch. The hint of a piece of meat, a snippet of onion, a morsel of carrot or sweet potato transformed the normal stuff we now ate from food to "delicious food."

Operating the *Oranje dapur*, as we called it on account of its location, was a challenge since it lacked a water supply and had no provision for waste water disposal aside from proximity to the Tjihapit *selokan* that flowed nearby. Such kitchen waste that found its way into this ditch would hardly affect the quality of the water, since it had already become an open sewer. More serious was the lack of a toilet for use by the kitchen staff; they had to avail themselves of the facilities in the nearest homes; doing so unfortunately now always required queuing. The kitchen boasted an electric light, important because cooking operations had to start before daybreak. Tables suitable for food preparation and distribution were found in Tjihapit.

Older boys were recruited to do some of the heavy lifting in the *dapur* and for collecting water in the drums from one of the nearby houses. They lifted the drums on and off the fires using bamboo poles passed through iron rings welded to the sides. Women and girls looked after the fires, prepared the food, stirred the huge drums and dished out the food to the waiting crowds.

The kitchen immediately proved inadequate for meeting the demand for food. How many mouths could it feed? Nobody knew. When it was constructed it was viewed as a supplementary food source for the seven thousand internees, but by the time the kitchen began operations our ability to cook for ourselves had vanished. It thus became obvious that more facilities were required or we would starve. Notwithstanding the strict rationing of food, the volume required was so large that the army had to build sheds outside the main gate where food could be delivered by merchants. From these storage sheds, daily supplies could be brought into the camp in accordance with approved rations; for a short while coolies were still permitted to do this work.

The construction of two more kitchens a month or so later coincided with the prohibiting of the coolies from entering the camp. The new kitchens were no improvement over the *Oranje dapur*; the one that we called the *Doekoek dapur* had no electricity supply at all, and the other one, the *Saninten dapur*, although having a paved floor because it was built on a piece of roadway, was worse off for water and waste. It was on such indifferent facilities that a population soon to approach thirteen thousand souls began to depend for their daily nourishment. In addition, a foraging party drawn from the remaining teenage boys in our midst now had the daily task of transporting the bags of rice and baskets of vegetables from the storage sheds to the kitchens. They took over the coolies' two-wheeled carts and had fun giving each other rides when the empty carts went out through the camp gate, but it was heavy work bringing the loaded carts back into the camp.

The growing camp population, combined with a deplorable lack of civic engineering maintenance, rapidly made the lack of sanitation a serious problem, because the sewage system had not been designed for the current population density. One could no longer just go to the toilet at will, but had to line up to await one's turn. When one did finally make it to the head of the queue, before disaster fell (as happened to me in a most embarrassing episode—have you ever been carried down a public road by two running women, holding your feet in the air so that the turd would not drop out of your pants?), one often found the toilet blocked and overflowing. The entire system throughout the camp was heavily overloaded and ample use had to be made of open ditches. A growing water shortage moreover prevented proper flushing and by now there was a frequent need for the drainage system to be unblocked with the help of sticks manhandled by work parties. The results were there for everyone to see and fear: an escalating incidence of disease, especially dysentery.

General Harada set upon his daunting task with vigour and within two weeks of his arrival we began to notice the concrete results. On June 6 elements of the new grand plan for the disposal of foreigners became known in Bandoeng; on that day the civilian men interned in the LOG (my father among them) were moved to Tjimahi, where space had become available thanks to POWs having been sent abroad as slave labourers. Governor Komiyama began working on an action plan for moving the much larger group of women and children living in Tjihapit. For this he needed to know the scale of the task. Komiyama found thirty-nine typewriters in a house that had formerly served as a typing school and had these transported to the Ladies' Office in Tjihapit, where he told Mrs. Diepeveen to prepare a register of internees. This was to take the form of four sets of index cards: a set for the Red Cross, a set for Tokyo, a set for the camp, and a fourth set for Batavia. The cards recorded each woman's name, date of birth, husband's occupation and names and ages of children.[5]

Mrs. Diepeveen subsequently posted a notice seeking the help of thirty-nine typists with this bait: "Soup will be provided as compensation." My mother, having had secretarial training, briefly considered this opportunity because the kitchen work, involving the huge cooking drums, had turned out to be physically demanding.

"I will stay working in the kitchen," she told Emmy. "There's more food to be had in the kitchen work."

---

5. Personal communication from Amelia de Visser.

"I'm damned well not helping the Japs with their bloody typing work," Emmy responded.

For various reasons other women, including Amelia, our former neighbour, took up the secretarial challenge and carried out this work until the very end of the war.

Outside the camp, in the rest of Bandoeng, a more complicated initiative commenced—dealing with the *Belanda Indo* population. This was a formidable challenge, given the sheer size of this population (estimated at twenty-five thousand) and the conflicting objectives—Indonesian aspirations for jobs and the Japanese need for continued economic performance, tempered by security concerns.

Komiyama addressed the problem with re-registration of all those over seventeen years old living in Bandoeng, but this time classifying each individual by racial purity:

Group 1: *Totok* father and Eurasian mother
Group 2: *Totok* mother and Eurasian father
Group 3: Eurasian mother and Eurasian father
Group 4: *Totok* father and Indonesian mother
Group 5: *Totok* father and *totok* mother
Group 6: Indonesian mother and *totok* father
Group 7: Indonesian father and Eurasian mother
Group 8: Indonesian father and a non-Indonesian, but Asian mother[6]

New *pendafteran* cards were now issued, with the group indicated by means of a large number written in blue pencil and formal standing established with the help of a new *tjap* (stamp).

It was a curious approach, the sole purpose of which seemed to be the internment of half of the remaining Eurasian population. Inspection of the scheme in light of an elementary knowledge of genetics will quickly indicate gaps in the range of possibilities, and although not stated, it was clear that a person's name had an important bearing: a person with a Dutch name was guaranteed closer scrutiny than one with an Indonesian name. However, the officials charged with the execution of this registration system were given plenty of leeway in interpreting the evidence presented to them by those needing to be classified. It was certain that groups 1, 2 and 5 would be interned, and that blue eyes and blonde hair guaranteed classification in one of these groups. The cards carried the comment, "child of troubled parents," but more alarming was the additional threat to family cohesion, more devastating in its impact than had been the case with the *totok* because in these families, members often had contrasting appearances—a dark-haired, brown-eyed mother and a blonde,

---

6. Bouwer, *Het vermoorde land*, 189.

blue-eyed child or vice versa. In addition, the Japanese policy of segregating male children from the remainder of the family had become rumoured and so a large number of *Belanda Indo* mothers took their family with them into hiding, spending the remainder of the war years under constant threat of discovery and abuse.

Tojo Seeks Friends

On July 7 Prime Minister Tojo arrived in Batavia to smooth the ruffled feathers of the Indonesian nationalist leaders. His mission was made more tricky by the week-old American offensive on Japanese positions; on June 30, 1943, General MacArthur had commenced his advance on the Philippines. This had taken Tokyo by complete surprise, since it began a year earlier than the Japanese military experts had anticipated. Japan's policy-makers had to accommodate the new reality hastily and further increase the emphasis on defence, an awkward message to deliver to the skeptical Indonesians.

Tojo was welcomed with full honours in Batavia by a huge, well-organized, flag-waving crowd. However, Indonesian wags quickly nicknamed him "*pisau tjukur*" (the razor) because of his previous role as head of the *Kempetai*.[7] Tojo delivered two messages in Batavia: Indonesians would be drawn more closely into governance functions, particularly on Java, but at the same time the Nipponization of Java would proceed apace. In order to harness the huge Indonesian manpower, he sought to ensure the adoption by the Indonesians of Japanese organizational attributes, Japanese attitudes and of course the Japanese language. He flattered his audience with assurances of their importance and offered them senior positions, but always subject to Japanese control. A *Shimon Kikan* (an advisory council also known as *Cho Sangi-in*) was to be created, but only a minority of the members could be elected.[8] The majority were to be appointed by General Harada; this council therefore was remarkably similar to the *Volksraad* used by the Dutch before the war. In addition, Japan took ownership of all industrial concerns and private property. Henceforth, those who had owned their houses outright had to pay rent to the *Hudosan Kanrikokan*, an agent of the occupational authorities.[9]

A week later Komiyama initiated the elimination of the remaining Western presence from Bandoeng streets, stimulated by news of Allied landings on Sicily. Young Indonesian volunteers delivered messages to the homes of the remaining members of the Red Ball brigade, the *totok* Nippon workers: their

---

7. Bouwer, *Het vermoorde land*, 192.

8. Reid and Akira (eds.), *The Japanese experience in Indonesia*, 113–125.

9. Bouwer, *Het vermoorde land*, 187.

days of relative freedom had ended. European doctors, nurses, pharmacists and dentists were allowed two days to pack their belongings and dispose of their households. The doctors had to hand over all medical supplies and surgical instruments to Japanese authorities because these were required by the Japanese doctors, who had finally arrived.[10] Their arrival coincided with an outbreak of a smallpox, prompting General Harada to order a week of house cleaning for all of Java.[11] Needless to say, that order did not penetrate the bamboo walls of Tjihapit, where the overcrowding made house cleaning an impossible and futile task.

More bad news followed for the Bandoeng citizens still at liberty: all church organizations had to cease functioning forthwith and any religious discussion had to be conducted in Malay. Komiyama furthermore decreed, as expected, that everyone carrying a *pendafteran* class 1 or 2 was to report to the "Protected Area." This decree mostly affected women, because the men with this classification were either already interned or continued to be important Nippon workers. These people, some of whom as former residents of the Tjihapit area had already been forced to relocate to other homes, were now no longer deemed acceptable as part of the liberated Indonesia.

Implementation of this decree was assisted by the recently established Indonesian police force, the *Keibodan,* working alongside the existing youth corps, the *Seneindan.* These quasi-military units, bearing Japanese names and staffed by young uneducated and unemployed Indonesian men, had no qualms about giving the overtly racist policies enthusiastic support. Camp Commandant Boenjamin, armed with a list of names prepared at the Bandoeng town hall, allocated the new arrivals to addresses in Tjihapit.

On Tuesday, July 20, Ank dropped by our house looking for my mother. "Why not come with me to the gate?" she suggested. "A good friend of Ben and mine, Landa, the wife of Dr. Bosman, has apparently just arrived with her children."

"No dentistry work today?" my mother inquired, for Ank had told her how pleased Juultje Boersma had been to find in Ank an experienced assistant who knew how to pedal at a steady speed while Juultje drilled out a rotten bit of tooth.[12]

"No, the relief assistant I am training is pedalling right now—she is getting better."

We hurried to the camp gate, taking a shortcut along the *gedek*, and, sure enough, inside the gate stood two *grobaks*, each pulled by a pony and loaded

---

10. Bosman, *Kamp dagboek*, 55.

11. Brugmans, *Nederlandsch-Indië onder Japanse bezetting*, 53.

12. There were two female dentists in Tjihapit; Dr. Boersma had managed to retain her equipment.

with suitcases, boxes, furniture and bags. It was an impressive load, but Landa had five children, two older girls, two boys and a baby, barely two months old. "Landa has always been a packrat," Ank quietly muttered to my mother. An Indonesian guard was casually inspecting the load for contraband, or anything else that might be useful to him. A suitcase with clothing lay open on the ground and he held up a Kodak Brownie camera. "*Tidak boleh*," he grunted and placed it on a table along with a pen knife and a hunting knife that must have belonged to one of the boys. The big girl looked glum at the loss of this prized recent gift.

Landa smiled when she saw Ank. We were quickly introduced, and since the inspection appeared to be complete, we followed the two *grobaks* into the main street heading northeast, where we stopped under some trees. The big girl, still upset at the loss of her camera, muttered darkly while surveying the neighbourhood, saying, "We at least don't have to live next door to dirty *inlanders* here."

"Now, now," Landa interjected disapprovingly, undoubtedly thinking back to her days as the wife of a mission doctor.

"What's happened to Heleen?" Ank inquired, ignoring Anneke's observation.

"She was diagnosed with appendicitis and has just been operated on. She will come in a few days," Landa answered.

"Where did Friso go?"

"Tjimahi, I think."

"Do you know where you are going?" Ank asked, looking thoughtfully at the huge pile of stuff that the Bosman family hoped to accommodate.

"We were assigned to 9 Houtmanstraat. That would have been *gezellig*, for we would be with friends, but I have just been told that the camp commandant—what's his name?"

"Boenjamin," someone helpfully answered.

"—Boenjamin has found better accommodation for us in the Tjihapit area."

"Bastard," Ank muttered under her breath, knowing that Landa was a gentle person and abhorred strong language.

"The house in Houtmanstraat would have been better," my mother, who also knew the district quite well by now, remarked. "Those buildings along Tjihapitweg are really little better than *kampong* dwellings with sewage and electricity. The rooms are tiny."

"Much of Tjihapit is like this," Ank added. "I bet you that's why the Japs chose this area for a camp. Boenjamin knows that Friso is a doctor and is just being mean and petty."

We accompanied the procession to the address, where a small welcoming party gathered in the narrow street, flanked by small cottages with pantiled roofs. Landa had thoughtfully brought along on behalf of friends some essentials, such as bars of soap, and these were now distributed to eager hands. We inspected the modest room that had been set aside for this large family. It had a concrete floor, but thin walls made of *gedek* covered with plaster. Outside, along the narrow yard, there ran a passageway, a sort of alley to ensure an emergency thoroughfare for firefighters; it had a narrow opening through the *gedek* camp wall, thus providing access onto the main portion of the Tjiliwoengstraat outside of the camp.

"It's guarded," one of the women living there commented, nodding towards the tantalizing opening to the outside world.

As we departed, leaving Landa to sort out her living arrangements, my mother remarked, "I don't see how she will accommodate her family in that room along with all the *barang* they brought along."

"Uh-huh," was all Ank could say.

A week later Mrs. Diepeveen posted a notice on a makeshift bulletin board in the middle of the camp: "ALL LIVING ROOMS MUST BE CLEARED, PLEASE HELP ACCOMMODATE MORE PEOPLE."

By the end of the month a stream of people had come through the camp gate. They were the *Belanda Indos* whose turn for internment had come. My mother and I went once more to the camp gate in the hope of seeing a familiar face.

"I wonder if *tante* Emmy is coming," she said as we ambled along the road. She was referring to Emmy Jochems, whom she hadn't seen for over a year. "The last time I spoke with her she was sure that her day to be interned would also come."

Mrs. Diepeveen was standing inside the camp gate checking off names on a long list as new arrivals came through, carrying or dragging what was left of their possessions after rough inspection by the camp guards. "Is Emmy Jochems on your list?" my mother asked her.

"Is she *pendafteran* 1 or 2?"

"I don't know."

"This list won't help," she answered, after a hurried glance over its full length. "It's full of errors—names misspelled, children's names wrong. The town hall lost the original list and this has been hurriedly thrown together," she added with a disdainful shrug. Nevertheless the list was long, containing over two thousand names. With about four hundred houses in the camp, it was obvious that each cleared living room would have to accommodate five people.

We hung around for a while to see whether Emmy might turn up, and other women joined us. People were always leering hungrily at the food supplies and material possessions the new arrivals brought with them, but with these arrivals being Eurasians a new dimension was added. *"Bah—kampong kippen* [chicks]!" they shouted with a mixture of envy and contempt. *"Kakkerlakken* [cockroaches]!" One unfortunate new arrival had her cart with her baggage on it turned over on the street, and my mother dragged me away from the scene in disgust. During the night of July 29 fights erupted between some of the new arrivals and long-term residents. The atmosphere within the camp had become as ugly as outside the camp, where General Harada's divisive racial policies had split the Eurasian community in two.

Landa, on the other hand, tried to capitalize on this new upheaval by seeking better accommodation. She had discovered that space would now after all be available at the Houtmanstraat address to which she had originally been assigned. Unfortunately her attempt to move to that address caused an uproar, because the room she had wanted to take and which had been cleared for the new arrivals, was adjacent to a room accommodating ladies branded as "Nazis." Landa now found alternative accommodation in a tiny house in the Rijpwijk. Although as small as the Tjihapit *kampong* homes, these houses were built of brick and were better able to withstand the terrible storms that sometimes swept through the Preanger.

Elsewhere in Bandoeng many *Belanda Indo* women, confronted with the evident chaos at the town hall and the rumours of unpleasant scenes in the camp, redoubled their efforts to remain hidden in the suburbs with what was left of their families. The promise of a hefty reward for betrayal was too tempting for some and so the *Kempetai* weeks later rounded up more of them and dumped them in our midst with no possessions. Within the space of two months the Tjihapit population had increased from seven thousand to about 9,500 and the average house occupancy had grown from seventeen to twenty-four.

The American counter-offensive of July 1, starting with the softening-up of Japanese defences in anticipation of the reconquest of the Philippines, had visibly rattled the Japanese soldiers. Repeated aerial bombardment of Soerabaja, the nearest strategic target on Java within range of Darwin-based planes, formed part of this operation and forced the Japanese navy to withdraw to Tandjong Priok. General Harada assumed that an attempted American conquest of Java was imminent, and on August 10 he paid a visit to Bandoeng to make sure that appropriate defence measures had been implemented. Curfews were reinstated with strictly enforced blackouts, and all houses had to be equipped with air-raid shelters, preferably in the front yard so that passersby, if caught by surprise, could also seek shelter. Harada did not deem such precautions necessary for the residents of Tjihapit.

Air-raid sirens once more howled, almost on a daily basis, over Bandoeng and the Preanger valley. Sometimes one or two fighter planes took to the air from Andir, but never more, because planes, fuel and pilots had become scarce.

Japanese nervousness seemed to peak during the nights in the middle of August, when the moon was full. One night the planes seemed to remain in the sky constantly. Inside our ghetto, we ignored the alarms; they were often very confusing, with the "all clear" signal coming first instead of last. Besides, they portended the long-awaited rescue operation by the Allies. The Japanese now took the regular precaution of parking their army trucks inside Tjihapit, hoping to thereby safeguard them from Allied bombing raids. The vehicles were an incongruous mixture of old KNIL Chevrolet army trucks and recent adaptations of passenger vehicles, with the rear part of the passenger compartment replaced by a wooden platform.

On August 20 Komiyama ordered that the Bloemenkamp be cleared. This was a neighbouring "protected area" characterized by streets named after flowers (*bloemen*), located across Riouwstraat from Tjihapit. This area had for a while been reserved for Nippon workers and their families. The men were now shipped to a men's camp and the women and children, along with some old men, joined us in Tjihapit. To make room for the newcomers more of the treasured pieces of furniture so many had initially brought with them into Tjihapit now had to be abandoned to the elements. Those who had brought paintings into Tjihapit cut them from their frames and rolled them up; the frames became firewood. The Tjihapit population grew to over eleven thousand.

Perhaps as compensation for this inconvenience Komiyama approved sending letters overseas via the Red Cross. For the occasion a Chinese photographer had secured temporary access into Tjihapit, and my mother managed to have our portrait taken. She placed a print in an envelope addressed to her parents.[13] Juf wanted to send a copy to my father as well. "Bou would be so happy," she murmured while gently shaking her head, and she was undoubtedly prepared to sacrifice part of her remaining modest hoard of silver coin for this, but my mother demurred, replying, "The camp office advised against even trying this. They said it would be a waste of money."

"If only we could get a postcard from Bou," Juf persisted. Near the beginning of August some lucky women had received a card but had been unable to send a reply. Juf and my mother often fretted in guarded tones about the lack of news from my father. Did he even know where we were?

---

13. The photograph reached its destination after the war.

Food, Food, Food

Our daily concerns were dominated by our alimentary canal—providing it with food, the unsatisfactory and often unsuccessful digestive process itself, and finally getting rid of the waste products; that is what life had come down to. We were obsessed by food, and being dependent on the soup kitchens, which delivered food as poor in quality as in quantity, aggravated our obsession. The evidence of malnutrition waxed obvious around us, with growing incidence of ulcers that would not heal because of lack of vitamins, and starvation oedema.

The *dapur* had become the unchallenged focus of our lives. My mother and Emmy alternated in working soup kitchen shifts; one week my mother had the morning shift and the next week Emmy had it. Those who did not work in the *dapur* were employed elsewhere; everyone except the old, the sick, the very young and mothers of tiny infants had to do something to try to maintain the functioning of our community. A committee of women was charged with the purchase of foodstuffs within the constraints of prescribed rations (officially two hundred grams of rice per day per person for three meals). The task of securing the necessary supplies was difficult because of the collapsing economy throughout Java, with food shortages everywhere and mounting corruption. We in Tjihapit could not fathom the food shortages elsewhere in the country we had known to be so bountiful before the war, but we knew that corruption was rife and that we inevitably were the principal victims.

To ensure the orderly distribution of food, the camp population was divided into groups and each family was issued a card with a group number, a family name and number, and the number of children. Someone at the serving table at each kitchen had lists of names that were checked off to make sure that no one got two helpings. Standing in a queue waiting one's turn to get a small helping of boiled rice, *sajur* and starch constituted a daily social event. Getting anything different in one's tin, such as a piece of onion or sweet potato or a tiny piece of meat, was a major thrill. Sometimes Corrie Vonk helped with the dishing out of supplies. Everyone knew the tiny vivacious Corrie, who could not stop cracking jokes as she handed out a dollop of sticky rice or *sajur*. She provided a never-fading star of hope and good humour. But the food supplied by the *dapur* was so tasteless and unappetizing that my mother and Emmy and countless other women spent hours struggling over an *anglo*, trying to turn the gooey stodge that the kitchen provided into something slightly more digestible. Aside from ingredients it took time and ingenuity to produce anything edible from cassava flour.

In early September a *toko* (shop) was opened to replace the banned Indonesians and their *pasar*; this shop, providing a second modest source of food, was housed in the small pre-war concession shelter on the Oranje Plein and had the glorious name, *Toko Lux Vincet*. The supplies, however, were erratic, the choices limited, and the prices high. One was unlikely to find much else besides soap, occasionally some bacon, fruit, sugar and salt. Still, it was a shop, and our ability to benefit from this source of food depended on our ability to eke out, or add to, our dwindling hoard of money. A successful trip to the shop, no matter how minor the purchase by today's standards, was cause for a major celebration. The diarist Anneke Bosman, for instance, recorded on October 8, "This afternoon we had a delicious pudding with sauce. Yesterday was our *toko* day; we obtained milk, smoked meat, soap, sugar, *gula Djawa* [brown sugar made from palm fruit], *pisang* [banana], papaya and *djeruk Bali* [pomelo]." It sounds like a sumptuous shopping trip; the list, however, is complete. That was all there was to buy, and the quantities, rationed of course, were tiny—a teaspoon of this or an ounce of that, a single egg or piece of fruit to be shared between two or three mouths. There were two more limitations on shopping expeditions: the shop was available to each family only once a month and one needed money—the right sort of money. Only the pre-war NEI guilder, available as bank notes and as coin, still had real value, even though it was no longer legal tender. The Japanese paper money received in exchange for pre-war guilders from the Yokohama *Specie* Bank was distrusted; the notes were flimsy, and those of small denomination, a cent for instance, quickly disintegrated. Those of us who had complied with instructions to deposit our savings in the bank immediately saw the money lose ten percent of its purchasing power because of this, while the recent Japanese military setbacks had eroded the worth of this currency on the black market by another twenty percent.

The one other item of value we still possessed, aside from guilders, was clothing. Throughout Java the supply of cotton had virtually dried up, and a clandestine barter trade was established between Tjihapit residents and those at liberty outside the camp, with used clothing being exchanged for food.[14] That trade was carried out through the *gedek* in remote corners of the camp, away from the prying eyes of the guards, preferably under cover of darkness and in spite of the risk of unspeakable retribution by the *Kempetai*. Increasingly we risked serious beatings and torture for food.

Also worrying was the rising cost of charcoal, essential for any supplementary cooking, when other sources of wood, such as doors, doorframes or window frames, had been consumed. A very few houses still had gas stoves, but their use was strictly prohibited and the gas supply was erratic.[15] Some women had with forethought brought electric hotplates into camp; when these were plugged into the electricity outlet the spiral wire embedded in a white ceramic plate got red hot. These had been declared contraband and my mother

---

14. Before the war Java exported cotton to Japan and imported cotton material. This trade stopped through lack of shipping.

15. Coal (for making gas) came from Sumatra: this supply was no longer available.

therefore only dared use hers when no one was looking, for one never knew whether one might be betrayed or found out.

The slightest success in modifying our boring diet was now quickly lauded with adjectives like "tasty." A bit of salt in hot water made a delicious bouillon; ground-up cooked *keongs* were deemed delicious croquettes; a bit of sugar had become a treat worth discussing. The collecting of recipes became a popular pastime. Old magazines were scoured for articles and pictures dealing with food, and those who could began to fill scrapbooks with these items.

The weather at least was helpful, for late September could be very agreeable; the sky was often blue and the trees along Bengawalaan, now covered in bright fresh green, were at their best thanks to a recent sprinkle of rain. If there was a wind, it was refreshing and gentle, and birds twittered among the leaves. In the evening, the song of the Javanese thrush could be heard. The good weather permitted a kindergarten class to be held in the open air on the lawn of a house directly opposite our house. Its principal goal was to groom us preschool children for more demanding future tasks: we were ordered to cut the grass with scissors—my first vocation. The instruction did not last long, however, for more rains soon came.

On September 3, 1943, Hirohito got more bad news: that day General Eisenhower announced on the BBC that Italy had changed sides and joined the Allied cause. The next day he heard that American troops had landed at Huon on the north coast of New Guinea and were threatening the important Japanese base at Lae.

These events forced the Emperor to take a hard look at Japan's huge and ill-defined defence perimeter. General Murakami, accompanied by three members of the Japanese Diet, was sent to Batavia to discuss security issues with General Harada.

Heavily Westernized Java was a key Japanese acquisition, but also had presented thorny problems from the very start of the Japanese occupation. Notwithstanding all the propaganda about Asian brotherhood, questions of loyalty to Japan remained, and in addition the economy was grinding to a halt, creating hardship among the masses. General Harada resorted to even more dramatic initiatives.

He ordered all Europeans removed from the east coast, and thus the ill-conceived attempt to start a self-sufficient European agrarian colony at Kesilir was abandoned; its emaciated inmates were sent to other prison camps. In Bandoeng, all remaining Europeans who were not Swiss or Axis nationals and had thus far not been declared enemies were now rounded up in dawn *razzias* and sent to internment camps; they included Poles, Belgians, Norwegians and Danes and a few women with German or Hungarian ancestry who had married Dutch or British nationals. This seemed to confirm the rumour doing the rounds in Tjihapit that France, Belgium and Holland had been invaded. Thanks to the confusion in Italy, where the Allies were meeting with stiff opposition from the Germans, it took another month before the Italians on Java also got branded as enemies.

The deteriorating security situation made the time ripe for a new nationalist initiative on Java; *raden* Gatot Mangkoepradja sent General Harada a petition, theatrically written in his own blood, requesting the creation of an Indonesian army "that would not only help destroy America and England, but would also take upon itself the defence of Java. This would free up Japanese troops for other fronts."[16] The timing of this suggestion was favourable and on October 5 General Harada was able to approve this radical request, thus setting in motion the creation of an Indonesian army and paving the way for future independence. In Bandoeng the growing nationalistic fervour brought into being street choruses comprising young men and women cycling up and down streets while chanting slogans through megaphones: "*Amerika kita strika Inggeris kita linggis, Amerika kita strika, Inggeris kita linggis.*"

Throughout all this the complex *peranakan* (mixed race) loyalty problem continued to smoulder. A group led by P. F. Dahler, a former journalist, loudly proclaimed *Belanda Indo* loyalty to the Japanese, while other members of this population, accused of real or imagined sabotage, were interned. Dahler was now enlisted by the Japanese to urge, via radio broadcast, all Eurasians to support the Japanese cause, curiously departing from the prescribed Malay text by quoting in English, "God created white and black men, but the half-caste is a creation of the Devil."[17] The only way for these people to minimize the risk of internment was to surpass all other population groups in the ferocity with which they supported the cause of the Japanese occupation, but their interests were at cross-purposes with those of the nationalists, and hostility between these two population groups grew. These tensions threatened to undermine Harada's security initiatives.

Even more vexing was the Muslim issue. In a manner of speaking this too was a Western concept. General Harada made a determined attempt to win the Muslim population over, but his efforts were frustrated by religious divisions within that community and by the Japanese insistence on homage paid to the Japanese foot soldiers and Emperor Hirohito in a way similar to the homage paid by Muslims to the centres of Islam. When it came to bowing, there was always confusion about the location of Tokyo with respect to Mecca, and one somehow had to distinguish between Mohammed and Hirohito, which for devout students of the Koran was taxing.

---

16. Bouwer, *Het vermoorde land*, 207.
17. Bouwer, *Het vermoorde land*, 210.

Enthusiasm for the cause of the Greater East Asia Co-Prosperity Sphere was moreover being undermined by increasing hunger among Indonesians of all ethnic and religious persuasions. The Japanese could not even be sure how trustworthy "Asian brother" Sukarno really was. The contradiction inherent in the propaganda—Japanese invincibility in spite of widely reported military setbacks and obvious Japanese concerns around Allied invasion—might precipitate a change of heart among the Indonesians, perhaps leading to a bloody rebellion that could overwhelm the small Japanese army of occupation. The Japanese, moreover, had grounds to fear the outbreak of a potentially disastrous epidemic amidst the collapsing economy.

General Harada next addressed the management of the internment camps, a matter that was within his full control. To improve their security Japanese soldiers would have to take over from the Indonesian camp guards, but for this he needed a greater concentration of prisoners. This began almost immediately with the movement of the two to three thousand men out of remaining Bandoeng locations to Tjimahi, now that the POWs formerly interned there were all gone, leaving the Japanese army guards at Tjimahi under-employed. Proper staffing of the women's camps was another matter.

Arsad Takes Over

On October 10 Camp Commandant Boenjamin was relieved of his duties. Disturbing rumours circulated widely, not only within Tjihapit but also in Bandoeng, that he had girl friends in the camp—as many as fourteen according to some. This alleged fraternization suggested to Komiyama not only a shocking undermining of morality, but also a threat to Japanese control. Then there were even darker rumours that some women had fraternized with the remaining teenage boys in the camp. General Harada's inspection trip a couple of months earlier had resulted in a scathing report demanding sweeping changes in the way the camp was run, but what finally brought about Boenjamin's demise was the discovery that he had absconded with camp money.

Arsad, Boenjamin's Indonesian replacement, was an improvement because he tended to keep a distance between himself and the camp inmates, and that suited us just fine. As a result of the July smallpox epidemic all of Bandoeng now had to be inoculated, and Arsad promptly got this project under way in Tjihapit. The women in the camp office prepared an injection roster for all 11,100 internees and posted it on a notice board on Barendszstraat, in the middle of the camp. Then the *hanchos* and *kumichos* had to make sure the internees under their authority presented themselves in front of a nurse seated at a desk on the corner of the street. It was a huge task, and we spent hours waiting our turn.

Arsad also ordered the creation of an official camp hospital to replace the existing makeshift arrangement. Until now, those who were in serious need of medical attention had still been sent to Borromeus, one of the city hospitals, which henceforth was for the exclusive use of the Japanese army; the existing Borromeus patients had been sent home. Space for a camp hospital was made available in one of the houses in Tjihapit, and its former occupants were told to find accommodation elsewhere. Since the hospital could immediately be filled with patients, an urgent request was broadcast through the camp for spare beds and linen, although medicine, instruments, dressing material and sterilizing facilities remained absent. Ten European doctors were found in other prison camps and transferred to Tjihapit to do what they could; the blame for further infections or disease could then be placed on their shoulders. When Landa Bosman heard of their arrival, she hurried to the camp gate to see whether Friso, her husband, was among them, but returned to her home bitterly disappointed.

The doctors needed medicine and permission was therefore granted for a trusted individual to secure medicine once a week from a pharmacy operated by Chinese. Elsa Kleist, who shortly before the capitulation had briefly served on General Wavell's staff, an experience that had endowed her with an air of competence and who moreover had an excellent command of Malay, volunteered to take on this task. Henceforth she was permitted to make regular trips to the pharmacy to get a list of prescriptions filled, and return with her delivery cart to distribute the medications to patients throughout the camp.

Arsad pursued more reforms. Two days later, on October 12, he ordered all boys between thirteen and sixteen to present themselves at the camp gate the next morning at nine o'clock. Each was allowed to bring a suitcase and bedroll. The order caused consternation, for it was far more sweeping in its impact than had been the previous orders, when the sixteen- and seventeen-year-olds had been evicted.

"Why do they want to send these young boys away?" someone asked.

"They want labourers," Emmy opined.

"I think they just do not like seeing men in a women's camp," someone else offered. "Have you not noticed how Arsad was upset to see Mr. de Bruin leading the technical task force?"

"Yes, that's right. Arsad said that a woman should take command."

De Bruin was a recently-arrived elderly gentleman who had agreed to deal with plumbing and electrical problems in the camp. He had been assisted by one or two boys and a couple of young women.

The following morning, we all gathered on the street in front of our house to wave goodbye to a boy who had been living in our house. His mother and younger sister, both crying, accompanied him to the main gate, while the boy, with his school backpack on his back, put on a brave face. Three hours later the mother and the girl came back, their eyes still red.

"The kitchen staff was wonderful," the mother said between sobs. She blew her nose and added, "Each boy got a peanut butter sandwich before they got into the bus." (The mother used the term *peanut butter sandwich* casually, but it did not resemble the pre-war version of the same. Peanuts were available in limited quantities and therefore could be ground up using a meat grinder, but the bread part was little more than two thin slabs of hard, grey rubbery material, shaped indeed like a piece of poorly made, tacky bread. It took effort to chew through one of these sandwiches). The boys nevertheless were grateful for the kindness—peanut butter was rare treat.

"Did you see them leave?"

"No—there were too many police and Jap soldiers, and all the windows of the bus had been blocked up as though the boys were dangerous criminals. It must have been stifling on that bus under the hot sun."

"Were there many boys?"

"We made sandwiches for 214 boys," Emmy, who had just come back from the kitchen, interjected. "That was the number of names on the list."

"It took a long time to load up the buses. Do you know where they went?"

"Someone thought they would go to Tjimahi, but Mrs. Diepeveen did not know."

For well over a month, my mother had been busy making a birthday present for Juf, who would soon be turning seventy years old. My mother had only been able do this during daylight hours, for in the evening we were not allowed to have any lights on; besides, the number of functioning lights was rapidly dwindling. From old sheets and shirts she had removed the worn pieces and reassembled the remainder into a portable toilet tidy, to be hung from a wall with the help of three rings sewn along the top edge. At the top was a pin cushion with a beautiful lady embroidered on it, and next to this she had embroidered the name of the camp, "Tjihapit," and the date, "18-10-2603." Below this my mother had sewn three bands of white material, each band forming three pockets in which personal effects could be stored. The upper row had pockets for a tin of talcum powder and face cream, toothbrush and toothpaste, candles and matches. The middle row provided storage for soap, hairpins and safety pins, and had a pocket for a nail brush. The lower row contained pockets for a hair brush, combs and a hand-held mirror. Such a toilet tidy had great practical value given our living conditions. Some of the pockets remained empty for a long time, until the opportunity arose to buy things like soap. My mother borrowed a hammer, found some nails and hung the cloth from the door of our bedroom. Juf was in tears when she received the gift. She knew how many hours my mother must have worked on this project, and the difficulty she would have had getting needles and thread.

A couple of days after Juf's birthday there was a terrible storm and we knew that more could be expected at this time of the year. A torrential rain instantly drenched anyone caught out in the open, while violent gusts of wind whipped around the corner of the houses and through the trees, bringing down branches. At one stage huge hailstones fell and it was a miracle that the *gedek* did not come down as well, because it swayed dangerously. That evening we heard that at the Stella Maris prison camp for *Belanda Indo* men, the wall had come down and the Japanese and Indonesian guards had had to go out in the storm to prevent escapes.

The following week, on Tuesday, October 26, we had another storm, even worse than the first one, and this time large sections of Tjihapit *gedek* did come down. The soldiers came to guard the opening while it was being repaired. Within ten minutes forty millimetres of rain had fallen and the streets had turned into rivers. The hailstones were huge and the Tjihapit *selokan* passing beneath Serajoestraat a few metres away from our house nearly overflowed its banks, its brown, dirty water loaded with an indescribable collection of debris, human and otherwise.

That evening, after the storm had abated, we went to the kitchen to collect our food rations. Normally I stayed behind with Juf, but her stomach was not well, and my mother feared that she had dysentery. When we arrived at the *Oranje dapur* a terrible sight greeted our eyes: there was mud all around the building with the rubbish dump rising from it like a small mountain; the kitchen itself seemed to be in chaos and turmoil. "We had a *bandjir* (flood) here," one of the distraught, dirty and exhausted kitchen staff wailed. Where there normally was a lineup of people collecting their food there now was utter confusion, with the serving tables turned over and bits of the *atap* roof and *gedek* walls lying in the muddy water. The fires were no longer even smoking—they had all gone out, except perhaps one. Emmy, her face blackened from wiping the perspiration off her brow, was furiously fanning a few remaining embers when we arrived. She saw us and came out, coughing, her improvised *kipas* still in her hands. She smelled of smoke and clearly needed to get some fresh air.

"Please come back in an hour or so," said one of the food-doling women, repeating the message over and over again. Children were crying with hunger.

"What's happened?" my mother asked.

"One of the fireplaces collapsed completely and we lost an entire drum of *sajur*. Someone is trying to clean the mud off the vegetables. It's a miracle that the building is still standing," Emmy replied.

"Do you need any help?"

"No! We have all the staff we can manage, but leave the food tins with me, and I will bring food later tonight."

We went back in the twilight, empty-handed. Near our house we heard from a stranger that the situation at the Doekoek *dapur* was even worse; they had lost all fires.

Late that night, Emmy finally arrived, sooty and tired, bearing a slice of sticky, grey bread for each of us. "We were lucky to have some bread in stock," she said. "Everyone could have one slice."

The stormy weather seemed to symbolize Japan's changing fortunes. The Japanese army could finally use the Burma Railway but by now it had ceased to be a vehicle for westward expansion towards India and instead only provided logistical support for defending Japanese positions in Burma. That notorious project had just been completed at an astronomical human cost. Of the forty-six thousand Allied prisoners of war who had been forced to work on its construction, sixteen thousand had died of starvation, malnutrition, disease, gross neglect and brutality. Also dying on the railway of death were more than fifty thousand Burmese forced labourers.[18] Burma had in the meantime gained its judicial independence, but was now more firmly linked than ever to the Japanese Empire by this blood-soaked band of steel. The completion of the project was the only good news Emperor Hirohito received in the fall of 1943.

On November 1 the Americans launched an offensive on the southwest coast of Bougainville Island in the Solomon Group; its defenders were taken by surprise through ineffective Japanese intelligence. The Japanese navy had to withdraw from an encounter with a much smaller American force. When Hirohito was first informed about this encounter it was described as a resounding American defeat. It was almost two weeks before a more accurate picture emerged in Tokyo. By December the American conquest of the Solomon Islands was complete.

At the same time, the food situation throughout Java had deteriorated to such an extent that rice had to be rationed to 160 grams (a spoonful) per day per person and price controls went into effect for other foods. From this perspective, conditions inside and outside the camp were converging, though our ability to offset the threat of starvation was practically nil. The disparity between food ordered (and paid for) by the camp and what was delivered grew. The only other staple available was "Asia flour," also referred to as "Flake," consisting mainly of cassava flour, but in practical terms useful only as a food supplement for the Westernized *Belanda Indo* population still at large. The Indonesians themselves, living in one of the world's best rice-producing areas, had to go hungry. Komiyama decreed that all European residents of Bandoeng

---

18. Gilbert, *A History of the Twentieth Century*, Vol. 2, 527.

(such as Germans or Italians still at liberty) had to make available six spoons of rice per week for the poor.[19]

To the misery of hunger the Japanese added more defence paranoia. On November 18 the Bandoeng air-raid sirens sprang to life because Soerabaja had again been attacked and Allied planes were thought to have appeared over the Preanger. Once more the Japanese authorities drove a couple of military vehicles into the camp, where they were parked until the "all clear" was sounded, and that evening took the additional precaution of having the municipal electricity supply cut off to ensure that the blackout was complete. A week later the Allies captured the Gilbert Islands in the middle of the Pacific Ocean, thereby facilitating air attacks on the Marshall Islands; this brought traditional Japanese territory within range of daily bombing sorties.

And so, the last month of 1943 made its entrance. The Japanese authorities, anxious to maintain the support of their Indonesian partners, decreed a week of festivities to celebrate the start of the Asian Liberation War, as it was now called. Each day would have a focus. December 1, a Wednesday, would be "Youth Day." Thursday was "Mother's day," Friday a day for celebrating "loyalty and service," Saturday dedicated to "racial harmony" (under Nipponese leadership), Sunday the day of "Assured Victory," Monday dedicated to "Volunteer Activities," and Tuesday the day for Greater East Asia.

In the camp, we were ordered once again to hand over all money except for twenty guilders. Arsad promised to deposit the money on our behalf in the Yokohama *Specie* Bank, where individual accounts could be maintained. Invariably such demands were followed up with house searches, so everyone was nervous. No one trusted the bank or Arsad, who in any case justified his call for money on the ludicrous grounds that the camp was there for our benefit and that we were expected to feed ourselves.

That night four young women ganged together to *bolos* (to escape) in order to leave money with trusted friends in town. News of this undertaking had been spread surreptitiously through the camp. Ank had inadvertently bumped into one of the conspirators, a rather exuberant person called Adri, whom she had recognized as a former patient of her husband, Ben. Ank also entrusted Adri with an addressed envelope containing some NEI hundred-guilder notes. My mother would have liked to have taken such a precaution, but all of the *Belanda Indo* friends she knew were already interned. Adri herself had no money, but was always ready to go on an adventure; on a previous occasion she had gone shopping in town by escaping from the camp over the roofs of houses along the Groote Postweg. Under the cover of darkness the foursome now stole out through Tjihapit *selokan* culvert and returned safely three days later, after "a

---

19. Bouwer, *Het vermoorde land*, 218.

pleasant stay in town." It was from such escapades that people still living at liberty in Bandoeng got an inkling of conditions inside the camp, incidentally strengthening their resolve to remain outside. Of course, those who had entrusted their savings wanted assurances that the money had been properly delivered and all were anxious for news and views about the outside world.

A few days later Ank came by and casually mentioned what had happened. She could not resist retelling an account she had from Adri. "Mrs. Helfrich, you know, the Admiral's wife, had given Adri an envelope with some money, but you know, she had then wondered what Adri would do if she were caught. Adri had told her that she would eat the envelope, and Mrs Helfrich had then asked her to remove the money before eating the envelope. Can you imagine what would have happened if Adri had been caught with that money?" And chuckling, Ank added, "Adri would have no hesitation about removing the money from the envelope when it reappeared, I can assure you."

Around the first of December Mrs. Diepeveen posted a notice saying that every household in Tjihapit was allowed to send a postcard to a husband or son. The message had to be printed in Malay, and we were allowed to choose up to three sentences from a prescribed list and add twenty words of our own choice. "A nice St. Nicholas gift," my mother commented dryly, but the choice of sentences offered for the prescribed text irritated her intensely. "They are all lies," she said. "We are in good health—we are very happy—my foot." My mother sought help from Ank in writing that all-important final sentence, and addressed the card to "B. A. J. van Oort, LOG, Bandoeng," hoping for the best. She was not allowed to specify her return address, beyond the name of the city, Bandoeng.

For the St. Nicholas festival that year the women of Tjihapit made another valiant attempt to give children a taste of normalcy. A woman dressed as a bishop in a shabby red cloak and a poor excuse for a white beard, along with a Black Peter, his (her) face covered with soot, made an appearance in various streets astride a velo. "St. Nicholas had to leave his horse at home," my mother commented laconically. The children were out on the sidewalk to see him go by, some of the smaller ones crying with fear, while the remainder attempted to sing appropriate songs, hurriedly taught by a cluster of mothers. Every child in our house got a small gift, a homemade puzzle or a golf ball.

As the end of the year was approaching Arsad subjected us to repeated upheavals. It began, sadly, when the *Kempetai* arrested Blackie the fox terrier. This friendly animal had become a frequent visitor to the camp and had appeared as mysteriously as he had disappeared. He was caught by a guard, who then discovered a message and some money in his collar and traced its ownership to a Eurasian family. The family promptly lost its freedom and appeared in our midst.

A bicycle *razzia* quickly followed; Komiyama needed to obtain a means of transportation for his newly established PETA (*Tentara Pembela Tanah Air* home defence) unit. The formation of this force was the fruit of the emotional letter *raden* Gatot Mangkoepradja had in September sent to the Japanese army. Enthusiasm among the young Indonesian men of Bandoeng had been wanting, but a *razzia* had solved that problem as well. The residents of Tjihapit did their best to frustrate the ambitions of the PETA by hiding a couple of bicycles for future use by the doctors and nurses and vandalizing the remainder before delivering them, with bent spokes, seats removed and tires slashed, to a dump near the camp gate. After the most usable bikes had been removed from the camp by a truck, a pile of handlebars, bent wheels and frames was left as a mute testimony to the bicycle *razzia*. During the weeks that followed, the PETA recruits, men in ill-fitting uniforms, many on rusty ladies' bikes, started patrolling the streets of Bandoeng in an un-martial spectacle.

To cap it all, the Japanese discovered a hole in Tjihapit's bamboo wall. All of the women living nearby were forced to stand under the blazing noonday sun for twenty minutes with their hands held high. The Japanese considered group punishment an effective and appropriate response. It might have worked among Japanese citizens, but not with us, for this approach simply encouraged more risk-taking by the desperate and audacious. Before the year was out, two other women had escaped through the *selokan* to buy some food outside the camp, but they were caught, taken to the *Kempetai* office and thoroughly beaten. Thereafter a guard was permanently posted by the culvert.

As a result of all this, nervous tensions rose throughout the camp. When days later the rice rations were once more lowered, this time to 140 grams per day, everyone assumed this was punishment for our misbehaviour.

The disastrous end-of-year food situation throughout Java precipitated the appearance all over Bandoeng of paper notices with the following message: "*Nippon mesti mati, kita lapar*" (Nippon must die, we are hungry).

The *Kempetai* promptly removed these announcements, but not before many had read them, and so General Harada felt compelled to organize a conference to discuss food provisions and immediately ordered, as a Christmas surprise, house searches for hoarded supplies—only to reverse this edict days after the conference by instructing Bandoeng households to lay up enough supplies to last a week. The succession of conflicting messages was confusing. The conference also recommended that all citizens of Bandoeng, both inside and outside the camp, become self-sufficient—every vacant plot of land should be used for food production.

In the internment camps of Tjimahi, prisoners already grew their own vegetables and reared their own pigs. In Tjihapit, it had been left to the initiative of the internees to do the same, but almost no land was available for this purpose; this city neighbourhood had been selected specifically for internment because of the dense housing. The tomato plants that my mother had so carefully nursed when we first came into the camp had died long ago, and at our new address, with so many more children and adults, it was difficult to grow anything; even if one succeeded one would have to guard such plants constantly because the temptation to steal a tomato, on the point of becoming ripe, had become irresistible to many among us.

In the New Year the food situation got worse. On January 7, 1944 (2604 by Japanese reckoning), rice rations distributed by the communal kitchen in town were further reduced to seventy grams per day, with a similar reduction implemented in Tjihapit. Searches for hoarded supplies among the houses and *kampongs* of Bandoeng were again conducted, resulting in the arrest of six Indonesians from the bamboo and *atap* hovels of a *kampong*. Two of the unfortunates were thrashed to death and the other four seriously injured, all left lying by the side of the road as a chilling example for others. Inside Tjihapit, hunger continued to drive women to desperate acts: early in February, four women were caught trading through the *gedek*. Arsad punished them by having them shaved; in Japanese eyes, this was akin to a mock beheading, but the women cheerfully went around camp wearing headscarves.

The deteriorating ability of the Japanese to keep supplies moving caused another emergency initiative to be launched on Java; the island had to become self-sufficient in lubricating oil for Japan's dwindling number of fighter planes. General Harada accordingly ordered castor oil seeds to be planted (fortunately we in Tjihapit were spared from this task). Officials went up and down the streets of Bandoeng, distributing six castor oil seeds to each household with instructions that they be planted in the front gardens. The nut of the castor oil plant was rich in oil, but it took ten thousand nuts to keep one aircraft engine running for one hour.[20]

This initiative coincided with a personnel change; on February 15 Yoshio Ichibangase, a middle-aged agronomist, replaced Komiyama as governor of the region. He was ordered to stimulate the considerable agricultural potential of the region and to stave off an economic catastrophe. The news prompted a typical reaction—he was immediately nicknamed "*bangsat nomor satu*" (rascal number one), which was derived from the Japanese meaning of *ichi* (one) and the Malay *bangsat* (rascal). The residents of Bandoeng were nevertheless relieved to see Komiyama go, for the reputation of wanton brutality he had brought with him from Semarang, his previous posting, had turned out to be accurate.

The Japanese were suffering one setback after another. During the first days of February, the Americans commenced landings on the Marshall Islands, which

---

20. Bouwer, *Het vermoorde land*, 234.

were psychologically significant because they had been long-standing Japanese possessions. By the middle of the month, the attacks on the Japanese positions in the Caroline Islands had become so successful that the Japanese navy had to abandon its base there and withdraw to Singapore.[21] Three days later, the important Japanese naval base at Truk was also taken by the United States. By February 22 the continuing stream of bad news from the front finally persuaded Hirohito to remove Sugiyama from office and to place more responsibility and authority in the hands of Tojo.

But elsewhere in Southeast Asia the war effort proceeded less smoothly for the Allies. The American victories at sea hardly helped Chiang Kai-shek and his embattled forces on the Chinese mainland, and there were differences of opinion as to what Mountbatten, now appointed Supreme Commander Southeast Asia (SEAC), should do. The Americans continued to urge him to use the forces at his disposal to press the Japanese positions in Burma, but the equipment Mountbatten needed was required elsewhere to finish off the Italian campaign. He nevertheless started working on Culverin, an invasion of lightly garrisoned Sumatra, for which he requested landing craft. This request was also denied by the Allied Chiefs of Staff because in their opinion it would do nothing to shorten the war with Japan.[22]

21. Brugmans, *Nederlandsch-Indië onder Japanse bezetting*, 58.
22. Ziegler, *Mountbatten*, 265.

7. PRISONER OF WAR

On the first of March, Camp Commandant Arsad made a surprise visit to the Ladies' Office to say goodbye and to let us know that a new commandant would be placed in charge. When Mrs. Diepeveen asked what the reason was for the change, Arsad merely shrugged his shoulders.

Three days later Murui, a Japanese soldier, presented himself to an astonished Mrs. Diepeveen. Amelia, still employed maintaining the camp inmate registry, dropped by to tell us about these events.

"What's Murui like?" my mother asked.

"Typical soldier but Japanese this time—rather heavy set, short, with hair no more than one millimetre long—the usual tall, shiny black boots and, of course, a sword and a revolver."

"I wonder why it's a Japanese soldier," my mother mused out loud. "Perhaps there is not enough for them to do."

"Mrs. Diepeveen was taken aback as well."

No one knew what to make of this, and a change in the familiar routine was worrying. The Indonesian camp guards had not all been satisfactory, but to some extent they were a known quantity. Some had spoken Dutch and with the others we had been able to communicate in Malay, but our contacts with the Japanese soldiers thus far had mainly been via the *Kempetai*, and those contacts filled us with terror. The change struck us as unpleasant, regardless of what else the Japanese authorities might have in mind.

An immediate practical communication problem arose for Mrs. Diepeveen; Murui spoke neither Dutch nor English and his command of Malay was poor. She therefore posted a notice on the board in front of her house in the middle of the camp, asking if there was anyone who could speak Japanese and help her in the office. A few days later my mother met Amelia and asked, "Has Mrs. Diepeveen found a Japanese interpreter?"

"Oh yes," Amelia answered, "Agnes Bouman offered her services; apparently she has lived in Japan for a few years and knows some Japanese."

"What did Agnes think of Murui?"

"She thought he was okay," Amelia continued, "but she thought that it must have been difficult to find a Japanese officer to take on the job. Looking after a camp full of women is humiliating for them. Yes," she added thoughtfully, "and Agnes thinks that he has a *Belanda* girlfriend."

"Here in the camp?"

"No, outside. The other day I also saw him walking away from the gate with a blonde woman."

Shortly after Murui's appointment he started to order changes, and it soon became apparent that we would have a lot to do with the Japanese in the future. But first Murui let it be known that he was only the second-in-command to a more senior figure; Lieutenant Susumo Suzuki would turn up later. When he did arrive, Suzuki seldom showed his face in the camp, and that was just fine by us.

The decision to place all civilian captives under direct military control had been taken six months earlier, when a succession of Japanese setbacks had increased Japanese concerns about security on Java; what if the Indonesians were to follow the Italian example and change sides? On November 7, 1943, Emperor Hirohito signed the decree that was to have a huge impact on our lives; on that day "Regulations on the Treatment of Army Internees" came into effect. Article 1 defined "intern" as "the detaining of enemy nationals or neutrals at a specified place with the purpose of restricting their activities and of extending protection to them," and "army internees" as "any enemy national or neutral interned."[1]

With a few deft strokes of his calligraphy brush, Hirohito changed the formal designation of "Protected Area" to "Army Internment Camp." His underlings nevertheless continued to describe our living arrangements as a form of imperial protection that from time to time necessitated severe physical punishment, starvation and torture. Implementation of that decision was delayed until now, and one can only speculate that this delay reflected practical difficulties, such as finding the necessary staffing resources.

Since then the Japanese security situation had continued to deteriorate, not only elsewhere in the Pacific but also on Java, where there were disturbing signs of anarchy, further complicating the Japanese position; Japan required a smoothly running economy and therefore civil peace. There was, for instance, a problem with the railroads. For some time this important transportation network had been plagued by unexplained mishaps—fires, derailments, and a distressing propensity for late arrivals. A service that once had been a marvel of punctuality was now in tatters, and evidence had come to light early in 1944 that a coordinated sabotage action might have been at work. The ringleaders seemed to be Eurasian and Chinese employees, with some collaboration from Indonesian staff. This news played into the hands of the Indonesian nationalists, who preferred to see all their half-caste cousins and Chinese eliminated from the good jobs, if not locked up. Such drastic action, however,

1. van Velden, *De Japanse burgerkampen*, 562.

would make the rail system more dependent on the indifferent skills of poorly educated Indonesians.

In addition, it had become obvious that the initial enthusiasm among Indonesians for learning Japanese had waned to an alarming extent. Only one quarter of the students who initially had enrolled were still willing to endure a Japanese examination, even as the pace of Nipponization continued.

In January 1944, hoping to resurrect the economy, the Japanese founded Djawa Hokokai (National Service Association). Its aim was to foster a united front, regardless of race, in support of the Japanese war effort. On publicity leaflets the title of this organization was printed over a background of the radiant sun, symbolic of Japan, with a map of Java centred on the sun disc.

The importance of this overdue initiative was further driven home on February 18, when an uprising took place in Tasikmalaya, one hundred kilometres east of Bandoeng. This was by far the worst of a series of incidents between the Japanese and Indonesians that had recently occurred all over Java. A fanatical *kiai*, a Muslim *imam*, had announced the time ripe for a *jihad* and had led five hundred followers to the local police station. The *Kempetai* was ordered to the scene, where two of its officers were *tjintjanged* (hacked into pieces). Then the Japanese machine guns came out and two hundred men, women and children died.

The Tasikmalaya incident, with its dark religious overtones, and the subsequent troubles on March 7 in Batavia leant further urgency to the task of increasing control. On the latter occasion General Harada, in a gesture of goodwill, had arranged to help the Indonesians celebrate Mohammed's birthday, but this had turned into a disaster. At the huge, solemn gathering of Indonesians on the Ikeda Square in the middle of Batavia, all those present were supposed to turn towards Tokyo to bow in deference to Emperor Hirohito, but hardly anyone did: the devout Indonesians knew where Mecca was, but were confused about the location of Tokyo; it was a terrible snub to His Majesty. This mark of disrespect had greatly alarmed General Harada and distressed some of the Indonesian nationalists present, who saw in this an indication of the short-sightedness of the ordinary Indonesian citizen: these simple folk placed more importance on the religious strictures of the Muslim faith than on the grand destiny offered to them as an *ade* (young brother) of *bung* (older brother) Nippon.[2]

General Harada had recently also become aware of rumblings of discontent within the newly-founded Indonesian PETA military organization. At issue were the relative rankings of Indonesian officers versus Japanese foot soldiers—who should be the first to salute? The Japanese soldiers clearly had a very low opinion of the Indonesian officers and the PETA officers grumbled

---

2. Brugmans, *Nederlandsch-Indië onder Japanse bezetting*, document 392.

that they had to walk around town almost continuously saluting, or risk a beating. PETA officers had also complained that their food was inferior to that enjoyed by their Japanese colleagues. If the loyalty to Japan of the Indonesian soldiers were to seriously falter, how could they be trusted to guard the *Belanda*? To safeguard Japan's position on Java, direct military control over a larger part of civilian life seemed to be urgently necessary. Thus we were to be converted into prisoners of war, while *Djawa Hokokai* was launched.

However, we were taken by complete surprise by the turn of events. A few days later, pamphlets were distributed throughout the camp with the following strange message:

> The internment camps on Java have been reorganized and I, the Commander in Chief, am in charge of your accommodation. It is my intention to protect you and in order to do that I have to constrain your freedom of movement. It is therefore inevitable that your daily lives will differ from what you enjoyed in peace time. You may understand this when you consider the current state of the war and the status quo of your respective fatherlands.
>
> I will justly promote your interests following rules of humanity, taking into account your customs and mores. It may be that the basis for my ruling differs from those that were in place previously, but I will do my utmost to treat you justly with firmness and determination even in unimportant matters. I am determined to punish without taking into account mitigating factors those who transgress my instructions or who act in a derogatory manner, or in other ways attempt to undermine my authority.
>
> You need to take careful heed of your current situation, refrain from preparations for liberation, or from careless actions, follow all regulations and orders, and you need to live an orderly life for the sake of your physical and mental well-being. As soon as you have accustomed yourself to various matters I am sure you will enter a happy future.

Colonel Masayuki Nakata,
Commandant, all internment camps of Java,
Djakarta, 22 April 2604.[3]

"The Japs have an odd way of protecting us," Emmy observed wryly. "I could do with a bit less protection."

The change in our daily camp life was quickly put into effect; by March 12, a week after Murui had arrived, the Japanese Economics Unit had formally

---

3. Brugmans, *Nederlandsch-Indië onder Japanse bezetting*, document 227.

handed off all control over Tjihapit to the Japanese military. From now on soldiers in Japanese army uniform stood in the small shelters on either side of our camp gate. Until that day it had been possible to smuggle notes in and out of camp to friends in Bandoeng with the help of the corruptible *heiho* guards. Henceforth we were even more isolated from friends and acquaintances in the outside world, while the dreadful *Kempetai* now loomed directly over our daily lives. In the following weeks we were subjected to a steady stream of new instructions, restrictions and demands without explanation. For example, an announcement dated March 2604, read :

ALL KUMICHOS HAVE TO HAND IN TO THE CAMP OFFICE LISTS OF NAMES OF RESIDENTS UNDER THEIR SUPERVISION. A NEW SET OF NUMBERS WILL BE ISSUED. THESE NUMBERS MUST BE DISPLAYED ON ALL CLOTHING AT ALL TIMES.

"What about babies?" someone asked. It was an absurd order because it was an absurd situation—army regulations seldom address the problems of babies. "You'll have to pin the numbers on the baby's diapers when there is an inspection," responded the house *kepalla* when one of the mothers raised this question. That day the camp office issued detailed instructions for making the number patches; every household had to hand in for each occupant a piece of white material, six centimetres wide and two centimetres high with finished, hemmed edges. This was an onerous request because white material and cotton were in exceedingly short supply, not only within Tjihapit, but throughout Java.

On March 18 the *kumichos* went around all houses to announce that an important visitor would come tomorrow, "and the camp should now be seen as a barracks. When the visitor comes," she continued, "you must bow properly from the waist, thus," and she gave a demonstration to each *kepalla,* summoned out to the street for the purpose. After that she concluded her recital with the comment, "The street in front of the house has to be clean, and there should be no children's toys, laundry or playpens in the front yard." After delivering the ridiculous message to a house full of children, the unhappy *kumicho* proceeded to the next house in her *kumi.*

Early the next morning Murui himself, accompanied by Agnes Bouman, made a hurried visit through parts of the camp close to the camp gate. At our house he noticed that a playpen with a toddler in it had been left out on the grass around the side of the house, but still visible from the road. It had rained the previous afternoon, and the mother was trying to clean up the veranda, where the playpen normally stood; the baby was happily enjoying the morning sun. With his sword Murui made a sweeping gesture at the playpen and its occupant and said something in Japanese, and Agnes told our *kepalla* that the playpen had to go. Early that afternoon Murui came round again with Lieutenant Suzuki and an unknown senior officer (who, it later turned out, was

Colonel Nakata), and after seeing our garden, smiled and said "*Semua bagus*" (all beautiful), a comment possibly motivated by the threat of another shower and the need for the officers to hurry or else get a soaking.

At about the same time a remarkable thing happened. It was totally unrelated to the imposition of military rule on our camp, but was one of those strange things that made one realize that the people who controlled our destiny had a degree of integrity after all. One of the ladies in the house came in holding a ten-guilder note.

"I never dreamt that I would ever see the money again after giving it to the bank," she said, "and look what has happened! Today I was allowed to withdraw ten guilders. This will last me for the month."

"Did you deposit Dutch guilders or Japanese guilders?" Emmy asked.

"Oh, Dutch guilders of course."

"You got diddled, because that is a Japanese ten-guilder note."

The lady stood still, staring at the note in her hand; it was indeed a curious thing, a promise written in Dutch that the Japanese government would pay the bearer ten guilders, but lacking the signature of an important person charged with the task of maintaining the value of the currency, with a curiously small serial number, and paper and ink that seemed to be poorly selected for service in a humid climate. As she tried to remove an ink stain from her finger she ruefully admitted that Emmy might have a point. The money we had spent on *toko* food during the previous two months could now be reclaimed from the bank, assuming that we had deposited our savings there, as instructed. We had also been told to keep a record of our food outlay from our ten-guilder allowance. Few of our fellow inmates had at the time placed any faith in the promise that the money would ever be returned, and had preferred to keep their cash supply under tight personal control, thereby running the risk of losing it all; besides, who had paper and pencil? One just never knew what to make of the instructions and promises. The tiny quantity of money in our possession had to last until an undisclosed point of time in the future, and had become a matter of life and death.

By now we had come to know quite well Emmy's sister-in-law, Charlotte, living on nearby Barendszstraat. My parents had met this family on a couple of occasions before the war, and it was at their house that Edu and Emmy got married. Since her neighbour, Mrs. Diepeveen, had a notice board in front of her house, we regularly went there hoping for news from men's camps, and in so doing, often encountered Lotte (as she liked to be called). She had three children, an eight-year-old boy, Rudolf, a younger boy about my age called William, and a two-year-old daughter, Alein. Lotte was a completely different character from Emmy, and tended to be somewhat melancholic and emotional.

She was a slightly built woman with a nervous disposition, and clearly was very unsure of herself. With her dark hair and beautiful dark eyes she must have been very attractive before the war, but the cares of family had taken their toll. Insecure at the best of times, Lotte was struggling because one of her children always seemed to be ill. My mother nonetheless found Lotte to be good company, partly because she could understand some of her own child-care problems, and so from time to time we wandered to her house for a visit, where my mother and Lotte enjoyed a cigarette—not a real one, of course, but the rolled-up dried palm leaves they referred to as a *strootje* (a straw).

The disturbing changeover to military rule was a prime topic of discussion for everyone—what did it really signify? And yet conversation with Lotte invariably returned to her daily preoccupation with her sick children and the challenge of survival.

"There are twenty-eight of us living here and almost everyday I get a complaint from someone about a child," Lotte moaned. Then, mimicking her tormentors with a sing-song voice, added, "Can't you stop your child from crying or coughing all night? or, Mrs. K., your child was so cheeky. If only I knew where Ru was—first someone told me he had been moved to Batavia, and then I heard that he was still in Tjimahi." After some hesitation she continued in a low, anxious voice, "Do you think Ru has forgotten about me?"

"Of course not," my mother replied, trying to be cheerful, and then adding, "Emmy has no idea where Edu is either. Many of the soldiers seem to have been moved elsewhere, and I have not heard a thing from Bou." Lotte, however, seemed perpetually to be on the point of a breakdown. "Before the war she was always very cheerful," my mother remarked to Emmy.

"Lotte complains too much," was Emmy's response. "Edu had no money to leave me when he was taken prisoner; she at least had some money."

"I think that's gone now. All she talks about is food and not being able to buy an egg." The price of an egg, at twenty cents (if available at all), exceeded by a large margin the *per diem* amount allocated to us under the military regulations for all of our food.

On March 21 there was another terrible rainstorm. We hoped it would be the last of the season, which seemed to have been unduly wet. The rain came down in torrents, instantly converting all the yards into shallow lakes and the road into a raging river, while incessant thunder rolled with deafening noise through the clouds above us. We had gone to visit Lotte and her children, and remained on the veranda to sit out the storm, watching the sheets of water falling from the overflowing roof gutters, pelting the footpath and the rapidly growing lake in the front yard. Once upon a time that instant lake would have had a grassy bottom and the rainwater would have remained clean, but now it was becoming a muddy expanse, and a swiftly flowing stream of dirty water had filled the gutters on the side of the road. Before the war such storms had been inconvenient, but now they brought a welcome distraction from the constant fear of the inscrutable Japanese soldiers, who had lately arrived in our midst and were now imposing such alien ways on us.

Lotte had heard more about Colonel Nakata's inspection trip from Mrs. Diepeveen, and raising her voice to penetrate the din of the falling rain was telling us about it, pausing whenever there was a flash of lightning and in anticipation of the thunderclaps.

"Everything was wrong in the Ladies' Office—the desks had to be re-arranged and the typists were accused of being shrimp-heads. The man has a nerve, don't you think? Oh yes, and you know what else? He had the nerve to ask Mrs. Diepeveen why women keep on defying the rules and buying food at the *gedek*. One of the typists blurted out that they and their children are hungry."

Another woman, perhaps in her early twenties and dressed in shorts, a sleeveless blouse and sandals, who had emerged from the house and happened to overhear the conversation, then butted in, saying, "Did you see the notice board today? We now have a dress code."

"You must be kidding," exclaimed my mother.

"No, the Japs don't want to see bare legs," Lotte interjected. "We may wear trousers, but they must be long. The Japs do not want to see more than ten centimetres of bare leg." We had heard about these views on public decorum when the Japanese first arrived in Bandoeng, but since our internment had been able to forget such strictures. Now we were once more threatened with forcible imposition of these alien norms of modesty and good behaviour.

It was getting late and the worst of the storm was over, so we started to make our way homeward. As we approached the bridge over the Tjihapit *selokan*, we met the two Poortman girls with their long dark pigtails, sheltered from the last raindrops by an umbrella.

"Mrs. van Oort, have you heard? A little girl fell into the *selokan*," one of them said in hushed tones, pointing over the railing.

We looked at the torrent of brown water below, in an attempt, I suppose, to see whether there was any sign of the unfortunate victim. The river had overflowed its concrete duct and risen up the grassy banks on either side to near the top and was probably two metres deep in the middle. The current was ferocious, and water draining from the street was adding to the flow on either side of the bridge. There was no sign of a child, just unspeakable amounts of rubbish, including human waste, floating downstream along with the leaves and branches. There was nothing we could do, and so we hurried home. There we found Emmy, soaking wet, having just returning from the kitchen.

"Boys were swimming in the water around the *dapur*," she said, "and the fires once more went out. The afternoon shift will have to start all over again."

Further changes to our daily camp routine followed one another in rapid succession. The coolies, readmitted after the boys left to transport the heavy bags of rice from the storage sheds outside the camp to the kitchens, were suddenly replaced by a number of European men. This of course drew excited interest from the women, eager to find a familiar face or hear about a loved one.

One day, Charlotte came by in an agitated state after a trip to the Ladies' Office. "I was shocked when I first saw those men come into the camp," she lamented, with evident emotion attached to the word *shocked,* which she kept repeating. After a brief pause to regain her self-control, she continued, "I did not dare talk to them because a rotten Jap was standing there with his sword, but I later heard they came from the 15th Battalion camp. They looked thin, worn-out and dilapidated—walking skeletons—I could not recognize any of them. And you know what happened? It was awful—a girl saw three boys among the men and said something to them and the Nip beat those boys to the ground. One was bleeding badly." After blowing her nose, she continued in a shaky voice, "—Terrible, terrible!"

"I wish I could ask these men about Edu," Emmy sighed. "If he knew I were here, I am sure he would have tried to join this party," adding, after a moment's reflection, "My God, I hope he is still okay."

These men henceforth made regular appearances in Tjihapit, always under the supervision of a Japanese soldier. They came mostly to repair the *gedek*, which always seemed to come apart whenever there was a storm. Their pitiful appearance soon earned them the nickname *kneusjes*, as though they were damaged, bruised fruit.

Ten days later, yet another order was posted on the bulletin board:

ALL FOOD SUPPLIES THAT HAVE NOT BEEN OBTAINED VIA THE TOKO OR DAPUR HAVE TO BE HANDED IN IMMEDIATELY.
EACH KUMICHO MUST DO A HEAD-COUNT IN THE MORNING AT 9, IN THE AFTERNOON AT 3 AND AT NIGHT AT 9.

Hand in food? Who would be so crazy? And what was this nonsense about being counted?

As the idiotic military orders followed one after another, the women in the camp chalked up a growing list of transgressions, each one of which, if found out, could bring them into the clutches of the *Kempetai*. There were a few women in the camp who had spent a couple of months in the *Kempetai* prison, and told terrifying stories. They had been crammed into a tiny cell along with seven or eight other women, leaving too little space for all to sleep, so they were forced to take turns. They had been denied spare clothing and often had the choice of either drinking their tea or using it to clean themselves. Their ablutions moreover had to be performed in the full view of guards and, worst of all, they had to endure the sound of other prisoners being tortured. When these women were finally let go and arrived back in camp, they were broken, both physically and emotionally. To avoid the attention of the *Kempetai* one had to be lucky and very careful. Notwithstanding the order and the fear of punishment, very little food was handed in.

The *dapur* food was so poor in quality and quantity that every opportunity was sought to get a little bit extra to augment the daily fare of rice, *sajur*, starch and indigestible rubbery bread. The bread that hitherto had been delivered (at our cost) from a Chinese bakery had by May become so bad that Mrs. Diepeveen began to explore alternatives. She heard that before the war one of the houses in Tjihapit had been used as a small bakery, and accordingly asked Lieutenant Suzuki's permission to restart the facility. Permission was granted and further shipments of the expensive but inedible bread were stopped. It took a week for the "technical team" to make the disused oven functional again and to improvise baking tins from empty food tins. Mrs. Diepeveen then sought volunteers to staff the bakery, which would have to operate around the clock with the help of three shifts to provide the camp with a modest daily ration; each shift required twenty women and four boys. The bakery began operations on May 19 but the only flour that could be procured was a mixture of tapioca, corn and cassava. Its composition changed unpredictably with each shipment, and so experiments were needed with each new batch to find an appropriate recipe.

The Economy Collapses

The situation elsewhere in town was not much better; in the two years following the Dutch capitulation the economic life of Java had deteriorated to an alarming extent. The shortage of medical supplies in Bandoeng, for instance, had become so acute that anyone needing to go to hospital had to bring along their own ether, cotton wool, dressing material, medicines and food. If a patient were unable to bring ether he would be operated on without anaesthetic, a common practice by now. The two Chinese surgeons still operating in town had sent out a general request for people to help provide them with Brooks' sewing cotton, the best substitute for surgical thread still available in this city of a quarter of a million.

General Harada accordingly struck a committee of senior administrative personnel to find ways of stimulating production. On May 19 the committee, consisting of thirty-two Japanese, eighteen Indonesian and two Chinese members as well as one (non-interned) *Belanda Indo* member, met and was charged with the task of gearing the economy to wartime requirements. Representation on the committee was, numerically speaking, inversely proportional to the ability of the population groups represented to do anything about the collapsing economy; before the war it had been the Eurasian and Chinese populations that had provided key management and entrepreneurial expertise, but their voices hardly counted now.

General Harada hoped that he would succeed by pursuing the Japanese pattern—increasing self-sufficiency by making use of substitutes. The remedies now presented to the committee spoke volumes about the sense of desperation that had descended so tragically and quickly on this magnificently well-endowed island. In order to deal with the desperate shortage of cotton he wanted to encourage textile manufacture from tree bark, while clothing was already being made from jute, the material normally used for potato and coal bags. A week later Sukarno, not wanting to be left out, proclaimed the need to collect old clothes for the *rakjat djelata* (the proletariat), and Camp Commandant Suzuki ordered the Tjihapit women to hand over all men's clothing, thereby stimulating a hurried modification of those clothes into women's garments.

At the same time a Java-wide scrap-iron collection campaign got under way. In March there had already been a request for "surplus iron, copper, steel and die cast materials." Now *kumichos* distributed to all the houses of Bandoeng written orders that each household had to make available ten kilograms of iron, and city residents were warned that a house search might be resorted to if the target were not met. The poles and street signs were being ripped from the streets of Bandoeng and all machinery from the factory that produced quinine, a strategic component in the struggle against malaria, had been removed.[4]

The call for scrap metal also went through Tjihapit, where the threat of a house search was never far off. On April 1 a new notice was posted on the bulletin board:

ALL ELECTRICAL APPLIANCES ARE TO BE HANDED IN WITH
NAME AND ADDRESS ATTACHED. ELECTRICITY WILL
HENCEFORTH BE FREE BUT A LIST MUST BE MADE OF EVERY
LIGHT BULB IN THE HOUSE.

The Japanese shipbuilding industry was in need of scrap iron. Fridges and electric stoves (now only used for storage), sewing machines, toasters and flat irons were dragged out of houses and piled up on the street, where the *kneusjes* picked them up in their carts to dump near the camp gate. Two days later the *kneusjes* loaded the pile onto their carts and wheeled it out of the camp to the waiting trucks. During the subsequent weeks and months periodic attempts were made by the administrative staff to reconcile the electrical consumption of Tjihapit against the theoretical load from the remaining light bulbs, but that proved impossible: somehow consumption was always higher.

---

4. Bouwer, *Het vermoorde land*, 251.

And yet, for a little while longer, neither the escalating conflicts with our Japanese captors nor the seriously deteriorating food situation could extinguish a burning, persistent urge for the inmates of Tjihapit to make light of our travails. Mrs. Schneider and Miss Richter, our two gifted amateur *cabaretières*, always ready to poke fun at the discomfort of our oppressors and ourselves, under the stage name "Tholen and van Lier," had arranged a Friday night show, which my mother and I attended. They had set up a stage in a garage they called "home," conveniently located in the part of the camp furthest removed from the camp gate. Now, donning their somewhat dilapidated top hats and tails, they proceeded to regale us with a song-and-dance routine. The performance started at five thirty in the afternoon, well after sundown, and included a large number of new songs composed with the latest camp developments in mind. The audience joined in lustily as usual when the refrains were sung:

Twenty chickens in a crate
Today arrived through the camp gate.
Twenty hens so plump and white
Truly a mouth watering sight.
Chicken soup! chicken soup!
Chicken soup for the second group!

We laughed, but while the mirth was a good tonic, it nevertheless was developing an edge. The food obsession had only grown during these last few months, and the communal kitchen operations provoked a continuing preoccupation with the fairness of the food distribution process, leading to rampant accusations of malpractice and favouritism. It was hard work for the kitchen staff, for they could never produce enough. Think what it takes to dole out an insufficient quantity of food to twelve thousand mouths, and imagine what would happen at the end of the process if food were left over, or if one or two people arrived at the end of the queue when the food drum was empty. It was nerve-wracking for all concerned, and tempers flared frequently. Lining up for food was moreover a time-consuming business, as time consuming as lining up for the few toilet facilities:

Hear a bell?
Run like hell
Come on time
Wait in line
Queue for an hour
With your neighbour
For soup or slop
Or something hot.

Unfortunately our brief period of merriment was brutally deflated the next day, when a camp notice advised that cards sent to the men's camp in early December had now been returned. Crestfallen and fearing the worst, my mother joined a huge crowd of women at the Ladies' Office to see whether her card was among them. It was, but it revealed no sign as to why it had not been delivered. That night we went to sleep deeply depressed.

A shipment of food parcels, arriving unexpectedly on May 25, provided some relief from our boring and inadequate daily rations. The labels on the parcels, marked "American Red Cross, November 1, 1943, Washington DC," were almost more important to us than the contents; someone far away knew that we existed; this constituted a psychological nourishment more precious and long-lasting than the physical nourishment contained in the tins and boxes, which would soon be consumed. Our isolation had become so complete that this sign of a normal world beyond the cursed bamboo *gedek*, a world that cared for us and for other people, made an enormous impression.

At the Ladies' Office, one parcel had been opened and its contents put on display for everyone to admire. How delicious it all looked—packages of Chesterfield cigarettes, three tins of butter, two tins of ham and eggs, three tins of corned pork, one tin of pâté, one tin of Kraft processed cheese, four packages of soap powder, eight boxes of OXO soup cubes, a package of dried prunes, a tin of orange juice, a box of cookies, a box of sugar cubes, a tin of Kup Kafay (instant coffee), a tin of Baker's cocoa, and a tin of Milko powdered milk; it was mouth-watering. The two bars of soap were much appreciated as well. Such a parcel had been intended for four persons, but would have to be shared among nine. The parcels had been shipped via Lourenço Marques on the East African coast, and had taken seven months to reach Tjihapit. After the boring and tasteless fare that we had consumed for a year, these tins and boxes contained nothing less than gourmet items. After deep deliberation as to how to ensure fairness, the contents were distributed among all the families, who then rationed individual future consumption as they saw fit.

That evening all of Tjihapit was in a festive mood, enjoying the cool night air. The veranda of our house, facing the street, was already packed with women and children, and so we sat on the steps around the back, enjoying our treats. While Juf was sipping a cup of coffee with condensed milk and I had a small cup of delicious hot chocolate, my mother and Emmy smoked a cigarette. It was a dark, moonless night, but there were millions of stars in a sky, clear as glass after the numerous recent downpours.

"You know something," whispered my mother. "I am beginning to feel human again."

Emmy stared intently at the wispy curls of blue smoke rising into the still evening air from the glowing tip of her cigarette. "The smell of this cigarette is

1. Lombardy East, 1936. Today the house is lost in the middle of a sprawling suburb of Germiston.

2. Juf (Margaretha Elizabeth Eisenberger Tau)— Passport photograph taken for her voyage to South Africa in 1936.

3. Boudewyn van Oort and Wilhelmina Boland, wedding photo, July 14,1937.

SEND-OFF TO HOLLANDERS.

4. *Johannesburg Star* press photo, May 22, 1940. Edu is leaning out of the train carriage window, facing the camera.

5. *Straat Soenda*, May 26, 1940. John Fisher is crouching down behind the bollard. Behind him, from left: Rein Jessurun, Boudewyn junior, Juf, Helmer Siegers, my mother, and Bessie Fisher. Justinus Heldring is at the very back and on the far right is Captain Koning. My father took the photograph.

6. 1 Serajoestraat, July 1940. This house was one of the better-quality homes in the Tjihapit camp. The yard in the foreground belongs to 3 Serajoestraat.

7. Front entrance of the KMA complex, Bandoeng, May 1941. My father is in the second row, third from the right. This military academy is still in use.

8. Our house in Dennelust, nearing completion, December 1941.

9. "The Indonesian has gone up in the world since the Japanese invasion." (*Djaga Clatik* guards against rice birds; *Djaga Moesoeh*, guards against enemies.) By M. G. Hartley, Tjimahi.

10. The *Oranje dapur* (kitchen), Tjihapit, 1944. A reworking of the original sketch by Lieske Stroobach.

11. Counting under the new Nipponese military administration. Original caption: "Yes indeed it checks—2 working, 1 sick, 3 at the PID=11 of the 17 persons."

12. "Dress Rehearsal for Transport," by Adri Bontekoe, November 1944.

13. The author (left), September 1945. The domestic water supply lies at my feet.

14. A Tjideng house, September 1945. Note the omnipresent chamber pots in the foreground. More shelter has been improvised with some *gedek,* on the right.

15. A family's living space, Tjideng, early September 1945.

16. The Tjideng coffin factory.

17. Destroying the *gedek* (bamboo wall), September 1945. The tall woman in the middle wearing a white blouse is probably my mother.

18. Tjideng guards, late August or early September 1945. After the arrival of the *Cumberland* in mid-September 1945, they were replaced by British marines. Later my father also stood guard here.

19. Sone on trial in Singapore, greeting his court, September 1946. Elsa Kleist was among those who testified against him.

20 and 21. Edu and Emmy at Ismailia as refugees, February 1946.

22. My family on the Durban beach, Christmas 1945 behaving like tourists.

23. Discussing politics, Vereeniging, Unitas Park, 1949. From left to right, Edu, Ina, my mother, my father, Ernest Zastrosny, Betty Zastrosny, Emmy.

24. My father's house in the forest (his "cathedral") at Robert's Creek, Sunshine Coast, British Columbia.

taking me right back to the past—to those evenings in the game reserve at Pretorius Kop," she replied. "Can you still remember the smell of the smoke from those fires? When there was no wind in the lowveld the smoke could also curl lazily up like this, as though it were alive."

A week later we received our official numbers. The pieces of cloth we had handed in were returned with a *tjap* (a stamp with Japanese writing), a number and the camp we belonged to (in our case, camp Bandoeng II). My mother became prisoner 17817, and I was 17818. At the same time Mrs. Diepeveen informed us via the notice board that we had to accommodate an additional nine hundred persons arriving from the Rama Camp. This camp contained older men and women, many of whom were ill, and was located on the western outskirts of Bandoeng. It was immediately clear that these new arrivals would add to the strain on the social services we had been able to provide for ourselves. None of the new arrivals could be expected to lend a hand with the heavy work. To accommodate them, thirty houses had to be cleared. Our house on Serajoestraat, being one of the better-quality homes, with a convenient location, was among those selected. We had to move and find space elsewhere. Some residents objected to the eviction order and refused to move, but the mere mention from Mrs. Diepeveen of her ultimate sanction, assistance from the Japanese guards, quickly solved the problem.

June 1944

On June 6 the Normandy landings got under way; the operation was so vast that the Japanese made no attempt to downplay its importance, and the news spread through the camp like a *taufan* (typhoon*)*. The event did not alter our immediate position, but provided a huge tonic of hope, while stimulating among the Japanese and those Indonesians who had irrevocably allied themselves to the Japanese cause increased fears of an invasion of Java. In response, the army set up a huge searchlight on the grounds of the Dick de Hoog High School, right outside the Tjihapit *gedek*, and established permanent machine-gun emplacements nearby. A week later the Americans launched their assault on the Marianas, and on June 15 they landed on Saipan. This made what had been a long-standing Japanese nightmare a reality: occupation of these islands made routine bombing sorties to Japan possible. The invading American armada was huge, and Japan threw the bulk of its remaining naval forces against it in a hopeless attempt to blunt the attack. Hirohito refused to accept the inevitability of defeat and urged Naval Chief, Admiral Shigetaro Shimada to pull off another miracle "like the victory against the Russians in 1905."[1]

These momentous world events seemed to stimulate strange happenings in Bandoeng, distractions perhaps from the drama unfolding far away on the battlefields; everyone in town was talking about the "dwarf mystery." In the middle of the month, both a *Belanda Indo* boy and an Indonesian ice merchant claimed to have seen four dwarfs coming out of a hole in the ground among the roots of a large Banyan tree standing in the middle of the Tjitarum square, a block away from the northern boundary of Tjihapit. An investigation unearthed (literally) not four dwarfs, but four frogs. It then became a widely accepted notion that the dwarfs had transformed themselves into frogs, and so for several weeks hundreds of curious spectators came to the square hoping to see the dwarfs. Naturally it also caught the attention of those inside Tjihapit, with internees peering at the commotion through narrow slits between the bamboo strips and perhaps hoping to trade some goods with passers-by without being caught by the guards. The situation got so bad that traffic had to be diverted, and six policemen were posted near the tree to keep order.

Even sober newspaper editors seemed to lose their perspective. The editor of the *Tjahaja* published an opinion piece on the front page, next to a detailed account of the dwarf/frog phenomenon:

> All American ships that are still afloat should be handed over to the victorious Japanese and the transportation costs should be borne by the Americans. All American military bases in the United States must be destroyed, oil production restricted, and all privately owned banks, trusts and monopolies must be banned. Private agricultural sector must be eliminated and all trade unions disbanded.

The good news from Normandy, heard via two contraband radios in the camp, had on the other hand filled Tjihapit with elation and defiance. "Once Holland is liberated, we will be next" was the general sentiment. But outside the camp attitudes hardened; there, in a fit of nationalistic zeal, police arrested a pair of six-year-old *Belanda Indo* children for speaking Dutch among themselves while playing on the street. Since the conquest of Holland by Germany, the Japanese had contended that we *Belanda*, having lost our fatherland, our place in the universe, had become stateless and therefore humiliated creatures not deserving of the benevolence bestowed upon us by the Emperor through his protection. The prospect that the Netherlands might soon be liberated, thereby undermining this rhetoric, was clearly unsettling them.

General Harada's response was to contrast the struggle on the Normandy beaches with the one under way on Saipan. Germans, being Europeans, did not

---

1. After the Saipan disaster Admiral Shimada was dismissed; he could not deliver miracles.

have what the Japanese had—superior spirit. The Nipponization process, designed to improve the performance of the Indonesians as Japanese allies, was accordingly accelerated by the introduction of more Japanese institutions and nomenclature under the guidance of *Djawa Hokokai*. Outside our *gedek*, in Bandoeng and elsewhere on Java, a daily propaganda war predicting the defeat of the Americans at Saipan, got under way. The broadcast losses of American ships and planes quickly exceeded by a wide margin previous Japanese estimates of total American military strength; for anyone keeping track of the statistics the situation had become ludicrous. The barrage of misleading propaganda could only be sustained by drawing on more and more senior Japanese military spokesmen, such as aged Admiral Nobumasa Suetsugo, to predict the day of American defeat; he made a comparison between the failed efforts of Kublai Khan trying to conquer Japan in the thirteenth century and Admiral Nimitz's current effort: "Both were far from home."[2]

Before the month was out the Japanese fleet had been so severely damaged that it no longer offered an impediment to the American advance over the Pacific. A key factor was the American's access to radar, allowing them to be warned of impending air attacks. By July 6, the battle for Saipan had become so hopeless that the two top Japanese commanders, Admiral Chuichi Nagumo and General Yoshitsugu Saito, committed suicide in order to encourage their troops in their final counterattack. Their example was followed to excess in an orgy of killing; all told, the numbers of Japanese lives sacrificed in the defence of this position were staggering: twenty thousand Japanese soldiers died, mainly in hopeless bayonet charges against the American troops facing them. General Saito had ordered his soldiers to make a final mass attack, with "each soldier to take seven enemy lives in exchange for his own."[3] Over four thousand killed themselves rather than be captured by Americans, the ultimate humiliation. Obsessed Japanese mothers jumped off cliffs (today called "*Banzai* Cliff") with their children in their arms, or walked into the sea to drown.[4] Five thousand Korean labourers working for the Emperor of Japan were executed by the Emperor's men for fear that they might turn on their masters. This epic struggle came to an end on July 7, when American forces emerged victorious and Japan had lost effective control of the air and seas everywhere in the Pacific.

The capture of Saipan placed the Japanese home islands within range of American B-29 Superfortress bombers and caused certain American Chiefs of Staff to question the value of invading and capturing the Philippines. In their view it was preferable to bypass the Philippines and to commence attacks on

---

2. Bouwer, *Het vermoorde land*, 270.

3. Liddell Hart, *History of the Second World War*, 649.

4. Gilbert, *A History of the Twentieth Century*, Vol. 2, 1933–1951, 591.

places such as Formosa, Iwo Jima and Okinawa. The Philippines invasion nevertheless proceeded in order to salvage American prestige, and especially the prestige of General Douglas MacArthur.[5] Neither Britain, France nor the Netherlands was able to do anything about their prestige in Southeast Asia.

On July 14 the first sustained American bombing raid on Japan occurred. It originated from China and the damage suffered was more symbolic than real. However, four days later Prime Minister Tojo handed in his resignation and Kuniaki Koiso took up the Prime Minister's mantle. The change merely accelerated Japan's bizarre decent into hell, because under Koiso the Japanese armaments industry pursued developments of "sure victory weapons," which meant the large-scale production of "body-smashing" or "special attack weapons" designed to exchange the life of a crew or pilot for a specific military achievement—in other words, suicidal *kamikaze* missions. On the home front, preparations were made for every man and woman to fight off a feared invasion with the help of bamboo spears. Koiso also set in motion steps to improve Japan's diplomatic standing in Asia with vague promises of power devolution.

With that do-or-die mindset, there is no reason to doubt that the hated Westerners and prisoners on Java were now as much part of Japan's military effort as the women and Koreans of Saipan had been. Had we known at that time what had gone on at Saipan, we would perhaps have been less enthusiastic about the prospect of an Allied liberation of Java.

We Get to Know Our Guards

We were oblivious to the demonic scene unfolding over the Marianas archipelago, but were fully preoccupied with the absurdity of the military regulations under which we were now living. The fatalism affecting the women of Saipan, making them choose death in preference to capture, could not be further removed from the mentality of the women of Tjihapit. To people like Emmy and my mother and almost everyone else around us, Japanese rules existed to be circumvented. In this way, the twelve thousand women of Tjihapit (we will ignore the five hundred or so children) gained a high degree of notoriety among the staff of Colonel Nakata overseeing all internment camps from steamy Batavia. The Japanese soldiers made our lives miserable, and we responded in kind. The situation was aggravated by the fact that some of these soldiers now lived permanently amongst us. What previously had been called "the Gentlemen's Office," a two-storey dwelling near the camp gate, was now doubling as a dormitory.

---

5. Liddell Hart, *History of the Second World War*, 649.

Heavy-set Murui, the chief guard, had several soldiers to help him. They were a mixed bag: we had come to know scary Hosjino first, but soon we also got acquainted with Tetsuka, a skinny man, and Ojama, who had a good voice and loved to sing "*Aka tsuki noh inori*" ("Prayer to the New Moon"). There was also a Korean, Yasuda, a good man in the opinion of some observers; he had been a schoolteacher in Seoul and gained fame as an outstanding linguist, not only fluent in Russian, but rapidly mastering Malay and Dutch. Then there was Oshinawa, known as the "Tiger of Tjihapit," whose terrible temper was attributed by some to chronic bouts of *malaria tropica*, and several others, including Iwamoto, Kawamoto (always wearing glasses), and Arai, who sported a moustache and a small beard. What most of them had in common was the expectation of absolute obedience and no hesitation in beating over the head anyone older than ten or so who ignored an order. In their own military training, physical punishment had been a routine pedagogical tool; absolute conformity to a set social pattern an unquestioned priority. "The nail that sticks up gets hit" is a common Japanese saying. This was the way they had been taught to think and such was their approach to us.

Of course, the disaster of Saipan and its subsequent fallout in Tokyo filtered through to General Harada and his subordinates on Java. Diminutive young Amelia came by our house one evening, visibly agitated. "I thought something terrible was going to happen to me this evening. The Jap—"

"What?" my mother asked. "You mean—?"

"Hosjino, you know, that horrible man—well, I was walking past the Jap office and he called me in. When he asked me to come upstairs to his room, I thought, 'this is it!'"

Everyone was listening in petrified silence as Amelia took a deep breath and continued, "He had a radio on, softly, a foreign station, it sounded like a news broadcast. Hosjino asked me something. At first I did not understand him, but then I realized that he wanted to know whether I could understand the language and what was being said. I guess he's worried about the war."

"Serves the bastard right!"

"Could you understand the radio?"

"No, and he let me go—he was also scared. He is not supposed to have a radio."

Notwithstanding the fact that an all-out assault on Java showed no sign of materializing, General Harada's men were tense; the yeast incident was perhaps an illustration of this. One July night Hosjino, doing his late-night rounds on his motorbike to ensure that the blackout order was strictly enforced, also came by the camp bakery, which needed to operate all night and where special precautions were in place. Through a window, he caught sight of a woman setting aside some yeast in a separate tin and hiding it. He got off his bike and stormed into the building, shouting, "*Maling gist, maling gist* [yeast thief]." He ordered the entire bakery staff to form a circle on the darkened street outside. Hosjino, beside himself with rage, tore off his helmet, dragged one of the women into the middle of the circle and began to beat her about the head, shouting "*saitei, teino!*" One of the ladies surreptitiously slipped away to the home of Sister Kramer, a nun, who was in charge of the bakery. Sister Kramer turned up just as the other women lunged at Hosjino, who was on the point of kicking his victim, now lying on the ground and bleeding profusely. The Sister put her arm around Hosjino and led him to her office to give him a cup of good coffee. She had a tiny supply of real coffee set aside for important occasions such as this, and was a very wise lady. This interlude permitted some of the other workers to take the bleeding and limping victim home. When Hosjino had finished his coffee and was ready to dole out more punishment, the woman was gone, so he got on his motorbike and returned to the camp gate. It took several days for the woman to recover. She had indeed stolen some yeast, which is rich in Vitamin B, on behalf of a friend who was then suffering from terrible open sores that would not heal.

Such intemperate reactions on the part of the Japanese soldiers now regularly in our midst made our lives more miserable yet. The biggest, most widely felt irritant under the new regime, however, was the thrice-daily *appel*, or *tenko* (roll-call), a means for ensuring that all prisoners were accounted for; nothing is more important for any prison warden than to prevent escapes. If there was any hint of trouble the camp guards would not hesitate to order an additional *appel*, regardless of the time of day or night and regardless of the weather.

Three times a day, the *hanchos* rang the *appel* bell as they walked up and down the streets of Tjihapit, ordering us out of our houses. We lined up on the street patiently awaiting the arrival of a guard to supervise the operation. As he ambled up in his shiny black boots, with the slap-slap as his left boot was hit by the scabbard of his sword, his revolver always on the ready at his right side, the *kumicho* had to yell out, "*Ki-o tsukete!*" and we all smartly came to attention. It was not always easy for the smaller children to comprehend the seriousness of these military orders and to react in proper martial fashion (figure 11). They preferred to lark about in the back, behind the legs of the adults. Occasionally they were distressed by a sudden bout of sneezing, a coughing fit, or an urgent need to pee. Then, as the representative of His Imperial Highness arrived in the company of the *hancho*, using a suitably stentorian voice the *kumicho* ordered, "*Kerei!*" Now we all bowed from the waist, our hands straight down by our sides, our upper torso at an angle of thirty degrees from the vertical, and stayed in that position until the next order was called, "*Naore!*" and we returned to a stiff upright position. Then the counting could begin, column by column. We soon got the hang of it, shouting out over and over again, "*Ichi! Ni! San! Shi! Go!*" For little children this ritual was not always easy, but the Japanese would never blame the child, just the mother, and there were plenty of incidents where a mother got beaten because of a transgression on the part of her child. That was the way it was in Japan, and whether we liked it or not we were now part of Japan. When all was done, the Japanese officer would thank us by saying "*Yasume!*" Only then could we relax.

The counting could take a long time, as each *hancho* had to account for all those from her *han* who were not present. With so many tasks involving shift-work—in the *dapur*, in the bakery, and in the hospital—the roll-call was always complicated by absences that needed to be explained to suspicious soldiers. There were always some sick people, some who had died, and some who had been hauled off to the *Kempetai*, also referred to as the PID or Police Information Department (a pre-war Dutch institution, gratefully taken over by the new regime). As military parades go, this spectacle was a joke. The women were clad in a variety of garments, many of them patched, and given the scarcity of material and the tropical climate, many were clad in the minimum that decency and our military masters would allow. It was also clear that the few elderly men who had recently arrived with their wives from the Rama camp, were not welcome at *appel* because their presence conflicted with the notion that this was a women's camp; they had to remain discreetly out of sight. Names were called and people answered, but whether it was their own name or that of a friend lying ill in bed was not always clear

Depending on the mood of the supervising camp guard, an indifferent bowing performance could result in a severe physical reprimand—being slapped about the face was the least one could expect. However, it took a considerable length of time for the Europeans to comprehend the seriousness of this mark of disrespect. Bowing had been a problem from the start of the occupation, two years earlier, but after internment we had been mercifully separated from the Japanese by the combination of Indonesian guards and the *gedek*. But since March, we had once again been brought into daily contact with our captors and their strange, intolerant ways. The Japanese saw bowing above all as a simple expression of courtesy. For us, bowing to a common, thuggish soldier was humiliating, while in Japanese eyes the soldiers were the personal representatives of the God-Emperor and demanded especial consideration. We suffered culture shock without realizing it, seeing in its stead an excessive display of Japanese arrogance.

The bowing routine nevertheless prompted a lighter reaction, particularly encouraged by the likes of Corrie Vonk, who accordingly sang:

Bowing is not yet okay
For a week we will have *kerei*
We bow too low, not low enough
We bow too late, or get confused by a cough
Look at the picture that hangs by the gate

227

Or ask a camp lady to demonstrate.

The entire *appel* process was intensely frustrating, and one can only speculate that it was equally resented by the samurai warriors who had to implement it. Sooner or later almost every regulatory transgression occurred, and it now became commonplace to have good behaviour reminders posted on the bulletin board. Thus towards the middle of June the following warnings had appeared, and now remained on the board as a permanent reminder:

CHILDREN AND ADULTS MAY NOT COME NEAR THE GEDEK
MOTHERS WILL BE HELD RESPONSIBLE
NO PORTIONS OF THE GEDEK MAY BE REMOVED FOR
FIREWOOD
DO NOT MAKE HOLES IN THE GEDEK IN ORDER TO SEEK
CONTACT WITH THE OUTSIDE WORLD
DO NOT CLIMB TREES OR ON ROOFS IN ORDER TO SPEAK WITH
MEN OF THE 15TH BAT (WORKING OUTSIDE THE CAMP WALL)
DO NOT STEAL ROOF TILES FOR YOUR OWN USE
IT IS FORBIDDEN TO COME NEAR THE SOUP KITCHEN THAT IS
BEING REPAIRED OR STEAL BUILDING MATERIALS
INFRACTIONS OF THESE RULES WILL RESULT IN BEATINGS OR
WORSE.

By now the implications of that last threat were well known and feared.

A few days later my mother and I encountered a terrible commotion as we were on our way to the soup kitchen: four European men dressed in rags came from a side street carrying a fifth, covered with a white sheet, on a stretcher. They were running in the direction of the camp gate, and behind them came sweating, fat Murui on his bicycle, shouting "*Lekas, lekas!* [hurry!]" It was a terrible sight. That night, while waiting on the street for evening *appel*, our *kepalla* explained what had happened.

"The men had been repairing the *gedek* and one of them did something wrong," she said. "Murui then beat him so severely that he suffered a brain haemorrhage—he was beaten over the head."

"What did he do wrong?"

"A woman had greeted him, and he had said something back," she explained. A muttering, liberally sprinkled with well-known Dutch four-syllable curses, flowed through the crowd of women gathered on the street, before the sight of the approaching soldiers and the *hancho* brought silence in anticipation of the bowing orders.

A week later another shock hit the camp. Mrs. Diepeveen posted a notice on her notice board:

ALL BOYS THIRTEEN AND OLDER AND ALL MEN BELOW 60
HAVE TO PRESENT THEMSELVES AT THE CAMP GATE ON THE
19TH AT 9 A.M. WITH A TIKAR [sleeping mat] AND A SUITCASE.

"Thirteen-year-old boys! That's terrible!" exclaimed Juf, when she heard this. "They can't look after themselves at all at that age."

Emmy knit her eyebrows and commented, "Most of them would not yet have started high school."

Earlier on we had had to contend with the sixteen-year-olds leaving, and that had been controversial, but this new demand from *tuan Nippon* involving much younger boys was alarming. We did not know at the time the contents of Article 8 of the Japanese Regulation for Treatment of Army Internees, which stated that the term *child* referred only to those younger than ten years of age. Boys and girls ten years and older were "adult." To evict boys thirteen years of age was therefore quite consistent with this policy of segregating men from women. It was an act of leniency on the part of our Japanese masters that those younger than thirteen were still allowed to remain with their mothers. Whereas girls stayed with their mothers, no attempt was made to reunite the boys with their fathers; the regulation had not specified this need and those boys were simply cast adrift. A tiny lucky number did get reunited with their fathers, but that was a matter of pure chance. Most of the others never recovered from the ordeal of having to fight for survival in an environment where physical size and deviousness reigned supreme.

On that Friday morning the party of old men and boys assembled at the gate. They were told to leave their luggage outside the gate and to return at a quarter to twelve. Three hours later the 110 boys and forty men reassembled at the gate and were marched out, and that was that. Among them was Marius, the boy we had met soon after our arrival in Tjihapit, and who had then been so badly maltreated by the *Kempetai;* the grim expression on his face betrayed deep anxiety as to what would befall him next. His mother was in tears. "First the rot Japs took my husband, then my money, then my house, and now Marius—I hope he'll be alright."[6]

Henceforth the girls would have to do more of the heavy work, such as lifting the food drums in the *dapur*, bringing the food into the camp, or wheeling the garbage cart out through the gate. Whereas the number of persons needing extra care and those incapable of work rose day by day, the numbers of those able to do the work shrank.

And just to make sure we did not forget our manners, Mrs. Diepeveen posted the following reminder on the bulletin board, reiterating her previous warning that we were not yet bowing correctly, under the heading "The Proper Greeting":

---

6. Marius survived, but suffered for the rest of his life.

WHEN WALKING YOU MUST STOP, OR IF ON A BICYCLE, DISMOUNT.

THE BOW MUST BE MADE TO 30 DEGREES FROM VERTICAL.

THE ARMS SHOULD BE HELD STRAIGHT AT THE SIDES.

THE FIRST PERSON WHO SEES A NIPPON HAS TO SHOUT "KERÉ."

WHEN ON APPEL, OR MARCHING, EVERYONE HAS TO BOW.

WHEN ONE SEES A NIPPON FROM ONE'S HOME YOU MUST ALSO GREET HIM.

YOU ARE NOT ALLOWED TO SING WHILE WALKING ON THE STREET.

The very next day there was another uproar, taking our state of nervous tension up another notch. "House search!" shouted the *hancho*, while furiously ringing her bell, summoning us onto the street. Forbidden items such as books, tools and electrical appliances had to be hurriedly hidden away. If one had just been busy trying to make some tea on the upturned flat iron, the water had to be dumped and the hot iron carefully but quickly returned to its hiding place.

"What on earth are they looking for now?"

A number of *heiho* armed with bamboo staves appeared and cordoned off the street to prevent people from leaving. All residents were summoned out of their homes, and a platoon of Japanese soldiers, accompanied by one of the ladies from the Camp Office, went down the street, entering one house after the other. While the woman glumly looked on, the soldiers ransacked houses, barking comments, emptying the contents of cupboards on the floor, emptying boxes, and roughly sorting through mountains of personal possessions. Since the houses had been tightly packed with people and their belongings, the resulting chaos was indescribable. Some rooms might have been occupied by a single family, a mother and several children, while many others were shared. By the time the inspection team had finished, debris was scattered everywhere, framed photographs crumpled and the glass broken, and clothes and mementoes of happier times littering the floor and trampled underfoot. There had been little enough privacy before this event, and now none remained.

The object of this search was scrap iron to assist the Japanese war effort, but inevitably other things disappeared as well. The soldiers emerged with their arms full of objects like tools and domestic appliances, such as fridges and stoves, which had been used as storage devices and had somehow escaped the previous dragnet. We were then ordered to help carry these items to the main gate. Most of them had been considered permissible so far and were of value for our survival, while items declared contraband had been carefully hidden.

This made the loss of the boxes of tools, table lamps, bicycle parts and axes even more painful.

Hunger

The food situation had become desperate; the additional supplies some had brought with them when they first entered the camp had been exhausted. Our daily ration now consisted of one cup of thin soup, three ounces of rice, half a pound of unpalatable stodgy bread, and twice a week two ounces of sugar and two ounces of salt. The quality and the quantity was well below any reasonable minimum standard, and the results were plain to see: there were widespread complaints of beriberi, thrush, swollen ankles and legs, hideous skin discolouration, malfunctioning taste buds and painful tongues, all indications of vitamin deficiencies.

The greatest scourge of all was dysentery. There were sixty water wells within the boundaries of Tjihapit that before the war had been used for watering gardens; we tried to rely on this questionable source to augment the faltering municipal supply, sometimes with disastrous results. The invitation "to enjoy a cup of tea" with a friend entailed the guest's bringing along the sugar and the hostess attempting to boil water in a saucepan placed on an upturned electric iron. Ironically, tea leaves had ceased to be available in the Preanger, the very centre of one of the most famed tea-producing areas in the world. The Dutch often drink tea without milk but with sugar, so hot water and sugar was the nearest equivalent to the pre-war beverage. However, boiling water on upturned irons was not only inefficient but also strictly prohibited and frequently not thorough, resulting in widespread amoebic dysentery. Visits for a cup of tea had become risky, but nevertheless continued.

On one such visit with Lotte my mother found her in tears. One of her boys was skulking outside by the road, looking miserable.

"What's the matter?" my mother asked Lotte.

"I can't stand it any longer," Lotte replied between sobs and wiping her eyes. "Last night Aleidje [her two-year-old daughter] cried nearly all the time because she was hungry—her stomach cannot stand this food. I spend hours trying to toast and cook the bread so that she can eat it—but all that crying last night and people around me complaining, telling me I am a bad mother." Lotte broke off to blow her nose before continuing, "You are lucky," she sobbed. "Boudy does not really know what's going on, but Rudolf knows and he blames me for not telling him that his father would not come back—he is blaming me for the loss of his dad. I shouted at him because I was so upset, and I know I shouldn't have done it, but I couldn't help it."

Lotte was right; the age of the child made a difference. Rudolf was four years older than I and for me my father had become a sort of myth like St. Nicholas, a person partly make-believe. Some mothers were driven to despair when their child addressed any strange man, even a Japanese soldier, who happened to come into sight as "*pappie*" (Dad).

And so the mothers were assaulted from two directions: on the one hand they faced an uphill struggle to keep what was left of the family intact and to keep alive the notion that one day we would return to a normal existence, while on the other hand they had to fight for sheer physical survival.

It had by now become clear to Mrs. Diepeveen and her management committee that our camp commandant, while perhaps well-meaning, was powerless to ameliorate our plight. On a number of occasions, accompanied by the heads of the kitchens, she had approached Lieutenant Suzuki over the terrible inadequacy of food supplies. The food had been ordered and paid for with our own money, but the delivery usually fell short in terms of both quantity and quality; often entire items of our limited request were simply not delivered. Rice might appear but no vegetables, or vice versa, and there were no refunds. Lieutenant Suzuki had then responded with a suggestion that we had heard before: the camp should cultivate its own vegetables. The military regulations even encouraged this.

Mrs. Diepeveen dismissed this suggestion as absurd, given the lack of suitable space; she instead drew up a petition dated July 31, 2604, and got it signed by the heads of families. It was directed not at Lieutenant Suzuki, but at the Commander-in-Chief of the internment camps throughout Java, Colonel Masayuki Nakata. To have gone over his head to General Harada had briefly been considered, but had been declared unwise. The petition, written in English, read as follows:

> The undersigned persons, all heads of families, interned in camp II in Bandoeng, respectfully beg the attention of Your Excellency for the following: the undersigned are aware of your Excellency's intention to render assistance to the internees in their difficulties and they also know that it is Your wish that everything shall be done to prevent illness and to cure the sick.[7]

Politeness was of course required in such correspondence, even if the message itself was outrageous. She was as well attempting to use what the Japanese refer to as *haragei*, the art of conveying one's thoughts without being explicit and by being elliptical, avoiding the need to say "No." The petition went on to inform His Excellency that the health of the internees was visibly deteriorating, and

---

7. *Tjihapit Boek*, 63.

attributed this sorry state of affairs to the combination of inadequate food, lack of vitamins and excessive labour. It noted that the recently made suggestion to develop kitchen gardens within the camp was impractical because the soil condition was poor and the water supply inadequate. In addition, the total quantity of land available in relation to the number of mouths to be fed was small. What's more, if this suggestion were followed it would only make matters worse, for the women were already weakened by the current labour expectations and it would be a long time before the effort expended might yield any benefits. The missive was accompanied by a second, more detailed statement analyzing the quantity and quality of food in terms of nutrients; such an analysis unfortunately defeated the *haragei* thrust first attempted, because *haragei* excludes analysis. The statistical summary supported the case that daily food deliveries fell well short of the theoretical target of 2,200 calories per person based on an optimal menu of available foodstuffs within the constraints of our daily pecuniary allowance of sixteen cents per person (a chicken could cost nine guilders by now). The shortfall of food shipped into the camp was of the order of twenty-five to thirty percent. About 2,200 calories were ordered per person per day, but the average delivery was less than 1,400.

This elegantly argued and detailed request was never answered by Colonel Nakata, and it is doubtful whether he was even made aware of it. The Japanese army made no allowance for requests or suggestions to be passed from lower ranks to higher ranks. On August 5 Lieutenant Suzuki went as far as he could go, acknowledging the receipt of the petition and promising to give this his fullest attention. That was all that happened.

The water supply was indeed inadequate, even without gardens, and this had been known for over a year. The personnel working in the Bandoeng municipal waterworks were having a difficult time coping with the extraordinary demands made on their system, as the local reservoir and the distribution system had become hopelessly overtaxed. Not only had the civilian population served by the local reservoir increased by a factor of seven, but this facility in addition also served the nearby KMA complex, which now housed a very large Japanese military garrison profligate in its water use. The civic authorities, moreover, were above all anxious to maintain system pressure in those parts of town where the Japanese officers had requisitioned dwellings that happened to be located at a higher elevation. The balance between water supply and demand had been stretched far beyond anything the municipal engineers charged with the pre-war design of the system could have envisaged. We were deprived of such water as was available in order to ensure an adequate supply for the soldiers. In a desperate attempt to compensate, most faucets had been relocated to ground-level, thereby lowering pressure requirements. Filling a kettle for a cup of tea or for a hot wash required lots of patience and always involved queuing. The water supply failed completely on August 27, leaving the entire camp population dependent for a full day on the polluted well-water, with the inevitable consequence of dysentery and a yellow fever epidemic in the following weeks.

The desire to survive nevertheless pushed us to take risks, including the pursuit of illicit trade in goods under, through and over the *gedek*. We were short of food but still had some money and clothing, while the *inlanders* and *Belanda Indo* on the other side of the fence had more food and less clothing.

The refusal of the two population groups to desist from this form of barter drove the Japanese to distraction, and it is a miracle that more people did not get hurt—or worse, killed. To counteract this, Japanese guards regularly patrolled the perimeter of the camp, to deter town dwellers from approaching the *gedek*. One August day two Japanese guards, Murui and Tetsuka, suspecting that some Tjihapit internees were looking for trade opportunities along a certain stretch of *gedek*, disguised themselves as Indonesian women in order to follow up this hunch, and headed for the suspect location. On hearing European voices coming from within, and perhaps noticing a knitting needle poking through the bamboo matting, they closed in on the spot and, placing themselves close to the woven bamboo, whispered, "*Ada spek njonja* [I have bacon, miss]." The women pulled out some bamboo strips, recognized Murui, noted the absence of his sword, and grabbed him; they pulled him through the flimsy bamboo matting and set upon him. Tetsuka then had to come in through the hole to rescue his companion, and the two started chasing the women, who disappeared among the houses. The angry Japanese denounced the women as *orang busuk* (bad people). They also confided that "*lebih baik berkelahi sama Amerika* [they fight better than the Americans]."

While we were gathered on the streets for the evening *appel* on August 22, our *hancho* confided to us that Paris had been liberated; this news was greeted with a muted "Hooray." Rumania, a member of the Axis, found the stars suitably aligned to switch sides, delivering more bad news for Tokyo, a blow especially disappointing for Hirohito, who had equated Rumania, the oil supplier for Germany, with the NEI, the oil supplier for Japan; it was a bad omen, especially for someone who set store by such things.

For some of the Tjihapit women the jubilation over the news from Paris was short-lived. A Japanese military inspection team discovered three homes that had "gas appliances" attached to the city gas system. For a long time the Japanese had harboured suspicions of foul play, because the actual quantity of gas used by the camp far exceeded the volumes that had been authorized for the hospital. These three houses were located on Houtmanstraat, running by the eastern boundary of the camp, as far removed from the main gate and the camp offices as was possible. The "appliances" consisted of curtain rods converted into crude gas burners by having holes poked into them with the help of a nail and a brick, and were attached to the gas supply by means of a bicycle inner tube. For a period of time, the residents had operated a "gas management scheme" whereby each house took turns using the gas burner while a girl was posted to keep watch. This operation had been spotted by chance when a pair of Japanese guards patrolling the back alley had surreptitiously poked their heads above the garden wall.

A Japanese officer now lined the women up in front of their houses, roped them together with their hands tied behind their backs, and beat them with a bamboo pole on their calves, their cheeks and other more unpleasant places, after which they were all marched to the main gate and locked up in a tiny cell. The officer stated that the women should be punished further, but being broad-minded, he offered a choice: (a) three weeks' confinement in a cell, or (b) removal to another camp. The women chose the former. In that way they would at least be able to return to their families and friends. The prospect of incarceration in a cell was grim indeed, a fact well known from the experience of others; that they chose incarceration spoke volumes about our mental state. That evening Mrs. Diepeveen managed to convince Lieutenant Suzuki that the women had been adequately punished, and late at night they were released from their cell, chastened in their respect for the rules under which we were living. When they returned to their dwellings, the gas burners along with some other possessions were gone.

August was also made memorable for a major night-time row between some of the women in Tjihapit. No one knows how it started, but it was symptomatic of our collective state of mind that the slightest disagreement between fellow prisoners could, within a matter of seconds, blow up into a riot that was totally out of proportion to its cause. About sixty or seventy women ended up fighting with one another using sticks and stones. The commotion reached the ears of the guards and at one o'clock in the morning all the *hanchos* and *kumichos* had to appear at the camp office, where they were told to get everyone out on the street for a nighttime *appel*. The lights were turned on in the nearby houses so that the miscreants could be identified and punished.

A week later there was more good news; Lieutenant Suzuki allowed a school to start up, using a church hall as a classroom. I joined a class of about twenty children for two hours of instruction per week, because the room had to be shared by classes of older children for whom this reprieve was more important. For three months we sat at desks left over from pre-war days, and practised our ABC's on old-fashioned slates, because paper, pencils, pens and ink were unobtainable. The slates were interesting because they had been well-used by many predecessors and the wooden frames were battle-scarred. Also, if one pushed the stone "pencil" at a particular angle over the surface of the slate it could make the most ghastly screech. The classroom was still decorated with pictures linking the letters of the alphabet to common objects, mostly with a distinctly local flavour—images of palm trees, tropical fruit, and *kampong* scenes.

We also got permission to send postcards, but this time Mrs. Diepeveen advised us to add our camp numbers "so that we could get a reply." This drew some sarcastic comments from those who had remembered the previous fiasco; they nevertheless complied, for one could not afford to let such an opportunity slip by. The limited range of permitted Malay sentences could include such stilted observations as "our health is excellent" and "it will be wonderful when we see you again," but the physical object, the handwriting, and the knowledge that a loved one had actually held this small card was worth so much—and there were always those tantalizing twenty words, an opportunity to mention names, providing assurances that a loved one or a friend still lived. For my mother, it was difficult to add anything to the standard text because her command of Malay was limited, while it was impossible for poor Juf. Both sought help from Landa, who on the other hand complained bitterly about the frustrating choice she had to make. "I may write only one card, so should it be to my husband or to my son?" It is in retrospect a miracle that so many of those cards reached their destinations, some even as far away as Manchuria; none of the writers knew the addresses of their loved ones and the route inevitably was tortuous. During the previous year a huge civilian movement had taken place all over the archipelago, with the emptying of hundreds of smaller camps and the arbitrary transfer of their occupants to places like Tjihapit, while families were perfunctorily split apart through the periodic eviction of boys and old men to separate destinations; it was a gigantic human winnowing operation. Under these circumstances the writing and sending of a card was a desperate act of faith on the part of the internees.

Our Society Crumbles

While the citizens of Brussels were greeting the Allied army of liberation with flags and breaking out carefully hoarded bottles of champagne, another riot exploded in Tjihapit, this time over the operation of the camp shop, the *toko*. On Saturday, September 2, 1944, a piece of bacon was discovered, buried in the *toko* garden. How the discovery was made is to this day in hot dispute. Was it a stray dog, following a keen sense of smell, or was it the activities of children, aimlessly digging in what used to be a lawn? The discovery was made in the afternoon and quickly caught the ear of the entire camp, the account gathering some additional colour on its way. Soon women and children were running from all corners of Tjihapit to the scene of the "crime," for that was what it was called. It was promptly concluded that Mrs. K., who was in charge of the shop that day, had stolen the bacon and hidden it in the garden. Mrs K. heard the commotion in front of her house and hid under her bed with her children. She was discovered and hauled out to face her accusers, where she protested that the bacon was spoiled. The women, who by now had formed an impromptu vigilante committee, inspected the supposedly stolen goods and concluded that the food was still usable, for the word "inedible" had long before left our vocabulary. A Japanese guard arrived to disperse the crowd, but as soon as he was gone the mob returned, angrier than before, and pelted Mrs. K.'s house with stones. The rioting crowd then moved to the camp office, bearing with them the evidence of the crime.

That night the camp administration issued a statement confirming that some of the bacon received by the *toko* had indeed been declared inedible, and that it was not clear whether or not edible bacon had been stolen, but that what was abundantly clear was that the camp no longer had any confidence in the honesty of the *toko* staff, and the entire staff had therefore resigned. Mrs. Diepeveen was now looking for volunteers who felt that they could command the respect of the camp and could spare the time to serve in the shop. She also admitted that the food situation was very serious and was unlikely get any better, and that loss of confidence in the *dapur* or *toko* workers would only make matters worse. She concluded the message with the statement that "she was not yet aware how the camp commandant would react to the uproar." She warned us to be on our best behaviour.

Lieutenant Suzuki reacted immediately by ordering an additional *appel* late at night, and Mrs. Diepeveen dutifully conveyed this to the *hanchos*, who went up and down the streets with their bells and gongs calling us out, the healthy, the sick and even the tiniest infants. There we all were, once more lined up on the dark streets, waiting to be counted. The *hanchos* warned us against more rioting because the Japanese guards and the commandant were in a devilish mood. Perhaps the guards had heard as well about the intense air attacks now being conducted by the Americans against Japanese positions on the Philippines, the islands where a once victorious Nipponese army had so brutally and successfully slaughtered the American and Philippine defenders. We were not allowed to return indoors until well after midnight and the rumbling of discontent among the camp residents did not cease, because a number of people automatically linked the *toko* staff to the overall administration of the camp. They argued that it was an autocratic set-up and that more democracy was required.

Perhaps Lieutenant Suzuki had noticed our morale problem, for a few days later he arranged a film show for our entertainment, to be held in the open air on the Oranje Plein. We were advised that the entertainment would not be suitable for young children, so those younger than sixteen were forbidden to attend, and furthermore, since it was impossible to accommodate more than a thousand viewers on the square, attendance would be rationed to one in ten adults. Very few went to see the movie, since those who could go were skeptical of the entertainment value, while older children, who were desperate to see a film, any film, were forbidden to attend; the fact that they were forbidden made the film all the more interesting for them. Those who went afterwards confirmed that it was a propaganda film, showing heroic Nipponese soldiers fighting to protect Asia from Anglo-American aggression and showing how the European population was enjoying itself in the protected areas set aside for them. There were scenes of European men playing volleyball or lounging in deck chairs, and women enjoying cups of coffee and chatting to one another, and all of course were smiling! One did not know whether to laugh at the absurdity of this film or cry over the way we were being taunted by our military masters.

A day or so later Mrs. Diepeveen, anxious to deal with the morale problem, asked *han* delegates to attend a meeting where measures to improve the administration would be discussed. The delegates were to be chosen democratically at meetings of all *han* residents on Tuesday, September 5. Nothing came of this initiative and the *toko* remained shut; who dared to shoulder the responsibility?

That same evening, however, there was more good news to relieve the gloom. The Allies had liberated most of Belgium and were within kilometres of the Dutch border, with the battle for Arnhem about to begin.

Prime Minister Koiso continued to pursue the tentative colonial devolution policy, and during those first days of September held secret discussions in Tokyo regarding the future independence of Indonesia. There is no doubt that the prospect of the imminent liberation of the Netherlands affected the timing of this development. It was not an easy policy shift to introduce and there were strongly entrenched diehard positions in Tokyo, particularly among senior navy officers who refused to countenance such a move; the *nanjo* (the southern ocean) had largely been "their" theatre. Koiso nevertheless made a declaration in the Japanese Diet that "Indonesia will in future gain independence as a member of the Greater East Asia Co-Prosperity Sphere."[8] An unspoken qualifier was that Japan would remain the centrepiece, the hub of such a commonwealth. That optimistic assessment was made while the runways on Saipan were being repaired for imminent use by the American B-29 bombers. A watered-down version of this policy shift appeared in the *Kan Po*:

NOTIFICATION OF THE SUPREME COMMANDER REGARDING
THE DISPLAY OF THE INDONESIAN FLAG, AND THE SINGING
OF THE NATIONAL ANTHEM "INDONESIA RAJA."

---

8. van Velden, *De Japanse burger kampen*, 317.

The Japanese Imperial Army permits the display of the Indonesian flag. It may only be displayed jointly with the flag of the Japanese Empire. When jointly displayed, the Japanese flag should be on the right when viewed from the building, and the Indonesian flag should be on the left.

A second announcement ensured that the Indonesian flag should be no larger than the Japanese flag, should be raised no higher up the flagpole, and might only be raised after the Japanese flag had been raised.

All the while the Japanese army was continuing its efforts to prepare Indonesia for the anticipated Allied landings. A key element of their strategy was the completion of the Pakanbaru railway line in Sumatra, which would improve the transportation link between Indonesia and Singapore, because Pakanbaru, located on the swampy north coast of Sumatra, was the nearest Sumatran port to Singapore; with the loss of control over the sea lanes, these land links gained strategic significance. The work had been commenced in 1943 and was now still months from completion. As with the Burma railway the Japanese were totally dependent on slave labour for the task, a remarkable situation given the sophisticated and impressive military hardware Japan had employed in its victorious campaigns. Due to the horrendous conditions under which the construction work was being conducted, and the high resultant loss of life, the labour force needed constant replenishment, with the associated logistical costs. Captured Allied soldiers and Indonesian *romushas* (so-called volunteers) were the slaves.

On September 14, an aged, rusty freighter, the 5,065-ton *Junyo Maru*, lay moored in the harbour of Tandjong Priok awaiting a fresh supply of labourers for the Pakanbaru project. Two groups of people would make this fateful voyage: one group had white skin and the other had brown skin. Justinus Heldring, the young Stellenbosch University swimming champion who had accompanied us from South Africa on our voyage from Durban to Tandjong Priok, found himself once more on this waterfront, having just arrived from Soerabaja in the company of Hans Lüning, who has left an account of the scene:

> We had to wait for quite a long time while the heat constantly increased. There was no shade to be found anywhere and food was not being provided. It was fortunate that we could get some drinking water from a tap along the quay. During the morning, thousands of *romushas* passed by. It was a pitiful sight to see all these poor devils struggling along, looking like skeletons. They were all chased into the hold in front of the bridge of one of the ships moored alongside the quay.

During our walk from the station to the harbour, as well as now that we were sitting there looking around us while waiting, we were struck by the desolate impression this once so thriving port made on us. Stacks of old iron were lying all over the place: piping, tubing, sheeting, boilers, bridge-railings, fences, and ships' masts, everything mixed up. It was all obviously waiting to be shipped to Japan. In the harbour nearest to us were, apart from the two black-painted ships, another two wooden boats. They were floating high on the water and with their terse shapes, looked heavy and unwieldy. We took them to be Japanese trawlers. For the rest there was, as far as we could see, not a single ship in the whole harbour. There was no trace of the so-called Greater East Asia Co-Prosperity Sphere.

At four o'clock in the afternoon, after having waited about ten hours in the glaring sun, we were to get moving and were driven up the gang-plank of one of the moored ships. This gang-plank led to the well-deck behind the funnel. As far as we could discover the ship was not named. The number 652 had been painted in large figures on boards placed on either side of the funnel. After the liberation I happened to find out that the ship was the S.S. *Junyo Maru*. The ship was in a state of complete neglect; everywhere the rust had set in and much of the metal had rusted through completely.

We were ordered to stack our luggage up against the railings, after which, with lots of shouting and brandishing of sticks, we were driven into the holds like cattle. Although I was still carrying my backpack, I managed to get down via narrow wooden stairs. Approximately two-and-a-half metre down, I reached a floor covered with tarpaulins. Along both sides of this hold, three- or four-high rows of bunks had been constructed, all about two metres deep. The distance between the bunks varied from fifty to eighty centimetres.

Notwithstanding the fact that the hold was already completely packed, more and more people were being driven down. At last all bunks were taken and on the floor one could only sit shoulder to shoulder with one's knees pulled up.

Lüning goes on to describe in great detail the awful conditions, before concluding the description of the vessel's load:

And that is how we sat there waiting for our departure. In both holds in the fore-part of the ship…and on the front deck about 4,500 *romushas* were crammed together. Lodged in both holds three and four were about 2,200 POWs—all told some 6,700 men.

The ship spent the next day waiting for its navy escorts while at anchor under a blazing sun in the roads of Tandjong Priok; it then left for a destination unknown to any of the passengers. It was only when the ship passed by the landmark volcanic island, Krakatoa, that the shipmates understood that they would be disembarking on the southwest coast of Sumatra, probably at Padang. But a British submarine, aware only that this was a Japanese freighter, torpedoed the *Junyo Maru*. Of the 6,700 slave labourers on board, only 880 were rescued by the Japanese navy and safely delivered to their horrendous destination. Justinus Heldring drowned while attempting to assist another victim. Of the 680 European survivors of the shipwreck only ninety-six survived the subsequent hell of the Pakanbaru railway. Of the two hundred Indonesian *romushas* who had been rescued and were then forced to work on the project, none survived.[9]

On the very day that the *Junyo Maru* was being loaded with labourers, Mrs. Diepeveen posted an ominous warning on her bulletin board, announcing that more men and boys would be called up in the near future. Two days later she was able to provide more details: "BOYS ELEVEN YEARS AND UP, AS WELL AS MEN OVER SIXTY YEARS OLD, WILL BE SENT ELSEWHERE."

My mother and Juf could not hide their dismay at this development. "Those are just little children!" Juf cried out. "How can they do such a terrible thing?"

Emmy pointed out that these children would normally enter the sixth grade of primary school. "They are barely out of kindergarten," she exclaimed.

My mother knew of a boy that age who still was not able to sleep through the night without the risk of bedwetting. "Rudolf will have to go, won't he?" she commented.

"There's no chance of him ending up with his father in camp—none of the sons of soldiers stand a chance of being with their fathers," Emmy responded. "He'll be on his own—poor child."

"How terrible, how awful for Charlotte," my mother sighed.

The rest of the day Juf went around the house with moist eyes. The idea of having birthdays and becoming older suddenly struck me as an unpleasant and frightening prospect.

The alarming situation electrified the camp. Groups of women immediately made their way to the Ladies' Office, where all agreed that something ought to be done, that this was too awful. "Surely the Japanese could not be so inhuman! Perhaps there is a mistake—you know how stupid these soldiers are!" The women agreed to organize a protest to deliver this message of outrage to the camp commandant's office. One of the women present, who had a penchant for the dramatic, pointed out that white was the traditional Japanese Buddhist colour associated with mourning and death. "All the ladies in the camp should

---

9. Lüning, *The Sinking of the Junyo Maru*.

join the protest dressed in white." An hour later hundreds of women, including Mrs. Diepeveen, all dressed in white, began to congregate in front of the Gentlemen's Office, lining themselves up silently, like ghosts. When Murui, the head guard, finally appeared, Mrs. Diepeveen read a prepared statement, a petition for leniency. Agnes Bouman translated the message into Japanese as best she could. Murui listened politely, and assured the ladies that he had known about this for many months, and had so far successfully managed to postpone this measure, but now it had to happen. "The boys have to learn to fend for themselves," he explained. That evening Amelia dropped by, and related some discussions that she had had with Agnes around this matter.

"Agnes said some strange things in the office," she began. "She says that Japanese boys are told that nothing is better than dying for the Emperor. She says the Japanese actually honour death. Apparently she had seen a play when she was in Japan. In the play the hero committed suicide."

"Some Italian operas are like that, aren't they?" my mother commented.

"Well, yes," Amelia continued, "but Agnes says it's different—in Japan suicide is not a tragedy but a celebration. She says the hero's friend stood by with a sword to behead him at just the right moment—when he was in greatest pain."

"Did Agnes like it?" Emmy sounded incredulous.

"No, Agnes confessed it had made her sick, but the Japanese audience loved it."

The Japanese seemed very strange indeed. For the time being there was no further word about the boy issue, and we were left in anxious suspense.

But this was not the only source of grief. All through these months death notices had become a daily occurrence; no one died just of old age, for the grim reaper responded to the urgings of dysentery, beriberi, hepatitis and jaundice and many sick also had open sores that would not heal. Sometimes the deaths were exceptionally tragic. On September 30, for instance, Mrs. Liesker died, leaving behind six children of whom the three older boys had already been sent away. Seven days later a large number of postcards arrived in the camp, including cards from this woman's husband and also from one of her sons. Who would look after her children remaining in the camp and ensure that they got their fair share of food? When would her husband and sons be informed that their letters, if delivered on time, might have encouraged her to fight for her life more vigorously? There had been an orphanage in the camp since the beginning of the internment, but it was now growing at an accelerating pace.

The total number of sick in the Tjihapit hospital had grown steadily over the last months; Elsa was accordingly kept busy delivering pharmaceuticals to the hospital and to the various houses where she had patients, but her employment soon came to an end. One day, she returned from the pharmacy to the camp gate with eggs intended for an extremely sick patient in the hospital.

The eggs had been provided by the pharmacy as liquid in a dark brown bottle labelled *emulsio ovorum*. Unfortunately the bottle dropped out of the bag during the inspection and broke on the pavement. Because the spilled fluid did not look like medicine but like food, the guards got excited and summoned the *Kempetai*, always on the lookout for troublemakers. They were as quick in drawing conclusions as they were in drawing their sabres, and before Elsa realized what was happening, they had struck her with the flat of a blade, while demanding an explanation. She got hit so hard on her head that she fell unconscious to the ground; her left foot was bleeding heavily where a sword had struck her. A lady from the office found a velo, our camp ambulance, and Elsa was carried to the hospital, where the nuns tended to her wounds, expending valuable sulpha compounds to prevent tropical ulceration, by now a commonly occurring scourge. Mrs. Diepeveen thereafter appointed another person to perform Elsa's essential medicine-delivery task. Elsa was fortunate in that her Achilles tendon had not been severed, but she lost the hearing in one ear and for years after the war needed operations on her left foot.

Early in the morning of October 24 news of another planned hunger demonstration rippled throughout Tjihapit. This coincided with an outbreak of dysentery in the camp, adding to our troubles and causing the improvised hospital, which had been moved several times since its inception, to be filled to overflowing. Emmy was working in the kitchen, but my mother went to the Orchidee Plein, a small square in the middle of Tjihapit, to join the protest. The occasion had been organized by Mrs. Gulik, a tall woman who now tried to address the gathering crowd, standing on a box and flanked by a number of supporters, among whom was Charlotte.

"We must be orderly when we go to the Gentlemen's Office!" she announced, straining her voice to be heard. "These mothers have agreed to help me deliver our message," she continued, gesturing to Charlotte and the other five or six standing by her. She got down and the procession got under way, with my mother following near the rear. Halfway down the Bengawalaan the guard Murui suddenly turned up on his motorbike. He stopped, got off and shouted, "*Tidak boleh, pigi, pigi!* [not allowed, go away!]," thereby bringing the procession to a halt. Mrs. Gulik, either unaware of the mental state of the Japanese or perhaps indifferent, straightened her back, drew herself to her full six-foot height, thereby taking advantage of being able to look down on Murui, and said something to him. Murui then led Mrs. Gulik and her companions to the Japanese camp office, while the others slowly followed at a distance.

Suddenly two Japanese soldiers armed with staves came running through the gate and indiscriminately beat the women who had gathered on the Oranje Plein. This commotion drew Mrs. Diepeveen out of the Ladies' Office in time to see the women fleeing from the scene. The soldiers returned to the gate, but then some women came back, this time shouting insults at their retreating backs. This brought the soldiers back in, and one had drawn his revolver and was waving it in the air. Mrs. Diepeveen, by now shaking with fear, climbed onto a chair she had dragged out and in a hoarse voice told the women to go home. "Mrs. Gulik has delivered her message," she shouted, "we can't do any more." This brought the protest to an end, but Mrs. Diepeveen immediately posted a warning on the notice board: "ACCORDING TO THE MILITARY REGULATIONS THE DEATH PENALTY APPLIES WHEN RIOTING OCCURS." Appended to this notice was the order that all those who participated in the demonstration would have to dig vegetable plots for punishment; a list of names had to be handed in the next day.

Charlotte turned up at our house the next day with her head covered with a piece of material.

"What happened?" Emmy asked.

"The damned Japs shaved us and locked us up. Mrs. Gulik did not even have a chance to deliver her message—it was terrible," she added, wiping a tear.

"The *Kempetai*?" Emmy asked in shock.

"No. We were locked up in an old *gudang* that had no roof and no windows. A guard asked us if we wanted food, but nothing ever came—they were just goading us. All we had to sleep with were some bricks on which to lay our heads. Luckily two Ambonese[10] took pity on us and brought us food, late at night, but they had to avoid the Japs, so one stood guard while the other climbed over the wall to give it to us. I owe my life to those Ambonese," she added, choking back tears.

This protest happened to coincided with the battle of Leyte Gulf, a last-ditch Japanese attempt to thwart the American landings on the Philippines. For the first time the Japanese resorted to *kamikaze* suicide missions. The previous day Admiral Onishi, a famous First World War veteran, had addressed the twenty-six volunteers with the following words:

> Japan is in grave danger. The salvation of our country is now beyond the power of the Ministers of State, the General Staff, and lowly commanders like me. It can come only from spirited young men like you. You are already Gods, without earthly desires.[11]

This first *kamikaze* mission, directed against the American ships, killed a total of 147 men, but did not disable a single ship; the tactic, however, created consternation among the American sailors. Never before had they seen persons pursuing suicide on such a scale, and then with such bizarre concentration, able to ignore the thousands of rounds of anti-aircraft fire through which they had to navigate their planes; but then the American sailors had never been

---

10. From the island of Ambon.

11 Gilbert, *A History of the Twentieth Century*, Vol. 2, 1933–1951, 622.

indoctrinated with the Zen philosophy that made these Japanese airmen so focused and single-minded. This naval encounter came to a climax on October 25, when nineteen American torpedoes and seventeen bombs finally sank the goliath-like battleship *Musashi*. No American vessel would have been able to withstand an assault from its eighteen-inch guns.

Radio Jakarta now had to admit that the wartime situation had become critical; the resulting tension was showing everywhere. In Bandoeng, street fights between *Belanda Indo* and Indonesian youths became commonplace. Some *Belanda Indo* youths, reacting to the growing evidence that the Eurasian population was no longer welcome on the island, formed a secret society with the threatening name "the Black Snake." It seemed as well that discipline among the Japanese was deteriorating, for there were now almost nightly incidents of drunken Japanese soldiers and civilians roaming the Bandoeng streets and abusing Indonesian and Chinese women.

8. TRANSPORTATION

Sacrifices in the service of the Chrysanthemum throne were required not only of an entire generation of young Japanese men, but also of the conquered subjects. The original "real" prisoners of war, the Allied soldiers, had long before been deployed in various army projects, such as railway and airport construction, or were labouring in the mines of Manchuria, Japan and Formosa. Now it was our turn.

Since March 1944 the Japanese army had been planning a role to be played by the civilian prisoners of war to thwart an invasion by allied forces. In Tjihapit, we had noticed only indirect evidence of this plan being implemented, in the form of a rising population; Tjihapit had become a human holding tank, a staging post. Now it was Tjihapit's turn to feel the full impact of the plan, and it involved a huge exercise in logistics.

On October 26, 1944, Yasuda startled the Ladies' Office with the demand for a list of five hundred names of persons to be transported. It was a surprise because hitherto Tjihapit had served as a preferred destination for European and suspect *Belanda Indo* women from all over Java. The news quickly spread through the camp, accompanied by our imagined rationale: "They are punishing us for our complaints, the fights and the demonstrations." It was difficult to find any other explanation, and Yasuda, when asked, either did not know or was not telling.

Amelia, one of the office women, was now charged with this task. She assumed that conditions at the destination, wherever it might be, could only be worse, and accordingly set about selecting those who might best be able to deal with more hardship. She therefore started out by selecting single, younger women. Hardly had this task been completed when another request came to the office; the number should be increased to 3,700 people. Any hint of an explanation or destination remained absent. An additional instruction demanded that "Women between the ages of eighteen and thirty-five were to be left behind." The initial list therefore had to be revised, and the new requirement further complicated the attempt to keep families whole.

A few days later, Juf received notice that she was to join this transport. She was in tears when the truth sank in that my mother and I were not to be part of it. Our family group would be split up. My mother promptly went to the camp office to complain.

"I am sorry, Mrs. van Oort, but we did not know she was your mother-in-law," one of the office workers apologized. Juf's name was therefore scrubbed off the list and another person was identified to replace her. Later that morning we heard via our *kumichos* that travel arrangement details were now on the notice board. The baggage allowance instructions read as follows:

ADULTS: TWO SUITCASES, ONE BACKPACK.

CHILDREN: ONE SUITCASE, ONE BACKPACK.

PER PERSON: TWO BLANKETS

TO BE SHARED BETWEEN TWO FAMILIES: A TIN WASH BASIN AND ONE BUCKET.

BOYS TEN YEARS AND OLDER, AND ALL OTHER BELONGINGS, WILL BE LEFT BEHIND.

There, in black and white, was the dreaded instruction that boys ten years and older had to go their own way, lumped together in this notice with all other mementoes of the past and discardable objects. The White Protest had been utterly in vain. A murmur went up among the women as they broke into little groups to discuss this news. Questions were showered on our *kumicho*: "How? When?" But she knew nothing more. The news was devastating, because it did not take much imagination to foresee the fate of these youngsters, given what had so far happened to us.

From the beginning of the Japanese occupation, two and a half years before, we had been subjected to a cruel process through which families tainted by European influence were torn apart; first the husbands had to go, and then the older and younger male members. We were being put through a monstrous race, sex and age sieve. In many ways, however, this last call was the worst of all. Since the change-over to military rule in March, another 1,800 souls had arrived, while eight hundred had left. The arrivals had been a mix of men, women and children. Those who had left had been almost exclusively older men and teenage boys, ordered out over the weeks and months in small groups. Leaving meant saying goodbye to loved ones, possibly forever. Now it was the children's turn.

The Japanese soldiers themselves had left their homes long before, since many of them had fought in China; this made us wonder whether family ties meant anything to them? Was this utter indifference to feelings purely a manifestation of military policy, or did it reflect Japanese society as a whole? With the benefit of hindsight and access to the Japanese military orders of the time, we now know that Murui had been right all along. The move to separate boys ten years and older from their mothers had been authorized under Japanese military regulations from the very outset of the occupation and appears to have reflected Japanese domestic social attitudes at that time. What was deemed good for Japanese boys was also deemed appropriate for European boys. Given the low opinion that the Japanese had formed of European soldiers' fighting capabilities, they were, in their own eyes, doing us a favour.

The wives and children of the military prisoners, the POWs, did not even know that most of their loved ones had left Java. There had been indications and rumours of large-scale transport of men, but the fact that they had become slave labourers, working under the most appalling conditions and scattered over a huge part of Asia, was unknown to us. For the unfortunate soldiers' wives in our midst it was perhaps a blessing that they did not know the awful truth about the whereabouts and condition of their husbands and sons; that knowledge might have robbed many of the will to survive. Hope for better times in the future was immensely important in sustaining us through the difficult present. That hope was regularly nourished with snippets of news about Allied advances.

As we awaited the first transport, the rumour mill feeding our anxieties and fears went into high gear. Some speculated that the Japanese intended to shoot us in revenge for the defeats they were suffering at the hands of the Americans. Others opined that the Japanese were going to send us to Borneo, release us in the jungle and let us die.

The origin of this rumour, which circulated around other women's and children's camps as well and was fervently believed, remains unknown. There were a small number of people in Tjihapit who had been to Borneo, either accompanying their husbands on pre-war business or as nurses and teachers, but there was little that they could say about the island and its mysteries. While living there they had kept themselves to the comforts of the clubs, the swimming pools and the tennis courts that had catered to the European community and that were located solely in the outskirts of half a dozen coastal towns, always at the edge of the immense jungle, and never in the jungle itself. One went from home to the shops, then to the clubs, sometimes via the school to pick up the children, and then back home.

Someone knew of a nun who had been in the interior, but nuns said little. Anneke, perhaps seventeen at the time, recalled her school geography lessons, and with a serious face explained that the interior beyond the coastal swamps was an impenetrable jungle "where the orangutan swung from tree to tree." *Orangutan* was a bastardization of the Malay *orang hutan* or "jungle man." The jungles were also inhabited by Dayak Indians, who still hunted with blowpipes, silently launching lethal darts from the undergrowth. Their longhouses were festooned with skull trophies celebrating their prowess. These Dayaks were mostly gentle folk, but they were not beyond cannibalism or head-shrinking when dealing with those perceived as a threat to their lifestyle. Abandonment in the jungles of Borneo ensured what appeared to us to be the most horrible, devilishly inhuman death that could be devised.

By the end of October, 1,300 people had been given transport notices. This first group had interpreted the travel instructions to mean that they could take as much with them as they could carry and began the process of reducing their possessions to fit this requirement.

"Can my baby carriage be taken along, and what about my mattress?" a young mother called Hannie asked our *kumicho*, who was on her way to the Ladies' Office to seek clarification as to who should now do her job, since she herself was to go.

The *kumicho* returned a while later with a positive answer: "You may take along the pram if there is a baby in it, and mattresses are also allowed." The young woman then experimented, packing extra items along with the infant.

The bad news was that each person could take only ten guilders with them and that the remainder should be deposited with the Yokohama *Specie* Bank. "There will be a luggage inspection before you leave," the *kumicho* added ominously.

Many of the inhabitants of Tjihapit, particularly those who before the war had lived in Bandoeng, had so far successfully retained most of their valuable and moveable pre-war possessions, and our houses accordingly were crammed. Almost everyone due to leave now had to make difficult choices—between things of sentimental and practical value. A lively trade in containers immediately sprang up so that residual supplies of oats, sugar and rice could be packed for the journey. It was a heartbreaking process for many; they had gone through so much to hang on to these material reminders of happier pre-war times—the photo albums, the collection of records, the family silver and crystal—and now they were forced to abandon these heirlooms with the prospect of an unknown, frightening future. Not only had these goods been a source of emotional comfort, but they also represented a valuable potential means of acquiring additional food, and in the case of furniture, firewood. Everywhere there was furious activity improvising backpacks from scraps of material and festooning them with pockets.

"Do you think they will weigh the suitcases?" Hannie wondered out loud, for she had to pack and carry not only for herself, but for her child as well. Her suitcase, held together by leather straps and clothesline, was very heavy.

"Nothing has been said about weight," her friend replied.

On Tuesday, October 31, Mrs. Diepeveen announced that all those identified for transport were to appear with their *barang* at Oranje Plein in two days' time for a "dress rehearsal."

That day, the prospective travellers, accompanied by friends, made their way from all corners of the camp to the Oranje Plein, where pandemonium broke out. We stayed away, but Ank afterwards explained what happened. She had offered to help Adri, whose sister Klaske "was really too sick to travel," Ank said. "Adri and Klaske seem to have lost all relatives in the fighting in eastern Java. It was chaos at the Oranje Plein, with Tetsuka and Murui shouting at Mrs. Diepeveen and Mrs. Diepeveen shouting at us (figure 12). They finally managed to get everyone and their *barang* organized into two huge groups—a Red and Blue group—and I guess they will travel separately."

"How many are going?"

"I don't think Mrs. Diepeveen knows yet. I got our *kumicho* to explain to Mrs. Diepeveen and Murui that Klaske is not in a fit state to travel, and Murui, who seems to be in charge, then insisted on finding a replacement. Someone from the Ladies' Office then complained about the difficulty she had had in preparing the list, and told Adri off for not giving an earlier warning about Klaske's medical condition. She said they would have to find two new names, because Klaske could not stay behind if Adri went. So then damned Murui insisted that if no substitute could be found then Klaske would have to go on a stretcher."

"Did he say where they are going?"

"No, he says he doesn't know."

"He knows—he just wants to bug us."

"What did they do with the *barang*?"

"*Barang*? Oh, that was another drama. Murui decided that there was too much, and particularly too many buckets and baths, and he said that only one backpack was allowed per person. He then got some men to carry all the luggage approved for transport out of the gate, to be loaded on trucks that turned up—it will be a miracle if half of all that stuff doesn't get stolen. He said the *barang* would be sent ahead to the unknown destination—can you believe it?"

"And the rest?"

"They took it back home with them, but they don't know when they are supposed to go. So Klaske and Adri are back with only those belongings that were refused by Murui or that they were carrying for the journey itself. They don't even have a bed to sleep on now."

"Did you see what happened to *tante* [aunt] Truus?" asked a woman who had just joined us and turned out to be Ank's *kumicho*.

"Murui had been sorting out what could and what could not go. With his stick he hit *tante* Truus's bag so hard it flew open and her chamber pot rolled over the grass. Murui got so mad he kicked it. *Tante* Truus ran after the pot to get it back, and Murui drew his sword and ran after the woman. It was funny," she added with a subdued giggle.

"But not for *tante* Truus," Ank added dryly.

"Lieutenant Suzuki came but did not stay long—I guess the spectacle was below his dignity. Anyway, with Murui, Hosjino, Tetsuka and the others we had enough Japs."

"Then everyone got organized into travelling groups of sixty to sixty-five people," Ank continued.

"Why?"

"For the buses, we think. They were also given new numbers."

Hannie had in the meantime also returned to our house with her baby and the perambulator, piled high with rejected travel possessions. The child clearly was in great distress, as was its mother, now close to tears and wailing, "How can I possibly look after the child for a journey to an unknown destination? I will have to carry him and somehow have to find a bed because the baby carriage was not allowed."

Five days later, the Red Group was ordered to the main gate. This time it was serious, and a cloud of depression hung over the camp as the travellers, loaded down with their travel packs and accompanied by a number of grim-looking young boys and well-wishers, trooped down the streets towards the Oranje Plein. We gathered by the side of the road to see them off. Ank and Elsa came along to support Klaske and help Adri with her *barang*. Emmy had gone to the kitchen early to help the staff prepare extra rations for the journey: sticky bread with whatever flavouring they could find—enough for five meals, for Murui had indicated that the trip might take forty-eight hours. Hannie had managed to cook some rice, which she had packed in her child's potty, hoping thereby to avoid a replay of Murui's anger. Now she set out with her baby in an improvised *selendang* strapped to her chest and the infant mercifully asleep. By chance my mother had heard that Vera Weeda and her children were in this party, and so we also set off for the gate hoping to see her and say goodbye. We had shared internment in this huge camp for almost a year without knowing it.

On the Oranje Plein it again was chaos, although my mother managed to make brief contact with Vera.[1] Murui was rushing about in a foul temper and swearing profusely. Again the travellers were lined up and again he inspected all of the baggage. One woman had tied two backpacks together, but the rope gave way, and another person hurriedly picked up the second backpack. Using a whip, Murui knocked a handbag out of the hands of an elderly lady. Someone else lost her food parcel for the trip through a similar blow. "That's for my children," she protested, but on top of the food parcel there was an item of clothing, and Murui stuffed it into her mouth, shouting "*makan, makan lekas* [eat, eat quickly]."

After completing the roll call, Murui ordered the party out through the gate. There were tearful, heart-wrenching farewells between three bewildered young boys and their departing family members. It was impossible to imagine how they might one day be reunited amidst all the chaos: it was like a death sentence.

---

1. The family survived the war, attempted to restart life on Java and finally left. Inga ended up living in California.

Outside the gate the 650 travellers were ordered to form rows, mostly behind the *gedek* and out of sight, leaving the farewell party staring in disbelief at the gate through which they had disappeared. Then, with a creaking of its rusty hinges, the great gate slowly swung shut.[2]

On Tuesday, November 6, the Blue Group left. Murui once more oversaw the departure, but this time ordered the send-off party away from the main gate before the party had left. Nothing more was heard from any of these former companions—they simply disappeared.

Perhaps Murui's exceptional bad temper reflected the bad news coming from beyond the shores of Java. Far away, in the United States, Franklin Delano Roosevelt was re-elected for an unprecedented fourth term of office, demonstrating a degree of political stability on the part of Japan's American adversary that contrasted sharply with the rapid succession of Japanese prime ministers in politically dysfunctional Tokyo. In addition, Japanese cities were now coming under daily bombardment from planes using the former Japanese airfields on Saipan. Japanese scientific advances were also suffering, for a meeting of top scientists in Tokyo had made it clear that Japan's efforts to make an atomic bomb would not yield results in time to influence the outcome of the war.[3]

The departure of these two groups of people left us deeply depressed. The sudden growth in numbers of orphans, for that is what the boys now left behind had become, left deep scars on all of us. In this and in other ways, the shared suffering had melded the Tjihapit population of thirteen thousand people—in other words, a medium sized town—into an extraordinary community, or perhaps into a giant family. As in all families, there was friction and there were squabbles, but after two years of internment, these had become like family squabbles.

To a remarkable extent the individuals thrown together in this camp community during those two years had also established, from scratch, a new civil society, catering to every conceivable social need in one improvised way or another. In addition to the hospital and shop, there was a technical maintenance group (electrical and plumbing), a bicycle repair group, a hygiene task force, police and even a quasi-judicial organization that could impose standards of acceptable conduct.

---

2. Adri and her sister, Klaske, ended up in Struiswijk, a prison located outside Batavia. The thirty-six-hour journey (in normal times it would have taken only four hours) was a further setback for Klaske. For another couple of months Adri nursed her sister, but the latter was finally sent off to the St. Vincentius Hospital camp, on her own, to die.

3. Gilbert, *A History of the Twentieth Century,* Vol. 2, 1933–1951, 625.

The recent stresses and strains had left a debilitating mark on this camp society, but we struggled on. Now, suddenly, there was a new need: caring for abandoned boys. For the time being, friends looked after them, but Mrs. Diepeveen sought out women willing to take care of the boys and to ensure that they continued to be accounted for in the soup kitchen roster, while the teachers of the provisional schools vowed to provide them with a rudimentary education. Mrs. van Dijk, our former neighbour, whose eldest boy, Marius, had departed in July, offered her services, while continuing to be burdened by the care of her remaining two children. But the respite was short-lived.

Two days later the *kumichos* sounded their gongs and bells; it was another announcement on the notice board: "THE CAMP WILL BE LIQUIDATED AT THE EARLIEST OPPORTUNITY." Below the message, Mrs. Diepeveen advised all in the camp to check the notice board regularly for more news. A second notice announced that each *han* was immediately obliged to deliver twelve wash basins to the camp gate. The number of these galvanized iron items that had turned up during the dry run the previous week had impressed Lieutenant Suzuki, and as he was still trying to meet scrap iron delivery targets, he might as well collect the excess basins now.

The very next day, the Ladies' Office sent notices to various houses regarding another transport. Two friends were notified: Charlotte Kerkhoven with the remnants of her family, and Landa Bosman, who had to bear the fact that two of her children, twelve-year-old Rob and eleven-year-old Friso, would be left behind. Friso was lucky, having an older brother to keep him company, and a relative who was not going promised Mrs. Bosman that she would do her best for the two boys. As usual there was speculation as to why these particular people had been chosen. A pattern was sought: was it by *kumi*? alphabetically? by *han*? by nationality?

The rumour that we were being sent to the jungles of Borneo for punishment refused to die down. The reason was simple: no other explanation was available. Having concluded that it simply had to be punishment, it followed that the punishment, and hence the Japanese who imposed it, were unjust. We had moved up the scale from beatings to a horrible death sentence, and we had also become accustomed to the lack of rationale for anything happening to us. Fear therefore stalked us every day, fear of staying under this vicious regime and fear of going away to an unknown destination.

The next group of seven hundred travellers had to present themselves at the camp gate at eight o'clock in the morning on Sunday, November 12. This time each person was allowed no more than one suitcase weighing twenty kilograms, a mattress or *tikar*, and bedding consisting of *kelambu* (mosquito netting) and blankets; only one backpack was allowed per family. This was much less than the previous two groups had been allowed to take. Landa Bosman complained to the camp office that Roelie, her youngest daughter, was seriously ill: how could she travel? The camp office replied that a doctor would also be going, adding, "If necessary she will be taken on a stretcher."

While these people were sorting through their possessions, trying to choose what was essential, a new camp commandant appeared. Lieutenant Ryochi Takahashi would prove to be somewhat more visible than his predecessor, and soon acquired a favourable reputation, particularly among the children. He was slightly built, wore wire-rimmed spectacles, had a little moustache, and appeared to be a more easy-going individual. He even encouraged the camp to organize entertainment; under Suzuki this had been forbidden.

The date of departure of the next transport was delayed until Monday. Once again the camp kitchen provided the travellers with food rations for five meals, enough for two days. The party said goodbye to their friends and assembled at the gate. Mrs. Diepeveen had asked *kumichos* and *hanchos* to advise mothers who were leaving children behind to say goodbye to them in the houses, where they could be looked after by friends; this would prevent disturbing spectacles from taking place at the camp gate. "You know how angry the guards get at displays of affection; punishment will just make matters worse," she confided to Emmy. At half past eight the travellers went out through the gate and all seven hundred women and children were gone.

Over the following weeks the call-up for transport came almost every other day. On December 3, Mien Aalbers came past our place with her young son Theo, sharing the news that they were to go the next day; it had come as a shock because she had nurtured a small hope, encouraged by the repeated delays in getting the dreaded call, that being *Belanda Indo* might allow her to leave the camp and return to the home of her parents, whom she thought were still at liberty. "At least we will stay together for now," she murmured with a sideways glance at Theo, who was roughly my age. Mien Aalbers's group turned out to be the last one to leave for a long time. We would not see each other again until three years later—on the other side of the world. All told, 7,400 women and children disappeared through the camp gate in November, and another 1,800 left during the first week of December—all of them for unknown destinations.

The almost weekly replay of tearful farewells between young boys and their mothers and siblings was very hard to digest. The fear of reaching the age of ten continued to haunt me in my sleep long after I had passed that milestone. The emotional damage those boys suffered is impossible to describe.

All attempts at schooling had now stopped, but suddenly another 250 young boys turned up from another camp. Three houses in the Bengawalaan were cleared to accommodate these newly arrived motherless boys, and this orphanage was subsequently referred to as "the boys' camp." Thus the role of Mrs. van Dijk and two other women expanded, though fortunately an elderly male doctor was appointed to help them.

Beyond our bamboo wall, beyond Java and its neighbouring islands, the Americans were relentlessly pursuing the onslaught on Japan; by the middle of November the Japanese army had been forced to move its southern headquarters from Manila to Saigon.

On November 24, the first B-29 bombing raids from Saipan over Tokyo took place; almost simultaneously Governor Ichibangase, displaying stoic determination and ignoring the gathering clouds of doom over Japan, ordered that preparations commence for festivities commemorating the beginning of Asian Liberation; every Bandoeng household once more had to display the *kokki* flag for a week. The occasion was also used by his superiors in Batavia to create numerous new governing positions to be filled with grateful and therefore loyal Indonesians; they had fancy titles but no real responsibilities, and they were forced to attend administrative training courses interspersed with other activities such as honouring the Japanese flag, calisthenics, clothes washing, cleaning their classrooms, *tenko* and swearing allegiance to Tenno Heika. Amidst all of this euphoria military exercises were organized in anticipation of an invasion, and a huge *razzia* was conducted throughout the town in search of radios. The contradictions inherent in all of this were startling. Once more, teams of cyclists went through town, shouting victory slogans in unison: *"Amerika kita strika, Inggeris kita linggis!"*

On December 8, the Americans avenged Pearl Harbor by starting the bombardment of Iwo Jima, a heavily fortified desert island halfway between Saipan and Japan itself. Its capture would facilitate a sharp escalation of American bombardment of Japanese cities. The defending garrison of this tiny desert island had recently grown to twenty-five thousand men, securely established in caves in anticipation of a lengthy, murderous siege that everyone on the island expected to be their last stand.

In Washington, General Leslie R. Grove briefed President Roosevelt on progress in the manufacture of an atomic bomb, anticipating the availability of a functional prototype by August 1.

For the unemployed masses on Java, life became more difficult. Commerce ground to a halt. The *pasars* were empty, partly as a result of a Japanese attempt to stamp out the black market commerce in contraband, such as spare parts for cars, electrical goods and medicine. Elsewhere in town the Chinese merchants closed their businesses to wait for better times. Inflation was rampant. The Japanese command held meetings with Indonesian leaders to discuss the devolution of power, while seeking to mobilize the native population for the Japanese cause, because it had become obvious that the *kampong* and *desa* dwellers were deeply disgruntled; the death toll of murdered Japanese soldiers rose steadily. By offering the educated nationalist leaders the promise of independence they hoped to ensure that the Indonesian masses, to whom the

255

notion of statehood was meaningless, would fall in line with the Japanese against the American and European imperialist powers.

In order to get co-operation from the humbler folk, General Harada created a new military organization called *Barisan Hezbollah*, or Allah's army; this consisted of young men willing to become *sjahid* (martyrs) in the fight against the *kafirs* (unbelievers). The only weapons made available for these new forces were bamboo spears. It seemed to have escaped the notice of General Harada that in the eyes of the *tani*, the rice farmers, the Japanese themselves might be considered *kafirs*.

Furniture Ladies

Since Tjihapit had lost two thirds of its inhabitants, there were many empty houses, providing a feeling of relief, for we now had a bit more privacy and it was easier to use the toilets. The accommodation that had become available in Tjihapit, however, also attracted the attention of the large uninterned but destitute Eurasian population of Bandoeng. Mostly these were women whose husbands had been imprisoned, and their children. Mrs. Douwes-Dekker, who had remained at liberty and was a member of a committee dedicated to the welfare of the *Belanda Indo*, approached the Bandoeng town hall with the suggestion that these empty Tjihapit houses might provide shelter for the uninterned *Belanda Indo*; the town hall told her that the houses first needed to be cleared and she would therefore have to wait.[4]

The house-clearing operation commenced in mid-December, when our *kumicho* ordered us to move. "You have been assigned accommodation in the Houtman *Plein,* number 6," she announced.

That same day an announcement appeared on the notice board, explaining that the camp was now divided into a northern portion, or the "upper camp," and a southern portion or "lower camp," and the upper camp was to be vacated. The new boundary was an imaginary line running through the Oranje Plein, eastward along the Barendszstraat to the Houtman Plein, semi-circular park abutting against the Houtmanstraat, defining the northeastern edge of the city. Our new house was just to the south of that line; the houses on the northern side of this small park remained empty.

My mother and Emmy found a cart and some willing helpers and we piled our belongings on this vehicle and moved to our new home. "This is not so bad," Juf remarked to my mother when she saw the place. "It's quieter here."

Yes, indeed, we were now close to the edge of town. Beyond the Houtmanstraat, to the north east, we could once more see, over the *gedek*, some

---

4. Bouwer, *Het vermoorde land*, 320.

of the hills in the distance. We also caught a glimpse of the KMA complex that my father had helped build.

As we entered the house to look for a room, Emmy mused, "I wonder if any of the gas appliances are still around?" She had realized that our new house was the one where there had been such a fuss about illegal gas fires some months before, and there remained in the house a lot of abandoned possessions: books, clothes, china, furnishings and furniture—but of course no signs of gas-burning implements. After a day's vigorous cleaning the women had managed to tidy the place a bit, and once more hung the zebra skin on a wall to give our new home a friendly feel—for a little while, at least. For the time being the transports seemed to have come to an end. And thus we entered 1945 (2605 by Japanese reckoning).

In the new year Mrs. Diepeveen assigned new tasks to the remaining inhabitants of Tjihapit. Since Takahashi had ordered all the houses in the northern portion of the camp to be cleared of abandoned goods, my mother and Emmy were now designated "furniture ladies," along with a large number of other strong young women and a few older boys. Part of the transportation pattern had now become clear: the old and the weak had been moved elsewhere and the strong and those able to do physical work had been kept back, along with a camp hospital filled with five hundred very sick people.

The furniture ladies were ordered to collect abandoned furniture from the vacated homes, sort it and store it in designated houses: all tables were collected in one place, all chairs elsewhere and so forth. It was heavy work, helped somewhat by the downward slope of the land from north to south. Worst of all was the task of moving the pianos, a back-breaking operation resulting in several injuries. All remaining items were to be dumped in piles at various spots in camp in anticipation of later removal. It was a huge assignment.

On the square in front of our house a mountain of abandoned household goods gradually began to take shape. We remaining children had the time of our lives sorting through this pile of stuff. What treasures it yielded! There were abandoned toys of all descriptions: electric trains and even Schuco cars— wonderful German wind-up toys that one could steer while walking behind them (the steering wheel that one held in one's hands was connected with a cable to the car itself, and the front wheels turned just like those on real cars). For a short while, I was the proud owner of a fancy electric train set, alas not complete and therefore never put in motion while in my possession.

Mrs. Diepeveen also set the older boys to work digging vegetable plots, a hopeless task as we all knew, but it kept them busy and out of mischief; she had also been ordered to help the Japanese army with clothing, and therefore sought volunteers for this task. The initial response was disappointing, so she had to become more demanding. But then it transpired that these new Nippon workers would get some payment in terms of additional food, and the promise of this reward created a wave of enthusiasm. As a result, Juf joined a group of ladies knitting socks, simple garments with no heel, while other women sewed uniforms.

The collapsing economy elsewhere on Java had a new impact on us: yeast ceased to be available, and without this ingredient it was impossible to convert Asia flour into digestible food. Fortunately, chemists interned in the Tjimahi men's camp had devised a method for making liquid yeast using urine as a feedstock. Not only was this product useful for making bread, but it also became a valuable source of vitamin B.[5] Mrs. Diepeveen heard of this development and requested a daily shipment of two hundred litres for the women's camp. Henceforth two *totok* men were allowed to use a small truck to make this daily delivery from Tjimahi into Tjihapit.

Shortly after this service had started, a teenage girl asked the men if she might also have a ride in the truck. Before military control had been established, such an escapade would have passed unnoticed, but now the girl was immediately apprehended by one of the Japanese guards and strung up by her arms from a tree so that her toes barely touched the ground, a common form of punishment. After the punishment, lasting an hour, she declared that it had been worth it.

About this time more men, women and children joined us from Karees, across town. These were the last of the Red Ball brigade to have been employed and were no longer required by the army of occupation; they could now be accommodated conveniently in Tjihapit prior to transport elsewhere.

Outside the camp the misery of a collapsing economy was compounded by increased Japanese demands and draconian clampdowns. On January 5 Ichibangase held a new *razzia* against unemployed young *Belanda Indo* men, who had been getting into frequent fights with Indonesian youth; the *Kempetai* rounded some up and tortured them in order to reveal the names of their collaborators before dispatching them to the Gunong Halu plantation in the Preanger as slave labour.[6] Three days later Ichibangase ordered all Bandoeng residents to hand over precious metals and jewels to assist the Japanese war effort. He set monetary targets for the principal population groups and for each suburban district of Bandoeng or *han*, with a deadline of January 20. The Chinese population of Bandoeng, for instance, had to donate two thousand carats in gold, and he threatened house searches where the targets had not been met. The Japanese were not simply stealing these precious materials: they "compensated" the owners—at a laughable 290 Japanese guilders per carat of

---

5. My father told me about this after the war. There are some humorous illustrations of the process in *Myn Kamp* by M. G. Hartley.

6. Bouwer, *Het vermoorde land*, 312.

diamond. A few weeks later each household was told to hand over five kilograms of iron to the authorities, a demand backed up with the threat of another house search. It was obvious that this was another attempt to compensate for the virtual cessation of tax payment since the occupation had started. And so another reign of terror began over the residents of the Greater East Asia Co-Prosperity Sphere.

In these first days of 1945 the Americans landed on Luzon in the Philippines, on exactly the same beaches where, three years earlier, the Japanese had made their landfall; the news quickly spread throughout Bandoeng. There was little the Japanese propaganda system could do to obscure this development, so a senior spokesman lamely claimed that the Philippines were worthless.

On Jan 28 another rebellion among the Indonesians broke out, this time at Blitar, a farming community halfway between Soerabaja and the south coast. A PETA unit of Javanese soldiers had taken control of a Japanese garrison and disarmed and imprisoned the Emperor's men. It took two days and some very firm action for the Japanese to regain control of this town. It then transpired that the uprising had actually been planned to take place later in July, but on a far greater scale.[7] In Bandoeng the Japanese authorities started another campaign to identify all "foreigners" whom they now considered a threat; *kumichos* were ordered to record the nationality of all the occupants in their *kumi*.

The situation in Japan was deteriorating even more rapidly; in early March the Americans abandoned precision bombing and began to carpet-bomb cities. On March 10, three hundred American bombers dropped two thousand incendiary bombs, set cities ablaze and killed 130,000 civilians, while the Japanese stationed in French Indochina took control and massacred the French garrison that had resisted.[8] Later that month, American marines raised Old Glory for the first time on a hilltop on Iwo Jima, having conquered this tiny, miserable volcanic island after a three-month struggle and twenty-six thousand American casualties; twenty-one thousand Japanese defenders died. Although the fighting was not to be concluded for another two months, this victory paved the way for the construction of airstrips, allowing the United States to increase the rate of devastation of Japanese cities.

---

7. Bouwer, *Het vermoorde land*, 325. (See also Reid and Akira (eds.), *The Japanese Experience in Indonesia*, 219–226.)

8. Gilbert, *A History of the Twentieth Century*, Vol. 2, 1933–1951, 650.

We Get Stripped of Our Remaining Possessions

The relief of enjoying a bit of space in Tjihapit did not last long. On March 20 we were told to move—from the southern part of the camp to the northern part. This was no ordinary house move, though: the camp office warned us that food supplies could not be taken along and that in future no family cooking would be tolerated at all; we were to become completely dependent on the communal kitchen. The announcement precipitated a hurried attempt to consume the tiny amounts of rice and brown beans that we had left.

The move was scheduled for March 30, and on that day soldiers were posted at the four crossroads giving access to the northern half of the camp. All too soon the purpose of this military precaution became crystal clear; the first few people who tried to make this trip found that the suitcases they had packed so carefully were ripped open and their contents dumped on the street for inspection. Above all the soldiers were looking for money and jewellery. Takahashi's men were now conducting the same search in Tjihapit that had been undertaken in January throughout Bandoeng, but here were able to use a more efficient and thorough method. In the process they confiscated anything else that was deemed illegal, including books and other written material.

Soon all those who had not yet traversed the inspection point took defensive action. My mother and Emmy hid their wedding rings and some coins in my teddy bear, a tatty old thing, and told me to hang on to the bear. Mothers with babies utilized diapers, while Amelia tried to hide her cache of coins in the bottom of a bucket of rice, hidden by clothing. Where we made the crossing, Tetsuka was seated on an Empire chair, closely supervising the inspection work of his team of *heihos*. If any of the booty had been for their own consumption, they might not have been so indolent. At first Amelia thought she would get through, but Tetsuka ordered the *heiho* to check Amelia's tin a second time and the *heiho* complied, again thrusting his hand into the tin, casually searching among the rice grains without finding her coins. Then Tetsuka lost his patience, thrust his own hand in, found a silver Dutch quarter and kicked the rice tin out of Amelia's hand; her small cache of rice and money were gone, but she was lucky that worse did not befall her. We followed and were luckier, for my teddy bear went through unscathed. Ank and Elsa had decided that careful packing was a waste of time, but had entrusted the cat along with valuables packed in a small bag to Ank's mother, who was scared to death of the Japanese and therefore extra polite, bowing frequently and deeply. Unfortunately they had not entrusted her with their supply of aluminium foil, hoarded to improvise (illegal) electric fuses, and this was confiscated. In this way the remaining residents of Tjihapit were stripped of their possessions even before leaving the camp.

No sooner had this move been completed than the work of camp-clearing started all over again, and my mother, Emmy and the other furniture ladies began to clear the houses in the southern portion of the camp.

Mrs. Douwes Dekker's quest on behalf of the destitute Eurasian population now received a double setback. Inspection of these recently vacated and cleared Tjihapit houses by the *Hudosan Kanrikokan*, the housing agency, revealed the buildings to be uninhabitable. On top of that, many Eurasians elsewhere in Bandoeng now had to leave their homes as a result of the huge military re-organization that General Harada had initiated in further preparation against an Allied invasion. Java had been divided into *gunseiribus*, military administrative districts that were to become self-sufficient in terms of food, fuel and defence needs. As a result, a large number of Japanese soldiers were concentrated in Bandoeng, now declared the capital of one of these *gunseiribus*, and they required accommodation. The obvious candidates for eviction were the *Belanda Indos*, thereby adding to the numbers of homeless people in this population group.

But we got a snippet of good news. On the last day of March Mrs. Diepeveen posted a notice advising all women to go to the camp office to check for mail. My mother came hurrying back, triumphantly waving a brown card at Juf and me. She was ecstatic. The card was written in Malay, and had been sent on February 11, 2605, only a month and a half before. My mother could not read the Malay text properly, but the message was predictable and so hardly merited translation. The important thing was the handwriting: the neatly printed block letters and the obvious architectural style—as though this were an inscription on a monument—were undeniably my father's.

My father had obviously received my mother's card, because he knew her registration number, but the address was two moves out of date. He had no knowledge of the upheavals we had been subjected to, but it didn't really matter, since street addresses had become pointless. His confidence that a house address was still relevant for us probably prevented him from being excessively worried about our condition, since it suggested a trace of normalcy. In the final twenty-five words he wrote that he had the company of Theo Aalbers, and he sent his love to "Willy, Boudy, Oma [Juf]." But where was he? The card merely said that he was prisoner 31580 and that he was on "Java CQ," whatever that meant.

A month later, after the southern camp had been cleared of abandoned goods, we were once more ordered to move, this time to the empty houses in the south, and we once again had to subject ourselves to the unpleasant search operation by the soldiers and their *heiho* helpers. We were warned that all papers we still possessed, such as birth certificates, passports and wedding licenses, had to be censored or they would be removed and burnt. Somehow my mother managed to retain my birth certificate, which was to prove useful later. It was in this way that we lost virtually all remaining personal documents, including the diaries that some had secretly retained. These frequent house moves, with the concomitant loss of possessions, were also disorientating, and only a confused blur remains in my memory of this period.

The furniture the women had collected ended up being demolished and sent to the remaining kitchen for firewood, because there was no other way to keep the fires going. Miraculously we stayed alive, but all other evidence of our existence and of our past had been eradicated.

At the same time the Japanese hold on Okinawa was undergoing rapid deterioration; fifty thousand US troops landed on its beaches in order to secure for American use an airfield situated halfway between Formosa and Kyushu; its possession would permit the United States to dominate the skies over China, Formosa and Japan. The Japanese knew this and defended Okinawa to the utmost. Aside from the Japanese garrison, deeply dug into caves, its defence relied on wave after wave of suicide missions using planes, manned bombs and even the huge battleship *Yamato*, which sailed forth on April 6 with only enough fuel to reach Okinawa; a concerted American airborne attack sank it well short of its goal, and so its immense cannons never had an opportunity to deliver their destructive potential.

On April 26 the Russian army made its way into Berlin, an event that for the first time since 1942 threatened to overshadow the Emperor's birthday celebrations as well as the usual cascade of new initiatives, including the replacement of General Kumakichi Harada by General Yosiuchi Nagano as the commander on Java. The news from Berlin spread through Bandoeng like the winds of the *taufan* that could molest these islands, and the *Kempetai* promptly swung into action, arresting seventy-six men for spreading rumours. But in seeking Indonesian support for their doomed cause, the Japanese nevertheless relented by changing the language they used. Indonesians would no longer be called *genjumin* (natives) but *Indonesia shimin* (Indonesians).[9]

That same week Roosevelt's death was announced in the local press, with the comment that "Roosevelt, who had spilled so much American blood, has himself now died from a haemorrhage: the blood was drained from his brain, the centre of his bad thoughts."[10]

The Shadow of Tarakan

In the second week of May, our stay in Tjihapit came to an abrupt end. However, this coincided with the end of the war in Europe and dramatic changes in the fortunes of war around Java.

9. Bouwer, *Het vermoorde land,* 336.

10. *Soeara Asia,* April 17, 1945, quoted by Jan Bouwer, *Het vermoorde land,* 334.

An Australian assault group and the Japanese occupiers were then engaged in a bloody battle for possession of Tarakan island, an oil-production centre off the east coast of Borneo. This could be interpreted as a step in the liberation of the NEI.[11] The Australian brigade included a company of KNIL soldiers, while the defending Japanese were being assisted by a company of *heiho*. Thus, in a small but significant way, a beginning was made in the looming struggle between the former colony and its former imperial ruler. Liberating Tarakan was a minor departure from the earlier Allied decision restricting such assaults to the eastern extremity of the Indonesian archipelago, in places like Timor and New Guinea; it was also a controversial decision.

Military operations in the eastern portion of the NEI—that is to say all territories to the east of the Sunda Strait—had since the early days of 1942 fallen under General Douglas MacArthur's command. The large island of Sumatra had then been made part of the Indian Ocean operations, assigned to Britain. But while the American war effort, enjoying the full backing of the American industrial machine, was focused on the defeat of Japan, Mountbatten was constrained by the limited resources he could muster from devastated Britain in executing his task, the eviction of Japanese forces from Southeast Asia. Consideration of Java fell outside of these Allied strategies: the task was not assigned to Mountbatten and was ignored by MacArthur. The decision to undertake the liberation of Borneo was based on tactical considerations and perhaps a bit of political manoeuvring—to deny Japan access to its oil and rubber, while giving the Aussie "Diggers" something useful to do.[12]

The Tarakan operation created a wave of excitement among the Indonesian population, and everyday they crowded around the office of the *Tjahaja* newspaper on the *Groote Postweg*, the main east–west artery through Bandoeng, to read the latest news posted on the walls, never more than two pages long owing to the shortage of newsprint. The struggle for Tarakan was, thanks to the tiny contribution of the *heiho*, and notwithstanding the impending defeat, the first concrete manifestation of nationhood for the Indonesian people. Thus the Tarakan operation cast a more complex shadow over future relationships in Southeast Asia.[13]

Shocked by the Allied landings so close to Batavia, Lieutenant General Nagano, the new commander on Java, sought to avoid the risk of more sabotage attempts in his backyard by firing remaining *Belanda Indo* from agencies such as the postal service and the railways. Colonel Takahashi, head of the Japanese information service in Batavia, made a radio broadcast in which he assured his listeners that Japan would not be defeated as easily as Germany had

---

11. Liberating the NEI was not contemplated by the Allies.

12. Liddell Hart, *History of the Second World War*, 719.

13. Australians are still wondering whether this costly operation indeed helped bring the Pacific war to a speedier conclusion.

been. But he also had a warning for Indonesians: "Indonesia is currently struggling to develop its capacity for independent action, a task for which other nations of Greater East Asia will render assistance. But Indonesia will only gain its freedom by being willing to fight for it."[14]

In Tokyo, aged Admiral Kantaro Suzuki, the new Prime Minister, reacting to the defeat of Germany, left no doubt that Japan "would continue to fight the Greater East Asia War, even though it now stood alone." His confidence in this course of action was partly based on the firm and not unrealistic conviction that the defeat of Germany would immediately bring to a crisis the conflicting aims of the Soviet Union and of the United States and Britain. But he also drew on the knowledge of his people's willingness to make the most extraordinary sacrifices to preserve the Emperor's throne. He began to implement his "*Ketsu-Go*" policy, redirecting Japan's entire armaments industry towards the mass production of suicide weapons.[15] There is ample evidence that the Japanese people were prepared to fight with religious fanaticism to the bitter end on behalf of their Emperor and Japan, and that an Allied victory, if that should be the outcome, would be dearly bought.

Goodbye Tjihapit

On May 5, 1945, Lieutenant Takahashi ordered Mrs. Diepeveen to make preparations for clearing the remaining 3,700 women and children out of Tjihapit. Mrs. Diepeveen posted the following notice: "TJIHAPIT WILL BE CLEARED DURING THE COMING WEEKS. ALL MEN AND BOYS (10 YEARS AND OLDER) WILL LEAVE TOMORROW. PLEASE CHECK THIS NOTICE BOARD FOR FURTHER DETAILS."

The blow came on May 8: our family group was ordered to be ready early the next morning for transport. My mother and Emmy were immensely relieved to discover that we would at least have the company of friends; Ank, one of the first friends we had come to know in Bandoeng, would be travelling with us, along with Elsa and both their aged mothers; another good friend who joined us was Hanna Poortman and her two daughters. We were extraordinarily lucky to retain their company on this awful journey. However, nothing had dispelled the rumours about our likely destination—the Borneo jungle. Nor had we heard anything about the fate of those who had so far departed; they had simply disappeared through the camp gate.

The list of items we were allowed to take with us was small. Each adult was permitted one suitcase weighing no more than twenty kilograms, and a bedroll

---

14. Bouwer, *Het vermoorde land*, 338.

15. Bix, *Hirohito and the Making of Modern Japan*, 494.

or mattress, and each child was permitted one backpack. Again the kitchen would provide food rations for the journey. Thanks to their occupation as furniture ladies, my mother and Emmy had obtained improved bedding, enabling us to abandon the two most worn-out of our canvas and wood folding camp cots. They would henceforth share a double spring mattress, a luxury, manageable as long as we remained together. Up to now my bed had also been a camp cot, but I had recently become the owner of an abandoned air mattress, which would be easier to carry, while Juf had selected the most functional of the camp cots for herself. We had to appear at the camp gate the next morning at nine o'clock, and there would be no dry run.

We spent the day sorting through our remaining belongings and carefully packing them. My mother and Juf had modified their housecoats by sewing in additional pockets, while Emmy had added a number of additional pockets to an abandoned backpack that she had procured. We did not know our destination, but a *kelambu* (a mosquito net) might be essential, if bulky; having a double one (for Emmy and my mother) also made for economical packing.

"What shall I do with this?" my mother wondered, holding up the zebra skin.

"Leave it behind," Emmy replied. "It's useless for *gedekking*."

"I wonder if we will ever see South Africa again," my mother sighed as she threw the skin on the discard pile.

The next morning at nine o'clock we were to muster for *appel* by the gate with our *barang*. Carrying our possessions all the way across camp from the eastern border, where we lived, to the Oranje Plein would have been terrible were it not for some friends who helped to carry the double mattress, which weighed a ton, in a cart. My mother had buried the Djokja silver bowls, wrapped in clothing and stashed inside the all-important potty, at the bottom of my improvised backpack, hidden by clothes from inspection.

It was a miracle that these bowls had so far not been confiscated. Their craftsmanship was of the highest calibre, the design elegant, and the detail of the ornate, deeply embossed flower and leaf patterns, beaten into the silver surface, was exquisite. These items not only represented a link to the happy days before the war and the wonderful vacations on Java, but also, if the right purchaser could be found, constituted a last potential source of money; the typical Indonesians who had come to the *gedek* to barter their food wares were more interested in items of immediate practical use, such as clothing. Aside from that, my backpack contained some eating utensils and toilet articles. To the outside of my backpack my mother had tied an aluminium army mess kit, recently salvaged from among abandoned possessions; it was rectangular and came in two halves, forming a box that was now stuffed with bread from the kitchen. In my hands I had to carry my rolled-up, floppy air mattress. Most children in our party carried rolled-up *tikars*, woven straw mats; they were light in weight but inclined to become infested with bedbugs.

My mother's suitcase consisted of two baskets of woven bamboo matting held together with a leather strap. In addition to clothing, a sheet and eating utensils, it contained a small number of precious items, such as my fathers' portrait, her remaining unconfiscated personal documents and a small quantity of cotton thread and needles. My mother was also burdened by a housecoat with its pockets stuffed with small essential items such as soap and a nail brush. Emmy had packed the double *kelambu* and some towels. It was very hard to cram the necessities for an entire household, including clothing, bedding, toiletries, and eating and cooking gear in a suitcase that weighed only twenty kilograms.

Juf had packed a small leather suitcase with the toilet-tidy that my mother had made and her collection of knitting needles, for which she had made a holder from a piece of cardboard covered with coarsely woven maroon material salvaged from an old curtain and decorated with embroidered flowers. She also brought balls of wool and cotton, unravelled from discarded sweaters and clothes. Most of Juf's things had been piled on the cart, but she was nevertheless weighed down, with her housecoat worn over her long dress. To shield her eyes, which seemed to be bothered by the strong sunlight, she wore her straw hat, firmly pinned to her hair by means of a wicked-looking pin with a pearl head. Walking to the main gate was difficult for Juf because she was far from well and her legs were badly swollen. Our travel gear was rounded out by a cloth shopping bag with two wooden handles, containing food and a bottle of water, which my mother and Emmy took turns carrying.

We could not help being excited, in spite of the ominous rumours regarding our destination and our fate. If the Japanese truly wanted to kill us, why go through all of this trouble? We would, moreover, finally get a glimpse of the world outside of the camp wall, the "normal world" that people living around us so often had talked about. As usual, a send-off party, though now very small indeed, accompanied us to the main gate, where Mrs. Diepeveen and some helpers from the Ladies' Office, including Amelia, stood waiting. They handed out temporary number cards and checked our names off a list. Here another familiar face joined our group: Mrs. van Dijk, our former neighbour from across the road when we had first arrived in Tjihapit, and latterly a house-mother for abandoned boys. The previous day she had to say goodbye to a second child, Bart, who was forced to go elsewhere with other boys. Mrs. van Dijk was in tears at the loss of a second child, while her youngest boy gripped his mother's hand tightly as we approached the gateway. All this misery made me very apprehensive about the prospect of one day becoming ten years old.

Murui arrived and the baggage weighing and inspection began, while Dr. Cramer went around administering medicine to a few sick travellers on stretchers, in the hope that this might ease their journey. Mrs. Diepeveen had dragged some scales out and in turn all the suitcases were weighed. We noticed one of the office ladies occasionally, and surreptitiously, placing her foot underneath the scale when it seemed as though a suitcase might be too heavy. The niceties of bowing were temporarily suspended in the business of getting us ready for the journey, but there was as usual a lot of shouting in Murui's gruff, staccato voice, "*lekas, lekas!*" in time with the slap-slap of his whip, an old riding crop, impatiently hitting his black leather boots.

My mother and Emmy had carefully observed the proceedings of the previous departures, and our *barang* passed muster, though luck also played a big part. The silver items would surely have been confiscated by Murui, had he known. To one of the women in our party, designated the leader, Mrs Diepeveen handed a small parcel containing a list of names and our share of the camp kitty, about two guilders per person, enough for eight days' worth of food supplies based on the official Japanese allowance. That was our share of the money that Murui and his colleagues had managed to extract from all of us with so much difficulty.

We finally left Tjihapit through the camp gate and saw the big doors closed behind us, permanently removing from view the place where we had spent three years of our lives. Murui got us to line up on the grass in groups of sixty-five. Here we were once more counted; we always had to be counted—*'Ichi! Ni! San! Shi! Go!'*—over and over. When Mrs. Diepeveen and Murui finally agreed that we were all present, we were allowed to sit down on the grass to wait for the buses.

By this time it was early afternoon. Mercifully, the usual afternoon rains did not materialize that day or we and our *barang* would have been soaking wet. Finally two trucks turned up, with some emaciated and shoddily dressed European men who started loading the mattresses and suitcases. The men were not allowed to talk with us on the grass, but worked silently under the scowl of Murui. When all the baggage was on the two trucks, they rumbled off with the men on top. Only Hosjino and Tetsuka, both fully armed, remained behind to guard us and to keep curious pedestrians at a distance.

We now found time to take in the local scene; Riouwstraat offered an unaccustomed sight to our eyes, for there were bicycles, *betjas* and even some trucks and motorcycles. There were Indonesian people, a few of whom were even smartly dressed, at least by our standards. We could not see far, just up and down the street, because across the way more *gedek* hid the Bloemenkamp from sight. Not far from us was a huge pile of stinking rubbish, mostly on the grass but partly spilling over the curb and onto the street itself.

"What a mess," Juf commented, while shifting her weight uncomfortably from one swollen leg to another. "Boudy and I used to go for a walk there before the war. Can you remember?" She shook her head with disbelief lamenting, "Och, och, och."

Mindful of the possibility of coming chaos, my mother had drummed into me a whistle signal. It was a simple semi-tone tune, "fa-so-fa-sooo," that could penetrate the hubbub of voices and traffic and provide me with a homing beacon. This signal had been perfected over the last few months, and we practised it softly while we waited for the buses. They finally arrived—green, belching black smoke, with the side and rear windows boarded shut.

"The Japs do not want us to see the city," grumbled Hanna, who had lived in this city her entire life, when she saw the blocked windows.

"The Japs do not want the city to see us," Emmy retorted icily.

The Indonesians we had seen riding or walking past us while we were waiting on the grass had certainly been curious in a friendly sort of way and had smiled.

We piled into the darkened, hot bus with our travelling bags. Of our family group, only Juf could get a seat. One of the soldiers pushed the bus doors shut, squashing a woman left standing at the very front next to the driver, and the buses lurched noisily into motion. As we drove through town, someone near the front called out familiar sights, but near the back, where we were, it was impossible to hear what she said. We bumped over some railway tracks, turned and came to a shuddering stop. It had been a short journey, bringing us to the front of a small brick building and a platform beside the railway line. The driver turned the engine off and for a moment it was quiet.

"Tjikoedapateuh!" one of the women near the front of the bus called out. "They might have taken us to the main station so we could leave in style."

The hubbub resumed after we got down from the buses and looked around.

"My God, what a change," my mother exclaimed, incredulous as she stepped down from the bus, gesticulating towards the street. "Did you see all those boarded-up shops?" Others used words like "decay" and "shabbiness."

Murui arrived on his motorbike and helped the men offload the *barang* from the trucks. This he did by simply throwing the bags and suitcases onto the ground; since some of them had contained water bottles, wet patches began to appear in the dirt. We were once more lined up in our groups of sixty-five, as a few passers-by stopped and gawked. Then Takahashi and Tetsuka turned up on their motorcycles. After a brief inspection, Takahashi disappeared into the station building and some *heihos*, armed with their sticks, turned up from somewhere, forming a cordon to keep a distance between us and the curious bystanders.

We waited outside the station building for what seemed like an eternity before Takahashi emerged, shouting orders to Murui, who now made us move onto the platform; a train pulled by a locomotive belching black smoke and sparks appeared out of a distant, smoky haze and drew to a squealing halt. The European men dragged a station cart loaded with *barang* from the street, and began to stow the *barang* in the baggage car as we began to board the empty train wagons, which were fourth-class coaches.

"I never dreamt I would see the day when I would travel *klas kambing*," Hanna exclaimed. "What a filthy mess."

"Did you see the toilet?" my mother cried out in disgust as she crowded in past a small, smelly compartment. "It's awful."

What she was referring to was a squatter by the entrance of the coach; once upon a time a door had offered some privacy, but the door was gone, exposing for all to see evidence of much distress on the part of previous travellers.

The entire train was dedicated to our party. Once upon a time, these carriages had been smartly painted in the maroon colours of the State Railway, but now the paint was peeling. Each wagon had a small platform at either end with a door that gave access to the interior. There were benches made of wooden slats with the backs to the windows on either side of the carriage, and in the middle a simple wooden bench with nothing to lean against. The windows, which normally would have been open to the fresh air, were now fitted with shutters made of woven bamboo strips; this train had been modified for the express purpose of transporting people who should be denied any contact, visual or otherwise, with the population of the land. The extent to which the Japanese were prepared to go to make us feel like vermin, unfit for human eyes, was unnerving. They were thorough.

By the time all of our company was loaded, each carriage was crammed so full that it was impossible to move in the gloomy, stifling interior. Someone had taken pity on an old lady who was clearly in physical distress and had with difficulty boarded our train wagon long after the seats had been taken. She was perspiring and sat down heavily on the seat offered to her. Juf also managed to find a seat, but my mother and I ended up standing just inside the door, close to the smelly toilet, while Emmy was squashed in one of the aisles next to Hanna and her girls; we lost sight of Ank and Elsa, who were in another coach. Takahashi came on the platform and shouted something, whereupon the doors to the outside were closed by the *heiho*. Then we waited.

With so little fresh air coming in and so many bodies packed together, the atmosphere soon became unbearable. The train eventually lurched into motion with a clattering sound as the coupling devices between the carriages were yanked taut, beginning near the front of the train and clattering past our carriage to the rear. With squealing wheels the train slowly made its way through town and then, after perhaps ten minutes, jerked to a halt with a noisy clatter as the buffers at either end of each carriage suddenly rammed into each other—bang! bang! bang! bang!—the racket starting at the locomotive end, approaching our wagon, and then fading as this signal was passed on to the wagons behind us.

"The main station!" someone shouted. "Hotel Homann, a block down the road on your left and Maison Bogerijen next door—enjoy your vacation!"

Someone snarled, "Oh, shut up."

We remained standing in the station for a long time. Some of the passengers speculated about where we would be going.

"Batavia!"

"No! Tandjong Priok!"

There was no way of divining the destination, apart from the fact that the railway through Bandoeng took one to either the southeast coast or the northwest coast. We seemed to be heading west, but the possibilities still were legion. Once again the train began to roll, with its clatter and squealing, and Bandoeng's station fell behind us. Fifteen minutes later, we arrived at another station. Those close to the windows peered through the cracks and the word "Tjimahi" rushed through the carriage—that was where so many husbands and fathers were thought to be.

"I wonder if Edu is here," Emmy muttered to my mother, adding with a miserable voice, "He won't know what's happening to us."

"Mien thought that Bou and Theo were now in Tjimahi. I am sure Bou would have mentioned Edu if they were in the same camp," my mother replied.

Outside there were many grim-looking soldiers, slowly patrolling up and down the platform's length with their rifles over their shoulders, sharp steel bayonets attached; they were clearly there to prevent escape attempts by any of us. What could these soldiers have been thinking, guarding a party of women and children on behalf of the Emperor of Japan, while five thousand miles to the north their homeland, now lacking any form of defence against daily air attacks, was being smashed by bombing raids? How could this demeaning, absurd activity on a small railway platform on Java affect Japan's survival? It defied common sense.

With the late afternoon sun beating down on our train, the atmosphere inside became thick with the smell of sweating human bodies. Someone had to go to the toilet, but that was impossible, and she asked for a potty. There was a clatter and lots of swearing. A patriotic soul, inspired by the struggle, tried to seek salvation in song, a solemn hymn from the time when the Dutch sought release from Spanish oppression, as though that might inspire fortitude in our time of need. The wobbly cracked voice rose with a tremble of emotion, but died when no one joined in. Then the train jerked, squeaked, and once more moved on. Someone lost her balance and the potty got upset, with more cursing. "*God ver-dom-me!*"

Tjimahi fell behind us. The thought of the widening distance from a loved one after such tantalizing proximity was too much for one woman, who began to sob, while my mother, stoic as always, also had trouble keeping a brave face. It was a blessing that I could not see Juf, for my father had been the nearest thing to a child that she had ever had. Her devotion to him had been unbounded, and that devotion was clearly reciprocated. The thought that our separation would now grow, with no end in sight, was very, very hard to bear.

A critical shortage of fuel made the large-scale relocation of prisoners of war difficult for the railways. After the Japanese invasion, inter-island trade had come to a complete halt, cutting off the railway system on Java from its supply of Sumatran coal, and the pre-war stockpile had long since been exhausted. The Japanese had attempted to exploit the coal deposits in the Bantam area of northwest Java, but the coal was of poor quality, and the railways had come to rely on wood. Rubber plantations and forests were consequently demolished. Aside from other delays, our progress was interrupted by the periodic need to replenish the wood supply for the locomotive. Numerous times the train started, only to stop again a short while later, having travelled only for a number of minutes, and each time we were subjected to the deafening clatter as the carriages bumped into one another or were yanked forward and we lurched against our neighbours. Sometimes it was clear why the train had stopped, for we would start up again soon after another train had either passed us or come the other way, but usually we just stopped. While the train was in motion we made attempts to open the windows to let in some fresh air and light, but then when the train stopped the windows were once again hurriedly shut, because soldiers patrolled both sides of the train at each station.

Night fell and mercifully the carriage cooled down. Outside, a peaceful landscape of mountains and jungle growth, hills swathed in the remnants of tea plantations or rice paddies, slowly passed by beneath a moonless night sky, but we saw nothing. All we got was a breeze, and soot and sparks from the struggling engine. Late at night, after a tortuous ride through mountainous terrain, we stopped at a railway station and someone in the carriage, peering through the slats, made out the name of the town when a Japanese soldier carelessly passed the beam of a flashlight over the station sign: "Poerwarkarta!"

After a long wait the train lurched forward again. At daybreak we reached another town, Tjikampek, and here we waited. Some Indonesians came to the station platform. Perhaps they always came whenever a train arrived; it might be an opportunity for business, for tending to the needs of travellers, but they also knew from the sight of the train wagons with their boarded-up windows that this was no ordinary passenger train, and they had probably seen more, perhaps many more such trains. While the Japanese soldiers were around, contact was impossible, but once they were out of sight there would be loud whispers, "*Njonja, njonja ada makanan!*" and invariably food would be offered in exchange for money or an item of clothing. A tray made of woven bamboo appeared by the doorway, where my mother stood. Through the partly opened shutters we could see small packages of food wrapped in banana leaves and neatly tied with a narrow ribbon of palm leaf: "*Njonja, Ada nasi tim ajam* [steamed rice and chicken]".

It was too good to be true! With difficulty my mother extracted a coin from a hidden pocket and then was able to buy two parcels. One parcel was passed on to Emmy to share with Juf, and the other one my mother and I shared. The smell was absolutely delicious. What a change from the awful glue that we had consumed for the last two years; we had forgotten what decent food could taste like, and the experience was overwhelming. There were real chicken bits mixed up with the rice, onions and spices, admittedly not much chicken, but it represented a memorable gourmet meal.

The train left the station with some of us feeling a bit better, but most of our supplies of water and bread had been consumed by now, since it was impossible to sleep and that made the gnawing hunger worse. Throughout the night there had been more accidents and the atmosphere within our partly-sealed carriage had become foul with the sour smell of urine, feces and vomit from dysentery sufferers. There was no avoiding it, one just had to let go and hope the potty, if one was available, was correctly positioned! It took skill and balance to avoid excessive contact with the filth on the floor as the train lurched forward or stopped.

By now we had emerged from the mountains and were rolling through a gently undulating green landscape. With daylight we could get glimpses through the crack in the shutters of the wonderful undisturbed countryside, a veritable paradise of tall palm trees, clumps of bamboo bushes and the rich green of the banana palms and flowering flame trees. An occasional bougainvillea vine graced a far-off, deserted plantation home, its rich purple colour like a splash of jewellery. And everywhere, rice paddies, miles and miles of rice paddies, with the water shimmering in the sun. Gracefully they curved around the slopes of the low hills, the blue sky and fluffy white clouds overhead reflected in the still, shallow waters, and the lush green sprigs of young rice plants thrusting through to the light.

"What a beautiful country this is," someone whispered.

The sun rose higher as the train continued its fitful, miserable journey down to the coast, while the atmosphere in our carriage became more fetid. We reached a big city and stopped in a railroad marshalling yard. There were lots of other trains around us, mainly freight trains filled with rusty scrap iron. We jerked backwards, and then forwards, and backwards again, seemingly going back where we came from, and finally travelled a bit further, past houses sheltered by big trees, and *kampongs* surrounded by dense growth of banana palms, and then, finally, drew to a halt. Soldiers came by, opened the doors, banging sticks on the sides of the wagons and shouting *"Turun! Turun!* [get out!]."

The unmistakable smell of humid maritime air greeted us as we stumbled, blinking, out of our lightless carriages onto a small station platform. A dilapidated sign read "Tanah Abang." Emmy and my mother helped Juf gingerly down the steps.

"We are in Batavia," Ank declared, emerging from a neighbouring carriage. "I spent my childhood not far from here—we are a long way from Tandjong Priok."

"Perhaps the Japs want to make us walk a long way," Emmy grumbled.

It was past noon, with the sun still near its zenith, and we stood exhausted, filthy, thirsty and hungry on the platform, where there was no shade. My mother and Emmy took turns supporting Juf, who was on the point of collapse. No one could tell us what would happen next. There was a commotion in a neighbouring carriage, from which two passengers had to be lifted: they were lifeless. Two *heiho* came by with a stretcher and carried them, one after the other, into the small station building. It was a miracle that Juf had survived. A trip that would normally have taken four hours had lasted twenty-four hours.

A week later the Tjihapit hospital was cleared of its five hundred patients, along with its complement of nurses and doctors. Those who survived the journey also ended up in Batavia, in the St. Vincentius hospital. One can only speculate about the horrors of that particular journey.

Our experience was hardly unique. Of the thirteen thousand women and children who had left Tjihapit, about sixty-five percent ended up in various camps in and around Batavia.[16] The remainder had been shipped to central Java, to camps in the port city of Semarang and in the interior, near a small town called Ambarawa, nestled in a valley between two volcanoes—the Merapi to the south and the Ungaran to the north—a picturesque location but with atrocious accommodation. Those voyages had lasted two days. Women and children had been moved to these two groups of destinations from all over Java.

The total scale of the operation, which only got under way after the original POWs had been sent abroad, was staggering. Over the course of the occupation the Japanese moved thirty-five thousand civilian men and 115,000 women and children, many of them several times.[17] This involved dedicated trains burning fuel that was in short supply and operated by staff with split loyalties. Some

---

16. Ernest Hillen and his mother left Tjihapit a week after we did and ended up in Kampong Makassar, a work camp where vegetables were grown by the internees for all prison camps in and around Batavia.

17. The analysis of this section is based on estimates of individual transports presented in *Geïllustreerde Atlas van de Japanse Kampen in Nederlands Indie, 1942–1945*, by Jan van Dulm et al.

transports had to contend with destroyed bridges that necessitated the passengers getting off one train, traversing a stream on a temporary bridge and boarding a second train to continue the journey. Civilian men from all over Java were herded together mainly in the Preanger valley, near Bandoeng, where they were accommodated in the large pre-war military complex at Tjimahi. By the end of the war, eighty-one percent of the twenty-seven thousand European civilian male internees were concentrated there.

The fate of the women and children was more complicated. The practice of moving trainloads of women and children across the length and breadth of Java had started as early as October 1943, to rid East Java, especially the naval base at Soerabaja, of all European influence. A few months later the focus had shifted to Bandoeng with its huge population of Europeans. Tjihapit served as a staging area, to which women, children and older men were brought from outlying districts, swelling its population to 13,400. It required seven months and the help of eighteen or nineteen dedicated, overcrowded trains to clear Tjihapit. By May 19, 1945, only thirty-one European women (the office staff, including our friend Amelia) were left in Bandoeng to carry out the final administrative tasks.[18] Of the total of forty-seven thousand interned women and children on Java, half ended up in the greater Batavia area; one quarter were interned in Semarang and the remainder in the primitive camps at Ambarawa, with the boys, ten years and up, living in separate camps. This summary cannot begin to convey the full impact of the misery, with thousands of women and children, many of them too weak or sick to walk, repeatedly packed for days in the foul trains, until weeks after the end of the Pacific war. An unknown number died.

This movement of people demanded the application of scarce resources: trains and Japanese military supervision. Its justification was our being part of the Japanese defence tactics. The women and children formed human shields at major marine centres such as Batavia and Semarang, and in the event of a successful Allied invasion, would have presented a humanitarian challenge to the would-be liberators. Concentrating the men in the Preanger highlands was a means to prevent them from assisting Allied invaders.

---

18. We encountered Amelia, the Tjihapit office girl, quite by chance forty years later in Vancouver.

9. TJIDENG

The nightmare that had begun the previous afternoon did not stop when we arrived at Tanah Abang: it only got worse. The earth in its normal spinning course requires 365 days to complete its trajectory around the sun, thus allowing us to shift forward the year's count on the calendar by another digit. But from May 11, 1945, time slowed down—the following months, and the daily miseries that filled that period, seemed to stretch on without end. So powerful was this perception that I could not shake it out of my consciousness for the next forty years—until Ank startled me by saying, "It only lasted five months."

Late in the morning we stood, dazed and tired, on the platform of a rundown suburban railway station near the western edge of Batavia. The heat was oppressive, the air thick with humidity, and perspiration ran freely down our backs, soaking our clothes. Although the sun's hot rays beat down from an almost cloudless sky, it was not blue, but light grey with moisture, and the air felt heavy and was difficult to breathe.

A road with foot and vehicle traffic ran along the far side of the station building and beyond it stood tall, broad-canopied trees, casting a cool shade; there some *inlanders* were crouched in the grass, casually scrutinizing us. Beyond them we could see houses that people like us might once have occupied.

"This is the Djati Baroeweg. Look! over there's the Tanah Abang *pasar*," someone called out excitedly, pointing to the right.

Indeed, in the distance we could make out among more shrubs and trees a bustle of people, while the road was crowded with *betjas* and *grobaks*. How tempting it was to escape that malignant sun and the soldiers with their guns and bayonets, herding us on the platform as though we were cattle; how tempting to join those fortunate *inlanders* in the shade. The stench from our hot, filthy *klas kambing* railway cars had followed us out into the open and clung to our persons; everyone in our party had soiled their clothes with urine or feces. This at least helped to keep the Japanese guards at a distance.

Poor Juf! With her long skirt and coat, she was on the point of fainting and had to be supported in turn by my mother and by Emmy, both of whom were themselves suffering under their bulging housecoats.

After what seemed like an age, two trucks arrived, carrying some young European women who were skimpily dressed in shorts and halter tops. One of the women was wearing what looked like a tea towel tied at her back; it needed periodic adjustment. They wore homemade sandals, and almost all had their hair wrapped in bandanas.

A Japanese soldier stepped down from the cab and conferred with the guards who had accompanied us, whereupon our group leader with difficulty began to order us into columns as for *appel*. In the meantime, the girls, looking thin and worn out, started unloading the goods wagon and transferring the *barang* onto the trucks. It was heavy work and they were obviously struggling, but plodded on with a sense of routine that betrayed frequent repetition of this assignment. All this took place under the watchful gaze of a couple of guards, periodically ordering "*Lekas, lekas!*"

A Blitzbuggy arrived, carrying a Japanese officer. He was perhaps twenty-five or thirty years old, with black leather boots, a sword dangling from his side, a brown leather Sam Browne over his chest, a revolver in its holster on his belt, and the usual ultra-short black hair visible under the sides of his *kepi*. His face was longer than some of the other Japanese soldiers, and he had heavily hooded eyes and thick, bushy eyebrows. His mouth, with a slightly protruding lower lip, betrayed a profound disgust at the sight of us. An impatient threatening gesture from him prompted our party leader, who clearly was unaccustomed to this role, to call us to attention. With a hesitating voice, she called, "*Ki-o tsukete!*" and then, realizing that most of us had not heard this, repeated the order, waving her trembling arms. Then she shouted "*Kerei!*"

This order, too, had to be repeated in a shrill, anxious voice, because some of the party were having trouble paying attention; the journey had been long and we were overcome by thirst, hunger, exhaustion and the awful stress of trying to control our bodily functions.

Then the counting began. How many had boarded the train? How many had arrived? The counting was complicated by the fact that two travellers had died, which the soldiers either did not understand or did not want to accept: two were missing and that was bad. When the officer was finally satisfied with the headcount he barked out some sentences in broken Malay, followed by the order "*Naore!*" and we understood that the counting was finished.

By this time the trucks, loaded with *barang* and girls, had rumbled away; the officer followed in his Blitzbuggy, leaving us once more waiting under the blazing sun, guarded by the soldiers.

Someone muttered, "What a nerve!"

"Yes—saying that we from Tjihapit are a bad lot, and that discipline is tight in Jakarta. Doesn't he know this is Batavia?"[1]

---

1. The Japanese administration had formally changed the name of the city but we continued to use the old name.

Two more trucks turned up, old Chevrolets with wooden sidings and iron frames for canvas covers. They were clearly former KNIL trucks, with faded camouflage paint and old military number plates still visible, though the regimental insignia had been crudely painted over. The soldiers barked orders for us to climb into the backs of the vehicles. It might have been fun for some of the older children in the crowd, were it not for the fact that we were so tired, hungry and thirsty. My mother and Emmy had to lift Juf up, for all strength had by now escaped her. Someone helped her to her feet, for there was standing room only. By the time the truck was full and the tailgate shut we were once more packed tightly together. Unfortunately there were not enough trucks to carry us all, so half the party was left waiting. The truck ahead of us wheeled onto the road, its horn blaring almost continuously, and we followed.

The road ran northward, alongside the bank of a canal with oozy brown water and here and there *babus* washing clothes and naked children happily splashing about but turning to wave at us at the sound of the truck horn. With us driving on the left, we could even hear some of their laughter. Across the road, behind the line of oncoming traffic were more trees and residential houses. Occasionally a tree provided a brief shady respite from the malevolent early-afternoon sun, so closely linked in our minds to the detested *kokki* sun disc of the Japanese flags. The glimpses we caught of the palatial-looking suburban houses, their front gardens filled with flowering shrubs, provided a startling contrast to the drab, rundown appearance of Tjihapit.

We did not have much time for sightseeing, however, because the truck swung frequently around slow-moving carts and other obstructions, making us lurch back and forth. The furious, almost non-stop hooting of the horn guaranteed that all *inlanders* on the street also got a good look at us.

Did those *inlanders* along the Djati Baroeweg realize that this was the first day of a liberated fatherland? Jan Bouwer, still hidden away in the backyard of his house on the northern outskirts of Bandoeng, had heard this news on the radio. Undoubtedly many people living in Batavia knew this as well, but we noticed no sign of this in the attitude of either the Japanese or anyone else around us; the dramatic events that had recently taken place in far-off Europe seemed to be totally irrelevant to the situation here. Even events closer to home seemed irrelevant: Tarakan, one of the main oil-producing centres of Borneo, had just been captured by Australian troops, and Okinawa, an island halfway between Formosa and Japan, would as certain as night follows day soon be entirely in American hands. The former privileged members of this society, having now become a humiliated public spectacle, were worth only blank, apathetic stares. It was as though this island had been transposed to a different universe; so draconian had been the imposition of Japanese control that even now, with the end of the war in sight, no one dared discuss imminent change. In our brief exposure to the outside world, there was nothing that suggested to us that the world was rapidly altering.

Nor could we know that Allied plans regarding our liberation were now also in a state of flux. MacArthur had not forgotten us entirely; he proposed to use the Australian troops that had successfully captured Tarakan to liberate lightly garrisoned Java by the end of June. In MacArthur's view such a move would enhance American prestige.[2] However, politics and grand strategy sank this proposal: in Washington there was no domestic political support for restoring European colonial rule, and the overriding American war objective was the defeat of Japan. For Britain, a new struggle emerged. Forced to relinquish to the United States the role of pre-eminent guardian against totalitarianism, Britain was now striving to retain relevance on the fast-changing chess board of the Pacific war. Playing an active role in the invasion of Japan took precedence over the restoration of Britain's own colonial position, which was furthermore being frustrated by Jawaharlal Nehru's vehement objection to the use of Indian troops for reinstating colonial regimes. The American Joint Chiefs of Staff recommendation that newly sworn-in President Truman should transfer the remainder of the NEI to Mountbatten's command would, if accepted, neatly let the United States off the colonial hook and leave our fate in limbo. The colonial era was obviously drawing to an end.

No one around us could imagine moreover that on that very day, when we arrived at Tanah Abang station, President Truman was being briefed on potential targets for the first atom bomb, an experimental weapon that few understood but the development costs of which had been so immense that Congress would inevitably demand concrete justification.

Our preoccupation was more mundane—preserving our balance on the bumpy, lurching journey through the suburban streets of Batavia, a journey that fortunately was not long. The trucks slowed down and with brakes screeching drew to a halt at an intersection. The refreshing breeze caused by the truck's movement stopped and, as we descended onto the pavement, an unpleasant smell began to be noticeable. Was this the canal by the side of the road, or was it from somewhere else? Ank thought that the canal was called the Tjideng *kali*.

"The word *selokan* is more appropriate," someone offered.

"It never was clean," Ank agreed with a dismissive voice, gesturing towards the water, "but I can't remember it smelling this bad when I lived here."

"I guess we are going into another camp," someone observed. The Borneo rumours were forgotten, and there was an audible small sigh of relief; our destination could have been worse.

---

2. de Jong, *Het Koninkrijk der Nederlanden in de Tweede Wereldoorlog*, 11b, 89.

At this intersection the road crossing our path also crossed the *kali* via a concrete bridge. The girls were still busy unloading one of the *barang* trucks and placing the bags in a long line on the pavement. Passengers were descending from the lead truck and under supervision of one of the guards collecting their bags before joining a queue going over the bridge. A street sign indicated that the road we had come to was called *Laan* Trivelli.

The heat of the tar pavement under my bare feet came as a shock when I alighted from the truck. Most adults still wore shoes, as did some of the smaller children, but I and a few others had bare *kakis* just like the *inlanders,* and it hurt. When we found the double mattress and lifted it on its side, the shade it cast provided a tiny bit of relief for my feet. With our *barang* we, too, could now join the lineup for the next stage of our journey, shuffling slowly over the bridge. Poor Juf needed constant support from my mother and Emmy, or she would have collapsed onto the hot tarmac, where glistening black puddles had formed. The trucks that had brought us now left to collect the rest of our fellow travellers, still waiting at Tanah Abang.

"What's the name of this camp?" my mother asked one of the girls, who had completed their task and were heading past us over the bridge.

"Tjideng," she replied.

As we slowly inched our way forward, it became possible to examine our destination. Ahead of us, beyond the bridge, where *Laan* Trivelli continued westward, there was a gate similar to but more formidable than the one in Tjihapit. It took a little while to understand why it was more imposing: the gate spanned *Laan* Trivelli but was positioned beyond a line of deserted bungalows with unkempt gardens facing us along the far side of the *kali*. Over the roofs of the houses we could make out the top of a high *gedek* wall liberally festooned with *kawat* and obviously running along the backyards of the bungalows. (In Tjihapit, the entire camp enclosure had been located along the roadside.) In addition, the doors of this gate were suspended from extra-large black poles. Somehow the lookout towers far to the right and left also seemed higher and more threatening than the ones in Tjihapit had been. To the left near the gate there was a guardhouse built of a bamboo frame covered with *gedek* and sheltered by an *atap* roof. On its veranda stood a formidable rack full of rifles.

"*Gedekking* is not possible in this camp," Emmy quickly observed. She was right; a house and its garden would separate anyone on the far side of the wall from *inlanders* on the street. We seemed to be entering a high-security prison. What lay beyond the gate was not clear, but the tops of tall trees visible over the *gedek* at least indicated that there would be some shade. How slow was our progress over that bridge, and how delightful the thought of shade.

As we shuffled, a step at a time, closer to the gate, each time lifting with difficulty the huge double mattress, which reached up to my shoulders, we became aware of a terrible commotion ahead of us. It was another *barang* inspection, but this time the young Japanese officer who had first addressed us at Tanah Abang was taking a vigorous personal interest in the process. The officer went about this task like a demon.

"I bet it's money he's after," my mother whispered to Emmy. "They always want money."

Each time a new person got to the head of the queue, he gave them a blow on the head if the bags they had with them were not opened immediately. If the suitcase on the ground had a lock that was sticking or a knot that could not be untied he kicked it, and invariably its contents spilled onto the dirty, tarry street.

"Ho-a! kuso!"

What were clearly choice derogatory terms came out in staccato bursts. From the moment we knew that our destination would be another prison camp we had hardly expected a friendly welcome, but this exceeded anything we had ever suffered in Tjihapit. It was obvious that the man loathed us.

His assistants, Japanese or Korean guards, worked gingerly around him as though he were an explosive device. A couple of grim-faced *Belanda* women were at work beyond the officer helping those who had been cleared through the inspection, reassembling their *barang*.

Finally our turn came. We were lucky again, because by now the officer was showing signs of fatigue. *"Ijiwaru basan!"* he growled when Juf did not open her little suitcase quickly enough and gave her a blow on the head that sent her staggering. Juf could no longer manage her suitcase, and I had to help pick up the contents, stuff them back in, and carry it all into the camp.

As we passed the guards I noticed on the left, beside the pole holding up the door of the gate, a cage on stilts with walls made of chicken wire. From within the cage peered two round, brown eyes. I had never seen anything like this creature, though it reminded me of some of the pictures I had seen during the short time I had been at school.

"A monkey," Emmy explained. With every shout and curse from the officer or cry of pain from a victim, the monkey uttered a high-pitched shriek, leaping to and fro in the cage. We passed through a gap between the two doors of the gate and ahead of us stretched a city street, flanked on either side by a row of tall, broad-canopied trees. Here the heat of the road was more bearable. Before the war this residential neighbourhood had evidently been a pleasant newer suburb of Batavia.

A few women had gathered inside the gate to survey our arrival. "A welcoming party!" Emmy called out cheerfully to my mother. "Perhaps they hope to see friends arriving!" However, as we struggled past, one of them spitefully called us "fatsos!" and "dirty Tjihapiters!"

After we were safely out of earshot, my mother and Emmy stopped to catch their breath and my mother said in a low voice, "Emmy, did you see how thin they are?"

Emmy cast a surreptitious, scornful glance over her shoulder and muttered "Uh huh," once again lifting the mattress and her suitcase. A cluster of new arrivals had gathered around a Tjideng woman, a *kumicho* or *hancho* to judge by her armband, who motioned us to pay attention, as flies gathered around our smelly, dirty bodies.

"The Jap commandant out there is called Sone," she said. "Watch out for him."[3] She then went on to explain that the corner house we had passed before entering the camp, on the left-hand side, was the "Jap office," and the corner house on the right of the gate was where the camp commandant lived. The two houses on either side of the road immediately inside the camp were the camp office and for storage.

"My name is Cornelisse, and I am a *hancho*" she announced in an officious voice. "We have cleared five houses for you Tjihapit people," she continued.

"Five houses! My God," exclaimed my mother. "That's terrible—120 occupants per house!"

So this was now to be our accommodation in Tjideng: houses that were no bigger than the ones we had left in Tjihapit, but that contained four to five times as many people.

Mrs. Cornelisse directed us to the second house on the left side of the street, where a number 91 was still visible on the once whitewashed stone pillar by the garden entrance. To get to the house we had to carefully step over a ditch at the side of the road containing sewage. Further down the road a small team of women and older girls were busy pushing the sludge in the ditch with sticks.

The house itself stood beyond what used to be a lawn, separated from the roadway and the sidewalk by a low garden wall. It was a typical single-family bungalow, with the customary veranda, a pan-tiled roof, and along one side, a driveway. A narrow stretch of garden separated the house on one side from its neighbour to the east, but directly ahead of us the driveway, flanked on the right by a garden wall, led to a garage, set further back. The property next door formed a sort of mirror image, with the two garages sharing a common wall. The arrangement was rather similar to the house we had occupied before the war in the Eykmanweg.

Once upon a time these houses, with their shady verandas, high ceilings, generous living rooms, dining rooms, kitchens, perhaps three bedrooms, and a roof with wide, sheltering eaves providing protection against the monsoon

---

3. Lieutenant Kenichi Sone was appointed commandant of all Batavia camps as of November 4, 1944.

rains, would have been attractive dwellings. However, they had suffered during the last few years: the woodwork around the doors and windows of this particular house was missing, and of the former lawn only patches of grass remained, leaving a yard mostly consisting of bare earth.

At the front of the property, near the road, some pipes stuck out of the ground, looking like a half-completed plumbing project.

"That's where you will get your water," Mrs. Cornelisse said as she waved us on, for she still had many others to deal with.

Juf was too exhausted to move so we left her sitting on the garden wall in the shade of the tree, while the rest of us hurried ahead as fast as we could to claim living space. On our way through the front yard we came past a hole in the ground that once had been covered with a cast iron lid; it looked as though someone had tried to access the septic tank. A disgusting smell wafted from the hole.

The living room was packed with new arrivals, so we pushed through to the adjoining former dining room, where others had already claimed a spot away from the window. Here we dropped the mattress, while Emmy and my mother checked out the bedrooms, only to find that they were also taken. Although the dining room was little more than a thoroughfare between the front and the back of the house, it seemed the best we could find. A space against the outside wall below a window and next to an improvised doorway to the garden, made by knocking out the lower part of the wall, was all we could find. There was just enough space for the double mattress and my air mattress, and this we now called "home."

"I hope this area does not get soaked when it rains," my mother remarked, looking thoughtfully at what was left of the window.

In the meantime Ank and Elsa had found space for themselves and their mothers in the garage of the house next door and shouted to us that there was also space for Juf. We helped Juf to the garage and assembled her cot so that she could lie down and rest. The arrangement was not ideal, for our family group was now split up, but at least we were neighbours, and it seemed to be the best that we could do.

All this time more of our fellow travellers had continued to come past our house, proceeding down the street in search of more cleared space, further from the camp gate.

What We Found in Tjideng

That first evening in Tjideng was chaotic. We were all packed tightly together, stumbling and falling over suitcases, backpacks and bedding, scrambling to get settled. Many children were crying. Those who had arrived after us had to make do with less desirable accommodation than what we had found; in the former kitchen children ended up sleeping under the counter, and even the bathroom had become a dormitory. We discovered the next day that we shared the house with about 110 others.

In the daytime we would have to store our suitcases on the beds to make more space available for those needing to walk from the lounge to the kitchen. The sole functioning toilet on the premises was a squatter in the former servants' quarters around the back of the house. It also now lacked running water and so required the use of a water bottle, not only to clean oneself, but to make a tiny contribution to the flushing.

The *kelambu,* which my mother and Emmy managed to hang from the ceiling, just covered the three of us at night; it would be essential when the mosquito plague peaked during monsoon.

"I'm not sure what's worse," Emmy growled as she tried to adjust the *kelambu.* "Borneo or this. I never dreamt such conditions were possible— *Godverdomme!*" she exploded when a nail she had tried to bang into the brick wall bent and fell out.

"If we can find a plant box we can grow something here," my mother grunted, pointing to the window ledge. She had just had an argument over a piece of the window sill with another woman, who had secured a small space between Emmy's side of the double mattress and the rear dining room wall. That woman had left in disgust to visit a friend. Almost in tears of frustration and fatigue my mother then sent me off with a pail to get water from the faucet near the road. "Just wait your turn," she added.

A little while later Mrs. Cornelisse, our *hancho,* came back to our house with a megaphone in one hand and a bell in the other; she climbed onto a box in the front yard and rang the bell. We gathered to hear what she had to say, discovering in the process that Hanna Poortman and her two daughters were also living here—that was a crumb of comfort. With a hoarse voice Mrs. Cornelisse explained that we should choose two people to go to the Tjimalaja *dapur* with a wash basin that could hold forty to fifty litres of food. This precipitated a frantic search through the house for a wash basin. Did any that we had brought with us from Tjihapit arrive here? A basin was tracked down and two women agreed to go. They returned an hour later with the heavy tub; the sago porridge it contained was enough to dispense about a cup of food to everyone. There were also some unappetizing lumps of bread, which with difficulty were cut into 110 pieces. The porridge was utterly tasteless, but we were so famished that not a drop was left behind and I watched hungrily as a little girl, whose mother had helped carry the tub, was allowed to wipe up the remaining film from the sides of the tub with her fingers; she then slowly and deliberately licked them clean.

That evening, as the sun was setting, Mrs. Cornelisse, armed with her megaphone, summoned us to *appel*. There she was, standing on the street in front of the house next door, calling us to start lining up a little further along the road, facing a building with the word "school" still visible above its entrance. Most of the structure was set back behind a lawn, but at either end a wing approached the sidewalk. "The hospital—the place where you go to die," commented a young woman standing beside us; she was evidently a long-time resident, to judge by her emaciated body. The *hancho* held a sheet of paper supported by a piece of cardboard and was trying to note names as people from our house arrived on the street, a task she periodically interrupted with anxious glances towards the camp gate. "Tomorrow you will get new numbers," she announced. "After *appel* please provide the office—" she pointed to the house next door to ours beside the gate, "—with a piece of cloth and your name and old number."

"Where is the office?"

Mrs. Cornelisse again pointed to the house behind us. "Next to the gate," she answered, as she tried to organize us into columns.

With curiosity we looked down the unfamiliar street, shielding our eyes from the setting sun, to witness an endless stream of people pouring onto *Laan* Trivelli from houses and side streets. At the end of our block, beyond the hospital, there was an intersection and people seemed to be coming by the hundreds from the left and right. The air was alive with the noise of people talking. In Tjihapit, *appel* had occurred in various places throughout the entire camp, but here in Tjideng it was a single massive gathering on what appeared to be the main thoroughfare.

"How many are there in this camp?"

"We think over ten thousand," she answered. Then, changing the subject, she ordered, "You must choose a *kepalla* for your house—I need a name before lights-out tonight."

"Are you the camp head-lady?" someone from a neighbouring column asked.

"No," she replied, and undoubtedly there was an explanation, but Mrs. Cornelisse sped away to deal with other houses and new arrivals.

"There is no *kaicho*," a woman standing next to us remarked wryly. "Sone fired the last one within a week of her getting the job—she was no good anyway." The conversation was brought to an end by an urgent "Shh!" from Mrs. Cornelisse's megaphone, because the gate had opened and a number of soldiers strode down the street. We recognized Sone leading the group.

Mrs. Cornelisse lifted her megaphone and shouted, "*Ki-o-tsukete!*" and then after a short pause, "*Kerei!*"

We bowed. Sone gave one of the ladies in the front row a slap on the back of her head that sent her sprawling, to his evident amusement. She hadn't bowed deeply enough, and now had to pick herself up from the road. After we had spent an interminable period bent over at thirty degrees, the order "*Naore!*" rang out and we could once more straighten ourselves. We had so often done the same in Tjihapit, but now the nervous tension was telling.

And then the counting began out loud.

"*Ichi!*"

"*Ni!*"

"*San!*"

"*Shi!*"

Over and over went this ritual, column by column. Sometimes a column had to be counted twice, even three times, before the next column of women and children could be checked. Finally Sone seemed satisfied and he moved on, followed at a respectful distance by Mrs. Cornelisse, who had to call the next group to order. And thus a succession of megaphoned "*ki-o-tsuketes*" and "*kereis*" rippled down the length of Trivelli, gradually drowned out by the resumption of chatter by the women and children around us. Long after our group had been counted we were still left standing, but at least it had cooled down, for the sun had set behind the trees.

The break from counting gave us a chance to make the acquaintance of long-term inhabitants. The woman who had addressed us before *appel* now introduced herself as "Lydia," and a small girl hid behind her skirts. Lydia had dark hair and alert brown eyes, and her skin was deeply tanned from years spent under the tropical sun. She spoke in short nervous bursts and one got the impression that she had always been thin. She had been in this camp since the beginning of the war and lived in the house next door. She helpfully offered some more background information. "At first it wasn't bad," she recounted. "But during the last year the conditions have worsened. Sone is a beast; he is mad—moon sick! When the moon is full he is really crazy. Kondo was alright—I wish he were still here."

"Who was Kondo?"[4]

"He was not a real soldier. He called himself an economist, but then he left and Sone came. Kondo told us that his father had been a doctor, and he had wanted to follow in his father's footsteps, but the war had interfered. He wanted to be home with his wife and children."

"How many are in this camp?"

"Until about a year ago, we were only 2,600 women and children, and the camp was much bigger, we even had some good times. You know Szymon

---

4. Hachiro Kondo, an economist, was camp commandant from August 1942 until April 1944.

Goldberg and Lily Krauss?[5] They gave us a concert performance—can you imagine Beethoven's Kreutzer Sonata in a prison camp?"

"Are they still here?" my mother asked with interest.

"No they left. Now there are fewer houses and more people," Lydia continued. "I think there are over ten thousand. The Japs keep on squeezing more in."

"The food seems terrible—even worse than Tjihapit."

"Yes? When we first came we had no money to buy food, but some *Belanda Indo* who were living in town helped us; they borrowed money from rich Chinese. Life was not bad then," she continued. "But one day Kondo told us that he had to become a military person and would have to alter his conduct, and he soon left. We had a farewell party for him."

"When was that?"

"March, I think—anyway, over a year ago. Then Lieutenant Sone came and our life has become a hell. People are dying here. If hunger and disease doesn't get you, he will."

"Why is it so crowded? There were more people in Tjihapit."

"That's Sone for you. He has made the camp smaller several times. Mrs. Willinge asked him once why the camp got smaller, and she got beaten up. Can you imagine? A simple question, and she got beaten. One of the other soldiers, a Korean, I think, told her later that Sone wanted to make the camp safer. I think it is to make it easier for him to keep an eye on us."

"Who is Mrs. Willinge?"

"She was the *kaicho*, the camp head."

Then, pointing to the building across the road, she continued, "That's now the hospital." After a short pause, she added, with evident emotion, "That's where we will all end up. If you get sick, that's where you go, not to get better, but to die."

She explained that the improvised hospital was served by four or five doctors and a small team of dedicated nurses, labouring against odds to make some of the sick whole and to ease the way to death for those beyond help. Mention of the hospital evoked in Lydia a memory; with a shaking voice she whispered, "You should have seen what happened in early March—it was awful. Sone had ordered all of the sick, about two hundred, to leave the camp, just like that! Many were dying. Can you imagine? Sick mothers had to suddenly say goodbye to their children. First the children were told that they could go with their mothers and then that they could not. Sick children also had to go, while the mothers stayed behind. He forced the sick into buses and even a

---

5. Violinist Szymon Goldberg was born in Poland, but in 1938 fled Europe for America. While he was on a tour of Asia with pianist Lily Krauss, war broke out and both were interned in Batavia. Both survived the war.

truck, and the poor children and mothers were left standing at the gate, crying. This street was full of crying people!"

After a pause to get her emotions under control, she continued, "We were not even allowed to lend a hand to those too sick to sit or stand and left lying on the ground, waiting in the sun for their truck to arrive."

"He can just get rid of people and send them elsewhere?" my mother asked in a shocked voice; the elaborate transport arrangements that had kept the Tjihapit Ladies' Office so busy was still fresh in her mind.

"Sone is in charge of all of the camps in Batavia. He does what he wants."

"Did you see those poor old men sitting by the side of the road?" This comment came from another woman who had joined the discussion. "They didn't know what was happening. I bet they are all dead by now! The Jap is a beast, a devil," she concluded.

"Why did he do this?"

"He did not want to see people dying in his camp—it would look bad on his reports to Tokyo. That's what Elly said, and she knows him quite well."

"How so?"

"Elly, my cousin, used to be the head of Grogol camp, a former insane asylum not far out of town."

"Was she dealing with mentally ill people?" my mother interrupted.

"No, there were a few, but mainly she was looking after a group of destitute people who had been imprisoned there. Anyway, Sone was boss there, too. When they were moved here Sone tried to get her to be boss in this camp to replace Miep Willinge, but she refused."

"Why?"

"She said it was too difficult," Lydia replied, lowering her voice. "Elly said she could handle Sone and the eight hundred people she knew by name and who trusted her enough to do as she ordered, but the difficulties of dealing with Sone on the one hand and ten thousand distrustful and rebellious women on the other hand was too daunting a task."

"How did she order them?"

"Oh, she insisted, for instance, that they dress modestly, even in the heat, just to keep Sone off their case. Yes, she sort of understood guys like him, but he respected her too. I sure could not do what she did." After a short pause she added, "Sone never touched her."

After standing on tiptoes to confirm that Sone and his party were well out of sight and earshot, another woman remarked, "You know, Sone once even made all of the sick and dying come out on the street for *appel*, and then he beat the patients whose number had been pinned on their *kelambu* and not on their pyjamas."

"Was that *appel* for punishment?"

"Yes, he was upset with the doctors. They were asking too many favours for the sick and dying."

"No, it was not the patients who got beaten up; it was Dr. Scheltema, because she dared ask Sone to excuse one of her patients from being moved onto the street. The poor soul had a serious abscess on her face. Sone then beat Dr. Scheltema until she was bleeding."

"Yes, and he left the sick on the street until midnight! If the doctors complain, he punishes their patients—that is how you stop complaints."

"Did you see the monkey cage outside the gate?"

"No," my mother answered. "I was too busy helping my mother-in-law; she was having a terrible time. She is in bed right now."

"Boudy and I saw it," Emmy interjected, "when we entered the camp."

"One of the women in this camp gave those monkeys to Sone. She was probably trying to win favours. Sone then placed the cage inside the camp to amuse the children—or so he said—and sometimes he let the monkeys out."

"Mrs. R., the bitch who gave him the monkeys, is now living with him! She is a traitor." The words were spat out with vehemence by the newcomer to our discussion.

"Those monkeys terrorized the small children. Sister Georgia complained to Sone, and you know what he did? He made her sit beside the monkey cage, in the sun, for hours each day to make sure that the children did not molest the monkey. Have you ever heard of anything like that? Sister Georgia, a highly educated nun, sitting next to monkeys—Sone can hardly read or write.

"Sone hates Christians!"

"Mrs. Ament—"

"Who?"

"—the administrative head then complained to Sone, and do you know what he did? He pulled one of the monkeys out of the cage and in front of her eyes smashed it against a wall. There was blood everywhere. She was lucky that Sone did not beat her, too."

"Why did he do that?"

"He said she was ungrateful for his gesture of goodwill in providing the camp with entertainment."

"Does he speak English?"

"Only a little. He usually barks in Japanese or shouts in Malay."

"Why is the cage now outside the camp gate?"

"I don't know. He moved it out to punish us, perhaps."

"No, Miep Willinge raised hell with him and called him a 'bastard.' She had guts."

"Did she get beaten up?"

"No, I don't think so, but in April she was sent away to Tangerang, along with other prominent ladies. That is when the cage was moved out of the camp."

"Who—what prominent ladies?"

"Mrs. Tjarda, the American wife of the Governor General and some others. Don't you know, Tangerang is a prison."

"Mrs. Tjarda is back now. I saw her the other day. She is living in a *gudang* at the far end of Tjideng."

"Wait 'til the Americans catch Sone!"

"Noda once told me that he thought Sone was *busuk betul* [rotten]."

"Who is Noda?"

"The assistant commandant, a Korean. He is over there with Sone right now."

Finally the *appel* was completed and Sone and Noda and their *heiho* assistants walked back to the main gate without looking at us, while we made a cursory bow, just to be sure. Everyone heaved a sigh of relief. Our little group broke ranks, but carried on the conversation. Emmy whispered to my mother that in Tjihapit, the head guard, Murui, had at least had the decency to tell us to be "at ease" with a curt "*Yasume!*" Even by Japanese standards Sone was boorish.

"I see you're in the boys' house," Lydia observed.

"Oh?"

"That's where the boys stayed before they left the camp. Yes," she added, "there was no trouble clearing that house this morning."

"That business with the boys was awful," the other woman, later introduced as Mrs. Stibbe, interjected, "and the dogs. That beast Sone first made my son help the other boys kill the dogs. They had been stuffed into jute bags," she added, starting to sob. "My Jac is such a gentle boy, and just eleven years old. He would not hurt a fly—he cried as much as the dogs."

"Kill them? How?"

"Beating them with sticks. He also made the boys dig a grave for the poor animals."

"But some dogs got away that time."

"Yes, and Sone brought in a truck and got the boys to load those last dogs onto the truck."

"Did you see how he hit the dog that tried to get off the truck? It was horrible. With a plank! He hit the dog so hard on the head that it bled and cried."

"Yes, and he thought it was funny!"

"I told you! Sone is a lunatic," insisted Lydia. "You wait until the next time the moon is full!"

"Last month I heard him crying when the moon was full—like a dog."

"I do not trust that Dr. Rijkebüsch. She is often with Sone."

"A friend told me that Annie gives him medication and it seems to help."

"Maybe. The bastard deserves a fatal injection!"

"Well, yes, but I admire her courage to even go near the guy."

Then Lydia gave a graphic description of the proceedings in camp just prior to our arrival that morning. She related how Sone, that very morning, had summoned the *hanchos* and told them to immediately identify five houses for clearance. The occupants of the house we were to inhabit left quite willingly because it was the one nearest to the gate ("*de poort*," as she called it with a slight tremor in her voice, as though it was a portal to heaven or hell).

"Sone then ordered a group of *heihos* into the camp to clear the other houses—bastards with their kicks and sticks—and all morning long people were forced to gather their stuff and to find another spot in another overcrowded house, where you have to push people out of the way to get a small space. We've gone through this almost every week—I had to move twice and each time I lost things."

"It was terrible during the monsoon. Several families had to sleep under the eaves and they got soaked," Mrs. Stibbe added wiping away some tears.

"And the soup kitchens?" asked Emmy. "Are they alright?"

"Oh my God, that was another Sone thing. When it was built—when was it?"

"In February."

"—Sone then wanted money. He said he needed four hundred thousand guilder. We thought he was crazy, and we knew he only wanted to steal the money, but he beat it out of us, literally."

"If we all stay alive that will be enough for one year. But we will starve—he'll make sure of that."

"Is there not a *toko?*"

"There was, but the people who ran it were corrupt. It's shut down now, but they say it'll start up again."

"Who is in charge of the camp, then?"

"Nobody. We used to have Miep. She was terrific, and got on well with Kondo and was not scared of the Japs, but when Sone took over he had her thrown out and her children were left here. Since then, an ineffective committee is running the show."

Night was falling; soon the lights-out order would come. It was time to go home. Thus our first day in Tjideng came to an end. The outlook for the future seemed grim.

Tjideng was located in one of the more modest but newer suburbs on the western edge of the city. The main street, *Laan* Trivelli, continued eastward through older suburbs, and its extension, the Museumlaan, led to the large grassy field in the middle of Batavia, then called the Konings Plein (now *Lapangan Merdeka,* or Freedom Square). The street was flanked by tall, older rain trees that provided generous shade from the burning tropical noonday sun. The eastern boundary was formed by the Tjideng *kali,* a drainage canal separating Tjideng from the main part of Batavia. Its northern boundary flanked an undeveloped, marshy rural landscape with some scattered *kampong* settlements among *sawahs* (rice paddies), more or less continuing to the shore of the Java Sea, seven kilometres further north. Its southwestern boundary (the camp had a triangular outline) ran along a railway line, a continuation of the track we had arrived on. Beyond the railway line, which was on a raised embankment here because of the low-lying, poorly drained land, lay more rice paddies and clusters of small *kampongs.* The northwestern portion of the camp contained modest dwellings, some of which had been intended for occupancy by single people, and before the war had accommodated a red-light district.

Clearly, in selecting this neighbourhood the Japanese had sought an area with a high density of buildings and small yards. The camp's total area was about a quarter of a square kilometre. At the start of the occupation, the camp had included not only the Tjidengweg itself, running alongside the similarly named *kali* or canal, but had also extended further eastward towards the centre of town.

During the previous twelve months Sone had periodically relocated the eastern and southern boundary, in the process removing a large number of larger, better houses and thus creating a smaller periphery that was easier to patrol. These changes also ensured that the house he now occupied, the first one along *Laan* Trivelli, was located outside the camp wall. Where the *gedek* did not run behind houses, Sone had built a second wall to create a no-man's land in between. Those living in the southern and northwestern extremities of the camp were so isolated from the gate by the intervening densely packed mass of humanity that they were oblivious to some of the dramas that often took place there.

This feature, combined with Sone's rages and the lack of coherent leadership, caused much disorientation, and contributed to the apathetic resignation that had become the hallmark of the residents. Children did not dare to play on the street. The camp inmates who lived in the northern area occupied some of the worst houses, where, during the tropical cloudbursts, flooding frequently occurred. They moreover suffered immensely from bedbugs and especially rats, cheeky and hungry enough to nibble at the toes of those asleep. Ank quickly discovered that the garage she and Elsa had found when we arrived in Tjideng was unoccupied because of a bedbug infestation. But the houses near the western edge of the camp had two redeeming features: not only were they isolated from the horrors that took place near the gate, but they could also offer a glimpse of the outside world; over the top of the *gedek* one could see the crowns of palm trees and gently swaying bamboo fronds marking the edge of a peaceful *sawah* infested by creatures no more threatening than rice birds. By climbing on a box or chair it was even possible to see in the distance the *alang-alang*, the tall sharp-edged grasses that spring up on untilled land and that grew along the railway embankment. Some houses that were elevated on account of the poor soil conditions enjoyed a limited view of part of the *kampong* and normal life itself, its inhabitants quietly going about their uncluttered rural lives.

That first night we nevertheless slept soundly after our two-day ordeal. Well, not quite soundly: unfortunately my air mattress had a leak and I woke up to find myself sleeping on the hard tile floor. The disturbance woke my mother, who reinflated my mattress. And so we slept for the remainder of the night.

It was still dark when we were woken for our first morning *appel*. After a drink of water and a small piece of bread left over from the night before, we set out from the house under an early dawn sky. It was surprisingly cold and quiet as we emerged from the building and gingerly picked our way through the dirty yard, past the septic tank. The unpleasant smell had abated somewhat during the night, but traces of it remained. We walked out through the garden gate under the tall dark trees and onto the street. Hundreds of people were already on the street, silently walking towards the hospital.

Juf emerged from the house next door, along with Ank and her mother. "Did you sleep?" my mother asked anxiously. Juf nodded.

"I had to help her to the toilet," Ank murmured. "She is not well."

Mrs. Cornelisse, easily recognized by her tall, gaunt figure and her official brown and red *hancho* armband, was already standing on the street with her megaphone in hand. We proceeded to our place, lined up and waited for the great man to arrive with his entourage. As Sone and his assistants strode down the street, our group fell silent. The *appel* routine of last night was repeated. Once again the hubbub of voices resumed when the counting party had moved further along the street. Someone standing near the rear grumbled, "Mrs. Cornelisse and the others—her English pal Nicholson—they are a useless quartet. They just do as Sone tells them."

To us it nevertheless was obvious that Mrs. Cornelisse was kept very busy. It was almost two hours before we were finally dismissed, and then she had to call out the order for each house to get bread for breakfast. Each day a different house went first to ensure that everyone got their fair share; this sort of thing had become very important.

Our turn came and this time my mother and Hannie, carrying an empty bathtub, set off along Trivelli towards the Tjimalaja *dapur*. An hour later they came back with a full tub. They had had to stop from time to time because the tub was heavy and the metal handles cut off the blood supply to their fingers.

They placed the tub on the veranda, and with 110 hungry faces crowded around, inspecting every move, the two women doled out the rations. We each got five centimetres of sticky, grey bread with a pinch of salt to give it flavour.

"I think we are lucky to be in this house," Hannie remarked. "Did you hear the complaints from the other women?"

"You mean from the Tjimalaja road—about having to carry a tub full of food, while straddling the poop ditch?"

"Yes, it must have been awful during the monsoon."

"Can they not use the road there?" another woman asked.

"Sone has positioned the *gedek* there so that the road is not accessible—just the poop ditch."

"*Bon appétit*," Emmy said as she tied a cloth around her dark hair.

After breakfast the rest of the day got under way; work parties were needed to clear the septic tank with a bucket and carry the contents to the ditch by the roadside and then to move the septic sludge along the ditch to where it disappeared under the *gedek* by the side of the main gate. Each house had to have its own crew to do this work. But Mrs. Cornelisse had also called for help for various other work parties—a "*kawat* team" to fix the *gedek* and *kawat* (barbed wire) wall, always needing repairs, a team to sweep the streets, and a team to help wash linen for the hospital.

At about noon, Mrs. Cornelisse signalled the food carriers—for the time being my mother and Hannie—to once more go back to the kitchen to fetch soup, which was really little more than hot water with some *kangkung* (water lily)[6] stalks floating in it and tiny morsels of meat. The food situation was curious—one never had enough, but it was so tasteless that one really did not want more. When the food containers had been emptied, the children were allowed to scrape out the remnants, which we called *kerak* (originally the Malay name for burnt rice in the bottom of a pot), because nothing was wasted.

After lunch, when the sun was at its hottest, many tried to get some rest, though it was difficult to find peace and quiet inside our overcrowded house, where one could hear absolutely everything, every burp, snore, cough, fart and quarrel, not only from our own room, but also from the other rooms, for there were no longer any doors to shut; we were living in the midst of non-stop chaos. In our room there were ten people trying to sleep, with only a narrow passageway left between the mattresses and *tikars* on our side of the room and those ranged against the opposite wall. We did not know our roommates beforehand and never got to know them well during our stay in this house; they were strangers with strange habits and thus our world had shrunk even further. Emmy's neighbour was fond of reading the Bible, which she had smuggled into the camp sewn into her coat, and she once tried to engage Emmy in a

---

6. *Ipomoea aquatica.* It was mostly the hollow stalks that we consumed.

discussion about the Book of Revelations, but Emmy was an atheist through and through; my mother was glad she did not have to deal with the woman. And thus began a hopeless quest for privacy.

With difficulty my mother had found a place for my father's photograph—the smiling face of a handsome young man in an open-necked shirt. "Do you think Bou has any way of knowing where we are?" she asked Emmy, without expecting any sort of meaningful answer that she did not already know.

"I worry that Edu is no longer alive. He was always so thin—Bou at least had some reserve built up before the war."

Never before had we become so conscious of the expression "no news is good news." The most common way of learning that a loved one in another camp had died was having a postcard come back to the sender with the curt message "Dead" written on it in pencil, and an upside down *tjap* (stamp) on it. There was no place where the recipients of this news could quietly mourn their loss; the combination of abrupt, commonplace death with the brutal environment of the survivors was undermining our capacity for feeling emotion.

An atmosphere of deep mistrust had moreover taken root, and the people crowded around us accordingly fell into two classes: a few, very few, close, trusted friends on the one hand and on the other hand, neighbours to be treated with deep suspicion. With the best will in the world it was easy to lose possessions in the midst of chaos, but desperate hunger also created a terrible incentive to assume that an unguarded item of clothing was a discarded item. The recent arrivals from Bandoeng quickly acquired a reputation for thievery, and the reason was simple: long-time residents of Tjideng had been able to retain many of their possessions, but the ones who had recently come by transport from elsewhere had arrived with almost nothing, creating, even in these pauperizing circumstances, a glaring disparity in wealth, measured in quotidian terms of spoons, cups, tea towels and garments. This led to rampant accusations of theft of clothing from clotheslines, because any piece of cloth, no matter how ragged, had become a potential bartering item for food or a means of maintaining a minimal sense of decorum and modesty in our dress. Tea towels had to serve as clothing when other garments had worn out. There was even a disparity in mementoes. Long-time Tjideng residents had been able to retain their diaries and letters; ours had all been confiscated. Those of us from Tjihapit had not only been forced to make difficult choices when we were transported, but also had been searched too many times to retain forbidden items.

The process of food distribution, three times per day, ensured that there were ample opportunities to vent one's feelings of suspicion, and was liberally accompanied by accusations of cheating: we counted the grains of rice and the drops of soup. The list of condemnatory epithets grew day by day: if one was not on one's deathbed, one was a traitor, a whore, a thief, collaborator or a Nazi. Being cooped up indoors just added to the risk of these unpleasant exchanges, but we children were lucky; since the monsoon had not yet started, we willingly escaped the oppressive daytime atmosphere in the houses by going out to lounge on the garden wall, beneath the trees along *Laan* Trivelli, always keeping a wary eye on the gate for the possible appearance of Sone.

In the bedbug-ridden garage next door Juf mercifully had a tiny bit of privacy, and during these initial weeks I spent a fair bit of time in her company. Some fresh fruit had arrived in the camp and thanks to this nourishment her health seemed to have recovered somewhat. She taught me how to knit, and for a few weeks I spent an hour each day with her, laboriously fiddling with two knitting needles and bits of wool trying to construct a face cloth for my mother. When not knitting, she sewed clothes for me from whatever leftovers she could find. And so we settled into a daily routine.

Of Coffins, Food and Medicine

The huge camp gate, "*de poort*" as we called it with awe in our voices, stood a mere twenty-five metres down the road from our garden gate, and immediately haunted our daily life. Through it we had entered the camp and through it we would leave, most likely sick or dead. Through it came what passed for food, but through it so many had also departed, leaving behind grieving, weeping, emotionally broken survivors. Inside was our known hell and outside a longed-for heaven, but guarding it, the arch-demon, Sone. Whatever drama unfolded in the camp usually occurred at *de poort* and therefore right in front of our house.

A week or so after our arrival I had a second encounter with Sone's monkey. I was in the front yard with a couple of other children, when a sudden commotion took place at the gate, which was partly open; a *heiho* came running in, pursuing the monkey, which scampered down the street to where one of the younger boys from our house was standing in the shade of the trees. For reasons best known to the fleeing animal, it jumped onto the boy's shoulder, causing him to scream with his arms flailing in an attempt to push the creature away. The monkey bit him on the ear before jumping down and carrying on with its flight along the street, thus infecting us with its terror. We ran to the safety of the hot, crowded house.

Every day the great gate would briefly open to let in the food trucks, always a welcome sight. A bread delivery van came every other morning and a meat and vegetable delivery truck early each afternoon. When the latter had offloaded its cargo of rice, greens and what was supposed to represent meat at the *dapur*, it usually stopped right in front of our house to pick up three or four boxes, brought out of a house across the road by a crew of teenage girls; they usually performed this task under the silent, watchful gaze of one or two adults and, from time to time, a child. An Indonesian helper who had come with the truck often assisted the girls with their heavy task of lifting the boxes onto the back of the truck. When this was accomplished, he would climb on the back of the truck next to the boxes, bang on the roof of the cab with his fist, and the truck driver then drove the truck out through the gate.

"What's in those boxes?" I heard Elsa from next door ask, shortly after our arrival.

"Corpses," one of the girls replied, wiping her forehead with her sleeve. Being a pallbearer was just one of the many tasks assigned to the teenage girls who were still relatively strong, because many of the corpses were heavy as a result of fluid retention. The girls carried the coffins from the morgue through the garden to *Laan* Trivelli for delivery by the truck to one of the cemeteries in Batavia. The morgue itself was in a house located next door to the hospital. A passageway, broken through the garden wall separating the former school playground from the neighbouring property, provided convenient access from the hospital. There was neither air conditioning nor refrigeration in the morgue, and since the deaths were almost always caused by amoebic dysentery, the medical staff had recommended prompt removal of the corpses.

A couple of months earlier, when deaths were less frequent, a hearse had still been employed, and then it had been possible for one or two relatives to leave the camp to witness the interment. Prior to Sone's arrival it had even been normal for one of the religious workers in Tjideng to hold a short service, but Sone had put an end to this, even though such a lack of respect for the dead ran counter to Japanese social custom. However, after the chance visit of a senior officer during such an occasion, Sone had been forced to retract this edict and it once more became possible for the recitation of a short prayer in the morgue.

A month before our arrival the hearse had been replaced by the vegetable truck. Days after our arrival the delivery of coffins ceased; instead, a truckload of bamboo poles and *tikars*, the mats commonly used for bedding, was delivered in front of our house. No one knows whether this change reflected a shortage of timber in Batavia, or Sone's discomfort with the high demand for coffins. The death rate of internees was a professional concern to Sone, because he was obliged to submit a regular account of his prisoners, and the shrinking numbers did not look good; the authorities in Tokyo could interpret them as successful escape attempts. His favourite solution for keeping the death rate down was simple: from time to time over the last few months, he had shipped the sick away to hospital camps; if they were to die there, it would be the fault of the medical staff, not his. In Batavia, the St. Vincentius Hospital provided this service and had the added advantage of being subject to his control. On these occasions grieving family members, either mothers or children, were always left standing in front of our house, watching the great bamboo doors of *de poort* swing shut after the truck had departed. No one ever returned.

Death nevertheless visited Tjideng at a rate of three or four per day, and Sone accordingly ordered Tjideng to become self-sufficient in the provision of coffins. Coolies hastily built a bamboo and *atap* coffin manufacturing shelter next to the morgue, and the *hanchos* went around Tjideng looking for coffin-making volunteers; they succeeded in finding five willing women, who immediately set to work. They made a frame from bamboo poles held together with string, and to it they attached panels made from *tikars*. Henceforth Tjideng boasted its own coffin manufacturing industry (figure 16).

Throughout the Japanese occupation, greater self-sufficiency had been a recurring theme. We were more successful with coffins than with the vegetable plots. No vegetables had ever emerged from the Tjideng vegetable plot, for reasons that had also applied in Tjihapit—lack of gardening tools, suitable land and water—but coffin construction proceeded apace. The technical demands placed on these containers were minimal: they needed to last only a few hours, from the time a corpse was entrusted into a coffin's final protective embrace until the moment the coffin left Tjideng on the back of the vegetable truck.

Within a month of our arrival, the demand for coffins had outpaced Tiding's manufacturing capacity, from time to time forcing the morgue staff to load two bodies into the same coffin. Handling these coffins was not only a heavy task but also a delicate operation, because they sometimes threatened to fall apart; in addition they were leaky, and almost always after the truck had left puddles remained on the street.

The departure of the deceased through the camp gate sometimes occurred before the next-of-kin were aware of the death, and so serious had the shortage of firewood for kitchen operations become that personal possessions of the deceased mother—her bed, for instance—would be surreptitiously removed and broken up while the children were not looking. On May 19 the soup kitchens, on which we were fully dependent, sent out an urgent call for firewood. Almost from their first day of operation a mere three months before, they had been plagued by a shortage of fuel, and the last available piano had been sacrificed. By the time we arrived, kitchen staff were having to scrounge for bits and pieces of furniture that had so far escaped burning.

"It's a relief that little Ankie is gone," my mother said to Juf one day in an attempt to console her, for the old lady was in tears. "That's one less worry for Jul [her mother]." Ankie was a little girl next door who had struck up a relationship with kind old Juf after her own grandmother had disappeared; then Ankie had contracted berriberri. Death came mainly to the very old and the very young.

One day the truck was being loaded under the sad gaze of three children, two girls and a boy. Emmy had gone out front to see what was afoot.

"Nobody has time to wash clothes for the orphans," she lamented upon returning to the house, adding, "They look dirty but they seem to get some food."

An attempt had been made to establish an orphanage, but all this meant was that a woman would try to keep an eye on the unfortunates in addition to fighting for her own family's survival. She could not be blamed for failing to wash clothes as well. My mother managed to wash some of my clothes every day—they were not much to look at, but they were clean. Washing took a considerable effort, for whatever supply of water was available had to be carefully recycled. The usual ritual was for my mother to pour water into a small tin bath, placed on what was left of the lawn, wash me first, and then use the same water to wash herself and, finally, our clothes. Mercifully, in the hot tropics few clothes need be worn. Such was our life, with everything out in the open: there was not a bodily function, not even dying, for which we had the privilege of privacy.

The high mortality rate of Tjideng resulted from a combination of the dreadful hygiene and poor nutrition. The entire island of Java had been suffering from a food shortage for several years, caused partly by a succession of failed rice harvests, and partly by the breakdown of the economy and the cessation of inter-island trade. Aggravating this situation was the decision made by the Japanese authorities on May 3, 1945, to stockpile rice for the anticipated final showdown with Allied forces on Java.[7] The most convenient way to do this was to reduce the flow of rice to the prison camps. Nor did the water supply meet the demand; water pressure was so low that all the original outlets had long since ceased to work, and jury-rigged faucets had been installed as close as possible to the water mains, just inside the garden wall and at ground level. The collection of water, drop by drop, from these sources became a full-time occupation. The best supply came at night, when the rest of Batavia was asleep. *Kepallas* accordingly had to organize water-collecting vigils. In Tjideng, the kitchens also being jerry-built, lacked their own water supply and a team of teenage girls and young women had the daily task of bringing water to the *dapur* in large drums.

The food shortage placed the doctors in a constant quandary. What advice should they give to the camp management: to convert the cassava and tapioca flour into porridge, or into a thing we called "bread" (a stodgy chewy lump, for there was no yeast in Tjideng)? What would be the easiest thing to digest? Another dilemma was what to do with the small quantity of nourishing food, such as the occasional shipment of *katjang kedelai* (soya beans) that came into the camp; reserve this for the sick in a desperate attempt to prolong life, or

---

7. Brugmans, *Nederlandsch-Indië onder Japanse bezetting*, 82.

distribute it among the whole camp in an attempt to slow down the rate of admission to the hospital?

I had a brief encounter with the hospital when I cut my scalp while fooling around on a stone wall after the counting of our *appel* section had been completed. Although the wound did not hurt, it bled profusely, and upon seeing this my mother picked me up and carried me past the startled Japanese guards to the hospital across the road, where my scalp was sewn back together with needle and thread. Since no anaesthetic was available for this sort of thing, my mother had to pin me down to let the doctor do his work, and the entire camp heard my reaction to this treatment.

The medical staff and their helpers were remarkable for their dedication to their work. Very often they were driven to asking Sone to exempt a particularly sick patient from *appel* or to request medicine; these requests were frequently rewarded with the blow of a fist and a broken jaw. The doctors as a group suffered more punishment than anyone else. They also had to improvise the manufacture of soap, ether and sterilizing solutions. It is a remarkable fact that they succeeded to the extent that they did, using the most rudimentary materials. Sugar was fermented into alcohol, which was then passed through sulphuric acid to produce ether, and where ether could be manufactured it was traded with other camps and with the Japanese military doctors for other essential medical supplies.

The only way the medical staff could hope to cope with the dysentery epidemic was to impose rigid isolation at the earliest signs of disease. However, this caused potential patients to hesitate in presenting themselves for diagnosis. For mothers with children showing the first symptoms, this was a particularly acute source of agony; once admitted to the dysentery ward, a child was unlikely ever to reappear and would almost certainly die without any chance of the mother being able to visit. The certainty of death increased the likelihood of the spread of the epidemic, since many mothers, fearing the worst, would withhold this life-threatening information.[8]

Overshadowing all of this and affecting everyone equally was a persistent, lingering hunger. Dealing with it was made all the more difficult by the various tactics our neighbours in the house used to bridge the gaps between mealtimes. Some consumed their rations immediately, while others, for one reason or another, tried to defer or stretch out consumption over a longer period of time; thus one was continually being reminded of food. We craved food of any kind and the slightest deviation from the dreadfully boring fare was a major event. The arrival of a shipment of brown beans was so remarkable that it stands out in my memory as a culinary highlight of our stay in Tjideng. To stretch the supply of beans, the kitchen staff had hollowed out the loaves of sticky,

8. Win Rinsema, *Dit was Uw Tjideng,* 72.

unpalatable bread, mixed the crumbs with brown beans and used this as filling for the bread shell. This provided a memorable delicacy. A rare treat for the adults was a liqueur made by fermenting banana skins. Rice was usually available, but the quantities were tiny, measured in spoonfuls. The most common vegetable was *kangkung* (water spinach), but any nourishment it might contain was limited by its sparseness.

Meat was sometimes dispensed in the form of a teaspoon of paste per person. The raw material for this was the entrails of cows or pigs, and occasionally other offal, such as hearts. Elly Campioni, contending with this for the first time in Grogol (a couple of kilometres west of Tjideng), recalls:

> I will never forget this occasion. I was always present when the daily food supplies were brought into the camp. To my horror they one day unloaded, instead of a piece of pig, a tin bathtub full of entrails and a heart. The heart did not bother me, but those intestines! Yes, and what are you to do? In my disgust I grabbed the end of an intestine and squeezed out the contents. This splashed in a green spray over the beautifully polished black leather boots of Sone. I was petrified with fear, but he had also been startled, and nothing came of it.[9]

After being cleaned, the entrails were cooked and ground to make a paste. My mother's experiments during the early days of our internment, with such revolting sources of protein as snails, had been good training. We all got used to everything.

On May 24 we were delighted to hear that eggs would be available: one egg for three people. These were duck eggs, and before the war many Europeans had refused to eat them. The egg shipment offered an opportunity for trade, especially for *gula Djawa*, a brown sticky confection made from palm sugar. A number of children had developed acetone poisoning from the lack of sugar, and a craving for sugar was a widespread phenomenon. Before the war, Java had been a prolific sugar producer, but now sugar was scarce: "Of the eighty-five pre-war sugar factories, only thirteen were still in production, but not all of them were producing sugar—several had been converted to the production of butanol for the manufacture of aviation gasoline."[10]

Finally, the twice-daily *appel* routine, in the morning and in the evening, ensured that each day would start and end miserably. Many were sick, the counting was difficult, and *appel* always took much longer in Tjideng, where we were forced into one huge assembly. If Sone was in a foul mood, he wouldn't hesitate to let us stand an extra hour in the sun for punishment. Many of us had to arm ourselves surreptitiously with potties to avoid embarrassment on the military parade; this, too, became routine, though for the sick, a horrible one.

---

9. Elly Campioni, unpublished memoir.

10. de Jong, *Het Koninkrijk der Nederlanden in de Tweede Wereldoorlog,* 11b, 529.

Curiously, a break from this ghastly daily routine created not elation but anxiety among the Tjideng dwellers. For instance, on May 29, when *appel* was cancelled and the *sjouwploeg*, the team of strong young women who did all manner of heavy work, were not called to the gate as usual for a new assignment, everyone got tense and nervous: what was afoot? There was never an explanation, so the anxiety only ended when we resumed our accustomed daily *appel* routine the next day.

On May 17, 1945, six days after our arrival, the American air force began to bomb the main islands of Japan from the newly constructed air bases on Okinawa, even while that island was still partly in Japanese hands. Up to now, the B-29s had to make the journey from the Marianas, over 1,500 miles away from their destination, a trip that had now been reduced by a third. A week later more than four hundred bombers left Okinawa for Tokyo and its immediate surroundings, raining death and destruction over a land bereft of almost all defences against air attack. In spite of this the war seemed doomed to continue, not only for us, but also for the inhabitants of Japan, who were expected to resist buckling under foreign pressure, regardless of the consequences for themselves.

In Tjideng we were oblivious to both the destruction that had been descending on the sacred land of our oppressors and to the fact that Japan's ability to wage any sort of war was being extinguished and our continued imprisonment was an act of stubborn defiance by an isolated band of Japanese soldiers. We were also oblivious to the lengths to which the Japanese soldier was then prepared to go, serving his God-Emperor by sacrificing his own life and that of any other person for what he saw as a sacred cause; all we saw was the brutality with which he treated us. The vision that we all clung to was the day the American army would triumphantly break down the camp gate and liberate us.

Our hope for an American invasion was matched by our captors' apprehension, and their preparations for dealing with the threat continued apace. In the previous week the Indonesian papers had made public preliminary plans to evacuate all children from the cities of Java because of fear of American actions. Dreadful stories were circulating about the atrocities committed by Allied troops against Indonesian *heiho* captured at Tarakan, a storyline quickly taken up by nationalist politicians eager to win converts to their viewpoint. On Sunday, May 20, General Nagano gave a major speech, expressing his disappointment that Indonesians had not been more enthusiastic in their embrace of the opportunity offered by the regime of *dai Nippon*. He did admit that some of his subordinates had been unwise in the zeal with which they had used Japanese disciplinary measures on Indonesians. The February uprising in Blitar had been attributed to this lack of cultural sensitivity.[11]

In Tokyo, thanks to the devastating daily air attacks, the Japanese High Command was changing its approach to the politics of occupation. They instructed Field Marshall Count Hisaichi Terauchi, overseeing all operations in Southeast Asia from his headquarters in Saigon, to seek the opinion of local commanders regarding independence proposals; General Nagano had recommended immediate action, but it was unclear whether this would apply only to western parts of Java or to other parts of the archipelago as well, since the Japanese navy, still in control of Singapore and Soerabaja, did not share this viewpoint. On May 28 a commission was nevertheless established in Batavia to lay the groundwork for Indonesian independence; its task was to prepare a detailed action plan.[12]

Almost concurrently the American nuclear physicist Robert Oppenheimer was trying to explain to a gathering of senior Pentagon officials what was meant by the "neutron effect" of an atomic bomb explosion. He described it as "dangerous to life, within a radius of at least two-thirds of a mile." The main purpose of the discussion was target selection, and it was agreed that the most desirable target would be "a vital war plant employing a large number of workers and closely surrounded by workers' houses."[13] It was an uncomfortable meeting because the scientists' initial willingness to develop this monster weapon had been stimulated by the fear that Hitler would obtain it first, but Hitler was dead now.

De Poort

De poort, the great gate and its malevolent guardian, continued to overshadow our existence.

During the early afternoon, most Tjideng inmates tried to get some rest indoors. Before the war, a midday siesta had been common practice throughout the Indies, but now it was absolutely essential for conserving energy. On a quiet Tuesday afternoon in early June, Sone chose to accompany the bread truck into the camp. He must have been in a devilish mood, for he kept himself hidden from view as the truck rumbled in. He then noticed that the truck, driven by an Indonesian, was being ignored by the few persons out on the street under the noonday sun. Nobody bowed to the driver, an employee of the Emperor of Japan; this was a clear contravention of the military regulations. Sone stood up, banged on the roof of the cab, and ordered the truck driver to stop, turn the

11. Bouwer, *Het vermoorde land*, 344.

12. Brugmans, *Nederlandsch-Indië onder Japanse bezetting*, 83.

13. Martin Gilbert, *A History of the Twentieth Century*, Vol. 2, 1933–1951, 692.

truck around and leave. Ten minutes later the great gate once more swung open and the delivery truck slowly re-entered the camp and proceeded up *Laan* Trivelli, only to make another U-turn and once more disappear, as though hell-bent on making us suffer: no bread!

A huge commotion now broke out in the camp. The *hanchos* were promptly summoned to hear Sone's complaint—the camp was displaying inadequate *hormat* for the Emperor and his servants, who, in defending their land against the wicked barbarians, needed more sympathy and respect than ever before, especially from the despised and degenerate European women. To punish us he would withhold food for three days. The *sjouwploeg* (work-team) girls were ordered to dispose of all remaining food in the kitchen; they also had to dig trenches and bury the supply of bread that had been awaiting distribution.

An astonishing scene then took place, with Sone himself participating in the destruction of food. He stomped up and down on the bread in the ditches to make sure it was indeed inedible and then, beside himself with rage, entered the kitchens, kicking over the drums so that the soup and porridge being prepared for ten thousand mouths oozed over the ground to turn into mud. Finally he hurled a brick at the electric clock hanging from the wall of the Tjimalaja *dapur*, destroying it; the clock had been important for the kitchen staff in preparing the food within the time allotted by the military regulations. And so the kitchen was shut down.

That night it was almost impossible to sleep. All around us in that terribly overcrowded house, there was crying from children and adults alike. The incessant crying of some distressed children drove their mothers to distraction. One woman in the far corner of the living room even shrieked at her child to be quiet; this was immediately followed by snarky comments from a woman lying on a *tikar* next to her.

"We must keep a supply of water handy," Emmy muttered, "and we must above all keep calm and rest." But it was difficult. A deep depression descended on the camp. Three days without food, and that on top of the usual hunger! Some people had tiny bits of emergency rations, left mostly from the shipment of Red Cross parcels received in the previous month. Those who had arrived later, including ourselves, had nothing. Mothers tried to let the children sleep as much as possible to avoid them wasting energy.

For two nights, almost no one in our house slept because of the crying of children. The diarist Anneke Henkes wrote:

> 4 o'clock, lying in bed—and I am thinking about food. I regret all the things in the past I had not eaten. Anne (her young daughter) is sleeping again. Almost everyone is staying in their beds. The children

are no longer naughty, but some adults are going crazy. Children are stealing bread, mothers are breaking into buildings.[14]

One never forgets such hunger.

Now that food trucks were no longer allowed into the camp, a temporary space problem arose in the morgue. One of the doctors plucked up the courage to remind Sone of the serious health risk he was incurring. The doctor was rewarded for his impertinence with a customary blow on the face, but a truck nevertheless entered the camp on the following morning, since Sone shared with his colleagues a dread of disease. Once again the morgue team was summoned to carry out their grisly task, now made even more onerous by the terrible hunger, the accompanying nausea and the resulting sleepless nights, along with the chagrin that the truck had come this time only to retrieve the dead. Outside, on the street in front of our house, the dreary daily ritual of loading the dead onto the back of a truck hardly lost a beat.

The medical staff tried to offer some relief by handing out minuscule quantities of bread and *katjang idu* (lentils) from the hospital emergency supplies, but that evening Sone ordered the camp to hand in all *anglos* so that no one could even think of surreptitiously cooking a meal. If a fire of any description was discovered at a house, food would be withheld for an entire week. We ground up the *katjang idu* and ate them with our tiny bit of bread. It was tasteless but provided some nourishment.

At the close of *appel* late in the morning of June 7, Sone gave permission for the kitchens to begin operations again. When he was out of earshot there was a muted "hooray." The *hanchos* asked everyone to bring whatever water they had to the kitchen to facilitate the cleaning of the large food drums, which were still partly filled with now mouldy food. And while the kitchen staff was thus occupied, we waited on our beds, because we were too hungry and weak to do anything else.

My mother managed to warm some water with a pinch of salt for flavouring in order to sustain Juf and me until the food was ready, and then she also went to the kitchen to help. The agony of waiting was made worse by people around us constantly talking about food, food and more food. Why could they not just shut up?

Finally, in the afternoon, the megaphones once again called the food carriers to the kitchens, and Emmy and Liet, her helper, hurried off with the bathtub. An hour later, when Emmy and Liet returned with our lunch, they were in a state of high excitement; they had heard the news (or was it a rumour?) that Sone was leaving. "We are not allowed to celebrate," Liet added.

"I don't believe it," my mother objected after eating her portion. After some reflection she wondered, "Is he being promoted or punished?"

---

14. Kemperman, *De Japanse bezetting in dagboeken: Tjideng*, 203.

Another woman in the house had been to the Ladies' Office and that evening, while waiting for *appel,* could confirm the news, adding that he would be replaced by a more reasonable man, "one who is more *manis* [gentle]. The first thing he'll do is give us back things that the Japs stole from us. It has something to do with the end of the war."

Lydia from next door commented dryly, "When Sone came he also was supposed to be *manis.*"

The next day the news of Sone's departure was dismissed as balderdash. There had been so many "good news" rumours before, and they had always resulted in increased suffering, the dreary daily routine always reasserting itself. Nevertheless on June 14 we were surprised when Ohara, one of Sone's assistants, turned up for morning *appel* accompanied by a new, smartly dressed Japanese officer with a beautiful shiny sword swinging from his belt. After *appel* the pair paid a courtesy call to Mrs. Stachouwer van Starckenborgh, the Governor General's wife, then living in a dank, almost lightless *gudang* in a remote corner of the camp accessible only by a path alongside her sewage ditch. This display of *hormat* to the wife of the Governor General of the Indies, living in such an atrocious, filthy environment, was curious. What were these two thinking?

In the meantime Mountbatten was planning the recapture of Singapore, a key step in the liberation of Sumatra. Operation Zipper would be an amphibious landing on the Malay coast facing the Bay of Bengal, where he expected to encounter formidable opposition from the defending Japanese army, entrenched in daunting terrain. Above all, he needed adequate air cover and he was hoping to get the use of light fleet carriers no longer needed for the protection of shipping over the Atlantic Ocean.[15]

An election was soon to be held in Britain, however, and the votes of servicemen would be important. The Secretary of State for War therefore announced that service abroad in east Asia would be cut from three years and eight months to three years and four months. The resulting loss of thirty-two thousand experienced veterans forced Mountbatten to delay Operation Zipper pending the necessary training of less experienced personnel. In addition, Mountbatten would soon learn that the light fleet carriers he had requested would instead be assigned to future operations in the Pacific in order to give the British component of a planned Japan invasion fleet greater weight in American decision making.

The perspective in Tokyo was also changing dramatically: the palace had inadvertently been bombed, and the strain of the situation caused the Emperor to become ill. His Privy Seal, Koichi Kido, now prepared a draft plan for

15. Ziegler, *Mountbatten,* 298.

"Controlling the Crisis Situation." The Kido plan called for help from the Soviet Union, which had remained neutral in the Pacific war. Kido was banking on the assumption that Russia would be quite content to let Japan wear down the Americans. As recently as June 8, an Imperial Cabinet meeting had persuaded itself that victory was still possible, despite the devastating American bombing.[16] In terms of withstanding the Allied onslaught, there was a huge difference between Japan's situation and that of Germany; mounting an amphibious invasion of Japan was far more difficult than sending tanks across the north European plains. Nevertheless, the willingness of Hirohito to countenance anything other than ultimate victory represented a startling change of policy.[17]

To all this we were oblivious, but Sone's imminent departure seemed to have become assured; the day after our introduction to Lieutenant Sakai, Sone ordered the slaughter of two piglets for a farewell feast and celebration of his promotion to captain. The resulting euphoria stimulated some long-time residents to organize their own celebration; on Sunday evening we were startled by the sound of music. It was very soft and came from the backyard of a house further up Trivelli, where a musical *soiree* was being held for about 120 invited guests. Mrs. t'Hoen gave a short violin recital followed by the singing of some *chansons* by Greta Beuk and Crince le Roy.

The next day, however, we once more witnessed the sad spectacle in front of our house of trucks being loaded with desperately sick people. Family members of the evacuees complained bitterly to the *hanchos*, and they in turn complained to Ohara, Sone's assistant, but he would question neither Sone nor Sakai: an order was an order. Both the reason for the order and the destination were left unexplained and undefined. As the trucks departed through the gate, a small group of distraught adults and bewildered children were left standing on Trivelli in front of our house.[18,19]

The following morning our new commandant, Lieutenant Sakai Sado, accompanied Sone with morning *appel*. We expected to hear a lengthy speech in Malay or Japanese, but all the man could utter was, "*Boleh pulang* [You may go home]."

---

16. Gilbert, *A History of the Twentieth Century*, Vol. 2, 1933–1951, 692.

17. Bix, *Hirohito and the Making of Modern Japan*, 508.

18. After the war we learned that this group went to Halmahera, a terribly overcrowded camp located in Semarang, three hundred kilometres to the east. It was a gruelling journey lasting two full days and one of the travellers died even before boarding the train. The total death toll upon arrival and during the remainder of the war is not known.

19. The total number of deaths in the civilian camps on Java is estimated at 6353 internees—see Utsumi Aiko, "The Japanese Army's Internment Policies on Dutch Civilians on Java."

"Sone's getting transferred because the Americans are coming. He knows they would hang him for what he's done," Lydia promised. "You just wait and see." That soon became the consensus throughout Tjideng. Everyone believed that Sone's departure was linked to the coming of the Americans. When Sone did not show his face inside Tjideng for the next two days, it became obvious that he was gone and the atmosphere in Tjideng became noticeably more upbeat. Late Thursday afternoon some young women were even tempted to try a bit of *gedekking*, trading for food through the wall, in the far northwestern corner of the camp, out of sight and earshot of the main gate. The *gedek* here bordered the end of the Burumaweg, which led eastward to the city centre; its westward extension was a footpath through an open *alang-alang* field, past a wind-blown coconut palm and then across the railway line and on through rice paddies to the hovels of a *kampong*. Buruma was therefore the main link between the poor country folk and the city. It was here, through a hole in the bamboo wall, that the smuggling got under way. It was not the first time this had taken place, but on this particular occasion the commercial transactions were undertaken with a good deal of upbeat noise and chattering, since the women had thrown all caution to the wind.

Elsa, who happened to be on duty in the Batanghari kitchen, not far from this spot, heard the excitement and hurried home to find items to trade, but when she returned was unable to get anywhere near the fence on account of the size of the crowd that had gathered. A *hancho* also got wind of what was going on and tried desperately to bring the trade session to a halt, but to no avail.

While the trade was still in full swing a drunk Sone returned from town, where he had been celebrating his recent promotion; upon his arrival his European girlfriend (who shared his house and bed) suggested that he take a look to see what was going on. He immediately headed for the Batanghari field, taking one of the guards with him, and he caught the *gedekkers* by surprise. He knocked the heads of two of the women together, and ordered the guard to find the *kumicho* for that block.

Mrs. Muthert-Vryer arrived on the scene at about three o'clock to find Sone using his fists to punish his victims, their faces black and blue and bleeding, and finishing the job by roughly cutting off all their hair; the woman he had in his grip was screaming in agony. Sone ordered the *kumicho* to immediately evict all of the residents of the entire city block adjacent to the fence and the field. Between six and eight small houses were involved, accommodating as many as two hundred women and children. One of those houses was occupied solely by elderly ladies. The *kawatploeg* (the team of girls charged with maintaining the camp wall) immediately began moving the *gedek* to deprive the already hopelessly overcrowded camp of this accommodation as well. To avoid the risk of the former residents also losing their possessions through this hasty action, the *hancho* quickly got the *sjouwploeg* (another team of girls) to help move the belongings out of the houses to safety, a couple of blocks down the road.

Around six that evening, Sone ordered all those guilty of *gedekking* to present themselves at his office by the gate. The *hanchos*, armed with megaphones, broadcast these instructions throughout the entire camp, but no one dared show her face. By this time all of us sensed that this was an extremely serious situation, because nothing so dramatic had ever happened before. Everyone hunkered down in their homes, not daring to raise their voices lest they carry to the camp gate and Sone's ears, but debating in whispers what was best—to obey or ignore the edict. During evening *appel*, Ohara, the tall Korean guard, warned us that the outlook was grim and advised a substantial turnout of volunteers in compliance with Sone's demands. "*Sone gila*," he said. (Sone is crazy.)

At the close of *appel*, the *hanchos* again went up and down the streets with their megaphones, urging a large turnout. This time fourteen or so, including Ank, who was suffering at the time from yellow fever, and Elsa, ventured onto the street to join a small group that had already gathered there. They lined up at the gate to await further orders, but Sone was dissatisfied: not enough had turned up. He made it clear that he especially wanted to see all those younger women living in *Han* II and that the entire *han* would be denied food for a day if not enough turned up. By eight o'clock another seventy or so volunteers had joined the group of women on the street and stood waiting in front of our house, while more women cautiously approached; eventually, almost five hundred stood there, waiting. Emmy, having no children to worry about and urged by whispers of "safety in numbers," had also joined this group.

Everyone in our house was clustered on the front lawn, by the veranda, anxiously peering through the dark, between the trunks of the roadside trees, and wondering what would happen next. The moon, nearly full, had just risen over the eastern horizon, and its beams, now shining through the open gate, bathed the crowd of women in an eerie glow.

Sone strode up and down the front row, where Elsa and her two older friends were standing, slowly looking each woman up and down. Elsa, still limping from her encounter with the *Kempetai* in Tjihapit, was seething with rage. Ank and Fien, a house-mate, had difficulty restraining Elsa from attacking Sone, and feared the worst if Sone became aware of their grip on her. He passed them by, but then stopped in front of the fifth woman in the lineup, dragged her out and began to beat her. It was not an arbitrary choice: he knew her from previous encounters and judged the time ripe to settle old scores. He picked out more women, including the *hanchos* and *kumichos* who had failed to exercise proper control, and marched them to the house diagonally across the road from ours, standing adjacent to the camp gate. The remainder of the party were left standing on the road.

The anti-air-raid building had a veranda along the breadth of its facade, lit by a single lamp dangling by a cord from the ceiling. In happier times before the war, the veranda would have been a pleasant place for the inhabitants, a family of perhaps three or four, to sit in the evening, savouring the relief brought by cooler night air and, on a cloudless, moonless night, the magnificent cupola of stars in an otherwise black sky. Here Sone, assisted now by *heiho* armed with staves and by Japanese soldiers, proceeded to the next stage of punishment. Some of the soldiers had helped Sone celebrate his promotion earlier that day, and were now looking for more entertainment or perhaps an opportunity to vent their frustration at being so far from Japan and their own homes, which were being bombed.

Sone began with a lengthy harangue addressed at the *heiho* in broken Malay, "Holy Japan is fighting the American barbarians, while protecting these ungrateful women, these sluts, and they disobey the Emperor's divine orders." He sometimes broke into Japanese, with "*baka, kusobaka*" and other choice words for which the Malay equivalent escaped him. He then ordered his first victim to advance towards him on her knees and began to accompany his harangue by beating her head, which soon began to bleed profusely. Every now and then, he succeeded in knocking the object of his wrath and fury down to the ground, but every time she managed to struggle to her feet; this seemed to exacerbate his fury. He grasped her by the hair and violently swung her around, causing the poor wretch to scream in agony. She collapsed once more and then tried to pull herself up on his uniform. It was hard to tell whether this was brazen defiance or she was simply dazed, but he responded by kicking her. Finally, he had had enough and ordered the *heihos* to drag her away and shave her head. While one held her another took a knife to her hair, a symbolic decapitation—to shame her. Then a third *heiho* with a hand-operated hair clipper completed the task, as the woman continued to shriek. By the time they were finished, the victim was covered with blue welts and blood was streaming down her face.

Sone repeated this with the other women he had so carefully selected, taking his wrath out not only on two confessed *gedekkers*, but also on Mrs. Muther Vrijer and her three fellow *hanchos*, along with the *kumichos* of *Han* II. From where we stood, the veranda light, swinging in a light breeze, cast a restless glow over the scene, with the shadows of the soldiers and the *heiho* executing a macabre dance over the house walls behind them, like demons in a traditional Indonesian *wajang* puppet shadow play.

As a finale, Sone demanded that all the women who had presented themselves at the gate hand over to him their rings, the only item of value that they still possessed. By now it was near midnight and the full moon stood high in the sky. Sone and his men left, while the remaining volunteers helped some of the victims to the hospital for first aid. But Sone had not yet finished. When we went to bed he went to the Batanghari *dapur*, where he expended the last of his wrath on the drums of food partially prepared for the next day's meals, kicking them over and spilling the contents onto the ground and, just to be sure, finishing the job by hurling dirt on the food pile. A few days later he wrote a letter to his parents, informing them of his promotion and his trials and tribulations: "The path to spiritual insight is difficult for those who are not holy, though I am constantly seeking that path."[20]

The woman who had been punished first lived in the house next door to us. The next morning, when her children woke up and saw the wreckage that was their mother, they began to scream hysterically. Elsewhere in the camp, once again made smaller, a group of women and children were on the move, looking for alternative accommodation. They had spent the night sleeping in the open on the dirty ground and were thankful that the monsoon season had not yet begun.

"I told you that the man is a lunatic," Lydia said later that morning. Her previous assertions to this effect, shortly after our arrival in Tjideng, had been questioned by Emmy and my mother, both of whom were down-to-earth characters.

"Did you notice the moon last night?" Lydia asked rhetorically, as though to say, "I told you so."

That same morning Dr. Lentjes went to the camp office to seek exemption from the starvation order for a group of children from *Han* II; they were lying in the hospital suffering from dysentery and their risk of death was very high. Sakai, our new camp commandant, for whose benefit Sone had perhaps carried out his final act of vengeance on the European women, whacked Dr. Lentjes over the head for her audacity, but then approved the reopening of the soup kitchen. That day three of the shaven *hanchos* dutifully carried out their *appel* tasks as though nothing had happened the previous night. Two wore headscarves and the third a wig, made available at short notice by a woman called Nel, who until now had kept her hair in a long braid but for the occasion agreed to relinquish her possession. One of the Korean guards, Noda, confessed to a *hancho* that in his opinion Sone was *busuk betul*, a very sick man.

That day, June 21, 1945, has gone down in the annals, recollections and camp diaries of the Tjideng internees as "St. Bartholomew's Night."[21] The link between what happened in Paris and what happened in Tjideng is tenuous; although what happened in Tjideng fell far short of anything resembling a mass murder, it nevertheless was traumatic for all of us and ensured that Sone would never return to his native land.

---

20. van Velden, *De Japanse burgerkampen*, 497.

21. On August 24, 1572, a catholic mob murdered Admiral Gaspard de Coligny, a Huguenot military leader, touching off months of religious violence resulting in the deaths of thousands of Huguenots.

On that same day, the Americans finally reached the Okinawa command cave where the two senior Japanese officers, General Ushijima and General Sho, "dressed in full ceremonial uniform and wearing their ceremonial swords, had been served a special feast, and then, kneeling on a clean sheet with their faces directed towards Hirohito's palace in Tokyo, killed themselves, using a specially sharpened sabre."[22] During the preceding weeks, that small Japanese island had changed hands, with the loss of 120,000 Japanese soldiers and eighty thousand to 150,000 civilian islanders, many of them committing suicide at the behest of the Japanese army.[23] American losses were a staggering 12,500 soldiers and sailors.

The Japanese nevertheless remained confident that an inevitable American invasion attempt on the home islands could be repelled by fanatical soldiers assisted by peasants armed with bamboo spears, and that Japan would be negotiating peace terms from a strong position. Hirohito had come to the conclusion that the week-old Kido plan for a diplomatic end to the war had to be pursued with all diligence, and on June 22 urged his Supreme War Leadership Council to follow this course. However, "neither Hirohito nor anyone else in the room was thinking of immediate capitulation," and a telegram was sent instructing the Japanese ambassador in Moscow to initiate peace manoeuvres on Japanese terms.[24] That signal was intercepted by both British and American intelligence and was ignored; since the Japanese initiative sought to forestall invasion of the home islands and to avoid unconditional surrender, planning for both an invasion and dropping an atomic bomb continued.

On the night of Monday, June 25, the moon displayed its dismay at the suffering inflicted by human on human by briefly disappearing from view; there was a full eclipse, visible over much of Southeast Asia. The spectacle precipitated great anxiety among the humble inhabitants of the *kampongs* and *desas* over Java. They were ignorant of the mechanics of the solar system and could only conclude that evil spirits, unleashed from the bowels of the earth, were responsible for hiding the moon. They now sought to chase away these spirits by going along the streets on the other side of our bamboo wall, shouting and banging on gongs and *tongtongs* (hollow blocks). Lieutenant Sakai also became anxious and at midnight ordered all the Tjideng residents, already awake on account of the noise, out on the street, while Kato, one of the Korean guards, was sent looking for a thief or perhaps an evil spirit in the camp; as a

22. Gilbert, *A History of the Twentieth Century*, Vol. 2, 1933–1951, 693.

23. Mass suicides had also been ordered when the Americans landed on the Kerama islands; there the Japanese army handed out grenades for the purpose. (*Asahi Shimbun,* editorial, June 23, 2007).

24. Bix, *Hirohito and the Making of Modern Japan*, 494.

precaution he was accompanied by two *heiho*. We enjoyed the celestial spectacle in the cool night air.

The next day, delegates in San Francisco signed the Charter of the United Nations. The preamble stated that "We the peoples of the United Nations determined to save succeeding generations from the scourge of war which twice in a lifetime has brought untold sorrow to mankind, and to reaffirm faith in fundamental human rights...have agreed to the present charter of the United Nations." Chapter 1, Article 1 furthermore undertook "to develop friendly relations among nations based on respect for the principle of equal rights and self-determination of peoples, and to take other appropriate measures to strengthen universal peace." Article 2 of that chapter stated the principle, "Nothing contained in the present Charter shall authorize the United Nations to intervene in matters, which are essentially within the domestic jurisdiction of any state, or shall require the Members to submit such matters to settlement under the present Charter." How "self-determination" and "domestic jurisdiction" were to be interpreted was not explained. Herein would reside future conundrums, and nowhere sooner than in the Netherlands East Indies.

Sone Is Gone

We never saw Sone again and gradually the Tjideng atmosphere became less tense. When not preoccupied with our tasks, such as catching flies (all children above a certain age had to catch ten flies each day and deliver them in a glass jar to the *kepalla*) or searching for something edible through heaps of discarded, rotting vegetables and fruit, the children began to venture out on the street, in the absence of traffic a perfectly safe place, where we once more played games.

One such game involved digging a hole in the bare earth beside the pavement, laying a short stick across it, using another longer stick to flick the short one into the air, and then attempting to strike the stick before it fell back to the ground. With skill and luck one could whack the stick right across the road. It was a sort of baseball or cricket game, but without a ball, because we had none. From discarded sewing yarn spools we made "tanks"; this involved cutting grooves in the raised wooden edges to ensure traction, slipping a piece of elastic band (obtained by cutting a slice off a discarded bicycle tire) through the hole, and looping it around a long stick on one side of the spool and a short stick on the other side. We then wound up the elastic band and placed the contraption on the ground, where it would slowly roll along. We also managed to play hopscotch with stones to mark the squares and we improvised stilts from tins. Empty tins were still available, thanks to the Red Cross shipment that had arrived in the camp in early May. Tins were highly prized possessions and the highest priority had been their conversion to domestic utensils such as sewage buckets or cups, but any tins left over were scooped up by the children. With a nail and a brick we made two holes near the closed end, through which string was passed and tied into a long loop. The idea was to stand on those tins, open end down, and hold the tins to the soles of one's feet by means of the string, and then to walk on the road, making a delightful clattering sound.

This relaxed atmosphere was reinforced on July 1, when *gula Djawa* became available from the camp *toko*. All children were given a one-ounce lump of the sticky brown stuff, a real treat, which we nursed all day long. I showed my piece of *gula Djawa* to Juf when I dropped by to work on my knitting project, to which I added a row of stitches each day. In addition, I needed to help Juf wind wool into balls, for she had joined the knitting brigade, as she had also done in Tjihapit. In Tjideng she got paid thirty-five cents for stockings that had to be thirty-five centimetres long. The socks needed a provision for a big toe, but a heel was unnecessary, and the Japanese soldiers were very pleased with the end product. There were other, incidental benefits to this activity, because the women soon discovered that the thirty-five-centimetre standard sock could be achieved faster and with less effort if a shorter product was soaked in water and then stretched with the help of a brick, providing as well a small surplus of cotton.

Several changes affected the lives of the adults. The upheavals of the last few days in the communal kitchens had rendered the staff either unwilling to carry on or incapable of doing so, and the *hanchos* were looking for a hundred new volunteers, so my mother and Emmy, neither of them shy of work when food and survival were at stake, put forward their names. In addition, Lieutenant Sakai asked the *hanchos* to find a *kaicho*, and Miss A. M. Roorda van Eysinga, a diminutive but patient former schoolteacher, agreed to take on this position. Under Sone she had been part of the management committee supervising the work of a group of teenage girls. As a result of this appointment, Sakai refrained from entering the camp, but stayed holed up in his office outside the gate and dealt only with Miss Roorda. Not everyone in the camp welcomed the new *kaicho*. Several women in the camp viewed the change with suspicion: Miss Roorda was "sweet and honest," but she did not have enough "push" in their opinion, and anyone selected by a Japanese camp commandant was bound to be a toady.[25] Hers was a difficult role, but she survived as leader until the end of the internment, thanks to her immense patience and Sakai's more reasonable behaviour; he was strict but "correct," and to everyone's surprise returned the jewellery that Sone had confiscated. When asked for modest improvements in our daily lives, he responded by not doling out blows with his fist, but by undertaking to "raise the matter with his

---

25. The military regulations specified that a *kaicho* had to be appointed by the commandant.

superiors." Almost every other day we now got a spoonful of cooked intestine paste, and *appel* was required only once per day, in the evening. Sakai nevertheless insisted that the sick should also present themselves on the street, with their numbers clearly displayed.

Despite these improvements, hunger, the onset of disease and the mortality rate did not diminish. Almost sixty percent of the population was suffering from enteritis, and even in our house, full of recent arrivals from Bandoeng, one could not miss the increased smell of diarrhoea. People sitting on a potty had become a common sight that one just shrugged off. Many took their potty with them to *appel*—just in case. Thus our situation continued on its downward spiral, driven by starvation and the relentless onset of disease. One of the older women in our house came back from her job of washing corpses and casually commented to my mother that her task was dangerous, because the bodies tended to release infected fluids, while water was in short supply and soap virtually unobtainable.

Every time the food carriers brought their tub of soup or slime-porridge the entire population of the house, some of them already suffering from dysentery, would stampede to the front yard with their billycans, *rentengs* (nest of aluminium pans) or plates, anxiously awaiting their turn. Usually the mothers were given helpings for the entire family, but increasingly some mothers no longer trusted their own honesty and asked one of the women doling out the quantities to make sure her children got their due. The incidence of jaundice, typhoid, beriberi and pellagra grew, while oedema had become widespread. Many thus afflicted lost their appetite for the food that was available; they were hungry and yet found eating difficult. On July 8 another group of fifty seriously ill persons was transported out of the camp to St. Vincentius, partly in response to the growing need for more hospital beds within Tjideng itself, where the entire population stood at risk of contracting dysentery unless the dysentery patients could be isolated. My mother had succeeded in finding a *tjabe rawit* plant, and I was now regularly fed some of the hot red peppers to combat vitamin deficiency and the onset of disease. She could only get a tiny quantity down my throat, but it made a difference, for I escaped illness.

Juf, however, now in her seventy-second year, had not been so lucky; her health had deteriorated relentlessly. Ever since she had arrived in Tjideng, she had remained in the garage next door, except when Sone had insisted that all sick turn up for *appel*. Her legs had become a terrible sight, but hospital care and doctors' services were strictly rationed. Suddenly, towards the middle of July, my mother announced that Juf was no longer next door; the time had finally come when the combination of weight loss and infection had made her a candidate for medical attention. Ank had called my mother over so that she could take possession of Juf's things—"Otherwise they will quickly disappear," she added.

Thus I had seen the last of Juf: she had vanished just like so many others had done over the last few months. To have to go to the hospital, where visits from family and friends were forbidden, was to be given a death sentence. In a healthy population of thirty thousand people, one could expect one death per day, since thirty thousand days corresponds to the average human lifespan. In Tjideng, the population was only ten thousand, but by the early days of August, four to five people were dying each day. The death rate, not counting the fate of the sick moved elsewhere, was therefore twelve to fifteen times higher than normal and was growing rapidly. Each day mothers inspected with great interest the contents of the potty for fatal signs of blood before tipping them into the septic tank or the ditch. Out in front of our house on *Laan* Trivelli, the number of corpses loaded onto the food truck each day continued to grow; unfortunately even one of the doctors had recently fallen victim. The hospital once more sought supplies, including eating utensils and cloth for bandages and for bed linen. Old supplies had either been worn out through frequent washing with poor or inadequate soap, or had been stolen. No one was convinced that Sone was gone, but the once-steady stream of beaten-up faces had finally come to a halt. Such was the stupor in which we lived that this clear reason for rejoicing never struck anyone.

Juf's departure for the hospital had been a terrible blow for my mother, who, ever since the day my father was taken prisoner, had felt it her responsibility to keep the remainder of the family intact. She moreover knew how devoted my father had been to his old nanny, and she appreciated the extent to which Juf had looked after me. Supporting Juf had long become an obsession, but in so doing a deep personal bond had also grown between my mother and Juf; now she was facing the probability of her efforts being in vain. Even Emmy, who had become closely linked to our family only during the last two years, was grieved and shaken by this turn of events. Now the stark prospect of death, a growing occurrence in Tjideng, was finally affecting us.

In the Pacific, the war had moved from island to island; every day brought a new disaster for the Japanese and a new but dearly bought victory for the Allies. On July 4, a day undoubtedly chosen with great care by the theatrically inclined General Douglas MacArthur, the latter announced the liberation of the Philippines. There was nonetheless every indication that the wider conflict could continue for another year. Although the Japanese were by now seriously out-gunned by the Americans, they single-mindedly defended each and every position with a tenacity that bordered on the fanatical; this, combined with the strategic commitments made by the Allied leaders, ensured an apocalypse caused by the complete breakdown in understanding between peoples.

Two and a half years before, in Casablanca, the Allies, or the "United Nations" as they now called themselves, had undertaken to extract "unconditional surrender by the Axis." The implications of this commitment had changed dramatically since then—from a puzzling relic of the American civil war to a redefined concept. Unconditional surrender had been achieved in Germany by a complete Allied invasion from the east and the west, the destruction of Berlin, and the death or capture of all German leaders. Applying this concept in the Far East implied the need for an Allied invasion of an island kingdom, a difficult military operation at the best of times, and entailed placing its God-Emperor under foreign control, an unfamiliar challenge for Western armies. The demand precipitated a theological debate in Tokyo.

The American army had thus far succeeded in conquering numerous former island possessions of the Japanese, tenaciously defended by troops long since cut off from their source of supply and reinforcement. Those "victories," if that is the appropriate description of these achievements, had become horrendously costly for both the victors and the vanquished. As long ago as January 1943, when the "unconditional surrender" strategy was promulgated, American generals had calculated that for battles such as Guadalcanal, the ratio of Japanese to American casualties was fifteen to one. The Japanese were conducting their own version of a scorched earth policy; and since every Japanese soldier was prepared to fight to the death, a huge number of American casualties was still required.

If it was now assumed that armed resistance on the sacred Japanese home islands, close to a large supply of manpower, would be equally fanatical, the cost of a future invasion, measured in terms of casualties, took on unthinkable dimensions: Churchill noted that a million American and half a million British casualties were predicted.

The genie of "unconditional surrender," released from the magic lamp two years before, had so far demanded thousands of lives, but could not be stuffed back into the lamp without devilishly complicated rhetorical manoeuvres, bound to affect the political fortunes of politicians facing elections. In the United States, the biennial tyranny of congressional elections, with its quest for simplistic popularity and its accomplice, mud-slinging, was never far away, and it was the Americans who bore the brunt of the struggle against Japan. Amidst all this, another spectre was re-emerging—the spread of bolshevism, feared equally by Japan and its Western foes. From the perspective of Britain and its European partners, the Netherlands and France, "unconditional surrender" had the unpleasant corollary of not necessarily entailing the liberation of former colonies; the combined task was beyond practical realization with the available resources. That was perhaps a good thing, and the European civilian men interned in the Preanger may have owed their lives to this turn of events.

A new factor began to affect the conduct of the Pacific war. At an Allied meeting to discuss the post-war governance of Germany, President Truman informed Churchill (but not Stalin) that the Alamogordo atomic bomb test of

July 16 had been successful. It is most likely that neither Churchill nor Truman understood the full significance of the atomic bomb—they knew only that it caused a big bang, and in Churchill's words, a "miracle of deliverance" was now at hand. Both saw the bomb as a possible alternative means for achieving Japan's unconditional surrender. An Allied invasion would in any case have required further intensive bombardment of Japan.

Plans to drop the atomic bomb accordingly went ahead. The first target, Hiroshima, had been selected from the shrinking number of unbombed candidates. Given the experimental nature of the bomb and its possible failure, it was agreed that no warning should be given.[26] For this reason it was also agreed to hold a conference for defining a strategy to achieve unconditional surrender; it was scheduled for August 5, 1945. There was no indication that Russia was ready to send its troops eastward, although its neutrality pact with Japan had by now expired.

Meanwhile the Japanese, confident that through successful defence of their main islands they could avoid the need for unconditional surrender, were moving ahead with plans for more *kamikaze*-style weapons to thwart Allied landings. This included the development of a torpedo guided by a human pilot, as well as "crouching dragons" (a mine that would be attached to a ship and detonated by a volunteer) and manned concrete bunkers packed with explosives to be detonated in the vicinity of landing craft. Hirohito was confident that his subjects had the stamina and mental discipline to carry out such tasks.

In the Netherlands, the repatriated Queen and her prime minister were preoccupied with re-establishing their authority, while contending with massive inundation of low-lying lands, partially destroyed communication systems, a major harbour city in ruins, and the huge problem of dealing with Nazi collaborators, alleged and real. One major challenge for which the country was woefully ill-equipped was reconstituting a Dutch army in order to participate in the liberation of the NEI. Such a task could be assisted through the use of the military facilities then available to the Dutch Crown in Queensland, Australia, where a parallel colonial government-in-exile, established in March 1942, had succeeded in making a tiny contribution to the Allied war effort in the Pacific, and from whence a returning Dutch administration had been launched on liberated New Guinea. Dr. Hubertus van Mook, the Lieutenant Governor General, residing in Brisbane, accordingly sought permission for the training on Australian soil of Dutch recruits for future military operations against the Japanese army of occupation. This request was turned down by an Australian government that was also heeding an electorate nursing pronounced anti-colonial feelings and, perhaps, lingering memories of Australia's failed attempt,

26. Gilbert, *A History of the Twentieth Century*, Vol. 2, 1933–1951, 692.

long before the disaster of December 1941, to procure full defence co-operation from the Dutch government.[27]

On the first day of August, postcards arrived in Tjideng; there was even a card from my father! The card had spent almost two months languishing in the post office. My father had no way of knowing where we were, and accordingly had directed the card to "Djawa C.Q.," the same *bunsho* he was in. A stranger had re-addressed the card to "Java C.R." Someone had very faintly written in pencil my mother's new camp number, 20462; it follows that several persons had puzzled over the correct destination for this humble communication between two persons, evidently constituting a high security risk to the Japanese army. It is a miracle that the card arrived at all.

My father wrote the following in Malay:

I have received two cards from you.
Why does Juf not write?
I am working hard with Theo in the kitchen each day,
Do not worry, I am in good health.
I hope that Boudy is also in good health.
Are you still living together with Emmy and Mien (Theo's wife)?
I send many kisses to Willy, Boudy and Oma.

Theo Aalbers was obviously unaware of what had happened to his wife and child; they were no longer with us and we did not know where they had gone. Once again, the most significant message was the handwriting itself—my father had still been alive two months ago.

"I must let Juf know," was my mother's prompt reaction. Somewhere she found a small piece of paper, borrowed a pencil stub and wrote a short note, which she hurriedly delivered to the hospital. After a while she returned, looking pensive.

"How is Juf?" Emmy asked.

"She's weak," my mother replied. "But the nurse said that Bou's letter had cheered her up."

Was it too much to hope that we might see each other again?

Of Bombs and Such

On August 5 the alternative tactics for achieving unconditional Japanese surrender were debated in Washington. The issue boiled down to this: what would be more effective—a blockade of the Japanese coastline or an invasion? The conference concluded that invasion, possibly by November 1, remained the

---

27. Bussemaker, "Australian-Dutch Defence Cooperation, 1940–1941."

best option, for it was evident that "the balance of demography and death lay in favour of the United States."[28] Bombing of Japanese cities should therefore continue.

That night, seven groups of bombers took off from Tinian Island (in the Marianas) and headed for targets in Japan. One of those bomber groups consisted of a solitary modified B-29, proudly dubbed the "Enola Gay" to honour the pilot's mother. It had a special mission and carried a single bomb. Although Truman was under the impression that the target for this bomb would be a military one, the Hiroshima population included "many more women and children than soldiers and sailors."[29]

Jan Bouwer, the Dutch journalist who had remained hidden during the entire war in a house in north Bandoeng, wrote in his diary entry for Tuesday, August 7:

> The American air force has dropped its first model of a secret weapon on Hiroshima. I do not know what an atom bomb is. I do know from news releases that an entire city has been obliterated from the earth's surface.

Weapons of mass destruction were hardly new. During the First World War, gas attacks had killed and injured thousands of soldiers at once. Mass killing of civilians, especially women and children, was not a novelty either: Guernica, Rotterdam, Warsaw, London, Hamburg, Dresden and many cities in Japan had all experienced this. The bomb that fell on Hiroshima was merely a more modern and therefore more efficient method of killing civilians. It had the added advantage of posing minimal risk to the person affecting its delivery, and would, in a manner of speaking, leave his hands clean. The advent of unmanned long-range missiles would in future take this technological progress a step further.

The monster bomb did not immediately generate the hoped-for reaction in Tokyo. At a Cabinet meeting on August 7 the event was discussed, and Truman's threat to drop more such bombs (another six were in the works) was dismissed by army spokesmen as "mere propaganda."[30]

The government in Tokyo continued to debate strategies for circumventing the demand of "unconditional surrender," and avoiding at all costs the threat of rebellion and the destruction of the *kokutai*, the sacred institution of imperial reign. With Roosevelt dead and Churchill out of office, the Potsdam declaration and its demand for immediate response was interpreted by Tokyo as a sign of American desperation to end the war. Nor did the Allied propaganda war, urging the Japanese people to "support their Emperor in throwing out the

---

28. Gilbert, *A History of the Twentieth Century*, Vol. 2, 1933–1951, 701.

29. Gilbert, *A History of the Twentieth Century*, Vol. 2, 1933–1951, 701.

30. Hasegawa, "The Atomic Bombs and the Soviet Invasion."

military clique," have the slightest impact in Japan, since it appealed equally to those opposed and to those supporting the military clique; it merely added confusion.[31]

The Japanese government also continued its cautious diplomatic moves aimed at paving the way to a form of Indonesian self-government, on the understanding that a quasi-independent Indonesia would remain firmly within the Japanese sphere of influence. Field Marshall Terauchi accordingly invited Sukarno for discussions in Saigon.

Within Indonesia itself, a sharper distinction was drawn between those whose loyalty to the nationalist cause (and by inference also the Japanese position) was questionable and those whose loyalty was considered beyond reproach. The key was genetics: were you or were you not a pure Asian? The times demanded a rough and ready criterion: the quasi-scientific method first used, based on percentage of Asian blood, was abandoned for the far simpler one of appearances. Some *Belanda Indo* with impeccable genealogies nevertheless had hair that was too blonde, and eyes that were too blue, and the genetic evidence that had been brought to bear on their claims of being *Indo* were now called into question. If one did not look like an Asian, how could one think like one? *Razzias* took place to round up these "pseudo Asians," as they might have been called, but the effort was constrained by the difficulty of finding space to house them.

The first atom bomb had far greater impact outside of Japan than within; it propelled the startled Russians into action. If a new super-weapon was going to bring Japan to its knees, Moscow had better hurry up and regain former Russian territories or face a possible American presence on its eastern coast. Two days after the destruction of Hiroshima the Soviets invaded Japanese-occupied territory over a wide front from Manchuria to Korea. This was a far more alarming development from Hirohito's perspective. At a stroke it invalidated his conviction that the USSR would remain neutral, and the Japanese Supreme War Council was summoned to discuss this development. "The news of the Nagasaki bomb was reported to the Japanese leadership during the middle of a heated discussion at the Supreme War Council."[32] It debated how a negotiated peace settlement that would not affect the status of God-Emperor could be reconciled with unconditional surrender. The United States peace offer had become the lesser evil.

That same day the three leading Indonesian nationalists, Sukarno, Dr. Mohammed Hatta, and Radjiman Wediodiningrat, oblivious to events to the north, began their cumbersome journey to Saigon to meet with Terauchi, in order to be instructed by him on the steps to independence.

---

31. Bix, *Hirohito and the Making of Modern Japan,* 500.
32. Hasegawa, "The Atomic Bombs and the Soviet Invasion."

Over the following days intensive conventional bombing of Japan continued unabated, while the Soviets moved southward, undeterred by Japanese discussions with the United States.

The news of these dramatic developments in Tokyo filtered through to some people on Java. On Friday, August 10, Jan Bouwer noted in his diary that a second atom bomb had fallen (on Nagasaki) and that the Japanese Cabinet had held an emergency session.[33] We, on the other hand, knew nothing. In Tjideng, on August 10, Mrs. Henkes Rijndijk, a consistent diarist living in the western part of the camp, merely remarked:

> Our food remains, though insufficient, slightly better. Curiously it seems as though our hunger has as a result increased. Liet [her daughter] is being prescribed her second dosage of acriflavine, but is doing poorly. Another person has gone from our house to the dysentery ward. Tomorrow another one, a Mrs. Visser, who is sickly, weak and emaciated will go to the normal hospital ward. I feel better, but Jan Olpert [her son] is having troubles with his intestines. Anne regularly suffers from pellagra with a high fever that comes and goes. Jetty Laverge received the announcement that Bert [her husband] had died on April 22. This was scribbled on the card she had sent him.

That was our world on this momentous day. A world of ten thousand people crammed within an area of a 15 acres, a community so isolated that it might as well have been living on a different planet.

---

33. Bouwer, *Het Vermoorde Land*, 369.

10. MY FATHER RETURNS

The end of the Pacific war came about in a most bizarre manner.

"At noon on August 15," writes the historian Herbert P. Bix, "the Japanese people gathered around their radio speakers and heard for the first time the high-pitched voice of the Emperor." Never before had an *okami,* a God-Emperor, directly addressed his people, let alone used a radio to deliver a holy royal message. In this speech Hirohito was enlisting the participation of all of the Japanese people in a *seidan,* a holy decision, using language drafted for him by two scholars of the Chinese classics. The message delivered in arcane, courtly language was far from clear to the man in the street, but in effect conceded defeat and accepted the Allied terms of surrender.[1]

That broadcast might not have happened. Before dawn on August 15, Yasuo Yanagisawa, the Tokyo broadcaster, was threatened at gunpoint by an Imperial Japanese Army major who ordered him not to air the Imperial announcement of surrender.[2] If that assassination had been successful, it would hardly have been the first and would certainly not be the last time that a Japanese zealot took matters into his own hands, thereby earning in Japanese society dubious but lasting fame for the sincerity of his convictions.

It is safe to say that very few living within the part of Asia that was subject to Japanese military rule heard this announcement, or if they did, understood it. Some people nevertheless soon knew its contents. Notwithstanding repeated Japanese efforts to control radio access, the news was heard through other sources, such as the BBC. In Tjimahi, for instance, my father and his friends knew the following day what had happened, and interned senior government officials immediately began to plan for a return of Dutch colonial rule. In Tjideng we remained in the dark; the one remaining radio in the camp was not touched as a result of a lingering fear of Sone's wrath. Sutan Sjahrir, one of the Indonesian nationalists who had kept a low profile during the period of occupation, knew as early as August 14 that capitulation was imminent, and started plotting the proclamation of an independent Indonesia.[3]

The Japanese military leaders' reaction to Hirohito's radio announcement varied. Aside from the Philippines and some other small islands, the army remained indisputably in full control of most of Southeast Asia; from their

---

1. Bix, *Hirohito and the Making of Modern Japan,* 526.

2. Jun Hongo, *Japan Times,* June 1, 2007.

3. Duchateau-Sjahrir, *Out of Exile,* 255.

perspective capitulation was a very disturbing development. Field Marshall Terauchi, for instance, on the following day sent Sukarno and his delegation on their way back to Batavia without betraying the slightest hint of Hirohito's announcement. Sukarno consequently arrived in Batavia with plans to convene meetings over the following months to pave the way for *dokuritsu* (partial autonomy). When he heard the news from Sjahrir he refused to believe it, and General Nagano did not go out of his way to set Sukarno straight either.

On the other hand, with the Japanese navy largely destroyed, Admiral Tadashi Maeda, occupying a luxurious villa in Batavia, saw the time as ripe for nationalists like Sjahrir or Sukarno to declare Indonesian independence. But the Japanese army and navy had often differed on policy matters, and the Japanese army remained largely undefeated; moreover, insubordination among Japanese officers was far from rare.[4]

Nevertheless another full day had passed before Sukarno finally declared the formation of the Republik Indonesia at a hastily arranged ceremony in the late afternoon of August 17 in response to considerable coercion by young, hot-headed Indonesian radicals in the *heiho* and PETA units. He was more concerned about the Japanese reaction than possible American interference. As independence declarations go, this one was most inauspicious: we in Tjideng were within two kilometres of this historic event and were as oblivious to it as was Mountbatten in his HQ in faraway Ceylon.

Behind the Tjideng bamboo wall, nothing changed for another full week. We were in limbo, suspended between war and peace.

Thursday, August 23 began for us like any other day. Early in the morning, well before sunrise, my mother, dressed as always in her shorts and a blouse with a clean cloth tied around her hair, had gone to the Tjimalaja *dapur* to help prepare breakfast. Hanna Poortman had helped her carry the tub of water collected during the night; a procession of women, similarly straining under the weight of tubs of water, could be seen emerging from the other houses down the street. It was the price we paid for breakfast, and indeed every meal. Since the beginning of August, breakfast had consisted of a starchy tapioca porridge, because the doctors had decided that the chewy bread the kitchen had been acquiring in the past was too difficult to digest for most camp inhabitants. Later that morning, when the bathtubs from the various houses had been filled with the appropriate number of ladlefuls of porridge, my mother came home as usual with a tiny bit of extra food, her reward for doing the heavy kitchen work.

She was tired and smelled of wood smoke. "If only we didn't have to start fires with wet wood," she complained. "The Japs are paranoid about the fire

---

4. Reid and Akira (eds.), *The Japanese Experience in Indonesia*, 299–324.

hazard, but we are careful; it is so difficult to get the fires going—my arms are ready to fall off from *kipassing* [fanning the flames]."

"Did you hear any more news?" asked Emmy.

"Ach! Some are convinced that the war is ended; they say that is why the food supply has increased, but others say it is only because Sakai is finally paying attention to the death rate."

Daily rice rations had been doubled, but our *kepalla,* quoting Mrs. Ament, the woman in the Ladies' Office responsible for food orders, ascribed this to the entreaties made by the doctors to Sakai. In the past, such requests to Sone had always been answered with a beating, and there had been so many requests and so many beatings that we had lost count. On August 18 Sakai had also approved a camp committee request to restore the camp to the size it had been prior to St. Bartholomew's night. The *gedek* could be moved back to its previous position and the six houses then vacated could once more be occupied. We had heard that some of those who had then lost the roof over their heads were still camping in the open, so this improvement came as a huge relief for them. For us nothing had changed—the house was still crammed and it was impossible to imagine the conditions in other houses where the crowding was worse; someone had recently complained of there being 180 inhabitants in her house.

There had been another puzzling announcement a few days earlier: Nippon no longer needed socks. Hanna, who had joined my mother working in the kitchen, had promptly concluded that this was more punishment, if only because the extra cash had been appreciated. Sakai had ordered that all half-finished socks and cotton thread were to be returned. We were used to these abrupt orders; it was just more of the same capricious, unexplained and therefore irrational Japanese behaviour.

And so the day went. Late in the morning the vegetable truck arrived, and the *sjouwploeg* girls as usual had to help offload its contents at the two kitchens. On the way back towards the camp gate it stopped, as always, in front of our house to pick up the corpses of those who had spent their final day in Tjideng. Once again the poor girls loading the coffins were struggling and sweating under the strain of the weight, the oppressively hot sun, the thick humid air, and the number of deceased, which on Thursday was eight bodies. My task was far less onerous: while the sewage ditch ladies spent an hour sloshing human waste towards the Tjideng *kali,* I had only to catch flies. The camp office was always very careful to preserve a sense of dignity by referring to such task forces as "girls" or "ladies," depending on whether they were over or under twenty-one years of age.

Late that afternoon, Lieutenant Sakai called Miss Roorda to his office, just outside the camp gate. This was not unusual, for the time shortly before *appel* had always been an occasion for the camp commandant to pass on his requests or orders. Living where we did, so close to the camp gate and next door to the

Ladies' Office, we were accustomed to the sight of the diminutive figure of Miss Roorda, always demurely dressed in a long skirt to avoid Japanese provocation, hurrying past our house towards the camp gate. Moments later we saw her coming out of the Ladies' Office in the company of two of the *hanchos;* Mrs. Cornelisse came into our yard looking for our house *kepalla,* Mrs. Bruinzeel, who hurried off with her companion after a short exchange. Mrs. Bruinzeel returned a short while later and called all the residents of our house together for an important announcement. We all gathered in the front yard, carefully avoiding the septic tank, always open, and the clothes-drying racks, while some residents muttered anxiously about the food supply, for it was almost time to go to the *dapur.* "Perhaps something has gone wrong and we will not eat tonight," someone wailed, but then Mrs. Bruinzeel started to speak. "I have good news," she announced. "There'll be no more *appel* required by Lieutenant Sakai, and blackouts at night are no longer necessary. We can get stronger electric light bulbs if we need them." The announcement did not seem very important, but it certainly was puzzling.

Appel of late had become a bit more relaxed, thanks to Sone's absence; he had not been seen in the camp for almost six weeks. Some women maintained that he was gone for good, but others were not so sure. Having *appel* only in the evening had been another improvement in our lives, for early morning *appel,* after a sleepless night, before breakfast and in the cold dawn air, had been miserable. Sakai's insistence on the sick turning up for *appel* was hard, but he had on the other hand been satisfied with the report from doctors that certain people could not be moved. Sakai moreover was always punctiliously correct in his attitude; when he was through with our group we could always count on his "*Yasume,*" the signal for him to move on to the next group and for the murmur of voices from chatting women and children to start again. Of late some women had actually complained that our *appels* had become somewhat sloppy, or unprofessional. One could be certain that these complaints came from the wives of military officers, feeling somehow that we had a need to be "correct" as well, so that "our husbands could be proud." Sone would never have tolerated the lack of precision in our falling to attention or bowing. His name was not mentioned, of course, but one suspected that there was a link. There were others who laughed at such remarks, with comments like "The rot Jap can go to hell; I do not need *appel* at all."

"There will be no more *appel,*" Mrs. Bruinzeel repeated with emphasis. "Lieutenant Sakai's formal announcement can be found in the camp office. I believe it says the war is over, but we must stay in the camp until the Allies arrive."

"I can't believe this," Emmy said. "Let's go next door."

In the office other women were gathering and one of them read aloud the statement written in English and pinned to the notice board:

After repeated requests by the Allies to stop the war, His Majesty Emperor Hirohito has ordered the cessation of hostilities. As a result, the status of the internees has been brought to an end on the understanding that their release from captivity will await the arrival of representatives from the Allied armies. The date of this arrival is not yet known.

For military political reasons you have been brought together here and that is why you have suffered the difficulties of the war; henceforth your circumstances will improve. Until the formal capitulation, the Japanese army will remain responsible for the maintenance of peace and order in the camps. In response to this requirement the existing regulations will remain in force. Now that the war has ended the provision of food will improve.

Money belonging to internees can be utilized to purchase necessary goods. The moneys taken into custody by the Nipponese authorities will shortly be returned.

General Nagano,
Commander Nipponese 16th Army, Jakarta,
22 August 2605[5]

It was a puzzling announcement.

"What does it say?"

"The war's over."

"Where are our boys?"

Mrs. Cornelisse had joined us, and advised us to stay calm and await further news, which would undoubtedly come soon.

"I wonder what happened," my mother said to Emmy on the way back home, looking forward to our meal of rice and *sajur*.

On August 15 General Douglas MacArthur had been assigned a new task; he was to secure Hirohito's signature on a ceasefire document. Admiral Mountbatten thought it appropriate for Hirohito to travel to Manila, but MacArthur had decided that the signing would have to take place in Tokyo Bay. By prior agreement Mountbatten took over responsibility for the liberation of the entire Indonesian archipelago. Neither MacArthur nor Mountbatten had illusions about the challenge facing them after seeing the aftermath of Rear Admiral Sanji Iwabachi's last stand in the defence of Manila.

Once he [Iwabachi] had decided to defend Manila (instead of following orders from his superiors to declare the city "open"), the atrocities began, and the longer the battle raged, the more the Japanese command

---

5. Brugmans, *Nederlandsch-Indië onder Japanse bezetting*, document 460.

structure deteriorated, until the uniforms of the Nipponese sailors and marines were saturated with Filipino blood.[6]

Given this pattern of behaviour, MacArthur determined that a formal surrender had to be signed by Emperor Hirohito before any further military activity was undertaken. Arranging the Tokyo ceremony required co-operation from Japanese officers who had the confidence of Hirohito. Prince Chichibu was dispatched to Saigon in order to seek assistance from Field Marshal Terauchi in appointing Japanese officers willing to undergo the face-losing exercise of travelling to Manila to work out logistical details. This all took a week.

Terauchi did not see an immediate need to respond to Mountbatten's repeated demands for a meeting to discuss security and the safety of POWs. On Monday, August 20, Mountbatten requested that Terauchi fly to Rangoon to make preliminary arrangements for an orderly transfer of responsibility and to accept interim orders for the care of the POWs under his control. Mountbatten at that stage assumed that the term *prisoner of war* referred only to the captured Allied soldiers, sailors and airmen. Terauchi refused to come unless ordered to do so by Tokyo.

By Tuesday, MacArthur's people had finally met the Japanese delegation in Manila and made arrangements for Colonel Charles Tench to fly to Atsuga airport, outside of Tokyo, to provide on-the-ground liaison. The next day General Nagano, prompted by his superior in Saigon, had finally signed the strange document, a copy of which was now pinned on the notice board in the Ladies' Office.

That evening it had been Emmy's turn to work in the kitchen, and when she returned she brought back an extra quantity of rice and some sugar. While we were eating, one of the women in the house asked, "Do you have any red, white or blue material? We want to make a flag tomorrow—we'll do it right here," she said cheerily, waving at the space around us in front of the garage before hurrying off to find more enthusiasts.

The two women rummaged around to see what they could find, prompting my mother to wonder out loud whether Juf had heard the news. "This might give her the courage to pull through," she thought.

That night we sat on the doorstep by the garage enjoying a treat, a cup of tea—some water surreptitiously heated on a small fire behind the house and flavoured with sugar. My mother opened her Djokja silver cigarette box and took out a cigarette.

"Can you please go to the *anglo* and light it?" she asked me.

I went to the *belekang* (the backyard, where the fire could not be seen by Sakai) and held the roll of dried palm leaves—for that's all it was—to the

6. Manchester, *American Caesar,* 414.

glowing charcoal embers, returning with the smouldering cigarette. Then we sat, while the two women took turns drawing in the smoke, causing the burning end to glow red in the dark and infecting us with an unfamiliar feeling of tranquility.

"The Americans must have invaded Japan," was Emmy's assessment. "I guess they will come here next."

The news of the war's end had come in such a peculiar fashion that we were lost trying to digest it. It was as though we had slept through Act III of a play and therefore could not link Act II to the final outcome in Act IV. The announcement we had heard hours before ought to have been so significant, and yet it seemed irrelevant to us.

Emmy continued her train of thought. "The war has ended and here we are still cleaning out the poop ditches and the Japanese are still guarding us: this is crazy." Then, changing the topic, she wondered, "Do you think Bou and Edu have heard the news?"

My father and Edu, the former in Tjimahi and the latter in the 15th Battalion camp in Bandoeng, had heard exactly the same announcement on the same day, but in their camps, where radios were still in use, the announcement had been greeted with howls of derision.

On the following day we got more good news: a shipment of wood had been delivered to the kitchen, which now had more food to prepare.

The next morning Mrs. Ramaer, who had worked for the Red Cross before the war, sought out Miss Roorda with a proposal to help reunite families. She suspected that the list of Tjideng camp residents had fallen into disarray after the numerous changes of the past few months and proposed bringing it up to date. Miss Roorda then announced the need for volunteers, and in response to this need, my mother quit one job and started another. Lieutenant Sakai made available a room in his office for this new administrative task.

A similar development got under way in Bandoeng, where Eric Wester, the Swedish consul, was successful in re-establishing a Red Cross presence; he furthermore obtained assurances from the *Kempetai* that Europeans could once more travel on trains without fear of arrest. The next day a train-load of women and children arrived unannounced in Bandoeng, after a terrible four-day journey from Central Java. Most were in dreadful physical and emotional condition and one woman was demented. This was the first hint of the huge and growing humanitarian disaster threatening to overwhelm whoever was charged with handling the aftermath of the war. Fortunately the Japanese army made available to the Bandoeng Red Cross two rundown ambulances to transport the sick and the dying.

Among the passengers on that train were Mien Aalbers and her son. They were able to move into a small *paviljoen* attached to Mien's mother's house in central Bandoeng. Their own house was now occupied by Indonesians and was therefore unavailable; in addition it stood next to the *Kempetai* office on the Heetjansweg.[7]

In the meantime, the flag-making party in our house set to work, a full week after Indonesia had declared its *de facto* independence. We were oblivious to the fact that there was now on Java a sort of flag competition. While some citizens outside our bamboo wall were furiously tearing off the blue portions of Dutch flags, my mother and Emmy enthusiastically joined the group of women feverishly sewing together a tatty replacement from an assortment of red, white and blue cloth fragments. There was a festive atmosphere out there on the driveway, accompanied of course by an awful lot of optimistic chatter; if the Americans were not going to mark the occasion by rolling in through the gate with their Camel cigarettes and chewing gum, then the women would create their own party.

However, the news of this activity reached Sakai, and he immediately ordered the *hanchos* with their megaphones to spread the word that Dutch flags should under no circumstance be displayed. The sewing work had to be stopped immediately, and no national anthems were to be sung on pain of severe punishment. Lieutenant Sakai, as usual, did not bother to append an explanation to this order. Perhaps he owed it to his newly established Indonesian hosts to suppress any indications of rebellion against the new order on Java.

Nervousness among several of Sukarno's colleagues regarding America's reaction to their independence declaration lingered, aided by the confusing attitude of the Japanese. Although Admiral Maeda had encouraged the independence declaration, General Nagano, prompted by Terauchi, became more conscientious in obeying Mountbatten's orders of the previous week, and got his men to storm the PETA and *heiho* barracks, sending the occupants packing with the words "*Perangan sudah habis, boleh pulang* [The war is finished, go home]"—summed up by a rueful PETA officer as "The war is finished and we have been duped."[8] Sukarno as a result found himself to be a head of state with no mechanism for maintaining law and order, and thus chaos began to overtake Java. Chinese merchants, fearing anarchy, once again boarded up their shops.

The majority of Indonesians lived in the *kampongs* and *desas* scattered along the volcanic slopes and river valleys of the island; they were rice farmers or *tani*, owing allegiance to the local Sultan and the *kepalla desa*. They did not even call themselves "Indonesians," but were "Javanese" or "Sundanese" and were Muslim, though retaining some Hindu and Buddhist attitudes and animist

7. Today called *Jalan* Sultan Agung.
8. Bouwer, *Het vermoorde land*, 378.

beliefs. These people also sensed that change was in the air, but were apprehensive about the future because they had heard that *keongs* (snails) were now found in urban areas: this was ominous. A report prepared by an Indonesian regarding the political situation in the interior, stated, "The press only reaches a tiny portion of this population. The majority of the population attaches far greater value to prophesies based on observations made in his or her daily life."[9] This was a cause for concern, for how then does a state, unable to rely on proclamations and without a disciplined enforcement system, exercise influence over its people? Looting and rioting began to rear their ugly heads among the Javanese in Semarang and Soerabaja, hundreds of kilometres to the east of Batavia and Bandoeng, the seats of foreign domination and power, whether Dutch or Japanese. Owing to the fragmented lines of communication, this development remained undetected by authorities in either city, let alone outside of Java, until the dam had truly burst.

On that same momentous Thursday, Lady Edwina Mountbatten "pinched" Sister Anne, one of Mountbatten's bombers, and flew to Sumatra to begin a tour of prison camps.

Meanwhile, in Tjideng, the vegetable truck had arrived that afternoon and, as always, left with a load of makeshift, leaky coffins. In addition, a new nutritional problem started to rear its ugly head. Part of the improved food supply included oil, and so starved had we been of this commodity that some were capable of drinking litres; and thus it went with other items that we had missed for three and a half years and that had now become available. Our stomachs could not handle the sudden change; the doctors became alarmed and warned the camp against overeating.

There was a group of people who thought that they owned the keys to the future; these were the former Dutch colonial administrators, who before the war had done such an admirable job of administering this marvellous collection of islands. One part of the group, under Lieutenant Governor General Hubertus van Mook, had been heading a government-in-exile from Brisbane, Australia, and the other part was languishing in a POW camp in the Bandoeng area, where they had entertained themselves by planning the return of a Netherlands Indies civil administration.

Van Mook attempted to exercise his imperial authority by instructing internees via radio broadcasts to remain inside their bamboo and barbed wire camps because of the inability of the Allies to provide immediate military protection. In the men's prison camps in Tjimahi (near Bandoeng), where this message was heard, it was greeted with defiance. In Tjideng, it went unnoticed; besides, van Mook was unaware that there even were such things as women's

---

9. Brugmans, *Nederlandsch-Indië onder Japanse bezetting,* document 448.

and children's camps. In Tjimahi Mr. H. J. Spit, vice-chairman of the former Advisory Council now demanded control of the government of Indonesia. His demands were ignored. Over the intervening years of Japanese occupation, both groups had lost all touch with political reality and convinced themselves and anyone who cared to listen that the Indonesian population would welcome the turning back of the clock and the re-establishment of Dutch colonial rule.

And so the first week of peace passed. We were still prisoners, wracked by malnutrition, disease and death. The mortality rate had only increased during these August weeks. The Japanese army was on the other hand kept busy destroying all documents.

Birthday

The morning of Saturday, August 25 was made memorable for a number of reasons. Our breakfast, for the first time that any of us could remember, included a hard-boiled egg. In addition, my mother handed me a present, a parcel wrapped in old wrinkled brown paper, and inside was an Indian suit— "For your birthday," she beamed.

In Tjihapit we had for a while celebrated birthdays as best we could, but with the mounting misery these sorts of events had been abandoned, so this was a novelty. The strange-looking garment consisted of a pair of long brown trousers and a long-sleeved brown jacket made of heavy cotton and decorated with a row of tassels along the arms and the legs. With it came a ribbon lined with coloured feathers. "An Indian headdress," Emmy explained. "Put it on and you will look like Winnetou."[10]

Until recently this garment might have represented a potential means of securing food from *inlanders* through the *gedek,* but now it served as a gift. Mrs. Henkes Rijndijk had given it to her son on the occasion of his birthday in July, and now it was my turn. The idea of wearing long trousers and a long-sleeved shirt made of heavy cotton in the stifling heat of Batavia was absurd, and it is clear that its previous recipient, Jan Hendrick, had formed a similar opinion to mine.[11] Who the next recipient was, I do not know.

Later that day, Liberator bombers with the markings of the Royal Australian Air force flew overhead, and red, white and blue parachutes drifted down among the houses in the city.

Good news came almost hourly; all of a sudden, several personal items that had been confiscated over the past months reappeared. A collection of electrical appliances was brought from one of the empty houses outside the camp gate,

---

10. A character in the popular children's books about Apache Indians, by Karl May.

11. Kemperman, *De Japanse bezetting in dagboeken: Tjideng,* 305.

after several people went there looking for lost possessions. Someone returned triumphantly with a gramophone and some records and began to play pre-war pop tunes. "Nippon has given us back our orange ribbons," shouted one of the older girls living next door. The ribbons had been confiscated almost a year before, when the *sjouwploeg* girls had attempted to celebrate the Queen's birthday by wearing them. Some later admitted that they had known it to have been a defiant gesture, but that was history now; within hours numerous girls were strolling up and down *Laan* Trivelli with orange ribbons in their hair. On Sunday, teenage *Belanda* boys wheeled large carts piled high with food parcels into the camp.

Liet, who had gone to the gate to help them with the *grobak*, came back saying that Noda (a Korean guard) was also looking forward to going home. "*Perang betul-betul habis* [the war is really, really over]." he had said. "I will miss Noda; he was a good man, especially when Sone was not around!" Liet added.

Far to the north of us, Mountbatten was struggling with his "post-surrender tasks," most of which had to be postponed until after the Tokyo ceremony, the date of which was determined by a number of unpredictable yet essential intermediate steps, including seeking shelter from periodic typhoons plaguing the vast area of operations. Although any military action was forbidden, Mountbatten was anxious to avoid the horror of chaos. After a week's negotiations, he had by August 27 managed to arrange a meeting in Rangoon with Lieutenant General Takazo Numata, representing Field Marshall Terauchi.[12] Finally the Japanese High Command officially recognized Mountbatten's so-called "status quo" order of August 15; this required the Japanese army to maintain law and order in the occupied territories and to disarm non-Japanese forces, and also made the Japanese army fully responsible for the welfare of their prisoners, which Mountbatten assumed would be about twenty-eight thousand on Java. He was still ignorant of the fact that the POWs had been moved elsewhere as slave labour, and that they had been replaced in prison camps by European and *Belanda Indo* civilians. Mountbatten was therefore unprepared for the nature and scope of the task that lay ahead. A corollary of the status quo order was that the prisoners had to remain interned so they could be protected and fed. Part of that earlier instruction had clearly filtered through to Tjideng, but now it was given the full force of Terauchi's formal undertaking.

The next day we noticed, to our amazement, that the *heihos* were gone, and that their place had once more been taken by Japanese soldiers. This promptly created another wave of despondency, for the clock seemed to have been turned back yet again. But the security at the main gate had nevertheless been

12. Woodburn Kirby, *The War Against Japan,* vol. 5, 237.

relaxed and curious strangers began to enter the mysterious camp that had been hidden from the rest of the city by the *gedek* and *kawat* wall, and from which emerged so many dead. Ripassa, a *Belanda Indo* photographer, who had retained his freedom during the war years, entered the camp and took a picture of the first children he saw, namely me and a younger friend, standing in the front yard of our house by the side of the road and next to the water supply. My pal had borrowed my Indian head dress (figure 13).

The increased food supply had stimulated a greater demand for wood, as people needed to cook their own food, and an obvious source of fuel was the hated *gedek* separating us from the world outside. On the far side of the camp, where the *gedek* ran along the Ogan field and was accessible, there was ample space to demolish it without tripping over peoples' belongings in yards, and that is where the activity took place. A large enthusiastic crowd of us had gone there to join the fun, and Ripassa had evidently followed us there. Demolition of one wall did not immediately give us a view of the *kampongs*, sheltered by the palm trees in the distance, but rather a view of the second *gedek* wall, demarcating the intervening "no-man's land." Some other children and I climbed a nearby tree to get a better view, but the branches broke. However, news of the destruction of the *gedek* reached the ears of Sakai and he immediately ordered its cessation (figure 17).

Other townsfolk, bearing gifts of food, arrived in Tjideng; these were more *Belanda Indo*, who had avoided internment and were now looking for friends and relatives, and some *inlanders*, former servants looking for their *njonja* and hoping for the resumption of pre-war duties in homes in and around Batavia.

Aside from these improvements, our life remained grim; we were still confined to our desperately overcrowded, unhygienic, stinking camp, while the doctors issued daily warnings about over-eating, warnings hard to heed after years of starvation: the death rate increased. On Thursday, ten makeshift coffins were filled with bloated bodies for transport to a cemetery. But even this macabre occupation was showing signs of improvement, for that afternoon a hearse, a real hearse, was for the first time allowed to remove the coffins.

All the while we were waiting for our liberators to replace the Japanese. The waiting seemed endless; years later, Mrs. van Starckenborgh, the last Governor General's wife, observed, "What sticks in my mind about the entire internment exercise was the endless waiting—waiting for food, waiting for the end of the war, waiting for *appel* and waiting for the Americans."[13]

The end of the month approached and with it the traditional celebration of the Queen's birthday, the most important Dutch annual holiday after New Year's Eve. Again the camp office forbade any display of patriotism or forms of

---

13. Rinzema, *Dit was uw Tjideng*, 102.

festivity. Several women could stand this nonsense no longer and took matters into their own hands: they left in search of family members and a new life. At the far western end of the camp the *gedek* was now partly demolished and there was no one to stop them from leaving. Ank and her friend, Elsa, joined this exodus. Years later Ank recounted the escapade:

> People in the *kampong* on the other side of the railway track were friendly and gave us some refreshment. Soon a truck came by, carrying labourers to town. We hailed it, the truck stopped and the driver cheerfully gave us a ride and even to Tjoekie's home in Krawang (part of Batavia). Tjoekie, being *Belanda Indo*, had avoided internment and was able to get me a train ticket to Bandoeng, where I tracked down Ben, who had just *bolossed* from his camp and was trying to re-establish his dental practice—he sure was surprised to see me and said "what on earth are you doing here?"[14]

My mother and Emmy had made no fuss about their departure. "We'll soon see you in Bandoeng," were their words of farewell. However, Emmy could not resist a jibe after they had left, sourly commenting, "She has abandoned us—pity, I would like to have gone as well to look for Edu." The "soon" got stretched out to a chance encounter seven years later, and then not in Bandoeng, but in Edmonton, Canada.

Elsewhere on Java the authority vacuum took on different dimensions. Malay-language newspapers had ceased publication and radio announcements had been replaced by martial music, so confusion descended over the entire island. There was talk of a Republik Indonesia being created, but the Japanese-trained Indonesian army had been disbanded. Bandoeng, though impoverished and dilapidated, nevertheless remained peaceful thus far. Around the huge men's camps a growing crowd of *Belanda Indo* women was seeking contact with sons or husbands; the camp management started making preparations for the prompt liquidation of the camps by compiling a registry to facilitate an orderly exodus, and the request that "those with homes in Bandoeng should present themselves at the camp office."[15]

However, in Soerabaja, on the eastern extremity of Java, totally isolated from Batavia, a thug-driven rebellion, thinly disguised as an independence movement, rapidly gained momentum; the rebellion waxed in violence, unhindered by any Allied directives from Mountbatten or Japanese constraints. Governor Sudirman authorized the inhabitants to celebrate independence for five consecutive days, during which murderous attacks on all non-Javanese persons, including the Japanese, grew in frequency.

---

14. Ank de Ridder, personal communication.
15. Bouwer, *Het vermoorde land*, 381.

On September 2, 1945, the surrender ceremony took place on the quarterdeck of the USS *Missouri,* which lay at anchor in Tokyo Bay, perhaps the same anchorage used by Commodore Perry nine decades before when it was called Edo Bay. General Douglas MacArthur, assisted by representatives of the British and Dutch Crowns and the governments of China, France, Australia and New Zealand signed a formal document with Emperor Hirohito's Foreign Minister and Chief of Staff of the Japanese Army. The Dutch Crown was represented by Admiral C. E. L. Helfrich and General L. H. van Oyen, undoubtedly seeing in the defeat of Japan the inevitable resurrection of Dutch Imperial rule in Indonesia; they were unaware of the two-week-old declaration of independence. However, the two main protagonists standing on the quarterdeck of the USS *Missouri* could quietly congratulate themselves on having achieved their respective war aims: Japan had rid Asia of European colonial dominance, while the United States had avenged its day of ignominy at Pearl Harbor and Bataan.

Now, finally, Mountbatten could take action. On September 5 the much-postponed Operation Zipper was launched and Mountbatten for the first time came face to face with the gruesome spectacle of internment camps in Singapore, while in the north, in Vietnam, part of his area of responsibility, a massacre of French citizens got under way. That same day Indonesian *pemuda* (youth) completed the occupation of all utilities on Java. Our tiny water supply in Tjideng was henceforth solely dependent on the goodwill and forbearance of the revolutionaries.

Simultaneously H. J. Spit, the former vice-chairman of the Advisory Council, took matters in his own hands and along with a group of senior government personnel and industry chiefs left his place of internment in Bandoeng and went to Batavia for another attempt to wrest control over the NEI out of the hands of General Nagano; Nagano promptly re-interned them, to their immense frustration.

Nagano, following Mountbatten's orders, restricted the growing exodus of interned men and women. His new-found concern for the welfare of the interned population was undoubtedly aided in part by the emerging issue of prospective war crimes trials and also by his full awareness of the potential scope for conflict between Indonesians thinking they were liberated from the colonial yoke and Europeans reclaiming their former homes and jobs; driving a wedge between these two population groups had been a consistent Japanese occupation policy. Nagano therefore faced a daunting peace-keeping challenge, now constrained by his inability to make accustomed use of the *Kempetai* against either population group. He had to take action. Careful implementation of Mountbatten's status quo order presented him with an attractive option: lean on the goodwill of the interned civilians to voluntarily prolong their ghastly internment. But for this Nagano now needed our help.

On that same fateful day the journalist Jan Bouwer, sensing the growing drama unfolding in Batavia, left his hideout in Bandoeng and boarded a train for the coast:

Seven hours in a packed second class railway carriage: the passengers were exclusively Chinese, Indonesians and British East Indians: a very pleasant journey. The only language we could all speak was Indonesian (Malay). The Indonesians shared with me the food that they had taken with them for the long journey. When the train stopped at a station, I bought fruit for the entire train compartment. In Batavia, the centre of nationalistic, anti-Dutch activities, I had no trouble finding a *sado* to transport me to a previously arranged address. The train journey itself: empty *sawahs*, forests felled to secure fuel for trains, poorly clothed, emaciated population, people in jute bags, covered with tropical sores, and a few red-and-white flags. Batavia not as rundown as Bandoeng— somewhat better streets, a more excited population as a result of the nearby nationalistic agitation and propaganda.[16]

There was thus a perception of relative peacefulness outside of the camps. Nagano requested a meeting on September 8, with representatives from the prison camps to personally explain to them the need to clamp down on escape attempts "for the sake of safety." Jan Bouwer was also invited to participate in this discussion and left us his account:

Gathered in the second floor ballroom of the Hotel des Indes were senior representatives of the Japanese army and delegates from the various prison camps in and around Batavia. The Dutch delegation consisted of camp leaders and Mrs. Tjarda van Starckenborgh (the wife of the Governor General).... Upon advice of *Jonkheer* Herman van Karnebeek, who had come down from one of the Bandoeng prison camps, I (Jan Bouwer, a journalist) also attended.[17]

On that same day a seven-man advance party of the RAPWI (Rehabilitation of Allied Prisoners and War Internees) organization, led by Major A. G. Greenhalgh, bravely landed by parachute on Kemajoran airfield in Batavia: their task was to pave the way for the start-up of a relief effort. That party was ushered into the meeting room in the Hotel des Indes just as the conference got under way. After General Nagano had explained that he was under orders from Mountbatten, the following happened, according to Jan Bouwer:

General Yamaguchi thanked Mrs. van Starckenborgh and Mr. Spit for their assistance in slowing down the leakage of internees from the

---

16. Bouwer, *Het vermoorde land*, 391.
17. Bouwer, *Het vermoorde land*, 396.

camps. Yamaguchi, however, complained that "Tjideng camp is very difficult to manage and in return for the trouble we have taken to protect them, the commandant of the camp suffers unbelievable mental torments." General Nagano referred to the growing unrest in the interior of Java and his obligation to Lord Mountbatten to keep the peace. He was able to assure the assembled company "that the Japanese army had from this viewpoint its own plans that would be effective."[18]

After the meeting, when Greenhalgh finally got his radio to work, he nevertheless signalled to Mountbatten "that few of the Indonesians had any interest in political movements here."[19] He was dead wrong.

During the coming weeks Nagano's undertaking to keep the peace would get added significance as heavy-handed Japanese military action conducted against Indonesian rebels was carried out at the behest of Britain and the Netherlands: it is difficult to devise a more unfortunate evolution of events. A few days later, the Vietminh proclaimed the independent republic of Vietnam, while in Malaya, conflicts between Chinese resistance fighters and Malayans who had collaborated with the Japanese or adapted to the Japanese occupation, a matter of viewpoint, also flared up. Nationalist uprisings and ethnic conflicts were creating a series of powder kegs throughout the entire region under Mountbatten's command, but:

> the Indonesians were more firmly entrenched than the Vietnamese and the Dutch weaker than the French. Nor was the French-oriented population anywhere as large as the Dutch one was. For both these reasons Mountbatten's problems were to prove more painful and protracted in Indonesia than Indochina.[20]

News of the RAPWI team's arrival quickly spread throughout Batavia and so did concern among certain Indonesians that this heralded the start of a determined campaign to reinstate Dutch colonial rule. Within days, slogans began to appear on the trams and buses of Batavia: "We are a free people, respect our institutions," or "Hands off Indonesia," and more provocatively, "What is good for the British Labour Party is good for us too."

The *pemuda* (young men) terror campaign gathered steam and in so doing metamorphosed from scattered acts of violence into an increasingly sharply focused, xenophobic rebellion under the banner of "nationalism." Initially, it was directed almost exclusively at the Japanese, but "the Japanese are now the policemen of the Europeans," Bouwer wrote in his first Associated Press

---

18. van Velden, *De Japanse burgerkampen*, 466.

19. Ziegler, *Mountbatten*, 333.

20. Ziegler, *Mountbatten*, 333.

dispatch sent out on Thursday, September 13, and thus the Europeans began to feel the wrath of the new phenomenon as this reality became obvious. Thus Indonesia was poised on the precipice of chaos.

The inmates of Tjideng were still isolated from these developments. My mother was busy organizing the growing stream of death notices coming from the slave camps in Manchuria, Korea, Japan, Burma and Formosa, announcing that corporal such-and-such or sergeant so-and-so had died. She had to hand the crumpled piece of paper over to a wife, a child or a mother who had just begun to savour the elation of a new future with an end to their own physical suffering, only to now bear a new burden. Room was made available in the Ladies' Office to give those who suddenly found themselves to be widows or orphans a place to grieve. This, combined with the news that Mountbatten himself had ordered us to remain inside Tjideng, guarded by the hated Japanese, caused morale to plummet to new depths. In Singapore Mountbatten had been greeted at the notorious Changi prison with the epithet, "Linger Longer Louis." In Tjideng many now started to use unpleasant language to describe the British, which they previously had reserved exclusively for the Japanese.

A Sign of Life

Where were my father and Edu? So far we had heard no news from Bandoeng. Emmy had not received any sign of life from Edu, and other soldiers' wives seemed to have lost all contact with their husbands as well.

On Sunday, September 9, Mrs. Ramaer, the provisional head of the Red Cross in Batavia, had come to the bold conclusion that the traffic of people escaping from the various prison camps could be utilized to facilitate the exchange of letters and family reunions. She undertook to meet anyone who arrived on the train from Bandoeng and might have knowledge of the camps there and bring him (or her) to her office to augment her lists of names. She also offered to have delivered by whatever means every scrap of paper, as long as the name of the addressee was clearly indicated, using her pre-war Red Cross contacts for this service. At lunchtime my mother came home with the exciting news that she had just written a letter to my father.

The next evening she came home full of excitement, waving in her hand two greenish-blue sheets of airmail paper with neat handwriting even written in ink. "From *pappie!*" she shouted as she came in through the doorway. "An answer to my letter!" She immediately started to read it out loud, as we listened:

Bandoeng 10/9

My dearest Wil,

You will be surprised by such a beautiful letter—no longer a rotten card with Malay garbage. I have escaped, together with Theo, and am now accommodated with the family Suyderhout (Theo's in-laws).

My father went on to explain that he and Theo had made use of the chaos created near the camp gate when a truck full of pigs entered the camp and the pigs, fearing the worst, escaped. His letter continued:

I am doing very well, and spend my entire day cycling through Bandoeng trying to run errands and looking for a place to stay so that when you return, we have a roof over our heads. Theo is in poor shape and is having trouble with his intestines, while Mien (his wife) is recovering from malnutrition, oedema. Little Theo looks fine, and I now hope that you and Boudy have also survived in good shape. In your last card of August 4 you wrote that you were working in the kitchen—that gave me much reassurance. I also received from you and from Juf the cards dated 29 August 1944. They were worth a lot as a sign of life, but beyond that they conveyed nothing. I had not expected that Juf would survive. Here in Bandoeng it is a mess. Women and children are arriving daily, but exclusively *Belanda Indo*. Is anything known at your end about release? I get the impression that release of Europeans is awaiting the arrival of the Allies, but when? Waiting is driving me nuts.

Internment of Eurasians had been a local (Bandoeng) policy initiative, and had not been authorized by Tokyo; their release possibly also reflected local initiatives. The letter continued:

One of Theo's Chinese building material suppliers has assisted us with money and a bike so that I don't have to be around Theo and Mien all the time. Everything is unbelievably expensive, so I have no idea how I will succeed with accommodation. About our beautiful camp life I would rather not write. It would spoil this first letter and I am also determined to forget about this crazy period as soon as possible. The future interests me more. I have made a thousand and one plans, but they remain dreams. I am anxious to see what we hear from the Netherlands and from South Africa. It will depend entirely on that information as to what we should do. I am also most intrigued to see what you make of all this. It is a pity we missed Boudy's birthday and yet the situation had by then improved. Now my girl, the days that we are still doomed to remain separated will last a damned long time, but hang on! Is Emmy still with you? Please send her my love. Say, Boudy, can you read this? And old faithful Juf, you stuck it out doggedly. All the best to all three of you!

The second piece of paper was labelled "Letter II."

My dearest Wil and Boudy,

I was on the point of mailing Letter I to Batavia, and then your lengthy epistle arrived. I tried, before quitting Tjimahi, to send you a telegram when that opportunity was made available to us, but that was a failure since you had heard nothing from me.

How is Juf doing? Your post-script came simultaneously with your long letter. I must say that when I received a card from you in March and not from Juf, and saw no mention of her in your card, I was convinced that she was gone. But it would be a tremendous pity were she to die now, within sight of liberation. I was just discussing with Theo the possibility of going to Batavia, but neither of us sees any value in that. In the first instance I am unable to get a train ticket because I do not have a *surat lepas* [an exit pass]. Please let me know if you are able to get permission to leave when I have found accommodation. Make sure that you do not leave the camp without a *surat lepas* because that is the only way of getting food and financial support. I would love to come to Batavia, but how could I find a roof there? I have a bit of money, but the prices are so high that we can forget about hotel charges. The best may be for me to find a room, perhaps with the family Hannay, our neighbours on the Eykmanweg; they still have a table and some of our chairs. Our house there is standing empty now, but still contains our gas stove. I tried to persuade Mrs. Raken to let us rent a garage or a *paviljoen* or even the house, but no luck. She has a hundred and one objections. She wants to keep the entire property free for her family. This morning I encountered Mr. Ploeg with wife and son: they are staying with the Biezevelds at Tjihampelas (a residential area north of Bandoeng). That's where I will go tomorrow: hopefully I can find something there. But I agree with you, we must have something where we can be alone: I am fed up with people. You asked about my plans. I have made thousands of plans, but I first need to talk with you. I have thought about New Zealand, old Holland and, of course, South Africa, but least of all about remaining here. Dear Wil, this letter must be sent off this evening. Please give Boudy a big kiss and encourage Juf to pull through.

Edu Returns

That same afternoon I was surprised when a strange, gaunt man, dressed in baggy khaki shorts and a sleeveless shirt, with a deeply tanned and lined face and a huge aquiline nose and what seemed like a frozen smile, accosted me in our yard.

"Do you know Mrs. Emmy Kerkhoven?"

"Tante Emmy?"

"Yes," and after a brief pause, "Are you Boudy?"

I showed him where we were living, and where Emmy was resting from a heavy morning's work in the Tjimalaja kitchen.

"How, how did you get here?" she stammered in surprise.

"I *bolossed* along with some others," he said as though implying, "I just ran away." That he had found Emmy in Tjideng was a miracle. "I knew that you had left Bandoeng," he added, "but I did not know whether you had gone to Batavia or to central Java."

Edu had made his way to Batavia with Lieutenant Lansink and some other escaped POWs in the hope of making themselves useful in restoring the Dutch administration and helping the large number of women and children who seemed to be here. He was cheerful but emaciated, a walking skeleton; he nevertheless immediately set to work in the kitchen, where the duties had become so much more onerous of late.

One cannot but marvel at the efficiency of the ad hoc postal service that had been improvised by the Red Cross. Two days later another letter from my father arrived, dated September 12, obviously a response to my mother's letter of September 11. My father explained as he had in the previous letter how he had tried to send a telegram and was worried that his two previous letters had not reached us and so he wrote yet again:

> I had sent two letters back with someone from Tjimahi travelling to Batavia, but since I was not sure those letters would arrive I am trying once more via the Red Cross. This business-like explanation was prompted by evidence that you were worried. I can assure you that I am fit and that my stomach and insides are in excellent working order well able to handle a sausage or bacon. I am thrilled that you are in such good shape. From Mien I had already heard much positive news. It is especially these last few months that have cost so many people their lives. The news of the capitulation reached us in dribs and drabs. I had always been well informed, but the "Hooray" atmosphere remained absent. And then we got better food and they began to liquidate the camp: first the *Belanda Indo* from Tjimahi and Bandoeng etc, but suddenly it all stopped. Then Theo's sister-in-law came for a visit with young Theo. Mien was unable to come because of her illness, and [her sister] invited us to come and live with them. We did not hesitate and the next day we took off. Now I read your plea to get you out of Tjideng. As a result of our escape we, Theo and I, have forgone

the opportunity of obtaining a *surat lepas* and so cannot get a travel warrant nor assistance from the Red Cross. So if you come, please follow the official route, otherwise we will starve. Another issue is accommodation. I have heard that if I can guarantee you a roof over your head, you can then get permission to leave Tjideng. So you can be assured that I am doing my best. Maybe we can get the *paviljoen* of the family Sloten. Our house in *Dennelust* is occupied, but that is too far away and too big in any case. Another problem is that we have no legal rights as long as the Allies are not here. You are completely dependent on the helpfulness of compatriots. Once again make sure that you do not leave the camp without a *surat lepas* because that gives you 25 guilders per week, rice, sugar and food from the communal kitchen.

Before the letter got sent, he received another letter from my mother, for he enclosed a second letter as follows:

Bdg 12/9/45

My dearest Wil,

Communication seems to be improving steadily because I have just received your last cry for help. I have not the slightest intention of returning to the camp, even though they supply that institution with a hundred pigs per day or whatever other delicacies. When we cleared out of the camp I left everything behind, otherwise the attempt would have failed. Theo had discovered among some lady visitors a pre-war acquaintance who had a bicycle outside of the camp that I was able to take charge of. Aside from that we stumbled into the arms of a Chinese building material merchant who recognized Theo and chartered a *betja* for him, since we had no money. And in this manner, we cycled and rode to Bandoeng. I had taken the precaution of packing my stuff and providing a forwarding address in case the opportunity arose for someone to ship it to me from the camp. Your letters were forwarded to me thanks to the labels on my suitcase. Your response "Yes" to my question whether we should leave this place is okay. I have the tentative plan to go to Holland, if possible via Durban, Johannesburg and Cape Town, in order to assess the situation in the old Transvaal, and in order to sort out my affairs in Holland. What I possess there [real estate] is too valuable to be ignored and if it has been ruined it will need to be rebuilt. I am sure that it is a mess in Holland, but it won't be such a lawless shambles as over here. How is Juf? You have not told me what ails her: her heart or oedema? I will enclose a short note for her: she will be happy with that. I fill my day with domestic tasks. This morning I spent a few hours ironing clothes and then I went to the soup kitchen, where you have to wait for a long time, but are rewarded with an excellent portion of food for 1 guilder. I fetch two portions using the *surat lepas* of Mien.

During the days that followed a rapid change overwhelmed Batavia and cities elsewhere on Java. The shrinking Japanese presence, reflecting a growing "self-internment operation" and a hands-off approach among the remaining Japanese soldiers, created an opportunity for the release of pent-up Indonesian frustration. Rebelliousness and riot spread, at the hands of growing bands of hungry, unemployed youth, stirred up by slogan-shouting and fiery speeches at mass meetings where the red and white Indonesian independence flag was displayed in growing numbers. Myriad groups with lugubrious titles like "the Black Snake" or "Black Buffalo" were competing in bloodthirstiness. Anyone, regardless of race, who attempted to haul down one of the red-and-white flags stood a chance of a severe beating. Here and there Japanese were caught and gratuitously *tjintjanged* (hacked to death).

On September 12, Lieutenant Colonel Nicholas D. J. Read Collins arrived in Batavia at the head of the RAPWI task force; its intent was to dispense assistance to an estimated twenty-eight thousand internees on Java. But Greenhalgh, who had visited Tjideng two days earlier, could tell him that the numbers were far larger and that the condition of the internees was far worse than had been assumed. Relief work could moreover not be undertaken without armed escort, of which there was almost none. The next day we nevertheless received another load of rations: individual parcels containing such luxuries as toilet soap, a towel, toilet paper, forty-five grams of coffee, a toothbrush, toothpaste and pencils.

A day later my mother wrote another letter to my father, her only one to survive the subsequent turmoil:

Tjideng 15-9-1945

Dear Bou

Let me just give you a report on what happened yesterday. We (a friend from here—Emmy could not because Edu is here all the time) and I first went to the gate in order to leave camp along an official route, but there we were held back, "Tjideng ladies not allowed to go outside." Then we just went elsewhere through a hole in the *gedek,* and took off. Outside we heard from some who had left Adek [another women's camp in Batavia] that friends of mine, a Dr. Wilkens and his wife, have just arrived in [Hotel] des Indes to take charge of the patient rehabilitation unit being established there for Tjideng women.

Read Collins, alerted by a Tjideng doctor to the fact that eight hundred patients were on the point of death, immediately arranged emergency removal of many of the sick, including Juf, from Tjideng hospital and installed them in the west wing of the hotel. My mother continued in her letter:

And so our first steps were directed towards des Indes [half an hour's walk from Tjideng]. We were greeted with a "hooray" by Mrs. Wilkens, who thought that we were in excellent condition, in spite of the fact that we came from Tjideng, generally referred to by outsiders as "the black flag." And there it was once again just like former times; we drank delicious coffee in grand style, in the company of officers, who offer you a cigarette [Hotel des Indes had become a temporary Allied headquarters], looking at passing traffic, *enfin*, you will understand that we once more felt human. From des Indes we went to Toko Ven, where we met some other escapees with whom we shared an ice cream sundae and a bottle of sherry. Then we took the tram to the lower [old] town, where we had a meal in a Chinese restaurant: a lot of *bahmi*, *fou yong hai*, and each two fried eggs and a beer. Then we saw a small *katjung* [Indonesian street urchin] enter with a bunch of bananas, and wanted to buy those for dessert. But it turned out that he had been asked to get them for a Chinese man sitting at a neighbouring table. When he discovered that we wanted those, he stood up and said, "It's yours, ladies," and he did not want us to pay him. The Chinese are tremendous here, and the *inlanders* too. We went to the *pasar* and noticed nothing about enmity or rebellion. I had just made plans with Hanna Poortman to go to Bandoeng tomorrow. Marius is also free and has resumed practice in the Borromeus Hospital and she also wants to talk with him. There is no way in which you can officially leave, but we can get to Bandoeng and I would then return on Monday. But Edu now tells us that we should not go tomorrow because the *Cumberland* is expected to arrive and we should wait to see what then happens regarding riots.

On September 15, HMS *Cumberland* had anchored forty kilometres outside of Tandjong Priok, awaiting assistance from the Japanese to navigate through the minefield and into the harbour. My mother continued:

There is truth in that, and so we will wait for a little while. People over here expect that once the *Cumberland* arrives, they will hurry up dredging out the troublemakers, so we will get our chance. Yesterday morning a Dutch pilot turned up and within five minutes we had to have letters ready for him to take to Holland. I was not here, but Emmy gave him a short note to my parents saying that we are all well.

The pilot, Captain van Emden, had come to retrieve his wife and son from Tjideng; he whisked them out of camp and into his Canso Catalina flying boat, moored in the harbour.[21]

> This guy knew Jan Butner and told us that he had died.[22] Last night, we had a film show. First Snow White for the children and afterwards the Sign of Zorro, a lousy, rotten film for the adults. Boudy had a wonderful time, and does not stop talking about Snow White.

Yes, indeed, the Disney film was memorable. At the crossroad in the centre of the camp, the RAPWI people had suspended a screen between light standards and placed a projector, powered by an emergency generator, on some boxes. We children, about five hundred of us, sat on the road. At six o'clock, the theatre lights went out as the sun dropped below the horizon and the dark tropical night engulfed us, and then the Snow White story unfolded before our enchanted eyes. It was sheer magic.

> Now I forgot to tell you that our trip into town ended with a glorious return here through the gate in a car. We live adjacent to the gate and we were dropped off in front of our house. And now I have celebrated the peace and a safe arrival home with our little family. Now I no longer need to go out before we can then repeat this celebration jointly. Are you already buying sausages at Anton's? Have you looked up Evert and Bouter? He is in Tjihapit.

That same day, Tjihapit, now converted into a men's camp, came under attack from Indonesians emerging from the *kampongs* beyond its eastern border. They were armed with *rantjangs* (sharp, fire-hardened bamboo spears) and *goloks* (machetes). My mother continued:

> Juf is making progress. She is causing amazement throughout the hospital at her appetite. She eats all the food that we send her. Bou, you are missing a lot, not being able to see all that is going on here. There are men everywhere with us in our rooms. Everyone sighs and pants because we have to be as well dressed as possible. In the past, when we were still "unmanned," we went about with minimal clothing, but now we are once more properly dressed. Men are streaming into the camp, all men with *bunkusjes* [baskets] of fruit for family members and friends. Fancy cars come and go, while we still walk around with our full

---

21. Captain van Emden had managed to escape with his Catalina aircraft shortly before capitulation in 1942 and had spent the war years flying anti-submarine patrols out of Colombo (Maarten van Emden, personal communication).

22. Jan Butner had died in an accident in Mississippi where he was training pilots. His name is on a war memorial at Hawkins field, Jackson, Mississippi.

chamber pots to empty them in the cesspit, because our toilet has not functioned for the last few weeks. Edu has already tried to clear up the drains with his arms, but the blockage is solid. But we lasted a long time. Do you know that ours was the only house with a usable toilet?

Edu was a very sick man, and henceforth Emmy had to nurse him. He quite possibly owed his life to the illness he had contracted early on during internment, for otherwise he might well have been shipped off to the Pakanbaru or Burma railway projects. The camp he had left had been the major transhipment point for thousands of doomed slave labourers.

H.M.S. *Cumberland*

On the morning of September 16, the slightly built, bearded, and very learned Charles Olke van den Plas, formerly the governor of East Java, a member of the Advisory Council and a fluent speaker of various indigenous languages, could look forward to setting foot once again on the land of his birth. He was a guest of Vice Admiral Wilfred Patterson, who was commanding a flotilla from HMS *Cumberland*. That morning the *Cumberland* weighed anchor to commence the final leg of its journey in the company of some minesweepers and a frigate into Tandjong Priok.

Van den Plas prided himself on his excellent relationship with many of the feudal Javanese rulers, and prior to his hurried departure from Java in 1942 had worked with some of these rulers to ensure ongoing anti-Japanese underground activity. Among the Dutch, he was sometimes accused of being too pro-Indonesian,[23] but to the Indonesians he was affectionately known as *pak djenggot* (bearded father). He now returned as a senior representative of the NEI government and political advisor to Patterson.

Three days earlier, he had informed a group of officers in Singapore that Sukarno and the Republik Indonesia had no credibility among the population, referring to them as "a bunch of desperadoes."[24] In his opinion, "there would be broad support for a return to Dutch colonial rule." The challenge van den Plas thought he was facing was simply that of purging Indonesian society of "collaborators and traitors," a process deemed to be no different here from what was at that time going on in the Netherlands and other countries formerly occupied by the Nazis. People would soon return to their old homes and their former jobs, and life would resume its normal course.

Arrival on earth by the man on the moon would have been no more bizarre than the return in this way of the Dutch colonial presence. The naval squadron

---

23. Bijkerk, *De laatste landvoogd*, 64.
24. de Jong, *Het Koninkrijk der Nederlanden in de Tweede Wereldoorlog*, Vol. 11c, 558.

was met at sea by a launch carrying two Japanese naval officers armed with charts and an interpreter. With the help of a Japanese pilot, the squadron was able to find a safe route through the minefields guarding the port and draw alongside a berth.[25] One could hardly describe this as a victorious entry by liberating Allied troops, trampling underfoot opposition from a hated Japanese army of occupation. To a casual local observer, unfamiliar with recent events far to the north, the scene would have appeared as a friendly welcoming gesture by the Japanese authorities on Java to visiting ships from a foreign navy.

The following day another squadron arrived, including the Dutch cruiser *Tromp*, another frigate and some minesweepers. That same day, Greenhalgh and two former internees briefed Patterson and van den Plas in the *Cumberland* wardroom with a first-hand account of the state of affairs on Java. What they had to say was unexpected and most disturbing.

Not only did this assessment contradict the assertions of van den Plas a few days earlier, but in addition Greenhalgh had to state how the political situation had deteriorated dramatically even during his brief stay. The recent spectacle of calm downtown Batavia, caused perhaps by the fresh memory of the heavy-handed Japanese military rule, had now given way to one increasingly marked by roaming bands of youth armed with a variety of weapons, and the display of independence flags. One of Greenhalgh's companions noted that he had encountered a growing reluctance on the part of Indonesians with a Dutch education to speak Dutch, and an anti-Dutch movement had become apparent. Seldom had a revolution exploded more abruptly.

That afternoon, van den Plas went ashore and managed to find a car to take him to Tjideng, where he found his own wife and Mrs. van Mook, wife of the Lieutenant Governor General. He had arranged accommodation in the Hotel des Indes for himself and these ladies, but his brief glimpse of conditions in Tjideng had made a deep impression on him. In a letter to van Mook he wrote, "We have been accommodated in Hotel des Indes, where we reside in a state of luxury that pains the heart, when one considers the women and children of those camps, the condition of which exceeds every conceivable imagined boundary."[26] The spectacle of van den Plas, tall, dignified, well-dressed and healthy, whisking his and van Mook's wives out of the camp in a shiny limousine made a most unfavourable impression on the women in Tjideng. Some could not hide their feelings of derision to see two of their own leaving in such style, and hurled abuse as the limousine left the camp gate.

Van den Plas, in his letter to van Mook, who was still residing in Brisbane, included a sober, troubling assessment of the political and economic situation. To his dismay, he had to admit that the country was in effect run by the

25. Woodburn Kirby, *The War Against Japan*, Vol. 5, 313.
26. de Jong, *Het Koninkrijk der Nederlanden in de Tweede Wereldoorlog*, Vol. 11c, 593.

Indonesians themselves, that the Japanese had done a thorough job of eliminating the European component from every facet of Indonesian life and that "to turn this clock back now would present a considerable challenge." Van den Plas did not stay long in Hotel des Indes, for the arrival of the *Cumberland* seemed to spark an increased rebelliousness among the Indonesian population. As a precautionary measure Patterson requested that van den Plas, who by now had discovered as well that his influential Indonesian friends had also become nationalists, relinquish his comfortable rooms in Hotel des Indes and remain out of sight, on-board ship.

Java's descent into a murderous anarchy gained pace. In the far eastern port of Soerabaja, no European could venture onto the streets without a heavily armed escort. There, a couple of Dutch soldiers, who had escaped from their camp and had tried to reclaim their pre-war military office, were ambushed and had their throats slit.[27]

To my mother the news that several ships, including the *Tromp,* were now lying in harbour at Tandjong Priok was on the other hand a clear indication that the Allies had finally arrived and that liberation would begin: this was too much for her and she had to see it for herself.

On Monday, September 17, she and a friend once more ventured out of the camp, walked down *Laan* Trivelli to the Hotel des Indes, where they caught a tram to Tandjong Priok. She returned triumphantly in the afternoon, bubbling over with a description of her wonderful experiences, including the welcome and the lunch she had enjoyed on the ship. But as far as I was concerned the two souvenirs were best of all: first she handed me a sailor's belt made of broad dark-blue cotton webbing with two short leather strips to buckle up and a shiny steel spring clasp hanging on one side from which a seaman's pen knife could be suspended; better yet was the buttered dinner roll, wrapped in a paper serviette. I thought this must be cake! Never before had I tasted anything so utterly delicious!

But my mother also came back rattled: "Everywhere on trams there are anti-Dutch and nationalist slogans. I could not believe how quickly Batavia had changed," she confessed to Emmy.

"Are there any Allied soldiers?"

"No, just sailors on the ships."

That afternoon trucks arrived in the camp with some large water tanks. One tank was offloaded and placed on the hospital grounds across from our house. Then the trucks went further up Trivelli to deliver the others to the camp kitchens. Another truck with a huge water tank came and was connected by means of fire hoses to the newly installed water tank in front of the hospital.

---

27. van der Post, *The Admiral's Baby,* 26.

"Thank goodness, no more hauling of water in bathtubs," one of the women standing by the side of the road sighed, as she watched this work being done.

"Yes," replied one of the men, "but we are also worried about the city water supply; there have been threats that it would be poisoned. This seems a bit extreme to me, but we are taking precautions."

More good things happened, arranged by Lieutenant Read Collins. Some Japanese men came in to clear the sewage ditches. They could not do anything about the toilet facilities, but the sewage ditch ladies were now finally relieved of their unpleasant task. A number of men also came to sweep the street and get rid of garbage. Another truck came loaded with petroleum stoves, which would be a huge improvement, because the poorly built and equipped soup kitchens could not handle the augmented food supplies that were now available. Individual women could now do some of their own cooking—if they could find a place for the petroleum stoves, and if they could stand the tedium of crouching over their pots. In the further reaches of the camp, where conditions were far worse, these improvements made scant difference.

That same day an RAF squadron of Mitchell Bombers and Dakotas arrived at Kemajoran, the Batavia airfield; its first task was to establish a repatriation office in one of the former government buildings on the east side of the Konings *Plein* (now *Lapangan Merdeka*—Freedom Square).[28] Repatriation of displaced persons was considered only for those who had British (including British Commonwealth) or American citizenship. The concept of repatriation for Dutch citizens had been assumed to be a non-issue: they would simply go home and revert to their pre-war lifestyles. As early as September 12 some of the Dutch POWs languishing in camps in Asia had indicated a desire to be repatriated elsewhere; they had been the ones who had in some haste joined the KNIL from places such as South Africa and Australia, and for them "home" meant either those countries or Holland. This now became a troubling issue, but although Mountbatten had no reason to deny the request, neither he nor the local Dutch commander was authorized to approve it. However, on September 18 Mountbatten, prompted by troubling reports from Lady Edwina, his wife, sought clarification from van den Plas as to the number of prisoners on Java: was it 123,000 or 59,098? Two days later he moreover became aware of the existence of civilian internees, who for one reason or another had ended up in places like Formosa and now balked at being sent to Java, where they had no other ties.

This coincided with a daily escalation of murder and mayhem, especially at night. On the evening of Tuesday, September 18, a huge crowd of youths and men armed with *goloks* and *rantjangs* marched through the town waving their red

28. de Jong, *Het Koninkrijk der Nederlanden in de Tweede Wereld Oorlog*, Vol. 11c, 561.

and white flags and making their way up *Laan* Trivelli (now called Jalan Tanah Abang 2) in an attempt to attack Tjideng. Screaming and yelling hysterically, they went around the back of the camp, where they marched along the railway embankment, beating *tongtongs* and starting to tear down the bamboo wall. The rapidly gathering dusk made it all the more alarming, and we fled inside our homes, a futile move given the fact that none of the houses had doors or windows.

It was a terrifying situation. A number of European men bravely took up a defensive position with whatever weapons they could lay their hands on, but many of these men were in poor physical condition. One of them, a medical doctor, went so far as to ask Lieutenant Sakai for the loan of his revolver. The latter hesitated to take action, but finally called up some reinforcements and sent them running down *Laan* Trivelli to the far side of the camp, where the crowd had gathered. A little while later we heard shots being fired, and that brought results: the crowd dispersed and the frightening sounds of wailing and banging diminished as the rioters returned in the dark to their *kampongs*.

"We'll take turns sleeping," Emmy suggested. "If they come again we may have to run."

The following evening, four Japanese soldiers were murdered in downtown Batavia, and in the outskirts of the city two more Japanese and a *Belanda Indo* met their end.[29] And thus, within the astonishing space of a week the role of the Japanese soldiers had changed from being our oppressors to being our allies and protectors. The dreaded and hated *Kempetai* once more established a command post in the European club, where the old pre-war name plate, *Societeit Harmonie*, still hung over the entrance, mocking the changed role of this erstwhile "pure European" establishment.

The next day, a huge crowd of excited Indonesians gathered in the middle of town on the Konings *Plein* to protest the return of Dutch rule. Patterson ordered the *Kempetai* to contain the situation; they manned all access roads to the square, confiscating a huge assortment of *goloks* and *rantjangs* from the participants, and ordered Sukarno, who was slated to be the key speaker, to cut the meeting short and disperse the crowd. That same evening a platoon of armed sailors from HMS *Cumberland* arrived at the Tjideng guardhouse to stand watch. The rapidly deteriorating security situation, coupled with the expectation that real troop reinforcements would not arrive for another two weeks, prompted the RAPWI team to start a food stockpiling program in Tjideng, but the lack of available space was a major stumbling block and bales of rice and sugar had to be left out in the open. At the same time our food rations were once more reduced. The real fear, however, was the water supply. Since the Indonesian nationalists were in complete control of the water supply, we were

---

29. Bouwer, *Het vermoorde land*, 403.

essentially at their mercy, and new threats that the water might be poisoned began to circulate.

A month earlier, a thin line of vicious Japanese soldiers had separated us from friendly Indonesians. Inexplicably, the Japanese suddenly became our protectors when the Indonesians stopped being friendly, and now a thin line of British blue jackets separated us from thousands of threatening Indonesians. It was a bewildering turn of events; morale once more plummeted.

Reunited at Last

Three days later, on September 23, it happened. The event sticks out in my mind as though it occurred only yesterday, and the thought of it still sends shivers up and down my spine.

It was roughly noon, for the sun stood directly overhead, and I accordingly was inside the house, resting on my mother's and Emmy's mattress, when a cry came from the front of the house, "Willy, your husband's here!"

I jumped up and ran through the sea of mattresses and personal belongings scattered about the room and out onto the veranda through the hole where the double French door used to be, onto the front yard, which was festooned as usual with drying clothes. There, just inside the low garden wall, underneath the shade of the trees that flanked the road, stood my father. He was wearing ill-fitting and much repaired khaki shorts, a shirt with the sleeves missing and improvised sandals. He did not look quite the same as the photograph my mother had carefully kept, for his face bore the scars of punishment, but it was him! Of that there was no doubt in my mind. He looked worried when I ran to him, grabbed him by the hand, and called him *pappie!* He did not respond, because, as he said afterwards, he did not recognize me at all and had been overcome by emotion, fearing that any child might run to him to call him "Father" amidst the chaos he saw around him in Tjideng. Could this really be his child, his son?

He had last seen me when I was a toddler, and children change mightily over the course of four years. I took him to my mother, who had been asleep, tired from the endless sorting of letters and compilation of names in the camp office. What an amazing experience this was.

"What happened? How did you get here? Is it not too dangerous?" The questions came tumbling out.

"I heard about the arrival of the ships and the setting up of the repatriation office, and I was worried about the threats to Tjideng, so I just came."

"My God," exclaimed my mother. "What on earth happened to you? I mean your teeth, your face."

"I'll tell you later," he replied, nodding mysteriously in my direction.

"What's it like in Bandoeng?" my mother asked.

"Terrible. Ank and Ben had to flee for their lives when *rampokkers* overran the neighbourhood where they were staying. I reckon that it is safer here with the navy in the harbour."

"But how could you get a ticket? Did you get a *surat lepas?*"

"I didn't bother with tickets—it's chaos everywhere. You only need tickets for first class carriages. I travelled *kambing*—you just need to squeeze in like everyone else." Then, glancing around the room, surveying the dense mass of humanity, the regular spectacle of someone walking to the cess pit with a pot in hand causing him to wrinkle his nose, he added, "I can see and smell why you want to leave Tjideng."

Having lost interest in a discussion regarding what I only saw as our normal situation, I left my parents talking while I crowed my good news to the other children in the yard and on the street. Much later I heard what had happened to him. He had failed to properly bow to a Japanese guard, who had promptly used a spanner he happened to have in his hand to wallop my father in the face, knocking out a number of teeth; he was lucky to escape without a broken jaw.[30] However, since he was in an otherwise reasonable physical state he was immediately recruited to assist with the guarding of the camp. In the following days, my father stood watch with a rifle slung over his shoulder and, as a result, was able to procure a *surat lepas*. The *surat lepas* permitted him to search around the district for accommodation, but in the meantime he slept in the guardhouse outside the gate.

Within a week of my father's arrival some Seaforth Highlanders and Gurkhas had disembarked in Tandjong Priok. They had been dispatched ahead of schedule largely as a result of the alarming reports Lady Edwina Mountbatten had personally conveyed to her husband at the conclusion of her surreptitious and brave visit to various internment locations. "The living dead," was the way she had described some internees. Command of these troops fell to tall, distinguished-looking Lieutenant General Sir Philip Christison, who arrived at Kemajoran airport on September 29, having being warned that his was a "tricky mission" on account of the political situation.[31] That evening, as he sat on the steps of his villa smoking a cigarette, a bullet whizzed past his head, not intended for him, he thought, but "probably to settle an old score," as he put it. Within a week he discovered that "instead of twenty thousand European

---

30. Thirty years later the experience still haunted my father. When his seven-year-old grandson bowed to him at the conclusion of a Suzuki violin recital, the man nearly assaulted the startled child.

31. Christison, *Life and Times*, 176.

women and children he was dealing with the safety of one hundred and eighty thousand, including Eurasians."[32]

The next day Christison held a press conference in front of the presidential palace with, as a backdrop, three flagpoles from which the Dutch, the American and the British flags fluttered in a display of solidarity. The Dutch flag hung from the central flagpole, somewhat higher than the other two "to indicate the senior partner in Indonesia." Indonesian wags quickly pointed out that the "Dutch flag was propped up by the other two flags." Christison made it clear that his first concern was security in Batavia, and that he was charged with the acceptance of the formal surrender of the Japanese troops, and their disarmament and repatriation. He announced the imminent arrival from Brisbane of Lieutenant Governor General van Mook, but recognized the fact that much of Java was effectively in the hands of the nationalists and that he would have to rely on Sukarno to help him maintain law and order by reigning in the *pemuda* terrorists.

This last statement, picked up by recently arrived journalists, caused an outcry in the Netherlands, for the Indonesian press gleefully concluded that the British government had recognized Indonesian independence. General Christison suddenly found himself in the midst of an international diplomatic row caused largely by the inability of ministers in London and the Hague to comprehend the reality of the situation now faced by him on Java: in his own words he was "stunned by the turn of events."[33]

Christison had a difficult assignment. He had to provide security, but at the same time keep out of politics in a country that was in turmoil. With the tiny force at his command he could only achieve a modicum of control in Batavia, but whereas the Japanese had made unrestrained use of ruthless techniques, Christison had to handle each threat with velvet gloves. In part, this reflected the policy directives from London, but it also reflected the Indian component of his force: Nehru had insisted that Mountbatten should not use Indian troops to thwart the ambitions of the nationalist movement in Indonesia, and the Gurkhas themselves could not be relied on to do otherwise if ordered to. Shortly after the press conference, Christison toured the city and was astonished at the new slogans smeared on walls and trams: "Death to van Mook" and "To hell with van Mook," and "What about the Atlantic Charter?"

The clocks of Java were put back one and a half hours from Tokyo time and Juf was moved, along with the other patients, out of the Hotel des Indes to the Tjikini hospital, located in the southern part of Batavia. This made it more difficult to see her, for the three-kilometre walk from Tjideng, well away from

32. Christison, *Life and Times,* 178.
33. Christison, *Life and Times,* 180.

the area now frequented by Allied troops and through a city with growing lawlessness, had become hazardous.

Elsewhere on Java, rioting escalated dramatically. Batavia remained a haven of relative security on a large populous island rapidly descending into a new hell, an orgy of killing and senseless violence.

11. FAREWELL TJIDENG

It was wonderful having our South African *kongsi* back together; we had all survived, though for two of us it had been a close call. Now our dear, seventy-two-year-old Juf was pulling back from the brink of death and Edu, nominally in the prime of life, was finally getting hospital care. The shared ordeal of the last three and a half years had moreover cemented the bonds of friendship first forged in South Africa during those weekend trips to Kruger National Park. Now we were jointly finding our way in a dramatically changed world.

Others did not fare so well. For the women, and especially for the mothers, the four-year-long burden of sole responsibility for children and elderly family members in the face of starvation, disease and brutality had been heavy indeed, made worse by the uncertainty of the fate of their husbands. The news that a loved one had died during the ordeal now came as a terrible shock, made worse by following so quickly on the heels of liberation and the hope for a better future.

But those families that had survived the war were also facing new difficulties. In the case of some family reunions, insurmountable tensions quickly arose. The elation of being reunited was soon to give way to the bitter realization that marriage bonds had become irreparably frayed; this second blow was almost more damaging. No longer could the wife revert to the pre-war role of submissiveness after having fought for survival against the Japanese, whereas the husband could think of no other relationship than the one he had been forced to break by the occupation. In some instances awful suspicions and allegations of misconduct, fed by whispers of sexual coercion and of opportunism, poisoned the atmosphere. The end of the war did not bring an end to the tragedies, and peace began with a spate of divorces. We were lucky.

Our real family reunion could only take place if we left the Tjideng hellhole, and my father set to work looking for accommodation. Within a week he had found a room not far from the Tjideng gate. This was part of a *paviljoen* attached to a larger house inhabited by a *Belanda Indo* couple, Mr. and Mrs. de Bruin. The small daily allowance my father was now earning could just cover the rental costs; the owners were more than pleased to have any additional income, and perhaps even more important, another friendly face on the premises.

"Yes," my father had mused thoughtfully. "The de Bruins are afraid. They managed to stay out of camp, but they are desperately looking forward to the arrival of the soldiers to restore law and order. Batavia is not what it used to be before the Japs came."

"Do you think it is safe to live outside of the camp?" Hanna enviously asked my mother when she heard of our imminent departure. She had repeatedly been talking about going to Bandoeng to find her husband Marius, who was once again working in the Borromeus Hospital, but she would have to take along her two daughters and that complicated such a trip.

"The de Bruins seem to be okay," my mother replied without too much conviction. "Anyway, I can't stand this place any longer—all those people and the eternal worry about hygiene."

With so few possessions, the move out of Tjideng was relatively easy. My father had been able to borrow minimal bedding requirements from our landlord, and Emmy, who would remain inside Tjideng for the time being, could keep the double mattress. I would remain sleeping on the air mattress.

"I can get the leak fixed," my father promised confidently.

Our departure from the house did not go unnoticed. "Leaving us in the shit?" someone pointedly asked with a hint of malice and envy, as Emmy helped us carry our possessions out of the house.

An official minding the Tjideng gate only wanted to be assured that we indeed had accommodation and that my father was staying with us before letting us through, past the spot where the notorious monkey cage had stood, past the guardhouse and Sone's house, and across the concrete bridge spanning the Tjideng *kali*, stirring in my mind memories of the awful day, five months earlier, when we had first seen that bridge and when for the first time I had had to endure the heat of that road under my bare feet. We walked on, down the *Laan* Trivelli in the direction of town, where the trees were older and taller and threw more shade on the villas on either side; strangely enough, the further we moved away from *de poort*, that awful gate, the longer seemed to be the time we had spent on the other side in the crowding, squalor and fear of Tjideng.

For my parents every step we took was a return to the promise of a remembered normal life; they were chatting about old friends, wondering what had become of them. The seeming calm of *Laan* Trivelli, the air of normalcy that prevailed in this suburban enclave, the orderly houses on either side, the sight of *inlanders* on bicycles or on foot and hawking vegetables to the residents, aroused in my mother the idea of moving into the house at *Dennelust*.

"You wrote that some of our furniture is still at the Eykmanweg address, didn't you?"

"Yes Wil, but Bandoeng is horrible. Over there it's impossible to safely walk on the streets the way we are doing here."

"Don't you think Christison will soon sort that out?"

"Wil, you would not recognize the place—not many friendly faces left there."

"Did you run into Ru or Charlotte at all?" Emmy inquired. "I wonder what has become of them." [1]

"I've heard nothing about either," my father answered.

We soon came to a stop in front of a two-storey house. My father pointed to a smaller building beside the house, set well back from the road. "That's our place," he announced.

For me the move out of the camp opened up a totally new and exciting world; camp life was all I had really grown to know, and the fleeting vision of a normal city we had had on the day of our arrival in Batavia was now replaced by the luxury of being able to study the scene at leisure.

Here we actually had a room all to ourselves—just the three of us. At first it felt unsettling—all that space. My air mattress, now repaired, was no longer right next to my mother's mattress. My father had managed to find a bicycle tire repair kit in the guardhouse and had fixed the leak. We now also had running water, a toilet, a wash basin, and a small kitchen all to ourselves. We did not have a proper stove, but managed to procure a terra cotta *anglo* and some charcoal and thus my mother was able to cook outside, on the steps. We even had matches, so lighting fires was no longer so time-consuming. With only the three of us living in this space it was unnervingly quiet. For well over three years we had shared each moment of the day with the sounds of other people—with coughs, cries, mothers scolding children, children and mothers crying, and people using their potties; now there was silence.

At night the road outside the house was deserted, for when the sun set, all traffic stopped, thanks to the recently imposed curfew. But in daytime the roadway here offered so much of interest to see. There were bicycles, *betjas*, *delmans* (four-wheeled horse-drawn carriages), *grobaks*, sometimes pulled by a horse, and occasionally a car or a truck going to or coming from the big city at the end of the tree-shaded avenue. *Inlanders* trotting down the street with their *pikulans* on their shoulders, hawking wares such as *pisang sisirs* (clusters of bananas) or baskets with fruit and vegetables or even chickens suspended by their feet from the ends of the pole became a regular sight. Watching the rhythmic gait of each of these men and their dancing bamboo poles was fascinating.

For a brief period of time, only a few weeks really, we savoured in this little place the novelty of normal life. My mother shopped with a daily allowance given to her by the Red Cross, cooked and did the washing, while my father worked and I gingerly began to explore our surroundings. It almost felt like peace, a misleading impression given the fact that around us Java had become a new battleground.

---

1. They were reunited after the war but later divorced.

General Christison began to address the security situation in three key cities: Batavia, Bandoeng and Soerabaja; to do more on this large and populous island was impossible given his resources. The reality he faced was absolute control by undisciplined, anarchic, rebellious *pemuda* over every aspect of life on Java— even in parts of Batavia, in spite of Christison's men, while Soerabaja was a disaster. Nationalist leaders such as Sukarno, Hatta and Sjahrir were holding press conferences, long on rhetoric and short on accountability. They seemed to be backed by a popular movement, but in fact had no control over the remnants of the Japanese-trained militia or the lawless bands of roaming armed thugs, the *pemudas* terrorizing the land. Already in August it had been clear that people like Sukarno were not so much leaders as figureheads, desperately trying to hang on to such semblance of authority as they could derive through their ability to whip up enthusiasm in large crowds predisposed to violent action. Johan Fabricius, a journalist accredited with the BBC and recently returned to the land of his birth, observed that "the armed *pemudas*, who were comfortably seated on Mohammed Hatta's porch, cheerfully smoking cigarettes, could hear each and every word this leader was uttering inside his house and they were not merely protecting him."[2] As far as they were concerned Christison's tiny force of men were little more than tolerated guests, while Sukarno and Hatta, both well educated, were concerned about reactions beyond the shores of Java but were beholden to their followers.

Identifying the *pemudas* was impossible because they had no uniform and made use of any and all tools of murder and intimidation they could lay their hands on. An Indonesian caught on the street with a suspicious looking *golok* (machete) in his hands near the site of a recent attack could with a great deal of earnestness claim that he was merely using the *golok* to cut coconuts in half, and would not dream of using it on someone's skull. The initial targets for the increasingly bloodthirsty *pemudas* were the hated Japanese, but since the Japanese soldiers were now taking orders from Christison, the European population had come under the same threat. A day or so later, Christison discovered in bookstores and on newsstands newly printed books advising readers as how best to kill Europeans, and he soon gained "ample evidence that those instructions were being put into effect."[3]

And so, even while we were trying to re-establish a normal family life in our tiny *paviljoen*, a second disaster was unfolding.

Emmy often visited us to let us know how Edu was doing. My father spent most days and even part of the night at the guardhouse by the Tjideng gate. He was not in uniform, but continued to wear his ragged and worn-out shorts. Sometimes he, but more often my mother, made the hazardous trip to Tjikini

2. Fabricius, *Een wereld in Beroering*, 121.
3. Christison, *Life and Times*, 180.

to see Juf. The risks attached to those visits grew day by day, but my mother shrugged them off, given three years' experience dealing with Japanese soldiers and the terrorism of Sone still fresh in her mind. From my mother's perspective the risk of violence outside the camp was overshadowed by the certainty of the crowded filthy horrors inside Tjideng. Besides, most of the older Indonesians seemed friendly enough and were as concerned about a resumption of normal, peaceful life as we were.

I spent a lot of time on the garden wall in the shade of the trees, watching people coming and going along *Laan* Trivelli. The trees were full of twittering birds; in Tjideng even birds had become scarce, but then we had perhaps bothered them too much with our catapults. One day an *inlander* came along the road pedalling a bicycle with a white box in front. He saw me, stopped and took the lid off the box, releasing a white a cloud of cold smoke that poured over the edge of the container and down to the ground. He reached in and pulled out two colourful *es loli*, long red and green popsicles on a stick. My mother came to the road and I pointed out to her some children further down the street licking the delicious-looking treats, but she refused to buy them and waved the vendor on, explaining as we walked back to our house, "They're probably made of *selokan* water." My mother had learned to be cautious. Moreover, we had very little money, and hygiene may have been a more convenient excuse than our poverty.

If these days were full of interest, the nights were magical. Our little dwelling was infested with the usual assortment of insects and insect-catching lizards and geckos. The only wildlife we had seen over the last year was that horrible monkey. In the camp, I had been assigned the task of catching insects, but here in the *paviljoen*, the *tjitjaks* and *tokehs* offered this service, and they were far more effective than I had ever been. The *tokeh* was bigger than the *tjitjak*, and my mother was not so sure she liked having them around. "They make a mess," she said, but they were also more colourful. In the camp, these larger, helpful creatures had long ago disappeared, probably eaten, but here, outside of the camp, they enlivened our nights when their activities and sound effects began—"rrrr, rrrr rrrr, rrrr, tjitjak, tjitjak, tjitjak," alternating with the reedy call from another part of the house, "tokeh, tokeh, tokeh." In addition, *kelip-kelip* (fireflies) danced through the nighttime air: if you caught a number and put them into a glass jar, they would cast an eerie, flickering green light as individual fly lamps turned on and off. After sunset and a delicious meal of *nasi goreng*, the three of us sat on the veranda steps enjoying the cool night air. I gazed, entranced, at my glass jar full of *kelip-kelip* and inhaling the pungent fumes of the smouldering *obat njamuk* (mosquito coil) that my father had obtained.

On October 2, a first small contingent of Dutch troops arrived in Batavia, but Christison ordered them not to venture beyond the boundaries of Kemajoran airfield for fear of further unbalancing a delicate situation and making it even more difficult to deal with the huge humanitarian challenge he was facing. That same day the *pemudas* occupied the munitions factory in Bandoeng, while Sukarno, wearing white robes and his black revolutionary cap, announced to the media that he wanted the same treatment for Indonesia as was being offered the Philippines—independence.[4] He was attempting to be diplomatic by making it clear to the world that in his opinion he had the full support of the sixty-three million inhabitants of Indonesia.

"Our republican government in fact rules Indonesia," he added—with some justification, since all the utilities and the railways (at least on Java) were controlled by armed *pemuda*. He omitted to say that he had no control over the rebels, and that they had no patience with *diplomasi*.

For the Netherlands government it was a matter of priorities. Which was to come first, "negotiation" or "law and order"? It chose the latter, thus pursuing a course of action that was eerily reminiscent of the previous Indonesian crisis, in 1784; the wars in Europe had also severed the lines of communication, and the stubborn directors of the Dutch East India Company refused to allow the authorities in Batavia to seek alternative export outlets for their growing stockpiles of unsold produce, thereby dealing "a death blow to their own company."[5]

The following day Lieutenant Governor General van Mook arrived by plane from Brisbane to re-establish Dutch colonial rule; he was determined to avoid any contact with the rebels. His arrival was an unhappy affair, for on that day *pemuda* murdered two Japanese guards at Struiswijk women's prison and more slogans indicating that the Indonesians no longer loved the Dutch appeared on the streets. The message "van Mook Go Home" greeted him, a sad spectacle for the man who had been born and bred in the Indies, had worked hard to make it a better place, and had seen his arrival at Kemajoran, the Batavia airport, as his return home from exile. The chaos, visibly growing almost hourly around him, added to his bitter disappointment.

By this time the Seaforth Highlanders had taken over from Lieutenant Sakai all responsibility for Tjideng; the Tjideng gate was once more firmly closed and my father had been reassigned to work in one of the Tjideng kitchens. In the following days anti-European feeling escalated rapidly. On October 5 a boycott of European customers sprang up in many *pasars*, effectively denying them the purchase of food. Two days later the Royal Air Force set up a headquarters in Batavia to facilitate evacuation of British Commonwealth and American

---

4. The US Congress had approved this step as long ago as 1934, deciding that colonial status was not worth the maintenance costs. The Philippines became largely self-governing in the following year.

5. Vlekke, *Nusantara*, 234.

citizens, but not the Dutch, whose home Java was deemed to be. That same day *pemudas* stormed Andir airfield in Bandoeng, killed the Japanese guards and secured rifles and grenades; throughout Java weapons from Japanese arsenals were now regularly leaked into the hands of Indonesian rioters, either with the assistance of the Japanese or simply by force.

Three days later Bandoeng descended further into murderous violence. An attempt by the Japanese to force the *pasars* to accommodate European customers resulted in a concerted *pemuda* attack on the city from three directions, resulting in turn in a bloodbath, as European and Japanese were hacked to death. Major Grey, who had just arrived to set up a RAPWI office, could do no more than order Major General Mabuchi to take action, which the two thousand Japanese soldiers under his command did with their customary efficacy.[6] Two days later General Hawthorne declared martial law for Batavia, with full support from van Mook, and henceforth the streets were deserted after nightfall except for patrolling groups of Seaforth Highlanders.

Outside of the three big cities nominally protected by the Gurkhas and Seaforth Highlanders the reign of terror increased, and Muslim hotheads declared the time ripe for a *Jihad,* a holy war. Depok, a small community of two thousand Christian Indonesians and *Belanda Indo* forty kilometres south of Batavia, was not spared. Johan Fabricius, visiting the place with a small Gurkha detachment shortly after a terror attack, provided the following account of the scene:

> A woman with eyes that radiated hysteria pressed forward and told us, "They murdered my youngest brother, sir, only because he tried to defend our house. He was already wounded and I threw my arms around him and begged for mercy—can you not see that he is only a child? But they stabbed on and on until he was dead! See—my hands." She held in front of us hands hastily wrapped with rags.
>
> The platoon began to conduct the survivors to safety, but this required reinforcement and was only partially successful. One of the columns of evacuees was attacked from the shelter of trees, leaving behind two small victims lying by the side of the road. A twelve- or thirteen-year-old girl no longer stirred and over her waxen face the first flies were crawling; a pair of bloody legs, frozen in a death cramp, emerged from her torn *sarong.* Next to her there lay a second girl, perhaps four years old with incredibly dark eyes. The doctor, who had accompanied us from Batavia, gave her a quick inspection, but declared that her end was near—a shot in the abdomen, clearly a dumdum bullet, had done its worst. The Gurkhas, having arrived in the country only a few hours earlier, stood staring at the scene in silence. They were

6. Bijkerk, *De laatste landvoogd,* 187.

used to fighting between men: a war against children was something new for them. One of the Gurkhas gave me a water bottle so that I could give the dying child something to drink. She managed to raise her head and with greedy hands reached for the neck of the bottle from which the cool water gurgled down her throat. She was exhausted by the effort and her head fell back. I saw from the rolling of her eyes that Death had already taken possession of her.[7]

What Now?

With the war ended, everyone wanted to go home; we did as well, but we had difficulties. The last place we had called "home" was the house on the Eykmanweg, now no longer available, since, as my father had found out, Mrs. Raken had other plans. There was the splendid house in *Dennelust*, but it had not yet been home to us, just a costly dream, and it was occupied by strangers. One evening my mother was discussing the future with my father, while cooking over the *anglo*. Emmy had promised to join us on the understanding that my father would escort her back to Tjideng afterwards. For us the only sensible option was to leave Java, but this would require evacuation assistance, because we were on an island; Java had in effect become a prison.

"I saw Hanna Poortman today," my mother related. "She has heard from Marius in Bandoeng that their furniture is still intact where it was locked away when the Japs came. Marius thinks that once the Allied soldiers bring law and order to Bandoeng, they will be able to move back into their house. It would be nice to live in *Dennelust*," she added wistfully.

"Marius has a practice in Borromeus [hospital], doesn't he?" was my father's response. "I guess there's lots of work for him, but there is no KNIL to hire me. I think I can get my job back in Roodepoort—at least get help from them. Yes, and before Marius can move back to his house he first needs to get legal confirmation of ownership—you know how the Japs simply confiscated property. It will be tough to get this sorted out."

"What will we do about *Dennelust?*"

"Sell it."

My father sounded resolute and determined, but the tears in his eyes betrayed his bitter disappointment. "We can only sell it if the legal system works again—sometime. Right now some bloody *inlanders* are living there."

"Did you talk with Theo about this?"

"Yes, he will try to start his business again and stay for Mien's sake and the rest of the Suyderhout family, but it's going to be tough."

---

7. Fabricius, *Een wereld in Beroering*, 171.

"What about his brother[8]—could you work with him?"

"Ach Wil, it's such a mess that he will be lucky to get any design work at all, and not for a long time. Besides, he's a sick man. The situation is hopeless here."

Emmy, who had just arrived, agreed that the future looked grim. "We want to leave," she said. "Edu thinks he can be rehired by Philips in Johannesburg. Even if the KNIL gets re-established here, he has had enough. But the authorities will not help us and will not allow us to go."

"Who told you?"

"Edu heard this in the hospital. He told someone he wanted to leave, but they said he couldn't since he was a Dutch citizen. Only Americans and the Brits can leave."

"What about New Zealanders?" my father asked in surprise.

"They're British subjects. I guess they're okay. Dutch citizens can leave only after all the others have been dealt with."

"Boudy is a British subject," my mother interjected. "I have kept his Germiston birth certificate—maybe we count after all."

"Hmm," my father mused. "Maybe."

"What about Juf?"

"I will discuss this with her," my father replied. "It would be best for her to go back to Holland, where Jurrema can at least help her with her pension."

The outlook for us on Java was bleak, because it was becoming clear that the island had become the focus of a new confrontation between East and West, and even of conflicts within the Western camp: instead of dealing with the Japanese, we were now embroiled in an ugly war of independence, where anyone with a light-coloured complexion was automatically branded as an oppressor, an enemy of "the people," and now there were difficulties with our allies, the impotent British and the unwilling Americans. We had always deluded ourselves that American military might would support "us," the Europeans, on these islands. That delusion reflected not so much shared interests as shared prejudices.

All of us had emerged from our isolation in the prison camps like Rip van Winkle, waking up from a deep, nightmarish sleep lasting three and a half years. For all that time we had dreamt of a return of *tempo dulu*, the good old days, but the world had changed and *tempo dulu* was no more. It took a while to comprehend the scale of the changes, and for many the first reaction to trouble was the imposition of military force: this would solve the problem as it had always done before the war. For those with deep roots in the country, the thought of the victors from the recent world conflict now letting the liberated land slip into a primordial state of unmitigated chaos seemed a betrayal of all

---

8. A. F. Aalbers, architect for the Savoy Homann Hotel, still in use in Bandung.

those who had died in the world conflict. With no reliable daily news coverage, no one in Batavia, let alone Holland, could yet fathom the extent to which the pent-up forces of rebellion and mayhem had now found sudden release throughout Java. And it was the changes not just on Java but in the entire world that took us by surprise.

In eastern Europe the changes of 1945 had been equally dramatic; ever since the final days of the conflict there, hundreds of thousands of people had been on the move with their cheap cardboard suitcases, looking for a place to live. We on Java were only beginning to see this reality. Almost all now emerging from the camps of the Netherlands East Indies, and many who had avoided internment, would eventually have to take such a route. For our Indies friends, Java was the only home they had known; many even had extensive family ties with Indonesians. For them the evolving situation was terrifying. The recent arrivals like us were lucky, not being so burdened by the past.

Leaving the country was impossible without official sanction. Only air evacuation was available and this was strictly rationed, based on citizenship. Our Dutch passports demonstrating former residence in a commonwealth country were gone, confiscated by the Japanese. However, my mother had managed to retain my birth certificate, issued by the Germiston municipality and printed in Afrikaans and English. Would that flimsy piece of paper have value as an exit visa from the hellhole we were now in?

"Tomorrow I'll go to the Displaced Persons Office on the Konings Plein," my mother announced.

Emmy immediately objected, "You can't go alone. I will come with you. Besides, Edu and I need to get to South Africa, too. See you tomorrow!"

12. REFUGEES

The next morning my mother began the process of achieving Displaced Person status for us, notwithstanding the official government position. My father left home early to visit Juf before reporting for kitchen duty in the Tjideng camp. Juf had understood the need for leaving, but my father had learned as well that she was now on a waiting list for evacuation by the Red Cross to Holland "as soon as shipping space is available in the New Year." In Holland she could get better medical attention, and once recovered she hoped to stay with her sister. My father promised her that we would see her again in South Africa.

On Emmy's arrival the two women left for the RAPWI office. They walked down *Laan* Trivelli, continued along its extension, the Museumlaan, to the large grassy Konings *Plein*, the great central open space in the heart of Batavia around which the government buildings were located. At noon the women returned, and my mother took me along to find my father in the Tjimalaja *dapur*.

"We are going!" she exclaimed triumphantly. "But we had a scare!" She was so excited that she had to pause to catch her breath. "As we started to cross the Konings *Plein*, Emmy and I began to panic when we heard rapidly approaching footsteps behind us. We started to walk faster. I must say, my heart was pounding. Neither of us dared look around. I was just hoping that some of the soldiers standing guard by the government buildings on the other side could see us. But then an English voice called from behind—two RAF officers. One of them told us we were crazy to be walking around town, but I told them what we were trying to do. The officers went with us, and their appearance must have created a favourable impression, for we actually got a chance to make our case. I told them how we came to Java and showed the RAPWI official Boudy's birth certificate, and one of the pilots said he still had room on his plane. He said he is with the No. 31 Dakota squadron and that they are here to help with evacuations."

"I reminded them that Boudy was a British subject," Emmy interjected.

"Yes, and then we got this letter," my mother added, triumphantly showing the document. They are going to pick us up around three o'clock. The pilot promised us limousine service to the airport. I told them where we live."

"You had no trouble getting back?"

"One of the guards conducted us to the Tjideng gate."

My father was immediately released from his duties and together with my mother returned home. We packed our few belongings; what we could not put in our one suitcase would be left behind with Emmy, who had come to see us off. The guard who had brought my mother and Emmy back arrived as promised with a scout car and accompanied by a turbaned Gurkha soldier, armed with a machine gun mounted on its side. We clambered on the back with our little suitcase, and the scout car rumbled off.

"See you in Joh'burg!" were Emmy's last words.

It was an exciting but unpleasant ride. We went fast and the road was in a poor state of repair. At the far end of town we were shot at by snipers sitting in trees. The soldier shouted "Duck!" and my mother pressed my head down on the metal floor as a bullet went zinging overhead. We also had to get around some unmanned temporary barricades, but we made it to Kemajoran, where we were driven up to a big, silver twin-engined military transport plane, stationed on the grass.

"That's a DC-3," exclaimed my father. "Remember, Wil, when *de Reiger* came to Johannesburg on that inaugural KLM flight with poor Jan Butner?"

A small group of people, including some nuns, had already assembled under the shade of the wing and were awaiting the arrival of the pilots. There was a small pile of suitcases and bags near the tail of the plane. About twenty or thirty of us were left waiting in the afternoon sun for departure clearance.

Finally a Blitzbuggy came bouncing over the field with two pilots and a driver.

"Sorry about the wait, folks," one of the RAF men sang out as he strode to the door of the plane and began to open it. "We had a little security concern but we can leave now. He propped the door open and swung down some steps, saying, "We'll place your baggage in the rear of the crate."

We climbed up the steps, entered the hot plane and found seats on the two rows of wooden benches that ran the length of the interior, with a wooden backrest attached to the ribs of the aircraft. We sat down over the wing; the glare of the sunlight was reflected from its surface through the small windows, making it impossible to look out, so we just sat and stared at the nuns seated on the other side. When we were all on board and the luggage had been loaded, the pilots shut the door, walked up the centre of the plane, told us to fasten the seatbelts and disappeared through another door in the front.

"That's the guy who took Emmy and me to the office this morning," my mother said, pointing to one of the pilots.

The plane's interior, already uncomfortably warm when we entered, now became hot and stifling and strangely quiet, for no one dared say a word. Then the engine on the right wing was started, and after it began to roar the other one was cranked into action; the noise was deafening. After what seemed an interminable length of time, the plane began to move forward over the bumpy ground; we taxied to the end of the runway, past other planes, some partly demolished Japanese fighters, crazily positioned with their noses on the ground and their tails in the air, and some heaps of junk. The plane turned around and then the roar rose to a crescendo, while the plane shook and vibrated and finally started to lurch forward.

We gained speed, there was a bump, and we were airborne, with the land falling away beneath us; some cooler air started blowing on our faces from vents above our heads in the ceiling. We rose over the city, above houses and streets that shrank in size by the second, and with that, the horrors of the last four years could be conveniently thrust into the darkest, remotest reaches of our memories. Then the emerald palm trees and glistening fish ponds lining the palm-fringed coastline rapidly disappeared behind us in an impenetrable haze, leaving below us the immense Java Sea, shimmering under the late afternoon sun.

Welcome to Singapore

The flight was uneventful. Occasionally we flew through clouds, and then suddenly the plane's interior got dark and my eyes had to adjust. It was so noisy that we had to shout to make ourselves heard, and then it was difficult to hear the reply. Mostly, we just sat silently and stared at the plane's interior. The nuns, seated across the aisle from us, had their eyes closed, their hands on their laps: were they praying or sleeping?

My father motioned to me to look out the window, and far below us, over the edge of the wing, we could see, through the haze, greenish land fringed by a white band of sand and surf bordering a sparkling sea, etched with a fine grid of thousands of tiny waves. "Sumatra!" he yelled at me. The land slipped away in the haze and all we had below us was the deep-blue sea, with here and there flecks of white foam. Large dark patches marked the shadows cast by the clouds.

The five hundred–mile journey took about three hours. Suddenly the noise level dropped and grey clouds flitted by the window as the plane lurched in the turbulence. Moments later we were flying beneath the clouds, then flitting over land and bumping onto the ground, with palm trees rushing past the wing tips. When the engines were switched off it once more became eerily quiet. The door near the front opened, and one of the pilots came down the gangway, walked past us and opened the door near the back.

"Welcome to Singapore," he announced cheerfully.

Outside, we could hear strange voices, and as we descended the steps saw some very dark-skinned people busy taking things out of the luggage compartment at the back of the plane and placing them on the grass.

"They do not look like *inlanders*," I observed.

"I think they are Tamils," my father answered.

My father found our *barang,* and then we waited with the other passengers and the pilots. A green and grey camouflaged army truck appeared and halted close to the plane. The Tamil men placed a box on the ground behind the truck and the pilots helped us climb onto the back. They closed the tailgate and one of the pilots, standing on the running board in the open doorway of the cab, made an announcement before sitting down and slamming the door shut.

"He said it will be a bumpy but short ride," my father explained.

As the sun was setting in a crimson and violet sky behind fluffy clouds over the Strait of Malacca, we began the next leg of our odyssey. The truck motor was prodded into activity, and with a noisy jerk we lurched forward, heading down a rough road alongside the emergency runway, made of metal strips with holes in it. The scene around us was not so very different from the one we had left behind on Java. Beyond the planes, palm trees and bamboo clumps were gently swaying in the evening breeze that was as humid and warm as the one in Batavia. The truck driver took us to a corrugated iron Quonset hut, looking like half of an enormous culvert, where some people, mostly women in military uniform and two in white nurse's uniforms, greeted us. Ceiling fans, some wobbly, silently directed a breath of air down on our heads. One of the uniformed women took down our names on a piece of paper; another gave us a bag with toilet articles: a toothbrush, comb, soap, toothpaste. It was like the Red Cross parcels we had received in camp, but now we all had our own and did not have to share. Then we had to line up in front of a nurse; she dipped a needle in a bottle and made scratches on the shoulder of each person in turn and covered the wound with a pink plaster. "Against smallpox," the nurse commented and my mother nodded her head. Each of us was inoculated in turn and given a folded piece of cardboard to record this event—our first travel document.

Then one of the uniformed women made an announcement, pointing with her hands in two directions. My father left us to join a group of men, leaving my mother and me once more with women.

"Where's *pappie* going?"

"He'll be staying at a different place, the Queen Wilhelmina Barracks, but he can visit us and we can visit him. They're putting us up in a hotel."

The six or seven men, each now clutching a small bag with their clothing and toilet supplies, boarded a waiting bus. My mother and I boarded another bus along with the other women and nuns. Soon we were rumbling through the gathering dusk and bouncing along a road in urgent need of repair. Tall palm trees could still be seen in the distance, silhouetted against thickening clouds in the western sky. "Looks like rain," said my mother.

By the side of the road, grim evidence of the war could still be made out everywhere: periodically, we passed the skeletal remains of abandoned, plundered houses, burnt-out vehicles, and, here and there, concrete gun emplacements that no longer housed guns or men. We passed small dwellings with the occasional electric bulb bathing the yard in dancing splashes of light, and soon more buildings appeared, shops and warehouses flanking the roadside. We entered a city with traffic lights and street lights and cars driving with their lights on; the road widened and we came past two- and three-storey office buildings. The bus came to a halt outside a large three-storey building with a grand entrance at the street corner, where uniformed men and women were lounging. The bus door opened and the RAPWI lady rose from her seat to make an announcement. My mother got up from her seat and reached for our suitcase on the overhead rack, saying, "I guess we get off here."

The street was poorly lit and the wind had picked up, causing a faded sign hanging above the entrance of the building to swing. One of the members of our party looked up and read the name, "*Oranje* Hotel," adding, "Hmmm, never heard of it." We all trooped up the steps and through the doorway. A Chinese man dressed in a dark suit and wearing glasses waited expectantly behind a high wooden desk. The RAPWI lady and the man had an animated discussion, after which everyone in turn had to register. Outside, a gusting wind had gathered strength and was lashing at the palm trees along the side of the road, but the hotel lounge adjacent to the entrance looked cozy and was filled with guests talking, drinking beer, sitting in chairs, chatting, or reading newspapers. The place looked grand to my eyes; I had never before seen so many people so relaxed, nor such a magnificent interior, with lots of pictures on the walls and potted plants. My mother, however, thought the place looked rundown.

A hotel porter attired in a uniform matching the hotel's pre-war pretensions—and to judge by the worn cuffs, its evident neglect over the last few years—with disdain picked up our bamboo suitcase and guided us to our room, up a flight of stairs and to the end of a long corridor. This room was far better than the one we had last used in Batavia: it had a bed with a bouncy mattress. My mother would sleep there, and she explained that the porter would bring a folding bed for me. There was a dirty wash basin in the room, but when my mother tried the faucet, it did not work; the porter directed her to a bathroom down the corridor.

"We have to get ready for dinner," she said, "but let's wash up first." The bathroom contained a toilet, which did seem to work, but there was no bottle of water with which to wash yourself afterwards.

"You have to use paper," my mother explained, pointing to a box hanging on the wall containing unattractive shiny brown paper that did not seem at all suited for the task. In the dining room our table was covered with white linen and there were silver knives and forks. It was a meal without frills, but oh, how delicious the food tasted, so different from what we had eaten in the camp. There were some other Dutch-speaking guests in the hotel who had arrived some days earlier. My mother, curious to know how they got here, was told by one of them, "Most English have been accommodated in the Raffles or the Seaview."

After dinner, when we went back to our room, a tropical downpour had started, and near the window the floor was wet. My mother pulled the window closed and now the rain splattered against the glass panes. It was fascinating to see the water dripping down the glass and catching the glow of the street lamps.

The next morning we went to the dining room for breakfast. The windows were open and a mixture of bird song and traffic noise from outside competed with a loudspeaker suspended from the wall, from which emerged the sound of a band accompanying a woman singing. Breakfast was even better than dinner had been. I got corn flakes and toast with jam, which I consumed while listening to the cheery lyrics:

> I'm forever blowing bubbles
> Pretty bubbles in the air
> They fly so high, nearly reach the sky
> And when they do, they fade away.

Singapore had seen some of the bloodiest fighting during the early days of the war, when the Japanese and the British fought for its strategic location guarding the sea route between the Indian Ocean and the South China Sea. Those subsequently imprisoned by the Japanese in this city suffered some of the worst excesses of brutality. However, the Strait of Jahore had shielded Singapore from the revolutionary fervour now sweeping the other former colonial territories on the Asian landmass to the north. Consequently it had become a haven of safety and was flooded with post-war euphoria, a far cry from the situation in Batavia, a city where a new wave of violence had taken hold. While chaos had a bloody stranglehold on the entire island of Java, Singapore was rapidly regaining its pre-war civility. In few other places in the Far East had the transition from occupation to peace been as complete; only the remaining decay and dilapidation served as a reminder of the grim past. The war was over as far as these folks were concerned, and they were looking forward to civvy street, happy days, and for the expatriate community, the voyage home. We merrily joined in when the loudspeaker belted out, "What's the use of worrying? It never was worth while, So pack up your troubles in your own kitbag and smile, smile, smile!"

The following day the Red Cross began to hand out more essentials for living. We were taken to a warehouse where people behind tables distributed items of clothing to a long lineup of ex-prisoners, many emaciated, clothed in ill-fitting garments, and casting furtive glances around while clutching tightly to their persons their new possessions, out of fear that someone might steal them.

My mother received a long white canvas "kitbag" and half a parachute, with the suggestion that she might somehow sew underwear from this. How she was to do so was unclear, for we had no sewing machine.

"Oh well, I can use it when we get back to South Africa," she commented, thinking of the Pfaff foot-pedal sewing machine she had left behind there. The parachute, and in particular its soft, pliable but strong nylon cords, for years thereafter was a regular household item. She laughed when a Red Cross worker handed her a blue woollen bathing suit. The idea of being able to go swimming seemed outrageous. The garment hardly made a fashion statement, but was gratefully stuffed into the kitbag along with the parachute and other clothing. Then it was my turn: we went to tables piled with boys' clothes, where my mother found me a pair of shorts, underwear, shirts, socks and a pair of black leather shoes with laces.

Back in the hotel we tried on our new garments. Lacing up the shoes was fun, but putting them on my feet presented a problem: after three years of walking barefoot, my toes had splayed out so much that my feet no longer conformed to the standard shapes used by shoemakers. The shoes pinched, a discomfort I stoically bore for the thrill of having tied, with my mother's help, my first bow.

That afternoon, we left the hotel in search of my father to show off our new acquisitions. Ignoring the rickshaws and pedicabs hawking rides outside the hotel entrance, we set off on foot in the direction of the old town across the Singapore River. I was clad in my new khaki shorts, a white shirt, and my new black leather shoes. The sun overhead was incredibly hot and with the gradual approach of the monsoon season the humidity was also close to a hundred percent, making the atmosphere oppressive even for us, who had spent half a year in Batavia.

At first the novel sights and smells of the city made us forget the heat. The streets were bustling with commerce; some enterprising vendors were selling Japanese paper money, stacks of it, for whatever one wanted to pay. "Look at all that material," my mother exclaimed, pointing to wooden racks set out on the pavement and festooned with colourful silks and cottons, a marvel of opulence and colour. It was hard to imagine that a few months ago, in Batavia, worn garments had been exchanged for food at great personal risk through the *gedek* with an *inlander* clad in jute. Elsewhere we saw road-gangs at work: what was curious was to see a British soldier supervising the labour of Japanese POWs, now partly naked, their upper torsos glistening with sweat under the noonday sun. They were easily recognizable by the hats they wore, with the flaps for their necks. Without their shiny boots and their swords, they now looked quite harmless. Somewhere in the old town among the Chinese shops my shaky love affair with the shoes ended. The discomfort of my cramped feet exceeded by far the discomfort of the hot pavement and so the shoes were taken off and tied together with their laces. Thereafter, I trotted by my mother's side once more on the hot pavement in my bare feet, carrying my shoes in my hands.

We found my father housed in an army barracks surrounded by barbed wire, but he was free to come and go as he pleased and was thrilled to see us. He had also been taken to the RAPWI distribution centre and now showed us some of his new possessions: a razor, a package of Gillette razor blades, some clothes and an army rucksack made of heavy khaki material to hold his things.

In the next few days there were several meetings with the Red Cross and RAPWI personnel. Our international standing continued to be a source of complication, and the Red Cross people were eager to clear us out of the hotel to make way for more refugees, whose numbers were rapidly rising. RAPWI agreed to send a telegram on my father's behalf to the Chief Engineer in the Roodepoort municipal offices in the hope of a helpful reply that might ease our way back to South Africa. Once again we played a waiting game.

To alleviate the boredom of the growing number of refugee children, the Red Cross arranged an outing. A bus came by the *Oranje* Hotel to pick us up, and after passing by various other hotels to gather more children speaking a variety of different languages, it headed out of town. The bus drew up at the ornate gates of an estate belonging to a wealthy Chinese citizen whose villa was set in elegant, spacious grounds, which included a formal garden laid out in a traditional Chinese style. It was a magical experience for all of us, a vivid contrast to the decay and depravity we had come to know. Here there were neatly laid-out gravel paths interlaced with miniature streams crossed with the help of stepping stones or fancy arched footbridges. The streams contained goldfish, and in among the manicured shrubs were colourful miniature pagodas of varying designs. The garden was a sort of fairy wonderland: a nature playground for children. But we were ill-disciplined ragamuffins and ran up and down the paths, and round and round playing tag, and did not always stay on the paths. It was a brave undertaking for the Red Cross and a generous gesture on the part of the property owner who made this memorable outing possible.

My father sometimes came to our hotel and ate lunch or dinner with us. Then my parents needed to talk without me constantly interrupting. A new Disney film called *Dumbo the Flying Elephant* was playing at the Capitol theatre nearby and there I was sent in the company of Tommy, another hotel resident roughly my age, with 1/6 (one shilling and sixpence) in my pocket for the ticket. For me the film was an uncomfortable reminder of the threat of separation from my mother that still haunted me: after the film ended I emerged from the theatre into the Singapore sunlight with wet eyes.

A pair of WRENS housed in the hotel also gave me an opportunity to leave the shadow of my parents, by inviting me for an afternoon's outing in a Blitzbuggy driven by a British soldier. Cars were still a major novelty and riding in one of these bouncy little vehicles with their rough-treaded tires, wartime camouflage paint, lights protected by steel grating, and best of all, no roof, was a huge attraction. We drove up Orchard Road and out of town through sugar cane fields. The only difficulty arose when I began to feel nature calling; however, a stop amidst sugar cane did the trick.

"Okay?"

"Okay!"—My first word of English.

On November 10, the RAPWI representative, smartly turned out in her khaki uniform, came to the hotel at dinner time and sought us out, finding to her pleasant surprise that my father was with us. "This will save me a trip to the Wilhelmina camp," she observed. She told us that we had to be ready to leave the hotel the next morning, since a ship bound for Europe would arrive in Singapore to pick up passengers. After dinner my parents were discussing the news.

"Where are we going?"

"South Africa," my father answered; another name, another place, but at least it was not back to Tjideng.

Orontes

After a Sunday breakfast of bacon and eggs, we packed our things and cleared out of our hotel room. In the lobby my mother left me looking after our baggage, now consisting of our bamboo suitcase and a kitbag, while she took our room key to the hotel desk. Quite a crowd of people had gathered; the uniformed RAPWI lady stood by one of the potted palm trees surveying the scene. From time to time she glanced at the clock above the hotel desk, finally calling for attention; she then began to call out names. People around us answered "Yes!" and "Here!" She then led our party out through the hotel entrance to wait on the pavement for a bus. We placed our kitbag and bamboo suitcase alongside a wide variety of bags, suitcases and cardboard boxes already standing along the wall of the building.

A camouflaged army bus came in sight at the end of the street, and when it drew up we could clearly recognize my father among the men sitting by the windows. A truck had pulled up behind the bus—"For your baggage," the RAPWI lady explained. A couple of men sitting near the front got out of the bus to help load our belongings on the back of the truck.

"What ship are we going on?" someone in the crowd asked.

"A British ship—a P&O liner, I think."

The bus, now filled to capacity, set off in the direction of the harbour, over the Singapore River, and thence through the streets of the Chinese district, familiar to us from our walks to the Wilhelmina barracks. It was a slow journey, for the narrow streets were clogged with vendors, rickshaws and bicycles.

At an intersection we passed another group of Japanese prisoners filling in trenches with picks and shovels. A man in the bus called out, "Look at them! The Aussies had to dig those trenches, but those poor bastards were all skin and bones; those Nips are still fat—they need to work a little harder." A Gurkha soldier wearing a turban and armed with a rifle was guarding them. That was our last view of our former oppressors.

We crossed some railway tracks and stopped at a gate guarded by another soldier wearing a turban, who checked the papers handed to him by the RAPWI lady and waved us through. We had arrived at the Keppel harbour, where a jumble of ships' masts and dockside cranes dominated the horizon. The bus stopped; we got out and retrieved our bags from the truck, while more buses drew up behind us.

Ahead of us lay a huge ship. Someone in our party asked a RAPWI official supervising our arrival, "What ship is it?"

"*Orontes*."

Nothing could better reflect the British Empire at the zenith of its prestige and might than the P&O liner RMS (Royal Mail Ship) *Orontes*, named after a river mentioned in Greek myths. The river rises in the great spring of Labweh near Baalbek and below the snow-capped peaks of Jebel el Sharqi on the east side of the Baka'a valley, marking the border of Lebanon and Syria. Thence the river flows north through the ancient city of Hama, and emerges on the plain of Antioch, before entering the Mediterranean at the port of Suedia, ancient Seleucia Pieria.

The ship's appearance in every way matched in grandness its illustrious namesake's historical richness. At twenty thousand tons, it was the largest P&O liner built to date, and had been intended for the England–Australia run, a long journey justifying extra attention to passenger amenities. When launched in Barrow-on-Furness, it had been hailed as the jewel in the P&O crown, offering the latest in luxury for five hundred first-class and eleven hundred third-class passengers, while boasting modern, oil-fired steam turbines for power. Wartime needs had caused some comforts to be compromised in order to accommodate twice that number of passengers.

The ship had just arrived from Saigon, where she had disembarked about five hundred French soldiers and officials, and had embarked about an equal number of passengers, most of whom were French military personnel and a few ex-POWs on their way home. By the time we arrived on the quay, the ship was in the final stages of docking. A smell of fish, tar and oil permeated the humid maritime air, which was alive with the shrill cries of seagulls fighting each other over bits of fish or bread lying on the ground. While waiting for instructions we watched how the ship's hawsers were being dragged by harbour workers onto the quay and slipped over enormous iron bollards. The ship itself was a splendid sight, with its black steel hull punctuated by three neat rows of portholes, placed in groups of twos and threes like a mysterious code. Above the hull, dominating the middle of the ship, stood the white superstructure, several storeys high. Stairs led up to three more decks, and behind the railings could be seen the windows and doors leading inside. The top deck was lined with lifeboats hanging from their davits; they were painted white and covered with orange canvas. Above the lifeboats towered two huge yellow smokestacks, and at either end of the ship was a mast festooned with wires and colourful bunting.

From the top deck a ship's officer, smartly dressed in a white tropical uniform, was leaning over the railing, high above the quay, surveying the activity of some men working with two ramps that looked like footbridges with white canvas sides. With the help of a crane they were lifting the end of one of these gangways up to a large doorway in the ship's side near the middle of the ship.

When the first one had been positioned, one of the RAPWI officials accompanying us went up the gangway and disappeared into the vessel, while another RAPWI official was urging us to form a lineup from the foot of the gangway.

We then noticed that another queue of uniformed soldiers and servicemen was now forming to the left of us, at the foot of the second gangway that had just been positioned in a gap in the railing near the ship's stern. These men and women were also carrying kitbags.

Finally the two queues of would-be passengers started to move up the gangplanks, where some splendidly attired ship's officers formed a welcoming party. "This is a better welcome than we had in Tjideng," my mother remarked happily. It was almost noon, and we were hungry and hot, once again waiting under a sun that burned through a hazy sky. But it soon became obvious that the soldiers were moving up their gangplank far more quickly than our line did, and the reason was equally clear: it was the men in white uniforms guarding the ship's side. Only one official stood where the soldiers entered the ship, but three officials were interfering with our progress. My solution was simple: I scrambled away from my parents, and joined the other queue, worming my way up between the legs and kit bags of laughing, easy-going soldiers, to the head of the gangplank, where I ducked the attention of the ship's officer and escaped up a flight of stairs to the boat deck. When one has spent three years learning how to scrounge for food while avoiding any encounters with Japanese and *heiho* on the lookout for troublemakers, a congregation of good-natured pommies and WRENS looking forward to their return home posed no problems.

From the lofty height of the boat deck I could lean over the broad teak railing, shaded by a lifeboat, and, like the captain, survey the scene below, waving to my parents while they waved back. It was all very jolly.

Aside from sorting out accommodation, the three ship's officers were worried about the risk of infectious diseases on board the ship. When my parents got near the head of the gangway it became obvious from the impatient motions of my father's arms that my presence was urgently required, and I managed to find my way down three flights of stairs and along confusing corridors to a lobby where, next to an office, my parents were by then engaged in a discussion with the exasperated officers, with my father, who tended to make ample use of his hands when talking, waving our travel documents in the air.

One of the officers wanted to look in my throat and another had a clipboard with numbers and was assigning accommodation. It was obvious that they were having difficulties dealing with us.

"These guys seem to regard us as tramps," my mother muttered under her breath in Dutch so as not to be understood. The contrast between their sharp-looking uniforms and our haphazard clothing was indeed troubling.

The purser assigned my mother and me to one cabin, while my father would share another cabin with another man; both cabins were on G deck, but not next to one another. "I'm sorry," said the purser. "That's the best we can do." The third officer introduced himself as the Chief Steward and handed us a small card on which he had jotted down the cabin numbers and our table number, "for the first sitting. We have sandwiches set out for lunch in the dining room."

The captain's report, filed upon the conclusion of the voyage in Southampton, indicated that he had managed to accommodate 322 RAPWI civilians, of whom 271 travelled first class and 103 tourist class. The remaining military personnel (about 1,200) travelled in what was euphemistically referred to by the captain as "ship's hold class." A complication was the fact that one of the holds had been damaged by a fire on the outward journey and some of the returning servicemen and women had to endure leakage through the temporary canvas hold-cover when it rained.

Although the *Orontes* was now serving as a troop and refugee ship, the ship's crew did its best to maintain some pre-war standards of elegance, contrasting sharply with the appearance of the passengers. The crew looked smart, well fed and well dressed, while we were in ill-fitting, worn clothing, with most children, like me, barefoot. The impression was confusing: shabbily dressed refugees accommodated like holidaymakers on a cruise.

"This is much nicer than the hotel," my mother exclaimed with a smile.

"It is much, much nicer than the Wilhelmina barracks," my father answered with a happy snort. "What I would really like now is an ice-cold beer and a pork chop."

We went to find our cabins, first looking for the one assigned to my mother and me, which was on the starboard side of the ship. We had to go down three flights of stairs and down a long narrow corridor with a wooden railing and numerous passages off to the right and left. At the end of one of those passages we found our cabin.

"An outside cabin," said my mother. "That's a relief—I can't stand closed-in areas." I do not know whether my mother had suffered from claustrophobia before the war, but she certainly did afterwards.

The varnished wooden cabin doorway had a high steel sill one had to step over. Inside, there were two beds with varnished mahogany sides, one to the right, next to the door, and another one to the left, below the porthole; a chair and a couple of chests of drawers completed the furnishings. Under the beds there was space for storing a large suitcase. The cabin door could be latched in an open position with a fancy brass hook. Above each bunk was an air vent, a metal sphere set in the bulkhead with a round hole out of which air blew. By rotating the sphere one could make the air blow in whichever direction one wanted. A brass porthole let in outside light, but not much because the quay was only a few feet away from the ship's side. I was anxious to see all the activity outside, and so my mother went to get some sandwiches while I went up on deck. My parents found me on the boat deck, and left me munching and watching all the goings-on, while they retired to the lounge.

Late that afternoon, my father and I were on the boat deck to see the ship being made ready for departure. There were some urgent last-minute comings and goings-on the gangplank before it was lowered to the quay. At about half past five, the ship's hawsers were slipped; one after the other ropes were slackened off and the men standing on the quay lifted the noose from the black iron bollards and let the ropes fall with a big splash into the dark oily water between the ship and the dock. On the other side two tugs had made fast to the ship with gigantic hawsers and gradually began pulling us away from the quay; their green, red and white navigation lights were on, giving them a fairy-tale look. Across the water, lights were beginning to appear on Sentosa and Pulau Brani Islands. At first the ship had been quite tightly jammed against some floating wooden rafts; then glistening, oil-covered streaks of water began to appear between the rafts and the steel hull, and before long a strip of water carrying bottles, bits of cloth and wooden crates separated us from shore. It was eerie to see the huge shell of steel moving ever so imperceptibly and noiselessly away from the dock. Finally, we began to head out towards the open sea, slowly sliding past *sampans* and even between one or two floating disabled mines: big ugly balls with spikes sticking out. Then the tugs let go and returned to shore in a wide arc, while the ship began to gain way. Plumes of smoke came from the funnels, and the ship vibrated to a gentle throb. Somewhere inside the ship a bell rang and a crackly voice came over the loudspeaker, "Ladies and gentlemen, first sitting please."

"Boudy, we must go down and get *mammie*," my father urged, pulling me away from the fascinating scene. It was too bad, because the activities had not yet finished: a busy little boat, fringed with a piece of thick white hawser to protect it from contact with ships, was coming alongside.

"That's the pilot boat," my father said. "Let's go down."

For Captain G. E. Nicholls, departure was saddened by the sight of a family of three sick refugees left standing on the quay. The ship's medical officer in the course of his hurried check had diagnosed the family with pertussis. They had promptly been set ashore, to be taken care of once again by RAPWI and the Red Cross. Captain Nicholls later complained that the entire embarkation procedure had been chaotic. When the ship had first left Tilbury early in October, it had taken on board a medical team and medical supplies for the express purpose of taking care of ex-POWs. However, on the outward journey the medical supplies had inadvertently been redirected to Australia, while the medical team had disembarked in Singapore. Now on the return journey the medical team, minus medical supplies, had rejoined the ship. At the conclusion of the voyage, the ship's medical officer, Dr. Royd Jones, reported that he nevertheless had "treated 181 passengers for scabies, measles, amoebic dysentery, septicaemia, beriberi, tropical sores, pulmonary tuberculosis, and myocardial degeneration, cases that should only have been sent by hospital ship."[1] Miraculously, no one died on the voyage.

The *Orontes* was a marvellous ship. In spite of the conversion to troop transport, she had many remaining amenities. There were two lounges, one for first-class passengers on the B deck and one for tourist-class passengers on the F deck adjacent to the dining saloon. There was also a reading room with a library, a writing room, a smoking room, and a bar. The children's saloon had been converted into sleeping quarters, but next door to that there was still a shop. It was a cut-glass-fronted treasure trove of goodies enabling passengers to simulate a shopping trip along London's Bond Street. Outside, on the boat deck, there were deck tennis facilities, and towards the stern on the D deck there was a swimming pool, partly filled with sea water.

To get from our cabins to the dining room, we had to go up the grandest staircase imaginable. It had soft, colourful carpets, a delight to walk on with my

---

1. G. E. Nicholls, *MV Orontes Voyage Report 19*, Pacific and Oriental Steamship Navigation Line (available at the Greenwich Maritime Museum).

bare feet, and the railing was of shiny varnished mahogany. The first part of the staircase was broad; then there was a landing halfway up, after which a narrower staircase to the next level went to the left and another one to the right. Over the landing there hung a large painting of the ship itself, but on the landing between the dining room and the E deck there hung a large, colourful map of the world.

This was really interesting. A thin ribbon stretched between pins showed the route we were following. On subsequent days the ship's noon position was marked by a tiny model boat, while a nearby notice board gave particulars about the voyage thus far: the noon position, the distance travelled and the weather conditions. My father explained where we were going, but most intriguing to me was his lesson in geology. "See, South America and Africa once were adjacent to one another. A geologist in camp had told us this. The Indonesians call geologists *tuan barrankali*—Mr. Maybe," he added with a grin.[2] The concept of drifting continents seemed perfectly logical to me. My father had become an inexhaustible source of information, and he answered my endless questions in a good-natured way.

The dining saloon was elegant beyond belief, with a ceilings supported by heavy beams that were festooned with medallions fittingly decorated with themes drawn from classical Greek history: ancient sailing ships and triremes plying the Aegean Sea. The floor was of polished wood with a parquet pattern of crossing lines. The tables, some for four persons and others for six, were supplemented by elegantly shaped chairs with brocade seats. Compared with the chaos of Tjideng and the dilapidated condition of the *Oranje* Hotel, we were now surrounded by opulence. There were no stewards to serve us, and once assigned to a table, we helped ourselves to food cafeteria-style, lining up with aluminium trays that had portion-sized depressions into which the cook ladled mashed potatoes, carrots and meatballs.

The mood in the dining room was festive. When we sat down at the table with its fancy white linen, silver knives and forks, serviettes, and best of all, dinner rolls and butter, we could only smile and had difficulty believing our good fortune. It was very hard to give the past, particularly *Laan* Trivelli and the Tjimalaja *dapur*, any further thought.

We shared our table with another family, which comprised a large man with very bushy eyebrows, his wife, who was thin and had dark curly hair matching her dark eyes, and two older children, a boy and a girl. The man introduced himself and his family as "Bob Williams, my wife, Adie, and my bairns, Robin and Chris." It was somewhat confusing, because Bob Williams had chosen to address my father in English with a strong Scottish brogue. Soon it turned out that the rest of the family spoke only Dutch, and when Mr. Williams spoke

---

2. It was another fifteen years before this concept was widely accepted by the scientific community.

Dutch, he sounded funny. Mr. Williams was noticeably more upbeat than Adie, his wife. Chris, the twelve-year-old boy, had a furtive, shifty look about him, as though he distrusted the situation he was in, and he clearly had scant regard for figures of authority; but his father, in his gruff way, seemed to have the measure of him and regularly called him to order. I was relieved to see, though, that he also was barefoot: we at least had this in common. Robin was a big girl, fifteen years old, almost grown up.

During dinner we swapped experiences. Mr. Williams had come from Scotland long before the war to work for a London-based firm, Harrison and Crossfield, on one of the rubber plantations in Sumatra. "The plantation lay between the hills near Brastagi, a great place, not so hot there," said Bob. My father told them we had come from South Africa to strengthen the defences of the Indies.

"Silly buggers—you should have stayed there. So should Adie and her folks; they also came from South Africa, you know."

Both Chris and Robin had been born on Sumatra and grew up on the plantation. After the Japanese came they had been moved from place to place. "Never stayed long enough in one place to find the pub," Bob had joked, but he had then been separated from his wife and children, and later Chris was sent away with nine other boys to a boys' camp. "He was a lucky lad, for he ended up with his grandfather and uncle in Si Rengorengo, a cluster of flimsy bamboo and *atap* sheds on the banks of a river in the middle of nowhere." When the Allies found the camp and evacuated its inhabitants, Chris was ill, suffering from glandular fever, and needed a month's recuperation in a Singapore hospital.[3]

"You are lucky with Boudy," commented Adie. "He has not missed much schooling, not like Chris. Robin at least had finished her primary education." Bob clearly was looking forward to a return to Scotland, but Adie had been sad to leave Sumatra. "I wanted to go back to the plantation," she said, "but Bob reckoned our life was finished there."

"With a labour government finally in power, Scotland must be better place than Sumatra," was Bob's opinion.

"Maybe in the future we can return, when things are better in the Indies," Adie added wistfully. "Scotland sounds so cold to me, and the children will have to learn English."

"Have you got any family left, Adie?" asked my mother.

"Yes, my father is still alive. He is hoping to meet us in Scotland when he is in a fit state to travel; he was badly treated by the Japs."

---

3. Photographs were surreptitiously taken in Si Rengorengo and survived the war.

After dinner, we went out on the boat deck to see and experience what it was like to be out at sea. A refreshing cool breeze blew through our hair and snatched our voices away. The deck and the various things it accommodated, such as railing and stanchions, were illuminated by the pale light of a new moon setting in the western sky; the ship's wake also glistened in the light. Here and there, the red glow of a cigarette betrayed a shipmate taking in the peaceful nighttime scene or relaxing in one of the deck chairs set out of the wind in the shelter of the superstructure. The horizon was still clearly discernible, and the land we had left behind was marked by the periodic sweep of a beam of light. A soothing symphony of sounds engulfed us; the wind hummed around the ship and through the rigging, offset by the surging rush of the ship's bow-wave, breaking in a steady pulse as the ship gently rolled and pitched over the ocean swell. Looking down from the height of the deck to the water below us, it suddenly struck me that the sea was displaying another form of light, not reflected moonlight but something almost as magical—a hypnotizing sight. The white foam that hugged the steel plates rushing through the water appeared particularly bright, but if one looked carefully at the waves, and particularly where they crested and broke, that puzzling light also appeared.

"What is that light from, *pappie*?"

"Plankton."

Somewhere above us, a seagull rose from its perch with a squawk and soared. That night, in our cozy cabin, we fell asleep to the throb of the great ship's engines and the rush of water against the ship's plates.

Captain Nicholls was concerned that the children on board needed "to be usefully occupied," as he put it. Realizing that about sixty-five of his young passengers had not been near a school for almost four years, he resolved to do his best to address the educational deficiencies and asked the ship's officers to organize classes. School commenced in the morning, while the ship was being cleaned. With the help of volunteers, the program began with physical exercises on the A deck, where there was lots of space and we could accordingly be lined up in columns and rows, a bit like *appel*, but with enough space in between to swing our arms and feet in and out. This session, lasting from nine o'clock to nine thirty in the morning, was an uncomfortable reminder of some of the better intentioned discipline we had been forced to submit to when the Japanese army had taken charge of the prison camps: enthusiasm was accordingly muted. Calisthenics were followed by "formal education" lasting from nine thirty to quarter to eleven. A nature study trip taking us to the ship's cold storage facility, "so that the children can get a feel for snow and ice," was arranged because the ship was due to reach its final destination, Southampton, not long before Christmas.

Mostly we spent the daytime on the deck marvelling at how the sea gulls could so effortlessly soar on the updraft created by the movement of the ship's superstructure, or skim the tops of the waves without getting wet. Sometimes we saw schools of flying fish emerging from the waves and soaring a few feet above the foam-flecked crests.

For Robin, the teenaged girl, the ship held quite different attractions, and soon a young Scandinavian swain regularly visited our table. "He had betterrr keep his filthy hands off my daughter," said Bob, with his Aberdeenshire brogue, speaking English so that Robin could not understand. But at night in the lounge there was sometimes music from a gramophone playing the latest Novello hits, and there we would catch a glimpse of Robin on the dance floor with her newfound beau, while a crooner sang,

> We'll gather lilacs in the spring again
> And walk together down an English lane
> Until our hearts have learned to sing again
> When you come home once more.

After four days' sailing, the *Orontes* made landfall at Colombo, on the west coast of Ceylon (today's Sri Lanka). Ahead of us lay a point of land with some sheds and a lighthouse, and beyond that, the sun glistened on the rooftops of the houses and buildings of a distant town. Low blue hills marked the horizon, and above that landscape, towering cumulus clouds were promising to drench the land as part of the same daily afternoon ritual we had known on Java. There was no sign of a tug, but suddenly we heard the roar of the chain spilling overboard as the anchor was let go. A swarm of little boats set out from the harbour to meet us: they were filled with more brown-skinned people holding aloft colourful pieces of material. Some of the servicemen lining the railing threw silver coins into the water, and then young men, almost naked, dived off the boats to catch the coins before they dropped out of sight. There was a lot of laughter and shouting.

"The little beggars want to clean us out," someone laughed.

The stopover in Colombo was a somewhat impromptu affair, arranged shortly before departure from Singapore. The captain, having failed to secure the proper medical supplies in Singapore, had made alternative arrangements with RAPWI to secure them here; he especially hoped to pick up vitamin B pills and cod-liver oil. A stopover would moreover permit more inoculations and incidentally facilitate the future distribution of more clothing to the refugees; RAPWI had asked the captain to prepare a "size roll," to be handed to the "Embarkation Commandant" at Colombo, so that clothing of suitable sizes could be distributed in Port Said in preparation for the journey into the northern hemisphere's wintry waters.

The Chief Steward announced over the intercom that all refugees were to go ashore. We gathered outside, on deck, where sailors were busy rigging up a staircase that had been lashed to the ship's side. Part of it was permanently attached to the ship with a hinge mechanism, and the men were lowering the other end down to water level from several davits. When the job was done the staircase consisted of two consecutive flights of stairs with a small landing in between. Meanwhile a strange vessel approached the ship from shore. It was a landing craft, a floating box with a small deck in the stern where the helmsman had a place to steer. The front of the boat sloped upward and could be used as a loading ramp to roll trucks and tanks from the craft onto a beach. A couple of sailors armed with boat hooks made the craft fast to the companionway, and we were told to go down the stairs in groups of seventy to board the landing craft and be ferried ashore.

Once on board the landing craft, we were very close to the water and, with the engine growling on its landward journey, spray from the waves bounced off the front and flew into our faces, providing me with a first taste of seawater. The landing craft took us to a floating jetty, where men with RAPWI armbands ushered us to a storage shed. There Red Cross nurses gave us more injections; to the children they gave coloured pencil sets as well. By the time we emerged from the shed the landing craft was on its way to the ship, and so we joined the party on the quayside waiting for our return journey.

Back on the *Orontes*, we were surprised to find a military band playing on the promenade deck. This, too, was a novelty, with the beautiful shiny brass and silver instruments, and the men in fancy uniforms! When the playing stopped, some of the ship's staff brought out lemonade and biscuits.

Late that afternoon another thousand serviceman were shuttled to the ship from Colombo. For hours the landing craft was busy going to and fro, bringing these men and their kitbags. They all had to find accommodation in the forward hold with the leaky roof. In the meantime the band had started up again and played until dinnertime, before returning to Colombo.

That evening, while we were enjoying our dessert in the dining room, the *Orontes* weighed anchor and set course for the southern tip of India. After three days' sailing we entered Bombay's harbour, where tugs nudged the ship alongside one of the quays. It seemed eerily quiet that night when we went to bed; we missed the sound of the wind and water and the vibration from the engines, and only the occasional tramp of feet walking up and down the corridor disturbed the silence.

The next morning, during breakfast, the purser announced over the ship's intercom that we would all go ashore for a couple of nights, while the forward ship's hold was being repaired. "Comfortable accommodation has been arranged in a hotel for the civilian passengers. Please prepare yourselves for temporary disembarkation at the purser's office on D deck, immediately after breakfast."

My father brought his clothes and toilet things to our cabin, where my mother helped him pack one suitcase to avoid us having too much to carry, a novel situation. We then proceeded to the purser's office, near the door to the gangway, where we joined a queue of passengers. Two military officers were seated behind a table; one was checking off names and the other handed out coloured tags to allocate us to separate buses. We left the ship and went down the gangway to the quay, where we set foot on Indian soil and were greeted by the typical harbour smells of oil and tar mingled with pungent odours of smoke and spices from food stands serving the harbour workers. A number of buses had drawn up, and after finding ours, we had to wait in its shadow for the remainder of our party to join us. The military passengers of the *Orontes* had also been told to disembark, but their destination would be Indian army barracks.

The bus journey was short and more or less followed the waterfront, finally bringing us to an esplanade where the harbour was teeming with fishing vessels and other small craft. We stopped in front of a huge Edwardian stone building several storeys high. "This is where you will be staying," one of the officers who had accompanied us announced, "Hotel Taj Mahal—not the real thing, but it will do." This last comment was supposed to be a joke, for some of the passengers laughed. Behind us, on a piece of land jutting out into the harbour, towered an ornate archway. Someone pointed to it and asked, "What's that?"

"Oh, they call that 'the Gateway to India,'" the RAPWI official answered. "Not quite in the same league as the Arc de Triomphe."

It was nevertheless an imposing structure, reflecting the grand history and wealth of an ancient subcontinent the size of Europe, the heart of a British colonial possession that in the grand calculus of humanity could overshadow its imperial master by a considerable margin from almost any perspective. My parents later confessed that the experience had been humbling: we were in a very grand part of a city in a very large country. "This is different from the Hotel des Indes," my mother mused. "This place is really chic." My father picked up our suitcase and we turned to the hotel. At the entrance we were greeted by white-robed, turbaned staff, whose elegance contrasted sharply with our rag-tag appearance.

Bombay had clearly thrived over the last few years, though the timepiece of fashion had not yet moved on from the Edwardian Imperial splendour personified in this hotel, which took up a city block. A postcard my father procured from the hotel desk explained that the hotel had been built by a wealthy Indian who had been refused entry into some of the other hotels frequented by Europeans, and in this manner tried to outdo the imperialists. Of the anti-colonial mood that had gripped this sub-continent, and the bloody civil war it would soon endure, we noticed nothing during our brief stay.

The elegantly robed concierge found us a room where the three of us could be together. The man, a monument to diplomacy, returned my father's toothless grin with a gentle smile, taking our dishevelled appearance in his stride. It must have struck him as passing strange to suddenly have appearances reversed—instead of serving the accustomed clientele of stylishly attired officials of his Majesty's Colonial Service, classically educated, well bred, titled, exuding a self-confidence that could only be gained on the playgrounds of certain British schools, he now confronted a hotel lobby full of refugees, whose appearance, aside from skin complexion, was not so different from his neighbours in one of the humbler parts of this huge and teeming city. We were nevertheless graciously welcomed.

The Taj Mahal prided itself on its superb cuisine, a feature that my parents could appreciate more than I; that night we dined on curried rice and lamb. My parents enjoyed this change from the somewhat stodgy, mass-produced fare we had been given on the *Orontes*, where quality had of necessity been sacrificed in favour of quantity. However, I found the jelly and ice cream served for dessert a treat. And thus the ocean voyage that had started in Singapore as an evacuation of displaced persons had metamorphosed into a vacation cruise.

Those two nights in the hotel provided all sorts of other novelties. The building was furnished with an old-fashioned lift that had iron folding doors. A smiling, deferential hotel attendant operated the contraption with the help of a big brass handle that he swung back and forth. The position of the lift was indicated above the door by a brass arrow that rotated over a brass dial. For us children this was a great attraction, and using sign language, we soon had persuaded the operator to give us rides to and from the top of the hotel. One of the boys, it might even have been Chris, had secured a packet of matches, probably through devious means, and chose the occasion of such a lift ride to demonstrate to the rest of us his skill at lighting them. Before long, the demonstration included a little campfire in the lift. This caused great alarm and precipitated complaints to the RAPWI representative who was overseeing our brief sojourn.

Aside from that, our stay in the hotel was uneventful, though punctuated by the arrival and departure of important people, the normal clientele, who moved about the big city in marvellous cars, their dark blue Buicks or long-hooded Packards drawing up under the entrance canopy to disgorge uniformed and bemedalled individuals. But there were also beggars drawn to the wealth and opulence, men and women in rags, covered with flies and invariably missing an arm, an eye, or a leg; hotel staff shooed them away. However, the moment one was gone another would turn up.

"At least in Tjideng we had not been beggars," my mother commented dryly while surveying this scene. The beggars approached the limousines hoping to get a penny or sixpence, but were grateful for a ha'penny or even a farthing.

A beach of sorts lay across the marine esplanade from the hotel, but the water was filthy, so we just strolled along to look at the fishing boats and the bustle of traffic, or walked up the grand shopping streets that ran inland from the water. The hotel concierge advised us that swimming was possible only at Chowpatty beach, facing the Arabian sea, but that was too far away, and taking one of the horse-and-carriage rides advertised at the foot of the Gateway to India was beyond our budget.

On the second night at the Taj Mahal, the RAPWI representative posted a notice in the hotel lobby for the *Orontes* passengers, stating that the buses would depart at nine o'clock the following morning.

The *Orontes* cast off from Bombay at about noon on Friday, November 23. We celebrated my mother's thirty-first birthday as we passed Aden. This was the first family birthday celebration in almost four years, and what a lot we had to celebrate. That evening dinner around the table was especially jolly, and notes were exchanged between the two families to keep in touch, for we would soon disembark, while our new-found friends would sail on to Britain. What we lacked on that occasion in terms of fine food and wine we made up for with cheer and laughter.

At the entrance to the Red Sea we briefly caught sight of the Arabian peninsula, barren, mountainous and forbidding; but although the land thereafter dropped out of sight, the hot, dry air suggested it was never far away, and the sunsets, a prelude to a cool evening, were spectacularly coloured in yellows and reds. The daytime temperature on-board ship grew noticeably hotter, and many of the soldiers could not stand the stinking hold at night and so slept on the decks under a sparkling night sky.

By the evening of December 1, the ship had reached the entrance of the Suez Canal, and was moored along a pier jutting out from the Egyptian coast. We stood on the boat deck to get a better view and watch the gangplank being raised to the entrance-way on the D deck.

"Is this Suez?"

The deck steward to whom my father had directed this question answered, "No, this magnificent city is called Adabiya, the harbour for Ataqa. Suez lies another mile or two to the north." All we saw, squinting against the setting sun, was a dusty collection of flat-roofed, one-storey buildings, now casting long shadows. They seemed to be made from concrete blocks or mud bricks, and beyond that lay a stark landscape desolate and forbidding, with hardly a tree or other form of vegetation. Looking in the other direction, across the water, we could make out through the late afternoon haze the rugged landscape of Sinai, illuminated by the setting sun.

"And Ataqa?"

In answer, the steward pointed to another cluster of one-storey buildings, three miles along the coast.

"I guess this is where we get off," my father commented, looking thoughtfully.

"What a God-forsaken hole-in-the-ground," Bob remarked, as he and his family joined us at the railing.

Beyond the few buildings and a railway track, a cluster of black oil tanks were the only other sign of civilization. Here and there, patches of smooth sand offered a reminder of the havoc winds could create in this landscape. Just then the chief purser's voice announced over the intercom that the *Orontes* would interrupt its journey here, "to permit RAPWI passengers to receive more clothing. Those who intend to journey to a different destination should contact a RAPWI official in the purser's office."

"I had better see to this," my father said, leaving my mother and me on deck with the Williams family.

A stranger joined us and, pointing at a barely visible valley, said, "Moses' fountain is there."

"Who is Moses?" I asked.

Inspired perhaps by our own journey, my mother began to share with me her scant biblical knowledge of Moses and the Exodus. She pointed in the direction of the setting sun, where the sky was red. "Moses came from over there, from Egypt."

"What happened at Moses' fountain?"

The man who had pointed out the site answered, "There was a spring there, but the water was bad, and could not be drunk; Moses threw the branch of a tree into the water and then the water was good. In those days the Pharaohs had a fortification there, on the Jebel Ataqa," he continued, pointing to one of the low rocky hills, a short distance inland.

A hot breeze began to blow from the west and the air smelled of sand and dust. We went down to the dining saloon for dinner.

The Desert Express

The next morning, the breakfast gong was followed by the purser's voice announcing that the ship would remain in Ataqa for the entire day and resume its journey that evening. "All of the civilian passengers are invited to go ashore to receive further clothing assistance from the RAPWI. Those passengers wishing to disembark in order to continue their journey to other destinations should visit the purser's office immediately after breakfast to obtain travel documentation to Cairo."

After breakfast, we said goodbye to our friends, and my mother and I returned to our cabin to pack our belongings, while my father went to the purser's office before getting his things. We met as agreed in front of the purser's office, where we had first entered the ship in Singapore. A crowd of passengers had already started to descend to the quay, where a ship's officer directed us to a goods train, waiting some distance off under the morning sun. There, an army officer in tropical gear urged us to step inside the goods wagons via a makeshift wooden platform. "Welcome on board the Desert Express," he cheerfully announced, and then, seeing the looks of dismay, added, "Only a short ride." The train quickly filled and, with the doorways closed by a makeshift barrier, rattled along for fifteen or twenty minutes before stopping at another platform near a cluster of buildings that were nothing more than large sheds. A small group of officers standing beside some army trucks welcomed us to "Ataqa, a fabulous holiday destination, noted for its turquoise waters," and directed us to one of the larger sheds. It was obvious from their relaxed demeanour that we were not the first refugees to have passed this way. Beneath the high ceiling of the shed it was mercifully cool, but it took some time for our eyes to adjust after the brightness outside.

Ataqa had served as a military staging post during the war, but had now been taken over by RAPWI as part of a larger "Civilian Rehabilitation Centre" set up in Ismailia. Our first stop was yet another medical inspection carried out by a Red Cross doctor and assisted by a nurse wearing a large white hood.

"Your medical cards, please?"

Some passengers were summoned to a walled-off area where they were scrutinized more thoroughly, but we were waved on in the direction of the "clothes parade." Large tables piled high with shoes, underwear, woollen coats, scarves, hats, sweaters and trousers were arranged in rows with signs attempting to classify the table contents according to size, sex and prospective use. Uniformed women hovered around the tables to assist with fitting and to maintain a semblance of order, while a man helped with the fitting of shoes. In a far corner of the shed a buffet had been arranged with rattan tables and chairs and piles of sandwiches, and near to it a play area had been cordoned off for children; it had a swing and a seesaw. We found some clothes that would be useful for the remainder of our journey to South Africa and that we could still fit into our luggage. Many of our fellow passengers were trying on heavy winter coats, but we could give those a miss.

After lunch we were ready to move on, along with about a dozen other *Orontes* passengers, to the next destination: Cairo. A railway clerk seated behind a temporary desk in a corner of the building gave us train tickets in exchange for our travel warrants, and directed us to wait for a bus to take us to the Suez train station.

The half-hour drive along the coast road and into Suez took us through an incredibly bleak landscape, unbroken by any colour other than that of dust. Even the small caravan of camels we passed seemed dusty, while behind us an immense cloud of dust quickly obscured all signs of Ataqa and its dreary ochre buildings. At the Suez railway station, we found room in a second-class train carriage, which we shared with strange-looking people, some in long flowing robes, others more conventionally dressed, but all wearing hats that looked like upturned flower pots with tassels dangling down in a jaunty fashion and all speaking a language none of us could understand.

The hundred-kilometre train journey to Cairo took us through more of the desolate landscape, with a few low-lying hills sparsely covered with shrubby vegetation. Here and there, isolated clumps of palm trees marked the location of oases. A hot blast of dry air came in through the open windows of the train and the only refreshment we had was from a bottle provided by RAPWI containing a warm and foul-tasting water. It was a boring journey until we came to the big city, where the train took us past the backs of houses and yards filled with junk, with, between us and them, a growing number of railway tracks bearing train wagons. We passed over viaducts, the roads below filled with traffic and flanked by buildings festooned with colourful signs and washing hanging out to dry, and finally entered a huge station with a glass-covered vaulted roof. On the platform we were greeted by a moustached man, smartly attired with a white pith helmet shading a ruddy face and twinkling eyes, a white open-neck shirt, a cravat, khaki shorts and long stockings, in one of which he had stored his pipe; he beckoned to us when we alighted from our carriage and made his identity clear with a helpful sign displaying the letters "RAPWI."

"Welcome to Cairo," he announced breezily. He then began calling our names from a list in his hand, checking them off one by one as we answered. When he had satisfied himself that we were all present and accounted for, he announced, "I have arranged accommodation for you in Hotel Victoria," adding as an afterthought, "I've provisionally booked you in for two nights on the understanding that you'll be making your own travel plans. If you need further assistance I can be reached via the hotel desk." He then led us to a small bus, parked outside on the street.

Hotel Victoria was located on Gomohreya Street. The five-storey building, though in the middle of town, had in front some green space with palm trees whose fronds were barely stirred by an evening breeze. We entered the hotel, tired and hungry, and the RAPWI man helped us deal with the reception desk. Above the receptionist, a man with shiny black hair, there hung a portrait of an important-looking person, also wearing a fez but dressed in a military uniform with lots of gold braid and large medals. His face, staring straight at us, was decorated with a beautifully groomed moustache. The hotel receptionist, catching my gaze, explained the portrait with the words, "His Majesty, King Farouq," while gravely nodding his head.

My father raised the problem of our need to stay longer than two days, depending on our ability to arrange transportation to South Africa. The RAPWI agent acknowledged that we still had a long way to go and that connections were uncertain; he urged my father to seek further assistance with repatriation from the Netherlands embassy.

The receptionist rang a bell and an Egyptian man wearing a white flowing robe and a red fez approached the desk, shuffling his slippers over the polished floor of the hotel lobby. The receptionist gave him some instructions and handed him a key, whereupon the man took our baggage and led us to the elevator, where yet another man in a flowing white robe (White Robe Two) opened and closed the folding steel gate. He pulled on a brass handle and the lift went up, stopping at the third floor, where White Robe Two opened the gate, jingling coins noisily in his pocket. My father thoughtfully gave him a coin with a hole in the middle. White Robe One led us down the corridor to our room.

The room was dark except for narrow slits of light coming from the street lights through a shuttered window on the far side. White Robe One placed our baggage on a bench and opened the window shutters, letting in the evening air and more light. Having checked the functionality of the electric light in the room, he then rattled some coins in his pocket, and my father obligingly handed him a coin, too. Not a word was spoken.

From the window, we could look down on the city street with its cars and carts and pedestrians setting about the evening's business in a leisurely fashion. Next door to the hotel was a small sidewalk café, where people were seated at tables, holding animated conversations assisted by tiny cups of coffee. Beyond them, further down the road, there were some illuminated words written in big letters on buildings.

"Neon lights," said my father. "Let's go down for dinner."

13. TOURISTS

The next morning, after breakfast, my father began to organize our journey to South Africa: he needed to get money and travel documents and secure passage. Although penniless and lacking passports, we were no longer refugees in the care of RAPWI; we were on our own.

The hotel receptionist gave us directions to the Cook's travel office and the Netherlands embassy. The former was located a short walk from the hotel in an elegant stone building with a classical façade. One of the large plate glass windows contained a beautiful model of a Sunderland flying boat, the type of aircraft that before the war had initiated the Imperial Airways London–Durban and London–Sydney services and had now resumed regular operations. The other window contained a model of an ocean liner. It quickly became obvious that our only option for returning to South Africa was by airplane, since all shipping was still dedicated to repatriating servicemen and women. The next flight would depart on December 5; space was available and the fare was about £100 per passenger. My father made his way to the Netherlands embassy to seek financial assistance and temporary travel documentation, leaving my mother and me to return to the hotel.

"At first they tried to brush me off," my father grumbled when he returned, "but they finally agreed to send a telegram to Holland to check on my bank account—can you believe that? I have to go back tomorrow afternoon. They looked at me as though I was dirt, and I had to explain to them where we had been—bunch of damned grocers."

The next day, my father did secure a loan, with the stipulation that it be repaid at the earliest opportunity. Armed with pounds in our pocket, with airline and hotel bill payment assured, we began to behave like tourists and hired a taxi for a trip across the Nile, to the west bank and the pyramids of Giza. The taxi driver, who doubled as tourist guide, took us first to a tiny Coptic church, St. Sergius, which from a distance was difficult to distinguish from the other brown buildings; the ornate entrance, visible only up close, gave way to an interior that was cool and dark, beneath a vaulted ceiling; at the far end stood a screen beyond which we were not allowed to go. There were other Coptic churches in this old part of town, but this one was the oldest, he claimed in broken English. Small windows with coloured glass and votive candles near the altar were the only sources of illumination. A black-robed, black-bearded priest guarded this shrine with his hand in a fold of his robe, jingling some coin, perhaps as a reminder that wealthy tourists like us should support this house of God. My parents lingered inside but I had caught a whiff of the dank air and of votive candles burning in the gloom, and preferred to wait outside in the shade. My mother emerged full of enthusiasm at the sight of the ancient frescoes on the church walls. The taxi then took us across the Nile, which was dotted with feluccas, sailboats with triangular striped sails, visible way upstream.

The sight of the Nile prompted my father to return to the legend of Moses. "When Moses was a baby he was hidden in a basket amongst the reeds, because Pharaoh wanted to kill him," he said.

The taxi driver chimed in, "The name 'Moses' comes from the Coptic words for water (*mo*) and saved (*uses*). The Pharaoh's daughter found Moses and rescued him."

In those days Cairo was still largely confined to the eastern shores of the river, and Giza was some distance upstream on an elevated plateau, standing in comparative solitude some distance away from the Nile. Along the west bank there appeared to be little other than mud-coloured, single-storey dwellings of uncertain age and structural soundness.

Soon we came to a place where only a hundred metres or so of bare earth, sand and rock separated us from the nearest pyramid, which now towered over us. The side of the road was dotted with shacks selling snacks and souvenirs. Some camels stood nearby, placidly munching their cuds, while their long-robed herdsmen, crouched in each animal's shade, waiting for tourists. Upon our arrival, they shuffled towards us, drowning us with exhortations, "You ride, sahib—cheap."

My parents showed not the slightest inclination for a ride, and the taxi driver/guide obligingly conveyed this message. Ahead of us, below the three huge pyramids and a cluster of smaller ones, there was an enormous stone lion with a man's head too small for its body.

"The Sphinx," my father explained, "a monument of great mystery—the head is not just smaller but also newer than the body. A man in Tjimahi told us about it."

Along the sides of the huge pyramid were some long deep holes cut into the rock. "That is where they found boats," said the taxi driver. "The boats were for carrying the Pharaohs' souls."

We walked to the second pyramid, which was even bigger than the first and was built of enormous limestone blocks, too big, I reckoned, for me to scale. Near the top, the pyramid was clad with shiny, smooth white stone.

"That's alabaster," the guide explained, and he proceeded to tell us how, long ago, the entire pyramid was clad with this material. "It reflected the sun's noontime rays far out into the desert—as far as Aswan."

"You, know," said my father, warming to the topic, "I heard a lot about this pyramid in the camp. The man in Tjimahi who had studied the thing gave a lecture about it. He mentioned that there was a mystery surrounding it—contradictions and riddles, mysterious measurements and proportions that related to the length of the year."

"That's right," confirmed our guide. "So far, no tombs have been discovered in it."

My father continued, "He also talked about a passage into its interior that foretold the future."

The guide, growing more animated, began to talk about mysterious air shafts, but my mother, recognizing my father's trait of letting a topic containing an intriguing element of mysticism wander off into a fascinating but tortuous and time-consuming discussion, tugged on his arm to remind him that we were paying the taxi driver for time as well as distance.

This drew my father from this absorbing topic and, responding to my mother with a "Yes, Wil," he brought the discussion to an abrupt end. We returned to the taxi, but not before stopping at a roadside stand to buy a miniature pyramid made of alabaster, the same material that once had covered the entire structure, and also a scarab beetle made of plaster of Paris, painted green and with hieroglyphic inscriptions on its base.

The return trip was marred by a lesson I had to learn about taxi doors, and their ability to inflict great pain on a carelessly placed thumb. We returned to the hotel, making liberal use of the taxi horn to shoo men, women, children and their goats and camels out of the way, and arrived just in time for dinner.

The following day we returned to the Cook's offices to finalize our travel arrangements. There I began to feel unwell, and by the time we arrived back at the hotel I had a fever. A doctor came and diagnosed German measles (probably caught from a passenger on the *Orontes*). He advised us to keep the illness secret, for otherwise we would be evicted by the hotel staff. Thus our stay in Cairo was inadvertently extended. My parents made grateful use of this forced sojourn to explore Cairo, including the nearby Place de L'Opéra with its statues, the famous Mohammed Ali Mosque and the even more illustrious Egyptian Museum. From my bed, I could only marvel at the stories they related each evening. However, they did not forget me, for over the subsequent days they spent some of their borrowed money on things to amuse me, and I was more than happy to occupy myself making Meccano models. After about a week, a second doctor's visit confirmed that I was ready to move on. My father paid a return visit to Cook's and secured passage on the next Imperial Airways flight to Durban.

Eight months later, a Dutch ocean liner, the *Klipfontein*, travelling from Tandjong Priok to Rotterdam, also stopped at Ataqa. Among its passengers were Emmy, Juf and Edu. Juf stayed on board to continue the journey to Holland, but Emmy and Edu disembarked, as we had done, along with John and Bessie Fisher, who in 1940 had travelled with us from Durban to Batavia. They spent a month in Ismailia (figure 20, 21) before the French merchant vessel *Felix Roussel*, forcibly enlisted in the service of the Allies for the duration of the war, was able to repatriate them to South Africa as its final contribution to the Allied cause.

Imperial Airways

We checked out of the hotel early on Saturday morning, December 22. In the small hotel garden, only the very tops of the date palms caught the sun's rays and glistened bright green against the dark walls of the courtyard. A taxi, summoned by the concierge, arrived and took us along a weaving route through the early morning rush hour to the Nile's east embankment, before heading south. From the road we caught periodic views of the river between the haphazard clusters of apartment blocks, some finished, most others half-built. The apartment buildings gradually gave way to mud-brick huts and animal enclosures, and in the far distance, beyond the Nile, the pyramids could once more be seen. We were proceeding upstream towards the flying boat service "airport" at Rod el Farag.

Shortly after we left the city we turned off the main road and drove a short distance to a small building, standing near the banks of the wide, sluggish river. Adjacent to the building stood a black and white mast supporting a limp, orange windsock. The building was the departure hall, waiting room, immigration and customs shed all rolled into one. My mother and I entered the building, followed by a porter carrying our luggage, while my father settled accounts with the taxi driver. Inside, we and our modest baggage were all carefully weighed, while a ticket agent dealt with the papers.

We then went into a lounge, where a dozen or so other passengers, some of whom had arrived on this plane the previous night, were seated. Through the windows we could see a concrete path leading through a neatly groomed lawn down to the water's edge, where a wooden jetty jutted out into the brownish-grey stream that gently flowed by. An open launch lay moored to the jetty, while its two-man crew, dressed in white shorts and shirts, sat patiently waiting under the shade of a parasol. Some distance away from the reed-fringed shore, a huge aircraft floated on the water.

"There's the flying boat," said my father.

There was nothing to do but look through the window to study this immense thing, as more passengers arrived. The magnificent flying machine, moored with a rope to an orange ball floating on the water, was fascinating, for its hulk was always moving with the changing current. It had four engines on its wings, making it a far more impressive piece of technology than the DC-3 that had taken us to Singapore. Suspended at either end of the wings, fairly close to the tips, were some struts holding a small float. Only one float could reach the water, while the other one was aloft. Occasionally the plane swung around and tipped the other way, lifting one float up out of the water, while the other float and wingtip dropped down. As the plane tipped back and forth the sun sometimes reflected off the pilot's windows above the nose, high above the water, and blinding sunlight flashed our way.

At about a quarter to nine, a man, smartly decked out in a white shirt and shorts and wearing a peaked cap, called us to attention and motioned us to follow. He led us out of the waiting room to the jetty and the waiting boat. Behind us came a cart loaded with suitcases and pulled by two workers clad in khaki. The boat could only accommodate twelve passengers, so at least two trips would be required. The officer called out some instructions and my mother pushed me forward to the boat.

"What did he say?"

"Passengers sitting in the rear of the plane will be loaded first."

The sensation of stepping into a rocking boat was a novelty, and yet it somehow felt very cozy and safe, notwithstanding the constant rolling back and forth when more passengers got on, because the boat always promptly righted itself. We were seated on a bench that ran around the side of the boat, with our backs to the gunwale. With the river water so close at hand it was tempting to reach down and touch it.

"Watch out for the crocodiles!" someone warned, but my father laughed and told me not to worry.

When the launch was full, the ropes were let go, and we chugged out onto the Nile. One of the boatmen stood in the bow with a boathook in his hand, while the other one steered the vessel to the airplane. When the boat's spreading wake reached the reeds along the shore, it created another green ripple travelling down the length of the river bank. As we came closer, the plane towered over us and it was impossible to imagine such a huge object being able to leave the surface of the water and become airborne. We slowed down and gently approached the aircraft until the man at the bow with his boathook could snag a ring hanging from the plane in front of the open door and pull the launch closer. The bowman made the boat fast to the plane and one of the officers helped us climb from the boat into the plane's interior.

Compared to the plane that had flown us to Singapore, this one was luxuriously appointed. There were two rows of forward-facing seats on either side of a narrow central passageway that ran down the length of the hull, and the sides of the plane were covered with grey, shiny material. Ahead of us the foremost seats were at a lower level, while beyond them one could see steps leading to the doorway of the pilots' cockpit. I ended up in a seat by a window on the left side of the plane, almost at the back, with my mother ahead of me and my father beside me. Hanging from the seat-back in front of me was a pocket containing some pamphlets, and a folded paper bag.

"What is this for?"

"In case you get air sick."

The launch made two more trips, bringing the remaining passengers and the baggage. The officer disappeared into the front after having shut the outside door and made some announcements. It got uncannily quiet, as though everyone was afraid of making a sound, but through the wall of the plane one could hear the waves of the Nile lapping against the plane's hull.

Then a propeller began to turn, slowly at first, and suddenly a deafening roar announced that one engine had successfully been fired up. After the remaining three engines were brought to life the plane began to move out into the middle of the immense river, while we just caught sight of the launch returning to its jetty. It seemed that we cruised up the Nile for ages, but then the noise level increased, making further conversation impossible, and the plane gained speed. Soon, all we saw out the windows was spraying water, which diminished as the plane lifted its immense bulk off the Nile. The water, the reeds, and beyond them the fields of wheat and palm groves sped by and dropped below us as we laboriously gained height.

Our course followed the river along its sinuous route through a narrow swath of green land. Beyond that, in the distance, an ocean of sand and rock stretched to the horizon. As the minutes of roaring grew to hours and the sun rose, an unpleasant sensation began to affect us. Every now and then the plane seemed to drop, making me lose contact with my seat, were it not for the seat belt, and then suddenly I hit my seat with a thump. Up and down we were tossed, and one could only marvel that the wings could withstand these terrible shocks; it was very uncomfortable and alarming.

"Air pockets," said my father with an air of authority on such technical matters.

I got sick, but managed to avoid using the paper bag by making my way to the rear of the plane, where there was a tiny toilet. It was a simple sanitary device, a seat over a stainless steel cone with a flap covering the hole. When one stood on a lever the flap opened and, while I bent over and retched, I could continue following the plane's progress over the desert, slipping steadily past us far below. The view of occasional palm trees, a rare group of camels, or sometimes the plane's shadow, clearly visible, added a degree of interest to an otherwise exceedingly unpleasant experience. I was not alone in my misery.

Virtually every passenger on the plane had to bend over paper bags or make the journey to the toilet, except for my parents, who seemed to enjoy the most robust of constitutions and never got sick.

After some three hours the plane began to lose altitude, and soon the river, like a silver band, slipped in and out of view between the fluffy clouds. We dropped down and suddenly water sprayed past the windows and then formed a huge surge as the plane suddenly lost speed and the nose pitched down. The plane's engines revved up on one side, making the great hulk turn around to face the opposite direction and then, with engines on both side roaring away and water splashing past our windows, we taxied along a shoreline marked by reeds, and beyond, a line of palm trees. The engines slowed down, a launch appeared and a few minutes later the propellers chugged to a stop. Once again a deathly quiet permeated the cabin, and after the ringing in my ears stopped, I could again hear the Nile waves gently lapping against the hull. One of the officers emerged from the front, announced that we were having lunch at Luxor, and opened the outside door, letting in a gust of hot, dry desert air, bright sunlight and Arab voices. While we began the process of boarding the launch, another boat appeared with hoses and men clambered up on top of the wings.

The boat journey and its gentle breeze gave a welcome relief from the noisy, bumpy plane, in spite of the hot sun overhead. We approached a wooden jetty providing access via a short walk to a one-storey building with a broad veranda sheltering rattan chairs and tables. Beyond the building lay a flat green landscape, but far in the distance there were towering ochre cliffs marking the edge of the Nile valley. We went up some steps past a couple of potted palms whose leaves were stirred by lazily turning ceiling fans, and sat down in the shade to enjoy a splendid view of the Nile and the plane's service crew, out on the water busy refuelling the Sunderland, while a number of waiters, tall, handsome, dark-skinned, and all wearing white robes and red fezzes, plied us with delicious salads, sandwiches and limeade. An hour or so later, we returned to the plane. We flew next to Wadi Halfa, on the border of the Sudan, where we stopped for tea. Then there followed a long hop to Khartoum. This leg of the journey took us away from the river and we crossed a seemingly endless expanse of desert, crossed the Nile at the fourth cataract, flew over more desert landscape and finally, towards dusk, landed once more on the great river, here coursing through a flat landscape. That day we had covered one thousand nautical miles in seven hours.

"The Nile splits in two here," my father said while we waited on shore for the next stage, "a Blue Nile and a White Nile"—but the water all looked brown to me. The bus took us from the flying boat base into town to the Grand Hotel, where we had dinner and slept. There was no opportunity and even less desire on the part of any of the passengers to go downtown for sightseeing; we were all too tired from the noise and the air pockets.

The next morning, after breakfast, we repeated the routine. The first section took us from Khartoum to Malakai on the White Nile and the dreadful air pockets again wrought havoc with my breakfast. At Malakai the land was flat, and here the Nile was fed by numerous meandering streams joining it from east and west. After lunch, we flew over a landscape that had become greener. The next stop was Juba, 274 miles to the south, where we arrived well after one o'clock. By now the landscape was slowly changing to savannah with intermittent scrub, but here along the shore of the Nile were big trees; we had left the palm trees behind. The next hop was to Port Bell on Lake Victoria. Over this stretch, the bleak scrub landscape gave way to more bushy land as we crossed over the Ugandan border and approached the northern extent of the great African lakes. Toward evening we landed and the captain informed us that we were on the equator, but 3,700 feet above sea level. This would be the highest point from which the plane would take off on its journey.

"Pity that we could not see Murchison Falls," a passenger sitting across the aisle from my father lamented after the engines had ceased roaring.

"Murchison Falls?"

"It is where the Victoria Nile flows through a very narrow cleft in the rock and into Lake Albert—a spectacular waterfall and, if the weather is good, the pilot would have flown over it so we could all see. I have made this trip before," he explained.

But we were now on a lake that seemed huge, like the ocean, and numerous fishing boats were on the water, their glistening nets, stretched out like butterfly wings, catching the rays of the setting sun. A bus took us to Kampala for a second night in a hotel. That evening, after dinner, we found our beds once again festooned with mosquito netting, while fans lazily moved the stifling but gradually cooling air.

Taking off from Lake Victoria next morning was a lengthy exercise. Because of the high elevation of the lake, the plane needed extra airspeed to become airborne. Fishing craft and dugout canoes slipped by us with ever greater speed while the plane threw out to either side a vast sheet of water from its hull, and then at last we were in the air again. An hour later, we landed on the eastern end of the lake at Kisumu to refuel, but this time we remained on the plane, staring at the bushy, gently rolling landscape along the lakeshore. There followed another lengthy take-off for the next hop, to Mombasa. According to the captain, this would be the longest, most demanding "hop," taxing the operating range of the Sunderland.

After about half an hour, a huge mountain came into view from my window. Although far away it seemed very high and its top was covered with snow. "That's Mount Kenya," my father shouted to make himself heard over the din, "always covered with snow."

Ten minutes later there was excitement on the other side of the plane. My father leaned back to let me look across the aisle past the passengers on the starboard side. There one could see, wreathed in clouds and much closer, another immense mountain. "Mount Kilimanjaro—bigger than Mount Kenya," my father explained, and I nodded in response. We then flew over Lake Navivasha, and the passenger sitting across the aisle from my father, the one who had also told him about Murchison Falls, shouted something to him. "Sometimes the plane lands there," my father then explained to me.

We arrived for a late lunch in Mombasa, on the Indian Ocean, and after taxiing into the harbour and finding a mooring on a buoy, made our way by launch to a shore. After lunch, the pilots, who by this time had taken an active interest in their human cargo, came over to our table and presented me with a model of an Arab dhow, which they had bought in the tourist shop.

"Merry Christmas," they smiled as they handed me the gift.

It was beautifully made from exotic woods, its hull polished to a high lustre and it had masts and rigging. Clutching this wonderful gift, I followed the party back onto our plane and thereafter was more preoccupied with my new prize than with the landscape outside.

From Mombasa, we flew over Dar es Salaam, and then on to Lindi for tea, where immigration formalities were required since we had left the British Empire. That night we stopped at the port of Mozambique for dinner and a night's rest in the Hotel do Lumbo. The next morning we took off for our final hops, again a long one to Lourenço Marques for lunch and then finally to Durban, where the plane landed in the shipping channel between two breakwaters and taxied to the far western end of the harbour, where the Congella Airport float plane base was. The 4,300-nautical-mile journey had required almost thirty flying hours spread over three days.

We were finally back in Durban, five years and seven months after embarking from this port on our ill-fated journey. That night, we found accommodation in the Parade Hotel, an eight-storey building fronting on the Marine Parade and with a magnificent view of the Indian Ocean beach. We were lucky because it was the beginning of the summer holiday season and soon Durban would be filled with holidaymakers.

The next morning, we unpacked our swim things and made our way across the Marine Parade to the beach. And so, a mere four months after being liberated from a Japanese prison camp, released from hunger, filth, disease and danger from marauding, bloodthirsty *pemuda*, we found ourselves sitting among a group of sunbathers on the sandy Indian Ocean shore, ringing in the jolly season of year-end festivities. Behind us on the road, a colourful crowd of Zulu rickshaw runners, decked out with extravagant feathered headgear, leopard skins over their shiny chocolate-brown torsos, and bells and rattles around their ankles, were trying to entice tourists into their ornate two-wheeled chariots. The happy atmosphere was heightened by the fairground in perpetual operation, with dodgem cars, coconut shies, cotton candy, ice cream vendors and a small zoo housing a reptile collection. In retrospect ours was an absurd, surreal situation: refugees one day and holidaymakers the next.

The beach and the rolling surf were novel experiences for me and I was not so sure that the water could be trusted with more than my ankles. My mother, for the first time wearing her sky-blue, woollen and somewhat unflattering bathing suit, also preferred to stay on the sand, but my father went for a dip, trying to entice us into the water as well. He also found it difficult to work up the necessary enthusiasm for frolicking so soon after the difficult years, and quickly rejoined my mother and me, building a sandcastle. He had, besides, caught sight of some beach hawkers approaching. One man was carrying a white box that contained cream-filled pastries, a treat my father could not resist: he bought three. While we were munching on this confection a photographer came by and wanted to take a family picture; the print could be picked up later that day from one of the kiosks near the road. We smiled for the camera, and the man clicked the shutter and moved on to the next party on the beach (figure 22). My father's smile did not last long after the photographer had done his bit, for as the latter moved off, my father gesticulated unwisely with his arms, shouting some parting words of gratitude. A seagull took advantage of the situation and neatly swooped down, snatching his half-eaten cream cake out of his hands— his first cream cake in four years!

A careful observer on the beach would perhaps have noticed that our swimsuits were somewhat worn, and that my father, who then was supposed to be a vigorous thirty-eight-year-old in the prime of life, looked distinctly unwell and un-South African, with his hollow cheeks and his gap-toothed smile.

We could not afford to stay longer than a day and next morning my father began to make arrangements for the next phase of our trip; for this he needed help from friends. Tracking them down was not easy; we did not know who might or might not have a telephone, still a luxury in those days, while sending telegrams to vaguely remembered pre-war addresses would have amounted to a pointless wild-goose chase. But after several long-distance calls and assistance from the Johannesburg telephone operator, the Wesselo family had been tracked down. During the intervening years they had moved to a new address in Auckland Park, one of the better residential neighbourhoods of Johannesburg. Joost was most surprised to hear my father's voice. "We heard so much bad news from the Indies that we were sure you had perished. Of course you are welcome to stay with us."

That same Boxing Day evening, we accordingly took a taxi to the train station and boarded the overnight train to Johannesburg, four hundred miles to the north.

14. IN THE OLD TRANSVAAL

The steward's voice, "Good morning, *goeie môre*," accompanying a discreet knock on our train compartment door, woke us up. My mother muttered "Yes," and opened the compartment door to accept a tray with cups, a steaming pot of tea, milk, sugar and biscuits. The train had stopped, and when my father lifted the window blinds we saw a deserted platform and, further along, a brick station building with a red corrugated iron roof. The early morning sun's rays filtered through the leaves of poplar trees standing beyond the station.

"Standerton," my father announced after peering up and down and finally finding a nameplate. "Welcome to *die ou Transvaal*," he added with emotion in his voice. "God, am I glad to see this place again!"

My mother and I got up to join him at the window, and I noticed rare tears on her cheeks, but then the train jerked forward, slowly leaving the station building behind and passing a stationary goods train, many of its wagons filled with coal. Beyond the tracks, we saw corrugated iron shacks, with some mangy dogs and dark-skinned children shyly staring at us, wide-eyed, from their doorways.

We had time to get dressed and enjoy breakfast in the dining car before reaching our destination. My parents were visibly agitated as we passed through towns like Balfour and Heidelberg, exclaiming these names in excited voices. The scenery was uninteresting and dreary; the landscape was almost treeless and the buildings were unimpressive.

"Germiston! That's where you were born, Boudy," my father exclaimed. We then passed huge piles of pale yellow sand, lit by the morning sun, glowing like golden mountains. "Look, mine dumps!" my father shouted. "We are nearly home!" In between them stood tall steel structures with enormous spinning wheels at their tops. Elsewhere, wires suspended from a series of towers carried steel buckets over the tops of one of the dumps, and beneath them some trucks were moving along dirt paths. Soon there were more trains alongside of us and we were obviously nearing a big city.

When the train finally stopped under the high arched roof of the station building, my father cheerfully called out, "Park Station! Off we get! I wonder if Joost is here to meet us."

We gathered our things, left the compartment and stepped down onto the platform, where we were immediately approached by a station porter who offered to carry our bags. My father hesitated, but handed them over, and we began to walk towards the exit. A middle-aged man, nattily dressed in slacks and a blazer and wearing an ascot tie, seemed to be waving at us from the exit gate. "Ha!—there's Joost," cried my mother, and waved back enthusiastically.

Smiling broadly, Joost Wesselo came briskly down the platform to meet us. "Bou, Wil, how good to see you!"

There followed an emotional greeting before I was introduced.

"We were all sure that you had died," he exclaimed. "The news coming from the east was so bad, and seems to be getting worse. People here will be most surprised that you have survived and returned." And then, after studying my father's face, he asked, "What on earth happened to you, Bou?"

My father explained in brief his unpleasant encounter with a Japanese soldier.

"Ruth will certainly write a story about you in *de Nederlandse Post*," promised Joost. This, he explained, was a monthly paper circulating among the Dutch immigrant community. Joost then expressed great admiration for my stature. "When I last saw you, you were only this big," he said, before continuing, "I wonder who is taller, you or Marijke?"

"Their little girl was born a month before you were," my mother explained as we followed the two men out of the station, with the porter bringing up the rear.

The buildings outside the station were huge, much taller than the Cathay building in Singapore that had stood not far from the *Oranje* Hotel. "Skyscrapers," my mother called them. "Johannesburg is a city of skyscrapers," she repeated as though it were a travel advertisement. Evidently the city had grown since she had last seen the place, and its growth stood in stark contrast to the wartime decay we had seen in the Far East. We left the rather grand station entrance and went to a parking lot, where Joost's car stood; it was a dark-blue Buick, just like the limousines we had seen bringing important-looking people to the hotel in Bombay.

My father was beaming. "Joost," he said, nodding his head for added emphasis, "it's good to be back on de Villiers Street. I tell you, there were times I thought never to see this place again."

Joost guided the porter to the rear of the car, opened it and said, "Put the luggage in the boot, man," and gave him a small silver coin. "Here's a ticky[1] for you." The smiling porter took the coin, touched his cap and said, "*Ja baas, baie dankie baas*," before returning to the station.

We got into the car and drove a few blocks down Eloff Street before turning onto another road. "Remember Bree?" asked Joost, but my father muttered something about all the changes that had taken place since he left in

---

1. South African three-penny coin the size of a Canadian dime.

1940. What a contrast this street scene presented to the shambles of Singapore and Batavia; it was clean and orderly and all the buildings were in good repair; Johannesburg had clearly thrived during our absence. When we passed by a huge truck, a strange sort of locomotive on rubber tires, belching smoke from a stack, my father laughed, "Do they still use those old steam-driven *poep* wagons? Wil, you could have used one in Tjideng!" My father then gave Joost a brief description of the sewage conditions we had left behind. It seemed that this clumsy puffing vehicle removed what was euphemistically referred to as "night soil" from some homes and businesses in and around Johannesburg.

In an area with one- and two-storey buildings, mostly dingy corrugated iron–clad, factories and workshops, we were stopped by a policeman directing traffic around a restriction in the road. It seemed that part of the road had caved in, and was barricaded off, leaving room for only one line of cars to pass this point.

"What happened here?" my father asked.

"An old mine working," Joost explained. "They came too close to the surface."

We carried on and finally left the industrial area, crossed some open, rocky land sloping upwards, and entered a residential district of modest bungalows. The road ascended a steep hill, and we finally turned off onto a driveway descending sharply between two larger houses, stopping on a paved area in front of one of them, a two-storey building with a prominent radio mast on the roof.

"Welcome home," Joost said, turning off the engine. He saw my father and me craning our necks at the radio antenna, and explained that he was a ham radio operator. "I will show you the stuff," he added, sensing my father's keenness.

Joost's wife, Ruth, accompanied by a girl my age and her two younger brothers, came out to greet us.

"Give *tante* Ruth a hand," my mother said to me.

Ruth warmly embraced us all, and there were more "Oohs" and "Ahs" when the children were introduced. "Ruth was the one who made your baby pictures," my mother explained. Ruth turned to the Bantu woman, dressed in a white uniform, who stood shyly in the doorway, and asked her to prepare some coffee, whereupon the latter scurried into the house with a "Yes, Miss."

Joost had to explain to my father the location of the new house. "We are actually on the edge of Auckland Park," he declared. "Our address is Surbiton Road, but that road does not exist here," and he pointed over the low stone garden wall at a steep slope below. "That's where Surbiton Road should be, but it's too steep here. That's Auckland Park," and he waved with a broad sweep of his arms at a mass of trees sheltering streets and houses stretching to the north below us.

"Yes, it has certainly changed a lot," my father commented. Seeing all these changes over the last six years drove home how costly those six years had truly been to him and my mother, but he did not complain.

Ruth led us up some steps to a balcony and then through French doors into the elegant and comfortably appointed living room. "You should have seen the living room in our previous house," my mother joked, and then, standing in front of the large window to admire a magnificent view stretching towards a distant northern horizon, she briefly described the conditions we had endured in Tjideng." It's beautiful here," she concluded.

"Yes. On a clear day you can make out the Voortrekker monument," Joost declared proudly. The nearly completed, massive cenotaph commemorating deeds from the past, both bloody and heroic, stood on a *koppie* some thirty miles north of Johannesburg.

"You can sleep in my studio," said Ruth. "I will ask Marie to set up a spare bed there for you two. Would Boudy mind sleeping on a camp cot with the other children?" Ruth motioned my mother to follow her and disappeared down a flight of stairs, while my mother protested that she did not want to evict Ruth from her studio. "I won't need it over the Christmas holiday," Ruth replied.

My father immediately began the task of reassembling life in South Africa by making contact with his former employer, the Roodepoort municipality, luckily finding the chief engineer at his post, while many of the employees were away on vacation; he promptly offered my father a temporary drafting position. They, too, had been surprised when they received my father's telegram from Singapore, and the chief engineer assured my father that a reply had been sent; that my father did not receive it did not matter now.

My father also managed to track down one of our pre-war belongings, an antique clock almost 250 years old, a prized possession that had been in his family almost since the day he was born; our former neighbour, Mr. Schoenzetter, had kept it all these years in his storeroom. With help from Joost and his car my father brought it back to the house, and we all crowded into Joost's workshop to admire it. My father called it a "*stoeltjes* clock" on account of its wooden base shaped like a chair, on which the finely crafted brass movement rested. Joost recognized it from the occasions when he had visited the house at Lombardy East. "You will be glad to have this back," he said. "That's a fine clock."

Two mermaids flanked either side of the clock face. The clock dial had black Roman numerals on a white circular band. A seascape filled the space above the dial and the two upper corners of the clock face; it portrayed a stormy scene with several sailboats heeling over amidst foam-scudded waves, one perhaps a fishing boat trying to gain the shelter of a harbour, guided by a church steeple. In the middle of the dial the artist had painted a rural landscape, with a small castle set in a large pond. Above the clock dial, and partly filling the space below the canopy, was an ornate transom cast in lead, but gilded; in its middle was an escutcheon, which was still partly coloured red.

"It used to have the year 1704 painted there," said my father, pointing to the area where the grey lead was now exposed, adding, "Pity it's worn off." He pondered the scene and then commented, "It's a Friesian clock and may well have once belonged to a merchant trading with the Dutch East Indies—those ships set out from the Friesian coast."

Mixed up with the movement there was a jumble of brass chains, and a heavy lead weight covered with a decorative brass skin.

"Let's hang it up to see if it still works."

After searching through some boxes and drawers in his workshop, Joost found an old coat-hook and attached it to a door frame in his workshop. The clock was hung and the two men managed to unscramble the brass chain, hang it over the sprockets and suspend the big weight from a brass pulley, but the escape mechanism immediately started to rattle in an uncontrolled fashion, and my father sadly noticed that the pendulum was missing.

"I think I can make one," Joost reassured. "At least it will run. Perhaps Schoenzetter can find the original one in his house."

After some more rummaging through tins and boxes, the two men were able to improvise a pendulum weight from an old piece of rectangular brass, to which Joost soldered part of a large brass electric plug that had a convenient hole and a screw originally designed to clamp electric wires. Finally, with the help of wire salvaged from a coat hanger, the remainder of the pendulum was manufactured, though it took some discussion before the two men had figured out how to suspend the pendulum from the steel support that jutted out from the clock's back just below the canopy. And then the clock once more ticked and tocked, though I was disappointed that neither the alarm nor the hourly chimes could be made to work. However, with a triumphant voice my father called for my mother to come down. "Wil, look! The clock works again!"

Ruth in the meantime had managed to track down a dentist who could see my father at short notice; the next day he pulled out the remaining damaged teeth and provided my father with a temporary set of false teeth, while a permanent set was being prepared. Already my father looked better and it certainly helped his eating.

My parents made contact with other pre-war friends, Wim and Bep Landzaat, who had more bedroom space in their house and who promptly invited us to move in with them. "But you will need a car if you come to live here, for we are out of town. Oh yes," Bep continued, "I will ask Tommy's school whether Boudy can join him, when school starts in mid-January." Our future was thus gradually taking shape.

Four days after our arrival we celebrated New Year's Eve in style in the company of our old friends at a big dining room table with a beautiful table cloth, candles, turkey and ice cream. Two weeks later our stay in Auckland Park came to an end, when Ruth needed to get her studio back for a wedding photography appointment. We loaded our belongings into the '38 aquamarine-coloured Oldsmobile my father had bought with some borrowed money, and set off for our next temporary home.

Northcliffe was a new subdivision of spacious lots on the northwestern outskirts of Johannesburg. Our host's house was an attractive whitewashed, thatched villa set well back from the road, which was unpaved but flanked by old bluegum trees festooned with weaver birds' nests. A small flower garden, stocked with canna lilies and sunflowers, lay adjacent to the house but the remainder of the property was the unaltered veld of a former cattle farm, with tufts of tall grass and red lateritic earth. It was a quiet and most agreeable location, with the only sounds heard in daytime being those of weaver birds flitting in and out of their cunningly-constructed grass nests dangling from the bluegum branches.

On the day after we arrived in Northcliffe I took the academic plunge. My first challenge would be to learn some English, and I would therefore start with the local Kindergarten in the company of Tommy, the five-year-old son of our hosts.

During the following weeks, my father tracked down more of our possessions, but not without difficulty because some of the valuable antique oak furniture, being bulky and therefore costly to store, had been sold during our six-year absence on the mistaken assumption that we had all perished. Since the status of these cherished items had unexpectedly changed from "abandoned" to "stolen," delicate and sometimes awkward transactions had to be carried out by my father. My mother nevertheless once more had her Pfaff foot-pedal sewing machine and could start turning the parachute she had been given in Singapore into underwear and blouses. She was an excellent seamstress, and after struggling for years to patch clothes with recycled material, now found it a relief to be able to work with good fabric. I could nevertheless see in her eyes the longing she felt for the carefree pre-war days, when sewing had been a source of diversion rather than an essential undertaking.

We spent eight months living with these friends in Northcliffe, while I made dramatic academic progress from Kindergarten and then into the neighbouring primary school called Blackheath, first into Grade 1 and then a month or so later into Grade 2, gradually bringing me into a class with a more or less compatible age group.

By September we needed to move, because our kind hosts would soon take possession of a new business venture, a commercial laundry servicing Johannesburg hospitals and hotels and located well outside of town, at Sterkfontein, about ten miles to the east; henceforth they would be living on the laundry premises. Fortunately this fitted well into our plans, for my father was being interviewed for a better-paid, permanent position in another municipality. This change moreover seemed to be a good time to make the long-desired visit to Holland; he needed to deal with the remnants of his real estate, discuss the future with Juf and finally become better acquainted with his parents-in-law. My mother also felt such a visit was overdue; she had left Holland so abruptly eight years ago, and the traumatic intervening period had transformed her youthful urge to rebel and seek adventure into sober anxiety for her aging parents. Besides, she was curious to see how her younger sister, Ina, had fared.

"She was barely sixteen when we left in '37, and is twenty-five now, and still single," she mused, wondering perhaps if she herself had, after all, been too impulsive.

My father managed to find new temporary accommodation in Roodepoort itself, almost within walking distance of his place of work. It was a furnished bungalow available for a short-term rental until the end of November 1946. Finally, for the first time since 1942, we were living in a normal way, in our own house; at last we had some family privacy.

Not far from the house stood Discovery Primary School, where I was enrolled in Standard 1 (Grade 3) for the final two months of the school year.

Juf arrived in Holland around this time and we once more had regular contact with her—every Sunday night was the time to write letters. She seemed to have regained her strength and, though she had recently turned seventy-three, was keen to join us in South Africa.

Emmy and Edu arrived in South Africa and went through the same process we had gone through—picking up the pre-war pieces of their lives. They also found temporary accommodation with the same pre-war friends who had helped us, but now in a guest cottage situated on the grounds of the Sterkfontein laundry. It was in this house where Beryl, their daughter, was conceived and brought into the world. On a number of occasions we made the trip from Roodepoort around the northern outskirts of Johannesburg to Sterkfontein, and inevitably the conversation between my mother and Emmy reverted to the final days in Tjideng.

"You know," Emmy reminisced, "after you had left, Sone one day returned. The British had captured him and brought him under armed escort in a Blitzbuggy into Tjideng for identity confirmation. You should have seen what happened!" she exclaimed. "A number of women walking on the street recognized him, and I swear that if the soldiers had not been there to protect

Sone, they would've *tjintjanged* him on the spot. The driver of the car made an immediate U-turn and left the camp."[2]

In the meantime our travel plans had been finalized. My mother and I were to leave by ocean liner for Holland in the last week of November, while my father stayed on until the middle of December to arrange the moving of our possessions to a storage facility in Vereeniging, a thriving farming and industrial town thirty-five miles south of Johannesburg: here he had secured a position as the municipal architect. He would then join us in Holland for a short stay, to remake contact with friends and family, deal with his affairs, ensure that Juf's pension was still properly managed, and make arrangements for her future move to South Africa. He had secured return passage on the Holland Africa Line ship *Bosfontein*, leaving Rotterdam in mid-January.

The Christmas stay in Holland, through a severe winter, was extended against our wishes when the *Bosfontein* caught fire while undergoing maintenance in the heavily damaged Rotterdam docks. With much difficulty my father was able to arrange alternative passage three months later for our own return journey to Cape Town, a trip that now necessitated a train journey to Marseille, where port facilities were intact. He also was able to arrange passage to South Africa for Juf later in the year.

A Fresh Beginning in Unitas Park

Vereeniging, our new home, was located where the railway from Johannesburg crosses the Transvaal border, defined by the Vaal River, to continue its journey via Bloemfontein, the capital of the Orange Free State, to Cape Town. *Vereeniging*, meaning "unity", was a name that contrasted sadly with the reality of South African history and future events. It was here, after a bloody three-year struggle, that the peace between Boers and Brits had been achieved in 1902, and where some of the first Canadian soldiers to serve overseas lie buried on a farm called "Macauvlei." But more recently, in September 1937, the town had been the scene of an ugly confrontation between police and "natives." That uprising, resulting in four deaths and numerous casualties, had been the culmination of resistance against the newly passed "Native Laws"; overnight, these laws (the intricate Pass and Liquor laws, the Masters and Servants Laws, and the like) had turned ninety percent of the Bantu population into statutory criminals and this had provoked the resistance. A subsequent Police Commission pleaded that:

---

2. Kenichi Sone was tried by a tribunal in Singapore, where Elsa testified against him. He was condemned to die on September 2, 1946. Tjideng continued to exist as a camp until the middle of 1946.

with so many inquisitorial laws to enforce, a South African policeman's life could not be a happy one, but admitted that many of the young country bred Afrikaners, from whom the force was now mainly recruited, lacked 'tact and consideration', and had an 'inaccurate outlook towards the urban native.'[3]

My father now occasionally referred to that event, which had caused such an outcry in the South African press at the time of his first setting foot in the country. Nothing much had changed since 1936, except that now, with the upsurge in the economy, the Vereeniging city fathers (in those days exclusively European, of course) undertook to do something about the harsh living conditions of the urban Bantu. One of my father's forthcoming challenges would be to design and oversee the construction of a subsidized municipal housing complex for the town's urban native population.

"You will be responsible for the development of the Sharpeville Project," Paul Klarer, the chief engineer and his future boss, had promised my father. Mr. Klarer was proud of this initiative, one of the first of its kind in South Africa, and he continued, "We are planning to build over three thousand houses, and ultimately we hope to get rid of the *lokasie* [location]. The *lokasie* is a breeding ground for disease and crime."

Every South African town had a *lokasie*, but the one he was referring to was a rapidly growing, miserable shantytown on the northern outskirts of Vereeniging, visible across a large open field from the main road leading to Johannesburg. It was a squatter camp, which even armed policemen hesitated to enter, an area where the constraints of tribalism and family had given way to an ugly quest for individual survival. Years later, long after we had left the country, the events of 1937 would be tragically repeated, paradoxically making Sharpeville, this progressive municipal venture, notorious for similar reasons and with similar results as in 1937, except that this time the world took notice and called it a "massacre."

To my father the assignment was a welcome challenge. Before the war, while in Bandoeng, he had had ample opportunity to contrast the progressive steps taken by the Bandoeng municipality in finding acceptable accommodation for the lower income groups, with the total lack of such arrangements in South Africa. Things were obviously improving in South Africa, and he was pleased to be able to play a part. Building subsistence housing could hardly be described as a test of his artistic skills, but there was a real purpose in providing quality accommodation for a cost that the municipality could afford. Besides, there was more in the works: once the Sharpeville project was under way, he would have to make a start with Duncanville, a low-cost housing project for the other social group in South Africa in need of government support, the "poor whites."

---

3. Walker, *A History of South Africa*, 647.

The house my father had bought just before Christmas stood in Unitas Park, a rural subdivision on the northern outskirts of Vereeniging. The house was unpretentious but comfortable, and lay within almost five acres of untamed veld; the little bit that was not veld was a poor excuse for an orchard. The only hint of style that the place possessed was the yard entrance. Its focus was a pair of ochre brick pillars set back from the property line and flanking a cattle grid made of round steel pipes. Cattle grids were an essential feature of this rural environment, where cows and horses occasionally sauntered down the dusty Japie Krige Road under the sometimes watchful eye of a Bantu cowherd. Attached to those brick pillars were two curved brick flower boxes, leading towards the roadway and the property line, otherwise marked by a north-south–running barbed-wire fence. The two curved structures created a welcoming funnel for those approaching the house from the road, but the flower boxes were devoid of flowers. The previous owners had also planted two cypress hedges along a curved trajectory inside the property, running from the brick entrance to the left and right and to the north and south edges of the land. These hedges enclosed two large quadrant-shaped and rather neglected peach orchards that through want of irrigation never produced edible peaches while we lived there. The house itself was whitewashed and had a red corrugated iron roof; it boasted a garage and a covered veranda, or *stoep* as we called it, that jutted out from the building.

My father immediately began to make improvements to the place. The first project was to replace the ghastly servants' quarters that stood some distance behind the house. It was a shack made of corrugated iron with a dirt floor and no running water. "A disgrace," my father called it. He immediately designed and had built a brick structure with two separate rooms and a common bathroom. It stood behind the house and was plumbed into the house water supply and septic drain system. It had a smooth concrete floor and its exterior was whitewashed.

"I wish our camp accommodation had been like that," my mother commented.

My parents hired two native "boys," as Bantu servants were then called: William for the garden and Josef for the housework. The existing corrugated iron shack was turned into a tack and feedstuff room for the animals my father planned to keep. He then converted the garage into an additional bedroom for future occupancy by Juf, and refurbished the dining room so that it could do justice to the antique furniture we once more had in our possession: a large eighteenth-century oak dining room table, with six matching oak chairs and a large oak armoire standing on ebony spheres. In the corner of the living room he built a new-fangled coal-burning fireplace with an iron firebox that could heat up the air "against the cold of highveld winter evenings." Next he added a wooden carport behind the house, a shed for bales of hay and beyond the tack room, a wooden stable block for three horses and two jersey cows. He built a chicken coop and a turkey coop, and then laid out a vegetable garden. This required the purchase of a gasoline-powered cultivator that was a demon for him to control as it thrashed away at the hard veld soil. My father furthermore acquired a solitary tethered ewe "to keep the grass down," but the poor animal fell prey to an attack by two neighbouring dogs and had to be converted to mutton. A swarm of bees established themselves in the tack room, thereby establishing my father as beekeeper. My father was enterprising.

My mother took pleasure in taking under her wing stray dogs, mostly of uncertain pedigree and not always well-mannered when there were chickens around. She soon found a secretarial job at Fick's Garage, the town's General Motors dealer. Aside from some welcome additional income and a stimulating working environment for her, this position also helped us to quickly secure a new car, a dark grey 1947 Chevrolet four-door sedan. Otherwise we would have had to wait for months to replace the unreliable pre-war Olds. Soon a piano appeared, and my mother got out her old books and enchanted me with her playing of Beethoven's *Appassionata* sonata, stimulating me to also take lessons. We even got a modern gramophone on which to play the collection of 78 rpm records we had left behind in 1940. The very latest in hi-fi technology in those days was bamboo rather than steel needles; when visitors like Ray Fone, a colleague of my father's, came to the house, bringing along his latest acquisition—for instance, a recording by Rubinstein—not so easily obtainable in a town like Vereeniging, there would follow a lively debate on the proper handling and preparation of the stylus, what grade of sandpaper was best, and how to ensure that the point was perfect in order to get the best sound without the slightest risk of damage to the valuable recording.

"I think *pappie* gets more enjoyment out of fiddling with the gramophone equipment than listening to the music," my mother confided to me. "He even stores the needle-sharpening gadget with his other gadgets—you know, the altimeter and that chart-measuring device."

And so, with a little help here and there, the family was remarkably quickly put back on its feet; the following years in Vereeniging were most agreeable. Inadvertently we had arrived at the right time to once more prosper in this land of plenty, for we now had a house, horses, cows and chickens, and went on holidays in the mountains, in the game reserve or at the coast. No one could have suspected the state of absolute pauperization we had left behind such a short time ago. My father all but forgot the personal fortune he had lost in the recent world conflict, for even the properties in Holland had suffered badly. Within the remarkably short time of two years, we had metamorphosed from penniless refugees to being comfortably off. Years later, in Canada, my father would refer to these halcyon days in somewhat sardonic terms: "People in North America pride themselves on their high living standards, but I can tell you that our (European) living standard in South Africa was way higher." If one pressed him on the issue he would admit that this was so because in South Africa, Europeans had access to an inexhaustible supply of "cheap (black) labour." It was cheaper to pay for Bantu muscle power than to buy or rent machines.

Our affluent situation neatly confirmed the claim of a government publication that came out in the very year that we established ourselves in Vereeniging. It bore the optimistic title, *South Africa, Land of Sunshine and Opportunity*. Those enticing words on the front cover had for backdrop a stylized painted landscape: a blue sky, distant mauve hills, and closer to the forefront, an image of a city, bright and sparkling with signs of industry—gold mines, of course. Between the city and the observer, there were farmers' fields, a stand of *mielies* (corn) and a grove of orange trees laden with fruit, while standing right in front, a smiling farm worker of uncertain race with a basket full of fruit at his feet. The first page made clear the book's purpose: "A Handbook of Information for Prospective Settlers." Inside, there were some apt comments from Prime Minister J. C. Smuts:

> Open wide the doors: if you can expand industry, if you can expand activity and production and employment on a large scale. No one will profit from it more than the citizens of the Union. We shall be calling reinforcements that we need very badly, with our small numbers fighting a great battle of civilization at this end of the Continent.[4]

The reinforcements alluded to were "European immigrants in large numbers"; this had been made clear in a parliamentary motion of March 1947 that accompanied the policy change and justified this booklet. To be fair, Smuts was deeply concerned about racial disharmony, but his solution was economic expansion to eliminate fear of poverty and the curse of racial envy, not only between Brit and Boer, but also between white, especially "poor white," and non-white.

And the policy shift? Immigration was a touchy subject with a long history. It was, after all, the immigrants of the last decades of the nineteenth century flocking to Southern Africa in search of gold and diamonds that had precipitated the Boer War, a clash between a "conservative agrarian" and a "progressive industrial" vision (progress sometimes takes odd twists and turns). But then it was easily forgotten that South Africa had always been a land of immigrants: even the bushmen, those stone-age hunters, now all but extinct, had come from elsewhere. We Europeans were merely the latest arrivals. This policy shift had partly reflected the new international scene: post-war Europe

---

4. McQuade, *South Africa, Land of Sunshine and Opportunity*.

was brimming with unemployed men and women seeking a future in what was then called "the New World."

The policy shift, on the other hand, tried to circumvent the consequences of the Pacific war, the establishment of the United Nations and the new political dynamic thus created—an era of self-determination and professed equality among peoples. The European colonial experience and the race-based societies it had spawned had entered its twilight years; the most outspoken critic of colonialism was Jawaharlal Nehru, and the country that attracted his most vehement wrath was South Africa, with its sorry record of race-based legislation. That its leader, Smuts, was a world statesman, added to the power of Nehru's rhetoric. How could a person who had drafted the United Nations Charter of Human Rights preside over a land where non-white peoples, especially immigrants from India, were second-class citizens? This criticism, painfully endured by Smuts during the opening session of the UN General Assembly, encouraged him to take the political risk of promoting large-scale immigration and to publish this little booklet.

It was in this new environment, encouraged by this same booklet, that my mother's younger sister, Ina, chose to join us in South Africa, as did her future husband, Tom, an unemployed metallurgical engineer abandoning his native Scotland to seek a better future. There were many who followed their example.

Smuts argued that the granting of rights to the non-white population was premature and politically suicidal. European immigration would reduce the existing white population's fear of isolation, while rapid industrialization of the economy by this influx of trained workers could have an economic trickle-down effect on the lot of the Bantu, help justify their education and eventually create a political climate permitting greater equality. Since South Africa was part of the British Commonwealth, immigrants from Britain were also enticed by the rapid granting of full citizenship status to British subjects. Smuts moreover could be confident that those newly enfranchised immigrants would strengthen the position of his United Party.

Dr. Daniel François Malan, Smuts's chief political opponent, accused him of sabotaging *Afrikanerdom*, of "ploughing the *Afrikaner* under a tidal wave of more *uitlanders* (foreigners)."[5] A significant part of the *Afrikaner* population, whose votes Smuts sought in order to retain power, were the poor whites, bankrupt subsistence farmers who recently had migrated into the cities; being poorly educated, they were unemployable in the new industries, and yet they possessed the vote. At its core the dispute was about the competing claims of two groups of needy people, a white minority and a black majority, both forced off the land and struggling to adapt to a rapidly changing world. A significant

---

5. Smuts, *Jan Christian Smuts by His Son*, 494.

difference was that the social problems this created for the Bantu were far more devastating, resulting in a skyrocketing crime rate.

The balancing act Smuts was attempting, by urging modestly progressive policies on his reluctant electorate without precipitating a voters' rebellion, was tricky. Yet so formidable was the standing within the country of this aged warrior that few could conceive any other future except one with him at the helm, and even those who in their hearts felt that his policies were wrong nevertheless might still be persuaded to vote for him. However, the parliamentary by-elections during the first half of 1947 gave an indication that Smuts's grip on political power was slipping.

The Good South African Life

For a short time my parents were far too preoccupied with their own post-war recovery to pay much attention to these developments. It seemed to them that not much had changed since the day we departed in 1940; in light of the Indonesian turmoil we had left behind and of the continuing upheavals in Europe and elsewhere in east Asia, South Africa did not seem so bad after all; in fact, it seemed like a haven of peace.

I made good friends at the local school, which happened to be an Afrikaans institution where English was taught as a second language. The nearest English school was three miles away, in town. First and foremost among my friends was Egmond Liebenberg, the son of the kindly, rugged-faced doctor who had assisted my mother with my birth nine years before in Germiston. By a strange coincidence, Dr. Liebenberg had moved his medical practice during the war years from Germiston to Vereeniging. Egmond was my age, lived in the same neighbourhood and attended the same modest school, notwithstanding the fact that on his mother's side he had illustrious forebears: nineteenth-century Boer statesmen. Then there was a tousle-headed boy called Wynand, who lived down the dusty road not far from our house. He was in my class as well, but in his case our families had nothing in common and indeed never met; it was a matter of outlook on life, a topic we avoided on the playground. The Afrikaans community was deeply divided, and here among my friends was an example of that division. I casually mentioned to my parents that the houseboy not only polished Wynand's shoes, but also tied them for him. "Maybe the houseboy knows how to do things Wynand can't do," said my mother. I did not know how to answer this, but my father was scandalized. "You damn well tie your own shoes," he growled.

My parents became active members of the Vereeniging Equestrian Club. Its doyenne was Elizabeth Klarer, the English wife of my father's boss, Paul, who also lived in Unitas Park; she gave riding lessons and organized the annual gymkhana. Occasionally the entire club would make an all day outing to Vosloo Park, on the banks of the Vaal River; it was a wonderful excursion across the open, mostly untilled land and involved fording two Vaal tributaries, the Suikerbos and Klip Rivers, shallow streams of sparkling water flowing over the rocky floor of gullies supporting the occasional small spiky *doring boom* (Acacia). In Vosloo park the party enjoyed a picnic on the bank of the sluggishly flowing, grey and therefore *Vaal* River, shaded by a grove of bluegum trees and weeping willows before making the six-mile return journey. Occasionally I also went, riding on Charlie, my pony. Charlie instinctively knew when he was going home, and along the *mielie* field we had to skirt I had to rein him in mightily so as not to damage the crop, but after May, when the corn had been harvested, we could gallop through the stubble to our hearts' content, past the cooling towers and coal stockpiles of the Klip River power station

Emmy and Edu had also settled in Vereeniging. With financial help from his father, Edu had acquired a sports shop called Vereeniging Gunsmiths, located on Market Street, the principal east–west artery of town and a few doors down from the intersection with Voortrekker Street. Over its wooden counter Edu sold hunting equipment and fishing gear. It was a thriving concern, because big game hunting was immensely popular in South Africa, and since Vereeniging was located on the banks of the Vaal River, there were also plenty of nearby fishing opportunities.

We often saw each other on a Sunday afternoon and sometimes reminisced about our life on Java, the good times we had enjoyed and the subsequent horrors and hardships we had endured. My father ruefully told Edu how he had managed to sell the house in Bandoeng, but the money was frozen in an Indonesian bank account. "The rupiah is worthless now," he moaned. "Each time they send me a bank statement, the capital is decreased because interest payments by the bank do not cover postage costs." My mother and Emmy's friendship, forged during the terrible camp years, remained as close as ever. My mother had often confided to my father that she might not have managed to carry the burden of the family through those war years were it not for Emmy's help, and she had been especially pleased when Emmy and Edu also came to live in Vereeniging.

Entertaining friends at home was popular, because, like all white South Africans, we were pleasantly freed from domestic chores by the likes of William, the Xhosa garden boy, and Josef, the Zulu. The latter now helped Juf (who had happily rejoined our family) in the kitchen and with the housework. Both Josef and William were great folk to have around.

Josef was barely thirty years old and conversed with us in Afrikaans. He was as handsome as he was shy. To him I was *die klein baasie* (the little boss). I could always count on Josef to help me with a bicycle tire puncture. With his strong fingers he could move the outer tube off and on the wheel-rim without damaging the inner tube. My father kept a close watch on these proceedings and frequently interrupted them, insisting that I do it myself. But if I undertook such a task by the kitchen door behind the house, while Josef and William were enjoying a cup of tea, sitting on the steps of their living quarters, I could always count on a friendly, willing pair of hands.

In many ways William was a more intriguing character. He was at least fifteen years older than Josef, to judge by the first sign of greying hairs showing around his grave but friendly face. On his days off he always left the house on his bicycle, neatly attired and wearing glasses. We knew not where he went or what he did, keeping instead a silence of mutual respect. We knew that Josef, for instance, visited family on his days off. William, however, professed to speak no European language at all, only Xhosa. This was slightly puzzling: a European name, the manner of a person with some education, but neither English nor Afrikaans? My father nevertheless got on well with William, and the two were often busy with the animals or the vegetable plot. In order to converse with William, my father learned to speak Xhosa, a language with difficult consonants, but similar in many ways to Zulu. My father's linguistic achievements always impressed me, but were by no means unusual in South Africa, where trilingualism was commonplace among all racial groups. We never resolved William's language enigma.

One day my father asked William to take Dotter, our Jersey cow, to the dairy farm from where she originally came. She was pregnant, and all facilities necessary for a successful delivery were available at the farm. On a Friday morning William, armed with a twig, guided Dotter out of the fenced-in pasture she had shared with the horses, around the house and through a narrow gate beside the cattle grid, and from there the twosome set off down dusty Japie Krige street.

It was my father's habit to always bring my mother a cup of tea in bed on Sunday mornings, but the following Sunday my father arrived in the bedroom, later than usual, carrying a beautiful brown-eyed Jersey calf, and deposited this on the bed beside my mother. Unfortunately the calf was not house-trained and quickly had to be removed to the nursing care of its proud mother, once more in the paddock with the horses.

Life was good, very good indeed.

May 1948

Within a year of settling into our new home in Vereeniging, my father's unease about the future in South Africa was given an unpleasant boost. A general election held on May 26, 1948, cost General Smuts his long-held parliamentary seat in Standerton, and gave a triumphant Malan a slim parliamentary majority. The shock of this turn of events was profound.

As a result of our experiences on Java, my father had come to set great store on the idea of the Commonwealth and our fortunate membership in this organization, but now South Africa's future in the Commonwealth was in question. During the run-up to this election Malan had kept cunningly quiet about his republican plans, but having emerged victorious, was now revealing his true intentions. He had capitalized on the anti-communist paranoia then sweeping the Western world, in effect accusing Smuts's United Party of condoning communists, if only because of the party's tolerance of trade union activities under the leadership of men like "Solly" Sachs, the Secretary of the Garment Workers Union, doggedly seeking a fair deal for his members regardless of their skin colour. The electorate was afraid of the changes then sweeping the world, especially elsewhere in Africa, but above all within the Union itself, and Malan's electoral rhetoric had preyed on these fears: where Smuts had shown a willingness to compromise, Malan offered a resolute commitment not just to maintaining the status quo, but to undoing what he termed "unhealthy concessions" made by the previous government. Malan moreover never left in doubt his feelings of contempt for Britain, and by implication, the remainder of the Commonwealth, now including India.

Malan drove home his commitment to a radically new policy direction by breaking with tradition in forming his first Cabinet, drawing only on Afrikaans-speaking MPs; this development was immediately followed by a flight of capital as nervous investors transferred their savings to other countries.[6] Unperturbed, he began to settle old scores by promptly releasing from jail Robey Leibbrandt, imprisoned in 1942 for an attempt to assassinate Smuts and stage a coup d'état in order to swing South Africa over to the German cause. So inflamed were the political emotions in the land that it even spilled over onto my school playground, resulting in turf wars, literally; our weapons were polls of tall grass, with the root ball attached, swung over our heads like a sling before being released in the direction of the "other side."

And so within three years of arriving back from Java the bright future in our new home was beginning to cloud over. Malan's electoral victory confirmed for my father the misgivings he had expressed to my mother shortly after our liberation from the Japanese prison camps, when he had considered options other than returning to South Africa. He distrusted the bible-thumping fundamentalists who liberally drew on Old Testament quotes to justify the most outrageous statements—that the black children of Ham were condemned to hew wood and draw water forever, that the Boers were Israelites and the Transvaal Canaan, and that justice entailed "an eye for an eye, a tooth for a

6. Smuts, *Jan Christian Smuts by His Son*, 514.

tooth."[7] Although many of our former fellow prisoners had in September 1945 noisily shared Malan's opinion of "perfidious Albion" and had expressed outrage at Mountbatten for "being thick" with Sukarno, my father had, thanks to his pre-war stay in South Africa, seen these developments in a different light.

"If men could learn from history, what lessons it might teach us!" My father was inclined to take Coleridge's words to heart, but it was difficult so soon after having made a new start in life. Aside from Malan's virulent hatred of anything British there was another worry: his native policy. The challenge of providing the Bantu with a place in South Africa's civil society had persistently overshadowed all other social and political issues of this country, but although the details of Malan's plans were far from clear, his determination "to keep the *kaffir* in his place," by whatever means and regardless of the cost, was well understood by everyone. Such stridency stood in contrast to the criticism *pak djenggot* (van den Plas) had endured on Java before the war.

The election results dominated the conversation of the Vereeniging Equestrian Club on the following Sunday. After the customary ride to Vosloo Park, our neighbours and horse riding companions, Ernest and Betty Zastrosny, along with their pretty daughter, Dirla, joined us for afternoon drinks on our *stoep*. Ernest, a tall, slightly balding civil engineer, was of Danish extraction, while Betty, his dark-haired wife, was English. Dirla was a shy, blonde girl a year or two younger than I. Emmy and Edu had also turned up.

Ernest, a card-carrying member of the United Party, offered a post-election analysis. "Smuts lost," he maintained, "because he was more concerned about the world situation than the situation here in South Africa. Malan outsmarted him and Smuts was stupid for recognizing Israel so quickly—that cost him many English votes."

My father was shocked to hear Smuts criticized so bluntly by one of his own supporters. "Do you think Malan can hang on to power?" he asked. "Business interests are obviously worried."

"They have cause to be worried, because the Sauer Report—you know, that Apartheid study that Malan wants to implement—will make it more difficult to hire natives. Malan is pro-farm and anti-industry."

"How's that?" asked Edu.

"He wants to stop the natives from living in our cities—they will have to commute to work, probably from a distance."

"But the *lokasies* are terrible. Would it not be a good thing to get rid of them?"

"Not if it wrecks the economy by moving them away from their jobs."

---

7. A sentiment to which I was liberally exposed at school.

"That's not going to happen, for Malan's bound to get thrown out at the next election, don't you think?"

"Not while Jan Hofmeyr is in charge of the United Party. I have heard, however, that the powers that be are not happy with his leadership—he is too liberal and scares the voters with his talk of giving the natives more rights. I also heard rumours that they are trying to get Smuts back into the Parliament— he is the only one who can rally support against Malan and put the *predikante* [preachers] back in their church."

My mother tried to introduce some jocularity into this discussion. "You know," she said, "there is a joke doing the rounds—at Fick's Garage on Friday, someone asked the question, Why is mutton so expensive now? and the answer was, *Al die skape is in die Parlement* [All the sheep are in Parliament]."

"I know a better joke," Ernest retorted. "One day a *predikant* was walking along the road outside of town and a motorist stopped to offer him a lift. The motorist was smoking a pipe, and after a while the *predikant* said, 'If the Lord God had wanted you to smoke, he would have put a chimney on your head,' whereupon the motorist slammed on the brakes and showed the *predikant* the door, with the words, 'If the Lord God had wanted you to ride he would have put wheels under your feet.' "

That was amusing, but it was really difficult to figure out what to do in this complex situation. My parents often tried to compare the pre-war situation in Bandoeng with that of Vereeniging, but there were no gold mines on Java, just rice paddies, tea and rubber plantations. Nor had there been anything on Java resembling the crime-infested shantytowns around the cities, just peaceful *kampongs*. There was a world of difference, and yet look what had happened. The atrocities in the post-war conflict on Java had been devastating; if that could happen in what at the time appeared to have been an idyllic situation, what might the future hold here, on the southern tip of this huge, untamed continent?

When Parliament resumed in August 1948, Smuts was back as leader of the opposition, but now representing a different, "safe" riding, thanks to the stepping down of its MP, and Jan Hofmeyr had been relegated to the sidelines, where he nevertheless remained a powerful lieutenant in a political party dreadfully short of talent. My parents and most of their friends were confident that Smuts, in spite of his advanced years, would save the day.

Anxiety nevertheless began to take hold of some of our friends, who detested the arrogant, opinionated and self-righteous Malan and did not doubt the lengths to which he would go to retain power. The Zastrosnys had been long-time United Party members and now quickly persuaded my parents to join the party to help fight an upcoming by-election caused by the standing down of our local MP (and neighbour), Lieutenant Colonel Karel Rood, a long-time

Smuts supporter, who was seriously ill. "We can't afford to lose Vereeniging to the Nats," said Ernest, and my parents agreed.

Malan, who had in the meantime unfurled his reforming banner and promised to bring the racial situation "under control" by introducing his "Apartheid" program, nevertheless moved stealthily so as not to jeopardize his grip on power. A first step would be to ensure that the blacks and coloured folk of the Cape Province did not continue to have more rights and privileges than those in the Transvaal, even if this meant tinkering with a constitutional provision guaranteeing the limited franchise they now enjoyed. Doing this without running the risk of a reprimand from judges would take time. He took other steps to turn the clock back, ignoring Smuts's criticism while implementing minor administrative measures, such as establishing a Grievance Commission to compensate all those who had been punished by Smuts for opposing South Africa's role during the Second World War—in other words, those convicted of pro-Nazi activities. He also introduced job reservation rules in order to benefit the poor whites, shut down artisan training for the blacks and imposed on Cape Town the need for segregated railway carriages, buses and post office queues. He promptly reversed Smuts's policy of attracting immigrants, especially those coming from the United Kingdom; the man was thorough.[8] In the first days of December, Malan got unexpected help through the deaths of his most outspoken critics—Hendrick van der Bijl and then Jan Hofmeyr, two of Smuts' best lieutenants. From now on the aged General Smuts was left to lead almost single-handedly the remnants of the United Party.

The Vereeniging By-Election

The Vereeniging by-election was scheduled for February 1949, and in order to prepare for the event the local branch of the United Party, now reinforced by more members, organized a huge fête on the grounds of the Vereeniging Golf and Country Club. The fête was conceived around the theme of multiculturalism with a strong folk-fest element, and accordingly each residential district of the riding organized a stand selling typical "ethnic" foods. A platform was erected in the middle of the grounds for staging folk dances and other musical offerings.

Ernest and Betty Zastrosny were in charge of the Unitas Park contribution, and by sheer coincidence our neighbourhood's theme was Holland. A theatrical agency in Johannesburg provided costumes, including folksy garments for Dirla and me. My mother volunteered to bake *poffertjes* (small, traditional Dutch pastries cooked in a copper frying pan specially made for the purpose, with

---

8. Hancock, *Smuts*, 512.

depressions the size of a shallow cups to hold the batter while it rose and cooked). There were Scottish country dances, a performance of the Black Watch Highland Pipe Band, and Lebanese and even Indian stands selling snacks.

The highlight of the event was the ceremonial arrival of General Smuts in a baby-blue Cadillac convertible owned by Mr. Maxwell, the proprietor of Fick's Garage. The aged warrior delivered a bilingual address lasting well over an hour; he spoke alternately in English and Afrikaans, mainly about the threat to civilization around the world from the growing aggressiveness of Soviet Russia, now engulfing the hapless countries of central Europe, and the disturbing developments in China, where the Kuomintang were on the point of defeat. He also spoke of his vision of making South Africa strong economically and advancing the welfare of the Bantu population to prevent the country from descending into the sort of chaos that was now affecting places like Indonesia, Malaya and French Indochina. It was a moving performance, partly because of the age and patrician bearing of the speaker, but Smuts failed to stem the growing tide of the National Party's electoral appeal. He said nothing to placate the poor white voters of Vereeniging who feared being swamped by the rapidly rising population of better-educated black workers. The only thing Smuts could wholeheartedly share with the electorate was fear itself: Smuts feared the demise of Western civilization and they feared *die swart gevaar* (the black danger).

Notwithstanding our efforts at the UP fête, the by-election of May 1949 went to the "Nats," whose candidate, Dr. Johan Hendrik Loock, represented the district for the following four years.[9] Almost simultaneously Malan ensured a permanent electoral grip on Parliament by enfranchising white voters in the former German colony and now mandated territory of South West Africa,[10] in defiance of United Nations resolutions. Two months later Malan introduced the first of his Apartheid legislation: the Prohibition of Mixed Marriages Act. Since it applied to a tiny portion of the population it met with little opposition in the country, but this grotesque piece of legislation was a blow to the distinctive Cape Coloured community,[11] who were now confronted with the first step in a determined onslaught that would deprive them of such modest rights as they had enjoyed since the founding of the Cape Colony.

With the excitement of the by-election out of the way, our daily life reverted to its normal pattern; neither the abstruse and sometimes heated parliamentary debates nor the war of words in the newspapers really affected us directly. My mother continued to work in the office at Fick's Garage, answering letters and

---

9. Professor J. P. Brits (Cape Town University), personal communication.

10. Today's Namibia.

11. This predominantly Afrikaans-speaking community had forebears among the original European and Malay settlers, as well as the Hottentot and Bantu peoples.

keeping track of customer accounts, while my father was fully engaged in the Duncansville and Sharpeville municipal housing projects; our menagerie of animals was well looked after; and Juf puttered quite contentedly about the house, while I went to school. Living out of town, we were not bothered much by the threat of robbery, and so did not need iron bars in front of each window. The sky was always blue and wonderful vacations lay in store for us in the future: the game reserve, the Drakensberg mountain resorts and the Natal beaches.

Japie Krige Street, where we lived, formed an approximate boundary between the well-to-do and the humbler folk in their smaller homes. Across the road from us lived "Ma Tromp," as we cheekily called her; she was an elderly widow, as kind as she was large. Her home did not boast the convenience of a refrigerator (which we had), but she had a telephone, in those days a luxury that we did not enjoy. Out in her yard was a cool chest standing on stilts with a double wall of wire mesh holding in place small rocks kept wet by a constant dribble of water, and that was where she stored her meat and butter. Behind the house she had a chicken run. The only contact we had with Ma Tromp were to retrieve one of our pet dogs caught prowling around her chicken coop or, more rarely, to use her telephone, when it was absolutely necessary.

Next door to us, on a road running from our street to the highway, lived Dr. J. J. Joubert, our physician, and his daughter, Hilda, a tall, good-looking girl who was also in my class at school. Across the street from him, sheltered by a row of tall bluegums, was a large chicken farm that supplied the town with most of its eggs. These chickens were a magnet for snakes and we occasionally found the discarded silvery skin of a puff adder on our property.

My school, Unitas Park *Skool*, was located close to the centre of the population—in other words, near the western margin of Unitas Park, among the more humble homes. On the way to school, a slight detour would take my bicycle (a Raleigh three-speed racer bought for thirteen guineas[12]) past a small collection of shops in the very middle of Unitas Park; they were housed in an L-shaped, one-storey structure at an intersection. At the corner of the structure the builder had tried to provide a modicum of elegance by means of a gable fashioned in a style vaguely reminiscent of the charming eighteenth-century Cape Dutch farmsteads. Shelter from sun and rain was afforded to shoppers on the sidewalk flanking the shop by a corrugated iron roof supported by a series of square brick pillars. Under that roof, and next to the "bottle store" selling beer, was the shop where we spent our pocket money on school playground toys, such as marbles and coloured wooden spinning tops that one activated by winding a piece of string around the conical base and artfully throwing them onto the hard dirt ground.

12. A guinea was worth 21 shillings.

The Indians who owned and operated these stores lived somewhere else—where, no one knew nor cared as long as it was not in Unitas Park. In any case they kept to themselves. My school friends all lived near us and we mainly spoke Afrikaans among one another, although almost everyone was bilingual. The more anglophile friends of my parents, on the other hand, sent their children into town, either to a private school or to a so-called English Medium public school, but their children happened to be girls. For Egmond and me, arrangements were then in the works for us to complete our schooling at Grey College in Bloemfontein, a boarding school for boys, while Wynand undoubtedly would attend the local high school in town. In short the dwellings in Unitas Park housed inhabitants with a wide variety of outlooks and backgrounds, and the inadvertent phenomenon of segregation was clearly displayed with the wealthy cosmopolitan whites in the eastern section and the poor Afrikaners living in the west. Bantu and Asiatics were tolerated in our midst only when and where their presence was deemed essential, either as live-in servants or as shopkeepers commuting from somewhere else.

The roads traversing this neighbourhood made their own peculiar contributions to our colourful life. One day a horse, ambling along Japie Krige Street under the not-too-watchful gaze of his Bantu cowherd, had stumbled onto our cattle grid between the two brick pillars and had broken its leg. The police were called to help the poor animal out of its misery and before the night was out the horse carcass, now lying in our yard beside the driveway, had been butchered on the spot by an enthusiastic, uninvited influx of Bantus from the Vereeniging *lokasie*. It was not a pretty sight. The next morning, the municipality sent a truck and some labourers to pick up the remains. Life was interesting.

The semblance of peace in South Africa contrasted with the external world, where turmoil was common; it was a scary world, but most tensions were far away, in Asia and Europe, separated from us by the immense, partly uncharted and thinly populated African continent. In September 1949 the Russians tested an atomic bomb; two months later Polish independence was again snuffed out, followed within weeks by a complete victory of the Maoists in China.

However, in the new year, Malan introduced in the South African Parliament an avalanche of repressive legislation: the Group Areas Act, Immorality Amendment Act, Population Registration Act, and the Suppression of Communism Act. With so many worrying developments worldwide, foreign criticism of these South African legislative initiatives was absent. By the middle of the year, North Korea had launched its attack on the south, and in the United States Senator Eugene McCarthy had begun to look for reds under the beds.

Smuts, too tired to unite his party around a clear alternative vision, too tired to oppose Malan and his parliamentary steam-roller, nevertheless celebrated his eightieth birthday in grand style at huge gatherings throughout the country, but almost immediately thereafter was felled by a heart attack and died later that year, bitterly disappointed in the changed course of South African history. His death truly marked the end of an era. Now there was no one left to pursue a policy of interracial reconciliation (in the broadest interpretation of that phrase) as a political objective. Instead, the blurry racial segregation lines that had always been there were now being defined more sharply: accommodation had given way to rigid ideology born of fear, while parliamentary opposition had been reduced to brave, but very few, isolated voices.

My parents could not ignore these initiatives and changes. Within a remarkably short period, their feelings of optimism for a new future were eroded by the apparent loss of any government standard-bearer advocating moderation, a disturbing prospect of increased government repression encouraging more violence, and worst of all, international isolation. They had seen the remarkable transformation of Java from a seemingly peaceful paradise to a hellhole caused by racially based civil war. The prospects for South Africa, isolated at the southern tip of the huge continent, seemed far more threatening, and a bloodbath appeared inevitable. Their growing alarm was not fully shared by those who had always lived here and had long been accustomed to background noise of strife and repression.

1951

On a hot summer Sunday afternoon early in January 1951, I came home on my bicycle with my swimming trunks dangling from the handle bars and found a party seated on our *stoep*, enjoying drinks. Tom and Ina, my mother's sister and brother-in-law, had come down from Germiston for a weekend visit. Edu and Emmy had turned up with their three-year-old daughter, Beryl. She was seated in the shallow pond, playing with a homemade wooden boat and the lily pads. The sun had warmed the water and she wore nothing besides a pair of glasses.

A couple of years earlier my father had made the pond, a large round concrete dish sunk into the lawn. It had been stocked with goldfish, but a savvy, brilliant blue kingfisher had quickly discovered the prize and had established himself in the birch tree planted by my father conveniently (from the bird's point of view) beside the pond. The kingfisher had departed after he had made sure that the pond was free of fish. Little Beryl was therefore able to enjoy the water without concern about fish life. A more recent addition to their family lay in the pram, shaded by the same birch tree.

My mother thought that Beryl's defective eyesight might have been caused by her parents' failure to heed the warnings of the medical experts who had recommended the avoidance of pregnancies for five years by all women who had gone through the Japanese prison camp experience. However, she sympathized with Edu and Emmy; since their marriage had suffered such a bad beginning, one could understand their hurry to start a family.

Emmy, Edu and their two children had turned up unannounced, as was often the case. Seeing Beryl that afternoon reminded me of Joan, who was my age. I had very much enjoyed her company as a temporary boarder for a number of months in 1948, while her father, Hans Westenberg, was remarrying and building a new family home further up Japie Krige Street. However, Joan and her parents had recently sold their home and left town; they had become dismayed at the trend of South African politics and moved to Kenya, a marvellous land, richly endowed and facing a promising future run by an enlightened British colonial office. They were not alone. Others had left for Southern Rhodesia[13] for similar reasons, to escape the consequences of the 1948 election and the clear signs that a strict, doctrinaire social control policy was being implemented. Kenya and Southern Rhodesia were then bastions of liberal racial attitudes—at least that's the way it seemed from reading newspaper accounts. On the occasion of the Westenbergs' departure, my father's colleague, Ray Fone, who had served in Central Africa during the war, had wondered out loud whether Hans had been wise. "In spite of their supposedly liberal policies they seem to have some difficulties with the natives in Kenya," he said. "This fellow Jomo Kenyatta and his Mau Mau are causing problems."[14] If one looked beyond Africa it got worse: the war in Korea was going badly and there were more hostilities in French Indochina. In Europe Soviet power was expanding westward and the Cold War was in full swing.

As I joined the party on the veranda, my mother's tall and slenderly built sister, Ina, was describing her adventure on Charlie, my horse, whom she had borrowed that morning. She and her husband Tom had come for a weekend visit and the horse-riding trip had been successful, especially for her, because she had still been a bit rattled from her previous attempt to control Charlie. That was over a year ago, before her wedding. On that occasion, Charlie had stumbled when he stepped into a *dassie*[15] hole and Ina had taken a fall, breaking her arm. This time, she and my mother had again walked the horses down the length of Japie Krige Street to the north end of Unitas Park, from where they had easy access to the open spaces of the Transvaal veld. The gently undulating grassland belonged to a farmer, but his barbed wire fence was in poor repair and he did not seem to mind having strangers galloping across his fields. Ina had enjoyed her ride on Charlie and had commenced her account as a distraction from the otherwise serious mood that affected the company of friends, given the signs of a deteriorating international situation. When Ina had

13. Today's Zimbabwe.

14. The Mau Mau atrocities quickly escalated to a climax in 1952.

15 *Petromus typicus,* a rat-like creature living in burrows.

finished her tale, Emmy went to retrieve Beryl from the pond; they should go home. "Stay for dinner," my mother said. "We are having *nasi goreng.*" As she was saying that, another car, a green Hudson saloon, unexpectedly came down our driveway.

"Ach! There is Ray. How nice of him to come," my father exclaimed.

Ray emerged from the Hudson, dapper as always with his glasses and his neatly trimmed moustache, carrying in one hand his latest prized acquisition, a recording of the Litolf *Scherzo.* Clad in British army shorts, he was the very image of a fastidious gentleman officer. Ray had served with the *rooi lussies* brigade, and after his duties in Kenya had served at El Alamein; he liked to compare notes on his wartime experiences with Edu, who had served with the KNIL on Java. Ray jokingly referred to my father as *die vet kaas* and to Edu as *die maer kaas.* A person from Holland was commonly referred to as *kaaskop* (cheesehead) and after five years of good food my father had once more gained weight, whereas Edu had remained thin. As Ray closed the car door, he looked thoughtfully at one of the tires and gave it a kick.

My father chuckled at this sight and explained to Tom, "Ever since Ray had that flat tire in the eastern Transvaal, when the spare tire was also flat, he always kicks the tires." Having completed the tire-kicking ritual, Ray came to the *stoep* and was introduced to Tom. On a previous occasion, Ray had met Ina, and once there had even been speculation that he might have married her, but Ray was still a bachelor and gave every indication that this would be his permanent state.

"You must join us for dinner," my mother said. Ray accepted with alacrity. Bachelors in South Africa tended to have monotonous meals, unless they could find a really good cook. For Ina and Tom and also for Ray, an Indonesian meal was a novelty. In order to accommodate the new guest, my mother disappeared to the kitchen, where Josef was helping Juf.

Juf's English was poor and she therefore tended to shun these social occasions on the *stoep*, preferring instead to work behind the scenes. Besides, Juf liked working with Josef, and Josef had a high regard for Juf; at seventy-eight years of age, she was old enough to be his grandmother, and he treated her with great respect. Now the two were preparing a large *nasi goreng.* It would certainly not be a fancy meal, for it was impossible to get all of the necessary ingredients in Vereeniging, and the task would have been too taxing for Juf. The simplified version was, for most of the guests assembled, a rare treat, an exotic dish. The secret of its composition was one of the few assets (aside from the silver bowls, now filled with freshly roasted and salted peanuts) that we had brought back from our five-year stay in the Indies.

As the sun was approaching the horizon behind Ma Tromp's house, the atmosphere on the veranda moved uneasily between relaxation and concern. Tom started to fret. He was a thirty-six-year-old balding Scot from Aberdeen who had immigrated to South Africa in 1947, lured by the promise of ample employment opportunities. During the war he had been withheld from military service because of his metallurgical training and had been deemed essential for Britain's Lancaster bomber building program, but when the war came to an end, bombers were no longer needed and Tom became unemployed, like thousands of soldiers. Then he had caught sight of advertisements, placed by the South African High Commissioner, seeking immigrants. Tom had written for more information and had also received the booklet with the colourful cover and titled, *South Africa, Land of Sunshine and Opportunity*. Tom still had the copy, but had occasionally complained that the booklet had been somewhat misleading. This had become a hobby horse for him.

The booklet had explained that South Africa "is now a civilized country," and is no longer "dark" like the rest of the continent, but needed "powerful reinforcements of its European population," preferably from "parent stocks of the original pioneers." The booklet said nothing about the Bantu farmers who had long ago come from the north to populate the land, previously the exclusive domain of the aboriginal people we referred to as the "Bushmen." Tom observed, dryly, that the country was far less civilized than the booklet had made out; the "comportment" of many of its inhabitants was distinctly "uncivilized." Although the police force was mainly white, its behaviour had on a number of occasions been brutal, matching the behaviour of the *tsotsies*, the young Bantu thugs in the *lokasies* on the outskirts of Johannesburg and Germiston. The treatment of the trade unionists, who had recently attempted to agitate for improved working conditions, a perfectly normal phenomenon in Scotland, had in his opinion been disgusting. Tom worked in industry and had first-hand information.

"This economy runs on cheap black labour," he snorted. He came from a socialist family background and found this repressive aspect of South African society troublesome. But he was even more upset now, and after he had been introduced to Ray, a *rooinek*[16] who might sympathize with a Scot "from the old country," he said bluntly, "This bloody government has reneged on its promises!" He spoke with a distinct Aberdeenshire brogue. He had pursed his lips when uttering these words, enunciating each syllable clearly, and absentmindedly stroked his right arm, where he had an incurable skin complaint.

Now Edu joined the conversation. "Are you talking about Dönge's Citizenship Act?"

"I guess so," Tom replied, surly.

That new law with its far-reaching restrictions had been rushed through Parliament within an astonishingly short, one-week period and with minimal

---

16. Literally "redneck," a derogatory name for an English person.

debate.[17] Its introduction had been scheduled to coincide with a planned absence of General Smuts, who was being installed as Chancellor at Cambridge University (shortly before his death).

In an agitated voice Tom continued, "The Nats have driven one more spike into our ability to throw them out at the next election. When I came to South Africa the government promised me, as a British Citizen, South African citizenship within two years and hence the right to vote; that has been changed. The Nats want to keep immigrants off the voting lists because we might vote against them."

My parents had acquired South African citizenship prior to the passage of this act as a result of the previously existing liberal criteria, which had been designed to promote immigration and which also took our pre-war stay into account.

"Yes," Tom continued, "and it fits in with the aims of the Population Registration Act they passed last year. You know we will have to carry identity cards that indicate our racial classification. And now they are even forcing me to take Afrikaans lessons." From the way Tom uttered this last statement it was clear that he saw this as insult being added to injury.

"On this continent it may be necessary to have identification papers," Ray offered; he had spent enough time roaming Africa to have a feel for the immensity of the continent, the poverty of its inhabitants and the potential for chaos.

"Hey, van Oort, this is no different from a *pendafteran*, is it?" Edu remarked as he leaned towards my father. "Can you imagine the problems this will cause for some of Malan's supporters? I bet they do not want anyone to investigate their genetic background too closely. You know, in the camp I met a fellow called van der Post,[18] from a Free State farm—yes, and attached to the British army—a real *Japie*.[19] He admitted having native blood in his veins. I think he had a Hottentot grandmother, though he also admitted that he was a *rooinek boetie*,"[20] he added with a grin.

"What's a *pendafteran*?"

Edu explained the identity card system that had been imposed on us on Java during the Japanese occupation and had forced us into an eightfold racial purity classification system that had later been used as an arbitrary means of incarceration for political purposes. Emmy elaborated Edu's point, "Yes, and people were afraid. They tried to hide their ancestry, or spent a fortune trying to track it down. We had friends where husband and wife were suddenly forced to live apart because one party was deemed to be European and was imprisoned

---

17. Walker, *A History of South Africa*, 786.
18. Laurens van der Post.
19. Derogatory term for Afrikaner.
20. Anglophile—literally "redneck buddy."

and the other not. You could not tell the difference by looking at them and they never knew where they stood—they were imprisoned one day and the next day they were free again."

"Oh, the Population Registration Act is more flexible," commented Ray. "I believe it classifies a white person as one who obviously is white—and is generally not accepted as coloured, or words to that effect, though—" he hesitated, "I believe it also says that a person shall not be classified 'white' if one of his parents is classified coloured."

"Van der Post would be unwise to return to South Africa," Edu repeated.

"We had good *Belanda Indo* friends in Bandoeng," my mother added.

"What are *Belanda Indos*?"

"They're like Cape Coloured folk, Ray, people of mixed race."

This was hard for Ray to understand; such a situation was inconceivable in South Africa: no one would tolerate friendship with "coloureds." Even if one suspected on the basis of appearances that a friend might have had mixed ancestry, he or she was white and the topic of ancestry was avoided. The conversation was getting heated and my mother slipped away to the kitchen. She hastened back to announce that dinner was ready, so we all trooped inside and gathered around the large antique oak table.

My father asked me to get some extra chairs from the kitchen. There, Juf had assembled the dishes on a tea trolley and headed to the dining room with the *nasi goreng* garnished with strips of omelette, and side dishes of *ketimun* (cucumber), homemade *sambal* (red pepper paste), *pisang goreng* (fried banana), and *serunding* (roasted coconut). My father went off to get some beer, Lions Ale. While we were munching on our *sate* and fried rice the conversation continued to be dominated by the political situation.

"The future doesn't look good to me," said my father. "This government is swimming against a worldwide trend, and is using police-state tactics. You know, Edu, in retrospect the Indies felt a bit like a police state with all those guys, troublemakers, exiled to Boven Digoel. Was that not where Sukarno spent much time?" [21]

"Bou, I'm not sure we should go as far as that—police state—that's perhaps extreme. But Sukarno certainly learned to hate us, while becoming a martyr in the eyes of the Indonesians," Edu added.

"We need to work hard to get the United Party fighting this regime," said Ray. "A lot of the problems the Nats are trying to deal with reflect the growing incidence of crime, but they are only making it worse."

"You know," said my father, "I think we might one day have to flee this country."

"Why?" asked Ray.

---

21. On Dutch New Guinea (West Irian).

"I think the problems here are too difficult to solve."

"Sure! We have difficulties, particularly with this government, but to leave the country would be ratting out—ratting out—yes, I mean that—you can't do that! We must work to get the right politicians elected and set this country back on a civilized path." Ray then confided that he and many of his ex-servicemen were starting a political pressure group.

"A fellow called Malan, Sailor Malan, started it," said Ray. "He's no relative of the Prime Minister, oh no—he was a Second World War fighter pilot and was awarded a DFC."

"What do they want to do?"

"They want to rally support to defeat the Nats at the next election."

"Is he getting anywhere?"

"Yes, we think that membership might grow to a couple of hundred thousand, and some important people, including judges, are joining; it is called the Torch Commando."

"And if they succeed in getting the Nats out, what are they going to do? Give that young ANC fellow, what's his name, Mandela, what he is demanding—one man one vote?"

"Oh no! The Natives are not yet ready for the vote, but the Cape Coloureds should not be disenfranchised."

For the remainder of the evening, the conversation avoided the topic of politics. The discussion instead reverted to the game reserve and trips to Durban and other pleasant outings. Juf finally reached up to press the bell that hung from the wrought-iron chandelier over the table and Josef came to collect the dirty dishes. Juf disappeared with Josef to the kitchen to supervise and help with the cleaning up. Tom and Ina needed to get back to Germiston and left promptly. They were facing an hour's drive with a hungry baby, and tomorrow morning Tom would once more be at work at eight. Ray, who had drunk a bit too much and was tired, clutched his unplayed new record and took to his Hudson, driving home via the back roads. This left only Emmy and Edu seated with my parents at the table; Beryl had fallen asleep on the sofa and Edward was sleeping in his pram. They would stay a little longer…

Six months later, on a Saturday morning in June, the plans that my parents had hatched that evening with Edu and Emmy came to fruition. At breakfast, my father announced that we would make a trip to Johannesburg. My parents and I stepped into the Chevrolet, bade Juf goodbye, and set off.

Trips to Johannesburg were a treat for me; it was exciting being in the big city, and usually there was an opportunity to visit the zoo. I also enjoyed seeing the gold mines, the yellow piles of mine tailings, the huge winding gear with the vast wheels forever spinning, guiding the cables down through the deep mine shafts and either bringing gold ore up or moving the mineworkers to and from the rock face. The neon lights that were often on by the time we left for home and included animated images, fascinated me. As we turned onto the main road leading north, my father turned half around and said, "Boudy, we are going away, we are leaving Vereeniging. Where do you think we are going?"

The question stunned me. Not so long ago, we had been looking at houses to buy. We had visited a nice house halfway between Vereeniging and Johannesburg, a whitewashed cottage with a thatched roof, perched on one of the many ridges that ran over the southern Transvaal landscape, interrupting the two-thousand-foot descent from where Johannesburg was located on the Rand to the valley of the Vaal River. The view from the house had been breathtaking, and I had not questioned the practicality of living so far out in the country, away from schools, and away from my parents' places of work. The prospect of moving to that house had struck me as the beginning of another immense adventure.

"Aren't we buying the house we saw?"

"No, we are leaving South Africa, and today we are collecting our tickets and visas. Where do you think we are going?"

The most exotic place I could think of was Switzerland, the land of wooden chalets and wonderful mountains covered with snow. That country I had seen in 1947, while on the visit to Holland; we had spent two weeks there with my father's relatives to give my grandparents a break during that terrible winter when everything was in short supply and we had been stranded by the burning of the MV *Bosfontein*. That visit had made a deep impression on me.

"No, we are not going to Switzerland. Try again."

"New Zealand?"

In the past, my father had sometimes mentioned New Zealanders he had met in the internment camps and had been impressed by their being an earthy, unpresumptuous and friendly group of people.

"No, we are going to Canada," my mother said.

I was flabbergasted. I knew where Canada was from school geography lessons, but that was all.

A week later, the travel arrangements my parents had so surreptitiously and carefully made were quickly put into effect. We left our house in Unitas Park and took up temporary residence with Edu and Emmy. The house and all of its contents had been sold in advance. All that we took with us to Edu's house were some books, clothes, paintings and the antique Dutch clock my father had inherited from his father. He had tried to sell the clock too, but at the last minute the purchase did not go through, and so we left South Africa with one more item than planned. My father set about furiously making a good packing crate for the clock. He and my mother had planned this trip under an impressive shroud of secrecy to ensure that the maximum amount of cash could be generated from the sale of our belongings, for the trip was bound to be expensive. Juf would accompany us to Holland, where she would remain, sharing a home with her sister in Amsterdam. Whether she would later join us in Canada was unclear. She had some ailments that were worrying and she was nearly eighty years old.

"Emmy, Edu, Beryl and Edward are also leaving," said my mother. "We will see each other again in Canada."

To our friends, the sudden departure came as a tremendous shock. Ray Fone once more reiterated his disappointment that "we were ratting out" of an unpleasant political situation.

We Move Again

Moving halfway around the world in 1951 was a costly and lengthy undertaking. A Webster Airlines DC-4 took us from Johannesburg Airport to Rome, where we would transfer to a KLM Lockheed Constellation flying the Jakarta–Amsterdam route. At Livingston airport,[22] on a refuelling stop, the plane developed engine trouble, causing a twelve-hour delay. Since the airport building closed at eleven o'clock at night, the passengers had to return to the plane for the remainder of a freezing highveld winter's night, to await the completion of repairs and take off at dawn. Fuelling stops were also necessary at Nairobi, Cairo and Athens, and we missed our connection in Rome, so were forced to spend three days sightseeing, waiting for the next KLM plane to arrive. Juf was too sick to do anything other than remain in her hotel room, while my parents and I roamed around the Eternal City.

During our two-week stay in Holland, we saw Juf settled with her sister in Amsterdam and bought clothing for the expected Canadian winter weather, attempting thereby to make use of our Dutch savings; in this way my father circumvented the strict exchange control legislation that prevented him from taking the money out of the country.

The overnight Hook-to-Harwich packet boat service conveyed us to England, and by train we travelled from East Anglia to Southampton, with just enough time in London to spend a day at the South Bank exhibition, where the "Festival of Britain" was in full swing. In Southampton we boarded an immigrant ship, the Cunard Liner *Georgic*, which deposited us five days later at pier 21 in Halifax. An immigrant train then took us to Montreal.

In Montreal we met up with Edu, who had left Emmy and the two children behind in Holland, pending his finding employment and a place to live. With Edu we bought a second-hand station wagon and began the journey west,

---

22. In Zambia.

drawn by reports of the Edmonton oil boom and a desire to see the country, including the West Coast. This undertaking was made challenging by the failure of our travel agent in South Africa to secure a visa for the United States, where McCarthyism was in full swing. We therefore were forced to take the Trans-Canada Highway, then under construction, around the north shore of Lake Superior. The journey came to an abrupt end in Edmonton, Alberta, because the Yellowhead Highway, the only route through the Canadian Rockies, was washed out.

We rented a house from Mme Fortier, and shortly thereafter Emmy arrived from Holland with her two children. And so our *kongsi* was once again back together, under one roof. What a lot we had gone through over the fourteen years since we had first met.

That first year in Canada was difficult. Edu lacked specialist training and was forced once again to look for a position in commerce, but now without financial assistance from his father. Without a Canadian university degree, my father's options for work were restricted, and he initially had to make do with a draughtsman's position. The two families moreover were forced to share a single home once again—"a bit like Tjihapit," Emmy joked at the time, "but with running water, a stove we are allowed to use and functioning toilets."

Within the first year I nevertheless acquired a younger brother, Peter. My father had never forgotten the bewildered teenage lad he had taken under his wing in Tjimahi, and it was that bittersweet memory that prompted him to name my young brother so.

Shortly thereafter a government architectural position became available in Ottawa, and so we once more were on the move. Our departure from Edmonton was memorable on account of a bizarre, last-minute encounter with Ank and Ben. They had just arrived in town and by chance heard of our presence. At a dinner party given by the professor of dentistry under whose tutelage Ben hoped to acquire Canadian qualifications, a conversation took place between two other guests, one of whom wanted to go to South Africa, while the other one retorted hearing of recent arrivals from South Africa who had expressed misgivings about the place. Since Ben had also entertained thoughts of resettling in South Africa, he was curious to learn more about these people, and discovered it was us, former patients and friends from Bandoeng. We had not seen Ben since 1942, and had last seen Ank near the end of August 1945, when she escaped from Tjideng, determined to make her way to Bandoeng to find Ben, unaware that the Javanese countryside was on the point of exploding with the ugliest conflict imaginable.

What a bizarre world to enable such unexpected encounters at opposite ends of the globe, and what strange turns our lives had taken over those last twenty years.

EPILOGUE

On Friday, July 20, 1962 I bade my father, mother, brother Peter and cousin Ian farewell at the departure gate of Madrid airport. So far the summer vacation had been most enjoyable.

After a brief stopover in Lisbon my parents would return to Ottawa and home, where they would then make preparations for an upcoming visit from old friends: Emmy and Edu had promised to visit my parents as part of a trip also taking them to Syracuse, in New York state, where one of Edu's brothers had settled. They would be accompanied by their two children, Beryl, now fourteen years old, and Edward, eleven. It was exactly ten years since we had parted company in Edmonton, when we moved to Ottawa and they remained in Alberta. I had not seen Emmy and Edu for so long, and yet I knew that our relationship had been significant. It was a reunion I would unfortunately miss.

It was this jumble of thoughts that crowded my mind at the departure gate of the Madrid airport. Standing on my tiptoes I caught a last view of my parents; my father was fussing with the travel documents but my mother looked back, over the heads of other passengers, and gave a final wave.

Then they were gone, leaving me standing there, fiddling with the car keys in my pocket. There was an empty feeling in the pit of my stomach, a feeling I could not place. Was it the experience of suddenly being alone in a foreign place after spending the previous three weeks traversing Europe, packed together in a car? Or was it something else? Perhaps I was tired, for we had, after all, spent three days in Madrid being tourists: the Prado museum, the medieval town of Toledo, El Escorial monastery and, of course, the sidewalk cafés. The July days had been hot, and the nights short. The physical constitution of the Spanish, with their love of late nights and early mornings, struck us as formidable. It had been a fascinating but exhausting visit.

I slowly left the departure hall and walked back to the rented Ford Consul station wagon, puzzling over it all. I got into the car and consciously set my mind on the coming days, the long trip through northern Spain, France and Belgium to England and Oxford and the comforts of the familiar stone walls of College and the friendly, gruff greeting of Doug, the head College porter, who seemed to know each one of "the young gentlemen," especially their foibles. I was also trying to focus on the next adventure, a second trip through Europe with my recently acquired student friends. It had been a bit extravagant taking two trips, but there was little else to do. The College would not allow students to remain in their rooms during the vacation, and unlike most of my fellow undergraduates, I had no family home in Britain. The next summer "vac," I knew I would have to concentrate on my studies and start preparing for the final exams, but I would then move out of College and into "digs," taking a room in a boarding house or, alternatively, sharing a flat with other students.

It had been many years since I last enjoyed a vacation with my family. Increasingly, summer employment had taken precedence over family functions. This trip had therefore been suffused with nostalgia and the pleasure of once more being united with loved ones, but had in truth been precipitated by my parents' desire to see me in my new university surroundings; the subsequent car journey had been a luxurious add-on, the icing on the cake.

The next trip with my friends would be different. Instead of staying in hotels it would be in tents in crowded European campsites. The travel plans for that trip would complement what I had seen thus far, for now we would head east to Italy, Austria and Germany. Paris I would see a second time, but then there was so much to see in Paris.

My new friend, John, from Cape Town, had taken the lead in planning the route and had already purchased a van, a Bedford "Commer," big enough to transport five with camp gear. Mike, an old school friend from Ottawa, had come over for his first look at Europe and agreed to join us on this expedition, as had Janet, John's South African girlfriend. In order to provide her with some female company we had advertised the trip in London and got an enthusiastic response from Beatrice, a footloose Australian girl. A swing through Europe in the company of four fellow students would be an exciting contrast to the trip I had just completed, and I was keenly looking forward to the coming adventure. Now, as I drove north over the hot, dry Castilian plain to Pamplona, the Pyrenees and the French border, there was plenty of time to think, to dream about the future and to relive the recent past.

After "Eights Week," Oxford had been at its best for my parents' visit: the weather had been glorious, bathing the ochre-coloured ancient buildings (at least those that had been cleaned of soot) with a golden light. The May trees sheltering the towpath along the Isis were still in flower, filling the air with their distinctive, pungent fragrance; the College gardens were beautiful, with some wisteria and japonica blossoms still on the vines hanging from the College walls, and the laburnum tree standing in the corner of the Merton Fellows Garden was still acting like a bright yellow homing beacon for those walking through Christ Church Meadows at dusk. In the Turf Tavern, snugly nestled beneath the ancient mediaeval town wall and accessible only through a narrow passageway, my family had met some of my new friends over a ploughman's lunch, while bells pealed the midday hour from numerous, somewhat uncoordinated church steeples. I had felt on top of the world, having just completed my first year in an entirely new, fascinating field of study and in the company of bright, entertaining, good-natured students. What was almost more thrilling was the success of our College First Eight on the river Isis, my very first sporting achievement. I had found student life in Oxford to be more idyllic than I had dared to dream.

Peter, my young brother, had clearly enjoyed the visit as well. I was glad that we had been able to find things to amuse a ten-year-old boy; punting on the Cherwell River had been great fun, particularly when he discovered how treacherous the floor of the Cherwell could be, with soft spots here and there in the muddy bottom catching you unawares as the punt pole got stuck, with you, the pole or the punt likely to part company.

My cousin, Ian, who had also come along from Canada, had also enjoyed the trip and had thoughtfully bought some gifts for his parents—for his mother, an old map of Holland picked up on the banks of the Seine from a second-hand bookseller, and for his father, a black steel Toledo dish ornately decorated with gold and silver filigree. Those had been good souvenirs, I thought. His parents, Tom and Ina, had stuck it out in South Africa for two more years after we left and had then followed us to Canada. For them, too, it had been difficult making a fresh start in Canada, but none of us had ever experienced regrets about leaving South Africa.

There was a sense of peace and security in Canada that was missing in South Africa, which had, not surprisingly, been turned into a pariah state by defiant, ideologically driven rulers brought to power by a frightened electorate. In March 1960, when the Ottawa *Journal* headlines screamed "Sharpeville Massacre," my father had been able to say, "I was afraid of that." The situation in South Africa had gone from bad to worse, very much as my father had predicted, although for the time being it was the blacks who were being killed, and not the whites, as he had expected would one day happen. That this unfortunate event had taken place in Sharpeville, the same Sharpeville he had designed, was pure coincidence; it could have happened anywhere in South Africa. The South African student friends I had met in Oxford were as aghast at the situation as I had been, but it was hard to explain to other friends, who did not know the country, how complicated it all was. My family had left those troubles behind, but it had been easy for us, for our ties to the land were minimal; it had also been that way when we left Java. For my South African friends it was more difficult; it really was their country and I felt heartily sorry for them: deep societal roots can simultaneously be a curse and a blessing.

On August 20, 1962, we arrived, tired and dirty, in Vienna after a hot day's trip from Klagenfurt. Admittedly the air of intoxication with which I had started out on my second European tour had begun to wear off. Venice had been a disappointment: the crowds of visitors overwhelming, the atmosphere beastly hot and humid, and the citizens seemingly rapacious. "A big tourist trap," John had called it. None of us had any familiarity with the Italian language, so we moreover felt defenceless. Although the city was stunningly beautiful, we began to see some of these European cities as glorified theme parks, kept alive solely through the tourist industry. Austria had been a welcome relief from Italy. In particular I enjoyed once more being able to communicate with the population, using my limited knowledge of the German language. This mountainous country with its pastoral landscape somehow seemed cleaner and more orderly. Upon reaching Vienna, which unfortunately was almost as hot as Venice, we planned to do a bit of sightseeing, more out of a sense of duty than with enthusiasm, but now refreshed by showers and a fairly comfortable night's rest—in sharp contrast to some of our previous camping experiences along the Mediterranean coast.

The next morning we woke up with the noise of holidaymakers all around us, consumed a breakfast of cereal, *brötchen* and jam, and after tidying up, departed for town. We drove to the *Kärtner Ring Straße*, Vienna's famous main street, looking for our first stop, the American Express office, to cash some traveller's cheques and pick up the mail, this being one of the few forwarding addresses we had given to family and friends.

After parking the Bedford under the shade of some linden trees we strolled to the office, watching the Viennese enjoying coffee at sidewalk cafés, and glancing at the beautiful displays in jewellery and fur shops. The clerk behind the counter took a list of our names to the back to check the mailboxes and soon returned with three or four letters. Among them was an envelope addressed to me, but with no postage stamps: inside I found a very short note, which read, "Dear Mr. van Oort: Please contact the Canadian Embassy."

The address and telephone number were included. The clerk allowed me to place a call, and a voice at the other end told me that there was bad news and suggested that I come over. The embassy was only a few blocks away, so while John fed some more *schillings* into the parking meter, the rest of us went ahead. At the embassy I was ushered into the presence of the consul, who introduced himself as Mr. Hardy and told me that there had been an accident in Ottawa, that my father had tried to contact me. The consul now offered me the use of the embassy phone for calling our home in Ottawa. My father answered the phone after a number of rings; later I realized that I had called him out of bed.

"Boudy, I have terrible news. *Mammie* is gone, she is dead."

His voice sounded broken, old. Thunderstruck, I stammered, "What happened?"

After a brief pause, my father explained about a car trip; he and Edu in one car "following *mammie's* car, in which Emmy was seated—a head-on collision— Emmy died instantly." For three days my mother fought a hopeless battle with massive internal injuries. Since my father did not know where or when he could reach me, he had gone ahead with the funeral. "It's all over," he said.

"And what about Peter?"

"He had gone to stay with Ina and Tom in Pierrefonds,"[1] my father answered.

"I am coming home—I'll send a telegram with the arrival time." I gently laid down the phone, too stunned to say anything more. Mr. Hardy eyed me with a concerned expression on his face.

Suddenly that final departure scene in Madrid came flooding back to me. Was it a premonition that had made me so sad? Mr. Hardy kindly offered assistance, but I told him that I would discuss what to do with my friends. I left the consul's office and conveyed to my friends, anxiously waiting in the reception area, the awful news. "You must go right away," said John. "We will get you on a plane somehow."

On the way to the Bedford, Janet awkwardly put her arm over my shoulder trying to comfort me. We returned to the campsite to pick up my belongings, and then found our way to Schwechat, Vienna's international airport, hoping that somehow an airline ticket to Montreal could be secured. The Air Austria ticket agent sprang into action and was able to arrange seats on three interconnecting flights, from Vienna to Zurich, Zurich to London, and from London to Montreal; I could board immediately. We paid for the ticket by pooling our financial resources, and I sent a telegram to my father to let him know my time of arrival the next day.

"Will you be okay for the journey home?" I asked John, for so much money had suddenly gone through our hands and I was too dazed to have any ability to think these things through.

"We'll be okay. Don't worry, Boudy."

Fortunately we had not long to wait; the agony of departure was short. I said goodbye to my friends, who had just become so much dearer to me, and I was the last person to proceed through the departure gate to board the flight. I found my seat on the plane, and sank down by the window. Outside, the merciless August sun shone on the hustle and bustle of the airport and radiated its heat through the window.

The broken voice of my father over the telephone haunted me, and the emotional memories of that day, almost seventeen years before, when I had first seen him after the war, came flooding back. There was nothing left to do now but think, trying to piece together life's puzzling fragments. Emmy and my mother, dying together, both gone—after all those bitter years, which I had long ago stuffed into the deepest recesses of my memory. For years, as a youth, I had thought of nothing aside from the future, and now I was suddenly forced

---

1. Near Montreal.

to contemplate the confusing past—bits of it were clear, events that had stood out in my mind as though they had happened yesterday, but the connecting threads were muddled and unclear.

My thoughts were interrupted by the air hostess instructing us in German, English and French to do up our seatbelts, and showing us how to put on our life jackets and bend forward in case of an emergency. The plane's engines started up, and my mind wandered off again as I tried to recall the few words spoken by my father: "Emmy died instantly, *mammie* died three days later." Emmy and *mammie!* They had shared so much. Emmy and *mammie* living in Edmonton, and before that in Unitas Park, where they had so often sat on the *stoep* talking about the old days on Java. And then there was that wonderful time when they met each other once again, after the war—where was that? Johannesburg? Sterkfontein? What warmth there had been after the shared hardships of the camp years! At the time I had found those emotions difficult to comprehend, because I was so young. Emmy and *mammie* in Tjideng, Emmy and *mammie* on the nightmarish train journey, Emmy and *mammie* in Tjihapit, Emmy and *mammie* as far back as my memory went. How tragic, I thought, that their relationship should have to end like this.

The flood of memories was interrupted by the plane having arrived at the end of the runway, turning around and readying itself for takeoff: next stop Zurich. I fumbled for my tickets, nervous that I might misplace them, my precious tickets and passport, and I studied the itinerary: how long a stopover? When would the BEA flight leave? Would there be enough time to make the connection? Then to London Heathrow, where I would have to make my way to the terminal serving transatlantic flights, to catch the Air Canada flight. I would have several hours' wait in London, plenty of time, I hoped, to make that vital connection. And then across the Atlantic, a ten-hour flight, with fuelling stops at Shannon and Gander, arriving in Dorval at noon the next day. I tried to figure out the actual travel time, but my mind could not cope with the arithmetic.

The plane began to move forward, then gathered speed. Outside the window the terminal building whizzed past, we sped past other taxiing planes, more runways, a blur of grass, and then we were up with the engines whining, and the whirr of the machinery pulling in the flaps and retracting the wheels. I closed my eyes and tried to rest, for it would be a long, tiring flight.

At Montreal's Dorval airport, my father, Peter and Oma (my maternal grandmother, who had joined us in Canada only four years before, after Opa, her husband, had died) were waiting in the arrival hall. How my father had aged in those last three weeks! The lines on his face betrayed many sleepless nights. Peter, too, had changed; the cheerful spunk of Madrid and the holiday trip was gone. He was quiet and looked bewildered. Little was said until we came home, and my father recounted the calamity.

Edu and Emmy and their two children, Beryl and Edward, had arrived on Friday, August 17 from Alberta. On the following day the two families went for a boat trip up the Rideau River. The *Sarie Marais*, the boat my father and I had built, was moored at Manotick, a small town along the Rideau River, some ten miles south of Ottawa. From there they had sailed upstream to Smith's Falls, a picturesque nineteenth-century town, before returning in the late afternoon. On the way home from the Manotick marina my mother was driving her little black Riley sedan, with Emmy sitting in the passenger seat and Edward in the rear seat, while my father followed in the Austin Westminster with Edu sitting next to him in the front and Beryl behind. After a few miles a Volkswagen came into view driving south from Ottawa towards Manotick. Coming up fast behind the Volkswagen was a large Chevrolet. The driver, John Edwin Molyneux, was in a hurry, but he was also drunk. Rather than slow down for the Volkswagen until the oncoming traffic had gone past, he chose to overtake it on the broad gravel shoulder to the right. When Molyneux tried to regain the pavement, the rear wheels spun and the vehicle careered over to the other side of the road, in front of the Volkswagen, narrowly missing it, but colliding head-on with my mother. Her little car crumpled and flew into the air before coming down in a cloud of dust and splintered glass. My father brought his car to a shrieking stop to avoid greater disaster. Molyneux was flung from his car by the impact. My mother and Molyneux's passenger suffered fatal internal injuries. "Both vehicles were mangled into masses of twisted metal by the force of the crash. Wreckage was strewn over the highway and some pieces were 100 feet from the cars," the Ottawa Journal had stated.[2] My father, Edu and Beryl had seen the entire ghastly drama unfold before their eyes.

For the second time in twenty years, my father helped my mother out of the wreckage of a car. Emmy was lifeless and Eddy was badly injured. For three days my mother clung to life in the hospital. She was anxious to know how Emmy was, but for fear of causing her any more stress, my father never told her that Emmy had died upon impact. So had Molyneux.

The last words my mother uttered were *"Onkruid vergaat niet"* (Weeds don't perish). According to my father she had smiled, almost cheerful, when she said that.

I returned to Oxford in time for the commencement of Michaelmas term and further studies; my father married Henny, a long-time family friend, and thanks largely to her efforts Peter grew up to be a fine young man. The family moved to Vancouver, where Peter flowered into manhood surrounded by the

---

2. *Ottawa Journal*, Aug 20, 1962.

mountains and sea. He became an avid skier, paraglider and sailor, and with every achievement my father's pride swelled. Peter was his joy: he was so much more like my father than I had been, perhaps owing to genes or reflecting the war's interruption. My father moreover had been able to follow and encourage every developmental step Peter took. At age twenty Peter trained to be a pilot; the financial wherewithal came from an insurance policy in my mother's name.

"Paying in this way for your flying lessons is a fitting use of that legacy," my father had said.

By age twenty-six, Peter had become the second officer on wide-bodied Boeing 737s flying on western Canadian routes. He loved his job, but it did not last long. On Wednesday, February 25, 1978, the phone rang early in the morning in my Edinburgh home. Outside, the snow lay thick on the ground and more was falling, and consequently I had got out of bed a bit earlier than usual, worried about getting to my office in Queen Street. My initial reaction was that Bob, my boss, had an urgent message for me, perhaps requesting me to attend a business meeting on his behalf in London, or advising me to stay home pending improvement of the road conditions.

However, it was my father's voice on the other end of the line. I could hardly make out what he was saying, for he was in great distress.

"Boudy, I have terrible news—Peter is dead. The plane he was flying had an accident while landing in a blizzard at Cranbrook[3]—snowplough on the runway."

I could not believe my ears. What a cruel fate had befallen this man, that he should have to deliver the same message twice within the space of sixteen years. This time I attended the funeral, a moving event because several of the plane's crew had died and a combined ceremony had been arranged; it was Canada's worst civil aviation disaster to date. My father's spirit was broken, and a goodly part of it never recovered. For Henny, his second wife, who had herself taken such a courageous leap into the unknown when she had married my father, the loss of Peter was equally devastating.

Two years later, Edu died after a terrible struggle with cancer. He and his new wife had also settled on the west coast of Canada, and from time to time my father and Edu had still been able to reminisce about the many shared experiences during those fateful years of the Second World War. Now only my father was left to nurse those memories, for Henny had endured the war in Holland.

But the human spirit is wonderful! For another ten years they enjoyed the company of friends and laughed in the beautiful chalet my father had so lovingly built on the Sunshine Coast, west of Vancouver. For ten more years

---

3. Town nestled in the mountains of eastern British Columbia.

they enjoyed glimpses of the sparkling waters of Georgia Strait through the tall Douglas firs and cedars, my father's cathedral.

Postscripts

Juf who had remained in Holland when we moved to Canada, died in 1954 after a struggle with cancer.

The Williams family, whom we met in November 1945 on the *Orontes*, found life in Scotland difficult. Their first venture, a hotel business, was a failure. Bob and Adie spent their remaining years managing a youth hostel on the Scottish west coast island of Arran. Robin married an American Air Force pilot and settled in America. Chris married a Scottish girl, but being unable to find employment in devastated post-war Britain, emigrated to Canada, served for many years with the Royal Canadian Air Force, and happily retired to a farm in the bucolic Comox valley on Vancouver Island.

Ank and Ben started a dental practice in Alberta, and finally retired to a cottage on one of the islands dotting the Georgia Strait off Vancouver Island.

Elsa escaped from Java in the back seat of a fighter plane, fell in love with flying and spent most of her life in the skies over Africa before retiring to Oxford.

Many of our other friends who had remained behind on Java because of family ties finally had to leave in 1957, and ended up scattered around the world.

Ray Fone admitted years later that my father had been right about leaving South Africa.

GLOSSARY

Note that for the spelling of Malay words I have adhered to the orthography defined in Kramer's *Kamus Belanda*, a Dutch-Indonesian dictionary prepared by Dr. Sudjito Danusaputro, professor of Medicine at the Universitas Indonesia, and published by G. B. van Goor Zonen, 1966.

For Japanese terms I have used the Random House *Japanese-English Dictionary*, 1995.

(Mal=Malay, Jap=Japanese, Afr=Afrikaans, Dut=Dutch, M/D Malay-Dutch.)

	Language	English meaning
ajam	Mal	chicken
anak	Mal	child
anglo	Mal	terracotta charcoal stove
apartheid	Afr	separateness
appel	Dut	roll call
atap	Mal	roofing material made from palm tree leaves
babu	Mal	maid—house maid, nurse maid
bangsat	Mal	criminal, rascal
bandjir	Mal	flood
barang	Mal	baggage
bebek	Mal	duck
Belanda	Mal	European
Belanda Indo	Mal	Eurasian
Belanda totok	Mal	pure European
bendi	Mal	two-wheeled horse drawn cart
betja	Mal	three-wheeled pedicab
bloemen	Dut	flowers
boerewors	Afr	farmer's sausage
bolos	Mal	quietly escape
braai	Afr	abbreviation for *braaivleis*—a barbecue
bung	Mal	brother
bunkus	Mal	packages, bundles
busuk	Mal	stinking, smelly; *pasar busuk* flea market
dapur	Mal	kitchen
dassie	Afr	*procavia capensis*—a small, ground-dwelling herbivore related to the elephant
desa	Mal	Javanese village, country district
diplomasi	Mal	diplomacy

djenggot	Mal	beard
djeruk	Mal	citrus fruit, *djeruk Bali*—pomelo
djongos	Mal	waiter (literally "boy")
donga	Afr	gully (Bantu word)
es loli	Mal	popsicle
gedek(n)	Mal	panels of woven bamboo strips used for house construction; the enclosure of prison camps made of this material
gedekking(v)	Mal	illicit trade through the camp enclosure
genjumin	Jap	native of an area
gezellig	Dut	cozy, convivial
gila	Mal	crazy, insane
golok	Mal	machete
grobak	Mal	two-wheeled cart, usually drawn by a horse or water buffalo
gudang	Mal	storage area ("go down")
gula	Mal	sugar
han	Jap	district; part of a town
haragei	Jap	literally "stomach art"—elliptical conveyance of true feelings
heiho	Jap	assistant soldier
hormat	Mal	respect
ijiwaru basan	Jap	nasty old woman
inlander	Dut	native
kaffir	Afr	Bantu, regardless of tribal links
kafir	Mal	unbelievers
kaicho	Jap	leader, chairman
kaki	Mal	feet
kali	Mal	river
kambing	Mal	goat; also the fourth-class train carriage
kampong	Mal	cluster of houses
kangkung	Mal	a type of water lily, also called water spinach
katjung	Mal	street urchin
kawat	Mal	wire—in this text, barbed wire
kawatploeg	M/D	wall-repair team (*ploeg* is pronounced *plugh*, rhyming with Scottish *Loch*)
kelambu	Mal	mosquito netting

kelip-kelip	Mal	fireflies
kepalla	Mal	head (of a household)
kerak	Mal	crusty, burnt food
kerei	Jap	salute (a superior)
ketimun	Mal	cucumber
kiai	Mal	Koranic legal expert
ki-o-tsukete	Jap	take heed!
kipas	Mal	Hand-held fan for fires
klas	Mal	class
klas kambing	Mal	goat class (fourth-class railway carriage)
klawang	Mal	large knife, machete
kneusjes	Dut	bruised ones (usually applied to fruit)
kokki	Jap	red sun disc—Japanese heraldic symbol
koki	Mal	cook, kitchen staff
kongsi	Mal	community
koppie	Afr	small rounded hillock
kraal	Afr	a settlement—usually huts forming a circle, or any other enclosure
kranse	Afr	rocky buttresses—literally "wreaths"
kumi	Jap	group or team
laan	Dut	lane or avenue
lekas	Mal	hurry
lokasie	Afr	literally "location"—shantytown
manis	Mal	sweet, gentle
mielies	Afr	sweet corn
moffen	Dut	derogatory name for Germans
naore	Jap	correct, restore
nanjo	Jap	Southern Ocean
njonja	Mal	married woman
obat	Mal	medicine
obat njamuk	Mal	mosquito coil
ossewa	Afr	ox wagon
pak	Mal	father
pasar	Mal	traditional Indonesian market
pasar busuk	Mal	flea market
paviljoen	Dut	guest cottage
pedis	Mal	hot, spicy

pemuda	Mal	young men, youths
pendafteran	Mal	registration card
peranakan	Mal	half-caste
pikulan	Mal	pole for carrying goods, supported on the shoulder
pisang	Mal	banana
plaas	Afr	farm
plein	Dut	town square or park—an open area
predikante	Afr	preachers—ministers of the church
raden	Mal	title, noble person
rakjat djelata	Mal	proletariat
rampokken	Mal	looting
rantjang	Mal	bamboo spears
romusha	Jap	labourer
rondavel	Afr	a round hut with a thatched roof
rooi lussies	Afr	red ribbons—a distinguishing mark for soldiers willing to fight outside of South Africa's borders
rooinek	Afr	literally "redneck" but in South Africa denoting "Englishman"
sado	Mal	a two-wheeled horse-drawn cart for two passengers seated back to back (dos à dos)
sajur	Mal	vegetables
sambal	Mal	hot red-pepper paste
selendang	Mal	carrying cloth—for babies, tied over the shoulders
serunding	Mal	meal condiment—fried coconut
shimin	Jap	citizen
sjahid	Mal	martyrs
sjouwploeg	Dut	heavy lifting team
straat	Dut	street
surat lepas	Mal	exit permit
stoep	Afr	veranda
tante	Dut	aunt
taufan	Mal	typhoon
tenko	Jap	roll call
tikar	Mal	sleeping mat
tjabe rawit	Mal	small red pepper

tjap	Mal	stamp, seal
tjitjak	Mal	insect-eating lizard
tjintjang	Mal	cut into small pieces
tjoep	Dut	slang—steal
telor	Mal	egg
tonari-kumi	Jap	neighbourhood team
tongtongs	Mal	hollow wooden alarm block
totok	Mal	pure (of race)
tsotsie	Afr	young male Bantu thugs
tuan	Mal	mister
uitlander	Afr	foreigner
vlei	Afr	valley
weg	Dut	way, road
yasume	Jap	relax!

BIBLIOGRAPHY

Note: Where English-language sources are quoted, including English text appearing in foreign publications and English-language publications incorporating translations from the Japanese or Malay, the page number in the source document is indicated. In several instances, I consulted published foreign-language texts, and translated them myself; where these texts are quoted, the page numbers are indicated. In the case of Dutch-language historical treatises, the document or chapter referred to is identified to assist those wishing to pursue a line of inquiry while avoiding lengthy translation projects. Where I accessed unpublished translations from Japanese, and where I rely on unpublished Dutch memoirs, only the original source is identified (without the page numbers).

Beynon, H. C., ed. Verboden voor honden en inlanders: Indonesiërs vertellen over hun leven in de koloniale tijd. Amsterdam: Jan Mets, 1995.

Bijkerk, J. C. De laatste landvoogd: Van Mook en het einde van de Nederlandse invloed in Indië. Alphen ad. Rijn, Netherlands: A.W. Sijthof, 1982.

Bix, Herbert P. *Hirohito and the Making of Modern Japan.* Toronto: HarperCollins Canada, 2000.

Black, Conrad. *Franklin Delano Roosevelt.* New York: Public Affairs, 2005.

Bosman, A. B. *Kampdagboek.* Privately published, 1985.

Bouwer, Jan. *Het Vermoorde Land.* Franeker, Netherlands: van Wijnen, 1988.

Brugmans, I. J. Nederlandsch-Indië onder Japanse Bezetting: Gegevens en documenten over de jaren 1942–1945. Franeker, Netherlands: Wever, 1960.

Buruma, Ian. *Inventing Japan: 1853–1964.* New York: Modern Library, 2003.

Bussemaker, Herman. "Australian-Dutch Defence Cooperation, 1940–1941," *Journal of the Australian War Memorial* 29 (November 1996)

Bussemaker, Herman. "Paradise in Peril: The Netherlands, Great Britain, and the Defence of the Netherlands East Indies, 1940–41," *Journal of Southeast Asian Studies* (March 2000).

Castle, Colin. Lucky Alex: The Career of Group Captain A. M. Jardine, AFC, CD, Seaman and Airman. Victoria, BC: Trafford Publishing, 2001.

Christison, General Sir Phillip. *Life and Times.* Unpublished memoir, Imperial War Museum, London.

Churchill, Winston. *The Hinge of Fate.* Boston: Houghton Mifflin, 1950.

Clark, Manning. *A Short History of Australia.* Fourth revised edition. Camberwell, Victoria: Penguin Books Australia, 1995.

Cribb, Robert. "'Indisch' Identity and Decolonization," International Institute for Asian Studies, *Newsletter* 31 (July 2003): 52, http://www.iias.nl/nl/31/IIAS_NL31_52.pdf.

Crocker, George N. *Roosevelt's Road to Russia.* Chicago: Henry Regnery, 1959.

Davis, Kenneth S. *FDR: Into the Storm, 1937–1940.* New York: Random House, 1993.

Deighton, Len. *Blood, Tears and Folly.* London: Pimlico, 1995.

Dreifort, John E. Myopic Grandeur: The Ambivalence of French Foreign Policy Toward the Far East, 1919–1945. Ashland, OH: Kent State University Press, 1991.

Duiker, William. *The Communist Road to Power in Vietnam.* Boulder, CO: Westview Press, 1996.

van Dulm, Jan, et al. Geillustreerde atlas van de Japanse kampen in Nederlands Indië, 1942–1945. Purmerend, Netherlands: Asia Maior, 2003.

Elias, W. H. J. *Indië onder Japansche hiel.* Den Haag: van Hoeve, 1946.

Emmerson, John K. *The Japanese Thread: A Life in the U.S. Foreign Service.* New York: Holt, Rinehart & Winston, 1978.

Fabricius, Johan. *Brandende aarde.* Den Haag: H. P. Leopolds, 1949.

Fabricius, Johan. *Een wereld in Beroering.* Den Haag: H. P. Leopolds, 1952.

Fuchida, Mitsuo, and Okumiya Masatake. *Midway: The Battle that Doomed Japan; The Japanese Navy's Story.* Annapolis, MD: Naval Institute Press, 1955.

Gilbert, Martin. *A History of the Twentieth Century.* Vol. 2, *1933–1951.* Toronto, ON: Stoddart, 1999.

Governor General of New Zealand. Telegram to New Zealand Secretary of State for Dominion Affairs, September 7, 1940. Document 15 in Section 1, "Relations with Japan, June–October, 1940," in vol. 3 of *Documents Relating to New Zealand's Participation in the Second World War, 1939–45,* in *The Official History of New Zealand in the Second World War, 1939–45.* Wellington, New Zealand: War History Branch, Department of Internal Affairs, 1949. Published electronically by the New Zealand Electronic Text Centre as part of the Official War History project, 2003. http://www.nzetc.org/tm/scholarly/tei-WH2-3Doc.html.

Griffiths, Owen. "Militarizing Japan: Patriotism, Profit and Children's Print Media, 1894–1925," *Japan Focus* (September 2007), http://japanfocus.org/products/details/2528.

Hancock, W. K. *Smuts.* Vol. 2 of *The Fields of Force.* Cambridge: Cambridge University Press, 1968.

Hartley, M. G. *Myn kamp, niet door Hitler.* Amsterdam: Amsterdamsche Boek en Courantmaatschappij, 1947.

Hasegawa, Tsuyoshi. "The Atomic Bombs and the Soviet Invasion: Which Was More Important in Japan's Decision to Surrender?" in *The End of the Pacific War: Reappraisals,* ed. Tsuyoshi Hasagawa. Palo Alto, CA: Stanford University Press, 2007.

Hillen, Ernest. *The Way of a Boy: A Memoir of Java.* Toronto, Ontario: Viking Canada, 1993.

Holmes, Linda Goetz. Unjust Enrichment: How Japan's Companies Built Postwar Fortunes Using American POWs. Mechanicsburg, PA: Stackpole Books, 2001.

Howarth, Stephen. The Fighting Ships of the Rising Sun: The Drama of the Imperial Japanese Navy, 1895–1945. New York: Atheneum, 1983.

Imamura, Hitoshi. "Java in 1942," in *The Japanese Experience in Indonesia: Selected Memoirs of 1942–1945,* ed. Anthony Reid and Oki Akira. Monographs in International Studies, South East Asia Series, 72. Athens, OH: Ohio University Press, 1986.

Jones, Mark C. "Escape from Soerabaja," *The Navy* (October–December 2001), http://navyleag.customer.netspace.net.au/fc_07so.htm.

de Jong, L. Het Koninkrijk der Nederlanden in de Tweede Wereldoorlog. Deel 9, London. Den Haag: Staats, 1985.

de Jong, L. Het Koninkrijk der Nederlanden in de Tweede Wereldoorlog. Deel 11b, Nederlands-Indië II. Den Haag: Staats, 1985.

de Jong, L. Het Koninkrijk der Nederlanden in de Tweede Wereldoorlog. Deel 11c, Nederlands-Indië III. Den Haag: Staats, 1985.

Kemperman, Jeroen. *De Japanse bezetting in dagboeken.* Amsterdam: Bert Bakker, 2002.

Klemen, L. "Massacres of POWs, Dutch East Indies, 1941–1942," www.geocities.com/dutcheastindies/massacres.html.

Krancher, Jan A., ed. The Defining Years of the Dutch East Indies, 1942–1949: Survivors' Accounts of Japanese Invasion and Enslavement of Europeans and the Revolution That Created Free Indonesia. Jefferson, NC: McFarland, 1996.

Lerner, Henri. *Catroux.* Paris: Albin Michel, 1990.

Liddell Hart, B. H. *History of the Second World War.* London: Papermac, 1992.

Lüning, Hans. "The Sinking of the Junyo Maru," http://www.members.iinet.net.au/~vanderkp/8transpt.html. Translated excerpt from *Herrineringen van een Landstorm soldaat: Belevenissen en ervaringen kort voor, gedurende, en kort na de Japansche krijgsgevangenschap, 1941–45.* Unpublished memoir (1980), Netherlands Instituut voor Oorlogs Documentatie, Amsterdam.

Mackenzie, Gregory J. *German Armed Merchant Raiders During World War Two,* part 2 of *Marauders of the Sea.* Ahoy – Mac's Web Log, http://ahoy.tk-jk.net/macslog/MaraudersoftheSea2GermanA.html.

Manchester, William. *American Caesar: Douglas MacArthur, 1880–1964.* New York: Little, Brown & Co., 1978.

Manning, A. F., and A. E. Kersten, eds. *Documenten betreffende de buitenlandse politiek van Nederland, 1919–1945; Periode C, 1940–1945; Deel 1, 10 mei–31 okt., 1940.* Rijks geschiedkundige publicatiën; grote serie, 157. 's-Gravenhage: Nijhoff, 1976.

Matloff, Maurice. *Strategic Planning for Coalition Warfare, 1943–1944.* Washington, DC: Center of Military History, United States Army, 1990. http://www.army.mil/cmh/books/wwii/sp1943-44/index.htm

McQuade, J. G. *South Africa, Land of Sunshine and Opportunity.* Pretoria: Immigration Council, Union of South Africa, 1947.

van Mook, H. *Indonesië, Nederland en de wereld.* Amsterdam: de Bezige Bij, 1949.

Morgan, E. B., and E. Shacklady. *Spitfire: The History.* Stamford, UK: Key Publishing, 2000.

O'Hara, Vincent P. "Battle of the Java Sea: 27 February 1942," http://www.microworks.net/PACIFIC/battles/java_sea.htm.

Parshall, Jonathan, and Tony Tully. *The Shattered Sword: The Untold Story of the Battle of Midway.* Washington, DC: Potomac Books, 2005.

Reeves, Ambrose. *The Sharpeville Massacre: A Watershed in South Africa.* African National Congress historical documents, http://www.anc.org.za/ancdocs/history/misc/shareve.html.

Reid, Anthony, and Oki Akira, eds. *The Japanese Experience in Indonesia: Selected Memoirs of 1942–1945.* Monographs in International Studies, South East Asia Series, 72. Athens, OH: Ohio University Press, 1986.

Rinzema, Win. Dit was uw Tjideng: Aspecten van de vertraagde afwikkeling van Japanse interneringskampen in Batavia. Utrecht, Netherlands: Stichting ICODO, 1991.

Sjahrir, Soetan. *Out of Exile.* New York: John Day, 1949.

Sjahrir, Sutan. *Indonesische overpeinzingen.* Amsterdam: Bezige Bij, 1945.

Sluimers, Laszlo. "The Japanese Military and Indonesian Independence: The Japanese Occupation in Southeast Asia," *Journal of South East Asian Studies* 27:1 (March 1996).

Smuts, J. C. Jan Christian Smuts by His Son. London: Cassell, 1952.

Snow, Edgar. *The Battle for Asia.* New York: Random House, 1941.

Stinnet, Robert. Day of Deceit: The Truth About FDR and Pearl Harbor. New York: Simon & Schuster, 2000.

Strachan, Tony, ed. In the Clutch of Circumstance: Reminiscences of Members of the Canadian National Prisoners of War Association. Victoria, BC: Cappis Press, 1985.

Thomas, David. *Battle of the Java Sea.* London: Pan Books, 1971.

Tornij, G. J. "De Seawitch bracht nog P40's naar Java," *Spinner* (Stichting Vrienden van het Militaire Luchtvaart Museum) 9 (June 2003).

Touwen-Bouwsma, Elly. "The Indonesian Nationalists and the Japanese 'Liberation' of Indonesia: Visions and Reactions," *Journal of South East Asian Studies* 27, 1 (March 1996).

Toynbee, Arnold. Mankind and Mother Earth: A Narrative History of the World. London: Book Club Associates, 1976.

Tromp, Sheri (Ed.). Four Years Till Tomorrow: Despair and Hope in Wartime Dutch East Indies. A Collection of 26 Eye Witness' Stories by Members of the August 15, 1945 Foundation. Langley, British Columbia: Vanderheide, 1999.

Utsumi, Aiko. "The Japanese Army's Internment Policies on Dutch Civilians in Java," *Journal of Sophia Asian Studies* 19 (December 2001): 1–31.

van Oosten, F. C. *The Battle of the Java Sea.* Annapolis, MD: Naval Institute Press, 1976.

van der Post, Laurens. The Admiral's Baby: An Extraordinary Episode in Twentieth-Century History. New York: William Morrow, 1996.

van Velden, Dora. *De Japanse burgerkampen.* Fourth printing. Franeker, Netherlands: Wever, 1985.

Vlekke, Bernhard M. *Nusantara: A History of Indonesia.* The Hague: W. van Hoeve, 1959.

Voskuil, R. P. G. A. *Bandoeng: Beeld van een stad.* Purmerend, Netherlands: Asia Maior, 1996.

Walker, Eric A. *A History of South Africa.* London: Longmans, Green & Co., 1962.

Wetzler, Peter M. Hirohito and War: Imperial Tradition and Military Decision Making in Pre-War Japan. Honolulu: University of Hawaii Press, 1998.

Woodburn Kirby, S. *The War Against Japan.* Vol. 5, *The Japanese Strategic Plans.* London: Naval and Military Press, 1969.

Yoshimura, Akira. *Zero Fighter.* Westport, CT: Praeger, 1996.

Ziegler, Phillip. *Mountbatten: The Official Biography.* London: Collins, 1985.

Zwaan, Jacob. Nederlands-Indië 1940–1946: Gouvernementeel Intermezzo 1940–1942. Den Haag: Omniboek, 1985.

Zwaan, Jacob. Nederlands-Indië 1940–1946: Japans Intermezzo 9 maart 1942–15 augustus 1945. Den Haag: Omniboek, 1985.

ISBN 1425151590

9 781425 151591